1001 HINTS & TIPS

FOR YOUR GARDEN

READER'S DIGEST

1001 HINTS & TIPS

FOR YOUR GARDEN

Reader's
Digest

THE READER'S DIGEST ASSOCIATION, INC.   PLEASANTVILLE, NEW YORK / MONTREAL

READER'S DIGEST GENERAL BOOKS

**Editor-in-Chief,
Books and Home Entertainment**
Barbara J. Morgan

U.S. Editor, General Books
David Palmer

Executive Editor
Gayla Visalli

Art Director
Joel Musler

Editorial Director
Jane Polley

Research Director
Laurel A. Gilbride

Library of Congress Cataloging in Publication Data

1001 hints & tips for your garden.
    p.   cm.
Includes index.
ISBN 0-89577-860-2
1. Gardening. 2. Gardening—Encyclopedias. I. Reader's Digest Association.
SB450.97.A15   1996
635—dc20   96-179

Printed in the United States of America
Sixth Printing, January 1998

Address any comments about 1001 HINTS & TIPS FOR YOUR GARDEN to Research Director, General Books, c/o Customer Service, Reader's Digest, Pleasantville, NY 10570.

To order additional copies of 1001 HINTS & TIPS FOR YOUR GARDEN, call 1-800-846-2100.

1001 HINTS & TIPS FOR YOUR GARDEN

STAFF

Project Editor
Fred DuBose

Project Art Editor
Carol Nehring

Senior Associate Editors
Alexis Lipsitz
Nancy Shuker

Associate Art Editors
Colin Joh
Bruce R. McKillip
With special assistance from Barbara Lapic

Picture and Editorial Research
James McInnis

Assistant Editor
Nancy Berrian-Dixon

Assistant Production Supervisor
Rose Ann Cassarino

Prepress Specialist
Karen Goldsmith

Quality Control Manager
Ann Kennedy Harris

CONTRIBUTORS

Editors
Ned Geeslin
Fiona Gilsenan

Research Editor
Leigh Newman

Art Production Coordinator
Tracey Grant

Indexer
Sidney Wolfe Cohen

Copy Editor
Virginia Croft

Principal Consultants
Thomas Christopher
Rosemary G. Rennicke
With special assistance from
Carroll Calkins *and* Jim Dwyer

Consultants for *Enemies of the Garden*
Roscoe Randell, Ph.D.
Malcolm C. Shurtleff, Ph.D.

Consultants
William D. Adams
Gwen Barclay
Nina Bassuk
Daria Price Bowman
Hank Bruno
James R. Brooks
Gregory J. Bugbee
Thomas Burford
Tom Burton
A. Wayne Cahilly
Mike Cannon, Ph.D.
Beth Castellon
David Cavagnaro
David Chinery
Maria T. Cinque
Ruth Rogers Clausen
Rick Darke
Tim Dillon
Arthur P. Dome
Thomas E. Eltzroth
A. Jenkins Farmer
Dora Galitzki
Wade Graham
Wallace H. Gray
Gordon Hayward
David B. Headley, Ph.D.
Madalene Hill
Matt Horn
George W. Hudler
Elizabeth Innvar
Rick Kerrigan
Peter J. Kool
Maureen B. LeMarca
Laura C. Martin
William B. McLemore
Roberta F. McQuaid
Joan Means
John T. Mickel, Ph.D.
Stephen A. Morrell
Shepherd Ogden
Lee Reich, Ph.D.

Bruce K. Riggs
Louise Riotte
Michael A. Ruggiero
Gray Russell
Roger Charles Sherry
Elsie Sydnor
Daniel J. Tennessen, Ph.D.
Carl A. Totemeier
Eliot Tozer
John N. Trager
Peter Trowbridge
John P. Van Miert
Charles E. Voigt
Mobee Weinstein
Janet Whippo
Christie H. White
Lucinda Winn
Priscilla L. Wormwood

Special thanks to
Bruce Adams
Thais Aguirre
C. Roy Keys
Mary Hoffman
Alice E. Knight
Karl Lauby
Norman B. Mack
John McClung
Mike McGarry
Maurice Paleau
Peter and Jean Ruh
Gammon Sharpley
Alice Starr
Ken Vetting
Olive Rice Waters
Peter Welcenbach

Preface

With its A-to-Z format, 1001 HINTS & TIPS FOR YOUR GARDEN works as a big, colorful dictionary. Just turn to the topic of choice, whether it's tulips or lilies, shade or shears. Covering everything from acid soil to zucchini, the hints and tips you'll find here have been culled from leading horti-culturists and accomplished home gardeners all over the country. Many of these nuggets are basic gardening tenets, while others are decidedly unconventional. (As we all know, no two gardeners do things in exactly the same way!) Any one of them, however, may prompt you to go outdoors and put your gardening talents to work.

The 320-page Garden Dictionary contains cross-references that direct you from one topic to related ones, making sure that you get the big picture. Many of the featured plants and flowers come with a sampling of their varieties and types; look for the green-tinted boxes. Additional boxes, tinted yellow, provide plant histories, lore, and fascinating asides.

Interspersed throughout are 12 special features. Three of them—on period gardens, wildflower gardens, and backyard habitats—might inspire you to try something different. A fourth considers fragrance as a perfumer would, helping you to best appreciate the world of garden scents. Two other features celebrate the revival of heirloom roses and vintage vegetables, while the remaining seven provide essential information on plant shapes, year-round garden color, tools, houseplants, and herbs, plus projects and crafts that you can make with your garden's rich bounty.

Following the Garden Dictionary is Enemies of the Garden, an illustrated guide to 108 common pests and diseases. A handy Garden Calendar, laid out month by month and divided into four broad climate zones, reminds you of the tasks you'll have to perform as the seasons change. Rounding out the book is a glossary, with concise definitions of common gardening terms. As a bonus, a list of garden information sources appears on pages 414–415. Happy gardening!

The colored bands in the table of contents at right indicate the Garden Dictionary's 12 special features and the introductory climate map. Vertical bands of the same color appear on the feature pages and are visible at the book's edge, allowing for quick and easy reference.

Contents

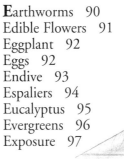

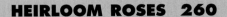

PROJECTS & CRAFTS 236

HEIRLOOM ROSES 260

TOOLS 294

VINTAGE VEGETABLES 312

WILDFLOWER GARDENS 324

Hardiness zones across the U.S.

The U.S. Department of Agriculture map on these two pages divides the country into 10 hardiness zones, determined by their average minimum temperatures. Be aware, however, that climates tend to overlap: many plants that grow in one zone will do well in the southern part of an adjoining colder zone, for example. Also take into account that temperature varies according to elevation, proximity to a body of water, and other factors. To be certain that a certain plant is hardy where you live, consult a local nursery or the Cooperative Extension Service.

For simplicity's sake, this book consolidates the USDA zones into four: cold, temperate, warm, and hot. This broad categorization is used throughout the book and applies to the Garden Calendar found on pp.354-379.

COLOR KEY

A hardiness zone is based upon an area's average minimum winter temperature.

- **Zone 1** below −50°F
- **Zone 2** −50°F to −40°F
- **Zone 3** −40°F to −30°F
- **Zone 4** −30°F to −20°F
- **Zone 5** −20°F to −10°F
- **Zone 6** −10°F to 0°F
- **Zone 7** 0°F to 10°F
- **Zone 8** 10°F to 20°F
- **Zone 9** 20°F to 30°F
- **Zone 10** 30°F to 40°F

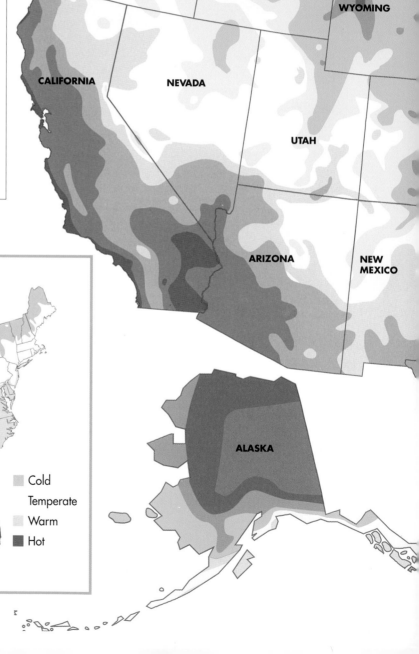

THE FOUR BROAD ZONES

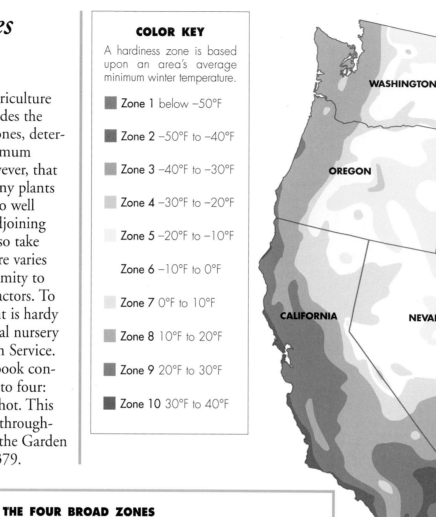

- Cold
- Temperate
- Warm
- Hot

CLIMATE

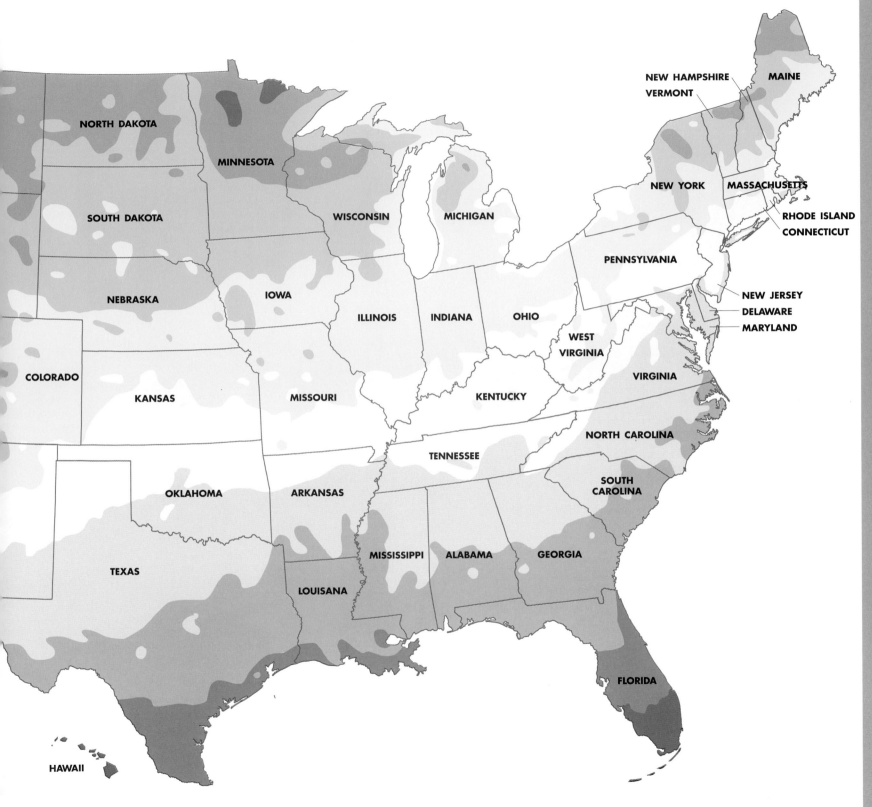

NORTH DAKOTA

MINNESOTA

SOUTH DAKOTA

WISCONSIN

MICHIGAN

NEW HAMPSHIRE

VERMONT

MAINE

NEW YORK

MASSACHUSETTS

RHODE ISLAND

CONNECTICUT

PENNSYLVANIA

NEBRASKA

IOWA

ILLINOIS

INDIANA

OHIO

NEW JERSEY

DELAWARE

MARYLAND

WEST
VIRGINIA

COLORADO

KANSAS

MISSOURI

KENTUCKY

VIRGINIA

NORTH CAROLINA

TENNESSEE

SOUTH
CAROLINA

OKLAHOMA

ARKANSAS

TEXAS

MISSISSIPPI

ALABAMA

GEORGIA

LOUISANA

FLORIDA

HAWAII

CLIMATE

The Garden Dictionary

The Garden Dictionary is a gold mine of hints and tips that combine to create an informative and entertaining guide to home gardening. Whether you're a seasoned expert or a beginner, the next 320 pages of hardworking advice will make it possible to solve almost any problem you encounter. And what could be easier than using a dictionary? The alphabetical order connects you directly to the topic you're interested in, while cross-references lead you to still more advice—proven and practical, but often delightfully offbeat. From Acid Soil to Zucchini, you'll find your answers here.

Interspersed throughout are 12 special features, each marked with a colored band. Here you'll find pages that provide a survey of essential herbs and favorite indoor plants, give you a glimpse of wildflower gardens in their many incarnations, and introduce you to heirloom vegetables (and roses, too!). You'll also learn how to best appreciate the fragrances in your garden—and even how to craft the plants you grow into useful items, pretty displays, or gifts.

ACID SOIL

Slightly sour. Because acids are produced when organic matter decays, most garden soils are somewhat acidic. They become increasingly sour as humus is worked in and chemicals are leached out.

Determine soil acidity before you plant. Acidity is measured by pH. A pH of 7 is neutral; any number below is acid and any number above is alkaline. Check the pH of your soil with a home test kit (available in garden supply stores) or send a soil sample to a lab. Your local Cooperative Extension Service can provide information on testing and sampling.

For a quick and easy soil test, wet a soil sample and add a pinch of baking soda. If the mix fizzes, the soil may be too acidic for most garden plants and vegetables.

To each its own. Most garden plants prefer slightly acidic soil with a pH between 6 and 6.5. This includes such fruits, vegetables, and flowers as apples and raspberries, beans and peas, and pansies and delphiniums. But other plants like more acid. Azaleas, foxgloves, heather, camellias, gardenias, and blueberries, for example, need a soil with a pH between 4.5 and 6.

To lower acidity in garden soil, apply 2½ to 10 pounds of dolomitic limestone per 100 square feet of soil, depending on soil type: a heavy clay soil will require more amendment than a sandy one. To raise the pH still higher, till the limestone into the top 6 inches of soil.

Ashes from the fireplace or a woodburning stove can also "sweeten" the soil. Spread 5 to 10 pounds per 100 square feet to raise the pH by one unit.

In regions with high rainfall, soils acidify more quickly as calcium leaches through the soil. Even if pH is at the right level, sprinkle the soil with limestone, which will slowly work its way downward.
▷ **Lime, Soil**

AGAVE

A persistent myth. According to folklore, the century plant (the common name for *Agave americana*) flowers once in 100 years. In fact, the plant may bloom its first and only time in 10 years, then dies.

If there's a danger of brush fires where you live, plant a few agaves, especially on hillsides. These succulent plants are not only attractive and drought resistant but also fire retardant.

A garden guardian. Plant the imposing agave around the perimeter of your property, underneath windows, or at the edges of other plantings. The needle-sharp leaves will discourage intruders and animals as well as resist fires. But keep them away from walkways; these big plants often overgrow path borders, where their sharp and spiky leaves can become a danger to friend as well as foe.

For erosion control, especially in arid areas, try planting agaves on banks. They also make excellent windscreens when planted around the borders of a large property. They're often unsuitable for limited spaces, however, since their large size can visually dominate an entire landscape.

Climate too cold? Grow agaves, hardy only to 40°F, outside as container plants in summer. When winter comes, store the plants in the basement and keep them dry.

Keep agaves neat and trim by regularly removing the untidy lower leaves. And remember that agaves die after they flower. Remove the entire plant once blooming is completed and the rosettes have died.

Patience is a virtue. Overfertilizing to speed up flowering will only risk damaging agaves without affecting bloom. And bear in mind that agaves grown in pots may take even longer to bloom than the 10- to 50-year span of outdoor plants.
▷ **Cacti & Succulents**

ALKALINE SOIL

Test soil with cider vinegar. Add a few drops to a soil sample. If it fizzes, the soil is alkaline. For a precise reading, contact your local Cooperative Extension Service to learn how to take a sample and where to send it. Or pick up a home test kit.

Reduce alkalinity by adding acidic materials such as peat moss, sulfur, or aluminum sulfate to your soil. To lower the pH by one unit, add 5 pounds of peat moss, ¾ to 2½ pounds of sulfur, or 5 to 15 pounds of aluminum sulfate per 100 square feet. Use the smaller amounts of additives in sandy soils and progressively larger amounts in heavier soils.

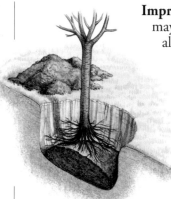

Improving drainage may help reduce alkalinity by allowing water to wash through and carry away alkaline salts. Put plenty of dead leaves, compost, or other organic matter into the bottom of planting holes.

Coffee grounds help reduce alkalinity too. Dig a good helping into the soil.

Blanketing the ground with an organic mulch prevents surface evaporation of water and the buildup of alkaline salts. Use straw or dead leaves.

In the Western states alkaline soils tend to be high in sodium, which makes them tight and sticky. Water the soil to loosen it. After it dries, dig in gypsum—about 2 pounds per 100 square feet of moderately clayey soil.

Make the best of it. Instead of acidifying your soil, consider growing plants that like it alkaline. Desirable flowers in this category include the madonna lily, purple coneflower, phlox, and candytuft. Alkalinity-loving shrubs and trees include lilac, crape myrtle, juniper, peach, and apricot.
▷ **Peat Moss, Soil**

ALOE

Warmth and sunlight are keys to growing these African natives, so place aloes in full sun—except those with speckled leaves, which need midday shade. Rich soil, good drainage, and regular summer watering are also important. Most species won't survive temperatures below 40°F, so frost protection is often needed in cooler climes.

❧ AN ALOE SAMPLER ❧

These sculptural succulents range from low-growing aloes suitable as ground covers to tree-sized plants that can dominate a yard. *Aloe vera*, the most commonly grown species, is prized more for its medicinal attributes than its beauty. A more comely plant is the stripe-leaved *A. variegata*.

Low-growing aloes, including *A. brevifolia*, *A. nobilis*, and *A. striata*, multiply into spreading clumps about 10 inches high. At the other end of the scale, tree aloes like *A. ferox* and *A. marlothii* grow to 10 feet. Even taller is the dramatic *A. bainesii*, with a 12- to 14-foot trunk topped by a symmetrical crown of spear-shaped leaves arching gracefully downward.

Homegrown salve. The gelatinous sap of *Aloe vera barbadensis* will soothe minor skin rashes and sunburn. Cut a leaf of the plant off at its fleshy base and split it open with a knife or razor blade. Scrape out the sap with a spoon and apply it to the skin. But be sure to handle it carefully; it can leave an ugly yellow stain on your clothes.

More attractive than the healthful aloe vera plant is *Aloe variegata*, with leaves edged in yellow. If you choose to grow it, never let water collect at the base of the leaves—it will rot the roots of this popular variety. The plant also has a strong dislike of chalky water.

Add year-round drama to your garden by planting aloes in large groupings. Many species—including *Aloe ferox* and *A. brevifolia*—flower during fall and winter when little else does, and mass plantings tend to emphasize the bright display of gold, coral, and orange flowers. Choose small to medium varieties and install them in rows, with each plant 18 to 24 inches apart. The plantings will expand into attractive large clumps within 2 to 3 years.

Leave the earth bare around aloes to highlight their striking sculptural quality. And regularly groom older clumps to keep offshoots from cluttering up the plant's inherent neatness and simplicity.

To grow aloes in pots, provide a moist, porous potting mixture by using 2 parts soil, 2 parts perlite or coarse sand, ¼ part bone meal, and ½ part dehydrated cow manure. Keep your potted aloe at a minimum of 50° to 55°F.
▷ **Cacti & Succulents**

ALTITUDE

Climate varies with altitude. If you live in a mountainous or hilly region, you move a full hardiness zone to the north for every 3,300 feet you climb. Elevation also affects the length of the growing season. A typical season in Pueblo, Colorado, for example, lasts 174 days; in Colorado Springs, 30 miles to the north but 1,500 feet higher in elevation, the growing season is 36 days shorter.

Terrace your plants. Mountainside gardens are subject to drought: rainwater runs off before it can sink in. Terraced plantings will slow down the runoff and absorb it.

Tall grasses and ground covers trap and hold rainwater for mountainside gardens far more efficiently than a clipped lawn.

North-facing slopes receive less sunshine than south-facing slopes and are considerably cooler. This can be a liability in winter, when plants on north slopes suffer more from cold. On the other hand, this difference can be an advantage in midsummer, when heat-sensitive plants such as alpines or ferns find the north slope hospitable.

Plants may need extra shade at higher elevations. On a clear day a garden at 3,000 feet above sea level will get 20 percent more sunshine that one at sea level. If you live at a high elevation, keep all plants well watered and avoid sun-sensitive species such as impatiens. But remember that tomatoes and many other vegetables thrive in the intense sun of high altitudes.

Add organic matter. Frequent doses of compost greatly benefit gardens on hillsides and in mountainous regions. Soils in these areas tend to be "young" ones—that is, composed mainly of weathered rock. The soils on steep slopes are almost always poorer than those in the lowlands.

"Frost dams" can be a liability or an aid. A common problem at high elevations is the creation of a frost pocket as cold air flows downhill and collects behind a solid fence, hedge, or row of trees. If your garden beds are sited on the uphill side of one of these obstructions, alleviate the problem by thinning out hedges and tree rows or using open mesh fencing. To protect beds on the downhill side, install a fence or hedge above.

Keep conifer branches from breaking under the weight of the heavy snow cover often found at high altitudes by tying them with rope.

Adaptable plants. Flowering shrubs and trees that thrive in high altitudes are French hybrid lilacs, highbush cranberries, the Colorado pine locust, and the hawthorn. *Rosa hugonis* and *R. rugosa* species of roses and their hybrids prosper at high altitudes. Adaptable annuals are cosmos and morning glory.

▷ **Exposure, Slopes**

ALUMINUM FOIL

Protect young trees from mice and rabbits. Wrap trunks loosely in sheets of foil to a height of 18 inches. The glittering, rattling surface keeps the gnawers away.

Use aluminum foil mulch to speed growth and protect against insects. Stretch it between rows of plants and use rocks or bricks along the edge to anchor. The light the foil reflects can increase yields, especially in cloudy regions, and speed the ripening of tomatoes or the blooming of a rosebush by a full 2 weeks. The foil also keeps thrips and aphids away.

A cheap substitute. If you're using large amounts of foil, save money by painting black plastic mulch with the aluminum-colored paint sold at hardware stores.

Foil scarecrows. Keep birds away by cutting patterns from cardboard—stars, circles, sea shells—and wrapping them in foil. Hang from the branches of ripening berry bushes and fruit trees. The flashing sunlight reflected from the fluttering objects will frighten birds more effectively than a stationary scarecrow does.

Boost winter light for houseplants. Cover a panel of cardboard with foil and and position it on a wall so that it reflects the light from a window onto your potted plants. It will not only boost their growth but will keep them evenly shaped.

Cones for bulbs. Give forced crocus and hyacinth bulbs the darkness they need by placing them on a chilly windowsill and covering with a cone of foil. Remove the foil when crocus shoots reach 2 inches and when hyacinth shoots reach 4 inches.

▷ **Grubs & Larvae**

Juxtaposing assorted species of annuals will give your flower beds brilliant splashes of color.

ANNUALS

PURCHASING
Keep your eye open for bargains. Young plants in six- or eight-packs of the same variety are often available at very low prices. The seedlings should be well rooted but need not be in bloom. If you wait a while to buy, you can save some money. Once planting season is past, however, beware of starved, dried-up leftovers.

Climbing annuals will quickly disguise a chain-link fence or the screening around

garbage cans. Morning glory, scarlet runner beans, black-eyed Susan vine, sweet peas, and hyacinth bean are some of the climbers that do the job nicely.

A few for shady gardens. Impatiens, monkey flower, nasturtium, California bluebell, and wishbone flower are shade-tolerant annuals.

For pots and window boxes, choose bushy or trailing annuals. Petunias, marigolds, verbenas, thunbergia, lobelia, and heliotrope are ideal. But avoid tall plants like sunflowers, which look awkward in small containers.

Be wary of "grab bags." Many seed stores sell small packets of seed mixes described as "fragrant," "mixed colors," "for shady areas," or "drought tolerant"—but too often they lack the specific information you need. Instead, buy individual seed packets labeled with advice on spacing and care.

PLANTING

The right place. A sunny location with good drainage is more important to most annuals than soil quality.

Use as fillers. Plant annuals in the empty spaces between shrubs, foundation plants, perennials, or rows of vegetables.

Sow half-hardy annuals indoors to give them a head start. To make sure they're evenly spaced, place chicken wire over your seeding tray and put a seed in each hole. This makes it easier to separate the seedlings for transplanting.

Flowers all season. While you wait for perennials to take hold, dress up the garden with annuals. Since they germinate, bloom, and die within a single season, there's no need to dig them up once the later flowers are established. You can also plant them at the base of a trellis while you're waiting for a perennial vine to flower.

Color considerations. Massing a single color will create an elegant, unified effect suitable for terraces, planters, and window boxes. Pastels—white, pinks, lavenders, yellows—show up best in early morning and evening light. If you want a multicolored effect, make a sketch and color it in; it will help you keep the colors harmonious.

MAINTENANCE

Good and wet. Plenty of moisture is essential when you set out young plants. First, soak them in a tub of water. Plant

only after the root ball is thoroughly wet. As extra insurance, soak the planting hole with a good watering as well.

Annuals don't like manure—even when it's well aged. Too much nitrogen results in plants with too many leaves, too many stems, and too few flowers. The only manure suitable for use on annuals is that which has dried for at least two years.

Pinching young plants delays blooming but helps them become stockier and bushier. Annuals such as clarkia, sweet pea, cosmos, godetia, coleus, snapdragon, nicotiana, red salvia, and petunia benefit from pinching. Use your thumb and forefinger to nip out the growing tip of the main stem just above a leaf or pair of leaves.

Which to deadhead. Use shears or scissors to remove dead flowers from annuals that bloom in flushes, like coreopsis, petunias, California poppies, and marigolds.

Put annuals into pots at the end of summer. Species such as coleus, impatiens, browallia, geranium, floss flower, and wishbone flower will provide attractive blooms in your home for several months. Inspect the plants carefully for insects before you place them with your indoor plants.

Annuals for drying. Traditional favorites include everlasting *(Helischrysum bracteatum)* and close relatives: winged everlasting *(Ammobium)* and immortelle *(Helipterum)*. Other candidates are statice, love-in-a-mist, globe amaranth, and bells of Ireland. Harvest when the blooms are just opening and air-dry upside down at 45° to 55°F.
▷ **Bedding Plants, Flower Beds**

⚘ SORTING OUT ANNUALS ⚘

HARDY TYPES

Sow directly in the ground whenever the soil can be worked—fall in mild climates, early spring in cooler regions. These tolerate cold weather and even some frost.	Annual phlox Chinese houses Godetia	Larkspur Sweet alyssum Toadflax

HALF-HARDY TYPES

Sow indoors and plant outside later. These tolerate cool temperatures but only very light frosts.	Butter daisy California poppy Knotweed	Morning glory Rainbow pink Spider flower

TENDER TYPES

Sow only in warm soil. In Northern climates, sow under glass and plant out only after all danger of frost has passed.	Floss flower Globe amaranth Impatiens Lobelia Marigold	Moss rose Petunia Potato vine Scarlet sage

ANTS

Pros and cons. Gardeners usually consider ants to be pests. Ants can loosen the soil around young plants, causing them to die. Some species shelter and protect aphids, whose honeydew they feed on. On the positive side, ants can improve air circulation in heavy soils, and their burrows improve water drainage.

To get rid of a colony, cover the anthill with a large flowerpot whose drainage hole has been plugged with a cork or tightly wadded plastic wrap. Heat a bucket of water to boiling and flood the surrounding soil, reserving a few gallons of the water. Wait a minute or two for most of the ants to find shelter in the overturned pot, then turn it upright and pour in the remaining water.

A mash of hot chilies and water will keep ants away. Another homemade repellent is a mix of orange peels and water puréed in your blender and poured directly into an anthill early in the morning.

Instant grits work too. Grits expand in ants' bodies and finish them off. Leave the grits in piles near the insects' pathways.

Inside the house, safely repel ants by sprinkling pennyroyal, camphor, clove oil, tansy, spearmint, or broken eggshells on a dish in closets and on shelves.

Boric acid mixed with sugar is an effective ant poison—but only in gardens with no children and pets. Spread it on a piece of wood or stone near the nest, then cover for protection from rain. The foraging ants will love it.

Wrap bands of paper coated with nondrying glue around the base of fruit trees to prevent ants from reaching the fruit. An easy way is to simply fold in half a sheet of adhesive paper—the kind used on shelving—with the sticky side out.

Ants hate aromatic plants like mint, lavender, chives, and garlic. Install these along borders or spot them randomly in clumps and pots around the garden.

Create an ant barrier around plants, on front steps, and between garden rows with a sprinkling of agricultural lime, bone meal, or powdered charcoal.

Fire ants, better known in the South as red ants, are tenacious little creatures with a vicious sting. They are especially partial to sun and sandy soil. If your yard is prone to infestation, provide shade with vine-covered trellises in a part of the garden where sun-loving plants won't be affected. And if you keep compost, store it in closed bins so that fire ants can't use it to build their hills.
▷**Pesticides**

APHIDS

Don't waste time. Get rid of aphids the first time you see them; these pests reproduce rapidly. They not only suck the nutrients from a plant but can also spread any number of deadly viruses, including bean mosaic virus and cucumber mosaic virus.

A simple and effective spray for aphids is 4 ounces of dishwashing liquid in 1 gallon of water. For another good spray, mix 1 tablespoon liquid soap and 1 cup vegetable oil, then add 2 teaspoons of the blend to a gallon of water—but don't use it on squash, cauliflower, or cabbage, which can suffer leaf burn. When using either recipe, spray the plants with the mixture and follow with a spray of water. Wait about 15 minutes and repeat.

Blender sprays. Use your blender to make organic aphid killers. Purée three or four jalapeño peppers, three cloves of garlic, and 1 quart of water; strain and use as a spray. A mixture of mineral oil and garlic also works. Better still, blend ½ cup of aphid bodies with 2 cups of water; strain and spray on plants. To avoid gathering aphids by hand, simply blend a generous bunch of infested leaves with the water.

Concerning chemicals. Rotenone- and pyrethrum-based sprays are effective against aphids and harmless to humans. But using them is something of a trade-off, since both kill earthworms and beneficial insects. Follow directions on the container. Spray in the evening and be careful not to contaminate the adjacent soil.

Sprinkle wood ashes over bushes and low-lying plants; they are caustic and will dehydrate and suffocate aphids. Use a large-hole shaker—the kind for grated cheese works well—or sprinkle them on by hand. After a day, wash away the ashes with a hose.

▶❙ APHID FIGHTERS ❘◀

▷ Praying mantises, ladybugs, and aphid lions (the larvae of green lacewings) are natural foes of the aphid. Obtain them from garden supply stores and catalogs. Release ladybugs at night so that they won't fly away.

▷ Hover flies and wasps kill aphids by injecting their eggs into them. Plant Queen Anne's lace to attract wasps and marigolds to attract hover flies.

▷ Lamb's quarters, a common weed, is an effective aphid toxin.

▷ Birds, especially chickadees and house wrens, consume aphids by the thousands.

A rhubarb insecticide. Soak 3 pounds of rhubarb leaves in 4 quarts of water for 24 hours. Bring the water to a boil and let it simmer for 30 minutes. Add 1 ounce of laundry soap flakes and allow to cool.
▷ **Pesticides**

APPLE TREES

To pollinate a tree—the first step toward an impressive crop of apples—find a neighbor with a compatible variety and ask for a few blooming sprigs. Place the sprigs in a bucket of water near your own tree and let the bees and butterflies do the rest.

The right forms. Productive trees should have open forms so that their branches have space to develop and are bathed in light and air. Train and prune your trees either for the open center form, with three or four main branches radiating up and out, or for the central leader form, shaped like a Christmas tree, with a single main stem and increasingly long side branches towards the base of the tree.

Bend vertical branches almost to the horizontal to make them produce fruit buds rather than shoots. Weight or tie the branches in spring, but be careful not to arch them; nonfruitful shoots may grow from the arch's highest point.

Use a pole pruner to remove high branches from a large tree. The pruner has a saw and cord-activated pruning shears at its end. Be sure not to prune your trees too much, especially the young ones; overpruning will weaken a tree and delay fruiting.

Thin out excess fruits as they develop so that those that remain will grow large and sweet. Thin right after the first small fruitlets set and after the "June drop" a few weeks later, when the tree naturally sheds its excess fruits. Leave the largest and healthiest fruits alone—but remove even some of these so that each apple has plenty of elbow room.

Coax an older tree to fruit by girdling it. Carefully remove a ring of bark about ¼-inch wide from around the trunk in spring, about the time that other apple trees have just finished blossoming.

Apples that are dimpled and tunneled with brown trails show signs that apple maggots, or railroad worms, have been at work. Trap egg-laying female maggots by hanging red croquet balls coated with a commercial insect adhesive in your trees. Use one ball per dwarf tree, four to eight per full-size tree. Hang at eye level, just within the canopy but not obscured by leaves.

Good hygiene, especially in fall and winter, will reduce insect infestation in spring and summer. Pick up and discard fallen fruit that is diseased or bug ridden. Prune away cankers—dark, sunken areas of bark—as well as any branches that are shriveled or blackened. Always trim diseased portions back to healthy white tissue.

Reduce codling moth infestation by installing a collar of corrugated cardboard around the trunk. The larvae will nest in the cardboard. Remove it periodically, burn it, then replace with a new collar. In the spring, rub loose scales of bark from the tree trunk to eliminate the crevices in which codling moth larvae can readily pupate.

Save work at harvest time with a fruit picker. The picker consists of a hook that dislodges the fruit and a cloth bag that catches it. It's especially useful for large trees.

Apples will stay fresh for months, provided they have enough moisture and are kept a few degrees above freezing. Put the fruit into plastic bags in which you've poked a few holes, and store in the refrigerator. 'Winesap' and 'Idared' are excellent varieties for long-term storage.

Dry some apples for healthy, tasty snacks. First, core the apples. Then slice them into ¼-inch thick rounds, run a string through the center of each round, and tack the ends of the string to the ceiling of your pantry. After the slices are thoroughly dry, store them in plastic bags. 'Golden Delicious' makes an especially tasty dried apple.
▷ **Orchards**

APRICOT TREES

A full-size apricot tree will fill about 15 to 25 square feet in the garden, making a nice shade tree, as well as bearing enough fruit for most families. If your space is limited, you can plant a dwarf tree, which will still bear full-size fruits.

Perfect drainage is essential. Apricots in particular need well-drained soil. If necessary, install perforated pipe in the ground and slope it away from the tree toward a nearby ditch. Or plant on a soil mound 1 to 2 feet high and 6 feet wide.

Plant on bare ground, which radiates more heat at night than ground insulated by lawn or mulch. Situate the tree in a cool, shady spot—near a north-facing wall, for example, so that blossoms will be less likely to suffer on frosty nights. To release more heat when frost threatens, hoe the ground lightly in the evening. If your tree is in bloom and frost threatens, drape cloth or plastic over it.

Paint the trunk white each fall. White reflects sunlight, keeping the bark from heating up during the day, then cools it rapidly as the winter sun dips below the horizon. Use either a limestone wash or a latex paint diluted with an equal amount of water.

In colder climates, plant two varieties. Even though many apricots are self-fertile, a second variety for pollination will encourage a heavier fruit set and lessen the damage caused by frosts.

Fuzzy gray fruits are infected with brown rot. Remove and dispose of any mummified fruits on the ground or still clinging to the branches in the fall. This year's mummies will carry next year's infections.
▷ **Orchards**

ARBORS

Placement is key. Tucked away in a secluded nook and sheltered by fragrant flowering vines, an arbor becomes a romantic hideaway. Set off by itself, it can accent the garden, offer an inviting destination, or command an imposing view. Arbors have utilitarian value as well. They provide shade in summer and serve as year-round screens for garden work areas as well.

A pergola is an arbor that you walk through. It can be a simple open framework or a series of arches that create a tunnel effect. Pergolas should have a focus— a destination, a view, or a path along a garden or across a lawn.

Design in proportion to the plantings your arbor will support. Anticipate the size of fully grown vines and climbers. Delicate latticework cannot support mature wisteria, while heavy timbers will dwarf a fragile clematis.

Check with a building inspector to make sure you'll be complying with local zoning codes and building regulations before you invest your time and money.

Use wood. The best woods for arbors and pergolas are redwood, cedar, cypress, teak,

oak, and locust. Use only heartwood, since sapwood will decompose rapidly.

Pressure-treated lumber is an inexpensive alternative that is useful when lumber must be in contact with soil. It tends to bow and split, however, and doesn't take stain well.

The right fasteners. Use rust-resistant fasteners made of brass, bronze, hot-dipped galvanized steel, or stainless steel. If your local hardware store doesn't stock them, try a marine supply store. Always predrill holes for nails, bolts, and screws to avoid splitting the wood.

Use waterproof glue on joints where extra strength is required. The new epoxy glues are extremely strong and will accept stains well. They are available at woodworking and marine supply stores.

Build with dimensional lumber—2 x 10, 2 x 8, 2 x 6, 2 x 4—for the upper framework of your arbor. Apply wood preservative and stain before construction to make sure the hidden areas in joints and intersections are protected. For tight, dry, long-lasting joints, clamp all the connections before you nail, screw, or bolt them.

To paint or not? After a few seasons, paint chips, blisters, and peels and has to be scraped, sanded, primed, and repainted. If you do paint, use an oil-base primer followed by latex or oil-base topcoats. Sand between coats for best adhesion. White or green is traditional for arbors, but you can duplicate the color of the trim on your house to create a unifying link between the house and garden.

Stains are better. Stains are easier to apply. They soak into and protect the wood, and they never blister or peel. Stains also enhance the wood's natural grain. For a weather-beaten, seashore appearance, use a bleaching stain; the wood will develop a silver-gray tone in 6 to 12 months. If you decide to use color, pigmented stains are a good substitute for paint and come in a wide assortment.

The natural look. Instead of painting or staining your arbor, simply apply plenty of preservative and allow the wood to weather naturally; it can be equally attractive.

Concrete piers. In areas with mild winters, tar the lower 2 to 3 feet of 4 x 4 posts and set them into concrete piers. The piers should protrude 3 or 4 inches aboveground to allow for drainage. In areas subject to heavy frosts, the footings, posts, and piers must be at least 3 feet deep to prevent the frost heaves that can upset the plumb and level of your structure.

Special metal spears, available at garden centers, make an easy job of setting posts—but are suitable only for moderate climates and relatively lightweight structures. Drive the spears into the ground with a sledgehammer. Leave the tops a few inches aboveground for proper drainage, then attach predrilled 4 x 4 posts.

Pave the area beneath your arbor with brick, flagstone, or gravel if the arbor casts dense shade. Grass cannot survive without sunlight.

Brick pillars project a formal ambience and can support heavy timbers. Scale your arbor or pergola accordingly. Be sure to provide a solid concrete footing.

Add lattice panels to your arbor to serve as trellis screens; simply cut them to size. Traditional arbor plants include clematis, jasmine, wisteria, climbing roses, ivy, and, of course, grapes—a favorite since the time of ancient Rome. Or you can hang baskets of flowering plants from your arbor. They not only add beauty and fragrance but also provide splashes of color to the arbor "walls."

▷ **Trellises**

ARCHITECTURAL PLANTS

The importance of shape in the garden

Think of your garden as an architect would a building—as a three-dimensional structure with line, scale, and texture—and of plants as the building blocks. For the framework you can choose from a vast array of "architectural plants"—hardy specimens with well-defined silhouettes that lend durable and dramatic form to the landscape in all seasons.

Such plants include trees, shrubs, and ornamental grasses, which come in myriad shapes depending on the growth habit of the stems and foliage. Whether standing alone or mixed in groups, distinctly sculptural plants can establish a boundary, minimize a defect, or provide an accent. Architectural plants can also set a tone: a symmetrical allée of upright arborvitae, for example, lends a formal look, while randomly placed stands of weeping cherries appear more relaxed.

Plant shapes can be used to achieve a variety of effects. In general, vertical forms, such as pyramids, columns, and upright ovals, are eye-catchers, drawing the design of the garden skyward. Horizontal forms, including spreading and umbrella shapes, act as anchors, linking the garden to the ground level.

Perhaps the most challenging—and rewarding—aspect of plant architecture is combining different shapes into a compatible grouping. Pairing strongly divergent profiles, such as a soaring pyramid and prostrate "fan," makes for dynamic contrast, whereas pairing related shapes, such as an egg and a globe or an umbrella and a bowl, results in a soft, harmonious design.

EGG-SHAPED, CONICAL, PYRAMIDAL

Little-leaf linden

European larch *Larix decidua*
False cypress *Chamaecyparis* spp.
Giant arborvitae *Thuja plicata*
Giant sequoia *Sequoiadendron giganteum*
Hybrid yew *Taxus* x *media* 'Hicksii'
Japanese cedar *Cryptomeria japonica*
Nordmann fir *Abies nordmanianna*
Spruce *Picea* spp.

Nordmann fir

Giant arborvitae

DECIDUOUS TREES
Alder *Alnus* spp.
Callery pear *Pyrus calleryana* 'Chanticleer'
English holly *Ilex aquifolium*
European hornbeam *Carpinus betulus*
Little-leaf linden *Tilia cordata* 'Greenspire'
Maidenhair tree *Ginkgo biloba*
Norway maple *Acer platanoides* 'Globosum'
Quaking aspen *Populus tremuloides*
Red maple *Acer rubrum* 'Pyramidale'
Scarlet oak *Quercis coccinea*
Silver linden *Tilia tomentosa*
Smooth-leaf elm *Ulmus carpinifolia* 'Dampieri'
Sweet gum *Liquidambar styraciflua*

CONIFERS
Arizona cypress *Cupressus arizonica* 'Conica'
Bald cypress *Taxodium distichum*
Dawn redwood *Metasequoia glyptostroboides*
Deodar cedar *Cedrus deodara*
Douglas fir *Pseudotsuga menziesii*
Eastern red cedar *Juniperus virginiana*

ORNAMENTAL GRASSES
Northern sea oats *Uniola latifolia* syn. *Chasmanthium latifolium*
Sand love grass *Eragrostis trichodes*

Maidenhair tree

TALL ROUNDED

DECIDUOUS TREES
Black walnut *Juglans nigra*
Box elder *Acer negundo*
Catalpa *Catalpa* spp.
Chestnut oak *Quercus prinus*
Chinese chestnut *Castanea mollissima*
Common horse chestnut *Aesculus hippocastanum*
Cucumber tree *Magnolia acuminata*
English oak *Quercus robur*
Flowering ash *Fraxinus ornus*
Linden *Tilia platyphyllos, Tilia x europaea*
London plane tree *Platanus x acerifolia*
Pin oak *Quercus palustris*
Shagbark hickory *Carya ovata*
Siberian elm *Ulmus pumila*
Silver maple *Acer saccharinum*
Sugar maple *Acer saccharum*
White willow *Salix alba*
Willow oak *Quercus phellos*

CONIFERS
Cedar of Lebanon *Cedrus libani*
Nootka false cypress *Chamaecyparis nootkatensis* 'Lutescens'

SHRUBS
Autumn olive *Elaeagnus umbellata*
Purple-leaved giant filbert *Corylus maxima* 'Purpurea'

Purple-leaved giant filbert

ORNAMENTAL GRASSES
Bottle brush grass *Hystrix patula*
Feather reed grass *Calamagrostis x acutiflora* 'Stricta'
Striped eulalia grass *Miscanthus sinensis* 'Variegatus'

London plane tree

COLUMNAR

DECIDUOUS TREES
Black locust *Robinia pseudoacacia* 'Pyramidalis'
English oak *Quercus robur* 'Fastigiata'
European beech *Fagus sylvatica* 'Dawyck'
European hornbeam *Carpinus betulus* 'Fastigiata'
European mountain ash *Sorbus aucuparia* 'Fastigiata'
European white birch *Betula pendula* 'Fastigiata'
Japanese flowering cherry *Prunus serrulata* 'Amanogawa'
Lombardy poplar *Populus nigra* 'Italica'
London plane tree *Platanus x acerifolia* 'Pyramidalis'
Norway maple *Acer platanoides* 'Columnare'
Sargent cherry *Prunus sargentii* 'Columnaris'
Silver maple *Acer saccharinum* 'Pyramidale'
Sugar maple *Acer saccharum* 'Columnare'
White poplar *Populus alba* 'Pyramidalis'

CONIFERS
California incense cedar *Calocedrus decurrens*
Common juniper *Juniperus communis* 'Compressa' and 'Hibernica'
Eastern arborvitae *Thuja occidentalis* 'Holmstrup' and 'Pyramidalis Compacta'

Lombardy poplar

Eastern red cedar *Juniperus virginiana* 'Glauca' and 'Skyrocket'
English yew *Taxus baccata* 'Fastigiata Aureomarginata'
Japanese cedar *Cryptomeria japonica* 'Cristata'
Italian cypress *Cupressus sempervirens*
Lawson false cypress *Chamaecyparis lawsoniana* 'Columnaris,' 'Lane,' and 'Witzeliana'
Monterey cypress *Cupressus macrocarpa* 'Fastigiata'
Norway spruce *Picea abies* 'Pyramidata'
Pond cypress *Taxodium ascendens* 'Nutans'
Scotch pine *Pinus sylvestris* 'Fastigiata'
Serbian spruce *Picea omorika*

SHRUBS
Nandina *Nandina domestica*
Tallhedge buckthorn *Rhamnus frangula* 'Columnaris'

ORNAMENTAL GRASSES
Giant Chinese silver grass *Miscanthus sinensis* 'Giganteus'
Ravenna grass *Erianthus ravennae*

Ravenna grass

ARCHITECTURAL PLANTS

ARCHITECTURAL PLANTS

GLOBULAR

DECIDUOUS TREES
Black locust *Robinia pseudoacacia* 'Umbraculifera'
European hornbeam *Carpus betulus* 'Globosa'
Red maple *Acer rubrum* 'Globosum'
Southern catalpa *Catalpa bignonoides* 'Nana'

CONIFERS
Colorado blue spruce *Picea pungens* 'Glauca Globosa'
Eastern arborvitae *Thuja occidentalis* 'Danica' and 'Gold King'
Eastern hemlock *Tsuga canadensis* 'Horsford', 'Gentsch's White Tip,' and 'Nana'
Swiss mountain pine *Pinus mugo* 'Mops' and 'Compacta'

Gold King arborvitae

SHRUBS
Crimson pygmy barberry *Berberis thunbergii* 'Crimson Pygmy'
Evergreen euonymus *Euonymus japonica* 'Albomarginata'
Japanese skimmia *Skimmia japonica*
Hybrid japanese holly *Ilex crenata* 'Compacta'

ORNAMENTAL GRASSES
Fountain grass *Pennisetum alopecuroides*
Large blue hair grass *Koelera glauca*
Pampas grass *Cortaderia selloana*

Black locust

UMBRELLA

DECIDUOUS TREES
Golden rain tree *Koelreuteria paniculata*
Kousa dogwood *Cornus kousa*
River birch *Betula nigra*

CONIFERS
Austrian pine *Pinus nigra*
Italian stone pine *Pinus pinea*
Scotch pine *Pinus sylvestris*

Italian stone pine

SHRUBS
Japanese witch hazel *Hamamelis japonica*

ORNAMENTAL GRASSES
Crimson fountain grass *Pennisetum setaceu*
Switch grass *Panicum virgatum*
Tufted hair grass *Deschampsia caespitosa*

Japanese witch hazel

WEEPING

Vanhoutte spirea

DECIDUOUS TREES
European weeping beech *Fagus sylvatica* 'Pendula'
European white birch *Betula pendula* 'Youngii'
Weeping golden chain tree *Laburnum subhirtella* 'Pendulum'
Weeping Higan cherry *Prunus subhirtella* 'Pendula' and 'Pendula Plena Rosea'
Weeping willow *Salix babylonica*, *Salix caprea* 'Pendula,' and *Salix alba* 'Tristis'

CONIFERS
Sargent weeping hemlock *Tsuga canadensis* 'Pendula'
Weeping blue Atlas cedar *Cedrus atlantica* 'Glauca Pendula'

Weeping Norway spruce *Picea abies* 'Inversa'
Weeping white pine *Pinus strobos* 'Pendula'

SHRUBS
Drooping leucothoe *Leucothoe fontanesiana*
Fountain buddelia *Buddleia alternifolia*
Vanhoutte spirea *Spiraea vanhouttei*

ORNAMENTAL GRASSES
Cord grass *Spartina pectina* 'Aureomarginata'
Maiden grass *Miscanthus sinensis* 'Gracillimus'
Moor grass *Molinia caerulea*

European weeping beech

MULTIBRANCHED

DECIDUOUS TREES
Cornelian cherry *Cornus mas*
Downy serviceberry *Amelanchier arborea*
Eastern redbud *Cercis canadensis*
European hornbeam *Carpinus betulus*
Full moon maple *Acer japonicum*
Gray birch *Betula populifolia*
Japanese maple *Acer palmatum* 'Senkaki'
Katsura tree *Cercidiphyllum japonicum*

Common crape myrtle

CONIFERS
Tanyosho pine *Pinus densiflora* 'Umbraculifera'
Swiss mountain pine *Pinus mugo*
Lacebark pine *Pinus bungeana*
Shore pine *Pinus contorta*
Japanese umbrella pine *Sciadopitys verticillata*

Japanese maple

SHRUBS
Common crape myrtle *Lagerstroemia indica*
Shadblow serviceberry *Amelanchier canadensis*

ORNAMENTAL GRASSES
Chino bamboo *Pleioblastus chino vaginata variegata*
Blue fountain bamboo *Sinarundinaria nitida*
Viridi bamboo *Arundinaria viridi-striata*

SPREADING OR CREEPING

DECIDUOUS TREES
Amur maple *Acer ginnala*
Common fig *Ficus carica*
Eastern redbud *Cercis canadensis*
Mimosa *Albizia julibrissin*
Oyama magnolia *Magnolia sieboldii*

Sargent flowering cherry *Prunus sargentii*
Saucer magnolia *Magnolia x soulangiana*
Siberian crab apple *Malus baccata*

CONIFERS
English yew *Taxus baccata* 'Repandens'
Norway spruce *Picea abies* 'Repens'
Russian arborvitae *Microbiota decussata*
Tanyosho pine *Pinus densiflora* 'Umbraculifera'

SHRUBS
Sweetfern *Comptonia pergrina*
Winter jasmine *Jasminum nudiflorum*

ORNAMENTAL GRASSES
Blue lyme grass *Elymus racemosus* 'Glaucus'
Ribbon grass *Phalaris arundinacea* var. *picta*

Common fig

UNUSUAL AND PICTURESQUE

Some architectural plants have contorted shapes or foliage so exceptional that they cannot easily be categorized.

Cut-leaf Japanese maple

DECIDUOUS TREES
Babylon weeping willow *Salix babylonica* 'Crispa'
  Weeping branches that sweep the ground
Black locust *Robinia pseudo-acacia* 'Tortulosa' Twisted branches, corkscrew shoots
Cut-leaf Japanese maple *Acer palmatum* 'Dissectum'
  Contorted branches
Dragon's claw willow *Salix matsudana* 'Tortulosa'
  Large, spirally twisted twigs
Strawberry tree *Arbutus unedo*
  Twisted branches and trunk

CONIFERS
Blue Atlas cedar *Cedrus atlantica* 'Glauca'
  Branches with silver-blue foliage arranged very irregularly from trunk
Hollywood juniper *Juiperus chinensis* 'Kaizuka'
  Small tree with divergent and irregular branches
Japanese white pine *Pinus parviflora*
  Bundles of needles on upper side of branches only; grows as wide as high
Monkey puzzle tree *Araucaria araucana*
  Twisted branches covered with scalelike leaves

SHRUBS
Black pussy willow *Salix melanostachys*
  Catkins are deep purple-black
Harry Lauder's walking stick *Corylus avellana* 'Contorta'
  Twisted branches

ORNAMENTAL GRASSES
Blue fescue *Festuca ovina* 'Glauca'
  Sky-blue foliage
Golden grass *Hakonechloa macra* 'Aureola'
  Bright yellow foliage
Zebra grass *Miscanthus sinensis* 'Zebrina'
  Yellow horizontal band on leaves

Monkey puzzle tree

ARCHITECTURAL PLANTS

ARTICHOKES

The hard truth. Artichokes usually take more than 150 days to mature from seed and are highly sensitive to extremes of hot and cold. Coastal areas where temperatures don't fall much below 10°F and rarely go above 75°F are the best places to grow them. In areas with cool summers and deadly winters, however, you can grow artichokes as annuals—and take your chances.

To grow artichokes as annuals, soak the seeds for 2 days at the end of January, then mix with moist sphagnum moss. Refrigerate for 4 weeks in an unsealed plastic bag. When roots emerge, pot the clumps in 6-inch plastic pots of sterilized potting soil and place in a cool but sunny window. Two weeks or so before the predicted date of the last frost, harden off the seedlings by setting them outdoors in a cool but frost-free spot during the day. Plant in well-dug soil, spacing 3 feet apart, when all danger of frost has passed.

For tender artichokes, speed the growth of the buds by keeping the plants well watered. Mulch with compost or peat moss and work some well-rotted manure into the soil.

If you grow them as perennials, get ready for winter by cutting off the large outer leaves and tying the center leaves together. Wrap in butcher paper and pile up sand, sawdust, or dead leaves as a protective screen against frost.

Keep artichokes fresh by arranging them like flowers. Place them in a large vase with the heads up and the stalks submerged in water.
▷ **Vegetable Gardens**

☙ AN ARTICHOKE SAMPLER ❧

New hybrids that are grown as annuals considerably shorten the time from germination to harvest. 'Imperial Star' matures 85 to 100 days after transplanting—about 80 days faster than the older 'Green Globe.' Another hybrid, called 'Violetta,' was developed for hardiness and has a lovely violet color.

ASH

Train to a single trunk. Ashes tend to grow double trunks that are liable to split apart at maturity. If two upright shoots sprout from the top of a young ash, prune off one of the shoots to keep the tree single-trunked and strong.

The winged fruit of ash trees can create a mess in the yard. To minimize the production of seed, don't mix male plants with female plants. Or try one of the new seedless clones: the white ashes 'Autumn Purple' and 'Rosehill' or the green ashes 'Emerald,' 'Newport,' or 'Summit.'

A fast grower. A compact green ash—*Fraxinus pennsylvanica lanceolata*—grows at about 1½ feet a year until it tops out at 50 to 60 feet. It's also one of the most adaptable garden trees, thriving even in nutrient-poor soils.

A tree for all seasons. The flowering ash (*F. ornus*) bears clusters of fragrant white flowers in late spring. In autumn the leaves turn soft yellow and lavender before falling, and in winter appears the appealing texture of smooth gray bark.
▷ **Trees**

ASHES

Ward off slugs and snails by encircling your plants with a ring of ashes about 6 inches out from the stem. The soft-bodied creatures will turn the other way.

Your fireplace is a built-in source of garden fertilizer. Use the potash-rich ashes for most vegetables and flowers—except for acid lovers like azaleas and heathers.

Keep them dry. Store wood ashes in plastic garbage cans or heavy trash bags. Many of their nutrients—including potassium, phosphorus, and calcium—degrade rapidly when the ashes are moist.

Make soil less acid by simply digging in wood ashes, which are strongly alkaline.

Fertilize with ashes a week or so before you plant. Spread 5 to 10 pounds of ash per 100 square feet over freshly cultivated soil or in furrows. Hoe in lightly. Don't mix ashes with manure or other nitrogenous materials, except for those already in the soil.

Heap a mound of wood ashes around the stumps of fragile plants like rhubarb, hardy fuchsias, and ferns to protect them in the winter. Rain effectively leaches nutrients from ash and supplies it to the root systems of the plants.

Don't add briquette ashes to compost! Chemicals make ashes from your barbecue off-limits, but wood ashes are fine.

Country gardeners who keep poultry can provide them with an ash bath. Birds flutter in ashes to get rid of parasites. Put the ashes in a crate and place it where it will stay dry. Change the ashes regularly.

An economical warmer. Shovel still-warm ashes into a covered metal container and place in the center of a cold frame. The ashes will radiate heat for about 24 hours.

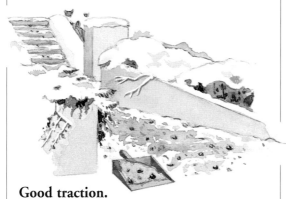

Good traction.
Spread ashes on icy walkways to provide traction; both wood ashes and coal ashes will work. But avoid salt—it can be harmful to the roots of nearby plants.
™ **Potassium**

ASPARAGUS

How much to plant? Put in about 25 asparagus roots for each member of your family—more if you'll be canning. Allow 25 feet of row for every 12 plants, with the rows spaced 4 to 5 feet apart.

If you can't plant immediately, keep the roots covered with damp sand or cloth.

A bleach bath. If you're not sure the roots you've bought have been disinfected, soak them for 15 minutes in a solution of 1 part household bleach to 3 parts water. Give them a good wash before planting to prevent crown gall.

The right depth. Plant each root about 8 inches deep—just enough for the crowns to be covered with an inch or two of soil. Place them 18 inches apart in the rows.

A bounty for years. Properly planted and maintained, an asparagus bed will yield a harvest for 20 years or longer. Just make sure the soil is rich in organic matter.

A mini compost pile. Mulch your asparagus bed every fall and spring to maintain a continuous 4- to 6-inch cover. Your autumn addition should include a 2- to 3-inch layer of manure as well. Not only will you keep weeds away and conserve

---

? AN ASPARAGUS SAMPLER ç

When it comes to asparagus, it's a battle of the sexes. Not surprisingly, two of the old open-pollinated varieties, 'Mary Washington' and 'Martha Washington,' are female. But many new hybrids are males, which are more productive, channeling energy into spear growth instead of the seeding that inhibits yields.

To make sure your plants are male, use 'Jersey Giant,' 'Jersey General,' 'Jersey Knight,' or other all-male Jersey hybrids. Another reliable hybrid is the productive 'UC 157.'

---

moisture, but you'll build a compost pile right on top of the dormant crowns, assuring your crop a long and productive life.

Mulches to avoid. Don't use sawdust or bark, both of which are too acid. Asparagus likes a soil near neutral, or pH 6.5.

No need to wait. Despite what you've heard, you don't have to wait until the second or third year to pick asparagus. The initial harvest should be limited to 2 to 3 weeks; add an extra week each year until the harvest is 4 to 6 weeks. Whatever the time period, stop harvesting when the average size of the spears declines to about the diameter of a pencil.

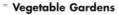

Cut off the tops in fall to prevent pests from overwintering. The lacy ferns become yellow-gold in autumn and are perfect for floral arrangements.
™ **Vegetable Gardens**

ASPEN

The quaking aspen, with its brilliant golden leaves, is the most commonly grown type. But don't overlook two equally colorful trees: the Swedish aspen, which shares the columnar shape of its Lombardy poplar cousin, and the large-toothed aspen, whose spreading crown of autumn leaves turns shades of yellow, red, and orange in fall.

A short life. Aspens can grow to 60 feet, but their life span is a mere 20 to 25 years.

Site with care. The roots of aspen are invasive and produce suckers. Don't plant the trees near sidewalks, sewers, or septic tanks.

Get rid of new suckers in the lawn by simply mowing over them. Larger suckers need to be undercut with a shovel or hoe.

A common pest. Look for the tiny, pale "crawlers" of oystershell scale insects. These newly hatched, pinhead-size pests attach themselves to the bark of aspens and suck enough sap to kill a tree. Control by treating trunks with a dormant oil in winter. If eggs hatch, spray with malathion immediately, before the pests' waxy covering makes them impermeable to insecticides.

▷ **Poplar, Trees**

AVOCADOS

OUTDOORS

The climate you need. Frost-free weather is essential for growing edible avocados. In the continental United States, the only places you can grow edible fruit are Florida and parts of southern California.

A warning. Commercial avocado trees are propagated by grafting to insure uniformity. Planted in your garden, the pits of their fruits will not come true to type, and your avocados will be of inferior quality.

Choose a self-fertile hybrid if you're planting only one or two trees. Nonhybrid avocados require cross-pollination, so commercial growers plant different varieties. You can achieve the same result by grafting several varieties onto one plant.

The three main strains. Mexican avocados can survive cool weather, Guatemalan types like it hot, and West Indian types need a subtropical environment to thrive.

Planting tips. If your soil is heavy, try not to compress the earth around the edges of the hole. Digging with a fork instead of a spade can help. Cushion the plant on a raised mound. Don't soak the shallow roots; instead, water lightly and frequently.

INDOORS

A houseplant for free. Select an unblemished fruit. Remove the pit and wash it clean (there's no need to remove the seed coat). Plant in a 4- or 5-inch pot with a drainage hole, laying the pit on its side and almost burying it in porous soil. Water and store at 60° to 70°F until germination starts—in 1 to 6 months.

Another way to start avocados. Insert three toothpicks around the pit just above the base. Suspend over water with the base immersed. Change the water frequently and keep the level constant. Wait several weeks until the pit sends out a shoot and roots, then pot it. For a bushier plant, pinch off the tip of the shoot after it grows to about 6 inches.

Place in a sunny spot away from heat or drafts. If growth is too tall, pinch the leads after the first flush of growth. Fertilize regularly with diluted liquid fertilizer or use a slow-release brand at longer intervals.

Time to water. When the soil begins to dry out, water until the dish under the pot starts to fill. If roots begin to grow through the bottom of the pot, move your plant to a larger container.

Potted avocados can summer outdoors at temperatures above 60°F. But let the plant acclimatize gradually to prevent sunburn.

Troubleshooting. Aphids and mealybugs like the new growing tips of avocado plants. Wash off aphids with a heavy stream of water. Remove mealybugs with a cotton swab dipped in rubbing alcohol.

▷ **Grafting**

AZALEAS

Moderation in all things. Remember that azaleas and the other rhododendrons respond best to moderation in all aspects of cultivation: moderate light, moderate water, and moderate pruning.

PLANTING

Azaleas do best in mixed sunlight and partial shade but will blossom in full sunlight.

Some prerequisites for success. Good drainage, acid soil, and plenty of organic matter are essential. To ensure proper soil conditions—especially in heavy clay soils—plant azaleas in raised beds. Alternatively, place the plant directly on a spaded-up surface, then mound up three or four wheelbarrows of a humus-soil mixture around and over the root ball.

Don't fertilize when planting! The common practice of putting fertilizer directly in the bottom of a planting hole can be fatal to azaleas. Wait until the plant is established before you start feeding it.

The proper humus. Use decayed bark or sawdust for humus. Don't use hardwood or fresh pine, which deplete soil nutrients.

Open the root ball and spread it slightly before planting. When planting from containers, mutilate the root ball by cutting or teasing it out. This will encourage the development of new roots.

Adjust soil acidity. A pH between 4.5 and 6 is necessary; 5.0 is ideal. If the soil is too acid, correct with dolomitic limestone. If too alkaline, add iron sulfate or sulfur (don't use aluminum sulfate). Epsom salts can also be used to increase acidity. Scatter on soil at 1 pound per 300 square feet.

Mulch well. Azaleas like a 2-inch mulch of wood chips, pine needles, bark chips, salt

The striking flowers of Kurume hybrid azaleas are complemented here by delicate Spanish bluebells.

hay, or oak leaves to keep roots cool and moist. But don't use peat moss; it seals in water and can promote root rot.

MAINTENANCE

Fertilize sparingly. Azaleas often fall victim to too much fertilizer. For a good homemade fertilizer, combine 4 cups of dried coffee grounds with 1 cup bone meal and 1 cup granite dust.

For rapid growth and dark green leaves, apply nitrogen in spring and early summer. Good sources are cottonseed meal, ammonium sulfate, manure tea, and urea formaldehyde.

Adequate moisture is critical for azaleas until they become established—at least 2 years after planting. Once mature, they can survive drought, although they're more susceptible to disease, insects, and cold. Wilted leaves are a sign of drought stress; water with a deep soaking.

Ease up your watering in the autumn. Watering induces new growth, which may not harden off before the first freeze.

Prune young plants lightly after they flower to promote lateral branching and a compact form. Remove larger branches from the interior of older plants to allow light in; sunlight inhibits disease. Cut away dead or diseased wood below the infected area.

Rejuvenate old plants by cutting the entire plant back to 6 to 8 inches from the ground. Or prune over a 3-year period, cutting back a third of the branches each year. Prune in early spring, before new growth starts.

Disinfect tools thoroughly with alcohol or household bleach before and after using. And always complete pruning by early summer to avoid injuring flower buds.

Relocations. If an azalea outgrows its site, relocate it. Because of their shallow and fibrous roots, azaleas and other rhododendrons are among the easiest plants to move.

Signs of infection. Root rot and phytophthora are common fungus diseases of azaleas. Look for discolored stem tissue, branch dieback, and wilted foliage.

To rout fungus disease, cut out and burn diseased wood and spray the plant with a recommended fungicide. Sterilize the cutting tools afterward.

Insect pests. Yellowish speckling of upper leaf surfaces and black spots on the undersides indicate the presence of lace bugs or thrips. Get rid of them with an insecticidal soap spray or systemic insecticide. For whiteflies, use pyrethrum.

🐦 AN AZALEA SAMPLER 🐦

Botanically speaking, azaleas are rhododendrons. In the past, those plants called azaleas were deciduous, while rhododendrons were those that held their leaves through the winter. Today there are both evergreen and deciduous hybrid azaleas, as well as older standard deciduous species, so the lines are less precise.

EVERGREEN HYBRIDS

including Kurume and Southern India types
'Delaware Valley White'
'Gumpo Pink'
'Hino Crimson'
'Hot Shot' (orange)

DECIDUOUS HYBRIDS

including Ghent, Exbury, and Ilam types
'Brazil' (orange-red)
'Flamingo' (deep pink blotched with orange)
'Gibraltar' (burnt orange)
'Pasil' (white blotched with yellow)

DECIDUOUS STANDARDS

Flame azalea (orange, yellow, or red-orange)
Piedmont azalea (pink or white)
Pinkster azalea (white to light pink)
Royal azalea (pale pink; yellow and crimson fall foliage)

▷ **Rhododendrons, Shrubs**

BALCONY GARDENS

Before you build on your balcony, be sure you receive approval from your co-op board, tenants' group, local landmarks commission, or other authority. If your plan includes large potted trees or raised planted beds, you must find out the exact acceptable load limits of your rooftop or balcony and not exceed them.

More privacy. A row of thick, sturdy evergreens like arborvitae creates a year-round natural windbreak and doubles as a privacy screen. Another simple windbreak can be achieved by stretching canvas, burlap, or nylon tautly across an existing fence or railing.

Growing vegetables in containers on a balcony requires plenty of sunlight— usually 6 hours or more a day. What you choose to plant should depend in large part on your balcony's orientation to the sun. Tomatoes and beans thrive on a warm, light-filled balcony facing south or west. Lettuces and root vegetables do well on balconies having northern and eastern orientations, which get limited daily sunlight.

Outdoor rooms can be created by combining hanging plants with a row of potted shrubs to make a green wall. If you use climbers on a trellis as a windbreak, remember to secure them tightly to resist wind shear.

Place wood decking on a concrete surface for a user-friendly balcony floor. Wood won't transmit temperature extremes as concrete and tar do. A wooden deck stays cool in the hot months and helps insulate plants from the radiant heat reflected off floor surfaces; it's easy on bare feet as well. Decking will also help protect rooftop surfaces from day-to-day wear and tear.

Properly built decking will dry quickly after a hard rain or after watering plants. Position boards closely, using a tenpenny nailhead as a spacer. The spaces will allow for adequate drainage, yet won't trap shoe heels or furniture legs.

For durable planters with rustic charm, use halved whiskey barrels. These are inexpensive and available at garden centers and nurseries. Be sure to drill several holes in the bottom and fill the first few inches with a gravel-sand mixture to ensure proper drainage.

Winterizing. If pots of clay, terra-cotta, or stone are to winter out on your balcony, be sure to set them on wood blocks and cover them with a large plastic bag. This will prevent the frost heaves and water penetration that can crack and destroy your pot or urn. Fill the bag with a good helping of straw, plastic packing peanuts, sawdust, or leaves to insulate both the plant roots and pot from temperature swings.

Save branches from your discarded Christmas tree to shelter small perennials, bulbs, or dwarf shrubs on your balcony from winter exposure. For climbing plants, protect with a straw mat or a winterizing cloth.
▷ **City Gardens, Dwarfs, Planters**

BAMBOO

The giant grass. Bamboos are not trees or bushes—they are grasses and grow as such. A shoot, or culm, forms in spring and reaches its mature height and thickness in the first year, although it will continue to branch out and add more foliage. If the plant is adequately watered and fed, each year's new culms will generally be bigger and taller than the previous year's.

PLANTING

Ensure success by planting container-grown specimens that won't risk transplant shock. Even though healthy plants are usually marked by sturdy, well-colored leaves, remember that you are really buying the roots, or rhizomes, where the future of the plant lies. As long as there are fresh young culms, the plant will grow and do well.

Choose a sunny spot, sheltered from the wind if possible, in a rich soil that holds moisture. Don't plant bamboo in a water-logged or boggy area or the roots will rot.

For a dramatic landscape feature, plant bamboo in the corner of a courtyard, along a walkway, as a backdrop to other plants, or as an exotic-looking hedge or screen.

Give it space. This shallow-rooted plant needs room to spread out. Start with a hole twice the size of the root ball. In clay soil, dig an even larger area to loosen the soil. Soak the hole with water and let it drain before planting the root ball. Backfill the hole with compost, well-rotted manure, or some aged manure. Soak again; finish backfilling the hole. The resulting mound should be slightly scooped and dish-shaped on top. Mulch. Water daily to ensure a good start and lessen transplant shock.

MAINTENANCE

Mulch, mulch, mulch! A good mulching aids in water retention, giving bamboo more top growth. Spread nitrogren-rich grass clippings around the plant in spring and summer. In the fall, spread a thick layer of leaves around the base of the plant to protect the shallow rhizomes from freezing. Use soaker hoses or drip irrigation to provide adequate moisture throughout the growing season.

Winterizing your plants. Bamboo dies back in cold Northern climates, where freezing can last from 1 to 3 months. But if you keep the roots well mulched, the plant will send up new foliage in the spring. In winter, don't worry about a heavy layer of snow—it is an effective insulator and will keep the plant from drying out over the winter. The bamboo shoots will spring up again as soon as the weather grows warm and the snow melts.

Bamboo is a heavy feeder. Nutrient-rich compost and manure are the best fertilizers for bamboo, providing the valuable humus that also helps the soil retain water. In the spring, a handful of lawn fertilizer high in nitrogen is an excellent addition around each plant; just make sure not to use the weed-and-feed type. Sprinkle a handful of fertilizer after each rain until the new culms start to appear, and then don't fertilize again until the culms reach their full height and the branches and foliage are fully extended. At this point, a more balanced fertilizer is preferable. In early autumn, stop fertilizing altogether to allow the plant to harden off before winter sets in.

✥ GOOD CHOICES FOR THE GARDEN ✥

SMALL BAMBOOS	Description	Height	Diameter	Min. Temp.
Pleioblastus chino vaginata variegata 'Chino'	Variegated leaves; delicate	3'–6'	½"	−10°F
Pleioblastus pygmaea 'Pygmy'	Quick growing; dense	2'	⅛"	−10°F
Indocalamus tessellatus 'Tessellata'	Shade lover; largest leaves	4'–7'	½"	−5°F
Pleioblastus viridistratus 'Viridi'	Striped 2"x8" leaves	3'–8'	¼"	−10°F
MID-SIZED BAMBOOS				
Phyllostachys aurea 'Golden'	"Fishing pole" type; golden	10'–25'	2"	10°F
Phyllostachys bissetii 'Bissetii'	Hardy; dense foliage	12'–24'	1"–2"	−20°F
Psuedosasa japonica 'Arrow'	Cascading leaves; hardy; tropical look	8'–18'	¾"	−10°F
Phyllostachys aureosulcata 'Yellowgroove'	Grows anywhere, very hardy	16'	1¾"	−20°F
Phyllostachys flesuosa 'Zig-Zag'	Extremely hardy; flexible culms	20'–30'	2"	−10°F
GIANT OR TIMBER BAMBOOS				
Phyllostachys bambusoides 'Japanese Timber'	Sturdy culms for building and crafts	50'–60'	6"	0°F
Phyllostachys heterocyla pubescens 'Moso'	Largest; hardy; tasty shoots	60'	5"–7"	0°F
Phyllostachys nigra henonis 'Henon'	Small leaves; delicate look	24'–40'	3"–5"	−10°F
Phyllostachys vivax 'Vivax'	Hardiest giant; large leaves	24'–40'	5"	−10°F

Runaway bamboo. Unlike well-mannered clump bamboos, the invasive running types spread rapidly underground in search of food and water. Stop the sprawl one of three ways. One strategy is simply to encourage your plants to stay put by continually feeding and watering them. Another solution: in late summer, take a spade and sever any rhizomes the plant is sending out. Or you can contain the roots by erecting an impregnable barrier (polypropylene plastic, fiberglass panels, or rubber belting) set in a 16- to 20-inch trench. When the rhizomes reach the barrier and try to cross it, sever them or redirect them back inside.

Increase your grove by propagation. For clump bamboos, divide plants carefully into quarters or thirds. For the running types, take root cuttings of the outer rhizomes with their new shoots. Trans-plant immediately—without letting the roots dry out—at a depth identical with the parent plant. And be patient: small bamboos take 3 to 5 years of cultivation to reach full size, while the giants can take 10 to 12.

Pest free. Bamboos are seldom troubled by insects. If you do find scale or other sucking pests on your plants, cut and burn the infested stalks or spray with an insecticide.
▷ **Ornamental Grasses**

BANANA

Not a tree at all, the banana plant is in reality a perennial herb. In fact, the trunk of the plant is not a woody stem but actually scores of overlapping leaf stalks.

Grow bananas from divisions. To propagate bananas, first get a clean cutting from a friend or buy a growing plant from a nursery, making sure the soil the plant came from isn't contaminated with fusarium wilt. Cut a shoot, or rhizome, and divide it so that a growing shoot and part of the root and its rootlets remain intact. Gently separate so as not to injure or break off the growing point. Air-dry new divisions for a day to seal the fresh cut and prevent rot.

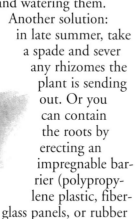

Bananas do well only in the hottest parts of the Southeast and at protected sites along the Pacific coast. They prosper in a very warm (80° to 85°F), humid environment in well-drained soil with full sun or partial shade and little wind. Thus they are a rarity outdoors in most of North America.

Dwarf bananas can be grown in containers in an indoor solarium or, in hot and humid areas, outside in a courtyard. The plants average between 5 and 7 feet high.

Containers for bananas should be at least 2 feet across. Water the plant frequently and fertilize heavily once a week with a solution high in nitrogen and potassium; the soil should have a pH around 6. Keep outdoor plants sheltered so that drying winds won't shred the large, tender leaves.

Bearing fruit. Allow only one stalk to grow the first year. Then limit the plant to three or four shoots. The oldest shoot should set fruit in 1 to 3 years. The fruiting stalk will eventually die; remove it after harvesting your bananas to let another shoot become dominant.

Pick before ripe! The taste and quality of bananas suffer measurably when they ripen on the tree. Harvest when still green —after 80 to 120 days of growth—and ripen in a warm spot (above 60°F).

Watch out for mealybugs, one of the few insects that bother bananas.

BARBECUES

Add real wood-smoke flavor to foods cooked on your gas grill with a handful of green twigs from garden trees or herbs. Toss them onto the fire just before you start barbecuing. Apple, cherry, and hickory twigs work well, and rosemary, sage, tarragon, bay, and thyme clippings add a special flavor; only use plants that haven't been sprayed with insecticide.

A temporary grill— one suitable for the needs of a single family—is easily built by stacking a few cinder blocks or bricks in parallel rows 1 foot high and 18 inches apart. Simply set your grill on a pair of steel rods laid across the blocks, ignite the charcoal, and enjoy your outdoor meal!

When building a permanent grill, the choice of location is important. Don't put it so close to the house that smoke wafts in through the doors or windows. Set the grill in a quiet corner of the landscape and make it accessible to the kitchen by a level paved path that makes it easier to bring food and supplies out on a butler's table or a cart.

If you use bricks to build a barbecue, make sure they have been fired at a high temperature. A test: when hit by a hammer, well-fired bricks make a ringing sound.

Stone gives a rustic look to a barbecue. Sandstone is an excellent choice because it withstands heat well. If you want to use other stones, be aware that limestone, basalt, shale, and granite may disintegrate when exposed to heat; line the firebox with bricks to protect these vulnerable stones.

Don't be stingy when you buy a portable barbecue. Constant exposure to the elements quickly wears down bargain sets.

Ignite charcoal without lighter fluid. Punch holes around the lower edge of a coffee can (2 pound capacity), then remove both ends of the can. Set the sleeve in the center of the grill and place a layer of crumpled newspaper inside. Fill the rest of the can with charcoal and light the paper through the punched holes. The can will act as a flue to draw flame up through the charcoal. When the coals are aglow, lift the sleeve with tongs, leaving the coals behind.

Coals are ready when they turn gray. To determine the medium heat you need for most barbecuing, place your hand about 5 inches above the surface of the coals and see how long you can hold it there. Five to 6 seconds means a low fire; 3 to 4 seconds means a medium fire; and 1 to 2 seconds is a sign the fire is too hot.

After cooking, it's a good idea to sprinkle the embers with salt—which will prevent the fire from flaring up again.

Smoke in your eyes is one of the least pleasant parts of a barbecue, and a fire fanned by the wind burns unevenly. Place your grill so that is is protected from the prevailing wind. A semipermeable windbreak such a hedge is far more effective than a solid fence or wall, which actually increases air turbulence on the downwind side. Just make sure you keep the grill at a safe distance from anything flammable.

Keep the grate clean of ashes. When rainwater mixes with charcoal ashes, they form lye, a powerful iron-corroding solution.
▷ **Patios**

BARBERRY

A hardy plant. Barberry is a tough, ironclad shrub that thrives in almost any type of soil as long as it is not kept constantly wet. The varieties with the most colorful foliage develop best in full sunlight, but many other barberries will develop quite nicely in full or partial shade.

The barberry culitvar 'Aurea' takes pride of place in this massing of dwarf conifers and hemlock.

Enjoy season-long color by planting one of the many Japanese-bred barberries, which range from the striking yellow foliage of 'Aurea' to vivid purple varieties.

No need to prune. Apart from the rare branchlet that grows astray, Japanese barberry naturally produces a near-perfect dome of dense branches.

Site thorny varieties away from paths and doors. They snare practically everything in their midst, including clothing, tree leaves, and trash. On the other hand, barberries make good barrier hedges and are among the best natural deterrents to hungry deer.
▷ **Knot Gardens, Shrubs**

BARK

Enhance your yard with beautiful barks. Placed separately or grouped together, trees like golden willows, paper birches, and red- and yellow-twig dogwoods add color and texture to any yard or garden year round.

Bramble bushes are notable for their decorative bark. Two to try are *Rubus cockburnianus,* which has lovely white and bluish branches in winter, or the cultivar *R. thibetanus* 'Silver Fern,' with off-white stalks. In summer, cut the branches at the bottom just before they flower to ensure that they renew themselves the following spring.

Protect young bark from rodents, sunscald, and weather extremes by carefully wrapping the lower trunk with the breathable tree wrap sold at garden centers.

Don't repair a tree whose bark has been torn off by painting the exposed area with orange shellac or an iron sulfate-based solution. Most trees can heal themselves.

The pocked white bark of the paper birch—also called the canoe birch—is the tree's most eye-catching feature.

Lawn mowers and weed cutters are the common enemies of bark. Put a sleeved protector at the base of tree trunks when you mow. These corrugated plastic guards can be bought at garden stores.

Mulch sparingly around the trunk. Too much mulch keeps a tree trunk too moist and makes it overly susceptible to problems like root rot, burrowing pests, and diseases such as canker.

Rabbits and other rodents often nibble on bark while hidden by the vegetation underneath trees. Protect the bark by wrapping a fine-meshed screen around the base of the trunk.

Bark mulch. The bark of coniferous trees makes superb mulching material. Adding nitrogen fertilizer to the mulch facilitates the decomposition of the bark.

Natural pest control. Ornamental pine bark mulch repels destructive garden slugs.

A flavor enhancer. Barbecue steaks over pieces of shagbark hickory bark to give the meat a deliciously rich, smoky flavor.
▷ **Mulch**

BASIL

Sow seeds in March or April in a standard starter mix with 85 percent peat or a combination of 1 part compost to 1 part sand. Cover the flat with a piece of glass; it will act as a mini greenhouse, providing the high temperatures that basil seeds need to germinate quickly.

Don't rush to plant basil outdoors during the first spell of warm weather. This acutely cold-sensitive plant dislikes any temperatures that drop below 45°F.

The secret of long production. Pinching back the shoots ensures the growth of bushy, long-producing basil. Pinch plants just above the point where two side branches leave the stem. Don't allow flowers to develop; they sap energy from the plant's leaves. Flowers and seeds should be encouraged only when propagating next year's plants.

Plant basil close to tomatoes. Folklore says these companion plants encourage better, stronger growth in each other.

Basil year round. Basil steeped in olive oil is a delicious year-round addition to sauces and soups. For more flavor, layer the leaves and oil in a container with dried tomatoes and top with a clove of garlic.

Frozen cubes. Another way to savor basil year round is to harvest the leaves before flowers develop, wash, and chop in a food processor. Pack them into an ice-cube tray, add water or olive oil, and put in the freezer. When using a recipe that calls for fresh basil, pop a cube from the freezer and add. Or simply make fresh pesto and freeze it in ice-cube trays for winter use.

⊰ A BASIL SAMPLER ⊱

'Sweet Genovese' is a favorite variety. But don't overlook the other types. 'Opal' and 'Purple Ruffles' have attractive purple leaves, and cinnamon basil and lemon basil are delicately scented. Note that lemon basil must be sown directly; it doesn't transplant well.

▷ **Herbs**

BAY TREES

The aromatic leaves of *Laurus nobilis*—commonly called bay laurel or sweet bay—impart a distinctive and unique flavor to stews and soups. Bay laurel also makes an excellent patio container plant. In harsh winter climates, bring it indoors.

Don't dry! Fresh bay leaves have better flavor than dried leaves. When harvesting a leaf, don't snip; pull it downward to break it off cleanly.

Bay as topiary. Clip your tree into a perfect ball or pyramid. Trim plants with pruning shears instead of hedge clippers, which will noticeably mutilate the foliage.

California bay has a much harsher taste than bay laurel and is better used for decorative rather than culinary purposes.
▷ **Laurel, Pruning**

BEANS

Beans like it hot. Sow bean plants only when the soil is very warm. Try this toe-tingling test: the soil is ready when you can walk barefoot in it without feeling the cold.

A pink alert. A chemical odor and a color on bean seeds—usually pink but sometimes blue or dusty white—lets you know they've been treated with a fungicide. Don't let children eat or handle them, and wash your hands after you've finished sowing the seeds. Better still, wear latex gloves.

The secret of long production. Beans like company. If you take their pods away, they feel obliged to make more flowers—and thus more beans. Once in production, pole beans should be harvested every 2 days. This is less true for bush beans, which prefer to be picked only once or twice a week.

Harvest beans young for maximum flavor and minimum toughness. Pick moist green pods that are tender and slightly filled out. Unless you're growing shelling beans, don't leave dried-out pods on the vines; they reduce the plant's production of new beans.

Never pick snap beans that are wet from dew or rain. Jostling a wet plant can spread the spores that cause one of the many mildews and blights that attack beans.

Enrich the soil for next year's crop. At the end of the season, cut off the foliage at ground level and leave the nitrogen-rich roots in the ground. Don't forget to rotate your vegetable crops annually to foil any diseases that are building up in the soil.

Enjoy fresh-tasting beans all winter. Parboil just-picked beans in boiling water for 2 minutes. Drain and run under cold water. Place in small freezer bags. The frozen beans will keep nicely until the next harvest. When ready to cook, simply prepare as you would fresh beans.

Keep shelling beans like great northerns and pintos on the plant until the foliage begins to wither. Then harvest whole plants and hang upside down in a warm place.

A dry bean test. Test dried beans for quality by biting a piece of this "poor man's meat." If it breaks cleanly, it is old and will be hard when cooked. If it gives way easily, it will be tender and tasty.
▷ **Bush Beans, Pole Beans, Vegetable Gardens**

BEDDING PLANTS

Bedding plants are usually annuals massed in beds for brilliant summer displays. Buy them in late spring to decorate flower beds and containers of all kinds. Discard at the end of the season or after they've been damaged by the first frost.

Taller accent plants provide a vertical dimension to bedding displays. Here red cannas fill the bill.

Low-key sage. Instead of planting the ubiquitous scarlet sage, which can look almost garish when massed, opt for the more understated varieties: Texas sage, which has a looser, more elegant appearance, or gentian sage, bog sage, and mealy cup sage, all in lovely shades of blue.

Use soft-colored foliage plants —summer cypress and dusty miller, for example—to offset such brightly colored varieties as coleus. Another way to tone down and lighten excesses of strong colors is to plant white flowers; try white cultivars of impatiens, petunias, geraniums, or nicotiana.

Play with color combinations in areas with partial shade. A cheerful combination of blue lobelia, white wax begonias or impatiens, yellow dwarf nicotiana, and purple verbena all work well together.

PURCHASING

Don't start too early. Young nursery plants are often forced to grow in the heat of greenhouses and may not be hardened off properly. Wait to plant until a few days after the last frost date in your area.

A bit of wisdom. Pick and purchase plants not yet in bloom. They'll flower longer. If you do buy a plant in bloom, pinch out the flowers and buds at planting time to encourage more profuse flowering.

Pay attention to variety names. Petunias, marigolds, geraniums, and other bedding plants come in a confusing number of varieties. Make a note of the ones you like so that you can narrow down and simplify your bedding selections the following year.

The healthiest plant. Look for bright or dark green foliage on short branching stems and a slightly moist soil. Avoid yellowed or drooping foliage, etiolated stems and leaves, roots that are bunched in drain holes, and dried soil that is pulling away from the edges or covered with algae or weeds.

Examine the buds of the plant you're ready to purchase to check the color— what is shown on package labels is often way off. Remember that buds may be slightly darker than the fully open flowers.

Infestation signals. Aphids leave a sticky residue, while woolly aphids look like small dabs of cotton, usually where the leaves join the stem. Whiteflies will fly up in clouds if you disturb the plant's leaves.

PLANTING

Carefully plot out large beds. Make allowance for the height and proper spacing of each plant. Put the plan on paper and color it in with crayons, pens, or paint to get a general idea of the overall effect.

Choose plants in pressed peat pots or biodegradable cardboard containers. Before planting, soak them in a bucket or basin until they are thoroughly moistened. For speedier root establishment, completely remove the bottom of the container before planting. Be sure to either bury or remove the rim of the pot or container; if you don't, it will act as a wick and draw water away from the roots.

Avoid planting in straight lines. Use staggered rows or trace curves in different directions. Or simply plant in clumps.

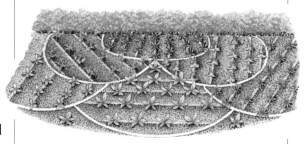

Provide height to your bedding layout by training tall plants as standards and using them as accent plants. Good choices are fuchsia, heliotrope, hibiscus, or angel's trumpet. Place them down the center spine of the bed or toward the back of a border. Plant as usual and later lift and repot to overwinter inside. Or simply bury the whole pot; this way, you can easily lift the plant and pot to bring inside at the end of the growing season.

Your favorite bedding plants don't have to be limited to the garden. On patios or balconies, plant them in containers in a mixture of coarse sand, a large amount of well-decomposed compost, and slow-acting fertilizer. This homemade mixture will dry out more slowly and provide the plant with needed nutrients for a longer period.

Decorate a terrace or balcony with the ready-to-use flower boxes that artfully mass plants together; they're available at most nurseries. Everything is included, from the box and soil to just the right mix of bedding plants. If you already have window boxes and planters, buy ready-to-plant seed combinations of your favorites.
▷ **Annuals, Flower Beds**

BEECH

Most beech trees are large, with a low-branching, densely leaved canopy. The two most common species are the native American beech and the European beech. The European species offer a wider range of choices for gardeners. The most visually striking cultivars include 'Pendula,' with its graceful weeping habit; 'Laciniata,' with its finely cut leaves; and 'Riversii,' with its gorgeous copper-purple foliage.

A beech hedge. For small yards, beech trees can also be planted close together and pruned into an elegant hedge.

Little will grow under beeches because of their water-thirsty, shallow roots and dense shade. Plants that don't mind include epimedium, five-leaf aralia, and goutweed.

The "I love you" tree. Its smooth, silvery bark makes the beech a nearly irresistible surface on which to carve a heart and two sets of initials. But it can also attract vandals. Discourage unwanted graffiti and trunk damage by planting the beech within view of the house or by strategically placing thorny plants and shrubs in the vicinity.

▷ **Trees**

BEES

The great pollinators. Bees are essential assets in any garden. In their search for nectar and pollen, they carry pollen from flower to flower, facilitating fertilization in many edible and ornamental plants. Attract bees to your garden by planting colorful, fragrant, nectar-rich plants; they're drawn in particular to contrasting colors, yellows, and anything on the violet end of the spectrum. But avoid planting tubular or trumpet-shaped flowers; bees don't like them because it's hard to reach inside.

Pesticide rules. When you treat plants for insect pests, protect bees in one of two ways. First, never use an insecticide on plants while they are in bloom—whether fruit trees, flowering shrubs, or vegetables; wait until the petals have fallen. Alternatively, control insect pests with *Bacillus thuringiensis* (Bt) or with insecticidal soap, both of which are harmless to bees.

On melons and cucumbers, blossoms are open for only one day. Apply an insecticide in late afternoon or early evening, when the bees have returned to their hive.

Which bees to attract? Bumblebees are more effective pollinators than honeybees, but by far the most efficient is the shy, unobtrusive horn-faced bee—actually a fly. Attract it with blocks of wood bored with 1-inch holes that simulate a woodpecker's. Or order the bees from an orchard supply or garden center.

Soothe the pain of bee stings by applying a paste of baking soda mixed with water or rubbing alcohol to the affected area. A folk remedy that may offer some relief is to gently rub the sting with a freshly sliced white onion or potato.

Avoid wearing perfume or cologne with a floral scent when you're outside working in the yard or garden. While it may attract bees, it also attracts wasps—especially the ubiquitous and annoying yellow jacket.

BEETS

For an early harvest, start your beets in a cold frame in pots filled with garden soil. Transplant as soon as all danger of frost is past. Then protect them outside with a geotextile row cover. Early beets are tastiest when they're the size of golf balls.

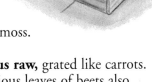

Late varieties keep several months if you harvest before the first frost. Let the roots dry for a day outside, sheltered from the rain. Twist the leaves off and shake the soil from the roots.

Have fresh-tasting beets on hand all winter by storing them in a root cellar or basement at a temperature of between 30° and 41°F. Place them in a case filled with sand or barely moist peat moss.

Beets are delicious raw, grated like carrots. The highly nutritious leaves of beets also make healthful cooked greens.

> ⊱ **A BEET SAMPLER** ⊰
>
> Not all beets are red. The white 'Albina Vereduna' is particularly sweet; 'Burpee Golden' makes a pretty salad; and 'Chiogga' is candy striped in pink and white.

▷ **Vegetable Gardens**

BEGONIAS

At the end of summer, transplant a few vigorous specimens from your flower beds into pots filled with potting soil. They'll continue to bloom indoors next to a sunny window for several months. Cut them back occasionally to encourage new shoots.

Don't get lost in this huge botanical group. Learn to distinguish the three most common kinds: *Begonia* × *semperflorens* varieties are tender perennials that are grown from seed as annuals. They can be used in flower beds, window boxes, and pots. *Begonia* × *tuberhybrida* are tuberous begonias, whose bulbs are planted at the end of winter for summer bloom in flower beds or window boxes. Rhizomatous begonias include the famous *Begonia rex* and its hybrid offspring. These are usually propagated from leaf cuttings and cultivated as houseplants.

BEGONIA X SEMPERFLORENS

Sow seeds by pressing them lightly into the soil, but not covering them. They are very fine and need plenty of light to germinate.

Water the seed-starting mix from below to avoid disturbing the seeds. Do this by soaking the base of the flat in a larger container of water. When the surface of the mix is moist, remove the flat and let it drip before putting it back in a semi-shaded spot.

Another way to water gently. Before planting seeds, put a peat pot or other porous container into the starting mix at the center of the flat, with drainage holes plugged. To water, fill the container. Moisture will slowly diffuse throughout the mix.

Wait until after the last frost to plant begonias in your flower beds and window boxes. They can't stand the cold.

If a late frost threatens, bring the begonia pots indoors for the evening and leave them overnight in a cool room.

Remove all spent flowers and any leaves that turn yellow. An occasional pinching back will encourage your plants to be bushier and to flower more profusely.

Darker foliage helps semperflorens begonias to tolerate more sun than those with lighter foliage. If you want to plant them in full sun, don't worry if some leaves scorch; they will fall off. The new set of leaves will be acclimatized to the greater light intensity, and your flowers will be all the more showy when grown in full sun.

TUBEROUS BEGONIAS

Don't skimp on the quality of the tubers. The bigger they are when you buy, the more flowers they'll produce. Take your pick of flower shapes: single and double blooms, either fringed or crenelated.

Plant the right way. To plant tubers, find the small point on the top; it will produce the stem. Orient it toward the surface (note: the top is concave, which may confuse you). Start tubers indoors in February or March. Place side by side in trays filled with equal mixtures of sand and damp peat moss. Place the top end just under the soil, since many of the roots are produced at the tuber's rim.

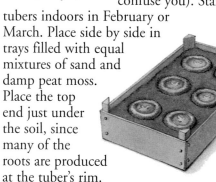

Side planting. If you can't identify the concave top, plant the tubers on their sides. The new shoots will grow their way up to the light at the surface.

For sunny locations, select the compact multiflora begonias, with single or double flowers. The other types prefer partial shade.

Tuberous begonias provide a colorful grace note to the top of a moss-covered stone wall.

Keep it wet. The rooting medium should be moist and kept at about 70°F.

Transplant time. When the shoots have two well-developed leaves, transplant tubers ½ inch below the soil surface, whether in pots or outside in the garden.

A few hours of sun in the early morning or late afternoon is to their liking. If grown in dense shade, begonias will grow tall and floppy and produce fewer flowers. Tuber-hybrida types appreciate cool nights to recover from daytime heat. In areas where summer nights stay hot, they suffer.

Let the leaves yellow after blooming. The life cycle of this bulbous plant calls for a period of rest. Water less, but don't let the soil dry out completely.

Dry tubers thoroughly on racks covered with newspaper for a few days after lifting them. If not completely dry, they may rot.

Winter storage. Dust tubers with a fungicide, bury them in peat moss, and store them in a cool location (39° to 50°F), such as a porch, basement, or garage.

RHIZOMATOUS BEGONIAS

Water sparingly. Rhizomatous begonias are subject to root rot. Let their soil dry out completely between thorough waterings. And remember always to use water that is at room temperature.

Repot infrequently. Indoor begonias prefer tight quarters; rhizomes often overgrow the pot edge. Shallow pots are the best choice.

To stave off powdery mildew, water early in the day and provide good air circulation around the pots. This plant disease is more prevalent when temperatures are low and humidity is high.

Treat with a fungicide those species most sensitive to powdery mildew: *Begonia maculata, B. corallina* and its hybrids, and the semi-tuberous *B. dregei*. Repeat the treatment every 3 weeks. Or spray foliage with a solution of 1 teaspoon baking soda added to 1 quart water. This changes the pH on the leaf surface, making it hostile to fungus.

Propagating from leaf cuttings. Select a healthy leaf and cut off the stalk. Place it flat on a small board and cut through it in several places across the major veins. Then place it directly on a tray of moist potting mix, with the top up, and keep it flat with a few stones. Plantlets will emerge at the incisions.

Increasing humidity helps you to propagate successfully. Good containers include plastic sweater boxes with tight-fitting clear lids. Or you can simply

---

⇥◀ A BEGONIA SAMPLER ▶⇤

There are thousands of different species and cultivars of the genus *Begonia*. Their leaves range from dime-sized to 24 inches across. One type grows to look like a few tiny blades of fine grass, while another towers over 9 feet tall. Flower colors vary from white to yellow, pale green, pink, red, and brilliant orange. Begonias have medicinal as well as ornamental uses. South American native peoples are known to use certain species to soothe teething infants or to treat colds and eye infections.

INDOOR CHOICES	
Rhizomatous types	'Cleopatra,' 'Norah Bedson,' and 'Masoniana' are popular compact plants.
Cane types	'Barbara Ann' blooms all year; 'Irene Nuss' is fragrant with coral flowers; 'Looking Glass' is a stunning plant with pewter-colored leaves and pink flowers. All may grow larger than other types.

OUTDOOR CHOICES	
Semperflorens types	Check with your local nursery for the types best suited to your area.
Tuberhybrida types	These include the striking camellia and ruffled camellia types.
Multiflora types	Profuse bloomers with a compact habit; tolerate sun and heat.
Pendula types	Drooping rather than erect blossoms; best for hanging baskets.
Picotee types	Flower petals are outlined with a border of another color.

TERRARIUM OR GREENHOUSE CHOICES	
Exotic tropicals	'Rajah' has deep mahogany leaves with green veins; 'Buttercup' is a creeper with tiny leaves and yellow flowers; *B. imperialis* is a small Mexican native with deep emerald, velvety leaves highlighted with silver.

place your cuttings in their containers inside sealed plastic bags. Make sure the plastic doesn't touch any of the cuttings.

Another way to start leaf cuttings. Cut the leaf into squares or triangles, each with a section of the main vein. Secure in soil by burying the bottom edge of each cutting in the potting mix. Plantlets will develop at the base of each leaf piece in 4 to 6 weeks.

Don't cut off the flower stalks of begonias chosen for their foliage. The pastel blooms, mostly white or pink, are a nice complement for the leaves. Remove the flowers when they die, however, to prevent seed formation.

BENCHES

A bench need not be new to deserve a place in the garden. A well-weathered bench that has aged gracefully over the years adds charm to any outdoor space.

Give it flair. Position your bench inside a bower of blooming roses, under an overgrown arched trellis, or beneath an arbor covered with fragrant flowers.

Build a bench from durable materials such as concrete, stone, or iron. Or use such expensive but long-lasting and attractive woods as cedar, cypress, teak, and oak.

Go for quality. When buying a bench, you indeed get what you pay for. Opt for solid joinery (mortise-and-tenon with dowels) and brass or bronze silicone fasteners.

Stain for color. If you want to color a wooden bench, use a high-quality pigmented stain instead of paint. A penetrating stain won't blister and peel the way paint does when left exposed to the elements for long periods of time.

Firm footing. Place the bench's legs directly on top of four flat, secure stones or blocks; this will help keep it level and prevent the legs from rotting. Position more large stones or slabs in the heavily trafficked area just in front of the bench. This will ensure that the foreground doesn't become a mud hole after rainstorms or extended wet weather.

A storage bench. Build your bench with a hinged seat cover that, when lifted, reveals a handy storage bin for small tools, gloves, potting soil, pots, and seed.

Blessed solitude. Build a bench around a favorite tree to use as a reading spot. Perch a bench on a knoll with a view or tuck it away in a quiet niche on your property as a haven for solitude and privacy.

Favored spots for benches are alongside a stream, near a fish pond, or beside a gurgling fountain.

The rustic kind. Make an inexpensive bench from half a fallen tree trunk, a large stump, or slabs of secondhand stone purchased from a local demolition company.

Increase the life span of your bench by protecting it from ultraviolet rays, harsh weather, falling debris, and tree sap. Simply sew a fitted cover of heavy canvas or use a large waterproof tarp.

BIENNIALS

A brief life. Biennials are plants that live for two years. As a rule, they produce leaves the first year, then bloom, set seed, and die in their second year. Some biennials, however, such as pansies, are grown as annuals; others, such as foxglove and silver-dollar plant, self-sow so prolifically that they are often treated as perennials.

PLANTING

Sowing cycle. Plant biennial seeds in pots in early summer. Plant out in the fall at least 6 weeks before the first frost or over-winter them in a cold frame. Pinch out any buds that form the first winter to ensure bountiful blossoms the following spring.

Water seeds well. Don't let germinating seeds dry out. Fit the watering can with a fine-holed rosette so that the seeds are not dislodged by a flood of water. Or water seed flats from below by placing in a container of water until the mix appears moist.

For successful transplanting, water the seedlings before and after, even if the weather is damp. In dry weather, thoroughly water both the seedlings and the soil into which they'll be planted on the day before you transplant.

Biennials and bulbs marry nicely in the spring garden. In the late summer or early fall, plant low-growing biennials (wallflow-

ers, stocks, and pansies) among tall-growing bulbs (tulips, daffodils, and hyacinths). Plant bulbs first; then intersperse them with biennials, following the recommended spacing guides. The bulbs will easily pop up, growing through a carpet of biennials.

An easy cutting garden. To avoid stripping your flower beds of blooms, site biennials for cut flowers in the vegetable garden instead. Biennials well suited to large-vase arrangements include Canterbury bells, foxgloves, stocks, and sweet William.

English daisies make a charming little bouquet in a small vase or a medicine bottle.

In wildflower gardens, especially those in mild coastal areas, try growing the evening primrose. Harvest seeds from wild plants along roadsides, near beaches, and on vacant lots. The beautiful yellow flowers will bloom throughout the summer.

Easy does it. Lighten your workload by planting biennials that seed themselves. At the end of the season, allow a few plants to set and drop seed before pulling them up.

MAINTENANCE

Deadhead hollyhocks at the base of the flower spike as soon as they are spent. This discourages seed-making and encourages reflowering the next season. Foxgloves should also be deadheaded at the base of the flower spike to encourage lateral shoots and another crop of flowers.

Protect windowsill pots of primroses and other flowering biennials from severe winter cold spells. Cover them overnight with homemade cardboard or plastic covers, and remove during the day. Then continue nightly until the weather becomes warmer.

Campanulas and other tall biennials can hide an unsightly wall behind a brilliant curtain of flowers.

Winter refuge. In chilly climates, place pots of young biennials such as wallflowers and stocks in a cold frame over the winter. Wait until the ground is workable in the spring to plant them out in a light, dry soil.

Bunches of silver. Grow the silver dollar plant, prized for its use in dried arrangements, in partial shade in summer. Let the plant set and drop seed in the fall, then cut the stems. After the seed pods have dried out completely, rub the flat discs lightly between your fingers to remove the brown outer membranes. With luck and a bit of practice, the bright silvery central membrane will be left intact for you to use in winter floral displays.

▷ **Flower Beds**

BIOLOGICAL CONTROLS

What are they? Biological controls are any biologically derived agents that help control garden pests. For example, some insects, called beneficials, feed on destructive bugs: ladybugs eat aphids, green lacewings prey on a wide range of undesirable insects, and praying mantises will eat just about anything they can catch. Critters from bats to toads are also exemplary bug-zappers.

Ladybugs and other beneficials are drawn to nectar sources like Queen Anne's lace, lamb's quarters, and goldenrod. Other "attractive" flowers and herbs include members of the daisy family (such as yarrow), members of the carrot family (dill, parsley, and fennel), and members of the mint family.

Supplement existing populations of beneficials with commercially available ones. You can mail-order ladybugs, lacewing eggs, and worms from suppliers around the country. Even nematodes are available; in many cases they can actually be helpful. For reliable suppliers, check with your local garden center or Cooperative Extension Service.

Put out a water dish. Be sure the beneficials visiting your garden have enough water to get them through a dry spell. Put out containers of water with rocks or sticks to act as perches. Change the water to keep mosquitoes from using it as a hatchery.

A natural insecticide derived from a common plant grown in India, *Azadirachta indica*, arrests the development of various insect pests. It is sold under various names, including Neemix and BioNeem.

Good bacteria. A bacterium, *Bacillus thuringiensis* (sold as Bt, Dipel, Thuricide, or BioWorm spray), controls cabbage worms and loopers, hornworms, and other damaging caterpillars. One of the most widely used and safest insecticides, it is available at most garden centers.

About toads. Toads are among the most efficient insect eaters, but be aware that they may consume as many beneficials as pests. Once you attract them to your garden, they'll need water and shelter. Sink pans filled with rocks and water into the soil. For shelter, simply place a broken flowerpot upside down in a shady spot.
▷ **Organic Gardening**

BIRDS

Lure birds to your yard with a seed table placed in a wind-sheltered spot atop a solidly planted post. Fill with white millet seed to attract ground-feeding birds like doves and sparrows, or raisins for fruit-eating robins and bluebirds. Black-oil sunflower seeds are popular treats for chickadees and woodpeckers. Other easy table food: unsalted peanuts, whole-grain breads, cereal, and small pieces of apple, pear, grapefruit, and orange.

Add a rodent guard to a feeder by placing an inverted cone, 36 inches in diameter, about halfway up the post. Or use a punctured metal or plastic garbage can lid.

A home improvement project. Transform your seed table into a fancier little house or bird pavilion. Add a rim to keep seeds from falling to the squirrels, then top with a roof to protect against wind, rain, and falling leaves.

Position your seed table about 10 feet from any nearby vegetation where cats might lie in wait for an ambush. The more open ground a cat must cover to reach the table, the better a feeding bird's chances of getting away. On the other hand, shrubs or trees within 10 feet of the feeder help hide feeding songbirds from hunting hawks.

Building materials. Supply your birds with little goodies with which they can build their nests. Tie onto a tree branch a plastic onion bag or meshed grapefruit netting filled with short string pieces, hair recovered from brushes, and snippets of scrap wool and cotton.

Home sweet home. Woo your favorite birds by building the houses of their dreams. Martins and swallows prefer apartment-style group houses. Wrens like sweet-smelling cedar homes. Bluebirds are drawn to lower houses—5 feet off the ground—set amid berry hedges. Place houses at least 200 feet apart, however, to keep the peace among these territorial birds.

The front door. Entrance holes should be properly sized to fit future inhabitants. A hole larger than 1½ inches invites pesky starlings, the noisy intruders who drive other birds from their nests. Perches also attract birds you may not want, so leave them out of the house plans.

Splish splash. Birds will flock to your yard if you offer them a pool of their own, available year-round and preferably placed at ground level. It can be as simple as a garbage can lid or a piece of plastic sunk into a depression. Birds don't like deep water, so fill the birdbath to no more than an inch or so.

Clean birdbaths regularly. Birds use them for both bathing and drinking. Keep birdbaths clean of algae as well: a slippery birdbath is an unused birdbath. Spread a little sand in the bottom for better traction.

Make a warmable birdbath for winter by turning over a large clay flowerpot, setting an upside-down metal garbage can lid on top, and filling with water. Place a low-watt bulb under the pot and use a ground-fault extension cord to run electricity to the light. You can also buy an inexpensive electric outdoor basin heater from your local pet supply store.

A dust bath. Many birds love to roll in the dust. Indulge them by placing a flat container filled with fine dirt, clean sand, or wood ashes in a sunny spot near a bush or some other natural perch.

Grow inviting hedges. Birds feed, nest, and seek cover in such attractive and low-maintenance hedge plants as honeysuckle, blackberry, beech, yew, and hawthorn.

Attract hummingbirds and orioles by offering a sugar-water solution. Use commercial feeders or try this homemade one: take a water bottle for hamsters, fill with sugar water, and suspend upside down. The mix should be 1 part sugar to 4 parts water. Add red food coloring if you like.

Woodpeckers love suet. But make sure that you put it out only in the cold-weather months; it becomes rancid above 70°F.

Leave the seed heads. Don't deadhead seed heads on such late-summer and autumn flowers as asters, sunflowers, cosmos,
verbena, zinnias, and coreopsis. You'll be rewarded with the sweet sounds and colors of seed-loving birds dining in your backyard even on the coldest winter days.

Friend or foe? Many birds suffer an unsavory reputation as crop-devouring rogues. Some, like starlings and blackbirds, enjoy making mischief in cornfields and blueberry patches. To repel birds and stop them from feeding on fruit trees and crops, hang aluminum pie plates from the tree's branches or from sticks in the ground so that they swing about in the wind. Stationary objects—even scary ones like scarecrows and models of owls—are eventually ignored by birds unless they are consistently moved around.

Cover your plants with the protective netting designed to keep birds from getting to your ripening crop. Netting is available from most hardware and feed stores.
▷ **Hummingbirds, Netting**

BLACKBERRIES

Enhance an archway or a split-rail fence with the lush foliage and pretty white flowers of blackberry plants. 'Chester' is a thornless variety that does the job well.

Create a fan espalier to best see stems and fruit. In early spring, prune fruit-bearing stems to the ground. When the new green stems appear in summer, train them in a fan shape by fastening them with plastic ties to a grid or trellis.

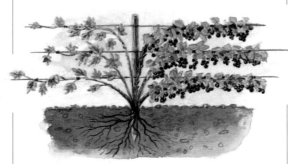

Simplify pruning. On fan espaliers, tie all the sprouts from last year off to one side and concentrate the new sprouts on the opposite side. Don't forget to turn the young stems in the right direction as soon as they come out of the ground.

Easy maintenance. Prune annually after the final harvest. Cut to the ground any canes that bore fruit. Except for long, trailing types, pinch off the tips of young canes in summer once they reach 3 feet in height.

Wear beekeeping gloves when pruning thorny blackberry plants. The glove's protective gauntlets reach up to your elbows.

Thin the bushes just before spring growth begins, leaving only a half-dozen canes on each plant. Shorten side branches down to about 18 inches in length.

A self-supporting variety. The thornless 'Navajo' blackberry doesn't need a trellis.

Want more plants? Bend the tip of a blackberry stem to the ground in spring and weight it down with a stone. Longer stems can be buried where you want new plants; by fall, the tip will have roots. Cut the plant from its mother and dig up the rooted tip for transplanting.

Weave trailing blackberry canes onto a homemade trellis of two to three wires strung between end posts. Young canes that have yet to bear fruit should be left to trail on the ground until the following spring.

Plant a new patch every 5 to 10 years, since cultivated blackberries pick up pests that lower productivity over time. Choose a new spot as far from the old site, and any wild brambles, as possible. Purchase only plants certified as virus- or disease-free.

In frigid climates, separate the blackberry stems from the support and spread them out on the ground. Cover them thickly with conifer branches or dried mulch to protect against severe frost.

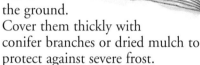

Summer pruning. Cut the lateral sprouts that form prematurely on young stems back below the second or fourth bud. Also get rid of all excess young stems. New buds will form in the fall on the axils of the leaves that remain.

BLANCHING

Want curly lettuce? Endive that's tender and not bitter? Blanch them by keeping sunlight from their developing leaves just before harvest. Cover with a plate, flowerpot, or bell-shaped piece of opaque plastic for 7 to 10 days. If you have persistent rain during that time, abort the blanching or the plants will rot.

Blanch other vegetables, including leeks, celery, and chard, by wrapping the base of the plants with newspaper or plastic. Or pile up soil at the base. Leeks can be planted deep to begin with.
▷ **Cauliflower, Endive**

BLEACH

Simple and effective. A solution of 2 tablespoons bleach and 1 quart water will disinfect several kinds of garden equipment, from flowerpots to pruning shears.

Clean flowerpots before reusing by washing the pots in the bleach solution. Remove caked debris with a scrub brush or nail brush. Leave the pots to soak for an hour or more, then rinse and dry. You can sanitize garden pails in the same way.

Remove mildew and other stains from your picnic hampers and garden furniture made of wicker, cane, or rattan. Use a stiff brush to scrub each piece thoroughly with the bleach solution.

Before restaining, prepare your outdoor woodwork—window boxes, plant containers, even garden sheds—by scrubbing well with the bleach solution. You'll remove dirt as well as mildew from the surface of the wood. Make sure the wood is completely dry before applying stain.

Eliminate slippery paths. Algae and moss can make brick or stone paths dangerously slick. Remove these hazards and discourage regrowth by scrubbing with a stronger solution: 1 part bleach to 1 part water.

Prolong the life of cut flowers by putting a few drops of bleach in their water. The stems in the vase will stay bacteria free.

Kill weeds and grass growing in sidewalk cracks by dousing with undiluted bleach.

Disinfect your pruning shears. Your pruning shears can easily spread virus and fungus diseases as you move from branch to branch and plant to plant. When removing branches that show obvious signs of disease—or have suddenly wilted for no apparent reason—dip the shears' blades into a bucket of undiluted bleach after each cut.
▷ **Lichens**

BLUEBERRIES

Acidity is essential. Blueberries must have acidic soil (pH 4.5 to 5) that's well drained and rich in humus. Mix one or two bucketfuls of acidic peat moss with the soil in the planting hole. If your soil is alkaline, dig a hole 3 feet deep and 6 feet across and fill with a mix of 1 part peat moss to 1 part sand. To fertilize, use soybean meal, cottonseed meal, or ammonium sulfate—all highly acidic.

After fruiting, these blueberry bushes flaunt their color in front of an evergreen mountain laurel.

Oak leaves and other acidic mulches—including pine needles, wood chips, or sawdust—make blueberries thrive. Spread an inch or two over the ground beneath your bushes to protect the plant's shallow roots.

Birds love blueberries, and the only sure way to thwart them is with netting—from the top of the bush all the way down to ground level. When blueberries are ripening, a walk-in cage covered with netting can measurably increase your harvest. Support the netting with a frame made from plastic plumbing pipe, which can easily be taken apart when the harvest is over.

A good ground cover. Low-bush blueberries make an attractive and productive ground cover. The plants grow only a foot high and blossom in spring with flowers resembling lily-of-the-valley's. Leaves glow crimson in the fall. In winter the reddish stems bring a touch of color to the yard.

For superior taste, don't pick the berries as soon as they turn blue. Let them hang on the branches a few more days to develop the best flavor. Then "tickle" the bunches; the ripe fruits will fall into your hands.

A long-term fruit bearer. As long as you harvest all the good berries and clean up or cover with deep mulch any damaged fruits, your blueberry bushes should bear year after year with no disease problems.

Plant more than one variety. Even though cross-pollination isn't absolutely essential for blueberries, planting more than one variety will make both bushes bear more and larger fruits than either would alone. Another plus: planting early, midseason, and later varieties enables you to have fresh blueberries for weeks on end.

Southeastern gardeners have better luck with rabbit-eye blueberries—large bushes that can stand more heat and require a less acidic soil than high-bush blueberries.

Sun lovers. Even though they grow in partial shade in the wild, blueberry plants bear more and better berries if exposed to full sun for at least 6 hours a day.

How much to water? Take special care to water regularly for the first year after planting. Give each new plant 2 gallons of water every week from the time growth begins in the spring until the end of August.

⇥ A BLUEBERRY SAMPLER ⥽

Extend the harvest in your blueberry patch by planting early, midseason, and late varieties. Early fruiters include 'Earliblue,' 'Ivanhoe,' 'Weymouth,' and 'Northland,' all ripening in June. Mid-season blueberries, including 'Bluecrop,' 'Blueray', 'Collins,' and 'Stanley,' fruit from early to mid-July. For berries in late July, plant 'Delite,' 'Dixi,' and 'Menditoo.'

▷ **Acid Soil, Birds**

BOG GARDENS

Pick a spot with naturally poor drainage for your bog garden, even if it doesn't stay wet all year. If it starts to dry out in the summer, provide extra water. Here you can grow any plants that thrive in damp soil.

If no wet area exists, create one. Dig out a spot 2 feet deep and line it with heavy plastic or a children's wading pool, pierced in a few places to allow slow drainage. Replace the soil, adding some peat moss.

For a tiny bog garden, bury a small plastic container with one or two drainage holes added. Hide the container's edges carefully so that they don't give away your secret.

Choose plants that grow naturally around ponds or lakes. Choices include marsh marigolds, water irises, flowering rush, and even some carnivorous plants.

Plant ferns. Exotic-looking ostrich ferns and royal ferns are among the feathery plants that adapt nicely to bog gardens.

Try primroses too. Many types thrive in damp soil. After the flowers have gone to seed, flood the area so that all the seeds are moved about. When they germinate next season, your primroses will be massed with an unplanned, natural effect.

Stay dry. Install stepping stones or a wooden bridge so that you can enjoy your bog garden and tend the plants growing there without getting your feet wet.

Dramatic and tall. If there's room, plant large, bold-leaved plants like the bog-loving *Ligularia dentata* 'Desdemona,' with towering stalks of orange-yellow flowers.

Too vigorous for gardens. Avoid planting cattails and wetland grass *(Phragmites communis)*; they can crowd out other plants.

▷ **Carnivorous Plants, Irises, Ponds**

BONSAI

The art of bonsai requires knowledge and patience. The cultivation of dwarf versions of mature trees and shrubs in small pots or containers is a work of true devotion. Don't take it up as a hobby unless you feel you can give it the attention it needs.

PURCHASING

Indoors or out? The ideal spot for a bonsai is outside on a patio or balcony. Never bring an outdoor species inside for more than a day or two; the leaves will dry out and fall off. In winter, don't bring the plant in at all; exposure to heat may trigger sap flow and prove fatal. Indoor species, on the other hand, come from the tropics and are better suited to a climate-controlled house. But they do need to be exposed to fresh air from time to time, either in the garden during warm weather or on a windowsill.

Choose a healthy specimen. Check the roots by examining the clump; the roots should spread evenly from the trunk and not overlap. The structure of the tree should look natural and untrained, and the leaves should be bushy. Deciduous trees, which lose their leaves in winter, should have a pleasing shape to their trunks and branches. Also check that the pot has unobstructed drainage holes.

Special tools. At first all you really need is a good pair of shears and a spray bottle. Later you may want to invest in special bonsai tools to create certain shapes.

MAINTENANCE

The best place for bonsai: on a pedestal. Place your bonsai up high, on a small shelf or stool (a revolving stand is best) so that it is easily accessible for its daily care. Give it plenty of light, but shield its leaves from scorching midday sun. Also provide protection from wind and cold drafts. Indoors, make sure you keep your plant well away from any sources of artificial heat.

Leaf drop may be caused by moving a bonsai around. Find the right place for your plant and let it stay put.

Freeze-wrap. In case of frost, wrap the pot in bubble plastic or several thicknesses of newspaper, burlap, wool, straw, strips of tarp, or old rags. Or place the tray inside a larger pot filled with peat moss to provide insulation. If your outdoor bonsai is completely covered with snow, don't brush it off; it makes excellent natural insulation.

Too much water asphyxiates the roots. If the soil is very dry, soak the pot in a pan of water and let it drain by propping it up on its side. Do the same for outdoor bonsai after a heavy rain.

Spray regularly, even daily, indoors, depending on the season. Saturate the soil, which can dry out rapidly in the shallow containers. During the summer, you may need to water twice a day.

Grow moss beneath your bonsai. Aside from being decorative, moss is a good indicator of the plant's water needs. When the moss appears parched, water the bonsai. Help moss grow by wrapping the pot for a week in a clear plastic bag, which acts like a greenhouse and maintains high humidity.

AN ANCIENT TRADITION

The word *bonsai*, which comes originally from two Chinese characters, is a combination of the Japanese *bon* (tray) and *sai* (plant). The practice of growing trees in containers began in China in approximately the third century B.C. But it was Japanese Buddhist monks who, over the centuries, eventually developed, codified, and perfected the art. They developed an extensive and complex classification system that categorizes all bonsai by size and shape.

Buy fertilizer that decomposes slowly, but never use it on young or newly transplanted bonsai. For healthy older specimens, fertilize fairly often in small increments in both spring and fall.

Prune the roots of evergreens every 3 to 5 years, deciduous plants every 2 or 3 years, and flowering or fruit trees every year. Cut off a third of the roots. Change the soil; for strong growth, fresh dirt is essential.

Pinch off the shoots of conifers from spring to autumn, concentrating on the offshoots on the trunk and at the base of the plant.

Deciduous trees such as elms and maples benefit from structural cuts in winter, while the plant is dormant.

Wire it up. Wrap a bonsai in copper or aluminum wire around the branches to hold them in the desired shape, whether contorted or straight. Take special care with young stems, which may be too tender to withstand much forcing. You can wire the plant anytime of year, but conifers are best done in winter. Once the plant has achieved the shape you want, simply remove the wire.

▷ **Moss**

BORDERS

Use string and a board to trace a straight border. Stretch a string between two stakes to mark the line. Cut the ground with a sharp spade or edging tool, aligning the board with the string as you work.

To trace a curved border, use a hose or rope to mark out the shape of the border, securing it in several places. Cut the ground with a sharp spade or edging tool, following the lines of the hose.

The right tools. A very sharp spade is generally sufficient (many gardeners prefer a spade with a T- or D-shaped handle). But special power tools to dig borders are also available. The job will go more quickly in light soil. Motorized edgers are most valuable for large lawns bordered by several big flower beds, but these electric or gas-driven tools are also useful for other cleaning jobs or small clipping work. On a smaller scale, manicure the edges of borders set in the lawn with special long-handled shears or an edging tool with a line.

Concrete edgings are efficient but expensive. Choose natural stones instead. Recycled materials such as bricks, stones, and cut stones are more economical. Railroad ties and landscaping ties are long lasting and can be cut to length and buried.

For homemade concrete edging, dig a trench about 4 inches wide and 4 inches deep along a flower bed or walk. Place thin planks every 3 feet or so and pour concrete into the trench. Remove the planks when the concrete has set; the spaces allow for expansion and contraction and prevent cracking.

A rustic trellis border. For a charming old-fashioned border, use this simple and inexpensive technique. Insert sturdy 12- to 16-inch wood stakes every 6 inches along the edge of your border. Then interlace the uprights with pliable vines or willow stems to create a lattice. The resulting trellis makes an especially complementary background and support for old-fashioned climbers, runner beans, strawberries, and herbs.

Discourage invasive plants such as St. John's wort, periwinkle, potentilla, or pachysandra from spreading beyond their beds. Dig a narrow slit trench and drive flat tiles, slates, or roofing shingles—lined up side by side—vertically into the ground.

Borders cut out of lawn must be well maintained to keep the grass from invading the flower border. They should be cleaned up at least twice each year.

To neaten lawn edges after a cut, dig a 2-inch-wide furrow around your lawn. Fill with a mixture of lawn-grass seed and leaf mold. Pack into the furrow and water. Use clumping grasses instead of trailing types.

A damaged edge? Cut out a rectangle of grass that includes the worn portion. Turn it around so that the worn part is on the inside of the lawn. Reseed if necessary; the wound will quickly fill in.

Keep it flat. Unless you're willing to clip lawn edges by hand, lay stones, bricks, railroad ties and other border materials so that they are level with the ground. Your mower will do the job.
▷ **Bricks, Flower Beds**

BOUGAINVILLEA

An unsurpassed climber in the subtropical areas of the country, bougainvillea is a striking covering for walls, pergolas, borders, and fences. It needs a strong trellis to support its heavy growth, and stems must be tied securely so that the plant's young shoots aren't damaged by wind.

In climates where frost is expected, shelter bougainvillea vines by planting them against a sunny, wind-protected wall. Or grow bougainvillea in containers and bring them inside during cold spells. Overwinter indoors in full sun and water just enough to keep the leaves from wilting.

Transplant with care. The bougainvillea's roots are especially intolerant of disturbance. When transplanting from a container to the ground, cut the container off the roots instead of pulling the plant from the pot.

Cultivars tend to flower continuously and are best grown where they experience no noticeable dry season. Feed and water your bougainvillea throughout the year.

A cold-weather variety. 'Green Velvet,' a variety of the *B. sempervirens* species, does well in Northern gardens and keeps its green color even in severely cold winters. It grows naturally round without pruning and produces fragrant flowers each spring. It is also resistant to deer.
▷ **Climbers**

A showstopper among climbers, bougainvillea brings a dramatic display of tropical color to the garden.

BOXWOOD

A low hedge. Stretch a string between two posts and dig a trench 16 inches deep. Put rotted manure or compost at the bottom of the hole. Plant a boxwood every 6 inches; don't remove the leaves at the base. Bury plants to about a third of their height. Firm the soil, then water. Mulch to cover the roots, but leave an open space around the trunk to keep stems from rotting.

Watering. Boxwood is famous for being drought resistant once it is established. If you water copiously the first year, you'll never have to worry about it again.

Boxwood takes well to pruning, from the simplest form to the most complex topiary. But be conservative; develop the shape slowly, permitting some extra growth each year.
▷ **Knot Gardens, Shrubs**

BRICKS

On hot days, hose down your brick pathway and walls. The bricks absorb moisture and cool down, helping to lower the surrounding air temperature. Keep in mind that paving bricks tend to be harder and less porous than building bricks.

Old bricks may look charming, but don't count on them for solid support or durable paving. They may be of varying quality and hardness, which can lead to splitting, chipping, and cracking. If you're lucky enough to find a trove of attractive weathered old bricks, use them for purely decorative, rather than structural, purposes.

A decorative border. Bricks can be used to create a solid and sturdy border around a planting bed. First dig a narrow trench about 6 inches deep. Then set the bricks in at an angle, positioning each one with care. And take your time: a hasty job can look a bit too "homemade."

▷ **Barbecues, Paths, Patios, Paving Stones**

BROCCOLI

Move broccoli to a new place in the vegetable garden at least every 4 years. Like other cabbage family members, it is subject to clubroot and cabbage worms; crop rotation foils both. This heavy feeder can also deplete the soil if planted in the same spot.

Cool weather is essential for broccoli. Make sure you time your planting to avoid the hottest months, since the plant will bolt in hot summer temperatures.

Pack more broccoli into the same space by planting only 8 inches apart. Although the heads will be smaller, the total yield will be up to twice that of the recommended 18- to 24-inch spacing. Use plenty of compost, add lime to the soil, and rake in 1 pound of 5-10-10 fertilizer for every 25 feet of row.

Sprouting vs. nonsprouting. When buying broccoli seeds, check to see whether the plant is a sprouting type. When the head of the main stalk on a nonsprouting plant is removed, no more lateral sprouts will form. A side-sprouting type, however, continues to produce new sprouts as you remove the developed heads. Always use an angled cut on  the stalks so that rain or other moisture doesn't collect on the butt of the stem and set into motion a plant-killing rot.

Pinch off flowers. Examine broccoli regularly to prevent it from flowering. Don't allow a single flower to go to seed.

⊁ A BROCCOLI SAMPLER ⊁

Two plants related to the familiar green-heading broccoli are gaining in favor in American gardens. Broccoli raab, from Italy, has succulent leaves and button-sized florets. The flowering gailon, also called Oriental broccoli, has leaves and buds with a sweet broccoli flavor.

▷ **Cabbage, Vegetable Gardens**

BROMELIADS

Water directly into the heart. Bromeliads that have a distinctive rosette or tubular shape, including the aechmea, vriesea, and billbergia types, should be watered in the heart. In cool conditions, reduce the amount of water

at the center of the rosette. Use a porous potting medium, not soil, and keep damp by misting. Plants of the tillandsia type benefit greatly from weekly 1-hour soakings underwater in a tub.

Encourage blooming by placing your bromeliad in a closed plastic bag with a few ripe apples or a ripening banana. The ethylene from ripening fruit will stimulate flower production.

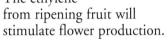

Carefully remove the lateral offsets, or "pups," that the plant usually sprouts just before blooming. Although the parent plant eventually dies, these offsets will grow into new plants of the same kind. Remove the pups when they are one-third to one-half the parent's size. Plant in a porous medium at the level of the bulge in the base and stabilize with a stake. Keep the heart watered. Roots will form in about a month. Keep damp and out of the sun; misting helps.

A tree with epiphytes. Put some bromeliads together on a large branch covered with moss. Secure with florist wire— green and thin, it disappears in the greenery. An even better mounting method is to use hot glue; but don't forget to let the glue cool to the point of tackiness. Keep these plants moist and apply leaf fertilizer from time to time. This popular method of growing and displaying bromeliads generally works best with the distinctive silvery-leaved types.

Cold-water humidifiers can help to keep your bromeliads healthier and happier during the winter—and your family as well!

BRUSSELS SPROUTS

A tasty latecomer. Don't sow this crop at the same time you sow its cabbage cousins: early spring. In temperate zones, sow in mid- to late June and plant out in July, protecting small plants from heat. Sprouts will develop in the ideal conditions of fall.

Leg room. Plants need a good 24 inches to produce well. Make use of the extra space by planting lettuces and radishes, which will happily grow to maturity in the gaps between the growing sprouts.

Remove the lower leaves a few days before harvesting by snapping them sharply downward. This gives the sprouts more room.

Simultaneous sprouts. To make the sprouts develop at the same time, lop off the top 6 inches of the plant 4 to 6 weeks before your desired harvest date.

For the tastiest sprouts, harvest when they feel firm to the touch and measure from ½ inch to 1½ inches in diameter.

✑ A BRUSSELS SPROUTS SAMPLER ✑

The hybrid 'Jade Cross' is the most popular variety in home gardens. Its tight little buds are extremely hardy—a plus with Brussels sprouts; their taste is actually improved by the first frost. Lesser known but equally good varieties are the Dutch 'Valiant' and the Japanese 'Prince Marvel'—both with the sweet, nutty taste of sprouts at their best.

Brussels sprouts also boast a colored variety, this one ruby red; scour your seed catalogs for the hard-to-find 'Rubine.' Whatever variety you grow, remember the cardinal rule after harvest: don't overcook! To bring out the best flavor, cook for 5 minutes or until just tender-crisp.

▷ **Cabbage, Vegetable Gardens**

BULBS

PLANTING

Plant early. Plant spring-flowering bulbs in mid-September to mid-October. They will establish faster and bloom earlier.

Plant in tiers. Whether planting in the ground or in pots, put in several layers of bulbs for more profuse blooming. Spread 1½ to 2 inches of soil between the layers. To get bulbs to bloom all at once, plant the same variety. Better still, overplant larger bulbs with minor ones that flower at the same time. An example: pair daffodil 'King Alfred' with glory-of-the-snow for a beautiful blue and gold combination.

For the best effect, always plant bulbs in groups, not singly in rows. For a naturalistic look, gently toss a handful of bulbs on the ground, planting them just where they fall. Some will fall close together; others, far apart. Siting your bulbs by this method will avoid an artificial or contrived look.

A good depth. A bulb should usually be buried at a depth at least twice its height, but there are exceptions: oriental or Asiatic lilies, which root all along the stems, must be planted three to four times deeper. An exception to the deep-planting rule is the Madonna lily *(Lilium candidum)*, which is buried with the top of the bulb almost even with the surface of the ground.

Feet on the ground. When you bury a bulb, make sure it doesn't remain suspended between the sides of the planting hole. The bottom of the bulb should be in firm contact with the soil. If there is an air pocket beneath, the bulb will not root properly and may begin to rot.

A special case. The bulb of the pretty crown imperial *(Fritillaria imperialis)* sometimes has a big central hole that is the remnant of the previous year's stem. Plant the bulb tilted slightly so that water will not seep into the hole and cause rotting.

Interplant bulbs with some bushy biennials, perennials, or leafy creeping plants, whose emerging summer foliage will help conceal the yellowing leaves of your bulbs. This is especially important for colchicum and crown imperials, whose dying foliage usually makes a most melodramatic exit.

Make transplanting easier by planting bulbs in plastic trays with large holes—wooden or plastic fruit crates will also do nicely. After the plants' leaves yellow, you can lift them from the ground all at one time. You can also take them out immedi- ately after blooming and put the crated bulbs, complete with their soil, in another corner of the garden.

The earliest flowers of the year. The snowdrop *(Galanthus),* with white bell-shaped flowers, makes its appearance in mid- to late winter. Shortly afterward comes the blue glory-of-the-snow, followed by the early crocuses and scillas.

The more the merrier. Don't be afraid to pack bulbs in a pot. It makes for a more colorful display. In a 6-inch pot, for example, use six tulips, three hyacinths, or up to a dozen crocuses.

Summer-long blooms are yours with gladiolus. Extend the blooming season by planting gladiolus corms every 15 to 20 days. Taller varieties of gladioli may need to be staked; simply tie them to bamboo canes with soft twine. Avoid planting them in windy spots or too shallowly in sandy soil.

Bulbs for fall blooms include hardy cyclamens, autumn crocuses *(Colchicum),* and *Amaryllis belladonna,* with massive trumpet-shaped flowers of pink or white.

Winter aconite. An early start is especially critical for winter aconite *(Eranthis hyemalis),* whose tubers quickly dry out and die. These buttercup relatives, which come up year after year and self-sow freely, are often in great demand. Starting in late August, check regularly with your local garden center to see if the shipment of winter aconite has arrived; the supply goes quickly. Before planting, soak the bulbs overnight.

MAINTENANCE
Weed by hand. A cultivator or other sharp-pointed tool can easily damage shallowly planted bulbs and their roots.

If rodents are a problem, place a mesh with large holes over the planted bulbs. This will discourage any unwelcome visitors. Mothballs also make good repellent.

STORAGE
Guard against rot. Store tender bulbs in dry peat, sand, or sawdust that is kept slightly damp. Arrange the bulbs in layers, being careful that they don't touch each other. Store in a dark place where the temperature is between 40° and 50°F. Your refrigerator will do just fine—if there's enough room!

Don't let your bulbs dry out. Dahlias, cannas, tuberous begonias, and caladiums are some of the bulbs that tend to dry out during winter storage. Check every 3 to 4 weeks and lightly sprinkle with water any that appear to be starting to shrivel.
▷ **Dividing, Flower Beds**

⚜ SOME RULES FOR GROWING BULBS ⚜

DO	DO NOT
▷ Buy bulbs at the start of the season, when there is a wider choice of varieties. Pick healthy ones that are firm to the touch. Larger bulbs yield more and bigger flowers.	▷ Buy bulbs and leave them in poor storage conditions (too much light, moisture, cold, or heat) and then plant them late.
▷ Plant spring-flowering bulbs in the early fall, when the soil still retains some summer heat; plant summer-flowering bulbs in April-May, when the soil has begun to warm up.	▷ Buy low-priced, small-grade bulbs. They will bear few flowers or none at all.
▷ Plant in well-drained soil. If your garden soil is clayey and drains poorly, add a good helping of sand, compost, and even a few handfuls of gravel at the bottom of the planting holes.	▷ Plant bulbs in heavy, very moist soil—except for arum and Jacobean lilies, which like to have cool roots.
▷ Form tight clusters of a single variety in a flower bed, in a dark patch of ground cover, on a piece of lawn remote from the regular path, and in pots and window boxes.	▷ Plant mixed bulbs that don't flower on the same date. The dramatic effect of massed blooms will be completely lost.
▷ Once the petals have fallen, remove the stems with withered flowers at the first leaf so that no unwanted seeds will form. Let the foliage yellow on the plant.	▷ Plant bulbs mixed together when you don't know their colors. Unplanned mixing of colors is suitable only in a cutting bed or a remote part of the garden.
▷ Add fertilizer (superphosphate, organic matter, special fertilizer for bulbs, or a tomato fertilizer rich in potassium) to the planting soil or mixed into water during the growing season.	▷ Plant bulbs singly in rows or spaced out too far apart. Doing so will undermine the colorful mass effect you want.
	▷ Pull off or cut the foliage after the petals fall. Bulbs need to rebuild their food reserves for the following season, and their leaves are the means by which sunlight is transformed into plant food. Do not remove leaves until after they have yellowed by themselves.

BUSH BEANS

No room for pole beans? No problem. Many of the best snap beans have been bred as bush varieties. Try 'Tendercrop,' 'Bush Blue Lake,' or 'Bush Romano.'

When to fertilize. When the plants are 6 inches tall, sprinkle a side dressing of complete fertilizer (10-10-10) down both sides of your row of bush beans, making sure none gets on the leaves.

Don't spray the plants. Direct watering can damage the flowers on a plant, thereby stunting its production of beans. Instead of wielding a hose or watering can, place a soaker hose between the rows—or simply poke more holes in an already leaky hose. Make sure the water pressure is low enough to keep the plants from being sprayed.

A BUSH BEAN SAMPLER

French filet beans are the slender, succulent beans that the French call *haricots verts*. If you grow them, be sure to pick the pods when they are no more than ⅛ inch thick. Among the varieties available through seed catalogs is the eponymous 'French Filet,' as well as 'Finaud,' 'Triomphe de Farcy,' and 'Vernandon.'

If you want colorful beans, don't be afraid to try the yellow varieties. The bland and waxy commercial ones you remember from long ago have been replaced by varieties like 'Roc d'Or' and 'Goldkist,' with delicate, buttery flavor. For bright purple pods, grow 'Royal Burgundy,' a tasty bean that happens to look beautiful in the garden as well.

Don't forget limas, even in cold climates. Although 'Fordhook 242' is the most widely grown large-seed lima and needs a fairly long warm season, cool-weather varieties like 'Geneva' and 'Thoroughgreen' have been bred for gardeners in the Northern states.

Bush beans yield their bounty for a shorter time than pole beans—usually for only 2 or 3 weeks in the summer. Because of their shorter maturation time—about 60 days, or 2 weeks earlier than pole beans—it's a good idea to plant them successively so that you'll have a constant supply of beans throughout the summer.

For once-over harvesting, cut off the bush at its roots or pull the whole bean plant out of the ground. Hold it upside down in one hand while picking with the other.

▷ **Beans, Pole Beans, Vegetable Gardens**

BUTTERFLIES

A butterfly house. Check garden centers and mail-order catalogs for the little wooden shelters that protect butterflies from birds and bad weather. Most come with a mounting pole, and all have narrow vertical doors that are too small for hungry birds to enter.

Showy displays of color attract butterflies. Plant flowers with blooms of vibrant purple, orange, yellow, and red. Single blooms provide better access to nectar than double blooms do. And avoid flowers that hang downward or have ruffled edges; butterflies will find them hard to sip from.

Plant in bunches. Butterflies are more likely to revisit a group than a single plant.

Overripe fruit is also attractive to butterflies. Leave dishes filled with mixes of mashed fruit, molasses, beer, or fruit juice

PLANTS THEY LOVE

Certain plants are irresistible to butterflies. One is so attractive to the colorful little visitors that it shares their name: the butterfly bush *(Buddleia davidii)*—a graceful shrub with showy clumps of vibrant purple flowers.

Happily, almost any plant with either brilliant colors or a sweet or herby smell will draw butterflies to your garden. Marigolds, nasturtiums, impatiens, zinnias, hollyhocks, and daylilies are among the flowers they love, along with sweet William, heliotrope, purple coneflowers, bright red bee balm, and—not surprisingly—butterfly weed *(Asclepias tuberosa)*. As for herbs, the most seductive are borage, dill, fennel, chives, and wild bergamot. Other good lures are wisteria, coreopsis, white clover, sweet alyssum, lantana, snakeroot, and sedum.

in the yard. Or soak dish towels in the mix and drape them over trees and shrubs.

A trade-off. Remember that when you create an environment hospitable to butterflies, you're also inviting them to lay the eggs that will become caterpillars. The cabbage white, for instance, is a destructive pest to nasturtiums, cabbages, and radishes. One solution is to plant enough for both you and the pests. Luckily, most other caterpillars are not excessively greedy. At worst, they munch a few leaves without doing much damage—a small price to pay for the beautifully colored wings they will bring into your garden.

In vegetable gardens butterflies are partial to beans, celery, and all the members of the cabbage family.

Tailor-made seed combinations designed to attract butterflies are offered by some of the larger garden seed companies.

▷ **Caterpillars, Moths**

CABBAGE

PLANTING

Double your crop. Plant several varieties with different maturation times. In milder climates you can grow both spring and fall varieties. Start autumn seedlings in June and plant out in late June or early July.

Transplant seedlings before the young cabbage sprouts its seventh leaf; the ideal number is between three and five leaves.

For more stable plants, bury them deep, sacrificing the bottom two leaves; new roots will develop from the buried portion.

Fertilize once a month unless your soil is especially rich; your cabbage will mature faster and taste better. Scatter a 6-inch-wide band of 10-10-10 fertilizer around the base of each plant. Or if you choose, dress with some organic high-nitrogen fertilizer.

Rotation is essential. When planting any members of the brassica family—broccoli, Brussels sprouts, cauliflower, collards, or kale—rotate the beds at least every 4 years to avoid exhausting the soil. All of the cabbage relatives are heavy feeders, taking up a giant share of your plot's nutrients.

Big or small? If you want small, tender cabbages, place the plants 8 to 10 inches apart. To raise bigger cabbages for stewing or stuffing, remove one out of every two plants to provide plenty of growing space for the remaining heads.

Grow your plants in spring and fall to produce the most tender and savory cabbages. The summer sun tends to harden cabbage and make it flower.

Plant fall and winter cabbages around the periphery of your garden. This leaves the beds in the center free for a thorough end-of-season spading.

MAINTENANCE

Prevent splitting. Cabbages have a tendency to split during hot spells or when moisture levels are erratic. If heavy rains follow a dry period while the heads are still forming, rotate each cabbage a quarter turn to break some of the roots. This slows water intake and inhibits splitting. Another way to deter splitting is to stop watering cabbages once they have formed a round head. Surround them with mulch or plant low-spreading flowers or vegetables between the heads.

Harvest a head by cutting about an inch above the soil. If you want smaller side heads to form, leave the lower leaves intact.

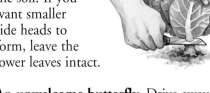

An unwelcome butterfly. Drive away cabbage white butterflies, whose caterpillars love cabbage, by applying *Bacillus thuringiensis* (Bt). This bacterial insecticide takes 2 to 3 days to work. Spray plants as soon as the moths are noticed and continue every 7 to 10 days as long as they are visible, especially after a good rain. A spray of the plant's leaves is all that's necessary.

Winter storage. Hang cabbages and their cousins, with their roots still attached, upside down in a root cellar, garage, or other cool place.

A common problem. Fattening of a cabbage's root indicates the presence of clubroot disease, a serious problem with all brassicas. Pull up and burn all infected plants immediately. Adding wood ashes or lime to the soil for next year's crop is a fairly effective control. But the best way to eliminate clubroot is by not planting brassicas in the diseased portion of the garden plot for at least 4 to 7 years.

⊱ A CABBAGE SAMPLER ⊰

Harvest fresh cabbage for months by planting varieties that mature at different times. Among the best choices for early types are 'Grenadier' and the heirloom 'Early Jersey Wakefield.' Mid-season varieties include the classic 'Stonehead' as well as 'Green Cup' and 'Cheers.' For harvesting late in the season, try 'Grand Slam' and 'Quisto.'

Also consider other cabbages. Fans of red cabbage will favor the burgundy hue of 'Scarlet O'Hara'—ideal in slaws and salads. Other reds are 'Ruby Perfection' and 'Meteor.' Savoy cabbages are notable for crinkly leaves and fine flavor, with 'Julius' a tasty choice.

Chinese cabbages combine the crunchy texture of lettuce with the taste of cabbage. They come in two forms: tall, cylindrical Michihli cabbages, including 'China Express' and 'Orient Express,' and the barrel-shaped Napa types, such as 'Jade Pagoda.'

▷ **Broccoli, Brussels Sprouts, Cauliflower**

CACTI & SUCCULENTS

Buy by the Latin. To make sure you're getting the exact cacti you want, learn their Latin names. Don't let Latin intimidate you, even if you're looking for the amply named Texas rainbow *(Echinocereus pectinatus dasyacanthus)*. Common names vary widely, even in the heart of cactus country.

OUTDOORS

Popular landscaping cacti in Arizona and other cactus-friendly states are the golden hedgehog *(Echinocereus engelmannii* var. *nicholii)*, fishhook barrel *(Ferocactus wislizenii)*, purple prickly pear *(Opuntia violacea)*, and the mighty saguaro *(Carnegiea gigantea)*. Choice outdoor succulents are agaves, aloes, yuccas, nolinas, and the desert spoon *(Dasylirion wheeleri)*.

Will they grow in the North? Cacti to try in drier temperate areas as far north as coastal New England are the fire barrel *(Ferocactus acanthodes)*, hedgehog *(Echinocereus engelmannii)*, and grizzly bear prickly pear *(Opuntia erinacea)*. Most yuccas do well too; many are hardy to 0°F.

Inspect plants at the nursery to make sure they're free of scale insects and soft spots. Note their stature: a plant that isn't standing straight in its pot is not well rooted.

Not only for show. Outdoor cacti and succulents are usually planted in raised beds covered with decorative gravel and surrounded by rocks or boulders—and with valid reason:

good drainage is essential. Fill the bed with a 50:50 mixture of soil and decomposed granite, pumice, or sand. Edge the bed with boulders placed close together and fill the crevices between them with concrete; the seams will be hidden once you fill the bed with soil. If you like, place a complementary ornament among the plants—perhaps an old wagon wheel or a bleached cow skull.

Don't overwater! Water cacti by drenching the soil and letting it dry out completely; it takes about a week. Succulents can tolerate more watering than cacti, even though they don't really need it. But they'll respond with lush growth if you water them daily when the temperature is above 90°F. Potted plants will need more water than those in the ground.

Moving large cacti. Whenever you need to move a large cactus, never drag it or roll it. Instead, grab it by the roots, loop a 6-foot section of old garden hose underneath, and lift with both hands. You'll need a helper for the heavier types.

INDOORS

Sow seeds in spring or summer on the surface of fresh potting soil and cover with a fine layer of clean sand ¼ inch deep. Set the pot in a pan of water until saturated, then cover with a plastic bag and place in a well-lit location—but not direct sun. The seeds of plants such as echeverias are as fine as dust and should be settled in with a light misting. Most cacti and succulents will thrive in this miniature greenhouse for several months.

Fertilize seedlings often for rapid and healthy growth. Transplant when large enough to handle, but be patient—it may take as long as a year.

Improvise a pair of cactus pincers with a large band of newspaper folded over several times. Wrap it around the plant whenever you're repotting or picking up the plant.

Water once a week. Overwatering is enemy number one. Water once a week in summer and only when soil is completely dry during winter dormancy. If your plant is kept in a heated room, however, water it once a month.

Repot cacti and succulents as soon as the roots start to snake from the drainage holes—usually every 2 to 3 years for fast-growing species and 3 to 4 years for slower growers. Always water before repotting.

Repotting brittle succulents. Some succulents, including sedum and burro's tail, are delicate enough to break when handled. To prepare these for repotting, stop watering several weeks in advance; the leaves will slowly crinkle and wilt, becoming more flexible. If the plant is drooping, place a large plastic bag over the head before you repot. Then remove the bag and water the plant. If any leaves have fallen, put them in pots; they will easily take root.

Dust your cacti gently with an old soft toothbrush or a worn shaving brush. In summer, shower them lightly afterward.

Fresh air. Open your windows or move your plants to an outdoor perch from June to September. But make sure they aren't exposed to chilly drafts.

Easily remove a cactus by pushing a pencil into the drainage hole of the pot. As long as you haven't just watered, the soil should come out in one clump.

Dealing with pests. A white woolly spot on your plant indicates the presence of mealybugs, while stems covered with small beige or brown bumps are a sign of scale insect infestation. If only a few of either pest are visible, kill them by dabbing them with a cotton swab soaked in rubbing alcohol. For heavier infestations, a thorough cleaning of the plant with a toothbrush and insecticidal soap may be required.

Easy propagation. Detach a cutting, or joint, from the mother plant. Let it dry for a week in a shaded place in the open air, then plant in well-drained soil.

Remove cactus prickles from your fingers with adhesive tape. You'll need a pair of tweezers, of course, for the more stubborn spines.
▷**Agave, Aloe, Yucca**

CALADIUMS

Shade lovers. These foliage plants offer a splash of color and pattern to any shade-filled spot in your garden. In the South you'll often see them around the trunks of spreading shade trees. They also do well in patio containers and pots, with their veined leaves spilling out up to 2 feet across.

Getting started. In May, buy dormant tubers and pot them in humus-rich potting soil with the tops of the tubers buried 1 inch deep. Carefully cut out the large main bud to encourage more shoots to form. Move the pots to a place where the temperature is 75° to 80°F. And keep the plants moist; otherwise, they'll go dormant.

Although caladiums crave shade, too little light may make them leggy and weak-stemmed. If you grow them indoors, place them near a north- or east-facing window.

Keep them warm. Caladiums flourish in heat and can't abide temperatures below 65°F. Even dormant tubers will rot if the temperature drops much below 60°F.

Keep them wet. Caladiums do well when they get plenty of water. If you have a garden pool, pot tubers in porous terra-cotta pots. Once the plants have developed one or two leaves, place the pots on a ledge or cement blocks at the pool's edge, with the rims just above water level. The plants will respond with lush growth.

Storing potted caladiums. To store your caladiums through winter, gradually withhold water from the plants in early fall; they will slowly go dormant. Keep the dormant tubers in pots or transfer them into peat moss that is kept slightly damp. Store in a dark place at no less than 60°F.

> ### ⇥| A CALADIUM SAMPLER |⇤
>
> Varieties are distinguished by the colors of their leaves and veins. 'Candidum,' probably the most popular caladium, has large snow-white leaves laced with green veins. Speckled 'Carolyn Whorton' has pink and green leaves with red veins, while 'Frieda Hemple' boasts both leaves and veins of vibrant red, surrounded at the edges by a border of fresh green.
>
> More delicate in appearance is the rare and lovely 'Pink Symphony,' its translucent soft-pink leaves etched with green veins. The dwarf variety 'Little Miss Muffet,' a miniature for borders, has lime-green leaves speckled with red; it reaches only 8 to 12 inches high.

The camellia, here trained as a standard, thrives in the humidity of the Northwest and coastal Southeast.

CAMELLIAS

The key to success. This evergreen shrub, with dark green foliage and delicate blossoms, prefers a humid climate like that of the Southeast and parts of the West Coast as far north as Seattle. Plant in soil that is slightly acidic or neutral—never alkaline.

If your soil is alkaline, grow camellias in pots, in raised beds, or in trenches filled with leaf mold. Team them with acid-loving azaleas and rhododendrons.

Shelter the bush from frost, wind, and full sun. One favorite spot is the sun-dappled shade of a rangy evergreen.

Mulch in spring and fall using a layer of well-aged compost about 6 inches thick. When the plant buds and flowers, apply ammonium sulfate at the rate of ¾ ounce per square yard every 3 weeks. Take care not to overfertilize.

Wrap a potted plant in winter. Plants in containers are more sensitive to the cold, and camellias are particularly vulnerable because of their shallow roots. When winter arrives, wrap the pot with thick plastic bubble wrap or several sheets of newspaper or burlap. Or bring the plant indoors to a greenhouse or well-lighted solarium.

Is it frost damaged? If your camellia has no leaves left, you have little chance of saving it. If there is only partial defoliation, prune severely above the healthy branches.

Water the plants from above in midsummer; camellias thrive in high humidity. Encourage flower bud formation by slowing down watering in September, moistening just the soil and using lime-free water.

Display in a bowl. To preserve camellias for as long as a month, run a length of thread through the center of the blossom and plunge into 145°F paraffin for only a second or two. Place face down on a few thicknesses of paper towels to cool. Pull out the thread and float the flowers in a shallow bowl. A couple of drops of floral perfume in the water enhances the effect.
▷ **Shrubs**

CARNIVOROUS PLANTS

Create an outdoor bog garden for your carnivorous plants, which need very damp soil. Dig a trench at least 1 foot deep and shovel in a thin layer of sand. Cover with a sheet of thick plastic—the kind used for building ponds—and pierce it with drainage holes 1 foot apart. Fill with peat-rich soil and install the plants. During hard

 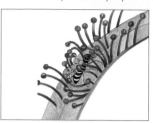 

⊱❘ FASCINATING TRAPS ❘⊰

Learn to recognize the methods that carnivorous plants employ in trapping their prey.

Passive traps, including those of the hardy and tropical pitcher plants, grow into little urns or cones. Insects attracted by the nectar lining the rim are prevented from escaping by downward pointing hairs. They eventually fall inside, drown in the liquid that fills the bottom of the trap, and are digested. Some tropical pitcher plants are large enough to catch even mice—and not let them go.

Semi-active traps, like those of the sundew and butterwort species, feature sticky leaves and glandular hairs. Insects become ensnared and, while struggling to escape, become progressively stuck in the adhesive. The leaf then gradually folds around the prey.

Active traps, such as that of the Venus flytrap, have leaves of two lobes that close together like jaws as soon as an insect touches the stiff glandular hairs found in the center. Hairs on the leaf's edge hold the prey inside until it dies and is digested. Note: Do not touch the leaf to make it close. It can close only five or six times before it loses the function and dies back. Overstimulation kills the plant.

freezes, protect the garden by covering with pine needles or peat. In cool climates, use hardy pitcher plants (genus *Sarracenia*), as well as butterworts *(Pinguicula)* and sundews *(Drosera)*. In warmer climates you can also grow the legendary Venus flytrap *(Dionaea muscipula)* and the California pitcher plant *(Darlingtonia californica)*.

Use portable planters for tender insectivores in cold regions. Fill a porous container with pure peat and install the plants of your choice. If you have a pond, place the planter at the edge so that it will be constantly moist but not underwater. When the weather cools, move the container to a greenhouse or warm windowsill. Alternatively, you can let the plants go dormant and store them in a cold frame, taking care to see that they never dry out.

Accustomed to the poor soil of their native bogs, carnivorous plants don't need a rich soil or extra feeding. Most will grow in pure unfertilized peat, while others, like pitcher plants, prefer a mix of sand and peat. For tropical species grown in hanging baskets, such as nepenthes, use a fibrous potting mixture like that used for orchids.

Maintain high humidity for indoor plants—but shade them from bright sun. Group pots on a bed of gravel soaking in 2 inches of water in a tray. In summer, be sure to maintain the water level. To provide constant heat and humidity, grow carnivorous plants in a greenhouse or terrarium.

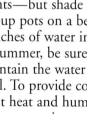

Use distilled water or rainwater—both of which have a neutral pH—as much as possible when watering indoor carnivorous plants. Keep the soil damp in summer, but water less when temperatures drop.
▷ **Bog Gardens**

CARROTS

PLANTING

Sow seeds in a row or a band as thinly as possible—about 3 to 4 seeds per inch. Planting in rows is preferable, since it makes weeding easier. Tamp seeds with the back of a rake to bury them ¼ to ½ inch deep. Thin out seedlings, leaving the strongest plant every 2 inches for small varieties and every 3 inches for larger varieties.

Mark rows with radishes. When you sow carrots, add a few radish seeds. The fast-germinating radishes will mark the row so that you'll know where to weed before the carrot seedlings emerge. Once the carrots are up, remove the radishes.

For straight, tender carrots, especially in heavily compacted soils, plant them in raised beds. Locate the beds in full sun except in the hottest climates, where a little shade and extra watering are advisable.

Match varieties to soil type. Follow this rule when choosing varieties: the heavier the soil, the shorter the root should be. Varieties sold as either half-long or baby types are preferable to long, slim carrots for clayey, compacted soil. In extremely heavy soil, plant the round varieties, which won't have to penetrate as deeply.

MAINTENANCE

To harvest sweeter carrots, apply a fertilizer rich in potash and poor in nitrogen. Too much nitrogen produces large, coarse, hairy roots that are devoid of good flavor.

A CARROT SAMPLER

A sweet, crunchy carrot is one of life's simple pleasures. The long-standing favorites are the Nantes types, which yield sweet, tender roots and grow in a variety of conditions. 'Scarlet Nantes' is a popular choice. 'Artist,' a variety crossbred from Nantes and Imperator types, is perhaps the sweetest carrot of all. 'Tendersweet' is a long, slim variety that grows well in deep, loose soil, while the 4-inch-long 'Short 'n Sweet' adapts well to heavy soil.

Baby varieties do better in shallow soils and short seasons. Try 'Thumbelina,' which is tiny, round (just over an inch in diameter), and ideal for canning. Another baby type is 'Parmex'— very sweet and nearly round in shape.

Water seedbeds carefully. If watered heavily and allowed to dry out, the soil may form a crust that makes it hard for carrot seedlings to emerge. Water regularly and gently until the seedlings are established.

A carrot pest. Control the carrot rust fly by covering beds with spun-bonded row covers immediately after sowing your seeds. The cover prevents the fly from laying eggs in the beds and is thoroughly effective in thwarting larval infestation. In Northern regions this remedy is necessary only for an early planting in spring. Otherwise, simply follow the old adage and wait until the apple trees bloom before planting carrots.

Harvesting without tools. Varieties for home gardens sometimes have weak tops that break off at the collar as you harvest the root. To remedy, push the carrot into the ground a bit before pulling it out; this breaks the rootlets that hold it in the soil and allows the root to come free. Or stick a pitchfork into the soil parallel to the row 2 inches from the plant. Lean back slightly on the handle; repeat on the opposite side. This loosens even heavily compacted soil so that carrots slide out easily.

THE MISFORTUNES OF CARROTS

SYMPTOMS	CAUSES AND SOLUTIONS
Roots are forked.	The soil in the bed either is too rocky or contains clumps of incompletely decomposed organic matter. Remove rocks and pebbles and do not apply fresh manure before planting carrots.
Roots are too short.	Plants are either placed too close together or have been damaged by extreme heat. Space correctly and provide shade on the hottest days.
Heart of the carrot is hard and woody.	The roots have either grown too slowly or have been harvested too late. For maximum tenderness, harvest roots young, even though their flavor may not be fully developed.
Roots are split.	Plants have been watered too heavily after a dry spell. Water moderately in times of drought and protect plants from sudden drenchings. Taste is not affected when carrots are split.
Carrots lack flavor.	Roots have been harvested after their bright orange color has peaked. Crops that mature in the bright sunshine and cool nights of fall usually achieve the best balance of color, texture, and flavor.
Shoulders are green.	Tops of the roots have protruded from the soil. Pack soil around developing roots early in the season. Remove the bitter discolored portion of the roots and use the rest.

STORAGE

Carrots in winter. Store carrots during the cold months in a root cellar, preferably buried in moist but not wet soil. Or leave in the ground and mulch the bed heavily.

Before any hard freezes in mild-winter regions, cut the carrot tops off and cover the rows with a band of wire netting over-laid with dead leaves or straw. When you're ready for carrots, simply lift up the cover-ing and harvest.

In hard-winter regions, place clear poly-ethylene over the carrots instead of metal netting, which may freeze in place. Secure with bricks. If you live on a farm, copy New England farmers and cover the beds with bales of hay after the carrot tops die down. The bales make perfect insulators.
▷**Vegetable Gardens**

CATALOGS

Made to order. Millions of gardeners annually buy their seeds, plants, and garden sundries from the glossy pages of mail-order catalogs. Shopping by catalog contin-ues to grow in popularity, even though materials bought by mail are not necessarily better or less expensive than those available in local nurseries or garden centers; it also carries the added costs of postage and han-dling. One advantage is that catalogs fre-quently offer many unusual, hard-to-find plants, as well as heirloom varieties.

Order in the fall. Many catalog companies will offer plants at a discount after their busy spring season is over. Or save money by pooling with your friends to order: some catalog companies will reduce prices on plants bought in quantity.

Read between the lines. Avoid vegetable varieties with "pak" in their name; they're bred with packing and shipping qualities that home-grown vegetables don't need. And be suspicious of tomatoes described as firm. That's often a tip-off that the fruits are meant for commercial growers, as are tomatoes characterized as "jointless," which were bred for mechanical harvest.

Look for the Latin. Be wary of catalogs that use only common names for trees, shrubs, and flowers, which often vary from region to region. Only the scientific, or Latin, name ensures that you get exactly the plant you are looking for.

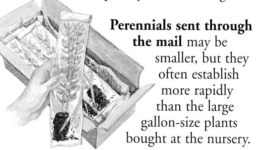

Perennials sent through the mail may be smaller, but they often establish more rapidly than the large gallon-size plants bought at the nursery.

Pretty pictures in catalogs may seduce you into buying a plant that's not right for your climate, soil, or site conditions. While cata-logs can help you envision a game plan for your garden, a plant will thrive only if its requirements are met. Good catalogs pro-vide essential growing information along with the beguiling photos.
▷**Latin Names, Nurseries**

CATERPILLARS

Caterpillars can wreak havoc in the garden. Many home gardeners are reduced to trench-warfare tactics in battling these pests. Treat the problem safely and effec-tively with a bacterial insecticide that specifically targets caterpillars, such as *Bacillus thuringiensis* (Bt). Harmless to animals, humans, and most other insects, Bt controls cabbage worms and loopers, hornworms, fruit-tree pests, and other crop-damaging caterpillars. It is also effective against cankerworms, fall web-worms, tent caterpillars, and gypsy moths.

To keep cabbage loopers from damaging cabbages and their kin, poke branches of fresh arborvitae or broom into the ground

between the plants. Or spread tomato suckers on the cabbages after pinching them off growing plants; tomato foliage emits a strong odor that for a time will repel egg-laying white butterflies. Cedar shavings and chips also make an effective mulch that repels insects, snails, and slugs.

A caterpillar cocktail. If a handful or two of your garden's cabbage loopers are chalky white and appear weak, your pests are infected with nuclear polyhedrosis virus (NPV). Put infected loopers in a blender with water and spray over crops. The remaining pests will die within 3 or 4 days.

Attract caterpillar-eating birds. The house wren, mocking-bird, warbler, and cat-bird devour the larvae of harmful moths and but-terfly caterpillars and numerous other tree- and shrub-attacking insect species. Install birdhouses in your garden or in nearby trees. Or erect seed tables and plant fruit-bearing hedges in the yard.
▷**Butterflies, Moths, Pesticides**

CATS

Make your cat happy. Cats find the scents of certain plants irresistible. Indulge them by devoting a sunny corner of a flower bed to growing the feline's favorites: mugwort, catmint or catnip, and the kiwi. Place cuttings of the plants where your cat likes to play. Or use the dried leaves to stuff a cushion that your cat can nuzzle up to.

Houseplant protection. Deter your cat from digging in large potted plants by placing inflated balloons atop the soil. After popping a few balloons with its claws, the cat won't be tempted to return.

Divert with sprouts. Offering your cat sprouts throughout the year may keep it away from your houseplants. Sow some cereal grains—wheat, barley, alfalfa, or rye—in pots. Cats often relish sprouts and will be able to graze at will.

Plants to avoid. Many house and garden plants are harmful to cats. If your cat is an inveterate leaf chewer, avoid the following plants: chrysanthemums, ivies, philodendrons, azaleas, delphiniums, daffodils, rhubarb, oleander, foxgloves, and wisteria.

With their thin skin and meticulous grooming habits, cats can readily absorb garden poisons. Use the least toxic substance to control pests and weeds and let any sprays dry at least 24 hours before letting your cat go near a treated area.

Felines are attracted to freshly dug earth. After you've been digging or cultivating, insert brambles or thorny prunings into the soil. The sharp branches will keep cats from getting too comfortable in your newly worked beds. If that doesn't work, try stretching some small-gauge chicken wire across the surface of the soil.

Protect the birds. Keep their broods out of the reach of your cat's claws by planting a climbing rose at the base of a tree trunk, on the sunny side.

Cover your seedbeds with holly branches or rose trimmings. Several small mesh bags of mothballs scattered along the soil will also help keep cats from intruding.

▷ **Conifers**

CAULIFLOWER

A sensitive brassica. This "queen of the brassicas" is also the most sensitive to frost and heat. Choose the earliest varieties for spring planting. Better still, grow cauliflowers in fall. Start from seed in July; protect young plants from heat and keep watered.

Plant out in fertile, well-drained soil and enrich the earth once a month with a high-nitrogen fertilizer like manure tea.

Blanch it white. Sunlight will quickly turn the creamy-white heart of a ripening cauliflower yellow or brown. Protect the heart—and retain flavor too—by blanching (covering the head of a plant to block out light). Blanch in one of two ways: once the curd has reached the size of an egg, break off a few outer leaves and place them on top of the heart, or simply fold the leaves over the heart and clip them together with a clothespin or rubber band.

Plant seedlings fast. Seedlings held too long in root-bound flats will produce smaller heads. Plant starters as soon as possible after buying them at the nursery or growing them at home.

Harvest cauliflowers before the curds start to separate—usually about 2 months after transplanting the seedlings.

⇒❘A CAULIFLOWER SAMPLER❘⇐

When it comes to cauliflowers, the faster they mature, the better. Try 'Snow King' (50 days) or 'Snow Crown' (60 days). 'Amazing,' a self-blanching type, takes slightly longer.

Or sample the more unusual cauliflowers. 'Cauli-Broc Hybrid,' 'Chartreuse Hybrid II,' and 'Green Goddess Hybrid' are "brocciflower" types, crossbred with broccoli. Purple types include 'Violet Queen,' a richly colored hybrid; its broccoli-like florets make good crudités.

▷ **Cabbage, Vegetable Gardens**

CELERY

A long season. Celery is a demanding crop, requiring highly fertile soil, plenty of moisture, and cool temperatures to thrive. But time and patience may be the key requirements: celery takes from 5 to 6 months to mature from seed. Start seeds 8 to 12 weeks before the frost-free date in your region. Better still, buy transplants in flats, which are sold in garden centers around May.

If soil is dry, grow celery in trenches 4 inches deep and 10 to 12 inches wide.

Run a drip watering system or soaker hose in the trench to provide the cool, moist conditions that celery prefers. Digging compost into the soil before planting will help it retain moisture.

Soil too shallow or sandy? If so, plant celery in raised beds with amended soil to retain moisture and promote fertility. Be sure to water regularly, since raised beds have a tendency to dry out faster.

For tender white stalks, try blanching. Two weeks before harvest time, wrap the stalk cluster in cardboard or black plastic tied with string, leaving the leafy top exposed to the sun. Or cover the bottom two-thirds of each plant with straw.

🎗 A CELERY SAMPLER 🎗

There's more to celery than just stalks. As satisfying as it is to bite into a perfectly crisp stalk fresh from the garden, don't overlook the varieties grown for the root (celeriac) or leaves.

The classic garden celery is 'Ventura,' whose brilliant green stalks have been bred to stay crisp longer. Another variety, 'Utah 52-70,' produces dark-green stalks that don't go to seed and toughen.

Celeriac is the celery cousin that is grown for its knobby root, used shredded in France to make the delectable *celeri remoulade*. Unlike celery, it is easy to grow—but its seeds can be hard to find in the United States. Scan catalogs for 'Diamant,' 'Brilliant,' or 'Apple.'

Leaf celery, sold as an herb, is grown for its leaves, which resemble Italian flat-leaf parsley. Two good varieties are 'Amsterdam Fine Cutting' and 'Dinant.' For curly-leaved varieties, plant 'Zwolsche Krul' or 'Par Cel.' A third celery relative is lovage, a 4- to 6-foot-tall aromatic herb. Its leaves are used in cooking, while its hollow stems impart an interesting flavor when used as straws or swizzle sticks in tomato juice or Bloody Marys.

▷ **Vegetable Gardens**

CHAIN SAWS

Be careful when starting. Never start a chain saw near a fuel can. Place it at least 30 feet away from the can to keep any sparks from igniting the fuel.

A common mistake. Don't pull the starter rope at an angle or it will rub against the starter housing and eventually break. The correct way to pull the rope on any chain saw is to draw it straight out of the recoil starter housing. Always lay the saw on the ground to start it, holding it firmly in place with your foot.

Sawing railroad ties. If you're landscaping your yard or garden with real railroad ties instead of commercially sold ties, pay special attention when using a chain saw to cut them. The ties often contain gravel and nails, which become dangerous flying objects if struck by the blade.

Prevent kickback. Start the chain saw before you make contact with the wood to prevent kickback. And always hold the saw with both hands, putting your dominant hand on the rear grip for best control.

Shake the fuel. Because a chain saw runs on a mix of gasoline and two-cycle engine oil, be sure to shake the fuel container gently for at least 1 minute before pouring fluid into the saw's tank. Open the cap slowly to release pressure inside the can.

Save time. Always have at least one new or sharpened chain, or cutter, in reserve, especially if you are working at a location that is far from home.

10 COMMANDMENTS OF SAFETY

▷ Don't use a chain saw unless you're in good physical shape.
▷ Wear gloves for a firm grip.
▷ Wear protective glasses, a safety helmet, earplugs, and boots with a solid tread.
▷ Avoid loose-fitting clothing. And leave your scarf at home!
▷ Clean the machine each time you use it to make sure that handles are free of grease and can easily be gripped.
▷ Make sure that the chain isn't touching any obstacle when you start the machine.
▷ Make sure there's plenty of space around trees before cutting them down or pruning.
▷ Always cut at a height below your shoulders.
▷ Keep children at a distance when you operate the saw. And put the blade cover in place whenever the saw is not in use; the sharp teeth of the chain can cut even when stationary.
▷ Shut down the motor when moving across rugged or uneven terrain.

▷ **Power Tools**

CHARCOAL

Never briquets! The charcoal used in gardening is produced from burned wood. It is not the chemically treated briquets used for barbecues. Scan specialty catalogs for horticultural or lump charcoal, which is often hard to find.

Condition the soil. Charcoal absorbs impurities in potting soil and neutralizes acid. Mix with a ½-inch layer of coarse gravel at the base of the pot. It works especially well with orchids, ferns, and bulbs.

Keep water fresh. Add a lump of charcoal to vase water to prevent mold and arrest the unpleasant effects of plant decay, including odors from rotting leaves. Charcoal also makes a good addition when you're rooting plants in water.

CHERRY TREES

Sweet or tart? Choose from the two types of cherries: sweet and tart. Sweet cherries are for plucking right off the tree and eating fresh; tart are for cooking and canning. The fragrant flowering of cherry trees begins as early as April. Sweet cherries are ready to pick by late June, while tart cherries ripen in late summer or early fall.

Both kinds of cherry trees need deep, well-drained soil—preferably alkaline. But tart cherries will thrive in less-fertile soils than sweet cherries will tolerate.

Spread a deep mulch of straw or wood chips around the base of the tree—but don't let it touch the trunk. The mulch will protect the shallow feeder roots.

How much water? Cherries can put up with arid conditions, so water only during long dry spells. Water only the soil—not the fruit—during the ripening process; water absorbed by cherries causes their skins to crack.

Fine netting is the surest way to discourage birds from devouring your crop. Cover the whole tree with the netting and remove it as soon as your harvest is done. Alternatively, string black cotton thread among the branches just before ripening begins. Take a spool of thread, grab the free end, and toss the spool back and forth over the tree to a helper; continue until the spool is empty. Birds will hit the invisible thread and find it too much trouble to return to the tree.

Cherries falling before maturity signal a plum curculio larvae infestation. Destroy them by spraying before they can burrow into the soil and begin metamorphosis.

Get pests stuck. Sticky substances like Tangletrap—an adhesive sold at home stores and garden centers—are useful in controlling cherry fruit flies, which lay eggs in young cherries in May. Hang red card-board cutouts coated with the substance on tree branches to alert you to an infestation. Then spray with carbaryl. Keep another common pest from munching on young leaves in the spring by ridding the tree of ants, which attract aphids. Wrap a collar around the trunk and coat with an adhesive. Inspect often for ant "bridges," created when straw, grass, or leaves stick to the coating.

Plant in a tub. Grow a dwarf cherry tree in a tub or large container. Select a tub at least 20 inches in height and width. Fill with a mixture of equal parts garden soil, compost, and perlite.

A CHERRY SAMPLER

'Bing' Sweet cherry with large dark red fruits and firm flesh; fruit cracks in wet weather; moderately hardy

'Compact Stella' Sweet cherry with medium-size dark red fruits; self-fertile and semi-dwarf; productive and moderately hardy

'Emperor Francis' Sweet cherry with yellow fruits that resist cracking; excellent flavor; productive and cold hardy

'Garden Bing' Dwarf cherry for container growing; fruits similar to 'Bing'; grows up to 8 feet when planted in the ground; self-pollinating; grows well in the West

'Montmorency' Tart cherry with bright red fruits of good flavor; fruits resist cracking; cold hardy

'Morello' Tart cherry with dark red fruits and bittersweet flavor; suitable only for cooking and preserves; self-fertile trees

'Northstar' Tart cherry with light red fruits; fruits resist cracking and keep well on the tree; moderate disease resistance; very cold hardy

'Sweet Ann' Sweet cherry with yellow fruits and a red blush; crack resistant and firm textured; excellent flavor; cold hardy

▷ **Orchards**

CHILDREN

Plant a mini garden. Make a space in the garden for a child to grow plants. Provide a child-size watering can and tools and place a sign with the child's name in the plot. And don't be too exacting—to a child, the thrill is in the process, not in producing something perfect.

Keep them interested by sowing plants that sprout quickly (lettuce, radishes, and marigolds, for example) or choosing different plants with staggered harvest times.

Blue potatoes? Plant varieties that bear unusually colored or shaped fruits—blue potatoes, purple broccoli, speckled bush beans, or rounded yellow cucumbers.

A tunnel of flowering climbers becomes a playhouse for children. Anchor wire hoops in the ground and plant an easy-to-grow climber such as honeysuckle.

Watch it grow. Lightly scratch your child's name or a silly face into a young pumpkin growing on a vine. Over time, the drawing will grow and take shape. Or plant your child's initials in the soil with garden greens; red- or green-leaf lettuce, chives, radishes, and garden cress will work nicely.

Make mint tea. Plant easy-to-grow mint. When it's ready, whip up a batch of solar mint tea with your child by filling a 2-quart glass jar with water and a handful of mint leaves. Cover the mouth of the jar with foil and let the jar sit in a sunny spot for 2 or 3 hours. Then pour into glasses, add ice cubes and a dollop of honey, and have yourselves a tea party.

A sneaker planter. Stimulate budding gardeners' imaginations by letting them use an old sneaker as a planter. Help your child poke a couple of holes in the shoe and fill it partly with soil. Plant little rosettes of hens-and-chicks in the holes, firming the soil with your fingers. Add soil to the shoe's top opening and plant more rosettes there. Then nestle the sneaker into the soil amid some flowers or herbs.

A sunflower room. Mark a square in the soil and plant sunflowers on the outline to make a private garden "room" for children. Be sure to leave a little space for the door.

Build a simple sandbox with treated wood, bricks, or paving stones. Line the bottom with small-size gravel or paving stones to let water drain through. To protect the box in bad weather, cover it with a tarp or a homemade canvas cover.

Avoid risky plants. Many plants are poisonous if ingested. Keep toddlers away from caladiums, philodendrons, English ivy, and many flowering bulbs.
▷ **Community Gardens**

CHILIES

Diverse and delicious, chili peppers are grown in much the same manner as sweet peppers but prefer slightly drier conditions. They can also be raised in containers to enliven a drab corner of the garden or the

---

⊰⊱ A CHILI SAMPLER ⊱⊰

The difference between chilies and other peppers is their level of capsaicin—the substance that makes them so fiery. Most can be used either fresh (preferably when unripe, or green) or dried. Best known is the jalapeño, which has become standard American fare. A larger, milder pepper with more culinary uses is the poblano, called the ancho when dried. Other types include the tiny, searingly hot serrano and the spicy cayenne, which comes in both red and yellow. The cascabel is a small round chili with brownish skin; dried, it sounds like a rattle when shaken. Seed catalogs often sell these and other chilies in seed mixtures.

Modern breeding has come up with varieties of chilies that offer heat at a comfortable level while retaining their distinctive flavor. Try 'NuMex Big Jim,' with 10-inch-long mildly hot peppers, and 'Tam Mild Jalapeño,' with only a tenth of the heat of the original.

---

house. Use chilies as a spicy condiment for sauces or stew or as the primary ingredient in zesty homemade salsas.

Hot weather breeds hot peppers. To grow the hottest chilies, plant in the sunniest spot in your garden and harvest during the warmest weeks of summer. Keep in mind that Southern gardeners should provide partial shade against the intense afternoon rays that may burn the pod. Northern gardeners should start chilies inside in pots to provide the long season required to ripen the fruits.

Hang them up to dry. This preserves the chilies for cooking and makes a decorative wall hanging. Easy to craft are traditional *ristras*—braided clusters of red peppers. Select only those peppers that have started to turn red. Bind peppers in groups of three with string and attach each cluster to strong wire or heavy twine. Hang from a rafter or door frame and braid the peppers around the twine.

Plant chilies and their bell pepper cousins in separate areas of the garden. If cross-pollination occurs, sweet peppers may end up spicier than you'd like.

Make a wreath of chili peppers as a Christmas decoration. Braid fresh red and green peppers around a florist's wreath. Or use a coat hanger that has been bent into a circle. Hang on a wall or door; the peppers will dry and last for at least two seasons.

The best defense against chili burns on exposed skin is rubber gloves. Wear them whenever cutting or peeling a hot pepper. If you do get burned, wipe the skin with a solution of 1 part bleach to 4 parts water. Keep your hands out of your eyes; the sting can be ferocious. If the chili juice does get in your eyes, flush with water immediately.

Put the fire out. To ease the burn when eating a too-hot chili, reach for the nearest starchy food instead of water. Because capsaicin—the chili's heat source—is an oil, it mixes better with starch.

JUST HOW HOT?

There are more than 200 varieties of peppers, including sweet and hot. Scientists have determined their relative heat by measuring their level of capsaicin. The selective list below ranks peppers from hot to mild and includes a new cultivar bred for mildness.

Heat rank	Pepper
1	Habanero
2	Chiltepin, Thai
3	Cayenne, Tabasco
4	Serrano
5	Yellow Wax Hot, Caloro
6	Jalapeño
7	Cascabel
8	Ancho, Pasilla
9	'NuMex Big Jim'
10	Bell, Pimiento, Paprika

▷ **Peppers, Vegetable Gardens**

CHIPMUNKS

A garden foe? While mostly harmless to the home gardener, chipmunks are known to feed on newly seeded garden beds. They can be a nuisance in rock gardens as well, where they burrow and disturb both rocks and your plants. Eliminate potential living quarters—hollow logs and rock piles—to discourage chipmunks from taking up residence.

A harmless trap. Trap and move chipmunks to another site. Place a Havahart or small box trap baited with oats, corn, or peanut butter by the burrow entrance. Check with a wildlife official to ensure that moving wild animals is legal in your state.

Keep chipmunks from burrowing in the garden by sprinkling dried blood on the soil surface; its odor repels chipmunks. The blood also supplies the soil with nitrogen.

Bulb eaters. Chipmunks have an appetite for newly planted bulbs—especially crocuses, hyacinths, and tulips. For protection, plant bulbs in wire baskets or sprinkle moth crystals on top. You can even plant bulbs deeper than usual and cover with coarse gravel: the animals usually give up digging when they get to the stones.
▷ **Rodents**

CHIVES

Hardy and decorative. Use chives' blue-green foliage and pastel flowers to best effect along low borders in vegetable gardens or flower beds. Alternate with bell-flowers or carnations for a pleasing look.

Divide clumps in early spring in temperate climates. In hot climates, wait until fall. Dig up clumps that are 12 to 18 inches across and separate by hand or cut into pieces with a knife. After replanting, cut the tufts to 2 inches tall. Fertilize and keep well watered. Pot extras and grow them indoor for winter use.

Mini bouquets. The flowers that look so dainty in borders or beds ultimately hinder production and harvest of the leaves. Cut the flowers off at the base when they are buds and make little bouquets out of them; either use them fresh or hang upside down to dry.

Harvest often for maximum growth, cutting tufts about 2 inches from ground level. If the tufts are large, harvest only half the plant at any one time. To prevent yellowing, don't harvest the leaves in small bits. Use scissors or a knife to snip off whole stems or portions of tufts instead; this spurs the growth of new leaves. Your chives will remain tender and fragrant.

The best way to store. Chives don't dry well for use later: freeze them instead. Harvest the tufts, being careful to keep leaves in the same direction. Pick through to remove yellow foliage, rinse, then dry with paper towels. Lift a small handful, fold it in half, and place in a small freezer bag. Never chop before freezing! The pieces will stick to your fingers and the plastic bag, and many will be lost.

Grow them in pots in cold-weather regions. At the end of summer, cut back a few of the tufts to the base and transplant the clumps into a pot with other herbs—perhaps parsley or basil. Bring them inside to a sunny spot. With enough light, they will last for weeks and even months.

Winter forcing. Lift the prettiest tufts in November and cut back the tops to an inch above the crown. Store them in a dry root cellar or a cold frame until ready to force. This period of rest is necessary before growth restarts. Bring them inside after 3 or 4 weeks at the minimum. Cut off the yellowed leaves at their base with scissors; prune the roots slightly and soak them for 12 hours in hot water.

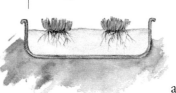

Transplant the chives into trays or pots and move them to a warm, sunny spot. Young leaves will quickly develop.
▷ **Herbs**

CHRISTMAS TREES

Buy only freshly cut trees. Fresh-cut trees are longer lasting and are less likely to become fire traps. To test for freshness, bend a needle or two sharply between your thumb and forefinger. If the needle is brittle, the tree is too dry; if it springs back to its original position, the tree is fresh.

Needle shed. Select the trees least likely to shed needles when brought indoors. The choices, from best to worst, are pine, Douglas fir, spruce, and hemlock.

Before setting up your tree, saw an inch or more off the base of the trunk to provide a fresh, absorbent surface for taking up water. Keep your tree stand filled with water. Set up the Christmas tree as far away from heat sources as possible to minimize drying and prevent fire hazards; because of their high resin content, dried evergreen branches are highly flammable.

A winter mulch. Branches from the tree make an ideal winter mulch for perennials, small border shrubs, and strawberries. Either shred with a wood chipper or lay pieces of whole boughs atop the soil.

Choose a living tree. Buying a living tree for replanting outdoors will enhance your landscape long after the holidays are over. Just make sure not to keep the tree indoors more than 8 to 10 days; otherwise, it may not survive when planted out. If your living tree has been balled and burlapped, pot it in a tub or planter. Fill in with sphagnum peat to keep the soil moist.

Decorate your living tree with strings of cranberries and popcorn. When the tree is planted out, it doubles as a bird feeder.

Mulch the planting site. In cold-weather regions where the ground freezes hard, blanket the site where your tree will go with a generous layer of mulch well before Christmas. This will keep the soil from freezing deeply and make it easier to work the soil and dig a planting hole. Before planting your living tree, acclimate it to the outdoors by holding the tree in an unheated garage or a garden shed for a few days.
▷ **Conifers, Evergreens**

Grown outdoors on a slope, chrysanthemums create a blanket of brilliant color in autumn.

CHRYSANTHEMUMS

Grow big potted flowers. Get big, showy chrysanthemums simply by pinching off all the side shoots—the lateral buds at the top of the stems—between April and June as the plant grows. Keep only the terminal bud at the top. For best bloom, choose the varieties called florist's chrysanthemums, large-flowered mums, or football mums; plant between three and five per pot.

Cascades of chrysanthemums. Train button mums or other small-flowered chrysanthemums to cascade over the sides of their pots by tying them to bamboo canes that are slanted progressively downward as the plants grow. In September, when the plants are ready to flower, remove the canes and let the plants hang down on their own.

Chrysanthemums as standards are possible with the most vigorous florist varieties. From early March, train to a single stem by removing all the side shoots and the basal leaves as they grow. When the plant reaches the desired height—about 2 feet—pinch out the top so that the branches of the crown can develop. Be sure you've retained enough of the higher side shoots to allow the top to form a full, lush crown. As the plant grows, maintain a balanced shape.

Colorful beds in fall. Many hardy perennial chrysanthemums boast a long and late flowering, even into November. They make colorful autumn companions for ornamental cabbage and kale. Look for them in catalogs under "garden mums."

Pinch out the growing tips of garden mums regularly until about the Fourth of July to encourage compact growth that will bloom heavily.

Shallow-rooted mums need extra winter protection to prevent heaving. After the first freeze, cut back the stems to ground level and mulch with about 3 or 4 inches of hay, straw, or shredded bark. This helps plants overwinter in temperatures as low as −10°F and escape the frost heaving that is caused by alternate freezing and thawing of the soil.

▷ **Flower Beds**

CITRUS FRUITS

Not just for warm climates. Citrus fruits can easily be grown in cooler regions—but only in pots or planters, which allow them to be moved inside when the weather cools. Dwarf plants are available that will grow and bear fruit in pots as small as 18 inches in height and depth. Move plants inside in autumn and back outside in May, after warm weather has settled in. Place the larger pots on wheels or move them in a wheelbarrow or a cart.

An adaptable tree. The trifoliate orange *(Poncirus trifoliata)* is a citrus relative that will grow even where temperatures drop as low as 0°F. The tree's leaves, flowers, and decorative fruits resemble those of true citrus plants, but the fruits are somewhat bitter; they're best used in marmalade.

An ideal choice. Kumquat is an all-purpose citrus with evergreen leaves, fragrant white flowers, and decorative edible fruits.

Watch for scale insects! These oddly shaped, immobile insects appear as a brownish or gray scale on stem, leaves, or fruits. Rub them off, dab them with a cotton swab dipped in alcohol, or spray if the infestation becomes severe.

Pretty plants. Citrus fruits are decorative as well as productive. Place on a veranda or within view of a picture window. When the first fruits wither or become ripe, cut with scissors, keeping a short stem.

Easy to sprout. Sown in a damp soil, citrus seeds sprout fairly easily. Repot them into individual containers when they become crowded. In no time at all, you'll have stocky and attractive green plants with foliage that grows prickly with age. Under ideal conditions, the plants may eventually bear edible fruits.

Yellowing of citrus leaves may indicate that the soil is too cold or too alkaline. To remedy, try adding ½ teaspoon of vinegar

to every quart of water that you give your plants.

Sweeten the air by drying a rind on a radiator or by throwing it into the fireplace.

Store the rinds in sugar. After peeling off the rind of lemons, oranges, or any other citrus fruit, cut it into small strips and place in a jar of powdered sugar. You can use it to decorate a cake or cocktail glasses or to perfume jams, fruit preserves, or compotes.

A closet freshener. Make a decorative pomander by piercing an orange or lemon with cloves and suspending it in a closet or armoire. The pomander will give off a pleasant fragrance after it has dried. It also acts as a moth repellent. Add a pretty ribbon, but only after the fruit has completely dried; otherwise, the ribbon will slip off. A pomander keeps for several years.

⇥ A CITRUS SAMPLER ⇤

Oranges, grapefruits, lemons, limes, tangerines, tangelos, kumquats—the list of citruses is a long one. Keep in mind that most of the edible varieties are not frost hardy. Among those that have been bred with some measure of frost hardiness are the kumquat 'Nagami,' a thumb-size fruit perfect for marmalades, and the lemon hybrid 'Meyer.'

Quality oranges include the juice-filled, seedless 'Valencia.' Grapefruits to savor are the meaty white 'Marsh' and the red-fleshed 'Redblush.' Try 'Mexican' or 'Key' limes for good juicy flavor. The tangelo 'Minneola' is tasty and keeps on the tree for 2 months.

▷ **Orchards**

CITY GARDENS

A matter of space. Some keen gardeners who live in the heart of a large urban center are lucky enough to have a small back yard or a courtyard, while others have only balconies or rooftops on which to cultivate plants. With a little effort, however, all city gardeners can grow ornamentals and food.

Don't be afraid to plant big. Small ornamentals in a small space may create an unwanted "dollhouse" effect. Taller potted plants, spreading evergreens, and flowering deciduous trees like the crabapple make good backdrops as well as eye-catching accent plants. On the other hand, don't clutter up a limited space and box yourself in.

Grow dwarfs for edibles. Dwarf fruit trees and dwarf vegetables produce fruits just as large as those of full size varieties, and are bred especially for growing in containers.

A tolerant rose. If you want to plant streetside roses, choose rugosa varieties, which are relatively immune to vehicle exhaust and pavement heat. This open rose is also undervalued by thieves, who prefer the tighter florist kind.

City-tolerant trees include the ginkgo, gray birch, little-leaf linden, sweet gum, red oak, and Bradford pear.

Grow rooftop tomatoes. City gardeners, too, can enjoy homegrown tomatoes. Dozens of varieties with cherry- to medium-size fruits have been bred to grow in containers. One of the larger-fruit-ing types is 'Better Bush Improved,' yielding 4-inch fruits. The smallest plant is the cherry tomato 'Micro-Tom'—small enough to grow in a 4-inch pot in a window box.

Create compost in your kitchen, on a rooftop, or—if the law allows—on a fire escape. A shallow 2- x 2-foot box is adequate for vermicomposting (composting with earthworms). If the box is placed outdoors, cover it with a tarp to insulate.

A window herb garden. Window boxes that get full sun will give you fresh herbs all summer long. Some easy-care choices are sage, chives, thyme, oregano, and basil.
▷ **Balcony Gardens, Community Gardens, Earthworms, Dwarfs**

CLAY SOIL

Know it when you see it. If you spot spontaneous growth of buttercups, sorrel, thistles, or chicory, your soil is clayey. Another sign: if a puddle remains on the soil's surface after a rain. Still another: if the soil makes hard clods when dry and is sticky when wet.

Try double digging clayey soil—especially if you're planting a vegetable garden. This technique is an especially good way to lighten and enrich the soil. First dig a trench about 2 feet deep and add a good helping of compost or aged manure. Then dig another trench alongside the first and shovel the turned earth back into the first trench, mixing it well with the compost.

Another solution. Gypsum—calcium sulfate—is an excellent conditioner for clay, improving soil structure and aiding air and water penetration. Spread and work in 20 to 30 pounds of gypsum per 100 square feet for a new garden bed. For planting holes, dig a few spoonfuls into the bottom and mix a handful into the backfill.

Using peat moss helps to retain air and moisture. For every 100 square feet, use 9 cubic feet of peat and 20 pounds of lime.

Make your spading easier by puncturing clay soil with a pitchfork and wiggling it slightly as you withdraw it.

Prevent cracking. Large cracks are common in clay soil in summer, especially in the hottest Southern states. Blanketing the soil with an organic mulch (leaves, compost, or pine straw) will enrich the soil with humus and keep it moist and crack-free. Replenish the mulch as often as necessary.

Keep off the clay. If you walk upon or till clay soil while it is still wet, you'll pack it even firmer. Instead, install permanent paths of brick or stone in garden beds to provide a place from which you can work.
▷ **Drainage, Soil**

CLEMATIS

Queen of the climbers, clematis is prized for its exceptionally long flowering period, variety of flowers shapes and colors, and tolerance of almost any conditions and climate. Equipped with twining tendrils, the plant will attach itself and rapidly grow through thin-lathe trellises, bushes, and even other climbers. If you want to festoon a tree trunk or other wide support, first attach a piece of plastic-covered mesh so that the tendrils can grab hold.

Submerge the root ball of a nursery-bought plant in a bucket of water and keep it underwater

until no more bubbles escape. Water the bottom of the planting hole (sited a foot or so away from the wall or support to allow for good air circulation) before planting. Fill in, firm the soil, and water thoroughly again.

Head in the sun, feet in the shade. The clematis grows best when its roots are kept cool and moist. Protect the roots with a thick layer of damp peat moss and straw. Or surround them with pieces of slate or roofing shingles or tiles laid flat. You can also keep roots cool by underplanting with any low-growing, shallow-rooted annual, perennial, or ground cover.

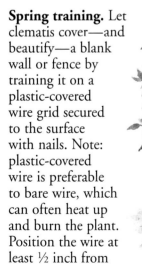

Spring training. Let clematis cover—and beautify—a blank wall or fence by training it on a plastic-covered wire grid secured to the surface with nails. Note: plastic-covered wire is preferable to bare wire, which can often heat up and burn the plant. Position the wire at least ½ inch from the surface so that the tendrils have room to twine. For smaller wall spaces, a thin-lathe trellis makes a good support.

The best thin supports include a coated-wire or steel-tube arbor or trellis construct-

The Argentine-bred cultivar 'Dr. Ruppel' twines over a harmonious trellis of bamboo canes.

ed from bamboo-stakes, twigs, or wrought-iron. The typical wooden trellis, with wide lathe lattice, is not suitable, since it necessitates tying the vine on with string or wire.

A happy marriage. Plant two different varieties either in the same hole or side by side for a spectacular bicolored flowering. Or, to prolong the floral display, plant adjoining spring and summer species with different maturation times.

Go wild with clematis. Use it to cover an arch, bower, or pillar. For an informal look and a double dose of color, let clematis climb up natural supports, as they do in the wild. For example, plant a clematis near a tall lily so that the vine can twine up the stem.

Withering away? If the foliage of your clematis withers and dies from a girdling stem canker at the soil line, it's a victim of a common disease: clematis wilt. Remove and burn diseased stems, cutting well below the infected area. Sow new plants in a new location and grow in moist, neutral soil that is well-drained.

Two for one. An evergreen hedge provides a good support for clematis, which offers in return a delicate, fanciful contrast. Allow the supporting plant to grow for 2 years before planting the vine at its feet. The clematis will then happily twine through its host.

Prune at the right time. Clematis that flower in spring do so on the previous year's ripened wood and require only light grooming. Late-blooming types flower on young wood produced the same year and require a hard annual pruning in late winter or early the next spring.

Easy cuttings. In summer, select a half-ripe branch from the middle part of a shoot. Cut below the bud and pull off the leaves and lower bark. Dip the end in rooting hormone and insert the cutting into a damp rooting medium. Keep shaded until roots form.

For winter decoration, leave the feathery fruits on your clematis. With the first frost or snow, the fruits will be transformed into dazzling little jewels. If you want to use them in a dried arrangement, cut them before they mature and fall from the plant.

THE BEGGAR'S HERB

The leaves of certain clematis have been known to cause violent dermatologic reactions when applied to the skin. In bygone days beggars used this to their advantage to gain the pity of passersby. It is for this reason that clematis was once called "beggar's herb" and symbolizes "artifice" in the language of flowers.

A favorite since the turn of the century, the morning glory 'Heavenly Blue' evokes a sweet nostalgia.

New life for an old umbrella. Slide the framework of an old umbrella into a metal pipe driven into the ground. Plant two clematis at the foot of the frame. The flowering vines will quickly blanket it.

Fragrant too. Many varieties of clematis are grown as much for their scent as their delicate blooms. The only one of the large flowering hybrids that has fragrance is the lovely 'Fair Rosamond,' which smells like violets. Fragrant small-flowering varieties include *Clematis flammula*, with tiny white flowers that sweeten the night air, and the almond-scented pink or white *C. montana*.
▷ **Climbers**

CLIMBERS

Beautify an ordinary barrier. Turn an otherwise dull wall or fence into a magnificent living barrier. Train such climbing plants as ivy, roses, Virginia creeper, and nasturtiums up the sides of walls, through the holes in fencing, or along latticework. Chain-link fences in particular benefit from this effective beauty treatment. To further obscure a fence, paint it green before the plants begin to grow and flower.

PURCHASING
A basic rule. Never buy a climbing plant with exposed roots. The odds are that the plant has suffered and the roots have dried out. Replanting may be difficult.

Why the cost difference? Price varies for members of the same species according to several variables, including the age of the plant, the number of stems, and how well rooted the plant is. Bare-root plants are generally less expensive. Some plants—often clematis or wisteria—have been grafted, and this delicate operation is always costly. These costs are then passed on to the consumer. The plus side is a plant that will flower quickly and one whose identity you are sure of—which is not always the case with plants grown from seed.

PLANTING
A shady place. Plant a low, shallow-rooted shrub, evergreen if possible, on the sunny side of the climber's foot. Its cool shade will help the vine establish itself and reach its full potential. Keep the soil around both plants cool by spreading a thick layer of organic mulch over the surface.

Keep the house cool. A climbing vine that covers a south- or west-facing wall provides insulation in summer, keeping houses cooler and air-conditioning costs down.

Don't plant ivy or other vines where they can climb on wood siding or clapboard; they can quickly cause the wood to rot.

Discover climbing hydrangeas. These plants make a lovely covering for a north- or east-facing or partly shaded wall. They need time to establish and a strong support to cling on. Your reward: spotless white flowers that appear in summer.

A climbing bulb. In summer, the climbing lily blooms with bright red flowers banded in gold. Plant it in full sun and provide a trellis or other support.

❧ GOOD CHOICES FOR THE GARDEN ❧

	ANNUALS	PERENNIALS	BULBS	
Sun	Chilean gloryflower (*Eccremocarpus scaber*)	Clematis	Star jasmine	Glory lily (*Gloriosa*)
	Hyacinth bean (*Lablab*)	Cup-and-saucer vine (*Cobaea*)	Trumpet creeper (*Campsis*)	
	Crimson starglory (*Mina lobata*)	Golden hops	Virginia creeper	
	Morning glory	Honeysuckle	Winter creeper (*Euonymus*)	
	Nasturtium	Kiwi	Wisteria	
	Sweet pea	Passion-flower		
	Porcelain vine (*Ampelopsis*)	Perennial sweet pea		
		Rose		
Part sun	Hops	Climbing hydrangea	Silver-lace vine	
		Ivy	Winter jasmine	

Trunk treatment. Some vines will climb a tree, adding color and texture to the trunk. Select vigorous species that can tolerate shade and tree-root competition and that can climb unassisted. Ivy, winter creeper, and cross vine are good choices. Install plants carefully around tree roots in humus-rich soil, and give extra food and water as needed. Train the stems by tying loosely to the trunk.

Heavy vines—such as those of honeysuckle and passion-flower—can be supported on strong copper wires. The wires will eventually oxidize to an attractive green that blends into the foliage.

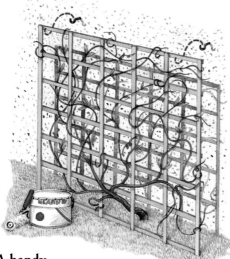

A handy removable trellis.
If you regularly repaint the wall on which you install a climbing plant, mount a trellis on hooks to make it easy to remove when the time comes to paint. Or put the base on hinges so that the trellis and plant can be folded down in one piece when you need to work on the wall.
▷ **Trellises**

COFFEE GROUNDS

As fertilizer. Coffee grounds placed in the planting hole encourage acid-forming bacteria, boosting the growth of such acid-loving plants as blueberries and evergreens.
But take note: once added to compost, the grounds no longer provide acid, as finished compost generally has a neutral pH.

Mix with mulch. Don't use coffee grounds alone as a mulch. Because they tend to cake up, your leftover grounds should always be mixed with dry materials like pine straw or dead leaves.

Use drip grounds instead of boiled grounds; they are richer in nitrogen.

Add heft to tiny seeds, such as those of carrots, lettuce, and radishes. When planting, mix the seeds with a small portion of dried coffee grounds. This will help keep the seeds from clumping, add weight, and give you a better "feel" in your hand.

COLD FRAMES

Indispensable. Often nothing more than a simple wooden box with the bottom taken out, a cold frame is an invaluable tool for starting seedlings, hardening off young plants, or storing bulbs.

Construct cold frames out of new or salvaged materials—bricks, wood, or metal. If you opt for wood, the pressure-treated type is the most durable.

A slanted lid or roof made of glass, fiberglass, or plastic will maintain warmth inside and help seedlings and plants establish themselves. In winter, use canvas, black plastic, or other protective covers to keep out cold and snow.

Make a movable lid to be opened during the warmth of day and closed at night. Or fashion a prop that will allow the frame to be opened to different heights.

An old window from a junk dealer makes a perfect cold-frame lid. Simply build the frame to match the window's dimensions.

Place the frame flat on the ground on well-drained soil. Place a layer of coarse sand or gravel on the bottom and top with good planting soil at least 6 inches thick. Height is important if the frame is used for housing larger plants.

Heat relief. Provide your cold frame with periods of partial shade during the hottest days. A light sheer voile fabric, netting, or a straw mat makes a good summer shade cover. It also keeps rain, wind, and animals away from your flowers and vegetables. Keep a large cover securely in place by weighting its edges with bricks on the ground. For a neater look, simply glue a triangular piece of Velcro to each corner of the frame and sew matching Velcro pieces onto the fabric.
▷ **Frost**

Enjoying garden color year-round

No matter where in the country you live, you can savor a garden full of color through all four seasons. Whatever your local climate, you can have sunny pastel buds usher in the first warmth of spring and bright paintbox-colored blooms signal the height of summer. You can draw on a palette of blazing orange, red, and gold foliage to herald autumn and, in winter, enliven the monochromatic landscape of cold and temperate areas with evergreens in a spectrum of greens and blues.

Not all of your garden's color comes from flowers and autumnal foliage. The many variegations of ground covers, grasses, and ornamental barks make a tinted backdrop for more prominent garden features.

Plan your garden season by season, with complementary colors in mind. Planting the same flower or shrub in masses creates striking drifts of color, while mixing and matching species and colors gives a less dramatic but more natural effect. As you work out a garden design, consider the differences in sunlight and shade during each season: a bed that gets good sun in early spring before deciduous tree leaves sprout may not be able to support sun-loving plants later, for example.

Use the chart on the following four pages to find plants that will grow in your climate—cold, temperate, warm, or hot—and provide the colors you want throughout the year. With some plants, you'll find that the species (spp.) blooms in its natural form in only one color, while its garden cultivars (cvs.) offer other hues as well.

WINTER

	COLD	TEMPERATE	WARM	HOT
PINK	David's peach tree	Daphne Lenten rose	*Camellia* spp. and cvs. Daphne Lenten rose Pansy cvs.	Bauhinia *Cyclamen* cvs. Freesia Poinsettia cvs.
RED	*Ilex verticillata* and cvs. Siberian dogwood *Viburnum* spp. and cvs.	*Cotoneaster* spp. Holly spp. and cvs. Red-twig dogwood Siberian dogwood	*Camellia* spp. and cvs. Coralberry Pansy cvs. Red-twig dogwood	Amaryllis *Cyclamen* cvs. New Zealand Christmas tree Poinsettia cvs.
ORANGE	Amur chokeberry	Japanese cedar Paperbark maple *Pyracantha* cvs.	Iceland poppy Pansy cvs. Paperbark maple Primrose	Bird of paradise Gerbera daisy Kaffir lily *Tulbaghia* *Veltheimia*
YELLOW	Arborvitae cvs. False cypress cvs.	Mahonia Stinking hellebore Winter jasmine Witch hazel	Mahonia Pansy cvs. Winter jasmine Witch hazel	*Acacia* spp. and cvs. Freesia Golden trumpet tree Panama orange *Veltheimia*
BLUE	Arborvitae cvs. Blue spruce Colorado blue spruce Creeping juniper cvs. Mugo pine	Arborvitae cvs. Blue atlas cedar Blue spruce Fir spp. and cvs. Juniper cvs.	Pansy cvs. Primrose	Baboon flower Cape primrose
VIOLET		Beautyberry *Iris reticulata* Lenten rose	New Zealand flax cvs. Primrose	*Fittonia* Fuzzy ears Glory bush
GRAY	Balsam fir Silver fir	Beech Lacebark pine Russian sage Serviceberry	*Artemisia* spp. and cvs. Olive Russian sage *Salvia* spp. and cvs.	*Artemisia* spp. and cvs. *Eucalyptus* spp. Russian sage *Salvia* spp. and cvs.
WHITE	Christmas rose White birch	Christmas rose Lenten rose Snowdrops White birch	*Camellia* spp. and cvs. Lenten rose *Michelia* Pansy cvs.	Amazon lily *Cyclamen* cvs. Freesia *Spathiphyllum*

COLORS

SPRING

COLD	TEMPERATE	WARM	HOT	
Cherry spp. and cvs. Crabapple spp. and cvs. Lilac cultivars Pansy cvs. Peony cvs. *Phlox* spp. and cvs.	Cherry spp. and cvs. Crabapple cvs. *Magnolia* spp. and cvs. Pansy cvs. Peony cvs. *Rhododendron* spp. and cvs. Tulip spp. and cvs.	Bleeding heart spp. and cvs. Cherry spp. and cvs. Crabapple spp. and cvs. *Magnolia* spp. and cvs. *Nemesia*	Holly flame pea Magic flower Mandevilla Myrtle	**PINK**
Pansy cvs. Peony cvs. *Phlox* spp. and cvs. *Potentilla fruticosa* cvs. Primrose	Crabapple cvs. Pansy cvs. Peony cvs. *Rhododendron* spp. and cvs. Tulip spp. and cvs.	*Anemone coronaria* cv. Crown of thorns *Dianthus* spp. and cvs. Shirley poppy	*Anemone coronaria* cv. *Banksia* Crown of thorns *Leptospermum* Red passionflower	**RED**
Crocus spp. and cvs. Iceland poppy Pansy cvs. Primrose	*Crocus* spp. and cvs. Daffodil cvs. *Euphorbia grifithii* and cvs. Flowering quince *Geum* spp. and cvs. Pansy cvs.	Buttercup cvs. California poppy Daffodil cvs. *Euphorbia grifithii* and cvs. Flowering quince	Blood red trumpet vine Holly flame pea Kaffir lily Marmalade bush	**ORANGE**
Basket of gold Daffodil spp. and cvs. *Forsythia ovata* and cvs. Pansy cvs. *Potentilla fruticosa* cvs. Primrose	Columbine Winter hazel *Crocus* spp. and cvs. Witch hazel Daffodil spp. and cvs. *Forsythia* spp. and cvs. Pansy cvs. Tulip spp. and cvs.	California poppy Columbine Cypress spurge Daffodil spp. and cvs. Japanese kerria Winter hazel	*Euphorbia* spp. and cvs. Golden candle Primrose jasmine	**YELLOW**
Bugle weed cvs. *Campanula* spp. and cvs. Forget-me-not Lilac cvs. Pansy cvs. *Phlox* spp. and cvs.	Bethlehem sage cvs. Pansy cvs. Bluebell cvs. Siberian bugloss Blue false indigo Columbine Forget-me-not Grape hyacinth *Iris* spp. and cvs.	*Anemone coronaria* cv. Bluebells Columbine Forget-me-not Grape hyacinth Lupine	*Anemone coronaria* cv. Australian bluebell creeper *Tillandsia*	**BLUE**
Crabapple cvs. Lilac spp. and cvs. Pansy cvs. *Phlox* spp. and cvs. Violet spp. and cvs.	*Crocus* spp. and cvs. Lilac spp. and cvs. Pansy cvs. *Phlox* spp. and cvs. Violet spp. and cvs.	*Anemone coronaria* cv. *Dianthus* spp. and cvs. Lupine *Osteospermum* cvs. Wisteria	*Hardenbergia* Queen's wreath *Tillandsia* Wisteria	**VIOLET**
Artemisia Creeping juniper Lamb's ears Snow in summer	*Artemisia* spp. and cvs. *Dianthus* spp. and cvs. Lamb's ears Lavender spp. and cvs.	*Artemisia* spp. and cvs. *Dianthus* spp. and cvs. Lavender spp. and cvs. *Salvia* spp. and cvs.	Artichoke *Eucalyptus* spp. Lavender spp. and cvs. *Salvia* spp. and cvs. *Senecio* spp. and cvs.	**GRAY**
Cherry spp. and cvs. Daffodil cvs. Labrador tea Lilac cvs. *Phlox* spp. and cvs. *Prunus cistena* Spiraea	Candytuft Columbine Peony cvs. *Rhododendron* spp. and cvs. Snowflake cvs. Tulip cvs. Violet spp. and cvs.	*Anemone coronaria* cv. Cherry spp. and cvs. Daffodil cvs. *Hebe* spp. and cvs. *Magnolia* spp. and cvs. Pacific dogwood	*Anemone coronaria* cv. California buckeye Madagascar jasmine Mexican orange bush Myrtle	**WHITE**

COLORS

SUMMER

	COLD	TEMPERATE	WARM	HOT
PINK	*Achillea millefolium* cvs. *Clarkia* cvs. Daylily cvs. English daisy *Lobelia* cvs. Oriental poppy cvs. Queen of the prairie	*Astilbe* spp. and cvs. Border phlox cvs. *Cosmos* cvs. Gayfeather Glossy abelia *Hydrangea* spp. and cvs. Purple coneflower	Crape myrtle Gayfeather Madagascar periwinkle Mountain laurel Showy evening primrose Spider lily	*Bougainvillea* cvs. Crape myrtle *Hebe* spp. and cvs. Oleander cvs. Spider lily
RED	*Achillea millefolium* cvs. Daylily cvs. *Lobelia cardinalis* Maltese cross Mask flower Oriental poppy cvs. Tassel flower	*Astilbe* spp. and cvs. Bee balm cvs. Daylily cvs. *Gomphrena* cvs. *Lobelia* spp. and cvs. Maltese cross Zinnia spp. and cvs.	California sweet shrub Cardinal climber *Hibiscus* spp. and cvs. *Lantana* cvs. Smooth sumac *Statice* cvs.	Cockspur coral tree Painted copperleaf Red cestrum Stiff bottlebrush Wax mallow
ORANGE	Daylily cvs. Marigold cvs. Monkey flower *Nasturtium* cvs. Oriental poppy cvs. *Potentilla* spp. and cvs.	Butterfly weed *Calendula* cvs. *Crocosmia* cvs. Daylily spp. and cvs. Marigold spp. and cvs. Mexican sunflower and cvs. Red-hot poker	Blanket flower Butterfly weed *Canna* cvs. *Phygelius* spp. and cvs. Shrimp plant	*Bougainvillea* cvs. *Canna* cvs. Frangipani *Lantana* spp. and cvs. Mexican flame vine
YELLOW	Black-eyed Susan *Coreopsis* spp. and cvs. Daylily cvs. Goldenrod cvs. Marigold cvs. Sunflower cvs.	Black-eyed Susan cvs. *Coreopsis* spp. and cvs. Daylily spp. and cvs. Goldenrod spp. and cvs. Sneeze weed cvs. Sunflower cvs.	Bush poppy Flowery senna Italian jasmine Mexican tulip poppy Moroccan broom Yellow cosmos	Bush poppy Canary bird bush Frangipani Mount Etna broom Tree lupine
BLUE	*Ageratum* cvs. *Campanula* spp. and cvs. Chicory *Delphinium* cvs. Edging lobelia Lupine cvs. *Salvia* spp. and cvs.	*Ageratum* cvs. Balloon flower Cape forget-me-not *Hydrangea* spp. and cvs. Perennial flax *Salvia* spp. and cvs. *Veronica* spp. and cvs.	*Ageratum* cvs. Balloon flower *Echium* Gentian sage *Hibiscus* cvs. Wild lilac cvs.	*Agapanthus* cvs. Cape plumbago *Ceonothus* cvs. *Hydrangea* spp. and cvs. *Salvia* spp. and cvs.
VIOLET	*Campanula* spp. and cvs. *Delphinium* cvs. Edging lobelia Heliotrope cvs. Lupine cvs.	Butterfly bush Lavender spp. and cvs. Meadow rue Russian sage *Verbena bonariensis*	Hyssop Lavender spp. and cvs. Rosemary Russian sage	*Brunfelsia* cvs. Glory bush Heliotrope cvs. Jacaranda
GRAY	Basket of gold *Dianthus* spp. Dusty miller cvs. Globe thistle Plume poppy	*Artemisia* spp. and cvs. *Eryngium* spp. and cvs. Globe thistle Lamb's ears Lavender cotton	*Artemisia* spp. and cvs. Cardoon Dead nettle cvs. Lavender cotton Lavender spp. and cvs.	Desert sage *Eucalyptus* spp. and cvs. Grayleaf cotoneaster Prickly poppy
WHITE	*Achillea* spp. and cvs. Baby's breath *Cornus canadensis* *Filipendula* spp. and cvs. Pearly everlasting Snow on the mountain	*Anemone* × *hybrida* *Astilbe* cvs. Baby's breath *Boltonia asteroides* Butterfly bush *Kalimeris (Asteromoea)*	African hemp California storax *Datura* spp. New Zealand daisy bush White fringe tree	*Bougainvillea* cvs. Calla lily Gardenia Rock rose *Yucca* spp. and cvs.

COLORS

AUTUMN

COLD	TEMPERATE	WARM	HOT	
Aster spp. and cvs. *Chrysanthemum* cvs. Ornamental cabbage cvs. *Sedum* spp. and cvs. Winged euonymus	*Anemone* × *hybrida* *Aster* spp. and cvs. *Chrysanthemum* cvs. *Dahlia* cvs. Heather cvs. Ornamental cabbage cvs. *Sedum* spp. and cvs.	Belladonna lily *Chrysanthemum* cvs. *Cyclamen* spp. and cvs. *Dahlia* cvs. Ornamental cabbage cvs. *Sedum* spp. and cvs.	Belladonna lily *Fuchsia* cvs. *Nerine* cvs. Wax plant	**PINK**
Chrysanthemum cvs. Ornamental cabbage cvs. Red maple *Rhus* spp. *Sedum* spp. and cvs. Sugar maple	*Aster* cvs. *Viburnum* spp. and cvs. *Chrysanthemum* cvs. *Dahlia* cvs. Maple spp. and cvs. Oak spp. and cvs. *Sedum* spp. and cvs Sorrel tree	Burning bush *Chrysanthemum* cvs. *Dahlia* cvs. Ornamental cabbage cvs. *Sedum* spp. and cvs. Tuberous begonia cvs.	*Bouvardia* Cigar plant Croton *Fuchsia* cvs.	**RED**
Apple serviceberry Blue beech *Chrysanthemum* cvs. Sour gum	*Chrysanthemum* cvs. *Cotoneaster* cvs. *Dahlia* cvs. *Fothergilla* spp. and cvs. *Pyracantha* cvs. Sweet gum	*Chrysanthemum* cvs. *Cotoneaster* cvs. *Dahlia* cvs. Lion's ear *Pyracantha* cvs. Red-hot poker Tuberous begonia cvs.	*Canna* cvs. Cigar plant Croton Frangipani Lion's ear	**ORANGE**
American linden *Chrysanthemum* cvs. *Ginkgo biloba* Goldenrod spp. and cvs. Poplar Quaking aspen	Birch *Chrysanthemum* cvs. Crabapple cvs. *Dahlia* cvs. *Ginkgo biloba* Goldenrod spp. and cvs. Poplar	Cape weed *Chrysanthemum* cvs. *Dahlia* cvs. Red-hot poker Tuberous begonia cvs.	*Canna* cvs. Cape weed Croton Frangipani Yellow bells	**YELLOW**
Aconite monkshood *Aster* spp. and cvs. *Salvia* spp. and cvs. Stokes aster	*Aster* cvs. Lily turf Plumbago *Salvia* spp. and cvs.	Aster cvs. Lily turf Plumbago *Salvia* spp. and cvs.	Billardiera Blue passionflower *Salvia* spp. and cvs. Tweedia	**BLUE**
Barberry cvs. *Chrysanthemum* cvs. Ornamental cabbage cvs. *Salvia* spp. and cvs.	*Anemone* × *hybrida* Aster spp. and cvs. Beautyberry Heather cvs. Ornamental cabbage cvs.	*Cyclamen* spp. and cvs. *Dahlia* cvs. Ornamental cabbage cvs. *Salvia* spp. and cvs.	Autumn crocus *Cyclamen* spp. and cvs. *Fuchsia* cvs. *Salvia* spp. and cvs.	**VIOLET**
Dusty miller cvs. Globe thistle Russian olive	*Artemisia* spp. and cvs. Lamb's ears Lavender cotton Lavender spp. and cvs.	*Artemisia* spp. and cvs. Lavender spp. and cvs. Rosemary *Senecio* spp. and cvs.	*Artemisia* spp. and cvs. *Eucalyptus* spp. and cvs. Lavender spp. and cvs. *Senecio* spp. and cvs.	**GRAY**
Aster spp. and cvs. *Chrysanthemum* cvs. *Lespedeza thunbergii* cvs. Ornamental cabbage cvs.	*Anemone* × *hybrida* *Aster* spp. and cvs. *Chrysanthemum* cvs. Heather cvs. Montauk daisy Toad lily	Belladonna lily *Chrysanthemum* cvs. *Cyclamen* spp. and cvs. *Dahlia* cvs.	Belladonna lily *Cyclamen* spp. and cvs. *Fuchsia* cvs. Rosemound	**WHITE**

COLORS

COLOR

Consider the surroundings. When selecting a color scheme for a garden, choose plants that contrast with their backdrop, not fade into it. A red geranium will blend with a red brick wall, whereas white or pink ones will sparkle. Against a white background—house siding, for example—use dramatic colors like magenta. On dark surfaces, peach-colored or pink blossoms stand out best.

Colors in shade. Dark colors tend to get lost in the shade. In spots that get little sun, plant light-colored flowers—white, light pink, or pale blues or greens. If you do use deep colors, provide contrast by interplanting with lighter hues. Surround burgundy-colored impatiens, for example, with pale green coleus.

Just the right color. When a plant is in full flower, tie a piece of thread or yarn of the same color to a branch. If you move, divide, or take cuttings from the plant during its flowerless period, the thread will indicate its color.

Repeat theme colors to unify your garden. For example, bordering all your garden plots with a row of yellow marigolds or creamy petunias can give the entire garden a unified look. Repeating colors using different plant types creates a similar effect.

A natural focal point. If you don't already have a visual centerpiece in your garden— a pool, statue, or fountain, for example— create one with color. Plant a mass of one color in the center of a bed and surround it with contrasting colors.

Work with the spectrum. Stick with complementary colors to avoid jarring visual clashes. On the color wheel, red is complementary with green, purple with yellow, and blue with orange.

To best see purples and blues, which tend to fade away in the garden, place them in full sunlight, mass them, or combine with dashes of white or yellow.

The illusion of space. Use warm colors— reds, yellows, and oranges—in large landscapes. Warm colors give the illusion of contracting space and make big spaces more intimate. Cool colors, on the other hand, give small areas a more expansive feel. Use cool blues and purples in courtyards and on balconies.

COMMUNITY GARDENS

Transform a vacant lot into a garden oasis. Before you start, make sure that you are operating within the law and have access to a reliable water source. If the lot is public property, get permission to use it from city officials, from whom you may reap more as well: government and private groups often offer support for fledgling gardens, providing soil, fencing, paint, seeds, and even manpower to clear land.

Organize through flyers, newsletters, or the neighborhood bulletin board. Elect a leader and establish clear rules for acceptable behavior (no ball throwing, for example). You may need to keep the garden locked; if so, provide keys.

Divided or not? Gardens can be designed as fully communal, like a farm, or may be divided into individual beds, with garden-

Shared work can transform vacant lots in the heart of cities into peaceful and bountiful gardens.

ers watering, weeding, and cleaning their own area. Personal plots help avert conflicts that may spring up over planting decisions.

Raise money for garden supplies or events by charging each gardener a minimal fee for the use of a plot. Or set up stands with surplus produce and ask for donations.

Swap seeds and cuttings with other community gardens. City parks departments may also sponsor giveaways of seeds, plants, and trees. Local garden centers often provide deals on bulk seeds, soil, or fencing.

A social center. Let the garden become more than just a garden. Use for children's storybook hours or poetry readings. Hang Japanese lanterns or strings of soft lights to illuminate the garden for evening barbecues. Designate open hours to allow the public to walk through.
▷ **City Gardens**

COMPANION PLANTS

Good neighbors. Certain specimens make good companions when planted together, yielding a variety of benefits: increased harvests, better use of nutrients, pest protection, and soil conditioning.

Lure harmful insects away from your vegetable crops by growing their favorite plants nearby. Plant nasturtiums, for example, close to beans, cabbages, or zucchini. Aphids will attack these flowers, leaving your vegetables to grow in peace.

Distract cabbage white butterflies by planting the herb hyssop in cabbage rows; the flies will flock to the hyssop rather than the growing vegetables. Hyssop is also said to boost grapevine productivity.

Plant mint between cabbages to discourage caterpillars and other pests.

Dead nettle, a member of the mint family and also called henbit, is believed by some organic gardeners to repel potato bugs. It is also said to improve the growth and flavor of many other vegetables.

Try marigolds. Although there is disagreement among gardeners and scientists alike, marigolds have been shown in some tests to keep nematodes away from growing vegetables when planted within a 3-foot radius.

Save space by pairing a climbing plant with a sturdy tall one. Stalks of sweet corn, for example, will support pole beans, letting you harvest two vegetable crops in a limited garden space.

For more snap beans, plant them next to sweet peas or morning glories, which will attract pollinating insects. Lima beans are said to flourish when planted near locust trees.

Plant green beans next to eggplants; the beans deter an eggplant nemesis: the Colorado potato beetle.

Sun screens. Install a specimen that needs shade underneath one that loves sun. Plant sun-shy lettuce at the foot of cornstalks, for example, or tender cabbage and spinach below trellised peas.

Shelter shade-loving cucumbers by planting sunflowers nearby.
▷ **Vegetable Gardens**

COMPOST

Turn kitchen scraps and garden trimmings into the rich organic matter known as compost. Packed with vital nutrients, compost is made by decomposing usable wastes in a pile or bin and then incorporating the finished product into the soil to improve its organic content. Fold the crumbly, sweet-smelling compost directly into the garden soil. Use as a mulch around trees and shrubs or to enrich houseplants. Or sift compost through a screen onto the lawn.

Build a compost bin from new or salvaged building materials, chicken wire, wooden pallets, cement blocks, or plastic. A garbage can makes a compact, manageable container. Even old refrigerator or oven racks can be put into service as sturdy compost walls. Whatever materials you use, be sure to build open slats or punch air holes to allow oxygen to enter and speed up the decomposition.

A good source for bins. The wooden pallets used for carting make ideal organic building materials for your composter. Assemble them like cubes without tops or bottoms. Place the structure in an unobtrusive corner of your garden. Plan at least two compartments: one for new wastes, the other for churning rotted compost and for use. A luxury composter has a third bin to separate semi-aged material from finished compost. Add boards to the front as the heap grows higher.

An easy alternative. Improvise a light-weight compost container by using large plastic potting-soil or garbage bags. Poke about 20 holes in the bag with scissors, fill with material, and tie off at the top. Leave the bag in the sun to allow heat to facilitate decomposition. Shake or turn the bag occasionally to mix. Bring the finished compost to the garden in a wheelbarrow and use right out of the bag.

The right consistency. If your compost doesn't heat up or is too dry, hose it down to achieve a damp consistency similar to that of a wrung-out sponge. If the compost pile is too damp, insert a few thin layers of an absorbent material; sawdust, peat, or cut hay all do the job well.

Turn compost materials regularly to provide oxygen for the organisms that induce decomposition. A pitchfork makes a perfect turning tool. If you're adding a big load to the composter, use a broom or rake handle to poke air holes in the pile.

Piles should smell sweet and fresh. A bad-smelling pile is your clue that compost is not getting enough air. To remedy, the problem, incorporate dry, carbon-rich materials like dead leaves and sawdust, turning them into the pile thoroughly.

Layer the compost heap with a mix of materials to ensure rapid decomposition. Alternate layers of high-carbon matter like dead leaves, straw, hay, or wood chips with layers of high-nitrogen grass clippings, trimmings, manure, and meatless kitchen scraps. Add new matter to the hot center of the pile to speed breakdown and hide it from flies. And never put a large quantity of any one material in the bin.

No room? Check on communal composting. If your garden is too small to accommodate a compost pile, you may be able to gain access to community composting bins. These are often managed by the city parks department or local gardening organizations, which offer compost to local gardeners at little or no cost.

Shredded or chopped materials decompose faster than bulky ones. Before you put materials into the compost bin, help the process along by chopping broccoli ends, apple cores, corncobs, citrus rinds, and other tough kitchen scraps with a sharp knife. Or use an old-fashioned meat grinder. Grind up branches, stems, and hedge prunings in a wood chipper, which can usually be rented from hardware or garden supply stores. Or burn the wood and save the ashes to add to the heap.

No chipper? If you have enough room in your garden or yard, put aside any large twigs and branches to create a "slow" compost pile. Occasionally layer the separate heap with grass clippings or nitrogen-rich manure to speed the decomposition process of the woody material.

Be adventurous with raw compostables. While all animal products except eggshells should be avoided, many other throwaways work fine. Among the materials you might try are shellfish shells, wine corks, used matches, chewing gum, nutshells, and the cotton balls from medicine bottles.

Compost needs liquid too. Pour vegetable cooking water, pickle and olive juice, water from cut-flower arrangements, and leftover coffee, tea, or broth into the compost heap instead of down the drain.

To prevent the heap from getting too wet in rainy weather, place a layer of hay, dried grass, or a piece of old carpet atop the pile.

Double duty. Take advantage of the rich soil around the base of the heap by sowing into it a few nasturtium seeds, which will scale the heap prettily and produce picking flowers. Planting squash or pumpkin seeds provides a bonus in fresh vegetables as well as decorative vining.

BLACK GOLD FOR YOUR GARDEN

Riches abound in the kitchen garbage pail and lawn clippings pile. Turn usable throwaways into invaluable organic matter that will enrich any soil with vital nutrients. You'll reap 1 pound of compost for every 10 pounds of trimmings.

Throw on the heap:	Keep off the heap:
▷ Chopped cornstalks	▷ Animal products
▷ Farm manure	▷ Diseased plants
▷ Grass clippings	▷ Perennial weeds
▷ Hay weeds	like bindweed,
▷ Hedge trimmings	mugwort, and
▷ Kitchen vegetable	other hard-to-kill
scraps	specimens
▷ Leaves	▷ Pig and pet manures
▷ Sod	▷ Vegetation treated
▷ Straw	with herbicides

Sift for a fine-textured compost. Make your own sifter by attaching wire mesh or fencing to a wooden frame and shoveling compost through it. Or remove the bottom of a wooden crate and replace with wire mesh, then sift by shaking. The finer the mesh, the finer your compost will be.

Store kitchen scraps on their way to the compost heap in the freezer. In many cases (with lettuce and tomatoes, for example), freezing will even help speed up the decomposition process.
▷ **Earthworms, Manure, Mulch**

CONIFERS

Not all evergreen. Although most conifers are evergreens, there are a few exceptions. The bald cypress, the larch, the dawn redwood, and the Japanese golden larch all lose their leaves in the fall.

Choose a well-balanced plant. Because most conifers are evergreens, they are more densely foliaged, making it difficult to spot imperfections. At the nursery, push the branches aside to inspect a tree. Never buy a tree with stunted branches or one that lacks a strong, straight main trunk.

Transplant conifers before growth starts in the early spring or after the tree has finished growing in early fall. If planting in the fall, make sure that roots will have time to establish themselves before the ground freezes. If you live in a region subject to early freezes, plant conifers in the spring. Stake newly planted trees.

The key to good growth is the aftercare given a new transplant. Water regularly the first year to establish a solid root system.

Spray the leaves to add extra moisture until the roots become strong enough to take in enough water for the entire plant.

Sun or shade? Most conifers need full sun for at least three-quarters of the day. Those planted in the shade—including even the shade-tolerant hemlocks, arborvitaes, and yews—sprout fewer branches and have a less attractive shape.

Poor drainage? Most conifers don't tolerate it. The deciduous Japanese golden larch, bald cypress, and dawn redwood are among the few exceptions. These conifers will grow well even in nutrient-poor soils.

Recycle pruned branches. Place the branches over newly planted perennials only after the ground has frozen; this protects the plants from the alternate freezing and thawing that can cause frost heaves, or shifting. Placing the pruned branches over the plants before the ground freezes won't prevent the frost heaves—but it may create a cozy nesting site for rodents.

Keep cats out of the garden and add mulch to growing vegetables by placing conifer branches among garden rows. The needles serve as a prickly barrier that keeps animals from digging in the garden, while the dropped needles provide mulch.

Needles as mulch. Rake up needles that have fallen from your conifers and spread

Dense and colorful, the foliage of conifers softens the stark winter landscape when all else is bare.

a 1- to 2-inch layer beneath shrubs and trees. Or tuck a layer around perennials, annuals, or vegetables. This protective covering not only hinders weed growth and preserves moisture but is attractive and fragrant as well.

A backdrop for flowering vines. Brighten evergreen foliage in summer by training such colorful climbing vines as clematis, nasturtium, morning glory, and cup-and-saucer plant to twine prettily on its south-facing side.

Reduce a conifer's spread by pinching back or pruning the new green shoots that appear each spring. Be careful not to prune past the point where leaves are growing, since only a few conifers can produce new growth from branches without live foliage present.
▷ **Dwarfs, Evergreens, Hedges**

CORN

Room to grow. Corn will take up a good-sized chunk of space in your vegetable garden—not only because the plants grow large but also because you'll need numerous plants, since each 5- to 8-foot stalk will produce only one or two ears.

Plant in blocks. Since corn is wind-pollinated, planting in blocks ensures that whichever way the wind blows, pollen from the male flowers (the plants' tassels) will reach the female flowers (the ears). Plant several rows so that each plant is more likely to be next to a plant that is in flower at the same time. The minimum for small gardens is 16 corn plants, planted in four rows of four plants each.

Extend your harvest in one of two ways. The first is to sow three varieties with different maturities—65, 75, and 85 days, for example—on the same day. Your corn crop should yield for 2 to 3 weeks, depending on the weather. The second method is to plant one variety successively, sowing new seed each time the previously sown seedlings have grown four leaves tall.

Don't rush it! When you plant corn, don't settle for conditions that are less than ideal. Wait until well after the last possible frost date, then listen to local weather forecasts or use a soil thermometer to make sure the soil temperature is 60°F or warmer.

Corn loves rich soil. Enrich the seedbed with compost, aged manure, and fertilizer before planting. When the plants are 1 to 2 feet tall, feed with a high-nitrogen fertilizer like manure tea or ammonium nitrate, sprinkling it beside the row.

Water first. Water the seedbed 3 to 4 days before planting and let it dry out to achieve the right moisture level. Watering freshly planted corn seeds directly will encourage rot in both seeds and seedlings.

Isolate all sweet corn—by at least 100 feet, preferably more—from any field corn, popcorn, or ornamental corn. If pollinated by these types, sweet corn will take on their starchy, tough characteristics.

Of the three kinds of sweet corn, sugary corn (SU) is the easiest to grow, since it is more tolerant of cool soil and moisture imbalance. Sugary enhanced (SE) is more demanding, needing soil that is neither too wet nor too dry and above 60°F at planting time. Supersweet corn (SH$_2$) needs even more pampering: it will not tolerate an imbalance in soil moisture or a soil temperature below 65°F. In addition, it must be isolated not only from nonsweet corn but also the other sweet corn types; otherwise, it will cross-pollinate and become inedible.

Is it ripe? Ears will be ready for harvest 20 to 21 days after the silk first emerges (exact time will vary, depending on the amount of heat the ears have absorbed through the summer). To check, look for silks dried to a dark brown. If still in doubt, slightly peel back the husk of an ear you suspect is ready, inspect the kernels, and puncture a kernel with a thumbnail; mature corn will ooze milky juice, not clear liquid. Once you become familiar with the way a ripe ear of corn looks, you can simply squeeze the tip of the ear to see if its time has come; it will feel plump and full.

Defeat corn earworms. The most effective prevention for these pests is a time-consuming one—but it's worth the effort to get a worm-free crop. A few days after the silk emerges from the developing ear, fill a medicine syringe with mineral oil and apply it to the base of the silk. Repeat the process every few days as the plant grows.

The best-tasting corn? Just picked. Boil the water while you're harvesting, shuck directly into the pot, and don't overcook! Sugary enhanced types hold their sugar content better than the traditional sugary types like 'Silver Queen,' but superiority in flavor is mostly a matter of taste.

To barbecue corn, leave the ripe ears unshucked and soak them in cold water for a half hour before cooking. The ears—husks and all—can then be banked up around the base of the fire, directly on the coals. When the husks are thoroughly charred, remove the ears, cool slightly, then shuck.

A CORN SAMPLER

Americans like it sweet! Hybrid corn varieties with a high sugar content have been preferred by home gardeners since the 1930's. They are listed in catalogs by their genotype (the genetic recipe), each with its own code.

Sugary hybrids (SU) have kernels with a sugar content of 5 to 10 percent and include a traditional favorite, the white 'Silver Queen.' Other popular choices are 'Golden Cross Bantam' (yellow), 'Honey and Cream' (bicolor), and—for short-season gardens—'Earlivee' and 'Early Sunglow,' both yellow.

Sugary enhanced hybrids (SE) combine the tenderness and complex flavor of traditional sweet corn with a higher sugar content: 15 to 18 percent. Good home garden types include 'Alpine' (white), 'Incredible' (yellow), and 'Peaches and Cream' (bicolor).

Supersweet hybrids (SH$_2$) have the highest sugar content of all (20 to 30 percent) but often at the expense of tenderness and flavor. Their advantage is a slower conversion of sugar to starch and thus a longer life. Three to try are 'Aspen' (white), 'Crisp 'n Sweet' (yellow), and 'Honey and Pearl' (bicolor).

Grow your own popcorn. A variety like the dwarf heirloom 'Tom Thumb' takes up less space than regular corn but is grown the same way. Don't forget to site it well away from other corn varieties to prevent cross-pollination. To dry, make sure kernels are fully mature before picking; the husks should be dry and brown. Pull back the husk, remove the silk, and hang or spread the ears out in an airy, mouseproof place to cure for several weeks. Kernels will rub off easily when the corn is ready to be popped.

Baby size. Unlike popcorn, baby corn—whose tiny ears are used for pickling—is not a distinct variety. Plants are simply placed closer together than usual and the ears are harvested just as the silks emerge. Choose a variety like 'Six Shooter,' which produces many ears on each stalk.

▷ **Vegetable Gardens**

CUCUMBERS

Trellis cucumbers to save space and fight foliage diseases. Getting them up high improves air circulation and allows the leaves to dry more quickly. It also keeps them off the soil, where they are susceptible to rust and rot. Gravity may help trellised fruits grow straighter, but the plants will need more water because of increased exposure to wind and sun.

Sow your cucumbers in peat pots instead of flats; the delicate seedlings won't tolerate any disturbance of their roots. Plant them out when they have grown two or three true leaves.

⊱ A CUCUMBER SAMPLER ⊰

America's favorite cucumbers are the dark green slicing types. Some examples include 'Marketmore 86,' 'Straight 8,' and 'Supersett.' All should be peeled before using. Slicing cucumbers that don't need peeling are the Chinese "burpless" types, which are longer, thinner, and more easily digested. Varieties include the original 'Burpless,' 'Orient Express,' 'Green Knight,' and 'Sweet Success.'

Pickling cucumbers are shorter, thicker, and lighter in color than the slicers. They typically produce more and smaller fruits—and all at one time, making them ideal for harvesting in large batches. Good choices include 'National Pickle,' 'SMR-58,' and 'Calypso.' A compact variety for small spaces is 'Picklebush,' with vines only 2 feet long.

Cucumbers also have their share of oddities. 'Lemon' is a sweet-tasting old variety with round yellow fruits that grow to the size of baseballs. An heirloom from Maine, 'Boothby's Blond,' is a pale yellow pickler with black spines. Scan catalogs for the rare 'White Wonder,' an ivory pickler popular in Europe.

An early start. Sow seeds 2 weeks before the predicted date of the last frost. Set the plants out 1 foot apart down the center of a 3-foot-wide raised bed covered with black plastic mulch. Cover with a floating row cover. As plants begin to flower, remove the cover so that insects can pollinate the fruit.

Encourage branching by pruning young plants as soon as they are carrying four leaves. Pick off the top of the stem, leaving two leaves at the bottom.

Grow better, stronger fruits by leaving only four fruits on a plant at the same time. When the tiny fruits begin to appear, thin them to four by picking them by hand; they'll pop off easily.

A guiding principle. Don't allow any fruit on the plant to ripen completely; otherwise, you'll limit the production of new fruits. Always pick the fruits young. If the skins have developed a golden yellow shading, you've harvested too late; by that time the cucumbers are overripe.

Space savers. If you lack room in your garden, sow compact hybrid varieties like 'Salad Bush' or 'Spacemaster.' You can even grow them in a large pot or halved wine barrel on a balcony or patio. Since cucumbers are mostly water, an ample supply is crucial; a water shortage will lead to problems with fruit shape and flavor.

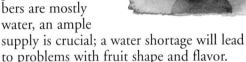

▷ **Vegetable Gardens**

CUT FLOWERS

A chicken wire holder helps your long-stemmed flowers stand up straight. Cut a piece of chicken wire, using about 10 square inches for a large vase. Fold it over two or three times, crumple it, and put it in the vase. Secure with floral tape if necessary and slide the stems into the holes.

Improvised holders. Use whatever you have on hand. Fill a soup tureen with sand or a clear vase with marbles, gravel, moss from the woods, or washed shells from the beach. Attach a pin holder with floral clay to hold flowers in shallow containers.

The best time to cut roses for indoor display is early morning or late evening. Most flowers, in fact, do better when cut at these times. Cool, cloudy days are ideal, since moisture loss is minimized.

Stems too short? Extend the length of the flowers by slipping their stems into drinking straws. Choose an opaque vase.

Prolong the life of cut flowers in any number of ways. The most reliable is to sprinkle Floralife or a similar product used by florists into the water. Lacking that, try a solution of 2 teaspoons medicinal-type mouthwash or a can of clear soft drink mixed with 1 gallon of water. Some gardeners keep flowers fresh by preparing a tea composed of about 20 foxglove leaves in ½ cup boiling water; let it cool before adding to the vase. Others swear by the addition of an aspirin, a sugar cube, or a little bacteria-killing laundry bleach.

Prepare the stems. Remove any leaves that will lie below the water line or they'll soon become slimy and rotted. On rose stems, eliminate any thorns. Cut the bottom of the stems diagonally so that they have a

larger surface to absorb water (this is best done underwater so that the vessels of the stems will not be obstructed by air bubbles). Asters, roses, and snapdragons in particular benefit from this treatment.

Cut soft stems neatly with a sharp knife or pruning shears; never tear or break them.

Smash the hard stems of trees and shrubs (redbud, mimosa, lilac, forsythia) with a hammer to enable them to absorb water more easily. Wash off or remove any loose pieces of stem before arranging the flowers. Then add a few drops of laundry bleach to the vase water to control bacteria.

A rejuvenating bath. Whether you've just picked flowers from the garden or bought

them at the florist, cut an inch or two off the stems, put the flowers immediately in a deep pail of water, and place them for a few hours in a cool spot out of direct sun. This conditioning period will help them last longer in the vase.

For fresh delivery when you're taking cut flowers to a friend, never place them in the back window in your car. Instead, wrap the flowers in damp newspaper or butcher paper and place them in the trunk or between the car seats, sheltered from the sun's rays, heating vents, and squirming children and pets.

Hollow stems, like those of daffodils, delphiniums, and amaryllis, live longer if you pretreat them to take up water. After conditioning the flowers in a pail, turn them over, fill the stems with water, and plug the base with a piece of cotton. Submerge the stems immediately in a water-filled vase.

Resuscitate wilted blooms by recutting the stems and plunging them into a few inches of warm water for a half hour. Then put them back into the vase along with fresh, cool water. If the room is hot, drop a few ice cubes into the vase. In the evening, cover the flowers with a damp paper towel to refresh and rehydrate the petals. Even better, place the flowers in a cool room or on a windowsill for a few hours.

A reservoir for water. Florist's oasis, the synthetic moss used for flower arrangements, retains moisture long after the water in a vase has dried up. Before inserting stems into the moss, give it a good soaking by holding it underwater for several seconds.

An unusual display.
Use florist's oasis to create your own original flower arrangements. Cut the moss with a knife according to your whim, changing the shape into a number, an initial, even a heart. Then attach it to a plate or dish with floral tape. Finally, soak the moss for several hours before inserting the flowers.

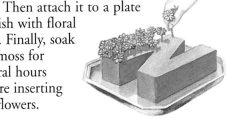

Camouflage florist's oasis by blanketing it with sphagnum moss. Moisten both before placing in your vase or container.

Cut lilies only every second or third year. Cutting the same plant in successive years tends to weaken the bulb.

Use hair spray. To keep blossoms from dropping off cut flowers, spray them lightly with an aerosol hair spray.

Keep it clean. Sparkling-clean vases ensure longer life for flowers. Wash vases thoroughly after each use and add a few drops of bleach to your rinse water. For narrow-necked containers that are difficult to clean inside, add half a cupful of dried beans or peas to the wash water and swish

them around to remove any vegetation that may be adhering to the surface.

Cauterize stem ends.
Daffodils, hollyhocks, hydrangeas, and poppies have difficulty drawing water from a vase into their stems because a milky, slimy substance inside seals the cut ends of the stems. The substance can have an adverse effect on other flowers in the same vase. Remedy the problem by singeing the ends briefly with a flame after you've trimmed the stems.

Mimosa in your freezer. Western gardeners who grow *Acacia dealbata* (mimosa or silver wattle) can delay bloom by putting cuttings in cold storage. Cut twigs that have tight buds and store in the freezer until ready to display; they will keep there for up to a week. The long panicles of fragrant flowers will bloom when the cuttings are put in warm water. To speed blooming, briefly dip the stems in boiling water.

Add fragrance to your flowers, whether fresh or dried, by soaking a small wad of paper towels in potpourri oil and placing it between the stems of the arrangement.

Add shimmering polymers—the soil crystals that retain up to 400 times their weight in water—to a glass vase for a decorative touch. Mix in a dash of food coloring if you like, and insert the cut flowers.

Repair a cracked or porous vase by melting some canning paraffin and pouring the hot liquid into the vase. Rotate the vase quickly to cover all the sides before the wax can cool. Another solution: rub a garlic clove along the crack inside the vase and let it dry.

▷ **Bleach, Charcoal, Chrysanthemums**

❧ SPECIAL TREATMENT FOR EACH FLOWER ❧

Clematis	Pour boiling water on the stems, then place them in cold water. The Japanese dip them in beverage alcohol (champagne works well) for a few hours before putting them out in a vase.
Daffodils	Cut them in tight bud or barely open.
Dahlias	Never cut in tight bud; they will not open.
Field poppies, poppies	Pick them still in the bud. Sear the base of the cut stems for a few seconds with a lighted match or gas flame, or plunge into boiling water.
Gladioli	Cut them when the lowermost floret is opening. Remove a few of the top buds.
Hellebores	Smash or split the stems before putting them in a vase. Or prick the stem in several places with a pin.
Lilies	Pick them in bud. As the flowers open, remove the anthers to prevent getting yellow stains on clothing.
Marigolds	Cut in early morning. Strip away lower leaves. Recut at a node where a leaf joins a stem. Put flowers in a quart of water with a tablespoon each of sugar and bleach. Let stand in a cool, dark place before putting out in a vase.
Pansies	Put the stems in a little water or in damp moss. Submerge wilting blooms in tepid water for 1 to 2 hours to revive. Pansies last better if one or two leaves are left on.
Peonies	Cut them when the buds are half open and coloring. Slit the stems 1 to 2 inches to aid in water uptake.
Tulips	Keep them from drooping by adding a few drops of vodka to the water.

DAFFODILS

Our favorite narcissus. The daffodil is also known as the trumpet narcissus. It is distinguished from the myriad other species of narcissus by the length of its central trumpet—as long as or longer than the surrounding petals. It comes in both single-petal and double-petal varieties.

Pinch off faded flowers with your fingernails or pruning shears, leaving the green stem in place. Removing the blooms speeds storage of the reserves the bulb needs in order to reflower next year.

⋇ A DAFFODIL SAMPLER ⋇

Home gardeners have a wide range of daffodil cultivars to choose from. Among the favorites are the classic 'King Alfred,' the most common variety in the trade. But many consider 'Dutch Master' the superior choice because of its ability to produce more than one flower per bulb. 'Little Gem' is a perfectly formed miniature version of 'King Alfred,' growing only 3 to 4 inches high and bursting with 1-inch blooms. The daffodil *Narcissus minimus* is even smaller than 'Little Gem,' peaking at 3 inches high. For those whose motto is "the bigger the better," there is 'Unsurpassable,' which requires a more fertile soil to grow the largest flowers of all—giant open trumpets of gold.

Leave the leaves, please! When its leaves become yellow, the daffodil can become unsightly. But as with all spring-flowering bulbs, be careful not to lift them from the garden until their leaves fully ripen. To shield them from sight, interplant the bulbs with annuals and perennials, whose foliage will mask the daffodil's dying leaves.

Daylilies make fine companions, because fading daffodil foliage will be neatly masked by daylilies' similar leaves. Other good screens are periwinkle and ferns.

The wild daffodil, or lent lily *(Narcissus pseudonarcissus),* thrives in damp meadows. Its trumpets are a full 2 to 2½ inches long.
▷ **Bulbs, Narcissus**

DAHLIAS

For midsummer blooms, start dahlia tubers in early spring in a warm (at least 50°F), sunny place, such as a sunroom or conservatory. Place in a shallow box filled with lightly damp peat moss, sand, or leaf mold, which let the shoots develop more easily.

Double your dahlias. When the shoots of tubers reach 6 to 7 inches, cut them 1 inch above the base and insert the cuttings in pots filled with a light mixture of damp sand and compost. Water and keep misted or cover with a plastic bag and keep them away from sun. In 3 weeks they will root— and you'll have twice as many!

The right depth. Larger dahlia varieties need a planting depth of 6 to 8 inches. Dwarf types need only 3 to 4. Plant outside only after all danger of frost has passed.

To get big flowers, choose cactus- or decorative-type dahlias. Remove the weakest stems, leaving only two or three of the strongest, when the plants are about 4 inches tall; support with stakes. As soon as flower buds have formed, pinch them off

Dahlias planted in groups bring dazzling color to the garden throughout summer and early fall.

or remove all the side shoots, leaving only the terminal bud. Water the plants well and feed regularly with a liquid 5–5–10 fertilizer.

Inconspicuous stakes. For tall dahlia varieties, stake when the stems reach 18 to 20 inches high. Select three or four bamboo canes of the same height as the mature plant and drive them into the soil beside the main stems. Tie the stems at two heights with soft twine and incorporate the new growth as it develops.

Prolong flowering by deadheading your dahlias—systematically removing all faded flowers. So treated, the small-flowered dahlia varieties are capable of flowering for a full 4 months or longer without interruption.

Easy does it. Don't tug on the stems when you lift dahlias. Delicately lift the entire clump with a spading fork to keep from damaging the tubers. Then let the tubers dry in the open air for at least a day, preferably in the sun, before knocking off the dry soil and storing them for the winter.
▷ **Flower Beds, Perennials**

DAYLILIES

Beautiful but brief. The colorful bloom of the popular daylily lasts only one day—hence the origin of its name.

Shop locally. Flower performance varies dramatically according to climate and conditions. A profuse bloomer in one climate may be a stubborn performer in another.

Look for two fans (young sprouts, or ramets) when buying a clump. It means the plant is more mature, which will greatly increase the likelihood of bloom in the first season.

Give them room. Place plants at least 2 feet apart. In the North, set them out in spring. In warmer climates, plant in spring or fall.

As erosion control. Daylilies planted on a bank provide good erosion control. Their vigorous roots help hold the soil in place.

Protect the reds. Plant red daylilies in a spot that gets relief from the hot afternoon sun, since these varieties tend to burn more easily than others. Or purchase plants advertised as "sunfast." Sunfast daylilies' petals are protected by a heavy waxy coating that makes them more sun tolerant.
▷ **Cut Flowers**

DECKS

The right place. Build your deck on the quiet side of the house and out of the neighbors' view. And site it for convenient access from the house: you don't want guests marching through the bedroom on their way to the barbecue.

Check your local building codes. In some cities or neighborhoods, you may need to apply for a permit from the local building department to attach a deck to your house. Freestanding decks, however, are generally accepted and rarely require an application.

A deck around a tree in the yard will give you hours of relaxation in cool shade during the summer months. The tree also offers shelter from sudden downpours.

Consider the wind. A trellis around the deck will help block harsh winds. Plant an attractive climber—morning glory, clematis, or jasmine—along the support to allow light breezes onto the deck.

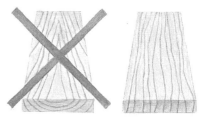

Wood is good. Much more forgiving than concrete and asphalt, wood doesn't transmit temperature extremes and remains relatively cool through the hot months. Bare feet will find it more comfortable.

Choose the right lumber. Never use flat-grain lumber when you build a deck. Moisture will eventually raise the grain and cause the boards to cup and splinter. Use vertical-grain lumber instead. Clear-heart redwood is an excellent choice, as is Western red cedar.

Stain, don't paint! When it comes to outdoor woodwork, staining is preferable to painting. Stains require less maintenance and penetrate the wood to create a soft patina that enhances the natural grain. Many have an acrylic latex base that allows for easy cleanup with soap and water. Paints blister and peel over time and need scraping, priming, and repainting.

A good paint substitute is pigmented stain, which offers tinted, virtually opaque coverage. Semi-transparent stains let the wood grain show through.

The weather-beaten look. Bleaching stains and weathering stains serve to accelerate the effects of sunlight on wood. They can create a convincing seaside silver-gray patina within only one season.

DELPHINIUMS

Long and lovely. Delphiniums, which are also called larkspurs, are tall, stately perennials with lacily toothed foliage and towers of white, blue, or violet flowers. Mature height on some types can reach 7 feet.

Plant only in rich soil that is deep, friable, and well drained. Don't expect dazzling flowerings in dry, stony soil. Delphiniums thrive especially in maritime climates; they're not suitable for the hot, humid, or arid summers of other regions.

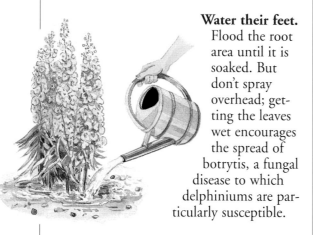

Water their feet. Flood the root area until it is soaked. But don't spray overhead; getting the leaves wet encourages the spread of botrytis, a fungal disease to which delphiniums are particularly susceptible.

For blooms all season on established plants, simply pinch out the growing points of the outer stems early in the season to stimulate lateral growth. The central unpinched stems will bloom first, followed by the shorter outer ones.

Staking is a must. Whatever you do, don't wait to stake. Do it as early as April. Only a few varieties—a handful of wild ones and small hybrids of *Delphinium belladonna*—can stand without any support.

An adequate stake must reach the base of the inflorescence, or floral axis, of the plant. Simple stakes suffice for low shapes, but medium-size delphiniums

need a special grow-through support. Place three canes around the plant and use string to create an outer ring and inner network.

Supporting the tallest. For the tallest delphiniums, make a cylinder of the required height using stakes encircled with a sheet of mesh or with string or wire. Or you can stake each stem individually with a bamboo cane.

Want a second crop? To enjoy a second flowering in September, cut back the stems of delphiniums as soon as the flowers have faded in June or July. Cut just above the basal leaves at a height of 4 to 9 inches. Water the plants copiously and apply liquid fertilizer several times throughout the course of the summer.

> ### ❧ A DELPHINIUM SAMPLER ❧
>
> While the Blackmore & Langdon and Giant Pacific hybrids—topping out at 7 feet—are hugely popular with gardeners, there are also smaller but equally striking delphiniums. Try 'Casa Blanca' for its chalk-white blooms, bushy 'Connecticut Yankee' for its prolific flowering, and 'Blue Mirror' for its brilliant hue.

▷ **Flower Beds**

DILL

Let some dill flowers go to seed. Doing so will give you plenty of seedlings every year. Dill seedlings are easy to move.

Plant among cabbage. The combined colors of dill and cabbage make a pretty picture. Dill's chartreuse-yellow flowers mix nicely with the blue-green of cabbage.

Succession plantings can be made, but don't plant dill until after the danger of hard frost in spring—about a month before the frost-free date in your area. In warm regions winter temperatures will rarely kill the plant, so you can plant in the fall.

Add to a border. Plant this herb, with its wispy leaves and yellow blooms, in your flower border for a lacy background effect.

Pretty flowers. If you decide to grow dill for the mature heads—which make wonderful fresh or dried material for flower arrangements—give the plants a foot of space all around, since they grow quite large. To use in arrangements, cut the head before the plant begins to brown. For dried arrangements or to harvest seed for flavoring, allow the heads to mature fully.

▷ **Herbs**

DIVIDING

Multiply your plants. Most herbaceous plants—those that increase in size by forming new stems and roots—can easily be divided. The process involves simply separating a big clump into several smaller ones, each carrying a few buds and roots. This type of propagation is well suited to numerous perennials and also to many bamboos, ferns, grasses, and herbs.

When to divide? Springtime is best for dividing perennials that flower in mid- or late summer: asters, chrysanthemums, sunflowers, and Japanese anemones. Those that flower in spring—peonies, columbine, euphorbia, bleeding heart, leopard's bane, and cranesbill, for example—are best divided in September or October.

A good time to fertilize. When you dig up plants for dividing, take the opportunity to enrich the soil at the same time by incorporating compost, bonemeal, aged manure, or other fertilizers.

Divide clumps of bulbs about a month after flowering, when the foliage is spent. Lift and gently separate the bulbs and replant them immediately at the same depth. Eliminate the smallest ones, which are not likely to be flowering size, or set them out in a seedbed to develop before planting in the flower bed.

Small division. You needn't pull up the whole plant if you want to separate only one or two small pieces for replanting. Gently loosen stems and roots on one side and cut the small plants off cleanly. Be sure to retain growing points or buds as well as roots on each piece. Then replace the soil around the remaining roots.

Impeccable borders. Keep edgings of chives, dianthus, and other border plants tidy by dividing them every few years at winter's end. Lift the clumps, cut each into three or four segments, and replant at 1-foot intervals. Use leftovers to extend the border's length.

To separate off a young plant, use a butcher knife, a grafting knife, old pruners, or a sharp spade. Where there are thick rhizomes, like those of bergenia and bearded iris, take care to make a clean cut.

To divide older plants, save only the outer fragments. Eliminate the woody or fibrous center, which will produce few shoots.

Divide the remaining clump into only three or four pieces; if you break it up any further, the fragments may be too weak and could be overrun by more vigorous plants.

Hands or hand tools? Use a fork or trowel to gently loosen the soil around plants that need rejuvenation before lifting the clump. Fine-rooted plants such as dianthus and bee balm can then be divided simply by pulling them apart with your hands. Use a knife or spade to separate those with tougher roots.

Having trouble seeing the buds? Knock off most of the soil and then wash the clump by plunging it into a bucket of water. Once the soil is rinsed off, you'll be better able to see the bud; cut off the desired portions with a knife.

Clean young plants before replanting. Remove any dry leaves, broken stems, and dead, rotting, or damaged roots. Inspect for any signs of pests or diseases—borers in bearded iris rhizomes, for example.

Replant immediately and water regularly to ensure strong, healthy regrowth. Heel in and keep watered any extra plants you don't put into the ground right away. Roughly repot those plants that you intend to give away or plant later, making sure to keep their roots moist.

Divide indoor plants too. When your houseplants start to look too dense and overgrown, don't hesitate to divide them. Those that divide easily include Chinese evergreen, asparagus fern, arrowroot, and African violets.

▷ **Propagation**

DOGS

Keep dogs away from your most vulnerable garden plants by fortifying the area with thorny hedges and plants. Roses, barberry, pyracantha, holly, or gooseberry are bothersome enough to deter the most determined intruders.

Use the sprinkler. If a neighborhood dog frequents your yard, train it to stay away by surprising it with a spray of water.

Keep your pet from roaming with an electrified fence specially designed for dogs. The dog is outfitted with a special collar that delivers a mild and harmless shock whenever he crosses the electric field.

A natural repellent. Sprinkle freshly ground pepper in your garden. Or plant common rue *(Ruta graveolens)* anywhere that dogs are a problem. One rue beside each tomato plant will discourage dogs from eating your harvest. A bonus: pesky ants are also repelled by this plant.

Store all insecticides well away from pets. Keep blood meal away too—dogs love it.

A compost concern. Never add dog droppings to compost. They may carry disease organisms, roundworms, or tapeworms.

Fence off the vegetable garden with wire fencing or, even better, a picket fence. Border the barrier with colorful flowers for a decorative effect.

▷ **Hedges**

DRAINAGE

Do it yourself. A large-scale drainage system that carries excess water from your yard is expensive, requiring professional help. But you can often take care of problems yourself with a few simple remedies.

Where to drain? Observe the areas where water collects after a rain and mark the sites with stakes. Then determine whether there is an outlet that is well below the area to be drained. If you have no stream or pond, check with the proper local authority to see if you can link your system to a town storm drain. If not, you must build a dry well.

Direct drainage trenches from the boggy areas to the lowest part of property. Dig the

trenches 2 to 3 feet deep and fill the bottom with a layer of coarse gravel. Lay in 4-inch perforated plastic pipe and overlay with more gravel. Then cover the pipes with topsoil. If the problem area in your garden is small—no more than about 25 by 25 feet—a single line of pipe will usually be sufficient. To achieve proper drainage for larger areas, lateral trenches (usually placed in a herringbone pattern) may have to be added.

IS YOUR SOIL WELL DRAINED?

Perform the following test to see if your soil has proper drainage. Dig a hole 1 foot wide and 1 foot deep at the lowest point in your garden. Use a garden hose to fill the hole with water. Then observe the results. If the hole empties quickly, the soil is too light to hold moisture and nutrients. If the hole still contains water after 24 hours, the soil is too heavy to drain well. If the water drains away in 30 minutes to an hour, all is well: your soil is adequately drained.

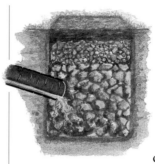

No outlet? Direct the water to a dry well, sited at the lowest point of the area to be drained. The well will hold runoff until the accumulating water can gradually seep down into the water table. Dig a hole 4 to 5 feet deep and at least 3 feet across. Fill it two-thirds full with stones, top with coarse gravel, and cover the gravel with topsoil.

A warning. Keep drains away from the invasive roots of elms, willows, and poplars, which are notorious for growing into pipes and obstructing them.

Plant on a mound. Planting a tree or shrub atop a mound of earth helps solve the problem of poorly drained soil. The mound should be at least 1 foot high. Its width depends on the eventual size of

the plant; it should be almost as wide as the spread of the branches at maturity.

A solution for small gardens. If your soil drains poorly, build a raised bed. Work into the soil plenty of organic material, such as peat moss or compost, then rake the surface until it is smooth and even. Keep the soil in place with borders of wood, stone, or brick. Alternatively, let the sides slope gradually enough to hold themselves up.

Make the best of it. Turn a poorly drained part of the garden into a haven for bog plants like marsh marigolds, water irises, and royal ferns. You need only to dig the bed a little deeper than usual. Conserve moisture with a top dressing of composted leaves in mid- to late spring. But take note:

if your bog garden is sited in a low-lying area, plants run the risk of being submerged during periods of heavy rainfall.

Houseplant drainage. The best way to ensure good drainage is to use a top-quality potting soil that suits the plant's needs. Although it is common practice to put a stone or pot shard over the drainage hole, a better solution is to place a small square of pantyhose at the bottom of the pot.
▷ **Bog Gardens, Clay Soil**

DROUGHT

Get a jump on dry spells. Plants develop shallow root systems and become more vulnerable to drought if you water them frequently. Instead, water less often—but slowly and deeply. This encourages deep root growth and makes plants better able to search out any moisture in the soil. Using a bubbler, soaker hose, or drip-irrigation system, wet the soil to a depth of 12 inches for flowers and 18 to 24 inches for trees and shrubs.

Test the depth to which the water has penetrated by pushing a ½-inch-thick iron rod into the soil. It will slide easily through wet soil—but will stop where the soil becomes dry.

Make use of compost, which goes a long way toward drought-proofing your garden. Use it as an amendment and mulch to help the soil retain moisture, ensuring that your plants will receive maximum benefit from watering and precipitation. Spread a layer about 2 inches deep over beds and dig it 12 to 18 inches into the soil before planting; add another layer as mulch afterward. To protect lawns, scatter compost over the top—about ¼ inch deep—and rake it in.

Surviving water restrictions. When watering is restricted by law, use "gray water" from the dishpan to irrigate your plants. Many ornamentals in particular thrive on the phosphates in detergents, which provide potash. The soap also acts as an insecticide. Just make sure that the detergent you use doesn't contain bleach, boron, or other toxic substances. Pour the soapy water gently over the plants, applying it to each spot no more than once a week. Alternate the applications with fresh water so that soaps won't build up in the soil.

No-no's for gray water are vegetables and other edible plants, ferns and similar shade-loving plants, and acid-loving plants like azaleas, rhododendrons, and violets.

Let your lawn go dormant. Dormancy is grass's natural defense against drought. If it appears that a drought is going to drag on for a while, stop watering your lawn. Once the grass goes dormant—usually in 1 to 2 weeks—give it only ½ inch of water every 2 weeks. The roots and buds will stay alive without resuming growth.

A clover lawn. Clover is more drought resistant than most turf grasses, staying green through the driest days of summer. Because it absorbs nitrogen directly from the atmosphere, it also works as a fertilizer, amending soil that may later be bedded with plants.

Don't give up your flowers. Keep color in the yard by planting drought-tolerant flowers. Annuals that withstand dry conditions include gerbera daisies, sunflowers, portulacas, marigolds, and zinnias. Perennials include black-eyed Susans, penstemons, coreopsis, evening primrose, and yarrow.

Keep it cool. Stave off the effects of drought by mulching plants in hot, dry weather. The insulation provided by mulch makes plant roots less vulnerable; a 3-inch layer of shredded leaves will keep the soil as much as 18°F cooler than any nearby beds that remain unprotected.

Consider xeriscaping. A more permanent way to fight drought is by xeriscaping—that is, growing drought-tolerant plants and minimizing watering. The idea is to use only trees, shrubs, ground covers, and other plants that are well adapted to the natural cycles of rainfall in your area. Don't worry about a xeriscaped yard looking drab and dry; if well designed, it can be full of color from flowers, foliage, and bark.

▷ **Lawns, Mulch, Xeriscaping**

DRYING

Pick flowers in dry weather—preferably after 11:00 A.M., when the dew has evaporated. Bunch the flowers into small bouquets and protect them from dust by covering with a sheet of paper.

Hang flowers upside down. To preserve their bright colors, hang flowers in a dry, well-ventilated place with very little light—an attic, garage, closet, or shed. Too much light causes colors to fade.

Drying herbs. Herbs used for cooking taste better when dried on paper towels or a wire screen; hanging them upside down can deplete their essential oils.

Prevent petal drop. To keep flowers from losing their petals while drying, pick them before they are fully open. And leave a sufficient amount of space between the hanging bouquets—at least 6 inches.

Replace brittle stems, like those of strawflowers, with metal florist's wire. While the flower is still fresh, thread a length of wire through the stem and bloom. Bend a small hook at the end and pull the wire downward into the bloom to conceal it.

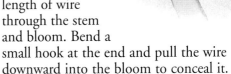

Fall foliage. Stabilize the colors of leaves by ironing with a moderately hot iron. Big leaves, such as those of beech, witch hazel, and maple, can be ironed directly.

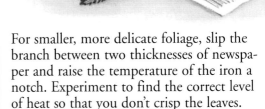

For smaller, more delicate foliage, slip the branch between two thicknesses of newspaper and raise the temperature of the iron a notch. Experiment to find the correct level of heat so that you don't crisp the leaves.

Old telephone books make good flower presses. Sandwich each bloom in tissue paper to protect it from colored inks and insert it between the book pages. Place a heavy weight on top to press the plants tightly. Leave them inside the book for up to 6 weeks or until they're completely dry.

Use silica gel crystals, sold in florist shops and hardware stores, when drying flowers with fragile petals—zinnias, pansies, and narcissus, for example—or tufted petals like those of carnations and roses. Place the flowers on a bed of crystals in a lidded tray and carefully sprinkle more on top until the flowers and stems are buried. Check them daily. Be aware that although the blue crystals will turn pink during the process, the changing color isn't a reliable indication that the flowers have adequately dried.

Try the microwave. To speed up the silica-gel technique, use a microwave oven. Select a container that is suitable for the microwave. Spread the bottom with silica gel, arrange the flowers on top, and add more gel to bury. Cover tightly. Use a medium setting—about 300 to 350 watts. Times may vary, but microwaving for 2 to 2½ minutes is usually sufficient. Repeat the procedure if drying is not complete. Once they're done, let the flowers stand—about 10 minutes for small, delicate types and up to 30 minutes for those with large petals.

Choose the right roses. Dried pink roses ('New Dawn,' 'Mary Rose,' and 'Queen Elizabeth,' for example) and yellow roses (such as 'Graham Thomas' and 'Peace') retain their color better than the reds, which usually deepen in color and may turn almost black. Single roses, like 'Betty Prior' and 'Dainty Bess,' don't dry as well as other types. White roses may become dingy.

Drying roses. Pick them when they're still in the bud stage or just barely open. Arrange them on a baking sheet or roasting rack in the oven at a very low heat—about 200°F—and keep the door propped open. Leave in the oven for about 5 hours. Once you have taken them out, pull off all the leaves and thorns.

Preserve branches of foliage—barberry, beech, oak, rhododendron, or magnolia—with glycerin, available at any drugstore. Don't wait to harvest until the leaves are ready to fall; cut in mid-season instead. Crush the stem ends and place the branches in a jar filled with 1 part glycerin and 2 parts water; there should be enough liquid to submerge the stems up to the leaves. Let stand for 3 weeks, until you can feel glycerin on the leaves.

To dry heavy-headed plants—such as thistles, alliums, and artichokes —make a simple rack out of chicken wire stapled to a cardboard box. Insert the stalks of the plants and allow them to dry for 1 week.

Bouquets aren't forever. Because dried bouquets quickly become dusty and aren't easily cleaned, they have a limited life span. Before you dispose of them, sort through the blooms and keep any that still look usable; you can rework them into another arrangement later.

▷ **Potpourri**

DWARFS

Why plant dwarfs? Dwarfs allow gardeners with limited space to enjoy varieties of their favorite plants. It also allows them the luxury of growing several different species in a small area. When space isn't a consideration, dwarfs are valuable simply for their charming miniature stature.

Trees are dwarfed in one of three ways: by genetic breeding, by grafting a normal-size tree onto a dwarf rootstock, or by pruning and training a normal-size tree, as in bonsai.

Identify them by their labels. Dwarf varieties often have the word 'Nana,' 'Pumila,' or 'Minima' in their names. For example,

The dwarf Hinoki cypress 'Nana Aurea' provides an elegant contrast to a border of red begonias.

Pittosporum tobira 'Nanum' is a dwarf variety of pittosporum; *Chamaecyparis lawsoniana* 'Minima Glauca' is a dwarf blue-foliaged variety of the towering Lawson cypress, which in its normal state grows to more than 100 feet.

Don't be fooled. Make certain that the specimens at the nursery are real dwarfs and not the slow-growing conifers that are sometimes sold as such. False dwarfs may eventually grow too large for a rock garden setting. Because of their stronger roots, they can be difficult to remove.

Ideal for the patio. Dwarf conifers are perfect for container culture. Try growing the dwarf American arborvitae 'Little Giant,' which is round and dark green, or 'Aurea,' a gold variety that turns bronze in winter. One of the smallest specimens is *Juniperus communis* 'Echiniformis,' which reaches a height of only 6 inches after 10 years.

Window box veggies. Grow dwarf tomatoes or peppers in a sunny spot on your balcony or windowsill. You can combine them with your favorite herbs.

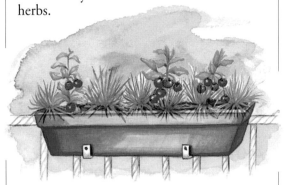

Essential for rock gardens. Dwarf perennials are mainstays of the rock garden. Choose among dwarf ferns and hostas, rock jasmine, sempervivums, saxifrages, campanulas, edelweiss, gentians, and creeping phlox.

Grow dwarf fruit trees in pots on your patio or balcony. You'll find dwarf varieties of most species at your garden supply store or in catalogs. Start them in small windowsill containers and move to bigger tubs as they grow. These small trees reach a height of 5 to 7 feet and bear fruit quickly. Plant with pollinating varieties unless the tree is self-fertilizing.

Prop it up. Support the branches of heavily laden fruit trees by using forked stakes to prop them up. Put a cushion between the fork and branch to protect the bark.

A culinary treat. You can cultivate miniature vegetables—also called baby or mini vegetables—in a corner of your garden. Some, such as squash, corn, and new pota-

⊱‖ DWARF EDIBLES FOR CONTAINERS ‖⊰

Dwarf varieties aren't limited to trees, shrubs, and flowers. You can grow a highly productive food garden within the confines of your patio or balcony simply by planting cultivars that have been specially bred to grow in pots and planters. Some of these dwarf plants produce the sweet and tender baby vegetables that are popular on the market today; others are bred to be sturdy and vigorous enough to handle normal-size fruits. Look for dwarf varieties in your local garden supply store or in specialty catalogs.

VARIETY	CHARACTERISTICS	VARIETY	CHARACTERISTICS
BASIL		**MELONS**	
'Dwarf Opal'	purple leaf; 6"–9" plant	'Minnesota Midget'	cantaloupe; 3' vines
'Fino Verde Compatto'	shrub form; 12"–15" plant	'Oliver's Pearl Cluster'	honeydew; 2' plant
'Greek Mini'	window box size; 6"–9"	'Sugar Baby'	watermelon; 3'–4' vines
BEANS		**OKRA**	
'Astrelle'	bush, mini filet	'Lee'	6"–7" pods; 3' plant
'Roc d'Or'	bush, yellow wax		
'Royal Burgundy'	bush, purple pod	**PEAS**	
		'Knight'	4" double pods; 2' vines
CABBAGE		'Super Sugar Mel'	sugar snap; 2'–3' vines
'Elisa'	green; 1–1½ lbs.		
'Fast Ball'	softball size; 1 lb.	**PEPPERS**	
'Promasa'	baby savoy; 1–2 lbs.	'Jingle Bells'	2" sweet; 16" plant
		'Mirasol'	3" hot; 2' plant,
CORN		'Petite Sirah'	2"–3" picklers; 2' plant
'Baby Blue'	4" blue ears; 5'–6' plant		
'Seneca'	mini Indian; 4'–5' plant	**PUMPKIN**	
'Strawberry'	2" red ears; 5'–6' plant	'Baby Boo'	3" white; trellis vine
		'Munchkin'	3" orange; trellis vine
CUCUMBER			
'Bush Pickle'	4" fruit; 3'–4' vines	**SUMMER SQUASH**	
'Salad Bush'	8" fruit; 1½'–2' vines	'Sunburst'	scallop, 2"–3"; 2' bush
'Spacemaster'	7"–8" fruit; 3' vines	'Peter Pan'	scallop, 4"; 3' bush
		'Gold Rush'	zucchini, 8"; 3'–4' bush
EGGPLANT			
'Bambino'	walnut size; 1' plant	**TOMATO**	
'Easter Egg' plant	egg size, white; 2'–3'	'Better Bush Improved'	4" fruit; 4' plant
'Purple Pickling'	tiny, purple; 2½' plant	'Red Robin'	1¼" fruit; 8"–12" plants
		'Yellow Canary'	1¼" yellow fruit; 6" plant

toes, will grow full-size fruits but are meant to be harvested when the fruits are young and tender. Others are bred to produce fruits that are small even at maturity; these include mini romaine lettuce, button-size carrots, baby pumpkins that will grow nicely on trellises, and serving-size heads of cabbage.

Dwarf houseplants. A number of common houseplants can be purchased in dwarf form as well. Among the favorite flowering specimens are miniature rose bushes and dwarf African violets. Popular choices for dwarf foliage plants include croton, assorted ferns, palms, and peperomia.

Dwarf no more. Don't be surprised if some dwarf flowering plants—especially poinsettias, chrysanthemums, and hibiscus—suddenly develop long stems after their flowers have faded. They are often treated with a dwarf-producing chemical called B-9, which makes them compact and early-flowering. If you want to keep them for next season, be aware that the plants will resume their normal nondwarf habit.

▷ **Planters**

EARTHWORMS

The good worm. A garden filled with earthworms is a healthy garden. That's because earthworms turn raw organic materials into a rich manure called castings. These slender coils of fertile humus can often be found by the entrances to underground tunnels. Scoop up the nutritive castings and use in pots, planters, or window boxes.

The different kinds. Of the thousands of species of earthworms, the gray-brown nightcrawler—*Lumbricus terrestris*—grows up to 12 inches long and is the most common type in North America. Another familiar species is the shorter redworm (*Eisenia foetida*), which is used for composting in worm bins.

Keep them fed. Earthworms need nitrogen in their diet and will appreciate a supply of compost as much as your plants do. Never use synthetic nitrogen fertilizer, however; the salts will repel them.

Spare the worms. To avoid cutting them up with your tiller, work in the middle of the day, when they burrow deep into the ground. When digging and planting, use a garden fork, not a spade. Contrary to popular belief, an earthworm that has been cut in half cannot regenerate.

Attract them with mulch, which provides them with food and keeps soil from becoming too hot and dry or too soggy and cold. Earthworms need an even temperature and moisture for their skin.

Make a worm bin. Composting with worms—called vermiculture—is a perfect solution for gardeners with limited space. A shallow box measuring 2 by 2 feet can comfortably handle the kitchen wastes of two people and can be placed in your kitchen or garage. The container should be free of any chemicals and well ventilated; leave the lid ajar to allow air to circulate or drill holes in the lid. To provide drainage, drill holes in the box's bottom and line with a sheet of porous fiberglass screening. Place about 1,000 redworms in the box,

along with compostables like vegetable scraps, shredded newspaper, or leaves—the more broken down, the better. Keep the bin moist but not soggy; compost will be ready to use in 2 months. If your worm bin is outdoors, provide insulation by wrapping it in burlap or plastic bubble wrap. Or sink it into the ground and cover it with a tarp.

A trap for fruit flies. If infestation occurs, place this homemade trap in the worm box. Pour ½ inch of regular (not diet) cola into a fast-food take-out cup. Push the straw through the lid so that it is above the surface of the liquid and cut it short on top. Fruit flies will crawl down the straw to reach the sweet liquid but won't be able to get out.

Harvest compost every 3 to 4 months or it will become toxic to worms. To save the worms while harvesting, dump out the pile onto newspaper under a bright light; worms will burrow toward the bottom. Scoop away compost until you reach the worms, then combine what's left with fresh materials to fill a new bin.

▷ **Companion Plants, Compost**

EDIBLE FLOWERS

Identify flowers before eating them—many are poisonous by nature. Check with a poison control center or reference guide before sampling any plant. Also keep in mind that flowers raised for the florist trade are often toxic from pesticides, and those found growing wild along the road are tainted with automobile fumes.

Unusual flavors. Try ornamental blossoms from your garden for a surprising array of tastes. Gladioli are lettucelike, and tulips taste like asparagus or peas. Clover reminds some people of honey, while daylilies have a chestnut flavor. Nasturtiums have a peppery bite, borage is reminiscent of cucumber, and dianthus tastes like cloves.

Grow your edible flowers from pesticide-free seeds or seedlings. Raise them organically and use only water, a homemade mix of dish detergent and water, or a commercial insecticidal soap for pest control.

Pick edible flowers just before you're ready to use them. They will not have wilted, and their flavor will be at its most intense. Harvested blooms can be loosely wrapped in dampened paper towels and kept in the refrigerator for about a day.

Always rinse flowers gently with water and pat dry or let air dry before using them. Be sure to inspect for insects.

Double crops. In addition to their fruits, zucchini and squash plants provide edible blossoms. Fry the flowers in batter, tempura-style, or lightly sauté them. Some people find the longer-stemmed male flowers more flavorful.

Make flower fritters. Dip acacia, elderberry, fennel, sweet cicely, squash, or fruit-tree blossoms—apple or cherry, for example—into your favorite fritter batter and deep-fry until golden.

An ordinary green salad benefits from the colorful and savory addition of nasturtium blooms.

To make candied flowers as dessert decorations, paint violets, pansies, or apple or rose petals with lightly beaten, slightly frothy egg white. Sprinkle with superfine (not confectioners') sugar. Let them dry on a baking rack or clean mesh screen and store in a tight-lidded container.

A sweet treat. Mix rose petals, lavender, or violets into cake batter or cookie dough.

Steam daylily blooms in a vegetable steamer until just wilted. Then toss with a little butter and grated Parmesan cheese.

Top fruit salad or sorbet with pineapple sage, rose, violet, lilac, or pansy blossoms.

Savory salads. Toss some blossoms from nasturtium, arugula, okra, chives, basil, marigold, fennel, mustard, or bee balm with your favorite salad greens.

Ice blossoms.
Trap violets, rose petals, or borage flowers in ice cubes to float in punch. First freeze an ice cube tray half full and then center  the blossoms on the cubes. Drizzle each with a teaspoonful of water, being careful not to move the flower; refreeze. Finally, fill the tray completely and freeze again.

Scented sugar. Layer a half-dozen leaves from a scented geranium, such as lemon, strawberry, rose, chocolate, cinnamon, or mint, in the sugar bowl. Use the aromatic sweetener for baking or flavoring drinks.

A spread for bread. Fold calendula, nasturtium, or arugula blossoms into soft butter or cream cheese for a tasty bread spread.

⊁ EDIBLES AND NONEDIBLES ⧏

DO EAT	DON'T EAT
Bee balm	Anemones
Chives	Azaleas
Daylilies	Buttercups
Dianthus	Clematis
Hollyhocks	Daffodils
Lavender	Delphiniums
Nasturtiums	Foxgloves
Pansies	Hydrangeas
Roses	Irises
Scented geraniums	Lilies-of-the-valley
Squash blossoms	Monkshood
Sunflowers	Oleanders
Tulips	Sweet peas
Violets	Wisteria

▷ **Nasturtiums, Zucchini**

EGGPLANT

Buy established plants. Because seedlings need 10 weeks of growth before transplanting and require the warmth of a greenhouse or other seed-starting arrangement, you'll be better off buying plants that are ready to be transplanted.

Make a depression at the foot of each plant to make watering easier. In cooler climates, space the plants 18 inches apart; in Southern climates, space them 24 inches apart.

Plant with their relatives. Planting eggplants, tomatoes, and peppers together in their own corner of the plot makes crop rotation easier. Move them the next year to an area where no solanaceous plants have been grown for at least 3 years.

Pinching. In areas with long growing seasons, pinch with your fingernail above the fifth leaf when the plant has six or seven leaves. This spurs the lateral bud to bear flowers and fruit. Then pinch each shoot above the leaf that follows the second flower. In short-season areas, a single pinching will suffice. Each plant is capable of bearing 8 to 10 fruits for picking in late summer through early fall.

The right conditions. Eggplant is miserable in cold, wet weather and the darker, moister areas of your garden. Put it in a sunny spot, where the soil stays warm. In short-season areas, protect with row covers.

An unwanted visitor. The Colorado potato beetle likes to stop and snack on eggplants on its way to the potato field. If you spot the beetles, crush them on sight. If the bugs lay eggs, remove and destroy as many egg clusters as you can find, then dust any larvae that hatch with rotenone.

Should you presalt? Cooks have long believed that curing sliced eggplant in salt before cooking will cut the bitterness. But modern plant breeding has made the practice almost obsolete. Most garden varieties grown today are less bitter—and ready for cooking straight from the plant.

▷ **Vegetable Gardens**

✥AN EGGPLANT SAMPLER✥

Good choices for home gardeners include 'Agora' and 'Black Magic,' with the bell shape and deep purple color of the typical store-bought eggplant. For variations in color, try 'Neon,' a pink-hued variety with semi-cylindrical, white-fleshed fruits, or 'Rosa Bianca,' an heirloom whose purple blossoms produce teardrop-shaped fruits mottled with rosy lavender and white. 'Ghostbuster' has oval, white-skinned fruits. A variety with a different shape is the early-ripening 'Ichiban,' with lean, 12-inch-long fruits of deep purple.

On the patio, put a 'Slim Jim' in a container and grow clusters of lavender fruits, each the size of a peanut. Or try 'Bambino' baby eggplant, which produces rounded, bite-size fruits that are ideal for stir-fries. The baby eggplant 'Purple Pickling' is perfect for canning.

EGGS

Seed pots. Eggshells make fine seed-sowing pots. Simply make a hole in the bottom of an empty eggshell half. Fill with a potting mixture, place in an open egg crate, and sow your seeds. When the time comes to transplant the seedlings, squeeze the shell slightly to crack it. The plant roots will push through the cracks and the shell will decompose naturally.

NATURAL COLORS FOR EASTER EGGS

Your garden is a rich natural source for Easter egg dyes. Vegetable scraps steeped in water can be transformed into colorful dyes, offering hues from baby blue to burgundy.

Place fresh eggs (preferably white) and some scraps in a pot filled with at least 2 quarts of water; add 2 tablespoons of white vinegar. Use separate pots for different colors. To produce yellow tints, use six onion skins; for pink, six beets; and for blue, half a head of red cabbage. Let the mixture come to a boil, then simmer for 20 minutes. Remove the eggs and let cool. Rub the eggs lightly with olive oil and buff with a soft cloth to bring out the highlights. For deeper, richer color, put the eggs back into the dye and let stand overnight in the refrigerator.

To add delicate floral silhouettes, place a fern, flower, or leaf on each egg and hold it in place with a nylon scrap that is porous enough to let the dye through; pantyhose works well.

Gather the corners of the nylon, pull it tight, and tie up with string. Then drop the eggs into water with the vegetable scraps and let them sit until nicely colored.

Fight pests. To repel cutworms, work bits of cracked eggshell into the soil. A sprinkling of crushed eggshells around the base of garden plants will also discourage slugs from feeding. Eggshell bits placed over rows of freshly planted seed beds will protect the seeds from birds.

A disposable funnel. No funnel within reach to pour chemicals into your sprayer? Improvise with an eggshell that has a hole punched into the bottom. When you're done, simply throw the eggshell away.

Extra calcium. Add eggshells to your garden to give it an extra dose of calcium. You can either sprinkle crushed eggshells directly into the garden soil or place whole shells in the compost heap.

ENDIVE

Chicory cousins. Endive is part of the chicory family and comes in three forms: the leafy salad green known as curly endive, the broadleaf endive called escarole, and the crisp, blanched sprouts called Belgian endive or witloof. Among the other relatives are the fashionable red-leaved chicories known as radicchio.

Too much heat causes bitterness. In regions with hot summers, pick the spring crop of curly endive and escarole young, before the heat has a chance to ruin the taste. Better still, plant in late summer to mature in the shorter, cooler days of fall.

Grow as you would lettuce. Give curly endive and escarole a sunny spot in humus-rich soil. Try planting them among tomatoes to provide shade from the scorching midday sun. Also make sure the soil is well drained, since endive roots rot easily.

Like all chicories, curly endive and escarole have a slightly bitter taste. Mellow the hearts of the plants by tying up the outer leaves as they grow.

Blanch Belgian endive to produce the crisp, mild-tasting sprouts called chicons. Wait until the plant is two-thirds grown—usually about 60 days. Tie the outer leaves upright loosely with rubber bands. Untie after rainstorms to prevent rot and retie when the plant has dried. Blanching generally takes 2 to 3 weeks; harvest only on a day when the plants are dry.

A root-cellar crop. Grow Belgian endive as a root crop in summer and take it inside for forcing during the winter months. Sow about 4 months before the first hard frost date in your area (25°F or below) and thin seedlings 8 to 12 inches apart. If they form seed stalks, cut them down and allow the plants to regrow. Once frost threatens to freeze the crown, dig the roots. Cut the vegetation above the neck and trim the roots, leaving them to 8 to 10 inches long. Place the roots upright in a box filled with moist earth and store in a darkened room or cellar. Pour an inch or so of water into the container so that just the tips of the roots are wet. Make

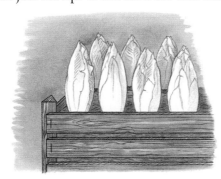

sure that the root cellar or storage room is consistently cool (around 50° to 60°F) and has steady 90 to 95 percent humidity. You will harvest chicons in 3 to 4 weeks.

No dark cellar? Put the roots in a box or crate covered with black plastic and keep it in a cool room. To prevent rotting, create a little space for ventilation.

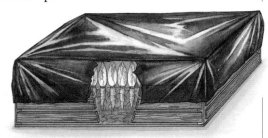

To harvest from the forcing box, cut the heads with a sharp knife just above the top of the root. They will regrow two or three times, depending on the strength of the root and the quality of the care.

A longer harvest. Produce chicons over several months simply by leaving a portion of the roots in cold storage and forcing only a few at a time, as needed.

After harvesting, keep chicons cool and in total darkness. If you expose them to too much light before they're eaten, there is a good chance they will turn both hard and bitter.

⊰| AN ENDIVE SAMPLER |⊱

Belgian endive is also known as witloof. Try 'Zoom,' 'Flash,' and the pale pink 'Robin.'

Curly endive is known to chefs as frisée and has delicate, finely cut leaves. Largest and hardiest is the slow-bolting, frost-tolerant 'Salad King.' Slightly smaller are the flavorful 'Galia,' 'Ruffec,' and the French 'Très Fine.'

Escarole has large outer leaves and a crunchy heart. Good choices are 'Cornet d'Anjou,' 'Sinco,' 'Sugarloaf,' and two self-blanching types: 'Nuvol' and 'Neos.'

▷ **Salad Greens, Vegetable Gardens**

ESPALIERS

The art of espalier entails training plants flat against a wall, fence, or trellis in a particular shape, such as a fan, U, V, T, or X. Plants are pruned and tied on supports to achieve the desired form. Espaliers are ideal

for gardeners who have limited space or want to beautify a blank surface with a "living wall." But take note: Espaliers need tending, so you'll have to make a commitment to enjoy this centuries-old art.

Pick your plant. While many supple-stemmed specimens are well-suited to espaliering, some lend themselves especially to certain forms. Fruit trees are good for tiered, U, and X shapes. Rockspray coton-easter and yew work well as fans. Forsythia and mock orange are appropriate for arched and curving designs.

The best supports. Use thin, solid stakes of bamboo, oak, or pine or heavy-gauge vinyl-coated wire to build the framework.

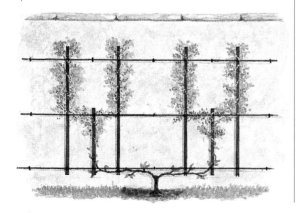

You'll also need soft string, raffia, or thin cloth strips to tie the branches in place, making a loose loop to allow for stem growth. Never use wire loops, which can cut and injure the plant.

Planting how-to.
Select a plant with flexible young stems; it should be no more than 3 feet tall. Dig a trench 2 feet deep and wide and set in the plant 6 to 12 inches from the wall to allow for air circulation. Spread the roots outward, away from the wall, and backfill with good rich garden loam. You can also use potted plants, making sure they are set out a bit from the wall surface.

Plot your pattern. Draw the design you want to create on a card and take it into the garden when training the plants so that you'll know which stems to bend, tie, pinch, or prune.

Breaking point. Train stems when they are young and flexible so that they don't snap. If a shoot is stiff, tie it to a length of wire and gently bend it a little at a time over the course of a few weeks. Remove the wire once the stem has matured in the desired shape—usually in about a year.

Pruning time. Cut back large stems when the plant is dormant. This is also the best time to see the overall shape. You can pinch out buds and shoots through late spring so that new growth can harden off by winter.

A vertical orchard. Fruit trees—especially dwarf varieties—and cane fruits like raspberries make fine espaliers. Pears and apples are easiest to grow; peaches, apricots, cherries, and plums are more difficult.

Harvest fruit earlier by placing the trees against a south- or west-facing wall—they will be protected from cold winds and bathed in sun. This works well for apple, pear, peach, and fig. Since the extra heat gives plants a head start, watch for late spring frosts that injure young buds. Also watch for heat stress in summer.

Fruit care. Pinch off the vegetative side shoots in June to encourage the formation of fruit buds, then thin out the buds to 3 to 6 inches apart to produce larger fruits.

The right height. If your wall is at least 8 feet tall you'll have no problem espaliering a fruit tree. If it is lower than 8 feet, however, you'll need to set in the plant so that the trunk is at a 45° angle to the ground.

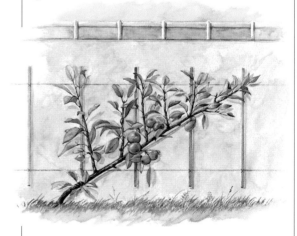

🦜 PLANTS TO ESPALIER 🦜

Certain plants lend themselves to espaliering. Deciduous trees and shrubs that perform well include dogwood, forsythia, laburnum, mock orange, ornamental cherry, redbud, rose, and viburnum. It you want your espalier to be in leaf all year, choose from the following: camellia, holly, lilac, pyracantha, Southern magnolia, winter jasmine, or yew. Fruits that espalier well are apple, blackberry, fig, grape, lemon, nectarine, pear, and raspberry, while good flowering vine candidates include bougainvillea, clematis, passionflower, and wisteria.

▷ Climbers

EUCALYPTUS

Big and fast. From the tiniest seeds, eucalyptus trees grow to become among the tallest in the world, with the largest topping out at 325 feet. They are also quick growers: in the Southwest, blue gums have shot up as much as 10 feet annually in the first few years after planting.

Tender giants. Most eucalyptus trees are native to Australia and are hardy only to about 30°F. Prized for their unusual foliage and pest resistance, these fragrant evergreens are used as ornamentals and for naturalizing in warm regions, especially in California. In the U.S. the tallest species reach 300 feet, while most of those used in home landscaping mature under 100 feet.

Inspect the roots when purchasing container-grown eucalyptus from a nursery. Reject any specimens whose roots appear overcrowded, whether they are coiled inside the bottom of the container or protruding through the drainage holes. Also watch for plants with bare spots on the branches or with evidence of heavy pruning. The best performers in the long run are small, young, vigorous plants.

Starting from scratch. Sowing seed is the most reliable means of propagating eucalyptus. In late winter or early spring, fill a shallow flat or pot with a sterilized soil mix; top with a ¼-inch layer of screened sphagnum moss. Sow the seeds directly into the moss and don't cover with soil. Place the container in a warm (55° to 60°F), well-lit location and keep moist. Germination should occur in 3 to 4 weeks.

Look for yellow leaves. While eucalyptus trees can generally adapt to various conditions, those grown in heavy, soggy soil are susceptible to chlorosis—a disease most often caused by iron deficiency that turns foliage a sickly yellow. To remedy, apply iron chelate to the soil or the plant.

Select a semi-hardy species. A few eucalypti can tolerate temperatures as low as 10°F in a sheltered location. Try the cider gum *(E. gunnii)* and the snow gum *(E. pauciflora* ssp. *niphophila)*—both of which have creamy white flowers.

Growing indoors. Place the plant in the brightest spot available—full sun in a south- or west-facing window is ideal—and where the nighttime temperature is about 65°F. If possible, move plants outdoors in full sun for the summer but bring back inside when frost threatens. Prune in spring every year or two to control size and encourage young growth. Remember that plants grown indoors seldom flower.

Battling the long-horned borer. Trees under stress are more susceptible to the

Only the largest gardens can accommodate the Tasmanian blue gum, which can grow to 100 feet.

eucalyptus long-horned borer. Symptoms include yellow foliage, a sparse canopy, and sprouting from normally inactive buds on the trunk. Avoid frequent watering, which promotes root diseases; during long dry spells, water at the drip line once a month. Use a sealant after pruning; the sap exuded from pruning wounds attracts pests.

Cut foliage for arrangements. Eucalyptus stems are attractive, aromatic additions to floral arrangements and last almost indefinitely when dried. Use the young foliage, which is soft and usually rounded; mature foliage is tougher and thicker. Three of the most popular species for cutting are the silver dollar gum *(E. polyanthemos)*, the round-leaved snow gum *(E. perriniana)*, and the silver-leaved mountain gum *(E. pulverulenta)*. While the leaves of all three are naturally gray-green, a preservative treatment is often used to turn them purple, red, or brown.

Savor their scents. When crushed, the leaves of some eucalyptus trees emit a distinctive scent. The lemon-scented gum *(E. citriodora)* has a sweet citrus fragrance, Nichol's willow-leaved peppermint *(E. nicholii)* gives off a minty scent, and the blue gum *(E. globulus)* smells like menthol. Another species, *E. melliodora*, blooms with honey-scented flowers.

Eucalyptus honey. Most eucalyptus species have blossoms that attract bees, which produce a heavenly honey from the nectar.

⚬ A EUCALYPTUS SAMPLER ⚬

Some of the most popular eucalyptus trees are those with spectacularly colorful flowers. When grown to maturity as outdoor landscape plants, the following species are sure to provide an eye-popping display of blossoms.

Coral gum *(E. torquata)* Vivid red blooms emerge from rose-coral buds shaped like little Japanese lanterns.

Red-cap gum *(E. erythrocorys)* Stunning bright red caps fall from the buds to reveal yellow flower clusters shaped like bottle brushes.

Red-flowering gum *(E. ficifolia)* The showiest of all eucalyptus trees in flower. Blooms are red, orange, pink, or cream, shaped in 1-foot-long puffs. Blooms sporadically through the year.

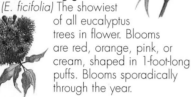

Rose mallee *(E. rhodantha)* Magnificent flowers of carmine red, some extending nearly 5 inches across.

▷ **Trees**

EVERGREENS

A catch-all term. Any plant—a tree, shrub, ground cover, vine, or perennial—that retains its foliage year round is an evergreen. The term is most often applied, however, to shrubs and trees. Semi-evergreens drop their leaves in cold areas but not mild ones.

Two types. Needle-leaf evergreens, like fir, have small, slender leaves, while broad-leaf evergreens have foliage in many shapes and sizes—from the spiky fronds of the palm to the broad, leathery leaves of the magnolia.

Dense and hardy, needle-leaf evergreens are generally very cold tolerant and make excellent hedges, good windscreens, and perfect backdrops for showier specimens.

Varied and versatile, broad-leaf evergreens usually have a looser, more open habit and are not as cold hardy. They often bear conspicuous flowers or fruit and are good for shrub borders and foundation plantings.

Play with shapes. Avoid planting symmetrical rows of matching evergreens unless you want a formal allée. Use their diverse habits, textures, and foliage forms to create graceful groupings in curved beds.

Clip art. Some evergreens, such as yew, box, and Japanese holly, lend themselves beautifully to topiary. The plants hold their shape and color all year long.

PURCHASING

Don't go bare. Buy evergreen trees and shrubs, which need constant moisture to replace the water lost through the leaves, either balled-and-burlapped or container grown. Bare-root plants can dry out.

No bargain. If you're buying evergreens from mail-order nurseries, make sure the plants are not bare-root. These may cost less but need more care to get established.

PLANTING

When to plant. Most evergreens like to be planted when partly dormant—in early spring or fall. Container-grown specimens and those balled-and-burlapped while dormant can also be planted in summer in the North and year round in the South.

Water in thoroughly and be sure to keep the plant moist during its first season.

MAINTENANCE

Winter mulching. In cold climates, protect evergreens with 3 to 4 inches of mulch. This inhibits frost penetration and allows the roots to take up water.

Water them well. Except for drought-tolerant specimens like the Arizona cypress or Aleppo pine, most evergreens need at least 1 inch of water weekly during the growing season. In hot weather, misting helps to refresh the leaves. In cold climates, water well before a hard freeze and anytime during winter when the ground is not frozen.

Go natural. Broad-leaf evergreens look best and require less care if allowed to assume their natural shape. Prune individual stems back about ¼ inch above the bud. This also promotes air circulation, which reduces pests and diseases.

Shape as a tree. Instead of cutting back overgrown specimens and risking disfigurement, remove only the bottom limbs to develop a more treelike shape. This works well on plants that have interesting bark.

Prune needle-leaf evergreens carefully. Some grow back slowly and most won't resprout at all if cut below green growth. Cut back broken or stray branches as needed. In spring, snip off the candles, or new tips, by half. Never cut the central leader or the tree will become misshapen.

No time to prune? Choose dwarf or slow-growing evergreen cultivars, which require little if any pruning.

Drastic measures. You can rejuvenate vigorous shrubs, such as yews and privets, that are overgrown by pruning severely in spring. If you're concerned about how the plant will respond, test first by cutting a few stems. If they resprout, cut the rest back to the ground.

How to feed. Fertilize in early spring and fall with a 10–10–10 mix. Many evergreens are acid lovers, so mix half the recommended amount of 10–10–10 with half an acid-forming source like coffee grounds.

A labor saver. A geotextile weed mat is a good way to eliminate maintenance chores in foundation plantings and shrub borders. Leave a clear space at the plant bases so that you can apply compost and fertilizer, then cover the mat with an organic mulch.
▷ **Conifers, Pruning, Shrubs, Trees**

EXPOSURE

Know your microclimate. Every garden has a distinct climate brought about by the topography of the land, the location of buildings, the proximity of a body of water, wind patterns, and similar factors. If you take this microclimate into account when planning your garden, you'll be able to expose your plants to the site's advantages and protect them from its disadvantages.

Telltale signs. Analyze your site to recognize subtle differences. Observe which plants are blown about by wind and which stay still. Watch where snow melts first and where it lingers. Note where soil dries quickly and where it remains waterlogged.

Don't fight your site. You'll save time, money, and energy by working with the microclimate instead of trying to combat it. In cool climates, for example, avoid planting in hollows, where frost collects; this will keep you from having to protect the plants in winter. In warm climates, keep heat-sensitive plants away from a south-facing wall, which gets intense sun; you won't have to counteract heat stress with extra water.

Hilltops are subject to drying winds and fast drainage, so use plants that can withstand drought and constant buffeting. At the bottom, where water collects, use moisture-loving plants that need protection.

East versus west. Grow plants that are vulnerable to sun damage on the eastern side of your house or another structure, since morning light is gentler than that of midday or afternoon. Reserve the west side for drought- and heat-tolerant specimens.

Southern exposure. If a plant is only marginally hardy in your area, it has a better chance of survival if placed by a wall facing south or southeast. It will stay warm and be sheltered from the wind in winter.

Frost dams.
Protect plants growing at the bottom of a slope from cold air by installing a hedge two-thirds of the way down the hill. Instead of settling on your plants, the cold will collect in front of the hedge.

Know your plants. Consider a plant's reaction to climatic conditions. How does it respond when exposed to sun, wind, frost, extreme heat or cold, rain, snow, humidity, salt spray, or airborne pollution? Azaleas and rhododendrons, for example, risk foliage burn from overexposure to sun. Accordingly, place them in filtered shade, like that cast by a tall pine.

Minimize moisture loss. Evergreens suffer in winter from the dry air; because the soil is frozen, the roots can't replenish water lost through the foliage. Plant them in a site sheltered from wind and intense sun. In fall, soak the ground with water and spray the leaves and branches thoroughly with an antidesiccant to help the plants conserve vital moisture.

Protect fruit trees that flower early, such as peaches and cherries, from late-spring frosts by planting them on the north side of the house or on a north-facing slope. This will help delay the tree's blossoming until the danger of frost has passed.

Another delay tactic. Site plants that blossom in winter or early spring, such as witch hazel, camellia, and hellebore, where they will receive no direct morning sun. A delayed exposure to light will allow the buds to thaw out gradually and risk less damage if they are nipped by frost overnight.

Plants on busy streets can be exposed to soot and other airborne impurities, which clog leaf pores. Keep foliage clean and healthy by spraying it with water weekly during the growing season. You can also wash large leaves with a damp sponge.

Block rain. Place delicate plants on the leeward side of a hill, building, hedge, or wall to protect them from hard rains. On the windward side, moisture-loving plants will be at home.

Siting houseplants. Because the light is more intense in summer than in winter, you may need to move sun-sensitive plants from a west- to an east-facing windowsill in the hot months. Also keep in mind that plants can tolerate more sun in the house than out; an indoor sun lover may scorch if placed outside in bright summer light.
▷ **Frost, Protection, Snow, Wind**

FENCES

Selecting a fence. Whether you need a fence for buffering wind, marking a boundary, or providing support for a climber, choose a material and style that harmonize with your garden and house. Consider the initial and lifetime repair costs, as well as the maintenance requirements.

WOOD

Lots of looks. Informal gardens are the right setting for rustic styles, such as the post-and-rail, picket, or split-rail fence. Formal gardens are better complemented with board, post-and-board, lattice, or basketweave fences.

Go for quality. A fence is a long-term investment. Select a durable, rot-resistant wood that will weather the elements—especially for posts. Wise choices include cypress, red or white cedar, redwood, and pressure-treated pine. For other components, you can use a less durable wood, such as spruce, hemlock, or fir.

Trim post tops to a point, slant, or dome so that they will shed water. Or buy the protective post caps sold at hardware and home stores.

Cap a board fence with a domed or sloped top rail to keep the end grain from absorbing water and rotting. Fasten with galvanized or brass nails or screws to prevent rusting, which will stain wood.

To prevent rot, apply a wood preservative, stain, or paint. Coat the individual pieces before assembling the fence so that all the surfaces will be covered. Check the fence at least once a year to see if it needs touch-ups, repair, or recoating, which should be done before the bare wood is exposed to the elements.

Anchor posts with metal spear connectors, available at home stores. Even though the spears can easily be driven into the ground with a sledge hammer before the post is attached, they will be sturdier if sunk in concrete instead.

Easy digging. Use a posthole digger to scoop out deep, narrow holes without disturbing the surrounding soil. Or use a soil auger, which bores neat holes with little effort. Dig 2 to 2½ feet deep for each post; in cold areas, dig to 3 feet—below the frost line.

Cutting uniform pickets. Clamp several pickets together in a bench vise and saw through them all at once to save time.

Proper spacing. When assembling a picket fence, use a spare picket as a spacer. Simply place it next to one that's already attached to the rails and set another picket next to it.

Rotted board ends? Repair by sawing out the damaged portions and attaching a 2 x 4 horizontally at the base. To prevent future problems, set the replacement 1 inch above ground level to let air circulate freely.

Sloping ground? A fence that follows the terrain will complement a naturalistic garden. Fencing in the stair-step style creates a more formal look. If you decide on stair steps, note that you'll need to level the grade between posts and fill in the open spaces between the bottom rail and the ground.

METAL

Don't skimp. As with wooden fencing, don't buy on the cheap. Select good-quality iron or heavy-gauge galvanized chain link, which also comes with a green-plastic coating to increase its longevity and help it blend with its surroundings.

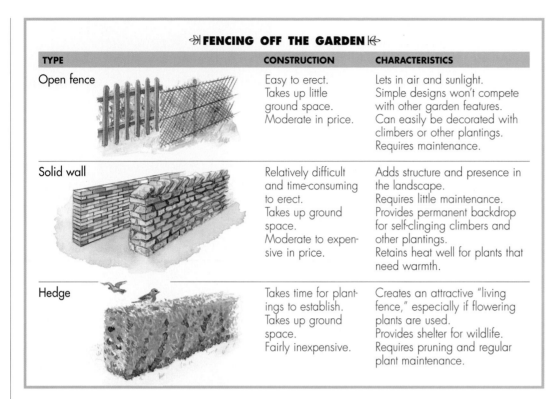

FENCING OFF THE GARDEN

TYPE	CONSTRUCTION	CHARACTERISTICS
Open fence	Easy to erect. Takes up little ground space. Moderate in price.	Lets in air and sunlight. Simple designs won't compete with other garden features. Can easily be decorated with climbers or other plantings. Requires maintenance.
Solid wall	Relatively difficult and time-consuming to erect. Takes up ground space. Moderate to expensive in price.	Adds structure and presence in the landscape. Requires little maintenance. Provides permanent backdrop for self-clinging climbers and other plantings. Retains heat well for plants that need warmth.
Hedge	Takes time for plantings to establish. Takes up ground space. Fairly inexpensive.	Creates an attractive "living fence," especially if flowering plants are used. Provides shelter for wildlife. Requires pruning and regular plant maintenance.

Coat an ironwork fence with rust-inhibiting paint before setting it up; repaint it about every 3 years. Watch for chipping or flaking that will leave the metal exposed.

Pest control. Bury the bottom edge of a chain-link fence 2 feet deep around garden beds to discourage raids from moles, rabbits, and gophers.

A disappearing fence. Let hedge shrubs or climbers grow through a chain-link fence to the outer side. They will envelop the mesh and help it fade into the landscape.
▷ **Hedges, Walls, Wire**

FENNEL

Fennel or finocchio? As a culinary herb, fennel (*Foeniculum vulgare*) is grown for its licorice-flavored seeds—a prime ingredient in Italian sausage and curries—and for its leaves, used in salads and fish dishes. Another variety (*F. vulgare* var. *azoricum*) yields finocchio, also known as Florence fennel. This plant is raised for its bulbous leaf base, which is eaten raw or cooked.

Grow fennel in well-drained soil in a sunny location; in hot areas, provide partial shade. If conditions are right, fennel will self-sow readily, so watch for volunteers.

For seasoning, use only the herb's young leaves and tender shoots. Harvest seeds just as the flower heads are turning from yellow to brown. Snip off the heads and let them fall into a paper bag to dry thoroughly, then just shake out the seeds.

Grow it for show. Fennel's lacy foliage and dainty flower heads make the herb handsome enough to deserve a spot among ornamentals. Mix it with roses and lavender, for example, or with any plant that has blue-green leaves, such as dianthus. Particularly pretty is 'Rubrum,' or bronze, fennel. Its reddish brown foliage is also hardier than the green variety.

A FENNEL SAMPLER

When growing fennel as an herb for its leaves and seeds, any variety will do. For choice finocchio, try the Swiss 'Fino,' the bolt-resistant 'Zefa Fino,' or the Italian heirloom 'Romy.'

Sowing finocchio. While finocchio is half-hardy, a heat wave can cause it to bloom without forming a bulb. In the North, sow seeds indoors and set seedlings out 2 weeks before the last frost date; protect from late spring freezes. In the South, sow seeds in July to harvest bulbs in October.

For white, tender bulbs, cover the young plants up to their necks with soil when you bed them out; water regularly. Once the bulb begins to form, cover with more soil. Harvest after 3 weeks. In moist climates, take care that the bulbs don't rot.
▷ **Herbs**

FERNS

PLANTING

Shades of preference. Most hardy ferns prefer dappled rather than deep shade. The amount of sun a fern tolerates depends on the moisture content of the soil—the wetter the soil, the more sun-tolerant the fern.

Multiply your ferns. Collect spores for propagation by cutting off a healthy frond whose spores are just turning dark and drying it on a sheet of white paper. The spores will fall off and look like fine dust. Remove the frond and crease the paper to gather the spores for sowing.

Sow the spores by tapping the paper to sprinkle them in sterile soil in a sterile pot; mist lightly. Cover the pot with plastic wrap and stand it in a dish filled with a few inches of water. Set in a warm spot in indirect light and maintain the water level until the soil surface is covered with the tiny heart-shaped growths called prothalli— in 6 to 12 weeks. Gently lift them out and transplant them in a soilless mix; keep moist until they have developed fronds and can be planted out.

Dividing ferns. Dig up root clumps in early spring and, depending on their size, divide into two or three pieces with your hands or a spade. Make sure at least one

---

⇥ A FERN SAMPLER ⇤

HARDY FERNS

Christmas fern Silvery new growth; very hardy.
Cinnamon fern Reddish-brown "cinnamon stick" fronds are followed by tall green ones.
Common maidenhair fern Dark, wiry stems and feathery fronds; must be kept moist.
Japanese painted fern Grayish fronds tinged with red and blue; needs light for best color.
Japanese red shield fern Coppery young fronds mature to green with red spores.
Ostrich fern Tall plumes; likes marshy soil.

TENDER FERNS

Bear's-foot and hare's-foot ferns Long, "furry" rhizomes at base of fronds.
Bird's-nest fern Rosette with lobed fronds.
Boston fern Long, narrow, yellowish-green fronds; easy to grow.
Japanese holly fern Shiny, leathery foliage.
Rosy maidenhair fern Soft, fanlike fronds are rose-red when young.
Staghorn fern Striking deeply lobed foliage shaped like stag antlers.

---

growing tip, where new fronds are produced, is present on each division. Transplant and keep well watered until established.

MAINTENANCE

Save time, save water. Each year at winter's end, mulch ferns with leaf mold or un-finished compost to keep soil cool and moist. Water ferns only during long dry spells.

Don't rake around ferns in spring or you'll damage the young fiddleheads; do your spring cleanup by hand instead. In fall, rake gently so as not to disturb the shallow roots. Let some leaves remain as mulch.

Should you fertilize? With most ferns, it's not necessary. Simply add compost to the planting hole and spread more on every year. It will provide nutrients and improve the soil's water-retaining capacity as well.

Don't cut back in winter—the dry fronds of deciduous ferns protect the base of the plant. Once the new shoots show in spring, prune old fronds off at the soil line.

INDOORS

The best tender ferns to grow indoors are the Japanese holly, hare's-foot, bird's-nest, staghorn, sword, Boston, and button ferns. All can tolerate the low humidity usually found at home.

To increase humidity, set the fern in a dish of pebbles and add just enough water to touch the bottom of the

---

The stately ostrich fern, at home in light shade and moist soil, provides an elegant garden backdrop.

pot. Mist occasionally and water regularly with water that's at room temperature.

Goodbye to old fronds. Snip out damaged or dying fronds in spring. If the fern has stolons, propagate new plants by pinning these runners to the soil with wire bent in a U until they root. Then cut the stolons close to the parent plant and pot up.

Slab culture. The staghorn fern, among others, prefers to grow on a piece of cork or weathered hardwood. Lay some sphagnum moss on the slab, then secure the fern's roots over it with fishing line or pantyhose strips. Once the fern is established, water by soaking the whole slab in the sink.

▷ **Bog Gardens, Shade**

FERTILIZER

The big three. For healthy growth, all plants require three important chemical elements: nitrogen for vegetative growth, phosphorus for strong roots, and potassium for flower and fruit vigor.

The others. Plants need three other major nutrients—sulfur, calcium, and magnesium—as well as minute amounts of trace elements, including iron, manganese, zinc, iron, and copper.

Know the code. Fertilizer labels list nitrogen, phosphorus, and potassium by their chemical abbreviations: N, P, and K, always in that order. Labels also indicate the ratio of each element to the total mass. A 10-6-4 compound, for example, contains 10 percent nitrogen, 6 percent phosphorus, and 4 percent potassium.

What kinds? Chemical fertilizers are made from inorganic compounds such as ammonium sulfate. Mineral fertilizers, like limestone, are mined from rock ground into powder or pellets. Organic fertilizers, including manure and bonemeal, are mostly derived from plant or animal matter.

THE PRINCIPAL NUTRIENTS

ELEMENT	PLANT PARTS AFFECTED	SYMPTOMS OF DEFICIENCY	HOW TO CORRECT
Nitrogen (N)	Foliage; helps branches, stalks, and stems form. Note: Excess nitrogen produces green growth at the expense of flowers and fruit.	Slow growth. Small leaves, branches. Weak, easily bent stems. Yellow or discolored leaves.	Use ammonium sulfate, ammonium nitrate, calcium nitrate, sodium nitrate (chemical); urea, fish emulsion, blood meal, cottonseed meal (organic).
Phosphorus (P)	Root systems; stimulates root branching and growth of root hairs. Aids in plant maturation.	Weak branches and roots. Parasite attacks. Poor flowers and harvests. Reddening of leaves.	Use superphosphate, diammonium phosphate (chemical); bonemeal, rock phosphate, guano (organic). Note: Apply to the soil around plant roots.
Potassium (K)	Flowers and fruits; promotes size, number, and color.	Leaf edges turn brown and crinkle. Weak stems. Reduced yield; fruits drop prematurely.	Use potassium chloride, potassium sulfate (chemical); wood ash, kelp extract, green sand, granite meal (organic).

OUTDOORS

What to choose? Do a soil test to determine the nutrient levels in the soil and watch for symptoms of nutrient deficiencies. Then select a fertilizer—either a simple or complete type—accordingly.

More is too much. Always follow the application rates recommended by the manufacturer. Using more fertilizer will not boost growth and may injure your plants.

Hot stuff. Some chemical fertilizers and fresh manures readily release so much nitrogen that they burn plants. Keep them away from seeds, seedlings, and foliage.

When to use. Plants vary in their requirements. Some, like herbs, need fertilizer infrequently; others, like roses, are hungry all the time. A rule of thumb is to feed most plants in early spring to stimulate growth but apply little or no fertilizer in fall so that top growth can harden off before winter.

How to apply. With new beds, incorporate fertilizer when preparing the soil; simply broadcast it over the bed or row and dig it in thoroughly. For single specimens, such as shrubs, dig fertilizer into the planting holes or work it into the surface around plants. For established plantings, side-dress by scratching fertilizer into the soil beside the plants. In each case, water the fertilizer in well.

A coffee-can spreader. Punch holes in the bottom of a 2-pound coffee can with a screwdriver to make a spreader for granular fertilizer.

SIX WAYS TO FERTILIZE

Broadcast Spread evenly over soil; rake in if desired.

Side-dress Apply in a ring or line beside a plant or row.

In holes Work into the base of planting holes.

Dig in Spread over soil and incorporate fully.

Top-dress Sprinkle on the surface of a bed.

Spray Apply liquid food directly on foliage.

Feeding a tree. Apply fertilizer where the feeder roots can reach it. Use an electric or a manual auger with a long large-diameter bit—at least 1 foot long and 1½ inches around—to bore deep holes. You can also use a crowbar or a stake pounded with a hammer. Space holes 2 feet apart around the drip line; make another ring of holes 2½ feet from the trunk. Funnel a slow-release fertilizer into the holes, using the amount recommended by the manufacturer for the tree's size. Plug the top of the holes with soil and water in well.

Mechanical spreaders, either the drop or broadcast type, make short work of fertilizing large areas. Use only dry fertilizers to avoid clogs and messy clean-up. Make sure to keep the shut-off mechanism clean so that it can close completely.

With a drop spreader, apply fertilizer in a crisscross pattern for complete coverage, going horizontally and vertically over the same area. Use half the recommended spread rate in each direction.

Station fertilizer bags around the area where you're working. When it's time to refill the spreader hopper, it will save you a long walk.

Have an aquarium? Gardeners who keep freshwater aquariums can recycle the contents in the garden. When cleaning the tank, save the nutrient-rich water to pour over plants instead of just sending it down the drain.

INDOORS

Use a liquid food for houseplants—it spreads evenly through the soil. Fertilizer stakes, on the other hand, provide nutrients to a limited area and can burn plant roots if the soil becomes too dry.

Halve the dosage. Feed your houseplants a dilute solution, cutting the manufacturer's recommended rate in half. Apply at 2- to 4-week intervals when the plants are making vigorous growth in spring and summer; let them rest in fall and winter.

Don't overfeed. If you miss a feeding, don't compensate by applying a stronger dose. And don't feed ailing plants—only healthy roots can take up nutrition from the soil.

Natural fertilizers. Mix tea leaves, coffee grounds, or even small pieces of banana peel into the potting soil and you won't need to feed for the first month.
▷ **Manure, Nitrogen, Organic Fertilizer, Phosphorus, Potassium, Trace Elements**

❧ CHOOSING A FERTILIZER ❧

Simple fertilizer
Contains only one of the three primary elements: nitrogen, phosphorus, or potassium.

Compound fertilizer
Contains more than one primary element.

Complete fertilizer
Contains all three elements; the percentage of each depends on the fertilizer. Some also contain various trace elements.

Chemical fertilizer
A chemically synthesized artificial compound. Acts immediately and can damage plants if overapplied.

Organic fertilizer
Made from plant or animal matter, although some include granite dust or other minerals. Acts slowly but lasts longer. Is weaker than chemical fertilizer but will not harm plants if overapplied.

Slow-release fertilizer
Chemical fertilizer formulated to break down slowly, depending on moisture and temperature, and release nutrients over a long period.

Foliar fertilizer
Water-soluble fertilizer sprayed on foliage. Is absorbed directly by the top growth, so acts quickly; won't harm plants.

FIG TREES

Fig trees aren't finicky about the soil they are grown in—as long as it's well drained. They like full sun, a mulch of well-rotted manure, and plenty of water their first year.

Semi-hardy figs can tolerate cold only to 10°F. In cool climates, plant them in spring after the risk of heavy frost has passed; in warm areas, you can also plant them in fall.

Winter protection. In the North, plant figs against a wall with a southern exposure to increase warmth and protect from wind. When the cold comes, prune stems to 6 feet and wrap them with twine to form a cylinder. Encircle loosely with burlap and stuff it with straw or dead leaves for insulation.

An easy orchard. Take cuttings 9 to 10 inches long and bury them 4 to 5 inches deep until they root. Protect them from winter freezes and replant in spring. You can also cut off suckers throughout the growing season and transplant them.

Pest protection. While figs are fairly resistant, you may need to cover them with netting to discourage thieving birds. To keep ants from marching up the stems, spread wood ashes around the plant base.

Wear gloves when picking figs or working on the tree. The fig's milky sap is irritating to the skin and mucous membranes. The leaves, too, can cause skin rashes.

Ready to eat? If a fruit doesn't break off easily when you bend it back toward the branch, it isn't ready; let it ripen for a few more days. Ripe figs are soft to the touch.

Drying figs. You can leave small fruits whole, but cut large figs in half to speed drying. Also prick the skin with a fork.

Pruning pointers. Figs generally need only light grooming. If you're growing one as a shade tree, train it to branch a few feet off the ground; then prune lightly when it's dormant. If you need to control its size—figs can reach 30 feet—keep it cut back to 15 feet or select a dwarf variety. Figs can also be trained as espaliers.

A patio plant. With its gray bark and lobed leaves that turn yellow in fall, the pretty fig can be grown in a tub as an accent for your terrace. Just make sure you clean up dropped fruits, as they are messy when squashed.

⇥A FIG SAMPLER⇤

Figs grow best in warm regions but can be raised where temperatures drop as low as –5°F if given adequate protection.

In California and areas with similar climates, 'Kadota,' 'Conrada,' and 'Mission' perform best. 'Neverella' and 'Lattarula' (the Italian honey fig) provide spring and fall harvests in the Northwest. For cold climates, try 'Celeste' and 'Magnolia.' 'Texas Everbearing' and 'Brown Turkey' are good for containers.

▷ **Espaliers, Frost**

FIREWOOD

Gathering wood. Pick diseased or damaged specimens first when cutting trees for firewood. By removing sick trees, you allow more space in your woodlot or forest for the healthy ones to grow and thrive.

The best firewoods are hornbeam, oak, beech, maple, apple, walnut, elm, poplar, and pine. Cut them to size between November 1 and Easter. To burn well, the wood should age for 2 years.

Avoid rot. Don't pile firewood against a wall or directly on the ground. Stack it on shipping pallets so that air can circulate. Stabilize the pile with a 4 x 4 post driven at least 2 feet into the ground on either side.

Place the largest logs on the bottom and make each subsequent row perpendicular to the previous one. Stop stacking at 6 feet for both stability of the pile and easy access to the top logs. Don't fill the spaces between logs with kindling.

Keep it dry. Cover the woodpile with a weatherproof canvas or plastic tarp. Anchor the tarp on top with a few logs or stones.

Direct deposit. If you store firewood in the basement of your house, let gravity do the work for you. Instead of lugging it down piece by piece, make a simple ramp or chute for sliding the wood through a ground-level window. Be sure to check logs thoroughly for insects before bringing any wood into the house.

Bag it. Store hard-to-stack kindling in paper shopping bags, placing in each bag just the amount of twigs needed to start a fire. When it's time to get a blaze going, put the whole bag in the fireplace, top with well-seasoned split logs, and ignite.

▷ **Chain Saws, Trees**

FLOWER BEDS

DESIGNING

Plot it out. Before installing plants, plot out your basic plan on a piece of paper and use tracing paper to make overlays for each month of the growing season. Note the bloom time for your perennials and blossom color for annuals, perennials, and bulbs. Then mark the overlays with the flower combinations you would like to use in the beds.

Consider style. Take the architecture of your house into account when designing a new bed so that both work in harmony. A Georgian-style or ultramodern house, for example, might look best with straight-edged, formal beds. A saltbox or ranch-style house would be enhanced with naturalistic beds in the cottage-garden tradition.

Bigger isn't better. "Praise large gardens, plant small ones," says a wise Chinese proverb. A small, well-designed bed with beautiful color combinations and interesting specimens can be just as attractive and satisfying as a large one—and easier to manage too. Plan your bed at a size that is suited to your property and the time you can devote to maintenance.

Put beds to work. Besides beautifying the yard, flower beds can serve many purposes. Accent your front door by framing it with beds of bright flowers. Hide the foundation with a double row of daylilies. Direct foot traffic with strategically placed beds.

Cutting a bed. For uniform straight edges, mark the bed with stakes and string before cutting with a spade or edger. For a curved bed, mark the contours with a piece of garden hose—it's flexible enough to assume any shape yet stable enough to stay put.

Dress rehearsal. Before cutting the bed edges and setting in plants, do a dry run. Mark the outline of the bed with lime or sand. Then put large stakes where the tall plants will go; for smaller plants, simply place them—still in their pots— in the desired locations. Stand back and take a critical look. If something doesn't appeal to you, now is the time to make a change.

A bed backed by a wall or hedge usually looks best when plants are arranged in decreasing height from back to front. This design gives an unobstructed view of all of the plants and lets each one receive sun. But be flexible; the occasional short plant tucked behind a tall one won't hurt.

In a true bed—that is, an island surrounded by lawn or paths on all sides— place the tallest plants in the center. Then use increasingly shorter plants as you move toward the edges. For a naturalistic effect, offset the center of the island slightly and accent it with a blooming shrub or a small flowering tree.

PLANTING

Picking flowers. Choose a variety of flowering ornamentals. Many bulbs provide early spring color, while perennials keep the garden's look changing from week to week. Annuals are steady performers, adding enduring color and filling in while hardy plants mature; because they last only one season, annuals also let you experiment with different schemes.

A progression of bloom. Keep your beds blooming from early spring to late fall by selecting and arranging plants according to their flowering periods.

Consider flower shape. In addition to color and bloom time, pick plants by the forms of their flowers. There is nearly infinite variety—from spikes to saucers to trumpets to bells. A mix of contrasting and complementary shapes will add interest to the bed.

Look at the leaves. Because there will be a less showy period when blooms are sparse, take into account the form, size, and color of the plant's foliage.

Mix it up. While flower beds are meant to be colorful—even when monochromatic—mix a few foliage plants in with the blossoming ones. An occasional spot of green provides a visual pause and makes the flowers sparkle all the more.

Group large plants in threes and smaller ones in fives or sevens. Odd numbers of plants look more natural than even-numbered groupings. Only a specimen plant used as a special accent should be planted singly.

When to transplant. Reduce transplant shock by setting out the plants in late afternoon or on an overcast day. Water them before you take them out

of the containers so that they will be easier to handle and their roots won't dry out.

Use a mat. Installing a geotextile mulch before planting reduces weeding chores for years. It lets you spend more time enjoying your garden instead of maintaining it.

Build a berm. If your land is flat, you can vary the terrain by building berms, or mounds of soil. Either raise the whole bed on one berm or make a few more to highlight various plant groupings.

Another way to add height is to accent the bed with climbers. Use a manufactured or homemade form in the shape of your choice for support. Sink it 4 inches into the soil and train a fast-growing climber such as morning glory, sweet pea, or scarlet runner bean to cover it.

MAINTENANCE

Don't forget to mulch. Protect roots, suppress weeds, and prevent soil from splashing up on your flowers by covering the bed with 2 to 3 inches of an attractive mulch— perhaps shredded bark or cocoa hulls.

Don't compact the bed. If your soil is heavy, wet, or sticky, lay down wooden planks to kneel on when tending flowers; you'll avoid compressing soil around roots.

Edged in stone. If your garden abuts grass, set a row of bricks or flat stones—slate, for example—along the edge of the bed. This mowing strip not only makes lawn maintenance easier but provides a tidy visual transition between the flowers and the lawn.

Path placement. Set a path made of gravel, shredded bark, or other loose material slightly below the level of the bed so that the material won't spill onto the soil. You can also prevent this problem by edging the path with wood or brick.

Avoid root competition. Keep shrub, tree, and grass roots from encroaching by sinking a rigid plastic or galvanized metal barrier 16 to 20 inches into the soil around the flower bed's perimeter.

Prolong blooming by deadheading; if you keep plants from setting seed, they will produce more flowers. When buds are visible along the stem, cut or pinch off the spent blooms just above the buds. When there are no buds on the stem, cut back to the base.

Tender loving care. Keep a close eye on your beds to keep them in top shape. Remove spent flowers and stake any weak stems. Pull up weeds and provide extra water for thirsty specimens or during long hot spells. Feed regularly, every 7 to 10 days, with a soluble fertilizer once plants begin growth, and continue until late July.

Save your favorites. Let a few nonhybrid flowers fade so that you can harvest seed once it's mature. Store seed in a cool, dry place and propagate the following year.
▷ **Annuals, Colors, Perennials, Shape**

FLOWERING TREES

All trees flower, even if their "blooms" are barely visible. While shade trees are grown for their dense foliage, those categorized as flowering trees are grown specifically for their showy displays of blossoms.

At home anywhere. No matter where you live or what your climate, you can plant a flowering tree that will grow and thrive—requiring no more maintenance than any other tree. Consult your local garden center or Cooperative Extension Service for a list of species suited to your region.

Good for small spaces. Because many flowering trees are of low to moderate height, they are ideal for gardens with little space. Plant one as an individual specimen to provide a colorful focal point.

In large gardens, plant several flowering trees in a group to create a dramatic cloud of blooms in the season of your choice.

Keep the yard in bloom from late winter to late fall by selecting species with different bloom times. Most trees remain in flower for 2 to 4 weeks.

Flowers plus! For visual interest all year, select trees that have not only beautiful flowers but also decorative foliage, intense fall color, ornamental fruit, or attractive bark and branching.

The right site. While most flowering trees need full sun, some prefer a shaded spot

---

THE INTRIGUING FRANKLINIA

A lovely but little-known tree is the Franklinia (*Franklinia alatamaha*), which blooms with 3-inch satiny white cups in late summer. If the name seems familiar, it's because the tree was named for Benjamin Franklin, a friend of the colonial naturalist who discovered the tree in a Georgia wetland in 1765—John Bartram. Considered the father of American botany, Bartram spent 40 years searching for native plants from Lake Ontario to Florida, collecting more than 200 species for his 102-acre garden in Philadelphia. While Bartram's garden has endured since 1728 and is now a historic site, the Franklinia, sadly, disappeared from the wild in 1803. Today's gardeners, however, are keeping the species from extinction—and honoring a pioneering plant hunter—by raising the descendants of Bartram's most famous find.

A springtime explosion of pink, the Eastern redbud blooms just before dogwood—together a pretty pair.

that resembles their native woodland habitat. Plant "understory" trees—those that grow under a forest canopy, such as dogwood, redbud, and Carolina silver bell—in filtered or partial shade to protect them from sunscald and summer heat.

Accent your flower garden with a flowering tree. Place it at the back of a border or slightly off center in the middle of a bed, where it will add a welcome vertical dimension to a horizontal look.

A living parasol. Make a 3- to 4-foot hole in your deck or patio and install a flowering tree for color and shade. You can also plant a tree beside a pond or pool; it will provide a shady place to sit while you admire the blossoms mirrored in the water.

❧ GOOD CHOICES FOR THE GARDEN ❧

TREE	FLOWERS AND FRUIT	CHARACTERISTICS	SPECIAL SPECIMENS
Crab apple	White, pink, or rose blossoms; red, yellow-orange, or purple fruits, 2 inches or smaller	Upright or weeping habit; green or red-purple foliage; some with good fall color	'Adams,' 'Barbara Ann,' 'Flame,' 'Rousseau,' 'White Angel'
Dogwood	White, pink, or ruby-red blossoms; scarlet-red or yellow fruits that attract birds	Good fall foliage color; some trees have peeling bark; graceful branching habit	'Cherokee Chief,' 'Rosabella Stellar Pink,' 'White Cloud'
Golden rain tree	Foot-long clusters of tiny yellow blooms; red, tan, or green seedpods that last through fall	Serrated, feathery leaves; rounded habit; no fall color change	*Koelreuteria bipinnata, K. formosana, K. paniculata*
Mimosa or silk tree	Clusters of fuzzy, bright pink puffs with white bases; flat peapodlike fruits	Open, spreading habit; finely divided, fernlike leaves; can be invasive	'Ernest Wilson'
Ornamental cherry	Pink or white blossoms, some double-flowered or fragrant; inconspicuous fruits	Upright or weeping habit; smooth, shiny bark, sometimes banded	'Kwanzan,' 'Sargent,' 'Weeping Higan,' 'Yoshino'
Redbud	Pealike rose-pink blossoms; also white and double-flowered forms; flat, winged fruit	Heart-shaped leaves; yellow fall foliage; multi-trunked; hardiness varies with species	'Avondale,' 'Texas White,' 'Withers Pink Charm'
Sourwood	Masses of small white pendulous flowers; fragrant; very heavy blooming; brown fruits	Large, glossy leaves; brilliant scarlet fall foliage; broad pyramidal shape	'Chameleon'
Stewartia	Large white camellialike blossoms; flowers in summer; fruits not ornamental	Flaking bark in brown, tan, and red; bright red and orange foliage in fall	Chinese, Japanese, Korean,

A tree of many names. Prized for its billowy white flowers in spring and bright foliage in fall, the serviceberry is also known as the shadbush or shadblow—so called because it blooms when the shad start spawning in Eastern rivers. Among the best species are the 50-foot-tall downy serviceberry (*Amelanchier canadensis*), the widely available Allegheny serviceberry (*A. laevis*), and the big-blossomed apple serviceberry (*A.* × *grandiflora*). All are hardy to –20°F.

A graceful specimen for moderate climates is the Japanese snowbell (*Styrax japonicus*), a 30-foot bushy tree that flowers in June with pendent white bell-shaped blooms.

Worth waiting for. The yellowwood (*Cladrastis lutea*), native to the South, can take 10 years to produce its first blooms. But be patient: you'll be rewarded with an abundance of long, drooping chains of fragrant white pealike flowers. Try the 'Rosea' variety for light pink blooms. Both trees boast beautiful yellow-orange foliage in fall.

High and dry. From the Southern Hemisphere comes the jacaranda, which thrives in the high deserts of Brazil and is used as a street tree in Australia. If you live in a hot, arid area, you can enjoy the jacaranda's white, pink, rose, or lavender funnel-form flowers from April to June.

City specimens. Several hardy, resistant flowering trees stand up well to air pollution. Try the hawthorn (*Crataegus* spp.), golden rain tree, saucer magnolia, or pagoda tree (*Sophora japonica*).

Disease-free dogwoods. The showy native *Cornus florida*, a garden favorite since the 1700's, has been decimated by anthracnose. Avoid heartbreak by planting the kousa dogwood, a resistant Asian native, or the newly developed disease-resistant hybrids.
▷ **Eucalyptus, Magnolia, Trees**

FORCING

What is it? To force a plant is to make it bloom out of season by manipulating the growing conditions. By staggering the starting dates, you can have plants flowering indoors through winter. Best for forcing are spring-flowering trees, shrubs, and bulbs.

Flowery branches. You can force many woody plants, including forsythia, pussy willow, fruit trees, witch hazel, spirea, wisteria, quince, and lilac. On a mild winter day, select several medium-size branches with well-formed buds and cut them diagonally above a bud in 2- to 3-foot lengths. Strip buds from the stem ends and crush the ends slightly. Set in tepid water and store at 60° to 70°F. Change the water every 5 days; the buds will open in 2 to 6 weeks. To speed blooming, keep branches warmer; to retard it, keep them cooler.

Poinsettias for Christmas.
To flower, poinsettias need about 8 weeks of short days, with less than 10 hours of light daily. Starting in early October, cover plants every night from 5:00 P.M. to 8:00 A.M. with a large box or opaque plastic bag supported on a hoop; don't let any light reach the plant. Stop covering once the top leaves turn red.

Forcing bulbs. Place tulips, narcissi, and other spring bulbs in a pot of fast-draining potting mix about 1 inch below the soil surface. Store at 40°F and keep moist. Let the bulbs root for 8 to 18 weeks; ask your bulb supplier for the required dormancy period. To stimulate sprouting, put the bulbs in a warm (55° to 65°F) spot in indirect light; keep well watered. When sprouts turn green, set in direct sun. Once the buds show color, move pots to indirect light to prolong blooming.

Crocuses and hyacinths can be forced in water. Use a narrow-necked bulb jar or vase that holds the bulb just above the water line, and put in a cool, dark place until roots form fully. Move to a warm, sunny room to flower after sprouts are 2 to 4 inches tall.

Paperwhite narcissus, with their spicy-sweet scent and pure-white starlike flowers, are the easiest to force, since they need no cold treatment or soil. Set bulbs in a shallow watertight container filled with pebbles, leaving ½ inch of their tops exposed; make sure they are well anchored so that they can support the long stems. Add water to ⅛ inch beneath the bulb base; never let water touch the bulb or it will rot. Place the container in a dark place until sprouts show (8 to 10 days), then move it to a sunny spot. The bulbs should flower in 3 to 5 weeks.
▷ **Aluminum Foil, Bulbs, Cold Frames**

FOUNTAINS

The different types. A fountain can be a free-standing structure, a spray issuing from a pool, or a wall-mounted spout that runs into a reservoir. In all cases, a pump is necessary to keep water recirculating. Kits sold at home stores and garden centers contain all the required equipment, including the fountain head, or nozzle, and a power cord.

What kind of pump? Submersible pumps are made for safe, quiet operation underwater. Surface pumps sit aboveground and must be concealed. Choose a pump slightly larger than needed so that you'll have more leeway to adjust the water flow.

A caution. Plug electrical pumps into a ground-fault circuit interrupter. The device will shut down power from the outlet to the pump when it senses any problems.

Consider style. For a formal garden, you may want a classic standing fountain. In a naturalistic one, a small pool with a softly dancing water jet might be best. Besides the straight jet, you can find nozzles that spray water in various shapes, including tulip, daisy, or mushroom forms.

Fountain placement. Make a free-standing or pool fountain a centerpiece by siting it prominently—in the center of a terrace or lawn or at the intersection of two paths. A wall fountain is by nature less conspicuous and becomes all the more charming with the element of surprise. Place it at the end of a walk or at the side of the garden and cover the spout with a carved relief mask.

Simple and soothing. Build your own small Japanese-style fountain in a quiet corner of the garden. Submerge a small pump in a stone bowl and use a hidden pipeline to connect it to a hollow bamboo pole. Add a second bamboo cane that will fill with water and tip down to spill its contents gently into the basin. Adjust the pump so that it issues a light trickle.

A fountain bubbling up through an old millstone provides a focal point in this shallow pebble pool.

Cool the air. In arid climates, fountains lower the temperature of the surrounding air—a bonus for overheated plants and people. The sound of the splash alone can seem refreshing on a hot day.

White noise. The persistent trickle of a fountain creates calming background music that can block out the rumble of traffic and other undesirable noises.

Keep kids safe. Wall and raised standing fountains are less hazardous for toddlers. Another safe solution is to sink a shallow pool or reservoir in the ground so that its sides reach a few inches below grade level. Add a small pump to force water up through a pipe. Lay a grill over the top of the pool, leaving a hole for the pipe, and conceal it with pretty stones.

Do not disturb. If you add water lilies or other aquatics to your fountain basin, keep them as far as possible from a submersible pump. Even though these plants like oxygen, they can't tolerate much movement.
▷ **Japanese Gardens, Ponds**

The subtle pleasures of garden scents

Learn to recognize and appreciate the world of fragrance in the garden. The key to understanding is provided by the vocabulary perfumers use to distinguish the three qualities, or notes, of a scent: head, middle, and base.

As a test, smell one of the older open-pollinated rose cultivars. First you'll smell the head notes, which dissipate quickly. Then come the richer middle notes, which last longer. Finally the forceful base notes appear, persisting even after a flower has dried up; it is these underlying notes that make potpourris a lasting pleasure.

Scents in the garden, from the most subtle to the headiest, come primarily from flowers—most often from open blooms but sometimes from the buds. Certain foliage plants, fruits, trees, shrubs, and even barks can also be richly aromatic. Some give up their fragrance all day, others at night, and still others only after a rain—but all bring yet another measure of gratification to a stroll through your garden.

The plants shown here are listed according to their dominant notes, then grouped by the scent they have in common. Plants are named either as a general group (herbs and hay), as a genus with more than one fragrant species (*Osmanthus* spp.), or as a particular species known for its scent (*Skimmia japonica*). Whenever possible, their common names are used.

Note that some plants whose fragrances are especially rich may appear in more than one place. An (F) indicates a plant with scented foliage only.

HEAD NOTES

The first notes you smell are the head notes—lively but fleeting.

CITRUS SCENTS

Bee balm (F)
Butterfly bush
Calamondin
Citrus bergamot
Damask rose 'Madame Hardy'
English rose 'Heritage'
Eucalyptus citriodora (F)
Gas plant (F)

Hybrid tea rose 'Fragrant Cloud'
Lemon
Mock orange
Orange
Osmanthus spp.
Pelargonium crispum
Skimmia japonica
Southern magnolia

HERBAL SCENTS

Allium spp.
Basil (F)
Bay laurel
Dill (F)
Lavender
Lemon balm (F)
Lovage (F)
Oregano (F)
Mint (F)
Rosemary (F)

Sage (F)
Scarlet sage (F)
Thyme (F)
Wormwood (F)

MIDDLE NOTES

The fragrant middle notes are longer lasting and somewhat more potent.

FLOWERY SCENTS

GREEN SCENTS

Culinary herbs
Ferns
Hay
Ivy
Leaves
Lichen
Mint
Moss
Sweet woodruff

FRUIT-SUGAR SCENTS

SPICY SCENTS

Anise
Apple
Carnation
Chocolate cosmos
Cinnamon
Clematis armandii
Clove current
Cloves
Cranesbill

Crossvine
Curry plant
Damask rose 'Kazanlik'
Fennel (F)
Ginger
Katsura tree (F)
Mexican orange
Moonflower
Pelargonium quercifolium (F)

Rugosa roses 'Blanc Double de Coubert,' 'Delicata'
Spanish broom
Spicebush
Stachys citrina
Sweet fern
Viburnum × burkwoodii
Wallflower

Alba rose 'Konigin
  van Danemark'
Cyclamen spp.
Daphne
Daylily
Floribunda rose
  'Escapade'

Honeysuckle
Hyacinth
Hybrid tea rose
  'Mr. Lincoln'
Jasmine
Lilac
Lily-of-the-valley

Orrisroot
Osmanthus spp.
Pelargonium
  graveolens (F)
Ptelea trifoliata
Tuberose
Wintersweet

Apple
Apricot
Bay laurel
Butterfly bush
Coconut
Crocosmia spp.
False acacia
Freesia
Garden phlox
Gorse
Iris

Jonquil
Laburnum
Lupin
Mahonia spp.
Mignonette
Mimosa
Peach
Pear
Pineapple sage
Quince

Rambler roses
  'Seagull,'
  'Kiftsgate,'
  'Bobbie James'
Raspberry
Snapdragon
Sweet box
Sweet pea
Viburnum
  bodnantense
Wisteria

BASE NOTES

Stronger and more persistent, the scent's base
notes are the last to appear.

RESINOUS SCENTS

Camphor tree (F)
Cedar (F)
Cherry birch
Douglas fir (F)
English roses 'Constance Spry,'
  'Fair Bianca'
False cyrpess (F)
Feverfew (F)
Gallica roses 'Belle Isis,'
  'Charles de Mills'
Juniper (F)
Madonna lily
Moss
Myrrh
Nothofagus antarctica (F)
Pine (F)
Rockrose (F)
Sandalwood
Wormwood (F)

BALSAMIC SCENTS

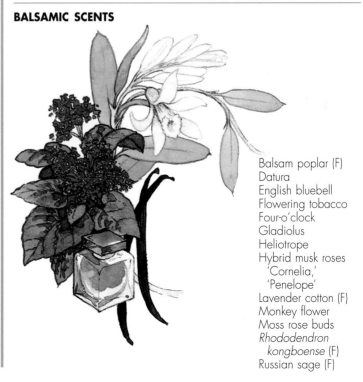

Balsam poplar (F)
Datura
English bluebell
Flowering tobacco
Four-o'clock
Gladiolus
Heliotrope
Hybrid musk roses
  'Cornelia,'
  'Penelope'
Lavender cotton (F)
Monkey flower
Moss rose buds
Rhododendron
  kongboense (F)
Russian sage (F)

FRAGRANCE

FREEZING FOOD

PREPARATION

Ready-to-use produce. To save time, prepare garden fruits and vegetables for freezing exactly as if you were going to consume them immediately: washed, peeled, dried, shredded, or cut into cubes or sticks.

Blanch veggies first. Before freezing, plunge carrots, beets, beans, diced carrots, and other vegetables into boiling water for 15 to 20 seconds. Drain in a colander and flush immediately with cold water. Blanching not only seals in the flavor but neutralizes vitamin-destroying enzymes.

Freeze by the piece.
The best way to store cut or sliced vegetables or fruits—apricot or plum halves, strawberries, carrot slices, or cauliflower florets, for example— is to freeze the pieces individually. Place the pieces on a tray, freeze, and put them in large plastic bags to keep in the freezer. You'll be able to take the food out by the handful as needed and thaw it more quickly.

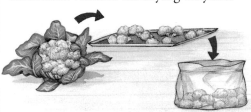

Add dairy products later. If you're freezing a hot dish for serving later, don't add milk, yogurt, or sour cream; they don't freeze well. Put a label on the freezer bag reminding you to add them in the correct amounts at final preparation.

Child's play. Save space when freezing green peppers by cutting off the tops and nesting the peppers inside each other like a child's toy. Cut the pepper tops into small pieces and bag and freeze them separately for use in soups and stews.

Ready-made succotash. Freeze a batch of homegrown 'Fordhook' lima beans mixed with a good freezing sweet corn—such as 'Early Sunglow' or 'Seneca Chief.'

Keep bags from bursting. If you are freezing food in water or broth, leave plenty of empty space. Freezing increases volume, and without extra space the bags or containers will burst.

More flavorful fruit. Thawed frozen fruit usually has less flavor than fresh fruit. Restore flavor by adding a few tablespoons of brandy or a corresponding fruit brandy. Honey may also help.

Ice cube surprises. In summer, put an edible flower, a raspberry, or a mint leaf in each square of an ice cube tray. Fill the tray with cooled boiled water—which has no air bubbles—and will make ice translucent. In winter, use bits of orange peel, some zest of lemon, or a brandied cherry instead.

Crispier pies. When making a pie with frozen fruit, which releases a lot of water as it thaws, keep the bottom crust from getting soggy by sprinkling it with granulated sugar, ground almonds mixed with an egg yolk, or plain flour. All of these will absorb any excess moisture from the thawing fruit like a dry sponge.

STORAGE

Should you buy a freezer? Modern refrigerators usually have enough freezer space for a family of four. If you have a large family or are economy minded, you may save money in the long run if you invest in a separate freezer. Buying food in bulk and freezing it for later use is ultimately thrifty.

An ice cube indicator. A bag of ice cubes placed on top of your other frozen produce bags can confirm that your freezer is functioning properly. If you notice that they've melted, other items probably have thawed out as well.

In case of a breakdown or a blackout, a full freezer holds up better than a half-empty one because air warms up faster than frozen blocks of food. If a power outage or brownout is announced, make sure to fill the freezer with bottles or bags filled with cold water as soon as possible.

For a freezer door that always shuts, slightly raise the front edge of the appliance with a thin scrap of wood. If you forget, or your arms are full, the door will shut itself.
▷ **Edible Flowers**

FROST

A three-season threat. Depending on your climate, frost can form on your plants and in the soil in fall, winter, or spring. This frozen moisture is most dangerous for young growth—like new spring buds or woody stems that have not hardened off sufficiently by fall. Signs of frost damage include puckered, distorted, or blackened foliage and blooms.

Not only frost but also alternate freezing and thawing harms plants. Woody stems may split, and roots can heave out of the soil with a cycle of frost and defrost.

Take note of the first frost-free date in spring and the last one in fall for your area and mark them on your gardening calendar. The period between them is the safe growing season for tender specimens.

The best defense for hardy plants against frost damage is mulch. After a killing frost, spread 3 inches of shredded bark, leaves, or straw to help the soil maintain a constant temperature. Cover with netting, chicken wire, tree branches, or drain tiles if wind threatens to blow the mulch away.

Water and weed. Keep your beds moist and free of weeds to head off frost damage in spring and fall. This treatment helps heat rise from the soil on chilly nights and warm the plants.

A paradox. Let a sprinkler play over tender plants all night when frost is predicted. Water gives off heat as it condenses to ice and will keep the plants warmer than the air.

Hill up your roses. Pile a mound of soil 10 to 12 inches high around the base of the bush to protect the roots and graft union from severe frost. Remove the soil in early spring but wait to prune until the tiny emerging buds indicate the extent of any injury.

Frost shade. Protect wall-trained vines, shrubs, and trees with a removable shade. Measure a sheet of canvas or nylon netting large enough to cover the plants completely and attach it to a stake. Mount the stake to the wall with hooks and eyes and let the shade hang; to promote air circulation, lean a couple of poles against the wall. Pull up the shade when it's warm and lower it in late afternoon to conserve heat.

A quick fix. If an unexpected light frost catches you unprepared, simply drape an old shower curtain, a tarp, a painter's plastic drop cloth, or unfolded newspapers over the plants before nightfall to trap soil heat.

A tailor-made muff. Wrap marginally hardy shrubs in an insulated burlap screen. Loosely stack oak leaves or straw around the plant; don't use maple leaves, as they will become soggy and mat down in the rain. Corral the insulation in a length of burlap supported by four corner stakes and tie with cord. Make sure to leave the top open for air circulation.

In the vegetable garden, protect young spring sprouts and maturing fall fruits with floating row covers. Lay the lightweight fleece right over the plants, although leaves touching it may sustain slight damage when the fabric freezes. Row covers are effective against frost down to 28°F.

Don't fret about carrots, cabbage, kale, and other frost-hardy veggies. They produce extra sugars to fight cold—and will consequently taste all the sweeter!

Face facts. Once a tender plant has been injured by frost, little can help it—so don't bother blowing hot air or pouring warm water over it. Just lift it and replace. For hardy specimens, prune back any frost damage down to healthy growth in spring.

Protect pots too. If you want to leave ceramic pots outdoors, bury them in a sheltered spot in a trench filled with sand, soil, or compost. This technique also provides frost protection for nursery stock or a proper chilling period for bulbs that you're preparing to force.

Encase a large container specimen in a topless, bottomless crate filled with straw. You can also make a "jacket" by packing straw between two pieces of netting or chicken wire. Make sure the pieces are tall and wide enough to encircle the plant. Stand the straw "sandwich" on one end and wrap it around the pot, leaving the top open; tie in place with cord.

Add some heat. If you have an outdoor electric outlet, you can help semi-hardy woody plants through their first frosts by burying electric heating tape 3 inches deep in the soil around the roots. The tape is available from specialty catalogs and garden centers.

▷ **Exposure, Protection**

FUCHSIAS

Delicate beauties. Because most of the 100 species and 2,000 hybrids of fuchsia are tender, they are raised as houseplants, annuals, or potted plants that overwinter indoors. Even the hardiest, *Fuchsia magellanica*—a shrub that can grow to 10 feet—needs protection to withstand temperatures to 10°F. All can take morning sun but prefer partial shade especially in hot climates.

Planting outdoors? Set out your hardy fuchsias in spring; they'll have more time to establish a strong root system and be better able to withstand their first winter.

For best blooms, plant in fertile, humus-rich, well-drained soil. Keep plants moist during the growing season —but don't overwater. Check potted plants for dryness every day and mist them when the leaves look limp.

Fuchsias are hungry plants. Feed with a balanced fertilizer when new growth starts and feed lightly once a week all summer—especially container specimens.

Pinching is essential. For lush fuchsias, begin pinching out the growing points when plants have three sets of leaves. As side shoots develop, pinch out the top set of leaves from each. After several weeks the plants will have produced more flowers and developed a symmetrical shape.

Mulch the crowns for winter. Frost will kill top growth, but don't worry; unless the soil freezes hard, a new plant will emerge in the spring.

Prune fuchsias between late January and early March, taking off about one-third of the growth. If the plant has died back com-

---

pletely, pull aside the mulch after danger of frost has passed and cut off the dead branches; new growth will soon start.

Perfect for baskets. Fuchsias' pendent flowers make these plants one of the most popular for hanging baskets, both indoors and out. They bloom through summer and often into winter. Use only one cultivar when grouping plants, since cultivars vary in vigor.

Multiply with cuttings. Take small cuttings, each with two to four leaves, in spring or fall. Dip the stems in a rooting hormone powder and place them in a tray of washed fine sand. Cover with glass or plastic to speed up growth. In 3 to 5 weeks the seedlings can be transferred to small pots or bedded outside.

Bring pots indoors. Overwinter tender fuchsias in a greenhouse, garage, basement, or an enclosed porch at about 40° to 50°F. If only light frost is expected, grouping plants close together next to a warm house foundation may be sufficient.

Overwinter care. Trim back any green tips or leaves and keep plants in low light; water only enough to prevent the soil from drying out. In spring, prune stems by two-thirds and repot the plants. Set in bright light in a warm place and resume watering.
▷ **Houseplants, Flower Beds**

FUNGICIDES

Know your enemy. To pick the proper fungicide, find out exactly what kind of fungus disease is attacking your plant. Among the most common culprits are verticillium wilt, fusarium wilt, clubroot, botrytis, powdery mildew, and rusts. Your local garden center, nursery, or Cooperative Extension Service can help identify the disease and suggest both the safest and the most effective method of control.

Is it really a fungus? Sometimes a problem you suspect is fungal disease is actually the result of overwatering, underwatering, or a nutritional imbalance in the soil. If so, a fungicide is of absolutely no benefit. Seek expert advice when in doubt.

How to spray. Treat all leaf surfaces thoroughly, even on the under-sides, and work your way up carefully from the lower leaves to the top of the plant. But apply the fungicide sparingly: an overdose can kill a plant. Read the manufacturer's directions and follow them to the letter.

Homemade fungicide. Painting or spraying leaves with a mixture of 1 teaspoon baking soda and several drops of vegetable oil dissolved in a quart of water helps control powdery mildew on houseplants and cucurbit crops. On roses it protects against both powdery mildew and black spot.

Think ahead. To work effectively, many fungicides must be applied before a disease starts to develop. Note which plants in your garden are attacked by fungus each year and use a protectant agent before any trouble begins.

LIMITING FUNGICIDE USE

▷ Many types of plants have been bred to resist fungus diseases. Choose disease-resistant plants; an example is the 'Donald Wyman' crab apple—resistant to apple scab, fire blight, and rust. Plant catalogs should indicate any resistance bred into their products; if you are unsure, call and ask before ordering.

▷ When sowing seeds indoors, use sterilized potting media or seed-starting mix to avoid damping-off disease, which affects seedlings.

▷ Prune overgrown trees and shrubs to encourage better air circulation around and through plants. Plant annuals and perennials far enough apart and away from hedges and buildings to allow good air circulation.

▷ Rotate each crop's location in the vegetable garden every year to stay one step ahead of any soil-borne diseases.

▷ Rake up all fallen leaves and fruit infected with fungi from around plants and dispose of them to reduce disease problems in the future.

▷ Water your plants early in the day so that the foliage will dry completely before the dampness of evening returns.

FURNITURE

Before you buy. Don't select garden furniture based on price alone. Also consider how you will use your furniture, what look you want to achieve, and how much maintenance you are willing to do.

Spruce up metal chairs and tables. Scrape off any rust or chipped paint with sandpaper or a wire brush. Remove stubborn blisters with a blowtorch and smooth with steel wool. Rinse well and let dry. To save time, pick a metal paint that doesn't require a primer.

Sponge, don't brush. Painting an intricate metal design can take hours. Speed the process by dabbing the paint on with an old kitchen sponge instead of a brush.

Retain the luster of aluminum furniture by applying a coat of liquid wax at the beginning of the season. Wipe down with soapy water occasionally and remove any stains with a light liquid abrasive.

New wood choices. In addition to classic teak, you can select from a wealth of newly available tropical hardwoods, such as nyatoh, bubinga, ovengkol, shorea, and iroko. Let these rot-resistant hardwoods weather to a silvery gray, or apply oil or stain annually to maintain their original appearance.

For a perfect match, paint wooden furniture with your leftover house paint. This way, even a ragtag assortment of Adirondack chairs will look like a matched set.

Reviving wicker. If your wicker furniture begins to dry out, refresh it with water.

⊰ BUYING GARDEN FURNITURE ⊱

Garden furniture is made from a variety of materials—from bent twigs to wrought iron. Consider the pros and cons of each before selecting what best suits your needs.

Wicker and rattan Traditional look; moderate cost; need protection from weather and indoor storage in winter; watch for mildew.

Metal Durable; usually needs cushions; cold to the touch. Steel and iron are costly and can rust; aluminum is more casual and cheaper.

Resin Inexpensive, light, and often stackable for storage; casual look; available in many colors; easily cleaned with soap and water.

Wood Comes in numerous styles. Weather-resistant hardwood can be left natural for low maintenance; durable but costly. Regular hardwood and pressure-treated softwood are inexpensive but need regular painting or staining.

Either spray it with a garden hose or moisten towels with warm water, wring them out, and lay them over the pieces for an hour or so.

Homemade picnic tables of pressure-treated wood weather the elements better if stained instead of painted.

The best fabric for cushions is vinyl-coated polyester, which resists stains, dries quickly, and is easy to clean with soap and water. Treat any mildew with a solution of 1 cup laundry detergent and 1 cup bleach mixed in 3 gallons water. Rinse well and let dry in the sun.

▷ **Benches**

GARBAGE CANS

Build a handy potting table that doubles as a garbage can enclosure. The sides can be brick, masonry, or treated wood; the top should be weather-resistant and big enough to work on—3 by 5 feet or so. Use the tabletop for preparing soil mixes and repotting plants. The space below provides storage not only for garbage cans but for pails, peat moss, and other gardening supplies.

Make a compost bin. Poke aeration holes in the base and lower walls of a garbage can. Set it on blocks and add compostables. Cover tightly and let "cook"; when it's finished, use the compost right out of the can.

A homemade shredder. Place dry leaves in a metal garbage can, filling it halfway. Lower your string trimmer into the can and chop the leaves for mulch or compost.

Collect rainwater for the garden by setting rubber or plastic garbage cans under downspouts and gutter drains.

Store a hose. Cut down a plastic garbage can to 2 or 3 feet high and coil a garden hose in it. Keep it in the basement in winter and an out-of-the-way place near the garden during the growing season. If you leave it outdoors, punch drainage holes in the base.

Stop wasps from trying to nest inside your cans; they love protein and sugar. Simply make sure that all can lids are snugly sealed.

Thwart animal raiders by using a bungee cord to hold the lid tightly on the can. Or link all of your cans together with bungee cords, making them more difficult to knock over. You can also squirt the can exteriors with ammonia.
▷ **Compost**

GARDENIAS

Gardenias love the South, thriving in hot, humid summers and mild winters. They are usually grown as border shrubs and hedges—especially close to the house, where the fragrance of their cream-colored flowers can be enjoyed by those indoors.

In the North, gardenias are usually grown indoors, where they decorate sunrooms and conservatories. To keep them from dropping their leaves and buds, give them plenty of light and humidity. Put them on

---

⚛ A GARDENIA SAMPLER ⚛

'Mystery,' growing a full 6 to 8 feet tall, is the most popular variety of this romantic Southern plant. More compact, at 2 to 3 feet, is 'Four Seasons.' Smallest of all and suitable as a small-scale ground cover is 'Radicans,' which grows to 6 to 12 inches and spreads 3 feet.

---

a tray filled with pebbles and an inch of water. But don't allow plants to get overheated, since new buds won't set in temperatures above 60°F. In summer you can move them outdoors to a lightly shaded spot.

A morning misting. Although gardenias need warmth and sun, whether growing indoors or out, they also appreciate having their foliage sprayed with cool water early in the day.

Rich and sour soil. To thrive, gardenias must have moist, acid soil enriched with plenty of organic matter.

Don't use a vase. Because the stems of cut gardenias don't take up water well, the delicate flowers are best displayed floating in a shallow bowl. Handle them gently to avoid bruising the petals.
▷ **Shrubs**

GARLIC

PLANTING
Buy bulbs from catalogs or garden centers. Don't use garlic from the grocer, which has been adapted for commercial production.

Plant in fall. The best time is around mid-October, so that cloves can establish a good root system that will withstand heaving.

For maximum production, plant only the biggest cloves from the outside of the largest bulbs; eat the culls and the runts. Plant in full sun in rich, well-drained soil.

Avoid planting garlic in the same place in your garden. Rotate every 2 years to prevent lower production and crop damage from soilborne diseases.

As a companion plant, garlic is said to enhance the growth of fruit trees, strawberries, tomatoes, cabbage, and roses. But garlic planted near peas, beans, and asparagus supposedly hinders their growth.

MAINTENANCE

Keep moist. Garlic likes evenly moist soil, so water well until the tops die back. Mulch to prevent drying and bolting.

Knot the stems, if you like, at the end of the season before the harvest. This helps the stems to dry out more quickly and is thought to concentrate more potent juice in the cloves.

HARVEST AND USE

Pull your garlic once three-quarters of the stems become dry and brown. Leave the crop in the sun for a day or two, then move it to a dark, dry place to finish curing for a week. Trim off the tops and store the heads in mesh bags at 40° to 50°F in relatively low humidity. Never keep garlic in a moist root cellar; it will rot there.

Eat the leaves, too. Snip the green sprouts as needed and use as you would chives.

Protect cats and dogs from fleas and ticks by putting a few cloves where they sleep and squeezing a bit of garlic juice into their drinking water.

In the kitchen, keep weevils and other household pests out of your dried beans and grains by adding a few cloves to their storage containers.

Pesticide and fungicide. Puree five or six garlic cloves in a blender with 2 cups water and a few hot chilies, strain it into a spray bottle, and add a few drops of liquid soap. Spray this potent homemade concoction directly on your plants to repel a wide variety of pests and to kill or prevent fungal diseases. Respray after each rain or watering.

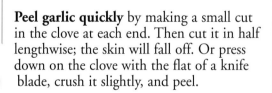

Peel garlic quickly by making a small cut in the clove at each end. Then cut it in half lengthwise; the skin will fall off. Or press down on the clove with the flat of a knife blade, crush it slightly, and peel.

Reduce garlic breath by eating fresh parsley leaves or chewing on a coffee bean.
▷ **Herbs**

GEOTEXTILES

What are they? Geotextiles are woven or bonded polypropylene "fabrics" that have been developed for agriculture and landscaping. Depending on their weight and permeability, they can be used for frost protection, mulch, or erosion control. Because they let water and air pass through, geotextiles are preferable to black plastic mulch.

Where to buy? Check garden centers and garden supply catalogs for geotextile mulch—also called weed barriers, weed mats, or landscape fabric—and for the lightweight, translucent textiles called floating row covers used to protect against insects and frost.

For weed-free vegetable beds, cover the prepared soil with a weed mat cut to size. Bury the edges in the soil or anchor with rocks. Cut slits where you want to plant and put in your seeds or transplants. The mulch lasts for years—so don't discard it after one season.

In shrub and perennial borders, cut circles or large crosses in the mat where plants will go to allow access for fertilizing. You can leave the mat in place permanently.

If you use organic mulch to cover the fabric, keep in mind that bark chips and the like decay into a fertile humus, and weeds can take hold. Their roots will entangle in the mat, making them hard to remove.

Use the fabric for weed control beneath a deck or under the stones or gravel on a path. Use it for erosion control behind a stone, block, or timber retaining wall.

Prevent erosion on newly seeded slopes with an open-weave mesh geotextile. The fibers gradually degrade upon exposure to light, at first warming and protecting the soil and then allowing seedlings to poke through and develop. The mesh will disappear after about 70 days.
▷ **Mulch, Weeds**

GERANIUMS

PURCHASING

Buying smart. The popular annuals and tender perennials sold in garden centers vary in price and quality. Generally, geraniums grown from seed are of less value. Those raised from cuttings perform better but cost more; they're also sold by variety rather than color. Before you choose a plant, ask the staff which type they sell.

Buy potted geraniums in the early spring. Look for bushy, well-rooted plants with one or two blooms so that you can be certain of their color.

A rainy climate? Single-flowered geraniums and those with darker leaves will grow better than double-flowered varieties in areas that have few sunny days.

PLANTING

Avoid big pots. Large, roomy pots encourage geraniums to produce a profusion of leaves instead of a profusion of flowers. Use medium-size pots instead.

Grow varieties from seed if you choose not to keep your geraniums from one year to the next. Start them in flats on top of a radiator or another warm spot in January for flowers by early June. Four to 6 weeks after they sprout, transplant the seedlings to medium-size pots and keep them in a cool but sunny spot. Move your plants outside in April or May, depending on your region's last frost date.

Propagate from cuttings. In late spring or early summer, take a healthy stem—preferably one with no flowers. Strip off the stipules and cut the stem into several sections. Make sure that each section has a leaf joint and one to three leaves; remove any flowers or buds. Dry the cuttings for about 6 hours, then dip the bottoms of each in rooting hormone and bury about halfway down in damp sand or well-drained potting soil. The stem sections should send out roots and be ready for transplanting to pots or window boxes in about 4 weeks. Mist lightly or cover the plants with large plastic bags to help increase the humidity around them.

MAINTENANCE

For more flowers, pinch back the stems of your newly purchased plants. More branches will grow, with each bearing flowers by summer. Pinch regularly, and you'll be rewarded with blooms right up to the first frost of fall.

Don't overwater. It causes root rot, especially if drainage is poor. With deeper pots you may need to water only once a week. Add fertilizer to the water, using a tenth of the recommended dose; applying small amounts of fertilizer often is preferable to larger infrequent doses.

Don't mist or sprinkle. Moisture on the flowers may cause them to rot.

Deadhead faded blooms. Snap or pinch them off by hand to prevent the plant from going to seed and to keep it looking nice and tidy.

Going on vacation? Keep your geraniums from looking spent on your return by dead-

heading the flowers and buds. Water and mulch just before you leave. If you're going away for 3 weeks—the time it takes for the blooms to form—a colorful plant will await your return. If you're going away for 2 weeks or less, don't cut the buds.

Rust removal.
If rust spots appear on the leaves, water the plant thoroughly, place it in a plastic bag, and set it outdoors in full sun. Rust-causing fungi will die at 90°F, which will be reached quickly in the bag. But beware: don't leave the plant in the bag for more than a few hours.

STORING
Overwintering. To keep potted plants from one year to the next, bring them inside. Put

---

GERANIUM OR CRANESBILL?

The plants Americans call geraniums are known as pelargoniums in the rest of the English-speaking world—from the plant's generic name, *Pelargonium*. Even more confusing is the fact that true geraniums—of the genus *Geranium*—are commonly called both cranesbills and hardy geraniums. The distinction between them is that so-called geraniums are either annuals or tender perennials and are often grown in pots and window boxes; cranesbills are hardy perennials and are grown in beds and borders.

---

them in a sunny, well-ventilated room and reduce watering. Give each plant 8 ounces of water every 2 weeks and turn the pots regularly for balanced growth. In early spring, start watering plants more frequently and cut back any scraggly stems.

If your basement is damp, try hanging geranium plants upside down there, wrapped in newspaper; if they're left

---

on the ground, they'll rot. Space them well apart to allow for air circulation.

CRANESBILLS
The true geraniums. Cranesbills have simple saucer-shaped flowers held over a bushy mass of foliage. Most bloom in spring and early summer; some will rebloom in fall.

Varied shades. These reliable bloomers produce lovely lobed cups in white, pink, magenta, blue, lavender, and violet—often deeply veined in a contrasting color.

What they need. Cranesbills will thrive in almost any well-drained soil. Most prefer full sun, though some will tolerate light shade. Taller types, like meadow cranesbill (*Geranium pratense*) and Armenian cranesbill (*G. psilostemon*), may need support.

A GERANIUM SAMPLER

Zonal geraniums have darker or lighter zones marking their round leaves. Two popular choices are the red-flowered 'Happy Thought' and 'Mrs. Cox,' with flowers of soft salmon.

Regal geraniums, also called Martha Washington geraniums, have serrated leaves and flowers similar to those of the azalea. Try the red 'Easter Greeting' or white 'Mme. Loyal.'

Ivy-leaved geraniums are trailing plants ideal for hanging baskets. Try 'Amethyst,' with purple-veined lavender blooms, and 'Crocodile,' with pink flowers and white-veined leaves.

Scented geraniums have smaller flowers and leaves that release a fragrance when rubbed —from apple to nutmeg. Try 'Mabel Gray' for lemon or 'Grey Lady Plymouth' for rose.

Cranesbills are hardy perennial geraniums that are planted outdoors. 'Johnson's Blue' is ideal for bringing bright color to your summer flower beds, while smaller cranesbills are perfectly suited for rock gardens.

▷ **Flower Beds**

GLADIOLUS

A succession of blooms. For an extended floral display, plant corms in full sun as soon as possible after the last frost. Then plant every 2 weeks, continuing until 2 months before the first frost is predicted.

Don't plant in rows. Add gladiolus to a mixed bed, where their long stems will enjoy the shelter provided by surrounding plants. As a bonus, they will flower a few weeks earlier than those in an isolated bed.

Plant them deep. To keep the top-heavy flower spikes from pulling out of the ground in sandy soil or on windy days, plant the corms between 3 and 8 inches deep, depending on their size.

Promote drainage by placing a layer of sharp sand or organic matter in the bottom of the planting hole. Press corms in firmly.

Stake each stem. Stake large-flowered gladiolus, which can grow 4 to 6 feet tall, with a bamboo cane and soft twine. Place the stake behind the flower spike as soon as you can tell which way the florets will be facing.

A GLADIOLUS SAMPLER

The flowers of "glads" come in all sizes—from miniatures to giants. Among the choice giant cultivars are 'Parade' (salmon and yellow), 'Prime Time' (cream), and 'Sharkey' (peach). Slightly smaller but equally impressive are the large 'Drama' (red and yellow), 'Showmate' (light yellow), and 'The Queen' (marbled pink). Medium-size cultivars include 'Brown Beauty' (brown and bronze), 'Jana M' (lavender and white), and 'White Ice' (pure white). For the smallest blooms, try 'Blue Bantam' (blue and white), 'Happy Time' (red and yellow), and 'Pink Flare' (pink and cream).

Hasten blooming. Gladiolus florets open from the lower part of the stem upward. Pinch out the top bud to speed the opening of flowers all along the spike.

Dig corms when the leaves begin to turn yellow—about 6 weeks after bloom. Lift the plants carefully with a spade, shake off the soil, and set them aside to dry for a few days. Then cut the leaves to 2 inches before storing the corms in a cool, dry place.
▷ **Bulbs, Flower Beds**

GOPHERS

Where they live. Gophers are bothersome rodents across America and serious pests in the western two-thirds of the country. The animals dig and live in a subterranean maze: a deep main tunnel contains the nest and food-storage areas, while extensive surface tunnels give them access to the underground plant parts on which they graze.

How to recognize them. Gopher tunnels often end in a distinctive fan-shaped mound of dirt. In contrast, moles push out soil from their holes in a circular pattern.

Gopher patrol. You basically have three choices when dealing with these destructive little diggers: install barriers to keep them away from your property and plants, kill or catch them in traps, or try to repel them.

Effective barriers. Erect a barrier around your yard or garden beds with ½-inch wire mesh. Make sure it reaches at least 2 feet high and is buried at least 2 feet deep (or 3 feet in light or sandy soil). You can also line each planting hole with chicken wire or the

---

bulb cages sold at garden centers. Protect tree bark with ½-inch galvanized hardware cloth. Sink the bottom edge underground and wrap completely around the tree.

The right trap. While rat traps work, there are traps specifically designed for certain regions and certain species. Check with your local Cooperative Extension Service.

Set up the trap in a shallow trench near the tunnel entrance and cover the trigger mechanism with a little soil. Sprinkle nuts, sunflower seeds, or grains over it, adding more bait inside the trap. Always wear rubber gloves when handling traps and bait so that you won't leave your scent on them.

Vibrating soil. Many garden centers and specialty catalogs sell devices designed to repel gophers and moles. One is wind-powered and looks like a windmill lawn ornament.

A kitchen-sink repellent. Soak rags in ammonia, drop them down a gopher hole, and seal all tunnel openings with dirt. The gophers will leave in a hurry. This tactic is most effective in spring.

Natural predators. Make your garden as safe and hospitable as possible for owls, hawks, gopher snakes, and king snakes. Dogs, cats, and skunks will also pursue gophers, but dogs and skunks are diggers too—they may cause more damage to your garden than gophers do.
▷ **Rodents**

GOURDS

Only for show. Gourds are unusually shaped vegetables in the cucurbit family, which includes pumpkins, squashes, melons, and cucumbers. While they are edible when young, gourds are grown chiefly for the ornamental value of their shells when mature and dried. Some boast brightly colored patterns of yellow, orange, and green and are often preserved with varnish or wax. Others, called lagenarias or calabashes, dry to yellow or tan and can be turned into dippers, bottles, rattles, or birdhouses.

Select by shape. The names of gourds suggest their form, such as Turk's turban, crookneck, bottle, dumbbell, club, ball, penguin, powder horn, and serpent.

Treat like tropicals. Sow these frost-tender plants where they'll get plenty of warmth and sunshine—against a south-facing stone wall, for example. They need up to 140 days till maturity.

A dry climate? Create a basin in the soil around the plant base to hold moisture. Mulch with straw or shredded dead leaves.

In wet areas, plant gourds in mounds spaced 5 feet apart. Mulch to prevent soil erosion and inhibit weeds, as the fleshy roots grow very close to the soil surface.

Prevent rotting by keeping gourds off the ground. Once the fruits form, put them on a board supported by four overturned flowerpots or bricks; leave in place until harvest time. Expect the bottoms to flatten out.

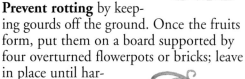

⊁ THE WASHCLOTH GOURD ⊰

The club-shaped luffa gourd is the source of a scratchy "sponge." To make your own, pick the gourd once it has turned brown, then soak it in water for several days. Peel away the skin to reveal the fibrous pulp; spray with water to remove any seeds and rinse out thoroughly. Squeeze, dry it in the sun for a week, and let it cure in an airy place for up to 6 months.

Save space. Plant gourds at the base of a trellis, fence, or wall and train the vines to keep them from sprawling all over the ground. Support heavy fruits in a net or cloth sling. Let dipper-shaped calabash fruits hang freely to straighten their necks.

When to harvest. Leave gourds on the vine until they are completely ripe, with hard, glossy shells and dry stems. Cut, don't pull, fruits from the vine, leaving 2 to 3 inches of stem attached. Handle carefully to avoid bruises, where rot can develop.

Cure gourds by washing them with a mild solution of vinegar or bleach. Let dry and harden in a warm, well-ventilated place for 2 to 6 months. Don't worry about any mold spots that develop on the surface—they won't damage fruits. Just scrape them off with a knife.

▷ **Cucumbers, Melons, Pumpkins, Squash**

GRAFTING

A happy union. Grafting is the method of propagating plants by joining a shoot or bud from one plant, called the scion, to the stem of another plant, called rootstock. If no shoots are allowed to sprout on the rootstock—that is, anywhere below the grafting union—the buds on the scion

will grow to resemble the plant from which they were taken. The plant's size, however, may be determined by the rootstock.

Why graft? This propagation method is used on woody plants, such as fruit trees and roses, that produce few seeds or will not grow true from seed. Grafting is also done to replace damaged branches.

Like to like. Grafting between species—an ever-bearing rose scion on a winter-hardy rose rootstock, for example—creates a healthy and often superior plant. A graft between genera—such as joining an apple scion to a pear root—may survive, but only for a few years. Grafts between families, such as apples and oaks, are doomed.

Key cells. In a successful graft, the cells of the rootstock cambium (the cell layer just under the bark) and those of the scion cambium divide and intermingle into a single unit. For this reason, you must align the cambium of the rootstock and the scion carefully.

A grafting knife must be able to take and hold a razor-sharp edge. Clean cuts minimize damage to plant cells and encourage quick healing. Look for a knife with a thin, carbon-steel blade; use it only for grafting.

Keep it sharp. Sharpen a grafting knife on a bench stone made of silicon carbide or aluminum oxide. Lubricate the stone with light household oil. With the cutting edge at a 25° angle to the stone, draw the blade across the stone from handle to tip. Turn the blade over and repeat the same stroke. Continue until the blade is very sharp.

Slipping bark. The type of graft you use often depends on whether the bark is

⇥ FOUR WAYS TO GRAFT ⇤

The four primary grafting techniques are shown below. In any graft, the rootstock and scion must be held tightly together while the union takes place. Seal exposed cuts to prevent drying out and infection, then loosen the binding material after 2 weeks. Never prune a shield- or chip-budded plant during or immediately after a graft. Wait until the following growing season, then trim the top to stimulate growth.

TYPE	TECHNIQUE	APPLICATIONS
Whip-and-tongue graft 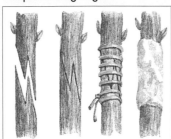	Cut diagonally across the top of the rootstock. Place your knife one-third of the distance from the tip and make a second cut extending just to the base of the first—without cutting all the way to the edge. Make two complementary cuts on the scion. Pull open the clefts resulting from the second cuts on both pieces and interlock the tongues. Bind with waxed string or grafting tape; you can also coat the graft with a latex sealant.	Use on dormant wood, usually when the diameter of the rootstock and scion are similar. If they are not, align the cambium on one side.
Cleft graft 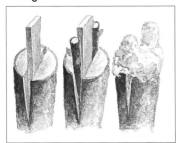	Make a vertical 2- or 3-inch split in the rootstock by pounding a heavy knife or cleft-grafting tool across the center. Hold the slit open with a wooden wedge. Choose two scions 3 or 4 inches long with two or three buds on each; hone the bottom 2 inches into a wedge, so that the cambium layer is exposed on two sides. Insert the scions with the bark facing out and the cambium touching. Remove the wedge and seal the graft.	Use on outdoor plants such as apple trees when you want to change the variety of fruit.
Shield or T-budding 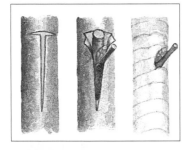	Prepare a bud stick by selecting a vigorous twig with leaves. Make a shallow cut above a leaf, then place the knife below it and slice the bark upward to meet the first cut. Pinch off the leaf blade, leaving a piece of stem for a handle. Make a T-shaped incision in the bark of the rootstock and insert the bud; make sure it's right side up. Bind the graft with plastic tape or a rubber budding band, leaving only the leaf stem exposed.	Use when the rootstock and buds are growing and the bark is slipping. It is ideal for stone fruit trees such as peaches and plums.
Chip budding 	Make a half-moon nick at a 45° angle in the rootstock, cutting ¼ of the way in. Place the knife an inch higher and cut downward to meet the first cut at the back, leaving a little lip; remove the resulting chip. Make an identical set of cuts behind a leaf bud to create a budwood chip that fits the rootstock opening; if the bud is smaller, align the cambium as shown. Insert the chip and wrap with tape, leaving a tiny opening.	Use when bark is not slipping. It's a popular technique in cold areas with short growing seasons.

"slipping." Bark is said to be slipping when natural lubricants make it loose—a healthy condition. When a tree is dormant, on the other hand, the bark is tight. Stress from drought or disease can also cause bark to tighten up, even in the growing season.

Seal it off. Old-fashioned hot or cold grafting waxes have been replaced by latex and plastic sealants that are easier to use and more tolerant to cold.

Secure it well. To bind a graft union properly, use the moisture-proof plastic tape designed for the purpose. It seals the graft for the required time and then disintegrates before it can restrict growth of the union. Freezer tape can be used as a substitute.

Timing is all. More grafts fail from bad timing than from sloppy technique. In temperate areas, do dormant wood grafting like whip-and-tongue and cleft on apples and pears in early spring; use budding techniques like shield and chip for propagating all fruits in late summer and early fall, just before dormancy begins.

Collect fruit tree scions for dormant wood grafting in winter from the previous year's growth. Graft sections ¼ inch in diameter with two or three buds to the rootstock. Collect budwood at budding time; it stores for only a few days.

Scion storage. Coat the cut ends of a scion with sealant to keep the wood from drying out. Wrap in barely damp paper towels and store in a plastic bag. Remove scions weekly to inspect for mold, let them air briefly, then rewrap. Don't store longer than necessary; scions lose vitality with time.

New graft care. Store newly grafted plants at a moderate temperature and keep the root system moist with a plastic cover. The buds of a successful dormant wood graft will begin to swell in a week or so.

▷ **Propagation**

GRAPEVINES

PLANTING

What kinds? European grapes are most often grown in the long warm-season parts of the West, while American species will grow in short-season areas. A third kind, the muscadine, is best suited to the South.

Plant vines in early spring or fall in a well-weeded, well-drained site amended with plenty of organic matter; they prefer a soil pH of around 6.0. Space vines 8 feet apart. If you plant in fall in a cold area, mound up the soil to prevent frost heaving.

Sun makes them sweet. To ensure that fruits develop a high sugar content, plant the vines where they'll receive the maximum sun and heat. Site vines against a wall or on a slope with a southern exposure.

Soak the roots in manure tea or in water mixed with a little bonemeal for 30 minutes before planting.

A vine-covered pergola over a deck or patio provides shade in summer. Keep in mind, though, that birds will peck unprotected fruit, which may then attract wasps and bees.

Plant grafted grapevines with 1½ to 2 inches of the graft above the soil line. To keep the union from drying out, cover it with a mound of sand for 2 months, then remove it.

Cultivate vines in pots for your balcony or porch. Fill large pots—at least 14 to 16 inches in diameter—with 2 parts garden loam to 1 part each leaf mold and coarse sand. Plant a non-vigorous variety, like 'Delaware' or 'Golden Muscat,' and set up a support for the vines. At summer's end, you may even reap a few grapes. Repot every 2 years in fresh soil when the plant is dormant.

Quick propagation. In autumn, take 8-inch sections of vine, cutting just above and below a node. Bury two-thirds of their length in well-drained soil or sand. To protect from cold, cover the exposed third with a mound of sand until the next spring. Transplant the cuttings in autumn.

MAINTENANCE

Cordon your vine. An easy and tidy way to grow grapes on a pergola is to train a single, permanent stem—called a cordon—overhead along the length of the structure. Fruiting canes will grow perpendicular from the cordon. Prune any canes less than 1 foot apart back to the cordon. Each winter, prune all canes down to two buds.

When to prune. Prune a grapevine anytime it is leafless. In areas with hard winters, wait until just before growth begins in spring so that you can recognize and remove any dead or damaged wood.

⊱ A GRAPE SAMPLER ⊰

Each of the following cultivars is good for eating fresh and for making juice, jelly, and wine.

'Aurore' French-American hybrid; sweet white fruits with slight pink blush; hardy to lower Midwest; mildew resistant

'Canadice' Large clusters of seedless red fruits; hardy to -15°F; resistant to black rot

'Concord' Adapted to Midwest, mid-Atlantic, and Northeast; prolific blue-black fruits; disease resistant; grown since the 1840's

'Edelweiss' Sweet greenish-gold fruits; cold hardy in north-central and Rocky Mountain states; disease resistant

'Interlaken' Heavy producer of nearly seedless golden-yellow fruits; cold hardy to -15°F; seedless; good for raisins

'Scuppernong' Muscadine grape grown in South; thick-skinned red-bronze fruits; needs cross-pollination; grown since the 1760's

---

Bleeding vines? Don't worry. Grapevines naturally bleed profusely when they are pruned in spring—but are not harmed.

Mulch early. Mulch in spring to give grapevines the moisture they need for good production. For best results, use plenty of well-rotted manure mixed with straw.

Keep them well fed. Grapevines quickly exhaust the soil. Side-dress each vine in spring with a 6-inch ring of a complete or high-potassium fertilizer. You can also add 1 pound of compost per 1 foot of row in late winter each year.

Protect fruit clusters from diseases, insects, and birds as soon as the grapes reach the size of a pea. Slip specially made bags of transparent paper or cheesecloth up to the stem and secure loosely. If you use plastic bags, punch holes for ventilation.

GRASS

The most convenient way to buy grass seed is in mixtures developed for particular conditions and uses. There are mixes for sunny and shady exposures, as well as for warm and cool climates. There are also blends for heavy traffic, as in children's play areas, and for a luxuriant putting-green effect.

Read the label. Seed labels list the combined seed varieties. To ensure you're getting quality seed, check that the varieties are listed by trade name rather than generic name: "Liberty Kentucky bluegrass," for example, instead of "Kentucky bluegrass."

Check and double-check. Seed labels also list the germination rate of each grass variety and the minuscule percentage of other ingredients, such as weed seed and other crop seed. Check that the germination rate is high—at least 75 percent for Kentucky bluegrass and 85 percent for most other varieties. Then check the amount of weed seed and other crop seed in the package; each should be no more than 0.5 percent.

A versatile variety. The popular turf-type tall fescues are especially adaptable, able to withstand cold temperatures and moderate heat, as well as drought, heavy traffic, and intense sun. They tolerate a variety of soil types and pH levels and need less nitrogen than most other grasses.

An improved Bermuda. Seeded Bermuda grass greens up 2 to 4 weeks earlier than other Bermudas and goes dormant later; it also has better color, uniformity, and winter hardiness.

A grass for arid climates. Buffalo grass—with its fairly fine texture and greenish-gray color—is native to the prairie states and is extremely drought tolerant, needing no water once established. Try 'Texoka,' 'Prairie,' or 'Sharp's Improved.'

Seeds to avoid. Be wary of "bargain" seed mixtures, which often contain low-quality grasses like redtop (*Agrostis alba*) or rough bluegrass (*Poa trivialis*). Such inferior lawn grasses can become weedy and quickly compromise the quality of your lawn.

Sod is quicker than grass seed—but it always must be installed within 24 hours of being harvested. To purchase sod, look in the phone book for sod farms. Or call your local Cooperative Extension agent, who can provide a list of suppliers in your area.

A common misconception. Many gardeners believe that grass clippings left on the lawn create thatch—a dense mat that keeps nutrients from penetrating into the ground. It isn't true: thatch, instead, is a layer of dead grass stems and roots that forms at the soil line. If you let the clippings decompose, they will release nitrogen into the soil almost continually, reducing the need for fertilizer by as much as 25 percent.

Recycled grass. "Grasscycling"—leaving grass clippings on the lawn instead of raking them up—is also environmentally prudent, helping to keep yard waste out of community landfills.

▷ **Lawns, Mowing**

GOOD CHOICES FOR THE LAWN

NORTHERN LAWNS	Varieties	Blade texture	Shade tolerance	Mowing height
Kentucky bluegrass	'America,' 'Freedom,' 'Liberty,' 'Monopoly,' 'Nugget'	Fine	Low/medium	2.5"–3"
Fine fescue	'James Town II,' 'Reliant,' 'SR 3000,' 'SR 5000'	Fine	High	1.5"–2.5"
Tall fescue	'Duster,' 'Mustang,' 'Olympic II,' 'Pixie,' 'Twilight'	Medium	Medium	2"–3.5"
Ryegrass	'Advent,' 'APM,' 'Express,' 'Manhattan II,' 'SR 4100'	Medium	Low/medium	2"–2.5"
SOUTHERN LAWNS				
Bermuda grass	'Midiron,' 'Tifgreen,' 'Tifway II'	Medium	Low	1.5"–2"
Seeded Bermuda	'Cheyenne,' 'Sahara,' 'Sundevil,' 'Yuma'	Medium	Medium	1.5"–2"
Centipede	'Au Centennial,' 'Georgia Common,' 'Oaklawn,' 'Tennessee Hardy'	Medium/coarse	Medium/high	1"–2"
St. Augustine	'Bitter Blue,' 'Floratam,' 'Raleigh,' 'Seville'	Coarse	High	2"–3"
Zoysia	'Belair,' 'Emerald,' 'Flawn,' 'Meyer'	Fine/medium	Medium/high	0.5"–1.5"

GREENHOUSES

Greenhouse culture isn't limited to professional plant growers. Because greenhouses are available in a range of sizes and prices, you can easily find one to fit your space, budget, and needs.

Consider the cost. When planning a greenhouse, take into account not only the price of the structure but also the long-term cost of operation—especially of providing heat. A "warm" greenhouse should be kept above 60°F, while a "cool" greenhouse must always be kept above 45°F.

Location is key. Site the greenhouse to receive as much sunlight as possible in winter. Attached types should have a southern exposure, while a free-standing house should be oriented north to south lengthwise. Protect it from prevailing winds with a hedge or berm.

Summer shade. To keep the greenhouse from becoming unbearable in hot months, block sunlight with blinds or fabric shades, which can be rolled into place with pulleys. Or use waterproof shade paint, which is inexpensive and easy to remove at summer's end. Apply it in a solid layer for dense shade or in intermittent streaks for part shade.

Homegrown shade. You can also add shade by planting deciduous trees nearby. Place them on the south side of the house, but far enough away so that falling leaves and branches won't create a problem.

An alternative: train any nonevergreen vine, such as clematis or morning glory, to climb up to the roof.

Winter warmth. Instead of heating the entire greenhouse, create a mini greenhouse in one corner for your tenderest plants. Install temporary walls with two sheets of plastic and keep it warm with a small thermostatically controlled electric space heater.

Save energy by installing a low-emissivity, or low-e, coating on the glass. This reduces heat loss without blocking out sunlight.

Keep glass clean to admit as much light as possible. Use a car-washing device, which hooks up to any hose; it eliminates the need for both hand-scrubbing and a ladder.

Go with the flow. A greenhouse needs ventilation to let stale air escape and fresh air circulate. To provide proper air flow, install at least one vent on each side of the roof and each side wall. Open them in the morning, when the temperature is rising; close them in the afternoon to conserve heat. Even on very windy or cold days, crack vents open slightly.

Eliminate guesswork in regulating air flow by installing automatic vent openers, whether an electric or nonelectric type. Activated by a thermostat, they constantly adjust the ventilation when cloud cover or other factors cause temperature fluctuations. They can also be operated manually with hand levers.

Water supply. Provide a faucet every 12 feet so that you can use short hoses, which are less clumsy to handle in a tight space than one long piece. Make sure that the faucets are threaded to accept a garden hose socket and are located for easy access. Install a mixing valve so that you can spray your plants with lukewarm water—at about the same temperature as the air.

Increase humidity by wetting down the floor of the greenhouse. While a concrete floor is the easiest to maintain, a gravel one holds moisture best. You can also spritz plants with a mister. Don't try to add humidity in winter, however; it will cause condensation on the glass and may promote the spread of fungal diseases.

Water plants in the morning so that they can dry off before sundown. Don't squirt them with a hard stream from a hose, which can dislodge or compact the soil; spray with a fine nozzle or use a watering can.

Test for dryness. Tap the pots to determine if your plants need water. If you hear a thud, the plant is moist enough; if you hear a ringing sound, it's time to water.

Organize your greenhouse for maximum convenience. Use tables, or "benches," that are about 30 inches high and 3 feet wide. These will let you work without bending over and reach to the far side of the tabletop comfortably. Store pots, soil, tools, and hoses underneath the benches to keep walkways uncluttered.

Maximize space by hanging plant baskets from the ceiling frame and shelves from the side walls. Make sure not to overload the shelves with heavy pots. Also cover any sharp edges with foam.

Organize your plants according to their cultural needs so that they will be easy to maintain. Keep plants with fuzzy foliage, which should be kept dry, away from those that like to be misted. Place sun lovers on the south side of the house and shade lovers on the north. Make sure that no leaves are touching the glass in winter.

No need to stake. Instead, hang strings from the greenhouse frame in strategic places. Twist the stems of young plants around the strings to give them support.

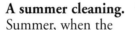

A summer cleaning. Summer, when the greenhouse is empty or sparsely filled, is the best time to give it a thorough cleaning. Wash down the glass and benches with detergent and disinfectant, which harms plants but helps combat insects and diseases. Use an algicide if slime has accumulated on the flooring and benches.

Housekeeping. Summer is also the time for routine maintenance. Check the glass for damage; you can repair cracks temporarily with glazing tape, but replace broken panes as soon as possible. Clean out gutters and downspouts. Repair any rusted metal or flaking paint on the frame.

Come September... Prepare plants for overwintering in the greenhouse about 6 weeks before you put them there—usually early September. Clean up damaged stems and foliage, pot up transplants, and treat for pests and diseases, which can spread rapidly in the confines of a greenhouse.

Keep it clean. To head off an epidemic, follow strict sanitary practices. Use sterilized soil; plastic, metal, or glass containers; and tools reserved just for the greenhouse. Inspect plants regularly for pests and diseases and isolate any problem specimens.
▷ **Cold Frames, Whiteflies**

GREENS

The greens scene. Greens comprise a range of vegetables grown for their leafy, dark green tops—each one distinctive and flavorful. Pick from collards, kale, broccoli rabe, or turnip, mustard, and beet greens.

Make a rich bed by turning rotted manure or compost into the ground as soon as it can be worked. Add 1 to 2 pounds of 10-10-10 fertilizer for every 50 square feet. Kale and collards prefer soil with a pH of 6.5 or above, so amend accordingly.

Fertilize again for maximum production of nutritious leaves and stems. Feed greens when they are about 6 inches tall by spreading a band of 10-10-10 fertilizer at the rate of 1 cup per 10-foot row.

Don't till kale under in fall. Let it grow through winter to be enjoyed as a fresh vegetable treat. If the leaves are frozen, don't thaw them before steaming or boiling. Some gardeners say that kale, as well as collards, tastes sweeter after the first frost.

Summer collards. Collard greens, usually grown in fall and winter, stand up well to heat. Planted in spring, they can make it through even the hottest months.

Vary your crop. To ensure a ready supply, plant a short row of the greens of your choice every 10 days in spring and summer. A staggered planting scheme means you can always harvest the leaves in their prime.

Harvest them young. Cut turnip greens and mustard greens while they're still young and tender. For tasty beet greens, harvest when the beets reach the size of marbles.

The best way to wash greens is to fill a large washtub or the kitchen sink with cold water. Put the greens in a colander, plunge it into the water, and swish vigorously to remove dirt. Let drain before using.

The sooner the better. Use greens immediately after picking them for the best taste.

To store greens for the short term after a thorough washing, drain them and wrap in paper towels. Seal them in a plastic bag and place in the refrigerator. But make sure the greens aren't too damp before storing; otherwise, they'll begin to rot.

Cook 'em right. Tender young greens can be stir-fried or steamed briefly before being served. Mature greens are tougher and should always be steamed or boiled before being sautéed or stir-fried.

Don't undercook. Even though cooking greens for a long time lessens their nutritional value, the nutrients of nearly raw greens can't be absorbed easily by the body. Undercooked greens are also hard to chew.

Not just for boiling. Raw mustard greens add a pleasant bite to salads. Clip leaves at 6-inch lengths. Be sure to keep plants well watered; their flavor becomes hotter and more bitter if the soil is allowed to dry out.

❧❙ A GREENS SAMPLER ❙❦

A turnip variety developed for its tender greens is 'All Top Hybrid.' For tasty beet greens, grow the heirloom beet 'Chiogga.' Collards lovers praise the flavor of 'Vates,' while experienced kale growers swear by 'Russian Red,' also known as 'Rugged Jack.' For the fastest-growing mustard greens, choose 'Tendergreen.'

▷ **Spinach, Swiss Chard, Vegetable Gardens**

GROUND COVERS

A green carpet of dwarf periwinkle will be dusted with tiny lavender-blue flowers in early summer.

Covering the ground. Ground covers can be bulbs, perennials, herbs, shrubs, roses, or vines—any low-growing, spreading plant that blankets the soil. They make an ideal lawn substitute, provide a foil for showier plants, and work well on difficult terrain.

Select suitable specimens. For best coverage, use plants that will thrive in your site. Determine the sun exposure and the composition, pH, and moisture level of the soil before choosing a ground cover. The right plant in the right place will take from 1 to 3 years to fill in.

Make the right choice. After you examine your site, consider what you want. Do you want an evergreen or a deciduous cover? Flowering or foliage plants? A smooth "carpet" or a textured look? Do you need to solve a specific problem—such as preventing soil erosion or filling in between stepping stones? Or do you simply want a low-maintenance alternative to a flower garden? You'll be able to find ground covers for every need.

PLANTING

Plant ground covers in the fall so that they'll be better established by spring, smother more weeds, and provide some winter interest.

Clear out weeds before planting any ground cover to cut down on competition. Particularly tenacious nuisances include Japanese knotweed, artemisia, and Canada thistle, all of which will grow back quickly.

Slope savvy. Ground covers are perfect for slopes, eliminating the need for mowing or heavy maintenance in an awkward space. To hold the soil while roots mature, lay down a permeable, biodegradable mat, such as jute netting. Cut planting holes, set in the plants, and mulch.

Slope too steep? Create planting terraces with boards, logs, or stones and install a

❧ GROUND COVERS FOR SHADE OR SUN ❧

	DRY SOIL	AVERAGE SOIL	MOIST SOIL
IN SHADE	Goutweed Ivy Lily-turf Epimedium Mock strawberry Mondo grass Solomon's seal Winter creeper	Ajuga Coral bells Dwarf periwinkle Bunchberry Lady's mantle Lily-of-the-valley Pachysandra Plumbago	American barrenwort Astilbe Foam flower Hosta Strawberry begonia Sweet woodruff Wild blue phlox
IN SUNLIGHT	Aaron's beard Blue fescue English lavender Lamb's-ear Lavender cotton Sedum Sun rose Thrift	Aubrieta Barren strawberry Campanula Candytuft Cranesbill Daylily Moss pink Speedwell	Bergenia Bog rosemary Houttuynia Japanese blood grass Knotweed Variegated manna grass Variegated sedge Variegated velvet grass

strong-rooted ground cover. Remove the supports once plants are established.

Plants for slopes. This special environment calls for strong-rooted specimens that can tolerate the dry conditions caused by constant water runoff. For shady yards, use ivy, lily-turf, or goutweed. For sunny ones, try Aaron's beard, lavender, lemon balm, thrift, or creeping juniper.

Annual aid. Plant colorful flowering annuals to fill in while ground covers mature; they'll keep out weeds and retard erosion.

Under-tree treatment. Shade and root competition make the area under trees an especially challenging environment, although a number of ground covers fit the bill. In dry, poor soil, use ivy, yellow archangel, periwinkle, or pachysandra. In moist, rich soil, try foam flower, lungwort, barrenwort, sweet woodruff, or ferns.

Plant under trees by breaking up the soil between roots as best you can with a trowel or hoe; incorporate a generous amount of compost. Set in plants, dividing the root ball if necessary, and mulch with leaf mold or compost. Keep well watered and fed, since tree roots will hog nutrients.

In the vegetable patch, use ground covers to cool the soil and suppress weeds between rows or at the foot of tomatoes, corn, and other large plants. You'll reap double rewards by installing edible covers, such as thyme, oregano, chamomile, and nasturtium. You can also plant strawberries beneath raspberry or gooseberry bushes.

Indoors, use small ground covers, such as creeping fig or Swedish ivy, at the base of large houseplants to dress up the bare soil. Choose a plant with the same cultural requirements as the houseplant and pot them at the same time.

Outdoors, keep the soil around a large potted plant—a lemon tree or datura, for example— cool and moist with ground cover; a blooming plant also adds color. Start with small plants and install them around the edge of the pot to limit root com-

petition. Try verbena or marigold in the sun and lobelia or impatiens in the shade.

MAINTENANCE
The no-maintenance myth. All plants need care, even relatively undemanding ground covers. If you treat them with the same attention as your other plants, they'll reward you with dense coverage and years of trouble-free flowers or foliage.

Mulch the beds while ground covers are filling in to smother weeds and keep soil moist. Use compost, wood chips, or shredded bark. Once they have grown, the plants themselves will act as mulch.

Keep them fed and watered while they mature. An easy way to fertilize large drifts is to use a soluble food that can be applied with a hose-end sprayer.

Restore vigor by pruning back any damaged, diseased, or bare stems. This not only improves the plant's appearance but also promotes new growth.

Tuft-forming ground covers, such as aubrieta or snow-in-summer, can become stripped in the center. To encourage them to root and send out new sprouts, pile some compost over the bare stems.

Increase your stock or fill in a bare spot by layering. While the stems of ground covers like ivy root naturally, others—including conifers and mahonia—need help. In spring, strip the leaves from a section of a young, flexible shoot near its tip. Bury it several inches in soil amended with compost, using a stone or bent wire to pin it down. Keep it moist until roots form; give a gentle tug or dig down to check for growth. Once roots are strong, sever the stem from the parent plant and transplant.

Slow down trailers and creepers. Keep an eye on ivy, winter creeper, sun rose, moneywort, and other ground covers that spread via creeping stems. Either give them room to run or hold them back by pruning.

Contain invasive roots. Goutweed, Aaron's beard, mint, sweet woodruff, ribbon grass, lamium, and the 'Silver' artemisias have rampant roots. Sink metal or plastic strips deep into the soil to stop their aggressive spread.

Clean them up. In early spring, cut back any evergreen stems that are too long or winter burned. Deadhead the blossoms of flowering ground covers once they're spent. For mass plantings, use either hedge clippers or a lawn mower with the blade adjusted to the highest setting; add the bag to collect the clippings. On slopes, test a string trimmer on a small area to see if it's powerful enough for the job.

A post-clipping precaution. Weeds that were previously shaded may spring to life after a mowing. Pull them up, mulch bare spots, or apply a postemergent herbicide that is safe for established plantings.

GRUBS & LARVAE

What are they? *Larvae* is the term for immature insects that undergo a complete metamorphosis on their way to adulthood. Most beetle larvae are called grubs, fly larvae are called maggots, moth larvae are worms, and butterfly larvae are caterpillars.

Identifying grubs. Grubs of the Japanese beetle, June bug, rose chafer, and other beetles are fleshy, gray-white, wormlike creatures about 1 inch long, with six legs and brown heads. They live in the soil, feeding on grass and weed roots; they need 1 to 3 years to become adults.

Turf trouble. If a patch of lawn is brown and spongy and can be rolled back like a carpet, it may be infested with grubs. Cut a square of sod about 4 inches deep and lift it up—five or more grubs are enough to warrant treatment with milky-spore disease, beneficial nematodes, or trichlorfon.

Let it dry. Water your lawn deeply but infrequently, letting it dry out in between. Beetles like to lay their eggs in moist soil; a dry lawn surface will discourage them and becomes inhospitable to any existing eggs.

A new vegetable plot? Before converting part of your lawn into a vegetable garden, inspect it carefully for grubs and treat as necessary.

Trap wireworms, which are the larvae of click beetles, by scooping out small holes in the soil in several places. Toss in chunks of potato and cover with boards—the "nests" will attract swarms of wireworms. Every few days, collect the infested potatoes and drop them into a pail of soapy water.

More solutions. Deter wireworms, which like moist soil, by improving drainage with organic matter or sand. Or plant mustard, buckwheat, or alfalfa in late summer and turn it under in spring. These green manures repel the pests and condition the soil.

Enlist your allies. Birds are hardworking grub eaters. Till your garden bed at least a day before you plan to sow or plant and let them pick it clean. You can help these grub fighters along by squashing any pests they miss. Or, if you prefer, drop the grubs into a pail of soapy water.

Country gardeners may have another winged pest fighter: the chicken. Turn the soil, and chickens will eagerly scavenge for cutworms, wireworms, and grubs.

Squash the squash vine borer. Find the worm's entry hole and poke inside with a piece of wire to kill it. You can also slit the stem open and remove the pest. Bury the wounded stem in the soil so that it will root, then destroy it after the harvest.

Band fruit tree trunks with corrugated cardboard to trap codling moth larvae as they move down the trees to spin cocoons. Check for and destroy any pests weekly.

Eliminate cutworms by tilling the soil as early in spring as possible to reduce weed seedlings—a favorite food. Also combat them with beneficial nematodes and trichogramma wasps.

Foil those cutworms! Before setting out tomato, pepper, or eggplant seedlings, wrap each stem with a 4-inch-square collar of aluminum foil; leave it loose enough to allow the stem to expand as it grows. Plant the seedlings with 2 inches of foil above the soil and 2 inches below.

▷ **Biological Controls, Japanese Beetles, Pesticides**

HANGING BASKETS

Give an old wicker basket a second life as a hanging basket. If you plan to hang it outdoors, varnish the outside to protect it from the weather; use an aerosol spray instead of a paintbrush to get the job done faster. Line the interior with transparent plastic wrap poked with drainage holes.

Convertible baskets. Make it easy to replant baskets by using removable pots. First rim the basket with ivy or ferns, leaving space in the center, then fill with 4-inch pots of your favorite flowers. When you want a seasonal change—from pansies to begonias, for example—simply switch the pots for a whole new look.

Use kitchen baskets. Convert metal-mesh food-storage baskets into hanging plant baskets. To contain the soil, you'll first need to install a protective lining—sphagnum moss or coco-fiber are both attractive and moisture retentive. Then add a permeable liner cloth and a saucer before setting the plant in potting soil.

Easy watering. Like most container plants, hanging baskets dry out readily. Water with a spraying wand attached to a garden hose. Position the basket where excess water can drip without harming anything or catch runoff in a basin.

Consider a pulley. Hanging your baskets with a pulley makes it easy to lower them for watering and other care.

Secure the footing. Most hanging baskets have a round base; if you set them on a flat surface when working on plants, they're likely to wobble. To keep them steady, place on top of an empty large flowerpot.

The invisible basket. If you want the plants—not the basket—to be the center-piece of your display, use plants with a trailing or sprawling habit that will eventually obscure the container. Swedish ivy, vinca, sweet peas, nasturtiums, and petunias will cascade profusely over the sides.

Splashes of color. Place hanging baskets anywhere you need a spot of color—a lamppost, tree limb, roof overhang, fence,

gazebo, or balcony. In all cases, make certain that the baskets are hung securely enough to withstand strong winds and the weight of wet soil.

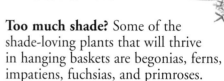

Lighten the look. To keep a basket containing several plants from looking weighed down, balance broad-leaf plants with lacy ones like asparagus or maidenhair fern.

Too much shade? Some of the shade-loving plants that will thrive in hanging baskets are begonias, ferns, impatiens, fuchsias, and primroses.

Scented geraniums, from lemon to strawberry to nutmeg types, are ideal basket plants, especially if hung where you can enjoy the fragrance—near a doorway, a porch swing, or outdoor furniture.

In hot, arid climates, use pendent or spreading varieties of succulents in your

Combine sprawling foliage plants with colorful flowers in your hanging baskets for a stronger display.

hanging baskets. Try the rattail cactus, Christmas cactus, and burro-tail sedum.

Not just for flowers. Try planting a few salad vegetables, aromatic herbs, cherry tomatoes, or strawberries in a hanging basket. Place them in full sun, watering and feeding regularly for best results.

An ideal bulb for baskets is the tropical achimenes. Plant bulbs 1 inch deep and 3 inches apart with tips facing outward; they bloom with large, colorful trumpets.
▷ **Houseplants, Pots**

HARVESTING

A handy tool. Check a specialty catalog or garden supply store for a long-handled fruit picker, usually equipped with a hook and a cloth bag. It's indispensable for harvesting fruit that is beyond your reach.

A homemade picker. Cut a "V"-shape into the rim of a 2-pound coffee can and bend the points slightly inward so that they will grab the fruit. Nail or wire the can to a broomstick or pole and lay a piece of carpet or foam in the bottom as a cushion for the fruit.

The right time. If you want to eat certain tree fruits—such as peaches, nectarines, apricots, plums, or cherries—out of hand, let them ripen on the tree for maximum flavor and juiciness. If you are going to can the fruits, pick them before they ripen completely.

Harvest pears when unripe, just as the dark green of the skin begins to fade to a yellowish green and the fruits separate more easily from the spurs. If allowed to yellow on the tree, pears develop gritty flesh and fail to ripen satisfactorily.

Falling pears or apples are often the result of pest infestation. To detect the presence of insects, set out pheromone traps, which attract and capture the male moths and butterflies that prey on fruit trees. An infested tree can then be treated with a carbaryl-based insecticide.

Don't be dismayed by "June drop." Young fruit falling in early June is a natural occurrence that rids the tree of poorly pollinated or badly placed fruit. Help reduce it by fertilizing the tree in March and watering regularly from the beginning of April.

Take it all. Harvest fruit trees thoroughly. Fruits knocked off by wind, as well as damaged fruits left on the tree, are an invitation to insects and disease.

Pick without staining. Many ripe fruits and berries are easily crushed and can stain a favorite basket. Before harvesting, line the basket with several layers of absorbent paper towels or napkins to soak up the juice.

Sun shy. Move containers of harvested fruits and vegetables out of the sun as soon as possible, since the absorbed heat promotes spoilage. This is especially true for dark-skinned fruits like black cherries and raspberries.

Harvest citrus fruits and grapes at late maturity for maximum flavor. Unlike other fruits, they will stop ripening after picking.

Picking strawberries. Don't pull off just the fruit. Take the whole stem by pinching it between your thumb and forefinger.

Easy does it. Take care when picking soft-skinned fruits and vegetables like tomatoes, peaches, and cherries. Placing them gently in the harvest container will help prevent bruising and prolong storage life.

Room temp is best. Keep harvested fruits and vegetables at room temperature. Chilling in the refrigerator will diminish their garden-fresh flavor. Tomatoes in particular should be treated this way.

Cut flowers for arrangements in the morning or evening or on a cloudy day. Picking in hot sunlight leads to faster wilting.
▷ **Cut Flowers, Orchards**

HEAT

To create shade for plants that are heat sensitive, construct a simple framework of new or salvaged lumber over the planting bed. Cover the structure with wooden slats, salvaged window screens, polyethylene plastic screens, or even reed matting. Burlap is suitable for temporary use, but keep in mind that it deteriorates rapidly.

Heat-intolerant vegetables. Let cauliflower, cabbage, radishes, beets, spinach, and peas mature during cool weather by planting them as soon as the soil can be worked in spring. Plant a second crop in late summer. In hot regions they can be planted in late fall for a winter harvest.

Shade providers. Plant tall sun-worshipping plants like corn, sunflowers, or cosmos south of those that need a little shade each day, such as lettuce, spinach, and beets.

Be careful with lettuce. Choose a heat-tolerant butterhead lettuce so that you can grow it all season. Plant a succession of seedlings at 2- to 3-week intervals.

Site heat-sensitive ornamentals on the shady side of buildings, next to taller shrubs, or beneath the overhanging branches of trees. Don't plant under shallow-rooted trees such as maple or beech.

Keep newly planted trees cool by painting their trunks up to the lower branches with white latex paint, which will reflect the sun's rays. Wrapping their trunks with burlap or crepe kraft paper will also help young trees escape the effects of heat.

Choose mulches wisely. Organic mulches like pine bark, wood chips, or shredded newspaper keep soil cool when spread 2 to 3 inches deep. Plastic mulches, unless covered with organic material, will merely make soil hotter. Any reflective materials, such as shiny pebbles, may contribute to foliage burn in hot or desert climates.

Take advantage of hot zones. Any paved areas near your garden, including walkways, patios, or driveways, will raise the temperature in the surrounding soil. To make the most of these hot microclimates, use heat-tolerant plants that wouldn't thrive elsewhere in your garden—portulaca, wormwood, or hedgehog and fire-barrel cacti.

Capture the heat. Place black containers, such as painted plastic milk jugs, next to early plantings or inside cold frames. The containers will absorb heat from the sun during the day and radiate it out at night, providing protection for young plants during early spring frosts.
▷ **Cold Frames, Exposure**

HEATH & HEATHER

Colorful evergreens. Heath (*Erica* spp.) and heather (*Calluna vulgaris,* with its many cultivars) are low-growing subshrubs that offer an array of foliage and flower color. Leaves may be green, gold, bronze, or silver-gray, and the bell-like blooms run from ivory to lilac to carmine.

Twelve months of bloom? It's possible to have heath and heather blooming in the garden throughout the year. Choose varieties according to their flowering period.

Pretty patchwork. Heath and heather look best when planted in drifts by themselves. Mass the plants in large swatches with complementary foliage or flower colors; use at least five plants of each variety and space at intervals of 12 to 18 inches. In a few seasons, the ground will be covered with a colorful patchwork. Spread an acidic mulch like pine bark or pine needles and keep the beds weed-free until the plants fill in.

The right stuff. Heath and heather prefer a light, poor, quick-draining soil that is slightly acidic—with a pH of 6 to 6.5. If your soil isn't suitable, set the plants in raised beds filled with leaf mold, peat moss, and sand.

Sun lovers. Plant heath and heather in full sun. In shade they bloom sparsely and tend to become leggy.

The right setting. Use the plants in rock gardens or as a "carpet" spreading before a conifer hedge. Accent them judiciously with dwarf conifers and azaleas.

⚘ A YEAR OF FLOWERING HEATH AND HEATHER ⚘

Species	June	July	Aug.	Sept.	Oct.	Nov.	Dec.	Jan.	Feb.	Mar.	Apr.	May
Calluna vulgaris		▬▬	▬▬	▬▬	▬▬	▬▬						
Erica carnea								▬▬	▬▬	▬▬	▬▬	▬▬
Erica cinerea		▬▬	▬▬	▬▬	▬▬							
Erica × darleyensis						▬▬	▬▬	▬▬	▬▬	▬▬	▬▬	▬▬
Erica vagans			▬▬	▬▬	▬▬							

In all four seasons beds of heath and heather create an ever-changing tapestry of foliage and flowers.

Prepare a hole at least twice the width of the root ball, but only deep enough to accommodate the shallow roots; the plant should "sit" in the soil at the same depth it did in the nursery pot. Backfill with soil amended with compost, peat, or sand.

Score the root ball. Scoring—lightly slashing the root ball in two or three places—often helps heather become established more quickly.

Watering wisdom. While the plants hate wet feet, they love moisture. Never let them dry out, especially when young, and water deeply as needed when it's hot.

Outdoors is best. Although some varieties can be grown in containers, heathers generally don't thrive inside the house—or even on a porch. If you're determined to try, plant them in a pot filled with peaty soil and place in a sunny location. To water, submerge the pot completely for 10 minutes in tepid water that's not alkaline.

A light grooming. Prune after flowering to stimulate growth and help plants retain their compact, cushiony shape. But don't

shear them into tidy mounds—they are slightly wild and "spiky" by nature. Cut back the stems just below the blooms. If pruning in fall, make sure plants have time to harden off before cold weather sets in.

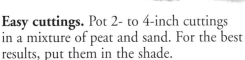

Easy cuttings. Pot 2- to 4-inch cuttings in a mixture of peat and sand. For the best results, put them in the shade.

Protect from winter woes. Heath and heather are susceptible to damage from drying winds, so cover with a layer of evergreen boughs in regions with hard winters. While straw is also an effective mulch, it's messy to remove. In spring, prune back any injured tips to promote new growth.

Mail-order heathers may arrive dried out. Submerge each pot in water until the bubbles stop rising. Keep watered until planting and dunk them again after the root ball has been scored.

▷ **Shrubs**

HEDGES

Multiple uses. Whether meticulously clipped into a formal shape or pruned only lightly for a looser look, hedges provide structure and a sense of permanence in the garden. They are practical for screening a deck or patio for privacy and buffering traffic noise and wind. They can frame a pretty vista or block an unsightly view. They can also mark property lines, define intimate garden "rooms," add dimension to a flat expanse, or be sculpted into topiary.

Start small. Use small plants set relatively close together when planting your hedge. The exact spacing depends on how quickly the particular species will fill in and what effect you want to achieve.

How to plant. When setting small plants close together, dig a trench the length of the desired hedge; the depth should be equal to that of the root ball or container in which the plants are growing. Mark out a trench for a straight hedge with two stakes and a string; use a garden hose to design the line of a curved hedge. After planting, water well until the plants are established.

Go easy on the fertilizer. The more hedges are fed, the more they will need to be pruned. Feed only if your soil is very poor. Use either well-rotted manure or a 10-10-10 fertilizer at the rate of 5 to 10 pounds per 100 feet.

Plant a windbreak. Minimize the damaging effects of wind by installing a barrier of hardy trees or shrubs. Site the hedge so that prevailing winds hit it broadside. The distance between the hedge and the area to be protected should be 10 times the plants' height; place a 5-foot hedge, for example, 50 feet away. Set plants in staggered rows; evergreens like fir, pine, and spruce or dense deciduous plants like privet and forsythia are good choices.

Pruning times. Prune deciduous hedges in the winter or just after they've flowered. Prune evergreen hedges in spring or early summer. In cool climates all hedges need to be pruned early enough so that any new growth will have time to harden off by preventing winter injury.

Sensible shearing. When trimming the flat top of a hedge with electric or manual shears, drive a stake at each end of the hedge and extend a string at the desired height. Then simply follow the line to make an even cut. For protection, wear work gloves, safety glasses, and sturdy shoes or boots and take special precautions with electrical equipment.

Keep a sheared hedge full to the very bottom by pruning at a slight angle, with the base wider than the top. This will let sunlight penetrate to the bottom branches and prevent dieback.

Tall hedges. An effective tall hedge takes a long time to establish, since regular pruning is necessary to create dense growth. Don't allow plants to grow tall and lanky at the expense of density; otherwise you'll end up with a thin and useless hedge.

Limit the height to between 6 and 8 feet. If the hedge is any taller, you'll need a ladder for maintenance.

A lilac hedge becomes one of the most prominent features of the garden when it flowers in spring.

EVERGREEN HEDGES

Fast-growing plants may not be desirable. While your hedge will become full and dense more quickly, you'll have to prune more often in the future to keep it in bounds. This is especially true with Leyland cypress, an evergreen popular in the warmer parts of the country; it can grow 3 feet or more in a single season.

Holly as a hedge. With their glossy, decorative foliage and prickly leaves, the evergreen hollies make superb hedge plants. But resist heavy pruning, which will remove most of the blooms and limit the number of colorful berries that grow on the female plants. To maximize berry production, prune holly lightly to keep at least a few of the blossoms.

Peace and quiet. Planting a dense, wide evergreen hedge on a mound of soil, or berm, can help block noise. Some open hedges may also create their own "white noise" as wind passes through the branches and rustles the leaves.

An evergreen hedge for warmer climes. The bright green broad-leaf cherry laurel makes an ideal evergreen hedge in warmer areas. Keep in mind that you must prune it carefully: use hand pruners to cut the stems one by one. Hedge shears can chop the large leaves to shreds, mutilating the plant and destroying its charm.

Use conifers. Conifers create handsome, dense hedges. Shape hemlocks, arborvitae, and yews by clipping the young sprouts, leaving ¾ to 2 inches of new growth. Or you can prune them lightly for a more natural look. Pines can also be hedged; prune them by removing one-half to two-thirds of the new candlelike growth with pruners in late spring or early summer. Most conifers perform best as a hedge when maintained in a roughly pyramidal shape, with the base wider than the top. Prune the plants slowly and carefully, stepping back every now and then to gauge your progress.

DECIDUOUS HEDGES

Tapestry hedges. Be adventurous in designing your living wall by using different plants or species that are compatible both aesthetically and culturally. The resulting "tapestry hedge" will add visual interest and let you use more of your favorite plants to provide blooms or attract wildlife. For a formal hedge, alternate green- and red-leaved beech trees and keep them tightly clipped. For a relaxed look, mix a shrubby dogwood, such as the gray dogwood, with winterberry holly and red chokeberry; prune lightly.

Keep out weeds, which are both unsightly and greedy in diverting water and nutrients. A geotextile plastic weed mat topped with organic mulch will control them as seedlings become established (it is preferable to plain black plastic, which doesn't allow air and water to penetrate to the roots below). Cut the weed mat the length of the hedge, lay it on the bed, and cut a hole or an "x" where a plant will be placed. Dig a planting hole and set in the specimen, then spread wood chips, pine needles, or shredded bark over the mat.

Winter cleanup. Prune out any dead, diseased, or broken branches in the hedge. Pull out the sprouts of any woody weeds or vines that have invaded the plants. Clean up debris around the base, but leave some of the fallen leaves to serve as a mulch. Also be careful not to disturb any bird nests you find—the owners may return in the spring or another family may take up residence.

Separate your vegetable garden from the yard and protect it from animals by growing a hedge of thorny fruits such as blackberries. Support them on a trellis around the perimeter. For extra color, interplant the brambles with morning glories, scarlet runner beans, sunflowers, or other climbing vines and tall annuals.

Discourage intruders. Use a thorny hedge as a barrier against dogs, opossums, and other uninvited visitors. Among the most unwelcoming plants are barberry, pyracantha, hawthorn, shrub roses, holly, and hardy orange. Another solution: install a double row of any hedging plant.

▷ **Beech, Evergreens, Pruning**

ᔥᕽ THREE KINDS OF HEDGES ᕽᔥ

As a strong structural element in the garden, hedges are most valuable when they retain their full shape year-round. In cold climates, many gardeners prefer hedges composed of coniferous or broad-leaf evergreens, which provide lasting beauty and color. Hedges of deciduous plants, however, also have advantages: they offer a wider range of leaf types and bring a different look to each season with their changing displays of fruits and foliage.

	COLD CLIMATES	WARM CLIMATES
DECIDUOUS HEDGES	American cranberry bush *Viburnum trilobum* Border forsythia *Forsythia × intermedia* Border privet *Ligustrum obtusifolium* Common lilac *Syringa vulgaris* Compact winged euonymus *Euonymus alata 'Compacta'* Japanese barberry *Berberis thunbergii* Japanese shrub rose *Rosa rugosa*	Bodinier beautyberry *Callicarpa bodinieri* Crape myrtle *Lagerstroemia indica* Japanese orixa *Orixa japonica* Japanese euonymus *Euonymus japonicus* Pomegranate *Punica granatum*
EVERGREEN HEDGES	Inkberry holly *Ilex glabra* Korean littleleaf boxwood *Buxus microphylla* var. *koreana* Meserve blue holly *Ilex × meserveae* Pyracantha *Pyracantha coccinea*	Cherry laurel *Prunus laurocerasus* Chinese holly *Ilex cornuta* Common boxwood *Buxus sempervirens* Holly-leaved osmanthus *Osmanthus heterophyllus* Nandina *Nandina domestica*
	ADAPTABLE TO ALL CLIMATES	
CONIFEROUS HEDGES	American arborvitae *Thuja occidentalis* Canadian hemlock *Tsuga canadensis* Eastern white pine *Pinus strobus* Japanese yew *Taxus cuspidata*	

An indispensable garden for cooks

Even the tiniest herb garden has its charms: brushing against a stand of lemon verbena and picking up its tart aroma; watching the chive buds burst into fuzzy pink flowerballs; savoring a fresh pesto sauce made with your own homegrown basil and garlic.

Luckily, growing an herb garden isn't difficult. Most herbs are hardy, pest- and disease-resistant, and not too fussy about soil. First choose a sunny spot—most herbs do best with 5 or 6 hours of sun a day. It can be a corner of the vegetable garden or the border of your flower bed. Or create a new space just for herbs; if it's near the kitchen door, all the better. The design can be as elaborate as a traditional knot garden or merely a random mixture.

Not all herbs are grown just for their flavor. Many, such as rosemary, thyme, and sweet bay, are also valued for the scents they give to potpourri and herbal wreaths. Others, like chamomile and ginger, have traditional medicinal as well as culinary uses. Some herbs with prominent flowers—dill and lovage, for example—make beautiful, fragrant bouquets to put in a guest's room or take to a friend.

Because there are hundreds of herbs you might consider, choosing the ones to grow may seem a daunting task. To help you get started, 25 culinary herbs are described on the following four pages. You can buy young plants at a garden center or through a catalog (growing from seed usually takes a long time). Once you have an established garden, you can swap cuttings and divided plants with other gardeners.

1. BASIL
Ocimum basilicum

A heat-loving annual, basil needs rich, well-drained soil and full sun. In addition to the broad-leaf sweet basil used for pesto sauce, try purple leaf basil, a handsome but less pungent variety, and globe basil, which grows in a mound with delicate green leaves.

Harvest young growth as needed; use fresh or preserve as basil oil concentrate or pesto. Add fresh basil just before serving.

2. CHAMOMILE
Chamaemelum nobile

Chamomile grows well in slightly acid soil. In cold and temperate areas, it is a hardy perennial that prefers full sun. In warm and hot regions, chamomile is treated as an annual and needs partial shade. It is easily grown from seed and will often self-sow if allowed.

Chamomile leaves and daisylike flowers smell and taste of apples. Picked and dried, they make a calming and fragrant herb tea that is served with lemon and honey. Homemade chamomile tea is tastier than store-bought.

3. CHERVIL
Anthriscus cerefolium

Chervil is an easy-to-grow annual that often reseeds itself if one or two plants are allowed to go to seed. In cold and temperate areas, chervil is sown in the spring. In warm and hot regions, it is sown in the fall to give the plants a cooler winter growing season.

Harvest outside leaves to encourage crown growth. Pinch back buds. Use fresh chervil leaves for cooking, adding them to salads, soups, vegetables, and grilled fish or poultry—but add just before serving; heat will destroy this herb's sweet flavor.

4. CHIVES
Allium schoenoprasum

A clumping hardy perennial, chives like rich cool soil and full sun, though they tolerate partial shade. Harvest stems to 2 inches from the ground; they will grow back all season.

Fresh chives add a delicate hint of onion flavor to omelets, stir-frys, salads, vegetable and cheese dishes, poultry, and seafood.

5. CORIANDER OR CILANTRO
Coriandrum sativum

Sow this annual herb—the source of both coriander seeds and cilantro—in fall in warm and hot regions; sow in spring in temperate and cold areas. It needs rich, well-drained soil and full sun to partial shade.

Pick fresh leaves (cilantro) as needed. Harvest seeds (coriander) when they are plump and changing color. Both leaves and seeds are used in many ethnic cuisines for marinades, meat and vegetable dishes, and baked goods.

6. DILL
Anethum graveolens

An annual with a tall, graceful profile, dill likes rich, well-drained soil in full sun. Sow in spring in cold and temperate areas; sow in the fall in warm and hot regions.

Harvest the lacy foliage by cutting off branches as needed. Harvest the seed heads when they plump up and change color. Add fresh dill to fish, poultry, cottage cheese, cucumbers, new potatoes, summer squash, and home-baked breads. Use dill seed in pickling.

7. FENNEL
Foeniculum vulgare

A tender perennial, fennel is often grown as an annual in cold and temperate areas. It likes full sun and some wind protection.

Use the young, licorice-flavored leaves in salads or on fish and vegetables. Italian and Greek cooks use fennel in pastries.

8. FRENCH SORREL
Rumex scutatus

Sorrel foliage dies back over the winter in cold and temperate climates but remains green where it's warm or hot. It prefers rich, well-drained soil in full sun and needs plenty of water during the hot summer months.

Take tender leaves for salad from the outside of the plant. Pinch back buds to keep it leafing. Cooked, sorrel gives a pleasant acidity to soups and sauces, especially those for fish.

9. FRENCH TARRAGON
Artemisia dracunculus

A hardy perennial, French tarragon likes loose, well-drained soil in full sun to partial shade. It requires regular feeding and at least 6 weeks of dormancy in winter, making it difficult to grow in warm and hot regions, except as an annual. The plant rarely blooms and doesn't set viable seed, so it must be propagated from cuttings. Russian tarragon looks similar but has none of the flavor or aroma.

Harvest the leaves during the season to use fresh in herb butters, sauces such as Béarnaise, and salad dressings. Sprinkle on poultry, seafood, and vegetables. Preserve leaves as oil concentrate or in vinegar.

10. GARLIC
Allium sativum

For all varieties of garlic, plant cloves, or bulblets, in the fall. Garlic prefers rich, well-drained soil and full sun to partial shade.

Harvest new bulbs the following summer when the foliage dies down. Then hang them up to dry; traditionally, the tops are braided and the garland hung in the kitchen. You can also freeze whole garlic heads in double plastic bags; this method will prevent a build-up of sulphides, which cause the bad breath for which garlic is famous.

Garlic is a part of many cuisines. If you find the flavor too strong, reduce the amount you use or roast garlic cloves before using them in a recipe. The pungent flavor will be reduced; so, unfortunately, will any health benefits.

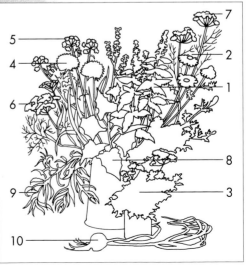

HERBS

11. GINGER
Zingiber officinale

A tender perennial with grasslike leaves, ginger grows best in warm and hot climates. It likes rich, well-drained soil in partial shade. Give ginger plenty of water during the summer. In cold or temperate areas, grow it in pots that can be taken indoors for the winter.

Harvest the roots after 1 year. Cut off as much as you need for cooking—you can store it in the freezer—and replant the rest.

12. LEMON BALM
Melissa officinalis

A perennial with a dormant period in cold and temperate areas, lemon balm is an evergreen in warm and hot climates. It likes plenty of water and a spot in partial shade.

Harvest the lemon-scented leaves just before using in salad dressings and fruit dishes, dessert sauces, and baked goods. Steeping the leaves of lemon balm makes a refreshing and healthful herbal tea.

13. LEMONGRASS
Cymbopogon citratus

An Asian favorite, lemongrass is a tall tender grasslike perennial that grows best in warm and hot regions. It likes rich, well-drained soil, full sun or partial shade, and plenty of water during summer. In temperate and cold areas, grow lemongrass as a container plant.

Snip fresh foliage or the fleshy portion of the lower stem as needed for Asian recipes. Harvest during the summer; cut the leaves and fleshy stem into small pieces for drying. Use in teas, soups, and poaching liquids.

14. LEMON VERBENA
Aloysia triphylla

Lemon verbena prefers full sun and normal garden soil in a warm or hot climate. A tender perennial shrub, it is grown as a container plant in cold and temperate areas.

Lemon verbena has aromatic leaves that are as welcome in potpourri as in salad dressings, dessert sauces, or cookies. It can also be used to make a refreshing tea and as a substitute for lemon grass in Asian cooking.

15. LOVAGE
Levisticum officinale

A hardy perennial in cold and temperate climates, lovage likes a cool, rich soil and partial shade. Treat as an annual in warm and hot regions.

Use tender young leaves in salads and soups—or anywhere you want to perk up flavor with a crisp, celery-like taste.

16. MINT
Mentha spp.

A perennial in cold and temperate climates and an evergreen in warm and hot regions, mint comes in several varieties. They all like well-drained soil in full sun but tolerate shade. Because mint sends out underground shoots to form new plants, it needs a location where the roots can be confined.

Harvest fresh leaves as you need them. Pinch off buds for bushier growth. Use mint leaves to flavor salads, sauces, grilled lamb, fruit compotes, and iced tea—and, of course, the classic mint julep.

17. OREGANO
Origanum vulgare

Oregano is a hardy perennial that prefers sandy soil in full sun or light shade. Depending upon the variety, the foliage gives off scents ranging from sweet to peppery. Be sure to ruffle a leaf and sniff before purchasing a plant.

In warm and hot climates, oregano leaves can be harvested year-round to season pizzas, cheese dishes, soups, vegetables, and salads. Oregano dries well for winter use in cold areas.

18. PARSLEY
Petroselinum crispum and *P. neapolitanum*

Curly-leaf parsley (*P. crispum*) and flat-leaf Italian parsley (*P. neapolitanum*) are biennials that prefer rich, well-drained soil and partial shade. In warm regions, sow in fall; in cold areas, sow in spring.

Harvest the outer leaves and stems as they grow. Use freshly chopped leaves or sprigs of parsley to season butter, sauces, salads, grilled meats and fish, vegetables, and soups. If you use it as a garnish, munch the sprig—it's especially high in vitamins!

19. ROSEMARY
Rosmarinus officinalis

An evergreen perennial shrub, rosemary likes warm, dry climates and hates hot, humid ones. In cold or temperate areas, it is a handsome container plant that takes well to pruning; it must be brought inside in winter. Rosemary prefers light soil and full sun.

Harvest branches all year long. Their strong, resinous scent and taste is delicious with grilled fish, meats, and vegetables.

20. SAGE
Salvia officinalis

A hardy perennial in cold and temperate areas, sage is an evergreen in warm and hot climates. It prefers dry, sandy soil and full sun.

Harvest fresh leaves for use with meats (many sausages contain sage), poultry, vegetables, soups, stews, and cheese dishes.

21. SAVORY
Satureja ssp.

Summer savory (*Satureja hortensis*) is an annual and may reseed itself each year. Winter savory (*S. montana*) is a hardy perennial. Both grow well in light soil and full sun.

Both have a slightly hot, peppery taste. Use the leaves with dried beans, poultry, and meat. Since its flavor is strong, use winter savory sparingly and add at the end of cooking.

22. SCENTED GERANIUMS
Pelargonium spp.

Scented geraniums are perennials in warm and hot areas, but need to overwinter indoors in temperate and cold areas. They like good drainage, rich loam, and full sun. Don't overfertilize. The flowers range from tiny pink to large, showy cerise with black markings.

The mimics of the plant world, scented geranium leaves flaunt fragrances of rose, lemon, apple, mint, and nutmeg. Add finely chopped leaves to cake batter and cookie dough, fruit compotes, and the poaching liquid for apples or pears.

23. SWEET BAY
Laurus nobilis

A tender evergreen tree, bay laurel, or sweet bay, can be grown outdoors in warm and hot regions; grow it as a container plant in cold and temperate areas. It needs rich, well-drained soil in full sun to partial shade.

Harvest bay leaves as needed and use in marinades for grilling meats, in soups and stews, and in patés. Discard the leaf before serving the food; it can stick in an unwary diner's throat. Combine bay, fresh or dried, with other herbs for rich seasoning blends.

24. SWEET MARJORAM
Origanum majorana

An annual in cold and temperate climates, sweet marjoram is an evergreen in warm and hot areas. It prefers rich soil and full sun.

A close cousin of oregano, marjoram is prized for its more subtle flavor. Use it in place of oregano to season pizzas, cheese dishes, grilled foods, soups, vegetables and salads.

25. THYME
Thymus vulgaris

A hardy perennial with a distinctive aroma, thyme can be a tiny woody plant, a creeping groundcover, or a bushy shrub. It is a sun-loving herb that needs well-drained soil. Small varieties do well in rock gardens.

Use thyme leaves in soups and stews, and with poultry, meat, and grilled dishes. Thyme, parsley, and bay constitute the classic *bouquet garni*, or bundle of herbs, used in traditional French cooking.

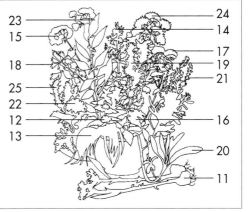

HERBS

HERBS

The right time for picking. Harvest flowers as soon as they blossom and are still only half open. Harvest stems and leaves just before the plant flowers, when herbs' essential oils are strongest. Harvest seeds when they have hardened slightly.

Harvest with care. Pick flowers, leaves, seeds, and stems only from healthy plants that haven't been sprayed with pesticides. Don't take damp plants, which can become moldy. Before drying herbs or using them fresh, sort out and discard any damaged pieces.

Pick in the morning after the dew has dried. You can also harvest in late afternoon. But remember that the sun's heat causes the amount of essential oils—the herb's source of flavor—to lessen.

Brew herb tea. Warm a china, pottery, or glass teapot (don't use metal) and put in 2 tablespoons of chopped fresh herbs or 2 teaspoons of dried. Pour in 2 cups boiling water and let stand for 6 or 7 minutes if using fresh herbs; for dried herbs, steep a minute longer. Strain, then sweeten with the honey of your choice.

Don't oversteep. Brewing herb tea for more than 10 minutes can make it bitter. For stronger tea, add more herbs but keep the infusing time under 10 minutes. Leaves and flowers are steeped off the heat, while

THE VIRTUES OF HERB TEAS

Tradition holds that herb teas have certain medicinal qualities. Here are some beneficial effects they are said to promote.

PLANT	PARTS USED
Calming; promotes sleep	
Chamomile	Flowers
Sweet marjoram	Flower heads, leaves
Tonic; fortifying	
Rosemary	Leaves
Sage	Leaves
Diuretic	
Fennel	Seeds
Parsley	Leaves
Peppermint	Leaves
Aids digestion	
Coriander	Seeds
Dill	Seeds
Lemon balm	Leaves
Parsley	Leaves
Thyme	Leaves
Eases coughs and colds	
Dill	Seeds
Fennel	Roots
Sage	Leaves

seeds must be gently simmered—but never boiled—for full flavor.

Storing herbs. The best—and safest—way to preserve the flavor of herbs is to chop or puree them in oil and freeze them. Use 2 firmly packed cups of leaves and tender stems to ½ cup vegetable or olive oil and process as fine as desired. Place the mixture in tight-lidded containers and freeze.

A warning. Keep your herb-oil mixture only in the freezer—never the refrigerator! Plant matter preserved in oil can develop botulism if not frozen.

Drying herbs. To dry large-leaved herbs, such as basil, mint, or sage, remove the leaves and place them in a single layer on paper towels or a screen. For small-leaved herbs, like thyme, dry the whole stem, then strip the leaves by sliding your thumb and forefinger down the stalk.

Drying in the fridge. Small amounts of small-leaved herbs or chopped large leaves can be dried in a frost-free refrigerator. Place on a plate or in an open plastic bag.

Don't heat herbs when drying; using an oven or microwave will destroy their delicate oils. Also note that drying herbs on trays is preferable to hanging them up.
▷ **Basil, Chives, Dill, Fennel, Mint, Parsley, Rosemary, Sage, Tarragon, Thyme**

HIBISCUS

A tender beauty. The lovely Chinese hibiscus, *Hibiscus rosa-sinensis,* is perhaps the best-known species, although it is hardy only in the warmest areas: Florida, the Gulf Coast, California, and Hawaii. It is prized for its large, disklike blooms of white, yellow, pink, and red.

A garden annual. Even if you live in a cool climate, you may be able to find hibiscus in the spring at a nursery or garden center. Once the weather warms, plant young specimens in a sunny location and treat as an annual. They'll flourish until the first frost, providing months of flowers that beautifully evoke the tropics.

To plant in containers, put each hibiscus in a 2- to 5-gallon pot. Place outdoors in a warm, sunny spot after the danger of frost has passed. To maintain deep green leaves and vibrant flowers where summers are torrid, provide some filtered shade.

Overwintering. When night temperatures drop below 50°F, move potted hibiscus indoors by a sunny window. Be careful not to overwater in this dormant phase; let the top inch of soil dry out before watering.

Shine your shoes! In Jamaica and other West Indian islands, hibiscus is known as "shoe flower" or "shoe black." The sap from the flower petals can be used as a polish for black leather shoes.

Hardy hibiscuses. Gardeners in cold climates can enjoy *H. syriacus,* a shrub known as althea or rose-of-Sharon. Another is rose mallow *(H. moscheutos),* a wetland plant with flower cups up to 12 inches across.
▷ **Shrubs**

HOEING

Hoe before a rain. Hoe hard, crusted soil before a summer downpour. Instead of running off quickly and eroding the topsoil, the rainwater will be able to penetrate deeply below the surface.

Don't hoe during a drought. While hoeing to uproot weeds, you expose more soil to the air, which lets more moisture evaporate. Combat weeds instead by spreading a water-retentive organic mulch.

Hoeing in the dark. Discourage light-sensitive weed seeds from germinating by cultivating the soil after sundown.

Hoeing know-how. Use a hoe with a handle at least 4½ feet long so that you can work standing straight—not bent over, straining the back. Keep the blade sharp and slide it below but parallel to the surface to loosen clods and sever weed roots.

Choose the right hoe. For delicate work, many types of small hoes are available, including heart-shaped, rectangular, or three-pronged ones. These narrow tools will penetrate everywhere and can be used between flowers and vegetables without the usual risk of bruising.

Should you hoe in winter? Yes, if the ground isn't frozen. Cold-weather hoeing gives you the chance to destroy grubs, cutworms, and other soil-dwelling pests.

One weed not to hoe is common purslane, a ground-hugging annual pest. Its tiny seeds remain in the soil and germinate if exposed by cultivation, and its fleshy, water-retaining stems can form new roots even after the plants are hoed up. Pull out seedlings by hand or treat with herbicides.

HOLLY

If the sharp spines of holly leaves bother you, select a variety that has either no spines or only a few on each leaf. These include Chinese holly, Japanese holly, and longstalk holly.

For profuse red berries, use both male and female plants. Only female specimens will produce berries—and only when pollinated by a male.

In cold climates with windy winters, plant hollies in sheltered areas to prevent leaf damage. Further protect plants by spraying

in the fall and winter with an anti-desiccant—a substance that keeps the leaves from losing moisture.

Not all hollies are evergreen. Winterberry hollies drop their leaves in the fall but compensate with a profusion of bright red, orange, or yellow berries all winter. In addition to providing spectacular color in a drab season, they are tolerant of wet soil and partial shade—and adapt to almost all parts of the country.
▷ **Shrubs**

HORSERADISH

To prevent forked roots, grow horseradishes in drainage-pipe sections placed vertically in the ground and filled with a rich soil mixture.  Roots will grow straight and thick until fall harvest.

A piquant condiment. Peel and dice the roots and purée in a blender with some vinegar or lemon juice. Check your cookbooks for recipes and variations.

Useful leaves. Horseradish leaves are known to have fungus-fighting properties—especially against brown rot, which attacks fruit trees. Mash the leaves to extract their juice, strain, and spray on plants.

A spicy salad. In the spring, harvest young, tender horseradish leaves to add a bite to green salads or spinach salads.
▷ **Vegetable Gardens**

HOSTA

Fancy foliage. These hardy perennials, prized more for their large, beautiful leaves than their trumpetlike flowers, are mainstays for shady borders and pondsides. They are also effective as a ground cover.

Beware of the sun. Hostas are sun-shy; the large leaves they produce to collect light will scorch if overexposed. Select their site with care, noting the amount of sun a prospective planting site receives before setting them out. In cool climates hostas can tolerate about 4 hours of sun daily; in warm climates, 1 hour of direct sun is the limit. Keep them well watered.

A common pest. Hostas are notorious for attracting slugs and snails. To thwart them, try growing the plants in wooden containers encircled with copper tape—which slugs are reluctant to cross. The tape is available through garden supply companies; simply staple several strips all the way around the container.

Lessen slug damage by keeping the plant's bed free of weeds and decomposing leaves. The improved growing conditions will not only strengthen the plants but also deprive the pests of nesting sites and make it easier to detect and destroy eggs and adults.

🦋 A HOSTA SAMPLER 🦋

Brighten dark spots in your garden with hosta varieties that sport the sunniest leaves, such as 'August Moon,' 'Golden Sculpture,' 'Piedmont Gold,' 'Sum and Substance,' and 'Golden Sunburst.' To soften the glow, intersperse a few variegated-gold varieties, such as 'Emerald Tiara,' *Hosta fortunei* 'Aureo-Marginata,' 'Gold Standard,' and 'September Sun.'

An aristocrat among shade lovers, hostas boast ornamental foliage in a range of colors and textures.

Sun-tolerant types. A few varieties can withstand sun better than most. Try the blue-green 'Aurora Borealis,' glossy green 'Royal Standard,' golden 'Zounds,' or white-banded 'Francee.' All produce white or lavender blooms around midsummer.

A rich diet. While hostas are adaptable, easy-care plants, they will thrive for years if given rich soil and plenty of moisture.

Good for cold climates. Because hostas need a period of dormancy, they grow well where the temperature drops below freezing for 2 to 3 months of the year.

To fill in spaces between hostas while they mature, plant impatiens, which share the same cultural conditions and will self-seed for a few years as hostas reach full size.

The bold, sculptural leaves of *Hosta sieboldiana* make a perfect foil for ferns and arrow bamboo (*Pseudosasa japonica*).

Multiply by division. For more hostas, divide mature root clumps in early spring or in fall, after the leaves have died back.
▷ **Ground Covers**

HOUSEPLANTS

PURCHASING

Be an inspector. Before you buy, lift the leaves gently to check for scale, mealybugs, whiteflies, or other pests. Then look under the pot. If roots are sticking out of the drainage hole, the plant will need to be repotted immediately. If you prefer not to transplant, select another specimen.

Waiting time. Before introducing the new arrival to your other houseplants, isolate it in a cool room for 2 weeks to make doubly sure it is healthy.

A reminder. Always keep the plant label even after repotting, so that you won't forget the plant's name or the care it needs.

PLACEMENT

The right light. Keep in mind three things when you're deciding where to put a plant: first, south-facing windows receive more light than north-facing ones; second, plants with brightly colored foliage need more light than others; and third, never put a plant where you can't read the newspaper without a light on.

For even growth. A half-turn of the pot every day or two will keep the growth of your houseplant even, since its foliage automatically bends toward the light.

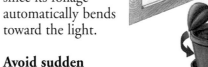

Avoid sudden changes. Don't move plants around from day to day. Sudden changes can cause droopy leaves, increase susceptibility to pests and diseases, and—in the case of flowering plants—promote bud drop. And take note: moving a plant from shade to bright sunlight can cause serious foliage burns.

Going on vacation? Water your houseplants thoroughly and arrange them, without saucers, on a dampened plush towel in your sink or tub; make sure the drain holes are in contact with the towel. Turn on the cold tap until water drips slowly onto the towel. Leave on; the moisture in the fabric will be drawn up by the roots.

Use ice cubes to water. Place them around the soil, but not touching the stem. The ice will melt slowly, releasing water gradually and evenly into the soil.

▷ **Aluminum Foil, Avocados, Begonias**

MAINTENANCE

Don't be too hasty to repot. A plant kept in a slightly undersized pot puts its energy into flowers and foliage instead of root development. It also dries more quickly after watering, allowing air to reach the roots.

Don't overheat your house. Your plants won't like it! The ideal temperature is between 55°F and 70°F, with cooler always better than hotter.

A good soaking. When the soil in your pot has completely dried out, wet it by placing the pot in a pail of water. Leave it until no more bubbles come to the surface. Drain well before putting it on a saucer.

Wash away dust, smoke, and other residues by giving your plants a shower with lukewarm water. You can also dislodge dirt, especially on fuzzy or prickly leaves, with a hair dryer set on cool or low.

⊰ KEEPING PLANTS BEAUTIFUL ⊱

▷ Regularly remove all faded flowers, dried leaves, and bare stems.

▷ When you cut brown tips, leave a small brown border. Cutting into live tissue will cause more drying and dieback.

▷ Fertilize your houseplants regularly during active growing and flowering periods—typically March through September. Reduce the dose to half of the recommended rate. Don't fertilize at all in winter.

▷ Don't use wax or shine products. They may give the foliage luster, but they can clog the pores. Another reason not to wax: it makes houseplants look artificial. For a natural glow wipe down the leaves with a wet sponge.

HUMMINGBIRDS

Pretty pollinators. Like bees, hummingbirds pollinate your garden. An extra bonus is that they're delightful to look at.

Build a trellis for trumpet creeper, morning glories, and honeysuckle. When the vines bloom, hummingbirds will arrive.

A simple feeder. Cut a red plastic plate in the shape of a hibiscus flower. Fill a hamster water bottle with sugar water tinted with red food coloring and insert it into the center of the "flower," securing it on the back with duct tape. Hang amid the flowers on your trellis or rhododendrons, whose blooms attract the birds. Even after the flowers fade, the birds will keep coming back.

Plant a "hot" garden. Hummingbirds like flowers of red, orange, and bright yellow. Bee balm, zinnia, salvia, daylily, penstemon, and red-hot poker are good choices.

▷ **Birds**

HYACINTHS

Plant fragrant hyacinths to perfume your spring garden. Their colorful spiked flowers mix well with tulips.

A LITTLE HISTORY

According to Greek mythology, Hyacinth was a handsome young athlete and an inseparable friend of Apollo, god of the sun. Zephyr, the West Wind, became fond of the young man, but Hyacinth spurned his affection. One day, as Hyacinth was throwing the discus with Apollo, Zephyr created a violent wind that blew the discus off course and into the young man's forehead at full speed. Hyacinth fell, mortally wounded, his blood staining the grass. Inconsolable, Apollo transformed the blood drops into the delicately fragrant flower that still bears his friend's name today.

Indoors or out? While hyacinths herald spring's arrival in the garden, you can enjoy them indoors in winter by forcing bloom. Plant bulbs with their "shoulders" exposed in a moist, well-drained potting mix and store at 40°F for 12 to 15 weeks before desired bloom time. To break their dormancy, move them to a warm (55° to 65°F), bright, but not sunny, spot until sprouts appear, then place in direct sun; keep well watered. Once buds show color, put plants in indirect light, which will help prolong flowering. Blooms will last about 2 weeks in a cool room.

Forcing in water. Always leave at least the thickness of one finger between the base of the bulb and the liquid. The humidity of this air layer is sufficient for proper development of the roots. The aerating layer also prevents rotting.

Flowers at Christmas. Garden centers sell specially prepared prechilled bulbs that shorten the forcing time, allowing you to enjoy hyacinths as early as December. But be sure to plant these treated bulbs as soon as you buy them. If they are exposed to warm conditions for too long, they won't produce the extra-early blooms you want.

Remedy short-stemmed blooming. If your hyacinths are flowering on short stems, force them to grow long-necked ones. Before the hyacinths bloom, place the cardboard rolls from paper towels or toilet paper over their stems to force them to elongate toward the light. When they reach the height you want, remove the roll; they will then bloom on their long stems.

Save used bulbs. Don't throw away your forced hyacinths after they've flowered indoors. Keep them well lit and well watered and feed with liquid fertilizer. After the foliage has yellowed and died back, plant the bulbs outdoors to bloom the following season. You may have only a few flowers the first year, but the spikes will become more robust with each succeeding year—and eventually bloom as beautifully as they did the first time.

Think small. When you plant hyacinths outdoors, the smaller the bulbs, the better. Small bulbs are less expensive than the larger, premium-quality ones. And although their flower spikes may be less showy, they grow even and full. They are also less likely than their top-heavy relatives to sustain damage from wind and rain.

Repair bulbs that have been damaged from digging. If the wound is superficial, dust with wood ashes or sand and let it dry. If the wound is deep—or even if the bulb is cut in half—store the fragments, cut sides up, in a cool, dry place. Small bulbs will develop on the surface of each piece. Plant them in the fall; they will grow large enough to flower in 3 to 4 years.

Planting delays? Place bulbs in the vegetable compartment of your refrigerator, where they will keep for 2 weeks. Wrap them in paper towels so that their pungent skins won't impart their smell to the food.

▷ **Bulbs**

HYBRIDS

Hybrid vs. standard. Although any plant crossbred from two different species or varieties is technically a hybrid, today the term usually refers to a first-generation (F_1) hybrid. This is an offspring intentionally produced from parents that were selected and bred specifically for a desirable trait, such as bloom, fragrance, or yield. Conversely, open-pollinated varieties, also called standards, develop naturally from two different parents that have been cross-fertilized by insects or wind.

Pros and cons. Hybrid plants offer many significant benefits, including improvements in productivity, hardiness, maturity period, uniformity, and disease resistance. The disadvantage is that hybridizing sometimes sacrifices one desirable trait to gain another, such as better bloom at the expense of fragrance. Some organic gardeners also reject hybrids because they prefer to let nature, not breeders, determine the development of desirable food and ornamental varieties.

Replenishing your stock. If you're partial to a particular F_1 hybrid plant and want to continue growing it, you will need to purchase a new batch of seed every season. Seeds gathered from these hybrids don't come true—that is, they revert partially or completely to the traits of their parents. An alternative to buying seed is to propagate the hybrids vegetatively, either by cuttings or other means.

You're probably already growing hybrids, purchased either as seed or as young transplants. Tomatoes, cucumbers, corn, squash, spinach, and broccoli are among the vegetables usually grown from F_1 hybrids. Flower hybrids include impatiens, petunias, marigolds, and geraniums. There are also hybrid perennials and shrubs, including daylilies, irises, and roses, but they are not available as seeds; buy stock at the nursery.

What is hybrid vigor? A term that is often seen in seed catalogs is *hybrid vigor*. Known scientifically as heterosis, this phenomenon means that a hybrid plant exhibits better and stronger characteristics than either of its parents—for example, in size, shape, disease resistance, or productivity.

Disease resistance. Many hybrid vegetables have built-in disease resistance. A tomato variety, for example, generally has any or all of three initials following its name, such as 'Better Boy' VFN. The V indicates resistance to verticillium wilt, a fungus disease; the F to fusarium wilt, another fungus disease; and the N to root-knot nematodes.

Interspecific crosses. Although most hybrids are made by crossing two different varieties within the same species, often two different species in the same genus are crossed. This "interspecific cross" is indicated by an *x* in the name of the resulting hybrid. For example, *Abelia* × *grandiflora,* the glossy abelia, was developed by crossing *Abelia chinensis* and *Abelia uniflora.*

HYDRANGEAS

The main types. Most commonly grown are the two types of big-leaved hydrangea *(Hydrangea macrophylla):* the hortensias (or mopheads), with domed flower clusters, and the lacecaps, with flat disks of tiny florets surrounded by

petals. Both flower in midsummer on the previous year's shoots. Another popular variety is *H. paniculata* 'Grandiflora,' which produces showy cone-shaped panicles up to 12 inches long. Unlike big-leaved types, it flowers on the current season's shoots.

Choose the right site. Plant hydrangeas in rich, moist soil with sun to partial shade and no competition from tree roots; water well during dry spells and keep mulched. Because some types bud early in spring, make sure that they are in a spot protected from frost. Hydrangeas look spectacular when massed, so select a place that will accommodate several plants.

The color of hydrangeas reveals the chemistry of your soil. Blue flowers indicate an acid soil (below pH 7), while pink indicates alkalinity (above pH 7). White varieties stay white, regardless of soil type.

Alter the hues of your hydrangea blooms by altering the soil. For blue flowers, acidify your soil with aluminum sulfate, iron sulfate, sulfur, or a store-bought bluing solution. For pink flowers, add lime or a phosphorus-rich fertilizer to the soil to raise alkalinity. And be patient: the treatments don't work overnight; they usually take several months before having the desired effect.

To obtain brighter colors, water the roots of each of your hydrangeas with a dilute solution of 1 ounce blood meal per 1 quart water. Repeat the treatment a month after the first watering.

The dried flower heads are not only beautiful, adding interest to the winter garden, but useful: they help protect the tender emerging buds from frost damage. Leave them on till early spring, then prune them back to just above a bud. Use spent heads for mulch or in the compost.

When to prune. Prune the panicle hydrangea *(H. paniculata* 'Grandiflora') in late winter or early spring, cutting the previous year's growth to right above the new buds. Big-leaf and other hydrangeas should be rejuvenated when the plant is dormant by pruning out 3 to 5 of the oldest stems at their base. For all types, also remove any dead, damaged, or spindly wood.
▷**Acid Soil, Shrubs**

HYDROPONICS

Grow plants without soil. Hydroponics entails growing plants in a liquid nutrient solution, sometimes supplemented with a soilless medium like pebbles or vermiculite. Use a ceramic or opaque glass container, a special double-walled hydroculture pot, or a watertight trough, whether homemade of wood or metal or purchased. Lettuce, tomatoes, peppers, cucumbers, radishes, and herbs are good choices for hydroponic gardens.

Hydroponics how-to. Plants grown in solution need support. Either place an inert medium in the bottom of a container for the roots to grab or plug the container with a stopper that has a hole in the center to hold the stem. Fill with the nutrient solution and make sure it doesn't dry out; otherwise the plants will die. Use a water-level gauge for an accurate reading. Keep plants in a warm place (65° to 75° F) and change the solution every 2 weeks.

Germinate a single seed in a folded strip of cotton fabric; a shoelace cut at both ends works fine. Place the seed in the strip and fold it over, securing with a pin. Lay the strip across the neck of a water-filled soda bottle or other narrow-necked container. The bottom of the lace should lie in the water to wick moisture up to the seed. As the seedling grows, its roots will reach down into the water and its stems will sprout up out of the fabric. You can transplant the seedling to a larger container as it fills the space.

Transplants from soil. Rinse roots well in clear water to eliminate traces of soil. Cut off any dead roots and, if necessary, prune the stems to balance the ratio of roots to top growth. You can also keep the plant in low light and cover it with a plastic bag to retain moisture until new roots form.

Give your plants oxygen. Hydroponic plant roots need plenty of oxygen for proper growth. If you're growing several plants in a tub, tank, or pond, use a fish-tank bubbler to pump air into the water. Your plants will grow considerably faster.

A special fertilizer. Use only fertilizers specified for hydroponics, available at garden supply stores. They contain the

---

FLOATING POND CULTURE

More than 500 years ago, the Aztecs used the science of hydroponics to grow fast-growing floating plant gardens out onto Lake Tenochtitlán, near what is now Mexico City. Today hydroponics—also known as pond culture—is employed in commercial crop production all over the world.

You can replicate the Aztecs' lush floating gardens if you have a pond or fish tank. Simply cut a "raft" out of 1-inch-thick rigid foam insulation, sold at hardware stores. The size of the raft depends on the size of the plant, although 5 by 5 inches is about average. Cut a ½-inch hole or slit in the middle and insert a rooted cutting or a germinated seedling; secure, if necessary, by wedging it with foam scraps. As it floats on your pond, the little green island will thrive.

---

essential micronutrients (iron, boron, and copper) and macronutrients (nitrogen, phosphorous, and potassium) for best growth. Be sure to follow manufacturers' directions exactly and to periodically monitor the pH in the solution; a level of 6.0 is best for most hydroponically grown plants.

Don't go to the max. To let air reach the roots and stimulate new growth, allow the water level to drop to the minimum indicated on the gauge before refilling.

A use for pretty bottles. Save a clear glass bottle or container with an interesting shape and use it to grow a houseplant hydroponically. A brandy snifter or an unusual liqueur bottle is a good choice. Fill the container with white or colored gravel, clay balls, or clear or colored marbles of different sizes. Your plant's roots will intertwine through the filler and look particulary decorative. Use a hydroponic liquid nutrient solution, changing it several times a year to keep it clean and clear.

IMPATIENS

Happy in the shade. Impatiens have earned their enormous popularity not only for their long-lasting displays of showy blooms but also for their ability to thrive with little sun. Plant beneath a shade tree or in borders or containers that receive partial to moderate shade.

Care and feeding. Impatiens require little special care other than rich, well-drained soil and plenty of water. Quench their hot-weather thirst often with deep waterings.

To propagate tropical or hybrid impatiens, cut a stem just below, not between, a node; (cuttings taken between nodes can rot). Then remove the lower leaves and root the stem in water; place in bright indirect light, not direct sun. Transplant carefully: the roots will be fragile.

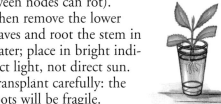

Hybrid impatiens grow fast. Sow seeds in March instead of January or February to produce plants that are ready to set out in June—in the warm (65°F), shady conditions they require. To ensure success, don't cover the seeds in the seed tray: they need plenty of light to sprout.

Easy-to-grow impatiens provide summer-long color in a shady flower bed and serve as sparkling edgings.

A tender perennial, impatiens will bloom year round in frost-free areas. In a greenhouse the flowers will bloom continuously as long as they are exposed to some light and steady humidity. Pinch their tips to encourage bushy growth.

For compact but well-branched plants that disappear under their flowers, pinch out the growing tips of your impatiens—even the squat varieties—before you plant them. To avoid having too few flowers at first, nip one out of every two plants, then the other 2 weeks later. Use the tips for cuttings to propagate new plants; they can be rooted quickly and used to fill out your groupings in a few weeks.

Delight your children by letting them grow touch-me-nots (*Impatiens biflora* and *I. pallida*) in their own corner of the garden. These Himalayan natives, also known as jewelweed, are hardy only in warm climates but self-seed freely. They produce an abundance of plump capsules that explode at the slightest touch, sending seeds on their merry way. With a single sowing you will always have plants, especially since they can adapt to any soil and exposure.

A wild impatiens. If you live in the Northeast, look in the woods for another touch-me-not, *Impatiens capensis,* which has naturalized in damp places. Bearing lovely large flowers spotted orange and yellow, this wild impatiens can thrive until frost in any cool soil. Collect its seeds and sow them in the fall.
▷ **Flower Beds**

Greening up the great indoors

It's difficult to imagine a warm and inviting home without any plants growing inside. Fortunately, it's simple to enhance any interior with indoor plants whose foliage and flowers can be enjoyed through all four seasons and over many years. Some of these plants are seasonal guests, like the zebra plant and poinsettia, which brighten up the winter months with decorative leaves or brilliant blooms. Others, such as the continuously flowering wax begonia, can easily be made permanent members of the household.

For healthy and problem-free plants, it is important to make your selections based upon exactly where in the house the plant will be located. Because most so-called indoor plants come from tropical and sub-tropical regions, how much light they will receive is vitally important. Also be aware that the intensity of sunlight indoors drops off dramatically as you move plants away from the windows.

The plants on these pages are grouped according to the amount of light they require. The full-sun lovers do best in an unobstructed south-facing window, which gets the strongest light for most of the day. Some other plants need bright light *without* full sun—that is, just inside a south-facing window hung with sheer drapes or on a windowsill facing east or west. Plants that prefer partial shade will be happy in a north-facing window or 6 feet away from a more brightly-lit exposure, while those that tolerate full shade will do fine in the middle of an artificially lit room.

INSIDE THE HOUSE

FULL SUN

BRIGHT LIGHT WITHOUT FULL SUN

PARTIAL SHADE

Crown of thorns
Euphorbia milii

Flowers between spring and fall.

Let dry out between waterings. Apply flowering plant fertilizer once a month at ½ strength, spring through fall.

Tip The brighter the sunlight, the longer the flowering season.

Crowding every surface in a sunny corner with flowering plants creates quite a show. Here geraniums share space with hyacinths.

African violet
Saintpaulia ionantha

Flowers between spring and fall.

Keep moist. Don't wet foliage. Water from below. Apply flowering-plant fertilizer at ½ strength, spring through fall.

Tip African violets do best when potbound.

Basket plant
Aeschynanthus

Flowers in spring and summer.

Keep it moist. Any excess or lack of water may cause the flowers to fall.

Tip In winter, keep in a cool place (55°F) and water lightly.

Kafir lily
Clivia miniata

Flowers at the end of winter and through spring.

Keep at 40°–50°F in fall and winter. Keep moist, though drier in winter.

Tip To gain extra blooms, don't detach the offsets.

Kalanchoe
Kalanchoe × blossfeldiana

Can be purchased in flower year-round.

Water enough to keep soil moist; let top half dry out between waterings. Apply flowering-plant fertilizer at ½ strength, spring through fall; withold feeding for 2 months after flowering.

Tip In September, give plant 6 weeks of 16-hour nights (total darkness). Expect blooms in 6 to 8 weeks.

Busy lizzie
Impatiens walleriana

Flowers in spring and fall.

Keep moist, though drier in winter. Appy flowering-plant fertilizer once or twice a month at ½ strength, spring through fall.

Tip Pinch back plants to keep them bushy.

Fairy primrose
Primula malacoides

Flowers at the end of winter or at the start of spring.

Water once a week when it is cool, keeping the leaves dry. Appy flowering-plant fertilizer once or twice a month.

Tip Flowering lasts longer at 50°–60°F and if fading blooms are removed.

Hibiscus
Hibiscus rosa-sinensis

Flowers in spring and fall—and sometimes into winter.

Keep moist. Apply flowering plant fertilizer monthly at ½ strength from spring through fall.

Tips Prune in late winter or early spring. Propagate from cuttings in spring or summer.

Jerusalem cherry
Solanum pseudocapsicum

Colored inedible fruits from fall to the end of winter.

Keep moist; avoid drying out or an excess of water. Fertilize monthly at ½ strength from spring through fall.

Tip Put outside over summer to encourage another crop of fruit. And be careful: the fruit is poisonous.

Bromeliads
Vriesea splendens or *Aechmea fasciata, Neoregelia carolinae 'Tricolor'*

Can be purchased in bloom year-round.

Water the growing medium sparingly but keep the "cups" in the center of the plants filled with water. Apply flowering-plant fertilizer monthly at ½ strength, spring through fall.

Tip The plant dies after the bright red "sword" fades. Grow a new plant from the offset next to the spike.

Cape primrose
Streptocarpus hybridus

Flowers between spring and fall.

Keep moist, though drier in winter. Apply flowering plant fertilizer monthly at ½ strength from spring through fall.

Tip Remove faded flowers to enourage blooms.

Flamingo flower
Anthurium scherzeranum

Flowers spring to summer.

Keep moist, though drier in winter. Apply flowering plant fertilizer monthly at ½ strength. Flowers last up to 8 weeks.

Tip Keep close to a slightly shaded window for healthy growth and to prevent leaves from elongating unattractively.

Moth orchid
Phalaenopsis spp. & cvs.

Several flowerings—each of a month or more.

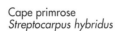

Keep moist. Apply orchid fertilizer every 2 or 3 weeks, spring and summer.

Tip May rebloom on old stems. Cut stem above the third or fourth node from the base; a new spike should develop in 4 to 6 weeks.

Orchid cactus
Epiphyllum spp. & cvs.

Flowers spring and summer.

Keep moist during spring and summer, drier in winter and after flowering. Apply flowering-plant fertilizer monthly at ½ strength from spring through summer.

Tip Keep cool in winter (50°F) to spur bloom. The white flowers are intensely fragrant.

Poinsettia
Euphorbia pulcherrima

Flowers in winter.

Keep moist, though drier after flowering. Apply flowering plant fertilizer monthly at ½ strength from spring through fall.

Tip Starting in mid-September, the plant needs 8 weeks of 14-hour nights (total darkness) to initiate bud formation.

Spathiphyllum
Spathiphyllum wallisii

Flowers between spring and fall—and sometimes in winter.

Keep moist. Apply diluted fertilizer monthly from spring through fall.

Tips Fairly easy to make flower, even in low light. Spray the foliage to raise humidity.

Wax begonia
Begonia × *semperflorens*

Can easily bloom throughout the year.

Keep moist, though slightly drier in winter. Apply flowering-plant fertilizer monthly at ½ strength, spring through fall.

Tips Pinch back regularly to keep plants full and bushy. Stem cuttings are easily rooted for more plants.

Zebra plant
Aphelandra squarrosa

Flowers usually in fall or winter.

Keep moist. Apply flowering-plant fertilizer monthly at ½ strength.

Tip This plant seldom flowers twice: cut back after flowering for a bushier, fuller look and more attractive foliage.

INSIDE THE HOUSE

INSIDE THE HOUSE

Aeonium
Aeonium arboreum

 Let dry between waterings. Apply all-purpose fertilizer at ½ strength monthly, spring through fall. Prefers cool winters (40°–50°F) but will grow at room temperature.

Tip Repot every few years in soil made porous with perlite or sand and enriched with compost.

Rebutia cactus

 Let the soil dry completely between waterings; water very little in winter. Apply flowering-plant or all-purpose fertilizer at ½ strength monthly through spring and fall. Same care applies to *Lobivia* and *Mammillaria* spp.

Tip To encourage flowering in winter, keep in a cool place (40°–50°F) and in bright light.

Jade plant
Crassula argentea

Let dry between waterings. Apply diluted flowering plant fertilizer monthly through spring and fall. Prefers cooler conditions in winter (50°F).

Tips Move into a pot one size larger only once every 2 years. Plants easily propagated from cuttings in a moist rooting mixture.

Aglaonema
Aglaonema commutatum

 Keep moist. Apply an all-purpose fertilizer monthly at ½ strength from spring through fall.

Tip The greener the variety, the more tolerant it will be of lower light.

Butterfly palm
Chrysalidocarpus lutescens

 Keep moist all year long. Apply an all-purpose fertilizer monthly at ½ strength from spring through fall.

Tip Spray or mist foliage frequently.

Croton
Codiaeum variegatum

 Keep moist. Apply an all-purpose fertilizer monthly at ½ strength from spring through fall.

Tip Keep warm in winter and mist frequently.

Dumb cane
Dieffenbachia

 Keep moist. Apply an all-purpose fertilizer monthly at ½ strength from spring through fall.

Tip Because the sap is toxic, always wash your hands after handling.

Parlor palm
Chamaedorea elegans

 Keep moist. Apply an all-purpose fertilizer once a month at ½ strength, spring through fall.

Tips Spray foliage frequently. Tolerates low light.

Polka dot plant
Hypoestes phyllostachya

Keep moist, though drier in winter. Apply diluted fertilizer monthly from spring through fall.

Tip Put pot on tray of wet pebbles to raise humidity.

Arrowhead plant
Syngonium podophyllum

 Keep moist, though drier in winter. Apply an all-purpose fertilizer monthly at ½ strength from spring through fall.

Tip Spray foliage frequently or place the pot on a shallow tray of wet pebbles to increase humidity, particularly in the drier winter months.

Boston fern
Nephrolepis exaltata 'Bostoniensis'

 Keep moist. Spray foliage frequently. Apply an all-purpose fertilizer at ½ strength monthly from spring through fall.

Tip Don't worry about the little brown dots on the backs of the leaves; they are spores.

Corn plant
Dracaena fragrans 'Massangeana'

 Keep moist all year long. Apply an all-purpose fertilizer at ½ strength monthly from spring through fall.

Tip Usually won't flower in pots. When it does, flowers aren't especially showy but are intensely fragrant.

Common philodendron
Philodendron scandens ssp. *oxycardium*

 Keep moist. Apply all-purpose fertilizer at ½ strength monthly from spring through fall.

Tips Use a hanging basket. Allow the plant to climb on a trellis or on a column of moss which is regularly moistened. Prune back bare stems.

Grape ivy
Cissus rhombifolia

Water enough to keep soil moist; let top half dry out between waterings. Apply fertilizer at ½ strength monthly from spring through fall.

Tip Promote branching by pinching out tips.

Japanese aucuba
Aucuba japonica

 Keep moist, though slightly drier in winter. Apply an all-purpose fertilizer at ½ strength monthly from spring through fall.

Tips Variegated forms are more colorful but less tolerant of low light conditions. The plants take pruning well.

Elephant's foot palm
Beaucarnea recurvata

Let dry between waterings. Apply diluted fertilizer monthly from spring through fall. Keep in a cool place (50°F).

Tips Also called the pony tail palm. Don't repot often; this plant likes close quarters.

Spineless yucca
Yucca elephantipes

Let dry between waterings. Water more sparingly in the winter. Apply diluted fertilizer twice monthly from spring through fall. Can tolerate temperatures down to 40°F.

Tip During winter, the cooler it is kept, the better.

String of hearts
Ceropegia woodii

Let dry out between waterings. Apply diluted fertilizer monthly from spring through fall. Cool temperatures (40°–50°F) are preferable.

Tip Propagate more plants with the little tubers that form on the stems.

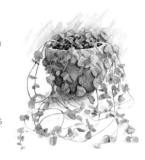

Striped dracaena
Dracaena deremensis 'Warneckii'

Keep moist. Apply an all-purpose fertilizer at ½ strength monthly from spring through fall.

Tip Can tolerate low-light growing conditions.

Umbrella sedge
Cyperus involucratus

Keep wet. Apply diluted fertilizer monthly from spring through fall.

Tip Mist foliage often during dry winter months.

Umbrella tree
Schefflera actinophylla

Keep moist. Apply all-purpose fertilizer at ½ strength monthly from spring through fall. Cut back the stems each spring to obtain a fuller plant. Repot young plants each year.

Tip Could happily spend the summer outside in a sheltered spot.

Golden pothos
Epipremnum aurem

Keep moist. Apply all-purpose fertilizer at ½ strength monthly from spring through fall.

Tips Give it plenty of light if the leaves turn green. Shorten any bare or too-long stems and root the trimmings.

Staghorn fern
Platycerium bifurcatum

Water by immersing the plant, container and all, for 20 to 30 minutes. Apply diluted fertilizer monthly from spring though fall.

Tip Repot in well-drained compost or mount on cork or bark slabs with a base of sphagnum moss.

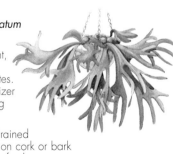

Unusual foliage can add an eye-catching point of interest to a room. Shown here is the polka dot begonia (B. maculata 'Wightii').

Snake plant
Sansevieria trifasciata

Let dry between waterings. Very tolerant of dry soil, especially in low light. Apply an all-purpose fertilizer at ½ strength monthly from spring through fall.

Tips Many cultivars available. Vigorous roots will crack pots when they need more space.

Tree ivy
Fatshedera lizei

Keep moist, though drier in winter. Apply all-purpose fertilizer at ½ strength monthly, spring through fall. Keep cool during winter (tolerates to 35°F). If room is warm, spray leaves.

Tips Prune in spring for a bushier plant. Variegated variety needs more light.

INSIDE THE HOUSE

INVASIVE PLANTS

What makes a plant a pest? Invasive plants travel rapidly by either underground rhizomes, aboveground stolons, or seed dispersal and crowd out less vigorous specimens. To become invasive, a plant must find conditions favorable for growth in its adoptive home. And limiting factors, such as insect pests or other aggressive plants, must be weak or nonexistent.

Which are the culprits? Aggressive invaders inhabit every corner of the country. Among the most notorious plants are the kudzu vine, Japanese knotweed, giant reed, and water hyacinths.

Discourage wanderlust. Curb rampant roots by sinking metal or plastic edging 1 foot deep around them in the soil. Or put the plant in a 2-gallon pot before setting it in the ground. If an invader is creeping under a fence, dig an 8-inch-deep trench along its base and fasten a plastic sheet to it; bury the rest of the sheet in the trench.

To remove an unwanted vine that has crawled up a tree, first cut it off at the roots. Leave the stems and foliage to wilt for a few days, then pull it out of the tree. A rake is a handy tool for snaring the wayward strands.

Beware of the trumpet-creeper, which is wildly invasive. It finds its way under paving stones, over fences, and across lawns to pop up far from the original rooting site. Sometimes the only way to eradicate the trumpet creeper and other stubborn invaders is to cut back emerging shoots and apply a recommended

---

herbicide to the cuts. When the stems have stopped growing, dig up and discard them.

Head off prolific self-sowers by deadheading the plants just after flowering. Also dig up any young volunteers as soon as they sprout. Among the plants that invade via seed are goldenrod, lamb's-ears, yarrow, asters, anchusa, and columbine.

IRISES

Sorting them out. Irises grow from bulbs or, more commonly, from rhizomes. The rhizomatous types include bearded irises—so called for the hairs on the down-turned petals—and beardless ones, with no hairs. Among the most popular in the beardless group are the hardy, heavy-flowering Siberian iris and the water irises.

A rule of thumb. Irises are most striking when massed; their blooms will look like a swarm of butterflies hovering over the garden. But it's best to group only one type—bearded, beardless, or bulbous, for example—together.

What colors? The iris lacks a gene for red pigmentation, but otherwise comes in many shades: from pale cream and yellow to deep blue, purple, maroon, and orange.

The contrasting bands, veins, and speckles on the flowers enhance their beauty.

BEARDED IRISES

All they need is sun and well-drained soil. Side-dress lightly with a low-nitrogen fertilizer in early spring and late summer.

Plant or divide irises as soon as possible after blooming—sometime between July and September. This gives the plants time to take root before winter. If you plant too late you'll get fewer blooms.

Prevent rotting stems. Plant the rhizome on a mound of soil amended with coarse sand to promote drainage. Spread the roots over the mound, fill the hole, and water.

Damage control. If frost heaves the rhizomes out of the ground in winter, don't push them back down. Instead, pile a small mound of well-drained soil or coarse sand around them—but be careful not to bury them.

Siberian irises are strong-rooted, heavy bloomers. Shown here is the graceful 'Orville Fay'.

In cool climates, guarantee regrowth by making sure that the top part of the rhizome remains exposed to the sun. In late summer, also cut leaves back to about half their length in a fan shape.

Watch out for weeds. Keep iris beds free of weeds, cleaning them thoroughly both before and after planting. But take care around the rhizomes—if you nick them with a hoe or cultivator, you'll provide a doorway for diseases.

Division is essential. Divide rhizomes before they become overcrowded and flowering lessens. Irises in cool-climate gardens may need to be divided only every 3 years, while those in warm climates may require yearly division. Check for soft, foul-smelling, or rotting rhizomes—a sign of borer damage. Make clean cuts with a sharp knife, dipping it in alcohol between cuts to avoid spreading disease. Keep only the healthy outer parts of the clump, with new growth. Let the cut rhizomes dry in the sun for several hours, then replant them 12 to 15 inches apart.

Be fastidious. Strict sanitary methods are necessary for the best bearded iris displays. Combat leaf spot, rust, or pests with fungicides or insecticides. Remove any yellowing or dying leaves promptly.

Pull off dry or damaged leaves carefully, holding them as horizontally as possible.

Pest control. Control thrips and aphids, which can spread virus disease and reduce vigor. At the first sign of iris root borers, remove the surrounding soil and any mulching materials and dispose of them.

SIBERIAN IRISES
Erosion control. With their tough, fibrous roots, Siberian irises will bind soil even on slopes. To plant, dig a deep hole and put manure on the bottom, below the root run.

Divide crowded clumps by first trimming back the foliage, then lifting with a fork. Break into sections with several shoots on each and replant. Don't let clumps get too large or you'll need an axe to divide them.

For bouquets, cut when the flowers are still buds. The blooms from this heavy-producing iris last only a few days in the vase.

WATER IRISES
Bog bloomers. Irises that grow in water or boggy soil include the Japanese iris *(Iris ensata)*, yellow flag *(I. pseudacorus)*, and several native species, such as Virginia iris *(I. virginica)* and blue flag *(I. versicolor)*.

Marginal magic. While some irises grow in water up to 1 foot deep, most prefer the shallow margins. Prepare a planting hole with coarse peat, leaf mold, or rotted manure and plant 2 inches deep in full sun or light shade. Mulch to suppress weeds and retain moisture. In cold climates, mulch also helps protect roots, but you will have to lift out tender types, like Louisiana hybrids, if the water freezes.

Know your species. Yellow flag has golden blossoms with brown markings; it is so hardy and vigorous that it can become invasive. Blue flag, with blue-violet blooms,

> **A SCENTED IRIS**
>
> The Florentine iris, with its large, almost white flowers traced in blue or purple, has been used for centuries for its scented rhizome, known as orrisroot. When dried, it releases a distinctive, long-lasting fragrance. Orrisroot is used in the perfume trade and, in times past, was added to laundry rinse water to perfume clothes. It is also an exceptionally effective fragrance fixer—hence its frequent use in potpourris. It can often be found in a pharmacy or herbalist's shop.

is better behaved. Rabbit-ear iris *(I. laevigata),* with white, pink, or blue-purple varieties, is a good choice for small ponds or bog gardens. The Louisiana irises, which include the copper-blossomed *I. fulva* and the giant-flowered *I. giganticaerulea,* grow wild in the Deep South, although some cultivars will tolerate cold temperatures.

BULBOUS IRISES
Cold-climate gardeners should lift the bulbs of bulbous Dutch and Spanish irises out of the ground after the foliage has yellowed and store them to replant in the early spring. In warmer regions these bulbs can remain in the ground all year.

If the foliage yellows during the growing season, the clumps may have become overcrowded. Lift them and divide by carefully pulling the bulbs apart, doing as little damage to the roots as possible. Replant the clumps, using wider spacing.

Watch out for black spot, which causes clumps to die off quickly. To stem the disease, plant irises in the fall in fertile, well-drained soil; avoid fertilizer. Check regularly for the symptoms: blackened bulbs and spots on the leaves. Remove infected plants and the contaminated soil.
▷ **Flower Beds**

IVY

The ideal ground cover for quickly enhancing an unattractive or little-used area, ivy grows well in even poor garden soil that is inhospitable to less vigorous plants.

Instant topiary. Cover a shape of your choice with ivy. The form can be created with a rough wood frame and covered with chicken wire. Prune only once a year, preferably in the spring, to preserve a well-defined shape.

Make a green carpet with ivy. For a quick covering, which takes 1 to 2 years, space plants 18 inches to 2 feet apart; if there's no hurry, 3-foot spacing is fine.

A natural insulator. Let ivy blanket a north- or west-facing wall for protection against rain and sudden shifts in temperature. Contrary to lore, it won't destroy the wall. But be careful: if the surface is already in poor shape, with cracks or bare patches, ivy will find its way in. Restore the surface of the wall as necessary.

Limit self-seeding by pruning ivy at the right time: after flowering but just before the fruit ripens to a blue-black color (generally in December). At this time it will be too late for the plant to produce more flowers and too early for the fruit that falls to the ground to sprout and spread.

Ivy-berry bouquets. Create pretty bouquets with ivy berries if you've let them form on the plant. They enhance cut flowers, especially the delicate blooms of roses, carnations, and tulips. Another plus: they're available in the winter. Don't pick them beyond early March; by that time the berries are overripe and will drop immediately after the stems are cut.

Up a tree? Don't allow ivy to invade your trees. It may be pretty—especially in its variegated forms—but it can often get the upper hand on its host, covering and smothering a tree's branches and blocking out sunlight. At most, let it climb up to the first fork in the trunk, where it can form a decorative "stocking."

Keep ivy in check by simply cutting it back with shears about 6 inches from any potential climbing surface; check new growth several times throughout the season and snip back as needed.

To root cuttings, don't take the long stems with aerial roots. Instead, use stems that have flowered but have no aerial roots or excess branching. Cut

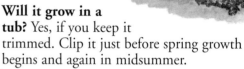

them in summer and root in pots filled with moist sand. Place them in a shaded cold frame—and plant out one year later.

Will it grow in a tub? Yes, if you keep it trimmed. Clip it just before spring growth begins and again in midsummer.
▷ **Ground Covers**

> ⊰| **AN IVY SAMPLER** |⊱
>
> English ivy (Hedera helix), with its dark green, lobed leaves, is the classic hardy ground cover and climber. For a different look, choose one of the variegated cultivars—such as 'Gold Heart,' with a yellow center, and 'Glacier,' whose white splotches turn pink in winter. In warm regions, try Algerian ivy (H. canariensis). Its stems are dark red, and its glossy leaves grow up to 6 inches; there are several variegated cultivars, like 'Gloire de Marengo.'

Fast-growing and hardy, ivy makes a handsome ground cover that will easily decorate a barren slope.

JAPANESE BEETLES

These pests aren't picky. Japanese beetles eat almost every part of almost any plant. They especially love raspberries, beans, and corn, but they're also fond of apple trees, grapevines, and roses.

Check corn daily once the silk appears because the beetles feast on the tender silk. Without the silk, no pollination can occur and no ears of corn will develop.

Plant garlic among your roses, fruit trees, and berry bushes to deter the beetles.

Cultivate soil deeply in spring and fall to kill grubs and to expose them to birds.

Handpicking can be effective in controlling adult beetles. Handpick in the cool of early morning, when they are sluggish and dew on their wings makes it harder for them to fly away. Crush them between your fingers or drop your catch in a small can of kerosene.

Invite birds into the garden by minimizing use of any broad-spectrum pesticides and by installing a birdbath, small pond, or fountain. Robins, starlings, and flickers, with the long pointed beaks needed for poking into soil, help control Japanese beetles by eating the larvae. Other birds, including cardinals and catbirds, eat the adult beetles. Make sure that fresh water is always available, but empty your bird feeders; you'll keep the birds hungry enough to snack on the beetles and grubs.

Try neem oil. An effective botanical control for Japanese beetles is neem oil, which comes from the neem tree of India. Applied to the soil, this substance kills grubs; applied to plants, it keeps adult beetles from feeding. Use it on ornamental and edible plants.

Two more natural controls. Milky-spore disease (*Bacillus popilliae*) is a beneficial bacteria that destroys beetles while they are still at the grub stage in the soil. You can also use nematodes (*Heterorhabditis spp.*), which are microscopic parasites, to combat grub infestation. Spread them on the lawn and they will begin infecting and killing grubs within a few days. Both controls are generally available from garden centers and mail-order sources.

Poisonous plants. Four-o'clocks, jimsonweed (*Datura stramonium*), dwarf and red buckeyes, and delphiniums all attract and poison Japanese beetles. But be cautious: both four-o'clocks and jimsonweed are toxic to humans and pets as well.

Pheromone traps usually give mixed results. These scented lures sometimes attract more beetles to your garden than would normally arrive. If you try them, set the traps at least 50 feet away from any of the beetles' favorite crops.

Raise the pH. Beetle larvae are known to dislike alkaline soil. Spread wood ashes or lime on the lawn and garden beds in the fall to raise the pH level—but first make sure that your plants won't suffer from the adjustment to soil acidity.
▷ **Grubs & Larvae, Pesticides**

JAPANESE GARDENS

The basic idea. The three essentials in a Japanese garden are water, plants, and stone—all combined harmoniously.

Ideal for small spaces. If you have a 50- to 200-square-foot yard, patio, or terrace, you have plenty of room for a Japanese-inspired garden. A pleasure to look at year round, it needs only pruning and weeding. By combining native and Asian plants, you can adapt this soothing garden style to your climate and location.

THE FIVE TYPES

Hill-and-pond gardens are generally made for viewing. As the name suggests, a body of water dominates. Plants and shrubs are usually used to suggest rolling hills and clouds.

Strolling gardens are based on the idea of a journey. The path itself is the garden. The placement of stones on the path articulates the journey, showing where to walk and where to stop.

Teahouse gardens are designed around a path leading to a simple teahouse.

Dry landscape gardens are the classic Zen rock-and-gravel types.

Courtyard gardens are usually in the entryway of homes. Often there is a basin of water for cleaning away the dirt of outdoors before entering the garden and then the home. *Shu-i-wa* is Japanese for this garden type. It means "point of energy," a term taken from acupuncture.

In a Japanese-style garden, the merging of water, stones, and plants soothes the eye and invites the stroller.

A Japanese corner. If you like the idea but are unwilling to transform your whole garden, lay out just a small area and define it with a bamboo fence or perhaps a living bamboo hedge. A Japanese garden can make good use of any rugged or hard-to-landscape spot on your property.

Don't overdo it. *Shibusa* is a word that the Japanese often use to describe their gardens. It has many meanings, but it mainly implies restraint, good taste, and elegant simplicity. Limit your choice of materials.

Look for contrasts when choosing plants, stones, shrubs, and trees. Use lighter shades against darker shades. Mix fine and bold textures. And remember that in Japanese gardening the emphasis is on foliage rather than flowers—although you can add a few flowering plants to punctuate the seasons.

Borrow from your surroundings—the hills behind your house or the large tree in a neighbor's yard, for example. Repeat colors and patterns. Use shrubs to mimic distant hills or gravel patterns to symbolize ripples in a stream. By borrowing, you unify your garden with its natural surroundings and make it seem larger.

A joy in winter. A Japanese-style garden is designed for beauty in all seasons. For this reason, make generous use of evergreens. In Japan many plants are grown simply because they look particularly attractive with snow on their branches.

Water is mandatory. Whether running or still, water is essential in a Japanese garden. Install a birdbath, a small fountain, or a tiny shallow pond with a few goldfish. Always make sure the water is perfectly clean.

Gravel guidelines. Use off-white instead of pure white, which can have a blinding glare. Smaller gravel holds patterns best. Before spreading, place a woven geotextile underneath. The plastic prevents weeds, as does black plastic, but lets air and water pass through. Rake carefully to make sure that no patches of the plastic show through the gravel.

Let a path meander. In a strolling or teahouse garden, the path becomes the garden. Stepping stones control the rate at which you proceed and the spacing of views. The long axis of the stones is generally perpendicular to the direction of movement. Interject larger stepping stones where you want to pause and view a special feature.

Using stones. Stones for the background should be fairly large and carefully chosen—either blocks of rock with a distinctive outline or large tablelike slabs laid on the ground. You can also add pebbles or river gravel, which are easy to maintain.

ZEN GARDENING PRINCIPLES

Asymmetry: No rules or formal arrangements

Incompleteness: A sense of things not being finished; carefully imperfect

Ordinariness: No hierarchy or showy specimen plants

Simplicity: Sparse plantings; uncrowded

Spaciousness: Freedom from hindrance

Spontaneity: Effortless and unexpected; a sense of playfulness and complete naturalness

Tranquillity: An oasis of calm

Crossing water. When you construct a pond, use large vertical stones with

flat ends or sections of sawn logs to make an elegant walkway across the water. Dig holes at least 1 foot deep and secure each stone or log firmly in the pond bottom. For safety, place them slightly closer together than you would on land.

Use local stone to help your garden harmonize with the landscape. Choose stones with similar traits, such as a smooth or coarse texture and a round or angular form.

Stock your pond with goldfish— called koi in Japan—for an authentic touch. They not only add color and movement to the garden but also are voracious insect eaters.

Add wind chimes. For a restful note, tie wind chimes to the branch of a tree, keeping them out of sight. To make the chimes, obtain four bamboo canes of different thicknesses and cut a 6-inch section from each. Using a 1/16-inch twist bit, carefully drill holes through the top of each cane. Then cut another 6-inch length to use as a hanging bar; drill four holes all the way through at 1¼-inch intervals. Attach each cane by running an 8-inch length of fishing line through the cane and tying it to the bar. To balance the bar for hanging, tie a string around it loosely and adjust it until the bar hangs plumb. Then drill a hole at the balance point, run a wire through, and wrap the wire loosely around a tree branch, tying it securely. As the canes clack softly in the wind, each will have a different tone.

The right furniture. Enhance your Japanese theme by choosing bamboo, rattan, or wooden garden furniture, all of which blend appropriately with the style.

▷ **Landscaping**

JERUSALEM ARTICHOKES

Not artichokes at all. Jerusalem artichokes—also called sunchokes—are actually perennial members of the sunflower family and are an American native. They are grown for their tubers—a tasty and low-calorie substitute for potatoes.

Keep them at bay. Tubers left in the ground will readily start another crop and quickly become a nuisance—especially if you've sown another vegetable nearby. It's wise to give them a permanent location where they can be contained. A good solution is to dig a 12- to 15-inch trench around the bed and install a barrier of heavy polypropylene plastic or rubber belting to stop the spread.

Dig as many as possible from the bed each year. Otherwise, tuber size and quality will soon suffer from overcrowding.

Keep their height in mind. In rich soil and partial shade, these plants can reach 6 to 12 feet tall. Pick a spot where their shade won't affect other plants. With their yellow fall flowers, they make a good screen for compost heaps or a cover for chain-link fences.

A shorter variety. The variety 'Stampede' flowers earlier, matures sooner, and grows shorter. In general, named varieties of Jerusalem artichokes produce tubers of larger size and higher quality than the more common tall-growing, late-flowering types.

Don't store the tubers. Since their thin skins allow the roots to shrivel quickly, it's best to dig up tubers only as you need them. They can be harvested in fall until the ground freezes, then again in spring as soon as the soil has thawed. In a heavily mulched bed, the tubers can even be dug from underneath a blanket of winter snow.

Problems to watch for. The tubers are often attacked by cutworms. And root-rot fungi may occur when the soil is too wet.

▷ **Vegetable Gardens**

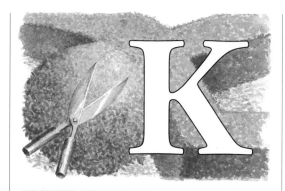

KIWI

Giant vines. Both the common (*Actinidia deliciosa*) and hardy kiwi (*A. arguta*) are fast-growing vines that need the support of a sturdy trellis or arbor.

Mix the sexes. The common kiwi produces the fuzzy fruits now available in many supermarkets; hardy kiwis yield sweet green grapelike berries that have a smooth skin. To ensure fruiting, use plants of both sexes; in general, you'll need one male for up to seven females.

Carefree. Kiwis need little extra attention besides pruning and regular feeding. Cut stems that fruited the previous year to 1½ feet in winter; control the shape with a light trimming in summer.

THE CHINESE GOOSEBERRY

The common kiwi, which has sweet, succulent flesh, was originally called the Chinese gooseberry. Although it is native to China, it was first grown commercially in New Zealand. There, the Chinese gooseberry was renamed after New Zealand's flightless national bird, whose feathers are quite fuzzy—just like the fruit!

KNOT GARDENS

Known since Elizabethan times, knot gardens were common features at monasteries and aristocratic estates. Today they are most often seen in public gardens, although they are enjoying a revival among home gardeners who have time for a creative challenge.

The basic design is geometric, with interlocking circles, squares, triangles, and other shapes defined by low, narrow hedges. The spaces inside the hedges might be filled with grass, mulch, gravel, herbs, or flowers.

A bird's-eye view. Because their pattern is best appreciated from above, knot gardens are often located to be viewed from a raised deck, porch, or balcony. They can also be planted in a sunken garden.

Start with a plan. Sketch your design to scale on graph paper to determine the shapes and the number of plants you need.

On the level. Before planting, make sure the ground is absolutely level—otherwise the pattern will be distorted. Then set the plants in position according to your layout. Exaggerate the design slightly so that it will keep its definition once the plants mature.

Selecting specimens. Knot-garden plants must be both hardy and tolerant of regular shearing. Popular choices are box, barberry, Japanese holly, gray or green santolina, lavender, germander, and rosemary. Use several kinds of plants with different colors and textures to accent the interlocking design.

Be wary of rue. Although it has striking blue-green foliage and is often used in knot gardens, rue (*Ruta graveolens*) can cause an allergic skin reaction. So handle with care.

Filling in. For color and contrast, fill the interiors with low-growing plants. Herbs, such as thyme, sage, and wormwood, give a subtle look. But you can add pizzazz with bright bloomers, like dianthus, marigolds, crocus, violets, or scented geraniums.

Add height by using shrubs or small trees either within the hedges or at the corners of the garden. Good choices are laurel, roses, heliotrope, rose-of-Sharon, figs, and citrus trees—all of which can be trained as standards.

Good mulches. Spread crushed marble, red shale chips, or pea gravel for a permanent mulch inside the hedges. Renew organic mulches, like shredded bark, annually. Use cocoa hulls with boxwood, which likes the potash that decaying hulls provide.

Keep knots neat by clipping plants lightly with sharp, thin-bladed shears every 3 to 4 weeks during the growing season. Clip conservatively at first so that you can judge the results as you proceed. Stop trimming 4 to 6 weeks before the first frost so that plants can harden off before winter.
▷ **Barberry, Boxwood, Pruning**

With its intricate pattern in green, a well-tended knot garden provides a captivating point of interest.

LABELING

Mark the spot. Don't rely on your memory alone to recall the locations and other details of hardy herbaceous plants—make weatherproof labels to mark their places. Use an indelible felt marker to record the name, color, height, and bloom period of the plant. On the back, add the name of the source—a nursery, catalog, or friend—and the date of seeding or planting.

Save your seed packets. Empty seed packets from vegetables and annuals serve as ready-made labels. Display them on small stakes stuck in the ground and cover with transparent plastic bags for protection.

Recycle. Convert plastic yogurt or cottage cheese containers into weatherproof labels; you can also use disposable aluminum pie pans. Simply cut them in strips and use an indelible felt-tip marker to write on them.

Cut index cards into any desired shape, mark them, and have them laminated. Punch a hole in a card, loop a piece of twine through it, and tie it to a stem.

Labeling trees and shrubs. Make it easier to find labels on trees and shrubs by always putting them in the same place on your plants—at head height on the north-facing side, for example.

Don't strangle trees and shrubs if you use wire to hold the labels. Loop a length of wire loosely around a branch and twist the ends to secure; loosen the wire periodically as the stem expands.

It's a natural. For labels that harmonize with the garden, use bamboo canes. Cut sections to the desired length, angling the ends to form a point that will go easily into the ground. Then write a plant name on each cane. You can also use seashells or flat, smooth stones, marking them with paint.

After lifting bulbs, use a felt-tip marker to write the plant name, bloom color, and other information directly on them. It will help you keep your collection straight come replanting time.

LADDERS

Before climbing a ladder, always check it thoroughly for damaged or bowed rungs. You can lay a wooden ladder flat on the ground and walk on the rungs—it's the safest way to find any weak ones.

Firm footing. On soft or unstable ground, support the base of an extension ladder on a sturdy platform, like a thick plank with a 2x4 nailed securely to one surface. To steady a stepladder, place its feet in four empty 2-pound coffee cans.

Handling extension ladders. An easy way to put a heavy extension ladder in place is to first lay it flat on the ground with the base against the wall. Raise the other end over your head and walk forward, grabbing the rungs hand over hand until the top of the ladder is leaning against the wall. Before climbing, ensure proper balance by pulling out the base until it's one fourth the ladder's length away from the surface.

On a slippery surface, keep the base of an extension ladder from slipping by propping a bag of cement or a couple of large cement blocks against it. Or attach a lower rung with a rope to a stationary object, such as a basement window grill or a tree.

When raising an extension ladder, brace the base with your foot. Pull the ladder away from the wall or tree and use the rope to hoist it to the desired height. Check for interference overhead from branches or power lines.

Be careful with tools. Before carrying tools, like pruning loppers or a chain saw, up a ladder, make sure you have a place to put them when you reach the top. Don't carry tools loosely in your pocket—they could easily fall out and cause injury.

Plant both feet on one rung close to the uprights—not in the middle, especially on an old ladder. Lean in and keep your weight on the balls of your feet—not on the arch—so that you can react quickly if you lose your balance.

Two cautions. Never paint a wooden ladder, as paint hides rot and damage; protect the wood with varnish instead. And always keep aluminum ladders away from power lines to avoid danger of electrocution.

LADYBUGS

A gift to gardeners. Ladybugs, also called lady beetles or ladybirds, dine heartily on pests in flower beds and vegetable gardens yet never damage the plants. But don't expect them to be a cure-all: their appetites are limited primarily to aphids, mealybugs, spider mites, scale, thrips, and whiteflies.

Attract ladybugs to your flower beds with marigolds, angelica, butterfly weed, yarrow, roses, and goldenrod. In the vegetable garden, good lures include cucumbers, peppers, eggplants, and tomatoes.

Buying ladybugs. Start with about 100 ladybugs per 1,000 square feet; if they have enough food and water, they'll stay and lay eggs in a few weeks. Make

≫⊱ HOW TO RECOGNIZE THEM ⊰≪

Among the 3,000 species of ladybugs, the most familiar to gardeners is the type with a black-spotted orange back (left). But they can also be black or yellow, with or without white, red, or yellow spots. Two of the most common are the intriguingly named twice-stabbed ladybug (right) and the convergent ladybug (below).

Ladybugs are voracious eaters, consuming up to 40 aphids in an hour; both the adults and larvae (below) are predators. While ladybugs have a "flighty" reputation, they will stay put as long as they have a supply of food and water—including nectar- and pollen-rich plants and their favorite soft-bodied insects—and are not harmed by pesticides.

sure you purchase healthy specimens: ladybugs can be infected with parasitoids, which kill their hosts and can spread rapidly through your ladybug population.

Release them in your garden in the evening when it's calm and they have dew to drink; if it's dry, sprinkle your plants first. Place a handful around the base of a plant where you see pests. Repeat every 20 feet.

If purchased ladybugs arrive before there is insect food in the garden, you can store them for 3 weeks in the refrigerator.

Keep ladybugs at home by offering a hibernation site. Pile dead leaves, hay, straw, or another organic mulch at the base of a fence or around plants to serve as winter lodgings.
▷ **Biological Controls**

LANDSCAPING

PLANNING
Divide by three. Think of your yard as having three distinct parts: public spaces, such as the front yard and driveway; private spaces, including patios, swimming pools, and children's play areas; and utility spaces, for items like garbage cans and firewood.

Take inventory. To begin planning your landscape, survey all the existing features. Take a pad and pencil outdoors and note plants, outbuildings, soil condition, slopes, sun positions, shade patterns, and bodies of water—in a word, everything.

A base map. On a piece of graph paper, draw to scale all the permanent structures, including house, driveway, swimming pool, outbuildings, and utility poles. Then, on a tracing-paper overlay, draw in features you want to keep, such

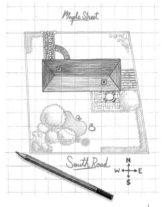

as trees, shrubs, or fences. Use successive overlays to sketch in your new ideas, whether for a vegetable garden, arbor, pond, greenhouse, or hedge.

Point and shoot. Snapshots of your property make a good substitute for a hand-drawn plan—they will save you time and portray your site accurately. Photograph the yard from different angles and have enlargements made, then draw your layout on tissue overlays.

Kits for home landscapers are often sold in the gardening section of bookstores or in specialty catalogs. The kits contain a large grid and self-adhering cutouts representing all the components of a garden. Once you mark off the dimensions of your yard and the existing features, you can arrange the cutouts to achieve the layout you want.

Have a computer? If so, check a computer store for landscape-design software.

Call city hall. To help you create your base map, obtain a copy of your property plan from your municipal records office or title insurance company. The plan will give the orientation of the property, its boundaries and dimensions, and building locations.

Mark it out. When it comes time to transfer your plan from paper to reality, use stakes and string or a garden hose to lay out new paths, steps, flower beds, fences, play areas, or anything else you've chosen to include. Then mark out the lines with ground limestone or sand.

A quick measure. If you don't have a yardstick or measuring tape handy, remember that a pace measures between 26 and 39 inches. The width of a hand, with fingers spread, is about 8 inches. With arms outstretched, the distance from one hand to the other is almost 5 feet.

Match the landscape to your style. If you like to work in the yard, a vegetable garden, rock garden, or perennial garden will provide hours of blissful distraction. If relaxed weekends are more your style, a few container plants on a deck or patio or a small patch of annuals may suit you best.

Integrate the house and landscape. Ease the transition between the "built" and the "natural" environment by combining plants with structural elements. Plan for flower-filled window boxes or tubs on the terrace

to help tie the house to the garden. Or consider letting climbers overrun a porch, wall, or doorway. You can also let plants soften the look of free-standing features like gazebos and fences—or even a lamppost.

Rooms with a view. Always take the view from indoors into account when designing the landscape. You may need to screen out some vistas with a hedge or enhance others with an eye-catching focal point, such as a as fountain, pond, or specimen tree.

A window on the world. Make your landscape seem larger by opening up the view. If your yard is

bordered with trees or hedges, plan to prune back or remove some foliage. You can also design a fence or wall, or modify an existing one, to include a window overlooking a pretty view.

In a small yard, you can create a beautiful landscape with container plants that can be redesigned at will. If you have a lawn, replace some or all of the grass with paving stones, brick, or pea gravel. Then select a variety of small trees, shrubs, and flowers that you can rearrange as their season of interest changes.

A corner retreat. Don't neglect the far corner of your yard: turn it into a peaceful retreat. Screen it off with a trellis or hedge and plant some colorful annuals. Add a lounge chair and a small tree for shade—and you'll have a private garden nook.

In a narrow yard, develop a design that diminishes the tunnel effect. Use curved instead of straight lines and plants with

spreading or broad, rounded shapes. Let a winding path meander into the distance and stagger plantings randomly on each side. Soften the linear look of walls with climbing plants or break up their surface with wall fountains or trellises. Also install a few focal points, such as a small pool or a pergola, to draw the eye horizontally.

CHOOSING PLANTS

Form, color, and texture. Three design elements are of primary importance when choosing plants for the landscape. One is the form of trees and shrubs (columnar, round pyramidal, or weeping, for example) and the various shapes of flowers and leaves. A second consideration is texture; foliage may be leathery, lacy, glossy, or fuzzy, while bark can be wrinkled, rough, or flaking. The last element is color: flowers, foliage, branches, and trunks can be any hue from soft pastels to ruddy neutrals to bright jewel tones. Artfully blending these three elements is the key to creating an appealing landscape.

Designing with foliage. Because leaves are usually visible longer than flowers, pay particular attention to a plant's foliage. Consider both the overall silhouette and the size and form of the individual leaves—whether they are needlelike, heart-shaped, serrated, or spiny. Also look at color: foliage may be green, red, yellow, bronze, blue-gray, or silver, either solid or variegated.

Exercise restraint. Resist the temptation to buy one of each plant you fall in love with—you'll find it difficult to combine them into a cohesive garden. Consult your landscape plan before buying and select plants based on their use in your garden and the growing conditions. Choose a few outstanding specimens to use singly as accents. Then buy odd numbers—threes, fives, or sevens—of "backbone" plants to install in naturalistic clumps.

A blank slate. If you're starting from scratch in a newly built house with no landscaping, plant fast-growing annuals—such as cosmos, nicotiana, impatiens, or California poppies—to fill in until hardy plants can become established.

If the terrain is flat, don't use conical or columnar trees by themselves: their rigid upright habit will merely draw attention to the lack of topographical interest. Instead, choose plants of varying heights with more natural, spreading form.

A low-maintenance landscape. If you want to spend less time gardening, choose your plants accordingly. Go with easy-care ground covers instead of grass, for example, and select shrubs with appealing natural shapes that don't require constant grooming. Raising perennials will save you from sowing and planting anew each year. And remember that vegetable gardens and fruit trees are generally time-intensive propositions.

CONSTRUCTION

Take it slow. If you've just moved to a new or neglected property, don't plunge in right away—let the site grow on you. Take time to develop your plan and get acquainted with your yard. Go through a growing season to determine how existing plants look in the landscape. Then go to work, regrading if needed and pruning, relocating, or removing plants. Take samples of unknown specimens to a nursery or Cooperative Extension Service for identification.

Time it right. The best seasons for major landscaping work are fall and winter, when contractors are more available and the absence of vegetation gives a clear view of the terrain. But keep in mind that days are shorter and that bad weather may delay work.

Take it in stages. If you are overhauling your yard, have all the regrading work done at the same time—it will save money and time if the contractor brings heavy equipment only once. Then you can implement your plan in stages, working near the house first and moving out to the property edges.

Be ready for mud. Soil exposed from regrading can be messy—especially after a rain—so set down planks to use as walkways. If there is an exposed or newly seeded slope, have tarps handy when rain threatens.

Allow for soil compaction.  After it has been worked or moved, all soil—whether light or heavy—will compact to about 80 percent of its original volume. Always supplement the volume of soil when backfilling planting holes.

Stockpile topsoil in a safe place when construction begins. It is one of your garden's most valuable resources and can be reused in the same spot or used elsewhere when work is completed.

If your soil is poor, amend it with topsoil or compost during construction for long-term benefits. Add at least 12 inches for a lawn, 18 inches for a perennial bed, and 24 inches for a shrub border or hedge.

Save stones—even small ones. Use them to cover a path or make a drain, lay out a rock garden or build a wall. Store them in an out-of-the-way corner.

Protect trees from damage by construction equipment. Encircle their trunks with planks secured with ropes or bungee cords.
▷ **Japanese Gardens, Paths**

LANGUAGE OF FLOWERS

A Victorian custom. In the 19th century it was popular to imbue flowers with a variety of symbolic meanings, including sentiments and character traits. Blooms were arranged in bouquets, or "tussie-mussies," to convey a message about the sender of the bouquet or to its recipient. Some meanings are still well-known—rosemary for remembrance, for example—while others have become obscured with time.

Be creative. As a gift to a special friend, make a floral arrangement that expresses the sentiments you want to convey. Push the stems through a doily and tie in place with a ribbon. Attach a pretty card that translates the meaning of the flowers.

Bone up. Several books on the language of flowers are available, giving the history of this charming custom and ideas for using it. Check with a bookstore or library.

SAY IT WITH FLOWERS

The guide below is a sampling of the symbolic meanings of popular flowers and herbs. The interpretations often vary from place to place.

Azalea	Temperance
Basil	Love, hatred
Camellia	Excellence
Carnation	Fascination
Chrysanthemum	Longevity
Clematis	Mental beauty
Dahlia	Instability
Daisy	Innocence
Dill	Irresistibility
Forget-me-not	Remembrance
Gardenia	Ecstasy
Geranium	Melancholy
Gladiolus	Generosity
Iris	Good news
Hydrangea	Boastfulness
Jasmine	Separation
Lavender	Distrust
Lily	Majesty
Marigold	Grief
Mock orange	Deception
Narcissus	Egotism
Orange blossom	Chastity
Pansy	Fond memories
Parsley	Festivity
Red rose	Love, beauty
Rosemary	Remembrance
Sweet William	Gallantry
Thyme	Courage
White rose	Silence

LATIN NAMES

Be not afraid. Latin botanical names may seem complicated, but they simplify gardening, letting you identify plants precisely.

Learn the system. Latin names generally have two parts. First is the genus (a plant group), written with an initial capital letter and in italic type. Next is the species (a specific plant within a group), written usually with a small letter and in italic type. These may be followed by a cultivar name, with a capital letter, regular type, and single quotation marks. For example, the full name for the white crested iris is *Iris cristata* 'Alba,' while the pyramidal Chinese juniper is *Juniperus chinensis* 'Pyramidalis.'

Named after whom? The surname of the person who "discovered" a plant is often used for the species name and given a Latin suffix indicating possession: *-ii* or *-i* for a man and *-ae* for a woman. *Prunus sargentii,* or Sargent's cherry, was named for the dendrologist C.S. Sargent. *Phlox henryae,* the Henry phlox, was named for the botanist Mary Gibson Henry.

Latin endings. Latin suffixes such as *-ense, -ensis, -anum, -ana, -icus,* and *-ica* are often added to a plant's place of origin to form the species name. The China rose, for instance, is *Rosa chinensis,* while the German iris is *Iris germanica.* The endings *-issimus, -issima,* and *-issimum* indicate the superlative degree and are used in species names to describe a particular attribute. *Lonicera fragrantissima* (winter honeysuckle), for example, is exceptionally fragrant, while *Salix × elegantissima* (Thurlow weeping willow) is one of the most graceful specimens.

WHAT'S IN A NAME?

Latin words found in the species and cultivar names often serve to describe a plant trait.

Latin	Meaning
alba	White
aurea	Golden foliage
contorta	Twisted
edulis	Edible
elata	Tall
grandiflora	Large flowers
grandifolia	Large leaves
japonica	From Japan
lutea	Yellow
maculata	Spotted
nana	Dwarf
occidentalis	From the West
odorata	Scented
orientalis	From the East
pendula	Weeping
purpurea	Purple
racemosa	Flowers in racemes
repens	Creeping
rugosa	Wrinkled
scandens	Climbing
sempervirens	Evergreen
stricta	Upright
sylvestris	From the woods
tomentosa	Downy

LAUREL

A classic for containers. Laurel, also called bay laurel or sweet bay, is perfect for containers—whether grown as a shrub or as the classic bay tree. While it can grow to 30 feet, you can keep it clipped to any desired height and shear it into formal shapes. This

aromatic evergreen is hardy only to about 20°F, so place plants against a south-facing wall in spring and fall for extra warmth. In cold climates, overwinter plants indoors in a well-lit spot; in warm ones, bring them inside whenever frost threatens.

In the garden. Plant laurel in rich, well-drained soil in full sun to part shade and enjoy its beautiful branching habit and long, lustrous leaves; the yellow-green flowers and black fruits are inconspicuous. Although slow growing, it also makes a dense hedge. Protect from low temperatures by wrapping the tree in canvas and spreading dead leaves or straw at its base.

If the leaves drop from cold, prune off damaged growth. A well-established laurel will usually rebound, sending out new leaves when warm weather returns. If stems freeze, cut them off at the base and be patient; it can take up to 2 years for regrowth.

When to water. Keep young laurels well watered. Even though mature plants can take some drought, never let the roots dry out completely—even during winter dormancy. Many winter losses are due to a lack of moisture instead of cold.

Beware of scale, which look like flat white or brownish ovals on stems and leaves. If you find the pests at an early stage, wipe them off with a swab dipped in rubbing alcohol. For heavy infestations, treat with an insecticide. You can also use a dormant oil spray before growth begins in spring.
▷ **Bay Trees**

LAVENDER

Give lavender full sun and light, well-drained, slightly alkaline soil. Aid drainage in heavy soil by adding a layer of coarse sand or gravel to the base of the planting hole. Feed and water sparingly.

Soften hard edges. With its mounding, slightly sprawling habit, lavender is an excellent choice for softening hard structural lines. Plant it at the corners of buildings or steps, at the front or edges of raised beds, or along paths and terraces.

Pruning pointers. Lavender needs a good clipping to prevent legginess. In fall or early spring, remove the dead flower spikes and an inch of the top growth; shape to form a bushy silhouette. Unless the plant is overgrown, avoid cutting into old wood, which may not regenerate.

Harvest for drying either when the buds just open or when they're in full bloom. Dry in a cool, airy spot and strip the stems.

In the laundry. Put flowers in a handkerchief, tie tightly, and toss in the clothes dryer. Your clothes will emerge perfumed.

Sweet slumber. Lavender is a prime ingredient in potpourri and is especially nice combined with rose petals. Folklore holds that a little bag of dried blooms slipped inside the pillowcase will help you sleep. To make sachets, fill handkerchiefs or tea napkins with petals and tie with pretty ribbons.

Make a wand. Clip a bunch of blossoming sprigs about 6 inches long and tie the stems with ribbon. Use this "wand" to freshen closets and drawers or slip it behind the corner of a bathroom mirror.

A winter air freshener. Sprinkle dried stems in the fireplace. As they burn, they'll gently scent the air.

In the kitchen. Steep lavender flowers in honey and use as a sauce for ice cream and desserts. Add a sprig to the jar when putting up apple jelly. Place some in the sugar bowl and use to sweeten tea. Lavender is also part of the delectable French *herbes de Provence,* an herb blend for flavoring meat, poultry, and stew.

In the bath. Sprinkle lavender blooms in the tub or in a foot bath to soothe, scent, and refresh the skin.

❧ A LAVENDER SAMPLER ❧

True lavender (*Lavandula angustifolia*) is the most common and is beloved for its gray-green foliage and spiky flower heads with their characteristic blue-purple—that is, lavender—flowers. The cultivar 'Hidcote' boasts deep purple blooms, while 'Jean Davis' has pale pink ones; these and 'Munstead' are hardy to −10°F.

Other favorites are French lavender (*L. dentata*), with fringed leaves, and Spanish lavender (*L. stoechus*), which has purple bracts atop the stems instead of the usual spikes; try 'Atlas' or 'Otto Quast.' For exceptional fragrance, plant the hybrid *L.* × *intermedia* 'Provence.'

LAWNS

Should you start over? Many landscaping professionals evaluate a lawn based on this 50/50 rule of thumb: if more than half of your lawn is infested with weeds, invasive grasses, fungus, or other intractable problems, it's usually less work to completely re-establish the lawn than to do spot repairs.

Lawn alternatives. You may find it easier to substitute a ground cover for turfgrass— especially if your yard has steep slopes or deep shade. Ground covers don't need mowing or frequent weeding once they're established. And don't overlook a second alternative: a wildflower meadow!

PLANTING

Test your soil. Get your lawn off to a good start by determining what nutrients your soil needs. A soil test will also tell you whether you need to adjust your soil's pH.

Till the earth. Tilling to a depth of 4 to 6 inches not only lets you work fertilizers, amendments, and pH-adjusting materials into the soil but also aerates the ground so that grass roots can take better hold.

Use the rake. After tilling, rake the soil well to remove any rocks and debris and to create a smooth, level planting surface.

Seed, sod, or sprigs? You can plant a new lawn in one of three ways: sowing seed, laying sod, or installing sprigs. Whichever you choose, firm the soil after planting by pushing a roller over the surface: it aids seed germination and ensures that sod and sprigs make good contact with the soil.

How much to sow? The seeding rate depends on the grass species used—so make sure you follow the recommendations on the seed package. Use a drop spreader to ensure even distribution over large areas and sow half the seed in one direction, then sow the rest at right angles to the first.

A velvety expanse of green lawn is all the more inviting when dappled with sun and shade.

Seed care. Mist seeds lightly with water daily to keep them from drying out. Cover with a thin layer of straw to retain moisture and protect seeds from wind and pilfering birds. The mulch will disappear as the grass grows, adding nutrients when it decays.

Sodding your lawn is not a quick fix— the soil must be prepared just as carefully as for seed. Make sure the surface is level and the soil is moist to encourage rooting. Lay the strips in a staggered pattern so that the end seams don't form a straight line; make sure the pieces butt together tightly. On a slope, run the strips lengthwise across the face. Trim the lawn edges with a spade, using a board or garden hose as a guide.

Planting sprigs. Sprigs are usually sold by the bushel or square yard. Make sure they are cool and moist when you buy them. Then plant as soon as possible in rows set about 1 foot apart. Dig a 1- to 2-inch furrow in each row and insert the sprigs 4 to 6 inches apart. Then roll or tamp the soil and water them in immediately.

MAINTENANCE

Wait to fertilize. Wait 6 to 8 weeks after planting for the first application of fertilizer. Unless a soil test determines a specific nutrient deficiency, use a complete granular fertilizer.

Don't overfeed. Excessive fertilizing stimulates blade instead of root growth, promotes thatch buildup, and "addicts" the grass to nitrogen so that it requires ever-increasing doses. Feed just twice yearly with a slow-release fertilizer formulated for blade growth in spring and root growth in fall.

Good sources of slow-release nitrogen are sulfur-coated urea, resin-coated urea, and formaldehyde urea. These chemical fertilizers provide nutrition throughout the growing season and won't burn grass. Organic sources of nitrogen—cottonseed meal, fish meal, and blood meal, for example—work equally well on lawns.

A compost treat. Just as it does in your garden beds, compost works wonders on lawns. Spread ½ inch of screened or whole compost over the grass each spring or fall.

Give it air. Aerate your lawn in early spring every year—especially if the soil is heavy. While aerating "shoes" are available from some garden suppliers, a mechanical core aerator is more effective.

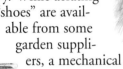

You can hire a lawn-care professional to do the job or rent a machine and do it yourself.

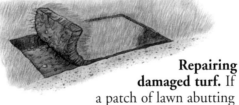

Another way to help your lawn thrive in heavy soil is to spread gypsum each spring; it lets grass roots penetrate more deeply and aids drainage. Depending on soil type, apply 4 to 5 pounds per 100 square feet with a spreader or by hand.

How much water? The basic rule: water heavily but infrequently. Your lawn needs about 1 inch of water per week during the growing season, either from rain or a sprinkler. After 24 hours, an inch of water soaks the soil to a depth of 4 to 6 inches in heavy soil and about 1 foot in sandy soil.

Water in the early morning so that the lawn can dry before sundown; grass that stays wet overnight is more prone to diseases. And never water in the heat of the afternoon, when moisture evaporates quickly.

A brown lawn may be caused by overzealous mowing instead of a lack of water. Recommended cutting heights vary by grass variety, but the general rule is to remove no more than one third of the blade.

Renovate an old lawn by overseeding in spring or fall. Mow the grass to about ½ inch and rake vigorously with a spring rake, removing thatch and weeds. Spread a layer of compost and sow seed at one and a half times the recommended rate for new lawns. Tamp to ensure soil contact, mulch, and mist to keep seeds moist.

Patch bare spots. Remove any dead grass and dig some compost into the soil. Rake smooth and at a level slightly higher than the surrounding lawn. Sow seed, then tamp with the back of a rake to ensure that the seed makes good contact with the soil. Mulch and keep moist until new grass sprouts.

Repairing damaged turf. If a patch of lawn abutting a path becomes ragged, cut out a section 1 or 2 feet square with the bare spot in one corner. Strip the sod out with a spade, turn it around, and reinstall it so the spot is in the opposite corner. Step on it to firm. Add a little soil to the bare patch to make it level, seed, and tamp to ensure seed contact with the soil. Mulch with straw and keep moist until new blades sprout.

▷ **Grass, Mowing, Watering**

▷ **Grass, Mowing, Watering**

LAWS

What's legal? Check to see what laws apply to your property. While many laws are created and enforced at the municipal level, county, state, and even Federal laws can also apply. Some housing developments also have sets of regulations for landscaping; check with the homeowners' association before making any alterations.

TREES

Forbidden species. In some areas, it's illegal to plant certain trees; they may be considered invasive, may attract nuisance wildlife, or may have been overplanted in the past.

Can you fell a tree? Some municipalities require you to obtain a permit before removing a tree.

Intrusive branches. It is often legal for you to prune the branches of a neighbor's tree that hang past your property line.

Unwelcome roots. If tree roots extend over a property line, they can often be pruned legally. But it's always wise to inform the tree's owner before taking action.

Falling fruit. Tree fruit belongs to the tree's owner. When it drops, however, it usually belongs to the owner of the yard it falls in.

Minimum setbacks may apply to trees or hedges planted near a street, a sidewalk, or your property line.

NOISE

Garden equipment, such as leaf blowers, chain saws, and lawn mowers, can be annoying, especially if several machines are operating at once. Some towns restrict the hours of operation, the number of machines that can be used, or the decibel rating. Separate laws may apply to homeowners and landscape professionals.

CONSTRUCTION

A building permit is needed for many garden structures. Even a deck may require one, depending on how high it will be off the ground; railings and steps may also have to conform to certain specifications. Check with your local building inspector.

Gazebos, sheds, and other outbuildings may require a permit if they're large, while smaller ones may not.

Fences and walls may or may not need a building permit, but there are often restrictions on their height, material, and style. Taller fences may be allowed in back and side yards, with only shorter ones permissible in the front.

Masonary structures, like barbecues and patios, are often exempt from legal control.

WATER

Wetlands over a certain size are often protected so that the diverse species living there won't be disturbed.

In arid regions, many communities have strict regulations about water use.

In the rest of the country, water restrictions usually apply only during times of drought.

Watering holes. You usually need to fence a swimming pool. And you should obtain a permit to divert a stream or add a pond—even for a small fish pool, depending on its depth.

PLANTS

Alien plants. Strict federal laws regulate the importation of plants to prevent the entry of pests and diseases. If you want to bring a plant back from your travels, check with government authorities—often found at the airport you're traveling from—well in advance of your departure date.

Check state restrictions. Many states outlaw certain plants. Minnesota, for example, has classified purple loosestrife as a noxious weed in wetland areas and forbidden its planting. If you're moving to a new state and want to take plants with you, check with the state's Department of Agriculture.

Endangered species. Plants growing in the wild may be protected by federal and state laws. It's usually best to leave them alone.

PESTICIDES

Landscape professionals usually need to be certified to apply pesticides, but homeowners do not. Professionals can purchase and apply restricted-use pesticides—which may be especially hazardous unless used with care—while homeowners cannot. The gardener must, however, follow all of the instructions listed on the pesticide label, which is technically a legal document.

LAYERING

Easy propagation. Layering involves burying a stem in soil to induce it to root while it's still attached to the parent plant. Spring is usually the best time for the job. There are several layering techniques, but in every case, choose a healthy stem that shows signs of recent vigorous growth.

The basics. Always strip foliage from the portion of the stem to be buried; otherwise the leaves will rot and slow down rooting. To aid root development, bruise the stem: either bend it to crack it slightly or make a shallow, 2-inch-long nick with a knife. Insert a toothpick to keep the wound open and dip in rooting hormone. Bury and always keep the soil moist. After the stem is well rooted, sever it and transplant.

Multiple layering. With some plants, such as evergreen azaleas and periwinkle, several stems can be layered at the same time. Bury about half the length of each stem in the soil; secure with stones or wire clips as needed.

Mound layering is particularly effective with shrubs. Before growth begins in spring, cut down all stems to a few inches above the ground to force new shoots. When the shoots reach 6 inches tall, cover half their height with a mound of soil and compost or peat; add more soil as they grow. Roots will form by fall.

For flexible stems—like those of honeysuckle or wisteria—use serpentine layering. Lay a stem along the soil and bury stripped portions under mounds; each one will root.

Air layering. If you can't bring the stem to the soil, bring soil to the stem with air layering. Make a slit on a branch between 6 and 18 inches from the tip; insert a matchstick to hold it open. Wrap a wad of moist sphagnum moss around the wound and cover with aluminum foil. Cover again with a plastic sleeve and tie the ends tightly. Check occasionally to see if the moss is still moist and roots have formed, which can take up to a year. Once roots are visible, cut the stem and soak the roots for a few hours before planting.

Strangle layering is a good technique for shrubs that are difficult to root. Tie a wire or nylon thread tightly around the section of the stem to be buried. In a few months, the stem's growth will create a fold where roots will form.
▷ **Propagation**

LEAVES

Learn your leaves. As the primary food factory for plants, leaves can indicate nutrient imbalances. Too little nitrogen, for example, turns leaves yellow, while excess potassium causes stunted growth. Learn to recognize the look of healthy leaves so that you can spot the onset of any problems.

Symptomatic signals. Leaves also indicate the presence of diseases and climatic damage, such as mildew, wilts, rusts, blights, scorch, drought, and frost exposure. Learn to read your leaves for symptoms.

Leaves are attacked by many insects, including leafminers, aphids, leaf rollers, leaf hoppers, scale, beetles, and caterpillars. Familiarize yourself with the damage they cause—like chewed leaves or discoloration—so that you can treat properly.

Pay attention to the various leaf forms and to leaf arrangement on the stem. Leaves help you identify plants and design pleasing plant combinations in the garden.

Cleaning up. An inevitable fall ritual is raking leaves. Since leaf burning has largely been outlawed, you'll need to decide on a disposal method. Some communities have special leaf-pickup requirements or a central leaf-composting site. The best solution is to use leaves for mulch or compost.

Easy composting. Fill black plastic bags with dead leaves; add a shovelful of soil and a handful of 10–10–10 fertilizer. Bounce the bags to mix and place in a sunny spot. In a few months you'll have rich compost.

Leaf mulch. Spread whole or shredded leaves over the soil as mulch, taking care not to pile them too close to plant stems.

Dig in. Turn dead leaves into the soil as a conditioner. Compost them first or add nitrogen fertilizer to the bed before planting.

Chop these first. Certain leaves are slow to rot. Sycamore leaves need up to five years, while oak leaves need three. Chop with a lawn mower, shredder, or string trimmer before using them as mulch or in compost.

Smoke out pests. Repel insects in a greenhouse by burning dead oak leaves in a large metal can punched with aeration holes.

Clean a pond. Tie a mesh screen over the tines of a pitchfork and use it to skim leaves from a pond. Or place plastic netting over the pond surface to catch leaves; lift it periodically to clean it off.
▷ **Compost, Mulch**

Once their autumnal show has played out, leaves can become a useful tool in the garden—and all for free.

LETTUCE

A cool customer. Lettuce prefers temperatures around 60°F to 65°F and bolts in the heat. It needs 6 hours of sun daily but likes a little afternoon shade to keep it cool.

To grow lettuce from seed, sow it ¼ inch deep in well-drained, moderately rich soil. Start heading types indoors about 6 weeks before you want to set them out; sow leaf lettuce outdoors 2 weeks before last frost.

Place indoor seed flats in the garage to sprout. The cool floor will hold them at the ideal temperature—about 65°F.

Hot-weather seeding. To help seeds germinate in high temperatures, sow them in a shallow trench early in the morning. Cover with soil, water in, and lay a plank over the row to protect seeds from sun. Leave the board in place until seedlings sprout, lifting it every morning to check on them.

Set out transplants 2 weeks before the last frost. Plant them 7 to 8 inches apart—you can measure with outspread fingers—and protect from cold with floating row covers.

⊱ A LETTUCE SAMPLER ⊰

Butterhead or Boston Loose heads with soft, buttery leaves. Try 'Buttercrunch,' 'Nancy,' 'Bibb,' or 'Gem.' Matures in 60–75 days.

Crisphead Cabbagelike heads with crisp, crunchy leaves. 'Iceberg' is the best known, but try 'Great Lakes' or 'Ithaca.' Matures in 75 days.

Looseleaf Spreading bunches of leaves; will grow back after harvest. Try 'Oakleaf,' 'Salad Bowl,' or 'Ruby Red.' Matures in 45–60 days.

Romaine or cos Long, narrow leaves form an upright head; good heat tolerance. Try 'Rosalita,' 'Apollo,' or 'Ballon.' Matures in 75+ days.

To inhibit bolting, wound the roots slightly to slow leaf growth. Use a spade with a sharp blade, piercing the soil and roots at an angle.

Water well. Lettuce needs constant moisture for good growth. If too much water washes away nutrients, turning leaves yellow, add some 15–10–10 fertilizer.

Rabbits and other creatures love lettuce. Fence in the rows with chicken wire or use a scent repellent to keep them away. Some gardeners swear by interplanting with marigolds.

Harvest heading lettuces by cutting plants at the base. With leaf lettuces you can pick the outer leaves when they are still young, which encourages inner ones to grow. You can also cut a young plant 1 inch above the ground—it will grow back in a few weeks.

Pick lettuce in the morning, when it is at its crispest. Eat the same day for best taste or store in the refrigerator for 2 weeks.

To ensure a constant supply of fresh lettuce, stagger your planting dates. Make successive plantings every 3 weeks until the weather turns warm.

▷ **Salad Greens, Vegetable Gardens**

LICHENS

Lichens consist of two organisms—a fungus and an alga—growing symbiotically on the surfaces of stones and trees. Found in many regions (even the frigid Arctic), they are used in medicine, dye, soap, and foods.

Only natural. If naturalistic is your gardening style, let lichens be. These colorful, interestingly shaped little plants add an appealing patina to walls, rocks, and trees.

Prevent lichens by rubbing tree trunks with horsetail rush *(Equisetum hyemale)*. While this treatment isn't foolproof, it helps discourage lichens from taking hold.

Remove lichens by scrubbing them with a stiff brush dipped in a solution of 2 tablespoons household bleach and 1 quart water. Make sure that the runoff doesn't come in contact with your garden plants.

LIGHTING

A spectacular effect. Illuminating a favorite specimen tree or shrub from below gives a whole new perspective on the garden at night. Simply direct a floodlight upward to highlight the comely shape of the branches and leaves. You can also use small uplights for garden statuary or a fountain.

Low-voltage lighting systems are available at many lighting and home stores. Using 25- to 75-watt bulbs, the lights are ideal for marking paths, steps, driveways, patio edges, and garden beds. The 12-volt system is powered through a transformer plugged into household current; it is economical, safe, and easy to install. Simply sink the spike ends of the fixtures in the soil and clip the fixture wires to the 12-volt line; you can bury the wires shallowly or hide them behind plants.

Designing a new garden? Consider traditional line-voltage lighting—the cables can be buried at a safe depth during construction. Make a plan first and let an electrician handle installation. Take photographs as work progresses so you'll be able to find the cables if you need to make repairs.

Don't overdo it. While light is needed for safety and beauty, leave some areas in shadow for contrast and an air of mystery.

Select fixtures that are inconspicuous— you want to see the light, not the lamps— and that are protected with a durable finish to withstand water, fertilizer, cold, and sun.

Match the light to the task. Floods and spots cast strong beams—good for uplighting and silhouetting. Spread lights cast a diffuse pool, which is preferred for illuminating walkways or highlighting a surface.

Cozy candlelight. Candles not only cast a soft glow but also draw fewer insects than light bulbs do. Protect the flame from wind with glass chimneys. Or use a pretty jar; weight the base with a flat stone and affix the candle with a few drops of wax.

Bulb color. The blue undertone in white light invites insects, whereas yellow light is less attractive. Bulbs with a red or pink tone make green plants look dull and lifeless; use a warm gold light instead.

LILACS

Combine with a climber. Plant a summer-flowering vine at the base of a lilac to add color once the lilac has finished bloomed. Try sweet pea, clematis, or passionflower.

A diverse plant. Along with the classic purple-blossomed lilacs, cultivated since the 1700's, are newer varieties, with white, pink, or blue flowers. Some lilacs are in tree form, while others are broad, mounding shrubs. All plants are fragrant and adaptable to various growing conditions.

Lilacs demand well-drained soil. If your site is wet, plant them in a mound so that surface water will drain off. They also need 5 hours of sun daily and an occasional dose of lime to keep soil slightly alkaline.

After planting, snip off the terminal buds and be patient: lilacs need a few years to establish and produce maximum blooms.

A blossom boost. Deadhead spent flowers immediately. Lilacs bloom on the previous year's wood, so cutting back after blossoming gives shrubs time to form new growth.

Painless deadheading. Clip plenty of bouquets for indoor arrangements—it will lessen deadheading chores and you'll have fragrant flower clusters to scent the house.

Prolong indoor blooming by smashing the woody stem ends with a hammer. This allows the lilacs to take up more water.

Lighten it up. Prune to allow both light and air to reach the plant. Remove all weak, dead, and damaged stems and thin out as needed.

To renovate an overgrown shrub, either cut the whole plant back to the ground or remove a third of the oldest stems each year over three years to promote new sprouts from the base. Conscientious annual pruning will make drastic measures unnecessary.

Look for white leaves. Lilacs are prone to powdery mildew in late summer, which covers foliage with white fuzz. Prevent the problem by pruning to promote air circulation. Also keep shrubs away from walls and reduce stress by watering and fertilizing regularly. Dust affected areas with sulfur.

Watch for suckers. If you're growing a hybrid grafted onto common lilac (*Syringia vulgaris*) rootstock, be sure to pull off any suckers as soon as they appear at the base.

Lilac borers attack older stems, tunneling into the bark and leaving a sawdustlike trail behind. Remove and destroy infected stems and spray plants with methoxychlor.

Increase your stock. In fall, propagate a favorite cultivar by grafting a lilac scion to a young privet or ash stem about the size of a pencil. Make a cleft at the top of the stem and insert a two-bud scion; bind and apply a grafting sealant. Bury the stem up to the grafting point in a partly shaded, sheltered spot and wait till roots form. Plant out the new tree while it's still young, burying the graft well.
▷ **Grafting, Shrubs, Suckers**

LILIES

The star of summer. Lilies are reliable summer performers, bringing color and fragrance to the garden when other flowers have faded. Keep beds blossoming through the season by selecting a variety of types.

PURCHASING
What to choose? Horticulturally, there are nine classes of lilies. One includes the species; the others the various hybrids: Asiatic, Aurelian and trumpet, and Oriental hybrids are the most available. The famous Madonna lily *(Lilium candidum)* and the Easter lily, hardy only in warm regions, are grown less today as hybrids gain favor.

Buy by bloom time. Asiatics and martagons bloom early—in June—followed by the Americans, Aurelians, and Orientals through August into September.

Buy flower form. Lily blooms can be shaped like trumpets, saucers, star bursts, or even tiny turbans, or "Turk's caps," with tightly reflexed petals. The flowers may face upwards, flare horizontally, or hang inverted in tiers from candelabra-like stems.

Buy by color. Flowers range from pure white to deep burgundy, with pastels and eye-popping hot hues in between. While some blooms are solid colored, many are freckled, spotted, or flushed.

Buy by use. Lilies lend themselves to various planting schemes besides the flower bed. Select dwarf types, such as the coral lily, for a rock garden and shade-tolerant specimens, like the meadow lily, for a woodland garden. Many hybrids are suited to containers and cutting gardens, as well as to shrub borders.

It's best to buy from mail-order suppliers and specialty growers who raise primarily bulbs. Lilies are sold in fall or early spring.

PLANTING
Their basic needs. Lilies like moist, loamy, slightly acidic soil. Pick a site with good air circulation, wind protection, and excellent drainage, to prevent rotting of the bulb.

Adjust the soil. If your soil is too heavy or light, dig very well-rotted manure, composted leaves, or other organic matter in the planting bed. Also work in some bonemeal or super-phosphate.

Plant deeply. Except for Madonna lilies, which are planted 1 inch deep, set bulbs three times as deep as they are tall. A 1-inch-tall bulb, for example, should be buried with its tip 3 inches below the soil surface.

When to plant. You can plant bulbs in fall or early spring. An exception is the Madonna lily, which goes in the ground in late August, before its rosette of leaves begins to grow.

➷ GOOD CHOICES FOR THE GARDEN ɭ

Lilies present a bewildering array of choices: there are some 80 species and hundreds of hybrids. The varieties below include examples from the largest, most popular hybrid classes and the species class.

ASIATIC HYBRIDS	Color	Flower Poise/Shape	Bloom time	Height
'Connecticut King'	vivid yellow/brown spots	upfacing/flat	late June	3'–4'
'Tiger Babies'	peach/chocolate spots	outfacing/recurved	late June–July	3'–4'
'Yolanda'	orange	upfacing	late June	3'–4'
TRUMPET AND AURELIAN HYBRIDS				
'Anaconda'	apricot/bronze flush	outfacing/trumpet	July–August	3'–4'
'Black Dragon'	white/purple flush	outfacing/ trumpet	July	5'–7'
'Moon Temple'	yellow	downfacing/ trumpet	July	5'–6'
'White Henryi'	white/orange	pendent	August	5'–6'
ORIENTAL HYBRIDS				
'Casa Blanca'	ice white	outfacing/recurved	August	4'–5'
'Journey's End'	crimson/white edging	outfacing/recurved	August	4'–5'
'Star Gazer'	deep red/maroon spots	upfacing/recurved	August	4'–5'
SPECIES				
L. auratum	white/gold band	outfacing/saucer	August–September	3'–5'
L. regale	white/yellow throat	downfacing/trumpet	June–July	3'–6'
L. speciosum	carmine/white edging	outfacing/reflexed	August–September	4'–6'

A tall order. Lilies range in height from 2 to 7 feet. Make sure you locate tall types in the back of the bed, where they won't block out shorter specimens and where the plants in front will hide their spent foliage.

Think in threes. For best effect, plant lilies in groups of three or more. Because of their tall, thin stems, lilies sometimes look awkward and bare when planted alone.

Add some friends. Underplant lilies with noncompeting companions, like primroses, violets, or baby's breath—these will keep lily roots cool and support thin lily stems.

MAINTENANCE

Keep lilies moist—but not soaked—until they bloom. Water less after they flower, but don't let bulbs dry out. To protect foliage from diseases, use a soaker hose to direct moisture to the roots, not the leaves.

Feed in spring, just as the "nose"—the asparaguslike shoot—appears. Gently scratch in a scant tablespoon of low-nitrogen fertilizer (5–10–10) around each plant, taking care not to injure the nose or shallow stem roots; water it in. Give the plants a light supplementary feeding just at bloom time.

To stake or not? Some gardeners prefer the look of a full-flowered stem nodding in the sun. But if you want to stake lilies, do so in spring, inserting a green metal or bamboo stake carefully by each stem so as not to injure the bulb. The stake should reach about 9 inches below the flowers. Tie in loosely with a figure-8 loop.

Warm head, cool feet. While lilies need sun to bloom, their roots must be kept cool and moist. Mulch with shredded bark, pine needles, leaf mold, or composted manure.

Once their flower heads unfold, lilies become the star attraction of the summer garden. Here the vibrant orange blossoms of the Asiatic hybrid 'Brandywine' shine against a backdrop of greenery.

Remove flower heads after blooming unless you want to collect seed. Cut the stem right beneath the blooms, leaving the stalk.

Off with their stalks! Cut off stalks after the foliage has withered completely. Doing so will help keep diseases at bay.

Seasonal protection. In cold climates, prevent frost heaves with a deep layer of straw, conifer needles, or chopped leaves. If shoots emerge prematurely in early spring, cover them with a cloche, basket, or other device. Work around the shoots gently—if you snap them off, you'll have no blooms.

Problems are few. Lilies are beset by only two serious diseases: lily virus, which is spread by aphids, and botrytis, a fungus that disfigures and kills foliage. To control aphids, water a systemic insecticide into the soil or spray plants with rotenone. To prevent botrytis, provide good air circulation around plants and spray with a fungicide every 2 weeks. Note that lilies are most susceptible to botrytis as they begin their early spring growth and their foliage is soft.

Cutting lilies. When cutting blooms for arrangements, leave at least one-third of the stem on the plant so that the foliage can replenish the bulb. Place right away in a vase of water; blooms will last a week or more.

A LITTLE HISTORY

Though less resilient than the new hybrid cultivars, the exquisite Madonna lily (*Lilium candidum*) remains the most fabled of lilies: it has been cultivated for 35 centuries. It was grown by the ancient Egyptians, while the Greeks valued it as an ornamental and a medicine—as did the Romans, whose soldiers carried bulbs of the fragrant flower throughout Europe. In the Middle Ages it was adopted as a Christian symbol; it was often included in paintings of the Virgin Mary to signify purity. Tended in medieval monastery gardens, it became a favorite among the English in the 1600's. Only in recent years has the Madonna lily been superseded by the more easily grown Asiatics and trumpets.

POTTED LILIES

Pot up in fall in a mix of 2 parts potting soil and 1 part pumice or vermiculite. Put a 1-inch layer in the bottom of the pot and set bulbs on top—close together but not touching. Fill the pot with soil and store in a cool place where bulbs won't freeze. In spring, move them outdoors into sun.

Pot considerations. Protect potted bulbs in hot weather by using light-colored pots, which absorb less heat than dark ones. To keep slugs out, set pots on wood blocks; air circulation will also be improved.

For the prettiest display, don't diversify—group only a single species or variety in each pot. Choose plants by their flowering time to achieve a sequence of bloom.

PROPAGATION

Propagate by scaling. Select a bulb with healthy, uninjured outer scales and detach them. Dust with fungicide and place in a plastic bag filled with damp peat or vermiculite; punch holes for ventilation. Store at 60°F to 70°F for 6 to 12 weeks. Once small bulblets have formed at the base of the scales and the roots are ½ inch long, place the bag in the refrigerator for 2 to 3 months. In spring, plant the scales with the bulblets attached in beds or pots. They will grow into bulbs big enough to bloom in 1 to 2 years.

Increase with bulblets. Most lilies form bulblets along the underground stem.

Gently detach them and plant in beds or pots to increase your stock.

A special case. The tiger lily (*L. lancifolium*) and some of its hybrids form beadlike bulbils in the leaf axils as well as bulblets underground. Harvest bulbils as flowers fade and plant in beds or pots.

Divide lilies only if they are overcrowded. Carefully lift the dormant clumps and separate the bulbs, planting each individually.
▷ **Bulbs, Flower Beds**

LIME

What's it for? Lime is most often used to add calcium to the soil. It raises soil pH, allowing gardeners with acidic soil to grow plants that need neutral or alkaline conditions. Lime also helps open up thick clay soil to water and air penetration and speeds decomposition of organic matter.

Do you need it? Some gardeners lime their lawns and garden beds annually, which is wasteful and can encourage weed growth. Have your soil tested; if the pH reading falls below 6.0, add 5 pounds of ordinary or dolomitic lime per 100 square feet.

Two necessary nutrients. If a soil test indicates a shortage of calcium and magnesium, apply dolomitic lime. Both nutrients are often deficient in sandy, acidic soils.

How to apply. Lime won't move upward in soil, so don't dig it in deeply. Apply by hand or spreader, then water in; use it in any season. Ordinary and dolomitic lime take 2 to 3 months to work, but the benefits last a few years. If you need to raise the pH drastically, make several applications over time, using no more than 5 pounds per 100 square feet at once.

A bad mix. Don't apply lime and manure to the same soil in the same year. Lime

interacts with the nitrogen in manure to release ammonia, which can damage plants.

Lime is caustic in all forms. Wear a dust mask and protective clothes when handling it and wash it immediately off your skin.

Dust plants with hydrated lime to fight pests and fungus. Apply with a coffee-can duster: punch small holes in the base, fill with lime, and cover the top with the plastic lid. To help it stick, shake lime over plants when their leaves are wet with dew.

In the fruit shed, sterilize the walls with hydrated lime. For a small room, apply a thick wash of lime and water with a brush. For a large room, strain a thin wash into a garden or paint sprayer.

The traditional way to protect fruit-tree trunks from heat and sun is to paint them with a thick wash of burnt lime and water. To make it last, heat the mixture and blend in a little flour.
▷ **Soil**

MAGNOLIA

The top two. Of the 80 species and hybrids, two are particular garden favorites. The Southern magnolia (*Magnolia grandiflora*), or bull bay, is a fixture in the Deep South. Growing to 80 feet tall, it features glossy evergreen leaves and fragrant, creamy-white, cuplike blossoms. The Japanese, or saucer, magnolia (*M. × soulangiana*) is a spreading deciduous tree that reaches about 25 feet. It flowers before the leaves appear, bearing elegant, tulip-shaped white blooms stained pink or rose-purple on the outside.

Other magnificent magnolias include the star magnolia (*M. stellata*), a shrubby type with double, starlike blossoms in white, pink, or rose. The sweet bay magnolia (*M. virginiana*) is a native that tolerates wet soil and shade and boasts a silvery felt on undersides of its leaves; its waxy white flowers are intensely fragrant.

Range of bloom. Species flower at various times from February to July, and the May-blooming Japanese type sometimes repeats in late summer. Select a magnolia that blossoms in the season of your choice.

Plant in spring. Magnolias tolerate movement only when their fleshy roots are growing—in spring. Transplant to the garden in March or April and never disturb the roots.

Planting pointers. Locate a magnolia in full sun; although many tolerate part shade,

they produce fewer blooms. Grow in deep, moist, slightly acidic soil and water new transplants regularly the first year. Prune lightly after flowering to maintain shape.

Brown blooms? The culprit may have been a late frost. Just remove the damaged blossoms and wait until next year. Avoid planting early-blooming types if spring cold snaps are prevalent in your area.

Rabbits like magnolias too. To keep these pests from nibbling the bark and destroying a young tree, wrap the trunk with a wire-mesh sleeve or a plastic collar.

Elbow room. Allow plenty of space for the graceful crowns to develop—especially with the large Southern magnolia. Keep trees at least 30 feet from your house, another tree, the road, a fence, or other structures.
▷ **Flowering Trees, Trees**

A potent perfume wafts from the voluptuous white flowers of the evergreen Southern magnolia.

MANURE

Raw vs. aged. Manure is invaluable as a soil builder and fertilizer, containing the three primary nutrients—nitrogen, phosphorus, and potassium. Some raw manure, like that of poultry, is so nitrogen-rich that it can burn plants; it may also harbor weed seeds. Let it age at least 6 months for "rotted" and a year for "well-rotted."

Where to get it? Ask at local farms, stables, or feedlots. City gardeners can check with a zoo. And don't forget to visit the circus—animal handlers are often happy to let you haul away manure. Make sure your source hasn't treated the manure with pesticides or the animals with medicines. Never use manure from pets. Alternatively, buy processed manure in bags at garden shops.

Aging manure. Put fresh manure in a pile and water it. Cover with a tarp to prevent nutrients from leaching out when it rains. Turn the pile occasionally to speed decomposition.

Heat it up. As manure decays it releases heat, which kills weed seeds. Measure the temperature at the center of the pile with a soil thermometer. If the reading is below 150° F, add water and a nitrogen source, such as soybean meal, and turn throughly into the pile.

Control odors. Add wood chips, sawdust, dead leaves, or another high-carbon material to aging manure, especially in summer. It will help alleviate the unpleasant smell.

Compost starter. Manure is a hardworking compost ingredient, helping to heat up the pile and speed decay. Just add a layer of raw manure to the other materials and turn in.

A three-year rotation. Enrich a third of your vegetable garden with rotted manure. In the first year, use the space for heavy feeders, like eggplant, cabbage, peppers, spinach, and squash. The next year, plant it with carrots, tomatoes, green beans, and other vegetables that need slightly less fertile soil. The third year, grow light feeders such as garlic, turnips, onions, and radishes.

A potent brew. Manure tea is a rich liquid fertilizer that gives plants a quick boost. Put a shovelful of raw manure in a permeable bag made of burlap or pantyhose, tie the top, and steep in a barrel or garbage can of water for a week. If you use it every time you water, dilute it by half. Use full strength to feed plants periodically, taking care not to let it splash on foliage.

Nitrogen content. Bird and bat guano are the "hottest" manures, with the highest nitrogen content. Rabbit, poultry, and sheep manures are a bit less hot, while those from cows, pigs, and horses are relatively "cold."
▷ **Composting, Fertilizer**

MAPLE

A rich diversity. With 110 species and countless varieties, the maple (*Acer* spp.) offers a range of trees and shrubs suited to various climates and soil conditions. They are grown as shade trees and for their beautiful leaf forms and brilliant fall colors.

Hedge maples (*A. campestre*), when planted in rows, make a good screen for hiding sheds and help to buffer noise.

With an almost unlimited number of growth habits and foliage colors, maples are a staple in the garden.

For a spectacular show, plant a red maple (*A. rubrum*), which boasts red flowers and fruits in spring and crimson leaves in fall. Try 'October Glory' or 'Red Sunset' for best autumn color. The 'Bonfire' sugar maple (*A. saccharum*) is also a good choice.

The delicate maple. One of the most graceful species is the Japanese maple (*A. palmatum*) and its cousin, the Japanese threadleaf (*A. p.* var. *dissectum*). These form spreading mounds of lacy foliage that needs protection from sunscald and drying winds. Plant in partial shade and keep soil moist; in extreme heat, shield with a row cover.

An invasive type. Though fast-growing and tolerant of pollution, Norway maples (*A. platanoides*) can become a nuisance. It self-sows freely and its roots are rampant. Give them space for the roots to spread pull up suckers as soon as they emerge.

The weaker species. While most trees have strong wood, the fast-growing silver maple (*A. saccharinum*) and box elder (*A. negundo*) are weak and brittle, and are easily torn apart by wind and ice buildup. Don't plant them too close to buildings or roads.

Feed maples annually with a high-nitrogen fertilizer and keep well watered in dry spells, irrigating deeply every 2 weeks.

Prune maple trees to develop a central leader and graceful branch angles. Prune only in late summer—otherwise trees will bleed profusely and create a mess.

What grows at its feet? Not much. Maples are shallow rooted and many—especially the sugar maple—have dense canopies. If you want to fill in around the base, plant euonymus, pachysandra, or periwinkle.
▷ **Trees, Unusual Plants**

MARIGOLDS

A summer staple. With blooms ranging from white to orange to burgundy, marigolds bring bright color and ruffly shapes to the summer garden. They are one of the most carefree annuals, performing well from seed or transplants in a warm, sunny spot and any well-drained soil.

Know their place. The compact signet marigold and the mid-size French types are suited to bed edgings and containers. The taller African marigolds are best for the back of the border or for a cutting garden.

Color combos. When planting different solid-color marigolds, mix in a few with bi-colored blooms to tie the scheme together.

Start seed indoors no more than 4 weeks before you want to set plants out. Otherwise the seedlings may become leggy.

Sow seed directly outdoors once the soil has warmed to near 70°F. Sow in shallow trenches and cover with ½ inch of soil. Keep moist; seedlings should sprout in about 2 weeks.

Water marigolds often until they are well established, then water only weekly if rainfall is inadequate.

Start pinching out blooms when they first appear to promote budding and a bushy shape. Deadhead and keep pinching until frost to keep marigolds flowering heavily.

A LITTLE HISTORY

French and African marigolds are actually mis-named. Marigolds are native to the American Southwest and to Central and South America. In the 1500s, marigold seeds were taken by Spanish explorers from the Americas to Spain. From there, seeds were transported to France and parts of northern Africa, where the taller types eventually became naturalized.

❈⊱ A MARIGOLD SAMPLER ⊰❈

African marigolds grow to 3 feet tall and have tight pompom blooms up to 4 inches in white, gold, or orange. Try the huge 'Climax' hybrids.

French types grow up to 1½ feet and have more open flowers. Try 'Golden Gate,' 'Queen Sophia,' or 'Naughty Marietta.'

Triploid hybrids are a cross between French and African marigolds. Because they are sterile, none of their energy goes into seed production—resulting in vigorous blooms. Try 'Fireworks' or 'Nugget.'

Signet marigolds form low clumps with lacy foliage and dainty 1-inch raylike flowers; the blooms are edible. Try 'Lemon Gem,' 'Golden Gem,' 'Starfire,' or 'Paprika.'

Prevent tipping. With their large pompom blooms, African varieties can tip over from their own weight. Instead of staking each plant, try deep planting. Strip the leaves from the bottom 3 to 4 inches of the stem, dig a deep hole, and set in the plant with the stripped portion below the soil line.

More stripping. Marigold foliage rots quickly in water. When preparing cut flowers for an arrangement, always be sure to strip off all the leaves.

Give it a try. While there is no guarantee that the roots of French marigolds will kill or repel nematodes, plant the flowers in your vegetable bed anyway. They attract hoverflies, which attack aphids, and they make any garden a more pleasant place.
▷ **Flower Beds**

MEALYBUGS

Mealybugs love houseplants, as well as certain fruits, vegetables, and shrubs. If you see small pink insects or white, cottony masses on leaf axils, the plant is infested. Always isolate newly purchased plants to ensure they are free of these common pests.

Remove them from houseplants with a cotton swab dipped in a mixture of water and vinegar or rubbing alcohol. Or wipe down the leaves with a sponge soaked in soapy water.

Outdoors, let the ladybug known as the mealybug destoyer (*Cryptolaemus montrouzieri*) prey on them. You can also spray plants with insecticidal soap or malathion.

Root mealybugs attack lettuce, cactus, and houseplants underground. Drench soil with diazinon or lift the plant, cut off the roots, and reroot in a soilless potting mix.

Sooty mold is a blackish fungus that grows on the sticky gel exuded by mealybugs. Wipe away the mold with soapy water or spray with a stream of water, then spray with fungicide.
▷ **Pesticides**

MEASURING

Two tools in one. Graduate the blade of a spade or shovel in 2-inch increments with indelible ink and use the marks as a ruler when you need to dig to a specific depth.

A handy yardstick. Mark the shaft of a shovel, rake, or other long-handled tool every 4 inches with indelible ink. When you need to figure spacing between plants, just lay it on the ground.

Measure quantities of pesticide or other chemicals with a set of plastic measuring spoons and cups reserved for garden use. Remember the following formulas: 2 tablespoons equal ⅛ cup or 1 ounce; 4 tablespoons equal ¼ cup; 5⅓ tablespoons equal ⅓ cup; 8 tablespoons equal ½ cup; and 16 tablespoons equal 1 cup or ½ pint.

Fertilizer featherweights. A pinch weighs about 0.1 ounce. A level spoonful of a granular fertilizer weighs 0.4 ounce, while a handful weighs about 1.75 ounces.

A watering can holds between 2 and 3½ gallons. Buy one with gradations marked on the side—it will make it easier to measure water when mixing soluble fertilizers.

Wheelbarrows generally have a capacity between 4 and 8 cubic feet. A 4-cubic-foot

---

THE BODY AS MEASURING TOOL

Your own body can help you make approximate measurements in a pinch.

▷ The length from the tip of a finger to the first knuckle is about 1 inch.

▷ The width of the index, middle, and ring fingers together is 2 to 2¾ inches at the second (middle) knuckle.

▷ The length of an index finger is about 2⅜ to 3½ inches.

▷ Spreading the hand fully gives you about 7⅞ to 9 inches from the tip of the little finger to the end of the thumb.

▷ A regular step covers 26 inches. Lengthen the pace, and you'll cover about 40 inches.

▷ If you extend one arm, the length between the tips of the fingers to the opposite shoulder is about 45 inches. If you raise both arms, you'll have 60 inches from hand to hand.

---

wheelbarrow will hold enough soil for you to fill about 30 1-gallon pots.

Water annuals by the yard. A square yard of annuals needs about 1.2 gallons of water daily—and as much as 5 gallons in hot, dry weather.

Sizing up the garden. Because the application rate for most fertilizers and soil amendments is based on 100 square feet, you will simplify gardening by making your beds and lawn a fraction of that measurement. For instance, if a bed is 5 feet x 5 feet, or 25 square feet, use one quarter of the recommended quantity for 100 square feet.

MELONS

Tip down. The seeds of all melons—watermelons, cantaloupes, and honeydews —sprout best when planted with their pointy tips facing down.

For a head start, sow seed indoors 4 to 6 weeks before last frost. Bury three seeds ½ inch deep in 3-inch pots filled with compost and sandy soil; keep moist and warm, at about 70°F. Thin to one sprout per pot and plant out 2 weeks after last frost.

Sow outdoors when the soil temperature reaches 70°F. Sow in hills, using five seeds per hill and thinning to two or three. Leave 3 feet between hills; allow 6 feet between rows for watermelon and 3 feet for all other types. Soil should be loose, loamy, and well drained; add a few shovelfuls of rotted manure or compost per hill.

Warm them up. Plant melons in the sunniest spot and cover with a floating row cover, which both protects against cold snaps and thwarts pests. Remove the covers once

---

plants flower so that pollinating insects can do their work and you'll have a crop.

Keep melons off the soil to prevent rot. Slip a board or flat tile underneath the fruits once they reach the size of an orange. Heat-absorbing tiles will also provide extra warmth in cool climates.

Mulch, don't weed. Because working around vines may disturb the transmission of nutrients to the fruits, stop weeding once the vines begin to sprawl. Just spread a heavy layer of straw around plants; it will adequately suppress weeds.

For the best fruits, allow only four or five melons to ripen on each plant. Cut off all the other young fruits; you can pickle those that have reached the size of a nut.

Give melons 1 inch of water weekly until 3 weeks before harvest; then withhold moisture to help concentrate the sugars.

Is it ripe? Press against the blossom end (not the end with the stem). It will give slightly and smell sweet when the fruit is ripe. Or you can knock against a watermelon with your knuckles; a ripe one will sound hollow.

✂ A MELON SAMPLER ✂

The cantaloupe, a type of muskmelon, is the most widely grown. For short-season regions, try 'Delicious' or 'Earli-Sweet.' In areas with long summers, grow 'Ambrosia' or a cantaloupe cousin, such as the Persian or crenshaw.
As for honeydews, try 'Rocky Sweet Hybrid,' 'Limelight,' or 'Snow Charm.' Among the best watermelons are 'Sugar Baby,' a small, round melon with crimson fruit, and the yellow-fleshed 'Yellow Baby' or 'Sunshine.'

▷ **Vegetable Gardens**

METEOROLOGICAL EQUIPMENT

Do it yourself. Always rely on your own temperature readings. Published or televised reports may bear little relevance to the weather of your locale or microclimate.

Where to put a thermometer? For the most accurate readings, put it in the shade.

Frost warnings. A thermometer set 5 feet above the ground can show a temperature up to 15°F higher than that at ground level. So, if the temperature reads 45°F, be aware that frost may strike overnight.

Use a rain gauge to measure precipitation levels accurately. Improvise with a simple homemade version. Cut off the top third of a large plastic bottle. Slide the top upside down into the bottle base to act as a funnel; tape the edges together. Mark off the measuring scale with narrow strips of waterproof tape or indelible ink, making the lines ¼ inch apart. If the bottle has the opaque plastic base common to many large soft-drink bottles, fill the base with water before setting the gauge outside. When it rains, check how far up the scale the water has risen. Note the amount, empty, and refill the base with water.

An ingenious tool. Use a maximum-minimum thermometer, available through specialty catalogs and some garden centers, to determine your garden's microclimates. With two separate gauges, it records the highest and lowest temperatures of a certain spot in a given time period. To see if a site for a new apple tree lies in a frost pocket, for example, place the thermometer there for 2 days. As the temperature rises, a red marker on one side moves upward and will remain stuck at the highest reading. A marker on the other side works the same way, registering the lowest temperature. To use again, press the reset button. The tool comes in handy in greenhouses or when checking the suitability of windowsills for houseplants.

Predict the weather with a trusty barometer, which gauges atmospheric-pressure levels. Note that it is not the actual reading that matters but how the reading changes over time. An example: if pressure levels drop rapidly, expect unstable weather.
▷ **Frost, Wind**

MINT

Plant mint in rich, moist, cool soil in part shade. In addition to peppermint and spearmint, add lesser-known types for variety and extra fragrance. Apple mint has downy foliage, orange mint emits a citrusy aroma, and the white-rimmed leaves of pineapple mint smell fruity-sweet.

A rambunctious grower, mint can quickly become invasive. To contain the roots, plant mint in a large pot and bury it, setting the rim slightly below the soil line. Or sink plastic edging strips 1 foot deep around the roots.

Corsican mint (*Mentha requienii*) is one mint that gardeners let creep to its content. With tiny—⅛-inch—leaves and whorls of lavender flowers in summer, this fast-growing species provides a peppermint-scented ground cover in warm areas. Use it to fill in around stepping stones or tuck it in a wall.

Snip away. Clip off young shoots regularly to promote bushiness. Prune established plants especially hard to stimulate growth of tender leaves.

Harvest mint until a few weeks before the first frost of fall. It has countless culinary uses—for teas, jellies, garnishes, marinades, salads, and, of course, juleps.

A fragrant repellent. Plant mint near entrances to your house—it will prevent ants from coming in. In the pantry, keep insects from invading jars of seeds, beans, and rice by placing a few stems of dried mint inside.

A mint cocktail. Drive aphids and caterpillars from the garden with a homemade pesticide. In a blender, mix 8 ounces of mint leaves with 1 quart water. Strain and spray on plants; repeat every 10 days.
▷ **Herbs, Invasive Plants**

MISTLETOE

A pretty pest. Christmas wouldn't be complete without this native plant, a traditional green used in kissing balls and other decorations. But mistletoe (*Phoradendron* spp.) is an invasive parasite that sucks the sap from its host tree, causing weakness or death. To get rid of it, pull or cut it out, removing all roots. Do it early—the smaller the plant, the easier the removal.

Be cautious. Mistletoe stems, leaves, and berries are all poisonous and should be considered dangerous. If you use the plant in holiday decorations, keep it away from children by hanging it from a doorway or ceiling.

To grow mistletoe, start by selecting a host tree that is at least 20 years old. Collect ripe white berries from mistletoe that is already growing on another tree of the same variety as your host. Find a branch on the host that is 5 feet off the ground and about 6 inches in diameter; smash the berries against the branch's underside. The sticky pulp will harden and help seeds adhere to the bark. After seeds have germinated, they will sprout and eventually invade the host.

MOLES

Moles can wreak havoc. While they don't eat vegetation, their constant tunneling for insects and worms mar your lawn and garden and upheave roots and seedlings.

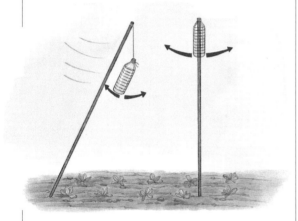

Good vibrations. Moles are sensitive to sound vibrations. Repel them by leaving a radio playing or using one of the commercial devices sold at garden centers. Or make your own: plant 5-foot metal stakes by the tunnels and attach empty plastic bottles to their tops so that they knock about in the wind. You can also insert a child's pinwheel into a mole run every 10 feet or so.

MOLES HAVE THEIR GOOD POINTS

Though a nuisance when they disturb seed beds and tunnel through the lawn, moles help maintain ecological balance in the garden. It is true, unfortunately, that moles eat soil-enriching earthworms. But they also feed on many unwelcome garden visitors, such as beetle grubs, wireworms, cutworms, and other larvae. In addition, the mole's tunneling aids in aerating the soil and in draining damp earth.

Scavenge soil from molehills for your seed beds and pots. It's light, aerated, rich, and as effective as any commercial potting mix.

Two repellent plants. Site the mole plant *(Euphorbia lathyris)* near tunnels to deter moles. The castor bean plant *(Ricinus communis)* also works, but be forewarned: since it is toxic to humans, never put a plant where it would be accessible to children.

An odoriferous cure. Place a few scoops of used clay kitty litter in the tunnel. Once the odor alerts moles that their territory has been invaded, they will disperse quickly.

Destroy their food source. Apply milky-spore disease or beneficial nematodes to the soil to kill grubs, cutworms, and mole crickets—all staples in the mole's diet.

To repair mole damage to the lawn, walk over the tunnels to press the grass roots back into the soil, then water in.
▷ **Rodents**

MOON

Gardening by the moon. Gardeners have for centuries been guided by the phases of the moon and its position in the sky as it passes across the constellations. "Moon signers," as they're known, hold that results are enhanced when planting and other tasks are done under a fruitful "sign."

Astrologically inclined? If you want to give moon gardening a try, refer to yearly almanacs or look for books on the subject; you'll often find them listed in specialty

Enthusiasts claim that gardening "with the moon"—planting, sowing, and carrying out other tasks according to the moon's phases and the constellations—pushes plants to their optimum performance in the garden.

catalogs or advertised in organic gardening or astrology magazines.

Be realistic. Don't "plant by the signs" and expect a miracle. Gardeners should always observe the basic rules of cultivation.

Plant aboveground crops when the moon is waxing (increasing) to make them more vigorous. Plant bulbs and root crops when the moon is waning (decreasing).

Pruning fruit trees while the moon is waxing is said to wake up the buds. So, in late winter, wait to prune until the moon is waning instead—there will be fewer buds exposed to potential frost damage.

Graft plants in winter when the moon is waxing to ensure vigorous bud growth. In summer, graft when the moon is waning.

MOSQUITOES

Their breeding ground. Mosquito eggs, larvae, and pupae all need water; only the adult is nonaquatic. If you eliminate all sources of still water near your house, you can reduce the number of young mosquitoes that develop into biting adults.

Repair, remove, or cover. Fix or get rid of any receptacle that holds stagnant water, such as a gutter that doesn't drain properly or a rain barrel you are no longer using. Also cover any receptacle that hold water permanently, including wells and cisterns.

Drain tree trunks. Remove water that pools in the holes of large tree trunks—a perfect mosquito breeding ground. An alternative is to coat the water surface with a small amount of vegetable oil to smother any developing larvae.

Don't forget these. Change the water in birdbaths at least once a week. And always empty children's plastic wading pools when they are not in use.

Dump the eggs. Don't let water sit too long in the saucers under potted plants after a rain or watering—adults may lay eggs there. Empty and rinse them out.

Cover rain barrels and other water receptacles with a custom lid. Attach a fine screen—with 14 to 18 wires per inch—to a removable frame sized to fit the container opening securely. Rainwater will pass through the screen easily but mosquitoes won't be able to reach the water surface to breed.

Sassafras and sweet basil are said to keep mosquitoes away. Plant them near house windows and doors or around patio edges.

Plant eucalyptus. Besides repelling mosquitos with their scent, eucalyptus trees take in a lot of water and can help dry up boggy areas where mosquitoes breed.

Stock your pond. Goldfish can be the perfect ally in the war against mosquitoes. But avoid mixing fish of different species and sizes in the same pond so that they will feed on insects instead of each other.

Dining outdoors? Mosquitoes are drawn to lights—especially, it seems, those illumi-

nating your patio or picnic table. Locate floodlights away from outdoor living spaces and use yellow bulbs, which attract fewer insects than white ones. On the table, use oil lamps, citronella candles, or wax candles; mosquitoes will either be repelled by the scent or zero in on the flame and die.

Homemade repellents. Steep pennyroyal or fleabane leaves in hot water and let sit for a few days. Strain this insecticidal tea into a spray bottle and squirt on plants around living areas. Or try garlic oil: simmer several cloves of garlic in cooking oil for about an hour. Cool, strain, and spray.
▷ **Pesticides**

MOSS

Blessing or curse? The fuzzy green plants that grow on lawns, trees, and stones can either be a pest or the start of a new type of garden, depending on your point of view.

A big family. There are about 23,000 different true mosses. Besides the common types you'll find in your yard or the woods, the best known is sphagnum moss, which grows in bogs. Partly decayed sphagnum moss is called peat moss. Spanish moss (*Tillandsia usneoides*), a tropical plant often seen hanging from trees, is not a relative.

ELIMINATION

Moss growing on your lawn indicates poor drainage, infertile or compacted soil, excessive soil acidity, or shade. Given the right conditions, including sufficient moisture, moss will also grow on tree trunks, clay pots, wood doors and shingles, and masonry paths, walls, and patios.

Correct conditions to make your yard less attractive to moss. Increase soil fertility with nitrogen and decrease acidity with lime. Aerate to combat soil compaction. Eliminate dampness by installing drainage tiles or dry wells and watering less. Remove or prune trees and shrubs that cast shade to admit more sunlight.

Banish moss. Treat moss on lawns, patios, decks, and other areas with a commercial eradicant that has a zinc, copper, or soap (fatty acid) base. Make sure the product won't stain wood, masonry, or plastic.

Up on the roof. Moss can thrive on wooden or slate shingles. Scrape away as much as possible or wash it away with a strong jet of water. Then treat with a commercial moss killer or ¼ to ½ ounce copper sulfate in 10 gallons water. Be careful near metal flashing, gutters, and downspouts, since many products are corrosive to metal.

Scrub moss from tree trunks with a stiff brush. But be careful not to damage the bark.

USAGE

Grow a moss lawn. Turn a moist, shady spot into a moss lawn—it's relatively resilient, evergreen, velvety to the touch, and low maintenance. A bonus: moss will often grow where grass will not.

Sour the soil to a pH of 5.5 to encourage moss growth. Use sulfur, aluminum sulfate, or ferrous sulfate on either bare soil or grass. These chemicals will kill grass, so just rake it up and add it to the compost.

If moss is present in the area, just be patient. Moss spores will blow in and establish themselves; it takes about three years for a "lawn" to fill in completely.

Transplant moss by lifting it gently with a sharp spade and relocating it to the desired spot. Press it firmly into the soil and mist lightly for the first two weeks.

Tuck moss between rocks to soften their edges. For added color, grow wildflowers in the moss— an ideal growing medium. Roll seeds in a bit of soil and press into a patch of moss. Put the moss between the rocks and mist to keep moist. Try foamflower, bloodroot, trillium, golden star, American columbine, violets, and creeping or wild blue phlox.

To encourage moss on a stone wall, spray the wall with a solution of 1 quart buttermilk in 1 gallon water. Or mix 1 quart buttermilk with 1 tablespoon corn syrup and 2 cups moss in a blender; pour or paint on the slurry wherever you want moss to grow.

Give a mossy patina to masonry planters, fountains, or walls. Combine 12 ounces of beer and ½ teaspoon of sugar in a bucket with a few patches of moss; purée with a hand mixer. Spread the slurry ¼ inch thick on the surface and wait for moss to develop.

A moss path is a soft, colorful addition to a woodland garden. Just acidify the soil and wait for moss spores to blow in, or transplant moss patches.

Moss maintenance. It's easy: don't fertilize or water. If you need to weed, do so after a rain, when the soil is loose. Hold the moss down with one hand and gently pull up or cut out the weeds with the other.

Don't let leaves pile up in fall or moss will decay beneath them. Use a broom (not a rake) to sweep them up. Or spread fine-mesh netting over the moss in early fall to collect leaves. Once trees are bare, roll up the netting and add the contents to the compost pile.

Sphagnum moss, which holds 20 times its own weight of water, has numerous roles in gardening. It's used in plant propagation and as a medium for sowing seeds. It makes an ideal liner for hanging baskets or base layer for terrariums. You can also use it to insulate a potted plant, protecting it from temperature extremes and keeping it moist. Line a large pot with sphagnum moss and place a smaller potted plant inside it.

▷ **Cut Flowers, Hanging Baskets**

MOTHS

The adult moths that gather around lights on summer evenings are not the gardener's nemesis—they feed primarily on nectar and do little damage. It is the moth larvae that chew on, bore into, and roll themselves up in plants—whether leaves, fruits, stems, or roots. The larvae, which are called caterpillars or worms, represent the second stage in the insect's life cycle, and they feed heartily to store energy for their development in the cocoon and eventual metamorphosis into winged adults.

Not all are harmful. Many moth species cause little damage and should be left alone. Also keep in mind that some caterpillars turn into butterflies. So be sure to correctly identify any larva you might encounter before destroying it.

ATTACK OF THE GYPSY MOTHS

In 1868 a professor returned to America from France clutching a package. Inside were a handful of gypsy moth caterpillars in a cage—the raw materials for the professor's dream of breeding a hybrid to make silk. Soon thereafter, wind blew open the cage, and the caterpillars escaped. Within a decade they were chomping a swath through oaks, apples, birch, and other favorite hosts, infesting millions of acres. The larvae are so destructive that they can defoliate a tree in two weeks. Numerous attempts have been made since the early 1900's to eradicate gypsy moths—with everything from DDT to beneficial insects—but they remain a serious pest.

You can often spot their brown egg clusters on tree bark or see—and hear—the caterpillars, which are spotted blue and red, feeding in early summer. Adults emerge in July; males are brown and females white. Larvae can be controlled with burlap barriers wrapped around tree trunks or by spraying Bt (*Bacillius thuringiensis*) every 14 days from April to June. Egg masses can be scraped into a pail of kerosene.

The worst pests on garden plants? Gypsy moths, webworms, leaf miners, budworms, and bagworms. Watch for codling moths, cankerworms, and leaf rollers on fruit; cutworms, borers, tomato hornworms, and cabbage loopers prefer vegetables. You can control moths as eggs, larvae, or adults.

Pheromone traps, which lure adults with scent, work in two ways. They capture moths in a sticky substance and also alert you when the pests are active; you can then time spraying to kill eggs or larvae. Just hang traps from trees likely to be infested.

Trick codling moths, whose larvae attack fruits, with fake apples. Save your burned-out light bulbs, paint them bright red, and cover with petroleum jelly. Hang them in fruit trees—the moths will be lured to these "fruits," get stuck, and perish.

A good bacteria. Bt (*Bacillus thuringiensis*) is effective not only against gypsy moth larvae but also bagworms, cabbage loopers, codling moths, and tent caterpillars.

Control larvae of codling moths, gypsy moths, and others with barriers that trap caterpillars as they crawl down trees. Tie a 6-inch strip of burlap around a trunk tightly with twine. Check under the fabric regularly and destroy any pests you find.

Squash them. You can control many moth larvae simply by picking them off plants and squashing them or dropping them in a pail of soapy water. Because some larvae have stinging hairs, be sure to wear gloves.

Hardworking wasps. Trichogramma wasps are beneficial insects that parasitize many moth eggs, including those that turn into armyworms and cutworms. Release wasp larvae in June when moths are laying eggs.

Woodpeckers will pick out eggs of codling moths and others from tree bark. Attract them to your yard in winter by hanging a feeder with suet and seeds in affected trees.

▷ **Butterflies, Caterpillars, Grubs & Larvae**

MOWING

Plan ahead. If you're designing a landscape from scratch, take this essential lawn-care chore into account. Decide on how much lawn you're willing to mow, then plan features to make mowing easier. For instance, design the lawn in a fairly symmetrical rectangle or oval. Locate benches and flower beds around lawn edges. If you plant trees on the lawn, select those with high branching so that you can mow beneath them.

Take a third. Remove only the top third of the leaf blade each time you mow. If the recommended height for your type of grass is 2 inches, mow when it reaches 3 inches.

When mowing a slope, always cut perpendicular to the incline. Straining to push a walk-behind mower uphill and restraining it on the downhill is not only exhausting but dangerous as well.

Don't mow when grass is damp with dew or from a watering or rain. The cuts will be uneven and clippings will clump up, forming clods that will smother the lawn. Wet grass can also clog the mower and makes a soggy mess around the mower blade.

Mow grass higher when it's stressed—whether from heat or drought. Taller grass blades encourage deeper roots and keep plant crowns cool. Cutting too short weakens the plant's resistance to disease and allows weed seeds to germinate by letting more light penetrate to the soil.

⚜ CHOOSE THE RIGHT MOWER ⚜

WALK-BEHIND MOWERS	Features	Surface to Be Cut
Push reel mower	Blades on a revolving reel give a precise cut. Requires no energy—except your own; is nonpolluting, low maintenance, quiet, and economical. Cut: 14–18 inches.	Lawns of a few square feet to ¼ acre. Good for fine-bladed grasses; hard to use in tall grass.
Rotary mower	The basic power mower, with one rotating blade; runs on gas or electricity. Models available with a rear or side bagger or a mulching mechanism. Cut: 18–24 inches.	Relatively flat lawns of ¼ to ½ acre. Better than reel mowers for coarse-bladed grasses.
Self-propelled rotary mower	Motor drives two wheels as well as the blade for ease of operation. Heavier and costlier than standard rotary mowers, but has similar features. Cut: 18–24 inches.	Flat lawns of ½ to 1 acre or on smaller lawns that are hilly.
VEHICULAR MOWERS		
Riding mower	Smallest type, with 6–12 horsepower mid- or rear-mounted engine and center or front mower deck with two or three rotary blades. Some with rear bagger. Cut: 25–36 inches	Lawns of ¾ acre or more or on smaller lawns if you want or need the convenience of riding.
Lawn tractor	Has front-mounted engine of 12–15 horsepower and center mower deck. Runs on gas, diesel, or battery. Cut: 36–42 inches.	Hilly lawns of several acres or more. Hard to use on small lawns.
Garden tractor	Has front-mounted 15–30 horsepower engine; mower towed at rear. Attachments for tilling, aerating, and other tasks. Cut: to 60 inches.	Estate-size lawns and the roughest terrain.

Mow grass shorter in spring, when the weather is cool and plants are growing. Keep shaded grass a bit shorter to stimulate growth. And make your final cutting of the season about ½ inch shorter than usual.

Provide a strip. Make it easy to maneuver the mower at lawn edges by cutting a turning strip first—either at both short ends of a rectangular lawn or all along the perimeter of an irregularly shaped one. You can also lay a strip of bricks at grade level along bed edges for the mower wheels to ride on.

Don't get stuck in a rut. Change the direction you travel with the mower every time you cut to prevent soil compaction and visible wear patterns.

Double duty. If the grass gets too long—when you're away on vacation or during prolonged rainy periods—mow twice. Adjust the mower blade to the highest setting for the first pass; cut again a few days later with the blade lowered.

Don't risk cutting the cord on your electric mower. Drape it over your shoulder or coil it around your elbow. Use a bright-colored extension cord so that it's visible on the lawn.

Watch your feet. Never mow barefoot; wear heavy shoes or work boots to lessen the risk of accidents. And don't wear light-colored canvas footwear unless you like green—grass can stain indelibly.

Split ends. Does your lawn look dull and gray after mowing? Examine the grass tips. If they have been shredded instead of neatly sliced, your mower blade needs sharpening.

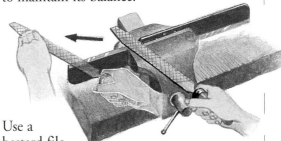

To sharpen a mower blade, put it in a bench vise and sharpen both ends equally to maintain its balance.

Use a bastard file and a toe-to-heel stroke to restore the original bevel—usually a 30° angle. Mower dealers and most hardware stores also sharpen blades.

All done? Turn off the power and clean the underside of the blade housing with a paint scraper. Removing debris keeps the blade spinning freely and prevents rust.

Take precautions with a power mower. Disconnect the spark plug before doing maintenance work, cleaning the discharge chute, or turning the blades, which will cause some mowers to start. If removing the bagger for emptying, be especially careful when the mower is on.

The finishing touch. Neaten the lawn edges around beds, fences, walls, paths, and trees with a string trimmer—which can reach where mowers cannot. Keep the cutting head level so that you don't scalp the grass.
▷ **Bark, Grass, Lawns**

MULCH

Why mulch? It insulates the soil from temperature extremes, keeping it warmer in winter and cooler in summer. Mulch also minimizes erosion, moisture loss, and weed growth. Perhaps its most important role is preventing frost damage. Not only will mulched plants not be heaved out of the ground by alternate freezing and thawing, but they won't be tempted to emerge prematurely during a brief winter warmup.

When to mulch. For perennials, trees, and shrubs, you can leave mulch in place year-round. For vegetables and annuals, wait until the soil warms. For vegetables and bulbs overwintering in the ground, wait till the soil freezes, then remove it in spring.

What to use. Many gardeners prefer ornamental mulches for year-round use or for flower beds. Shredded bark, wood chips, and cocoa or walnut shells are attractive but expensive. For seasonal use in the vegetable patch, hay, straw, chopped leaves, ground corncobs, even shredded newpaper are inexpensive and effective—and you can turn them into the soil at summer's end.

What not to use. Never use a mulch that mats down or cakes together—it will prevent water, air, and nutrients from penetrating the soil. Materials like coffee grounds, peat moss, grass clippings, or sawdust should be mixed with a less dense mulch before being used.

How much? Usually 2 to 3 inches are enough. If erosion or weeds are a persistent problem or if you're overwintering tender specimens, spread 4 to 6 inches. In permanent installations, just refresh the top each year to maintain the proper depth.

Match your mulch to the plants. Acid-lovers, including rhododendron and camellias, appreciate an acidic

---

❧ THE RIGHT MULCH ❧

Many materials make suitable mulch, as long as they cover the soil well and are "healthy"—that is, have never been exposed to toxic chemicals, insect pests, or diseases. Organic mulches allow water, air, and fertilizer to pass through, and they decompose to add nutrients to the soil; inorganic mulches are generally impermeable and durable. While you can purchase mulch in bags, bulk, or rolls, don't forget materials you might have on hand: chipped brush, pine needles, leaves, or newspaper.

ORGANIC	INORGANIC
Buckwheat, rice hulls	Aluminized or
Conifer needles	reflective plastic
Corncobs (ground)	Aluminum foil
Grass clippings	Black plastic
Hay, straw, salt hay	Brick chips
Leaves, leaf mold	Geotextiles
Newspaper, paper	Photodegradable
Nut, cocoa shells	plastic
Shredded bark	Stone, river pebbles
Wood chips	Volcanic rock

mulch. Try pine needles, oak-leaf mold, shredded oak leaves, or composted sawdust from cypress or oak. On plants that don't need acid, use neutral materials like buckwheat hulls, corncobs, or straw; if you're using an acidic mulch, add a little lime.

Dead leaves can be used in several ways. Spread small leaves right on the beds. Let large leaves age a year or so to make nutritious leaf-mold mulch. Or chop large leaves to make them easier to handle. If you don't have a shredder, run a lawn mower over a pile of leaves or pack them in a garbage can and chop with a string trimmer.

Good news. Newsprint is an effective mulch—as long as it doesn't contain colored ink. Chop it first with a lawn mower or shredder.

Live near a brewery? Ask the brewmaster if you can haul away the spent hops—the fine-textured mash makes an ideal mulch.

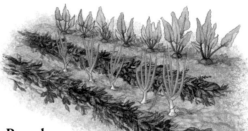

Recycle the leafy tops of root crops such as carrots, beets, and radishes—as long as they're healthy. Just lay them between the rows in your vegetables garden.

Don't forget compost and manure. You can use compost even before it's finished, but make sure manure is rotted before spreading; otherwise it may burn plants and hold weed seeds waiting to germinate.

Ask around. Arborists and utility companies that trim trees around power lines often have surplus wood chips ground from felled trees. Also ask your municipality—some have leaf-composting or brush-chipping sites and offer free mulch to the community.

Reflective mulch. Aluminized plastic mulch helps repel pests—insects passing by are confused by the light and fly away. Make your own mulch by placing sheets of aluminum foil around plants and anchoring them with stones.

High-tech mulch. The latest trend is geotextiles—permeable woven or bonded fabrics that blanket the soil and perform all the functions of organic mulches. They are particularly effective in suppressing weeds and are safe to use around permanent plantings like shrubs. Because they degrade if exposed to light and are unattractive, top them with shredded bark or wood chips.

Black plastic mulch is best for vegetable gardens. Its radiant heat warms the soil—up to 3°F higher than unmulched soil—and keeps dirt from splashing on plants, which can cause rot. Lay it on the bed and make slits for transplants or seeds; fold it up at season's end and reuse the following year. But take note: since rain can't pass through, you'll need to water beneath the plastic with a soaker hose or drip line.

Be aware that some mulches, such as wood chips and sawdust, deplete nitrogen from the soil when they begin decaying. Dig in ammonium nitrate, blood meal, rotted manure, or another nitrogen source before spreading these mulches.

Mulching doesn't mean you can neglect the garden. You will still need to weed, water, fertilize, and monitor pests and diseases. Also be sure to weed thoroughly before mulching.

Two don'ts. Don't pile mulch too close to trunks or stems. It can smother plants, promote rot, and let slugs, mice, and other pests hide near a food source. And don't use plastic mulch around shrubs and other hardy plants. Because it is not permeable, it cuts off air and water to roots; it also causes soil to heat up excessively in summer.

Keep your eye on wood mulches close to your house. They may harbor termites, mice, or other invasive pests.

Before mulching roses, soak mulch in a dilute solution of 1 ounce bleach per gallon of water for one hour. This will help discourage black spot.
▷ **Compost, Conifers, Geotextiles, Leaves, Manure**

MUSHROOMS

Become a mycologist. Study the various species so that you can tell if poisonous wild mushrooms invade your patch of cultivated fungi. Check in books and seek out a mushroom expert—called a mycologist.

Homegrown. You can raise your mushroom crop indoors or out. All you need is spawn, which are germinated mushroom spores, and a growing medium, like compost, sawdust, or newspaper. Buy spawn or complete kits from mail-order sources.

Where to grow. Most species prefer moist, dimly lit, well-ventilated conditions around 55°F to 70°F. Grow them in a garage, cellar, or tool shed or outdoors in the shade.

Button and shaggy mane mushrooms grow well on the lawn in a shady spot. Plant in late summer or fall with purchased spawn. Pull back a 15-inch square of sod and dig a trench 6 inches deep. Fill with horse manure rotted for 6 weeks and top with about 3½ ounces of spawn. Replace the turf and keep the area moist.

Grow shiitakes indoors on sawdust. Place a mound of sawdust in a container and add spawn; cover it with glass or plastic to increase humidity. You can harvest in about 2 months. To grow them outdoors, drill holes in oak logs, fill with spawn, and seal with wax. Stack the logs crisscrossed in a moist, shady spot. Mushrooms will appear in about 2 years and may keep growing for several years thereafter.

Fun for kids. Let children try this easy way to grow oyster mushrooms. Soak about 20 sheets of newspaper. Drain, lay flat, and sprinkle with spawn; roll tightly, tie, and slide into a plastic bag. Close loosely and store in a kitchen cupboard for 3 weeks. Open the bag slightly and place it near a north-facing window. Mushrooms should appear in 3 weeks.

Sweet and pure. Mushrooms need a sweet, or slightly alkaline, growing medium and pure water; use spring or rain water or let tap water stand for at least 24 hours.

Black gold. If you live in an area where mushrooms are cultivated, ask local growers about buying spent mushroom soil as a mulch or amendment. The dark-brown compost is weed-free and highly nutritious.

᎒ A MUSHROOM SAMPLER ᎒

Button *(Agaricus brunnescens)* The white, firm mushroom with a mild taste often found at the grocery. It can be eaten raw or cooked.

Shiitake *(Lentinus edodes)* A brown species from Japan with a smoky aroma. Use only the wide-brimmed, spongy caps in cooking.

Portobello A "grown-up" button with a tan cap and black gills. When grilled, it has a meaty texture and a rich, savory flavor similar to that of steak.

NARCISSUS

Beyond the daffodil. Although "daffodil" is often applied to all members of the genus *Narcissus*, it is just one of the many plant groups in this diverse bulb family. There are about 25 species and thousands of varieties blooming between February and May.

Range of blooms. All narcissus have a central trumpet, or corona, but its size, color, and shape varies from plant to plant. While the classic daffodil has a long, fringed, tubelike corona, the double narcissus has a flat, ruffled one. Colors of the petals and coronas range from soft white, lemon, and salmon-pink to vibrant gold and orange.

Like all daffodil relatives, the poet's narcissus 'Actaea' makes the grandest display when planted en masse.

The poet's narcissus (*N. poeticus*) is one of the most popular types. The scented blooms open in mid- to late spring with white petals surrounding a contrasting "eye" that is usually rimmed in red. Growing to 18 inches and naturalizing readily, they are best planted in drifts.

Sweet fragrance. The jonquil (*N. jonquilla*) has slender leaves and clusters of blooms with small cups that appear in late spring. The scented flowers, in white and yellow, are ideal for cutting.

Two for the rock garden. Angel's-tears (*N. triandrus*) flower in April with ivory cups dripping from backswept petals. The cyclamen narcissus (*N. cyclamineus*) has reflexed petals that resemble a cyclamen's and long trumpets with crinkled ends; it is one of the first narcissus to bloom. Both are dainty specimens that grow no taller than 1 foot.

Grow narcissus as you would any spring bulb. Plant in fall at twice the bulb depth in rich, well-drained soil. Note that they can tolerate more shade than other bulbs.

The best way to plant narcissus is in naturalistic drifts, with dozens of bulbs creating meadows of color. But keep in mind that narcissus foliage must be allowed to die back naturally. So locate bulbs where fading foliage won't interfere with lawn mowing or be a distraction. You can also overplant with a ground cover, ferns, or perennials.

Rodents hate them. Interplant narcissus with tulips, hyacinth, and other bulbs beloved by chipmunks, mice, and moles. Because narcissus are slightly toxic and unpalatable, pests will generally leave them—and neighboring plants—alone.

Deer, too. Narcissus are one of the few plants that most deer don't like. Plant several species: not every one is deer proof.

Prevent leaf burn. If a spring cold snap threatens to injure plants, protect them with a mound of dry peat moss.

Divide narcissus every 4 years in early summer, after the foliage has died back. Lift the clump with a fork, shake off soil, and let bulbs dry in the shade for a few days. Pull off the bulblets and replant.
▷ **Bulbs, Daffodils**

NASTURTIUMS

A colorful screen. Train a vining variety of nasturtium (*Tropaeolum* spp.) to adorn a blank wall—the 10-foot-long runners will cover a trellis with lily-padlike leaves and funnel-shaped flowers. Set the tender plants out after all danger of frost has passed in well-drained soil amended with compost. Select a sunny location but provide afternoon shade in very hot climates; water well till established. They will bloom until frost.

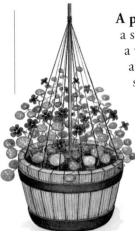

A pretty pyramid. Drive a stake into the center of a wooden barrel. Stretch about a dozen pieces of string from the stake to the edges of the container and fasten with tacks. Plant climbing nasturtiums around the barrel perimeter and train the vines up the strings. Use as a centerpiece in an herb garden or on a patio.

Pair with a potted citrus. Plant bush-type nasturtiums around the base of a potted lemon, lime, or orange tree. Their bright yellow, orange, and red blooms will complement the colors of the citrus fruits.

Mix with vegetables. Plant bush nasturtiums between rows of vegetables, spacing them at about 12 to 18 inches. They make a pretty ground cover and are said to repel some insects—and their blooms are edible!

Be direct. While transplants are readily available, nasturtiums are so easy to grow

---

THE TASTY NASTURTIUM

Native to South America, nasturtiums have a long culinary history. Conquistadors brought seed from Peru to Spain in the 16th century, and the plant soon spread throughout Europe. Seed pods were pickled in vinegar as a substitute for capers. Attempts were also made to cook the tubers of certain species—which are still eaten today by some inhabitants of the Andes. In America, the flowers are favored. With their peppery taste and tender texture, they make a colorful addition to salads.

The nasturtium's round leaves and bright blossoms bring beauty to the garden from June to September.

from seed that you can sow them directly in the garden. Sow once soil warms in ½ inch of average, well-drained soil. Thin seedlings to 6 inches; protect from frost.
▷ **Edible Flowers, Flower Beds**

NATIVE PLANTS

What are they? The word "native" refers to plants that grow in the same habitat in which they originated; "exotic" plants, conversely, are those growing in a different area from where they originated. Plants can be native to a continent, state, or region.

Be selective. Just because a plant is native to your area doesn't mean it's suited to your site. Always consider the plant's growing requirements before including it in your garden.

Never collect plants from the wild. More than 2,000 native American plants are endangered or protected—digging them up may be against the law. And many, like the lady's-slipper, are difficult to transplant

---

SAVING HAWAII'S NATIVE PLANTS

More than a third of America's endangered or threatened plant species are native to Hawaii, where naturalists are trying to restore a balance of nature upset by years of destruction. Because of the islands' remoteness, the native plants evolved over the centuries without defenses against "exotic" flora and fauna. A delicate harmony ensued: the i'iwi bird, for example, developed a half-moon bill designed to draw nectar from the long-throated native lobelia.

When the first Polynesian voyagers arrived in Hawaii some 1,500 years ago, they carried with them the alien species that would, over time, disrupt the islands' fragile ecosystem. In 20th-century Hawaii, feral pigs uproot shrubs, hollow out giant tree ferns, and distribute seeds of invasive Himalayan ginger. The goats imported by early explorers erode lush slopes and eat the endangered silversword, a plant that takes 50 years to bloom. In response, conservationists are now at work fencing out wild animals, destroying some exotic plants, and even pollinating native plants by hand.

---

from their natural habitats. An exception to the "don't touch" rule is made only when plants would be destroyed by development. Check with a wildflower conservation society about endangered species in your area.

You may collect seed from the wild, which helps a species spread. But take only small quantities—no more than 10 percent of the seed in a given area—so that the plants can replenish their populations naturally.

When buying native plants, make sure your source is selling stock propagated from seed or by vegetative means—not plants dug in the wild. Look for sales of native plants at local botanical gardens or from wildflower societies. Or ask them for a list of reliable mail-order suppliers.

Local is better. Plants that are native over a wide geographical range adapt to their specific microclimates. So be sure to select plants that grow in a region with climatic and soil conditions similar to those in your own garden.

Bringing nature to the backyard

A garden that teems with wildlife—tadpoles in the pond, chipmunks darting out of the brush, and hummingbirds drinking from the summer flowers—is a neverending source of pleasure for adults and children alike. Even a small sanctuary in a suburban backyard can become a wildlife haven. Animals, birds, and insects will not only visit: many will likely settle there if you provide a constant supply of food, water, and undisturbed shelter.

To create such an environment, you'll need to put up borders that will block out the hectic world outside and make wildlife feel welcome. A dense screen of trees and shrubs, for example, can provide ready nesting sites as well as edible fruits. A compact deciduous tree like the hedge maple offers summer shade and habitats for birds, insects, and small animals, such as squirrels, shrews, opossums, and raccoons. Planted in groups, nut- and fruit-bearing shrubs and trees—both deciduous and evergreen—will create thickets brimming with treats for birds and small animals.

You can provide other natural habitats with an old wall full of nooks and crannies, a fallen tree trunk or hollow tree, or a manmade brush pile in the garden. If you have no natural water source, such as a creek or a spring, dig and fill a pond, creating a boggy area for marsh plants around it.

Since a wildlife garden is unkempt by design, it makes an ideal site for some of the typical garden's less sightly necessities, including the compost pile, the rain barrel, and the tool shed.

ECOLOGICAL BORDERS
An informal cluster of shrubs such as elder, hazel, mountain ash, and blackthorn creates a hedge that will attract birds and insects with its nuts and fruits. Interplanting it with evergreens will provide year-round screening.

A mortarless stone wall is a natural home for lizards and snakes. In a sunny site, it makes a fine trellis for flowering vines, which attract nectar-loving birds and butterflies. In shade, the wall supports ivy.

A FALLEN TREE TRUNK
A rotting tree trunk can provide the base for a shallow bird table, which serves as a drinking fountain and birdbath in summer and a feeder in winter. Be sure the dish is fastened securely and won't tip or spill; you may have to squirrel-proof it with fine wire mesh at one end. Under the trunk, leaf mold and decaying wood make a fine breeding ground for earthworms, which keep the soil aerated. Upend a broken clay pot as a friendly toad house; toads prey on slugs and snails.

A POND
A strong focal point for any garden, a pond also attracts birds, aquatic insects, and even small animals like porcupines and foxes. Line the pond with plastic, reinforced concrete, or clay and slope the edges gently from a depth of at least 2½ feet at the lowest point. Two pool inhabitants are both beautiful and practical: waterlilies, which discourage algae by shading the water, and goldfish, which eat mosquito larvae and help to aerate the water.

A BRUSH PILE
In a quiet corner of the garden, make a brush pile by stacking cut tree branches of various diameters over a bed of rocks. Interlace the branches until the pile is 3 to 4 feet deep. The crevices in the rocks under the brush pile may serve as a hideaway for garter snakes and toads; chipmunks, rabbits, and field mice will likely prefer the brush structure as a nesting site.

A FLOWER MEADOW
Set aside a sunny open area to grow wildflowers such as black-eyed Susans, coreopsis, gaillardia, gayfeather, and Queen Anne's lace. Select species native to your region and cultivate the soil thoroughly before planting the seed in the spring. Add prairie or ornamental grasses—Canada wild rye or prairie dropseed, for example—as a contrast. The meadow will harbor insects, birds—possibly quail or pheasant—and small animals.

ATTRACTING POLLINATORS
Choose flowers that secrete nectar and have a long blooming season to attract pollinators like butterflies, honeybees, and ruby-throated hummingbirds. Good choices in the sunny border include bee balm, butterfly bush, cardinal flower, and goldenrod. Tuck in a few fragrant herbs such as lavender and rosemary and sow a patch of nettles as a breeding ground for butterflies. Don't forget flowering vines such as clematis, honeysuckle, and climbing roses.

FEATURES FOR A HABITAT

The diagram below is keyed to the garden features shown in perspective at left.

1 Compost
2 Clematis vine
3 Nettles
4 Hedge maple
5 Brush pile
6 Hazel
7 Shade plants under trees
8 Shed
9 Lavender
10 Rain barrel
11 Tree trunk and bird table

12 Climbing rose
13 Rosemary
14 Flower meadow
15 Elder
16 Sunny border
17 Mountain ash
18 Honeysuckle
19 Pond
20 Blackthorn
21 Stone wall
22 Ivy

NATURE

NETTING

A valuable tool. Netting protects fruits, vegetables, and ornamentals from birds, insects, rabbits, and other predators. Usually made of nylon or polypropylene, it is available in various dimensions and with various mesh sizes, from about ⅛ inch to 2 inches.

A deer barrier. Deer will eat almost anything—flowers, leaves, fruits, and vegetables. Protect individual shrubs by covering them with ½-inch mesh, securing it at the plant base with twine. To keep deer out of your planting beds, erect an inconspicuous fence with

black or dark green 2-inch mesh netting. Fasten it to stakes or trees; it must be at least 8 feet tall and enclose the area completely. Otherwise, deer will be able to enter but they won't have room to leap out. They will not only destroy your plants and the netting but may also injure themselves.

Cover berry bushes with ¾-inch mesh to keep birds from pecking the fruit. Build a framework to hold the netting 1 foot from the branch tips—so birds can't reach in—and staple the netting to the top and sides.

Protect row crops, like strawberries, from birds with ¾-inch mesh rigged over hoops. Tie the ends around stakes and anchor the

sides with bricks or stones. To protect against insects, lay the finest mesh netting over plants and anchor edges.

As a windbreak. Use durable, fine mesh netting to set up a wind barrier. The permeable netting will slow wind flow by about 60 percent.

An easy trellis. In the vegetable garden, use 2-inch mesh to support tomatoes, squash, and other vines. For ornamentals, use 1-inch mesh; you can tack the nearly invisible netting to pillars, walls, or fences.

A good catch-all. Use ½-inch mesh to collect leaves and other fall debris. Lay it over a bed, a ground cover, a pool, or the lawn till trees have shed. Then roll it up and deposit its contents in the compost pile.
▷ **Protection**

NETTLES

The two types. There are two plants with the name "nettle." Stinging nettle is a weed that nonetheless has several uses. Dead nettle is an ornamental ground cover.

A magical plant. Many claims have been made for the powers of the stinging nettle *(Urtica dioica)*—from hair restorer to hemorrhage halter. It's also hailed as a soil builder: its nitrogen-rich foliage decomposes to form a humus said to be as potent as manure. If nettles are growing wild on your land, plant there with confidence: the soil will be good and fertile.

A neighborly plant. Folklore holds that stinging nettles promote the growth of some vegetables and increase the quantity

of essential oils in herbs. Nettles also attract beneficial insects and help repel pests around fruit trees.

Protect yourself. Tiny hairs covering the foliage cause a burning and itching sensation as painful as a bee sting. Always wear leather or rubber gloves when touching the plant. To harvest leaves, pick from the bottom of the stem upwards.

Got stung? Rub your skin right away with an onion slice, sorrel leaves, or rhubarb.

A natural additive. Steep 1 pound of nettle leaves in 1 gallon of water for at least a week. Water plants with the solution—it's a rich fertilizer and a natural pest repellent.

Condition the soil. After nettles have shed their seed, place branches on top of a newly turned bed. Let decompose and dig in. You can also add nettles to the compost heap.

AN ALL-PURPOSE HERB

The hard-to-handle yet versatile stinging nettle has enjoyed many uses through the centuries. Remarkably, the prickly plant has been woven into fabric since the Bronze Age. Indeed, the Scots maintain that the linens their countrymen weave from nettles are more durable and beautiful than those made from flax. In ancient Rome attempts to cure paralysis included flogging afflicted limbs with nettle branches. And herbalists in 16th-century England recommended drinking nettle tea as an antidote to poison.

American Indians used both native nettles and those introduced by European settlers as a food and medicine. A tonic of brewed nettles remedied everything from chills to jaundice, while a nettle leaf placed on the tongue was said to arrest nosebleeds. Nettles were even used to treat the bite of a mad dog.

Nettles' virtues continue to be championed by many enthusiasts today. As the late naturalist Euell Gibbons said, "If even half the claims made for stinging nettles are true...this one plant can satisfy our hunger, mend our health...[and] delight our taste buds.... What a wonderful herb!"

Ripen stone fruits such as peaches and plums more quickly by laying them on a bed of nettles. You can also place the fruits in a plastic bag filled with nettle leaves.

Cook nettle leaves as you would spinach and season with butter and salt. Or brew them in water and use for soup stock. The foliage is rich in vitamins C and A and loses its sting when cooked.

The other one. Dead nettle *(Lamium maculatum)* is a vigorous ground cover that will thrive in part shade and poor soil and blanket a barren spot quickly. The heart-shaped leaves are variegated silver-white—ideal for lighting up a dark area in the garden—and the lavender, white, or pink flowers last all spring, then repeat in fall. Give it plenty of room to spread and fertilize only lightly.

NEWSPAPERS

Turn green tomatoes red. At the end of the season, pick your tomatoes as soon as they blush pink and wrap each one in a sheet of newspaper. Store them in crates in a warm spot. They will ripen slowly, giving you fresh-tasting tomatoes well into autumn.

Tuck in sleeping orchids. Protect the tuberous roots of hardy *Bletilla striata* and *Pleione* orchids through the winter with

a newspaper blanket. Lay sheets of newspaper over their beds and top with 4 inches of soil.

Protect a young tree from the elements by wrapping its trunk in newspaper secured with biodegradable twine.

Vacation care. Limit moisture loss of your potted plants when you're going to be away for more than a week. Cut a ring from several layers of newspaper and moisten it well. Water your plants thoroughly, then place a ring on the soil of each plant.

To guard against rust, clean and oil the metal parts of your garden tools at season's end. Then store the tools in newspaper.

Extra! Extra! Line the inside of a cold frame with sheets of newspaper to provide extra insulation whenever there's a risk of hard frost.

Chop newspaper with a lawn mower or shredder and add it to the compost. You can also spread it as a mulch.

Smother weeds or other undesirable plant growth with a newspaper mat. Wet several sheets of paper to help them cling together. Place the mat so that plants are completely covered and no light can reach them; anchor the edges with rocks or soil. Top with wood chips or another mulch to camouflage and remove once the weeds are dead.
▷ **Compost, Mulch**

NIGHT BLOOMERS

Flowering or fragrant only after sunset, night bloomers seduce moths, bats, and other nocturnal pollinators with their extravagant, richly scented flowers.

Most nocturnal plants are tropical natives and suited to warm areas. If you live in a cold climate, select hardy perennials. You can also grow tender specimens as annuals or overwinter them indoors.

Not all are exotic. Species of many common plants, such as daylilies, iris, cactus, gladiolus, and magnolia, either bloom or release their scent at night.

Light it up. Don't rely on the moon and stars to illuminate night bloomers. Show them off with small accent lights that cast a soft, diffused glow.

Indoor blooms. Cut a night bloomer with a ready-to-open bud just before sundown and bring it into the house. Place it in water and wait: it will open after sunset and release its perfume all night long.

Plant fragrant night bloomers by a bedroom window or an outdoor living space, such as a deck, porch, or patio, so you can enjoy the plant's flowers and scent.

Enjoy it while it lasts. The night-blooming cereus *(Hylocereus undatus)* has luminous, 1-foot-long flowers that last but a single night. The blossoms open so fast, usually around 8:00 P.M., that you can actually see the movement; by the next morning, they will have closed and shriveled.

The creamy white, trumpetlike blooms of the downy thorn apple seem to glow in the summer twilight.

The dazzling daturas. Often called angel's trumpets, daturas are tender tropicals that boast long, funnel-form flowers in various colors. Try the sacred datura *(Datura inoxia)*, which opens in late afternoon, or the downy thorn apple *(D. metel)*.

A "ballroom beauty." The evening primrose *(Oenothera biennis)* looks bedraggled by day, like a partygoer who stayed up all night dancing. But after the sun goes down, numerous little buds pop open with glistening gold cups.

An old favorite. Choose the old flowering tobacco species *(Nicotiana alata)* instead of the new hybrid cultivars, which are less fragrant and stay open during the day. Also plant woodland tobacco *(N. sylvestris)* and nocturnal tobacco *(N. noctiflora)* for scented star-shaped night blooms.

For evening gardens, plant evening stock *(Matthiola longipetala)*. A sweet, jasminelike scent wafts from its papery purple blooms. Or try the four-o'clock *(Mirabilis jalapa)*, which opens punctually in late afternoon, as its name suggests. The tubular flowers in red, white, or yellow smell like a blend of sugar and lemon.

Ideal for arbors is the moonflower, a morning-glory cousin whose 10-foot-long stems will twine around a trellis. Its pure white flowers open at twilight to emit a clovelike perfume. The seed has a hard coat and is slow to germinate. Soak it in warm water overnight and nick it with a knife or file before planting in well-drained soil and a sunny spot.

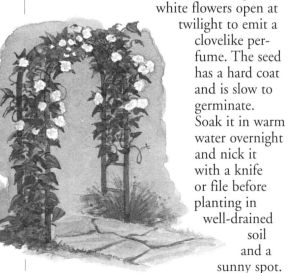

NIGHT-BLOOMING WATER LILIES

A number of tropical water lilies *(Nymphaea)* flower only at night. The blooms remain open until about 9:00 A.M. the next day and generally last three days. 'Missouri' is one of the most popular cultivars, with white blooms up to 14 inches. 'Red Flare' has deep red flowers to contrast with its mahogany foliage. 'Mrs. George C. Hitchcock' blooms with pink petals surrounding orange stamens. A novel relative is the giant water lily *(Victoria* spp.), whose leaves can reach 6 feet across; the blooms turn from white to pink and measure a mere 12 inches.

▷ **Trellises**

NITROGEN

A garden must. Nitrogen is one of the three primary plant nutrients. Although it is present in the air, plants must take it up through the soil—either from chemical fertilizers or from the breakdown of organic matter. Because nitrogen is rapidly depleted, it must be replenished regularly.

The best organic sources of nitrogen are manure, blood meal, cottonseed meal, hoof and horn meal, fish emulsion, and soybean meal. Good sources found in your own back yard are leaf mold and grass clippings.

Chemical sources of nitrogen include ammonium sulfate, ammonium nitrate, calcium nitrate, and sodium nitrate.

Read the label. Nitrogen (N) is the first element listed on a fertilizer label; the others are phosphorus (P) and potassium (K). The first number—as in 6–2–1—indicates the percentage of nitrogen in the total mass.

Green manures, like white clover and rye, are raised to add nitrogen to the soil. Sow seed wherever you want to enrich the soil and let grow until plants are 6 inches tall. Cut them to the soil line, then turn under. They will decay rapidly to release nitrogen, so wait at least a week before planting.

Feathery fertilizer. Poultry feathers make a nitrogen-rich fertilizer. Place them in a tub; top with a plastic screen and a few stones to hold them down. Cover with water and let steep in a shady spot. After 2 months, strain and use the liquid to fertilize plants.

Sour the soil with ammonium sulfate. Use it on plants needing acidic conditions, like rhododendrons, azaleas, and camellias.

Let it sit. There's no need to dig nitrogen fertilizer into the soil. Water it in or let the rain do it for you.

Get a jump on spring by applying an organic nitrogen source in late fall. It will break down slowly and be available in the soil by planting time the following year.

Heat it up. Add a chemical or organic nitrogen source—preferably manure—to the compost pile to speed decomposition.

How much is too much? You'll know you have applied excessive nitrogen if blossoms are sparse and foliage grows too fast and lush, which makes plants more vulnerable to pests, disease, and environmental stress. There is no antidote; rain and frequent watering will eventually wash nitrogen away.

Not enough? Plants deprived of nitrogen will look stunted and spindly, with pale foliage that eventually turns yellow and dies. Correct the shortage by adding 1 inch of rotted manure to the soil and by spraying foliage with fish emulsion weekly until symptoms disappear.

▷ **Fertilizer, Manure, Organic Fertilizers**

NOISE

A proven soundproofer. A tall, dense evergreen hedge has been shown to block noise by 40 to 50 percent.

Build a berm. Soil is one of the most effective sound baffles. Consider placing a gently rising mound along the edge of your property. The taller the berm, the more noise that will be reduced.

A better berm.
To make your berm more effective, plant at least one row of trees along its top. Sink deciduous trees in planting wells to bring their branches closer to the ground. Or plant them at the

---

NOISE AS A DETERRENT

Noise can be an ally when used to keep animals out of the yard. Everything from blaring radios to rattling pie pans have proven useful in driving creatures away. While some gardeners have resorted to blasting recordings of bird distress calls over a sound system to deter thieving birds, you needn't do anything so drastic. You can make moles and gophers relocate simply by sticking clattering pinwheels near their tunnels. Or try an empty soda bottle—the lonesome whistle made by wind blowing over the hole will keep critters at a distance. Night raiders, like raccoons and deer, may be chased off by a radio tuned to an all-night talk show. Whatever noise-maker you choose, you'll need to move it around or replace it with a new tactic frequently to extend its effectiveness.

NOISEBUSTERS

Dense-growing evergreens are excellent noise absorbers. Select stocky plants with full foliage and plant them close together.

COOL CLIMATES	WARM CLIMATES
Arborvitae	Boxwood
False cypress	California incense cedar
Fir	Cherry laurel
Juniper	Cotoneaster (evergreen)
Pine	Holly (evergreen)
Spruce	Holly-leaved osmanthus
Yew	Leyland cypress

recommended depth, then underplant with shade-tolerant shrubs like rhododendrons and azaleas. Evergreen trees can be planted at the usual depth. A solid fence or wall in back of the plants will further block noise.

Do not disturb. Locate noisy recreation areas—such as pools, tennis courts, or volleyball nets—as far as possible from your residence. If yard space is limited, plant evergreen trees or shrubs around the area to help keep the noise contained.

A soundproof nook. Train a hedge of yew, cherry laurel, or other densely foliaged shrub to form a cozy "U" around a garden bench. In time, you will have a quiet, secluded spot for reading and conversation.

Create a distraction. Use a fountain and wind chimes to bring pleasant music to the garden. They won't obliterate bothersome noises but may well reduce the annoyance.

▷ **Moles, Rodents**

NURSERIES

COMMERCIAL NURSERIES

Make friends. Establish a rapport with your local nursery: growers are an invaluable source of information on plant culture and the growing requirements and problems specific to your area. The best nurseries provide not only plants but also sound advice from experts, whose livelihoods depend on raising quality plants.

Seek out specialists. Besides large-scale general nurseries that stock everything from marigolds to magnolias, shop at specialty growers who restrict their business to one type of plant, such as bulbs, roses, or fruit trees. They are more likely to grow the rare specimens that you won't find elsewhere.

What to expect. Some nurseries merely sell plants, while others offer landscape services as well. You may want to buy a large specimen tree, for example, from a nursery that will also plant it for you.

Check guarantees. Policies on replacing failed plants vary among nurseries, so ask before you buy. Some growers will replace a plant for free, while others charge a percentage of the plant's cost; there is usually a time limit—perhaps 6 months or a year. Always retain receipts and make sure that your purchases are clearly itemized. And be prepared to explain why your plant died: if you didn't care for it properly, the nursery is not responsible.

Be an early bird. Find out what day the nursery receives new plants from wholesale growers; it is often a Thursday or Friday, in preparation for the weekend rush. Shop on these days to get a better pick of plants and avoid the crowds.

Tag it. Most nurseries will let you reserve trees and shrubs for pickup or delivery at a later time. In the interim, the nursery—not you—is responsible for your plant's care.

Buy in bulk. Discounts are often available on quantities of the same plant. If you're planning a large installation, such as an allée or hedge, buy plants all at once instead of over time. It will be expensive, but you'll save money in the long run.

Take a list. Just as you do when grocery shopping, bring a list of plants you want to include in your garden plan—and stick to it! It's easy to get carried away by the vast array of nursery specimens—many of which may not be right for your site.

Ask first. Examine plants carefully for any signs of pests, disease, or weakness. Ask growers how the specimens were propagated and raised and what conditions they will require. Also ask about the size at maturity—a pretty little shrub pruned back in a nursery display may grow into a monster.

Judge by the roots— a good guide to the plant's health and age. Pull the plant gently from the pot and inspect the roots; they should be healthy, vigorous, and evenly distributed through the soil—not cramped. If they are coiled around the base or poking out of the drainage hole, the plant is pot-bound and has been in the container too long. Such roots usually have difficulty growing out when transplanted into garden soil.

When buying a flowering plant in a container, select one at the bud stage so that it will bloom after being planted at home. If the specimen is already in full bloom, it will fade quickly after being transplanted.

Welcome home. Unpack plants and make them comfortable as soon as you get home from the nursery. Place them in the shade and let them get air; water if necessary. If you can't plant them right away, place them in a sheltered spot and keep moist. Sink larger container-grown plants in the soil— they'll need less water. On cool nights, set tender plants in a warm cellar or garage.

Mail-order nurseries open the door to the plant world, extending the range of plants available to you beyond the local growers. Because you can't inspect the plants, you'll need to look at other clues to determine what you're buying.

First check that you're dealing with a reputable nursery (anyone can put out a plant list!). Ask about refund and substitution policies and how plants are packed and shipped. Also see if you can specify a shipping date so that you'll be home to receive and care for your plants. You may want to place only a small order when buying from a nursery for the first time.

When it comes to catalogs, the more details, the better. The nursery should provide information on bloom time, cultural requirements, and mature size—plus the Latin names, so that you can select exactly the plant you want. Watch for nursery euphemisms such as "vigorous" or "self-sower," which can actually mean invasive.

Look for indications of the plant size and type being shipped. Bulbs, for example, are often sold by age, such as "one-year" or "two-year." Perennials are sold by age or container size. Trees and shrubs may be "bare-root," meaning they'll arrive dormant, with no soil around the roots. Fruit trees described as "unbranched whips" have only one stem. Don't shy away from young plants—they are easier to ship and transplant, may adjust better to your garden, and will cost less than more mature specimens.

HOME NURSERIES

Create your own nursery. A home nursery is an economical, enjoyable way to fill your garden or grow extra plants to swap with fellow gardeners. Many annuals and perennials are easily grown from seed or divisions, while woody plants may need to be propagated by cuttings or layering.

Where to put it? Establish your nursery in a sheltered, out-of-the-way spot. It need not be elaborate: any area that gets sun and has access to water will do. Set aside a corner of the bed for sun-shy or fragile plants and shade them with lath or shade cloth, a black mesh fabric.

Grow in pots. Don't plant your cuttings directly in the ground; they'll be more difficult to move around. Instead, plant them in containers instead. You can use the same plastic pots that commercial nurseries use, though any type of waterproof container —from metal food cans to plastic soda bottles—will do. Make sure you clean the vessel thoroughly, file off or remove any sharp edges, and poke a hole in the bottom for drainage. Lay down a black plastic sheet, gravel, or wood chips to discourage weeds.

Winter bedding. In cold climates, pots buried up to their rims can overwinter right in the soil. Dig a bed to the required depth and backfill with soil mixed with peat moss.

Mother young plants. Young trees, shrubs, and perennials bought from a commercial or mail-order nursery are usually inexpensive, but they may be too small to plant out right away in the garden. Raise these "babies" in your own nursery for a season or two until they are large enough to compete.

Labeling your stock is an essential practice for any busy gardener. Use waterproof plastic or metal tags that loop around the stems of woody plants. Alternatively, insert plastic labels into the soil. Write the plant's name in indelible ink.

Keep a journal to document how and when you propagated a particular plant. It will provide a handy record of comparison when evaluating your failures and successes. Also write down the names and varieties of the new plants you acquire; if the tags become lost or illegible, you'll have a plant list to use for reference.

▷ **Catalogs, Labeling, Propagation**

NUT TREES

What's a nut? Botanically, it's a one-seeded dry fruit with a tough shell that won't split when ripe. True nuts include acorns and beechnuts. But the term can be applied to any hard fruit, such as the almond, chestnut, macadamia, or coconut. All grow on trees or shrubs—except for peanuts, annual legumes whose fruits grow underground.

Nut-bearing trees are valued for providing not only edible fruits but also natural beauty, shade, and habitats for wildlife. While some types are messy or pest-prone, most are highly adaptable to a range of growing conditions and landscape sites.

The best trees for cold climates include walnuts, hickories, filberts (hazelnuts), and chestnuts. In warm climates, grow almonds, pistachios, pecans, and cashews.

PLANTING
Nuts or not? If you're growing nut trees for their fruits, choose selected cultivars that

Because its roots can be detrimental to garden plants, the black walnut is best set apart from your beds.

have been grafted onto seedling stock; trees raised from seed may not produce fruits of good quality. Nut trees used as ornamentals can be grown satisfactorily from seed.

Pick your spot. Keep in mind that the nut crop drops. So don't plant your trees where falling fruits will create a problem.

No fruit? Many nut trees, including pecans and most walnuts, require cross-pollination to bear fruit. For maximum harvests, plant pollinating partners of compatible varieties.

Don't transplant these. The deep taproots of black walnuts and hickories make them difficult to transplant. Purchase a nursery-grown tree no more than 2 feet tall and plant it in its permanent spot. Prepare a hole deep enough to accommodate the entire taproot without bending it.

Whither the chestnut? Devastated by a fungal blight, the majestic native American species has virtually disappeared. As a substitute, plant the smaller, disease-resistant Chinese chestnut. To get fruit, plant at least two varieties; this species is self-sterile.

THE ALL-AMERICAN TREE

The native hickory has long held a place in American history and folklore. Growing strong and stately, it symbolized the country's steadfastness and pride. Andrew Jackson, a general in the War of 1812, was so tough that his militiamen nicknamed him "Old Hickory." It is believed that many of the rails Abe Lincoln split were of hickory, which grew plentifully on the Indiana frontier. The tree also literally united the nation: the ties that held the railroad rails linking east and west were hewn from hickory timber.

Thomas Jefferson championed the largest member of the hickory family—the pecan—and planted 200 trees at Monticello in 1794. That year, he sent the nuts to George Washington, who planted a pecan grove at Mount Vernon. Sadly, none of the original trees still stand.

A warning. Give a black walnut plenty of space. The tree's roots emit a substance that is toxic to many garden plants. Happily, however, it won't harm your lawn.

The twisted branches of the hazelnut called Harry Lauder's walking stick (*Corylus avellana* 'Contorta') make it a striking landscape specimen. Give it a prominent spot in the yard. Children, especially, will delight in its corkscrew limbs.

Gourmet pine nuts. Piñon pines, natives of the arid Southwest, bear resinous nuts in cones. Plant the small, slow-growing trees in a rock garden in areas where temperatures don't drop below 10°F. Even more tender is the Italian stone pine, the source for the pignoli used in pesto. Northern gardeners can plant the nut-bearing Swiss stone pine, which is hardy to –10°F.

Want almonds? Related to the cherry, almonds are pretty flowering trees whose blooms—and fruits—can be devastated by spring frost. Plant them in a protected site where temperatures don't dip below 10°F.

I've got a lovely bunch of … Coconuts from your own tree are a luxury for gardeners in Hawaii and southernmost Florida and California. To start a palm from seed, bury an unhusked nut halfway in the soil. In colder climates, a lucky greenhouse gardener may get a few fruits from 'Dwarf Green' or 'Dwarf Golden Malay.'

MAINTENANCE

Easy care. Nut trees don't require much attention. Water young trees deeply once a week until established; otherwise the soil may pull away from the taproot. Mulch with 6 inches of compost to retain moisture. Prune to create a central leader, then groom any broken or dead branches.

Snap off suckers from the bases of grafted trees. They will weaken the top growth and diminish production of the nut crop.

When to feed. Don't feed nut trees the first year; it results in tender growth that is susceptible to pests and frost. Thereafter, spread a complete fertilizer between the trunk and dripline each spring.

Beat the squirrels. These nut-loving pests can easily clean out your crop. Beat them to the punch by picking up nuts from the ground at least once a day.

To harvest black walnuts without getting stained by their sticky juice, spread plastic sheets under the tree before you beat the branches. You can gather up the crop in the tarps without having to touch the nuts.

STORAGE

Drying hazelnuts. Spread these nuts in a single layer on a tarp and let them dry in the sun for a week. Otherwise the moisture of the shells will spoil the nut meat. Then store them in a cool (50°F), dry place.

Dry black walnuts in the sun to make them easier to hull. Lay them on a hard surface and stir them well with a pitchfork daily. Once dry, the husks will break more easily.

Store chestnuts in the refrigerator. Place them in a plastic bag with a little damp peat moss to keep them from drying out.

▷ **Squirrels, Trees**

OKRA

A tropical shrub that can reach a full 6 feet tall, okra is an edible cousin of hibiscus and cotton. It's grown as an annual vegetable for its tasty seed pods, which are preceded by showy, funnel-form yellow blooms up to 3 inches wide.

A hot-weather plant. Okra thrives in heat and sun. The seeds require warm soil (70°F) to germinate, and the plants won't set seed unless the air temperature is at least 75°F. Although it is a fixture in vegetable patches in the Deep South, okra will succeed in any region where corn will grow.

Prep the seeds. To encourage germination, soak seeds overnight in tepid water or nick them lightly with a file.

Sow seeds ½ inch deep in sandy soil and 1 inch in heavy soil at 3 inches apart; thin

---

⇥AN OKRA SAMPLER⇤

Brought to America in the 1600's from Africa and the West Indies, okra has been bred for easy culture in modern gardens. Many varieties no longer have prickly spines, so they won't irritate the skin; they also grow into compact plants with more fruits. Nearly all are early producers: they begin bearing about 60 days after sowing and continue until frost.

Good choices are 'Annie Oakley,' the first hybrid okra, and 'Spineless Green Velvet,' with pods up to 7 inches long. For variety, try growing 'Red River,' which bears bright red fruits, or 'White Velvet,' with pale green ones.

'Clemson Spineless' okra is a traditional favorite.

to 18 inches. Okra isn't fussy about soil, but it will respond well to fertile garden loam.

Reap twice. Southern gardeners can double their harvest by starting their first crop in early spring and their second in June. An alternative to resowing is to cut back the first crop almost to ground level; if watered and fed, the plants will regrow.

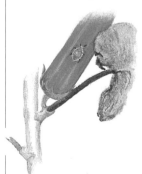

Watch out for stinkbugs—also known as the harlequin bug. They suck the juice from developing pods. Pick them off by hand and destroy them.

Basic care. During the hottest days of summer, give plants at least 1 inch of water each week. Once plants reach 6 inches tall, mulch heavily to conserve moisture and keep weeds under control.

A greedy eater. Feed okra heavily with a high-potassium fertilizer in spring,

---

especially if you're growing it in light or sandy soil. Then give it supplementary feedings once a month with manure tea or a side-dressing of rotted manure.

Harvest often. Pick pods every few days during the peak of the season. They are at their best when young and tender—about 2 to 4 inches long for most varieties. Mature pods tend to be tough. Clip with a pruner or sharp knife and wear gloves if the plant has spines. Remove and compost any mature pods you may have missed so that the plant will keep producing.

Once called gumbo, okra is a staple in the spicy Cajun stew that inherited its name. Use it as well in soups or casseroles; its sticky innards act as a thickener. Okra is especially delicious battered and fried.

Dried pods. Late in the season allow the pods at the top of the plant to mature until dry. Their interesting shape makes a novel addition to dried arrangements.

▷**Vegetable Gardens**

OLEANDER

A Mediterranean native, this flowering evergreen shrub is a favorite in warm climates—especially in coastal areas—because it tolerates heat, drought, wind, and salt spray. The tough, fast-growing plant requires little attention once established.

Give it room. Some oleander varieties grow to about 12 feet tall with an equal spread. Use the plant in hedges or as a screen and let it form a mound. If you must keep it restrained, try root pruning.

Decorate your patio with oleander planted in containers. Fill tubs with fertile, well-drained soil and plant with a specimen that flowers in the color of your choice: pink, yellow, white, red, or rose-purple. Some varieties even have double blooms or are fragrant. Dwarf cultivars like 'Petite Pink' and 'Petite Salmon' usually grow only 4 feet tall and are perfect for containers. Place plants in a warm, sunny spot.

Overwinter potted plants. If the temperature drops below 20°F in your area, you'll need to protect oleander from frost damage. Move containers indoors to a cool, bright spot and let the soil dry between waterings. In early spring, prune hard, removing any weak shoots and at least half the length of stems that flowered the previous year. Stimulate growth by exposing plants gradually to more warmth (to 55°F) and light; water regularly. Set outside once the days are warm and sunny.

Watch for scale. Gray or brown scale insects commonly infest oleander. Remove by hand with a soft brush dipped in soapy water, then rinse. Or treat with pyrethrum.

Painless propagation. Oleander roots easily. All you have do is put a cutting in a jar of water and wait for roots to form.

A pretty poison. Oleander is extremely toxic. The seeds, foliage, and flowers are all poisonous, and some people get a skin reaction even from contact with the leaves. Keep children and animals away from the plants and wear gloves and long sleeves when it's time to prune them.
▷ **Seashore Gardens**

ONIONS

Sets or seeds? Onion sets (young bulbs grown the previous year) are convenient, fast growing, and quick to mature. But only a limited number of cultivars—generally with a pungent taste—produce sets. Seed offers the largest variety of sweet onions, but plants can take five months to mature and are susceptible to disease.

Another option is to use transplants, sold at nurseries or in catalogs. These seedlings come in bare-root bundles; they look like scallions and will mature in 2 months.

More decisions. Pick from bulb and bunching onions. The familiar bulb onion may be white, yellow, or red and range in size from tiny pearls to outsized Spanish types. Bunching onions, called scallions or green onions, are grown for their top stalks and harvested before the bulbs form fully.

Long vs. short. In the North, plant long-day onions, which require as much as 16 hours of sunlight per day. In the South, use short-day types, which need only 12 hours.

Start seeds indoors in pots 8 to 12 weeks before the last frost. Sow four seeds per pot; water and feed. If you sow in trays, thin when plants are 4 inches tall to 1 inch apart. Outdoors, sow seed ½ inch deep and 1 inch apart in loose, fertile soil; thin to 4 inches. Start 2 weeks before the last spring frost or 4 weeks before the first fall frost.

Set out seedlings in early spring, as soon as soil can be worked and the danger of

---

WINTER FORECAST

Folklore has it that you can tell how brutal the coming winter will be by counting an onion's outer skins at harvest. If the layers are thin and few, winter will be mild; if they are thick and numerous, get out your heavy winter clothing.

---

frost is past; the soil should be at least 45°F. Space your home-grown plants, with four in a plug, 1 foot apart. Space individual purchased seedlings 2 inches deep and 4 inches apart. After 4 weeks, brush back a little soil to expose the tops of the bulbs; this will help them develop.

When planting sets, look for bulbs about ½ inch in diameter. Plant with the pointy tips up 1 inch deep and 4 inches apart. A pound of sets is enough for a 50-foot row.

Lots at first, a little later on. Water and feed with a high-nitrogen fertilizer—fish emulsion, for example—early in the season to develop large plants; it will encourage the growth of large bulbs. Cut back water and food at midsummer; bulbs will ripen better in the drier, less fertile conditions.

Weed carefully, as shallow onion roots are easily damaged. Pull weeds up and away from bulbs by hand. Or use a sharp hoe to cut them off—but don't dig into the soil. You can also spread mulch, but be sure to remove it when the bulbs start ripening.

Speed ripening by loosening the soil around the bulbs with a hoe 2 to 3 weeks before the harvest.

Once tops turn yellow, bend the leaves over with the back of a rake; this will divert the plant's energy to the bulbs instead of the stems. In a day or so, after tops have turned brown, lift the bulbs with a fork. If it's sunny, let them dry a little on the bed. Lay the tops of one row over the bulbs of another to keep them from burning.

Dry in a pail. To cure bulbs, drape the tops in a pail weighted with stones and let the bulbs dangle over the rim. Once the skins are dry and the tops have withered, in about a week, cut away the stems—they'll fall in the bucket for easy disposal in the compost pile. Don't forget to remove the stones.

Dry on a screen. If space is limited, fit a wooden frame with a large-mesh grill. Loop the onion stems through the holes to hold them in place. Once bulbs are dry, cut or pull them off as you need them.

A garland of onions. If the tops are long enough, you can braid them into a garland once the leaves are dry.

Store onions anywhere it is cool and dry to prevent rotting; always handle carefully to avoid bruising. Properly cured bulbs will last from a month to a year, depending on the variety.

For green onion tops year-round, place a bulb in the neck of a carafe or in a hyacinth vase. Roots will develop in the water, and you can harvest the stems until the bulb is exhausted.

No more tears. To peel an onion without crying, try one of the following tricks. Put a piece of bread on the point of the knife you're using. A second way is to peel the onion under running water. Or light three matches and blow them out; clench them with your front teeth and keep your lips closed around them while peeling.

Drive birds from fruit trees by suspending slices of onions in the branches; birds will be repelled by the odor.
▷ **Pantyhose, Vegetable Gardens**

ORCHARDS

Think it through. Having a home orchard yields delightful rewards—nothing is sweeter than sun-ripened fruit picked fresh from your own trees. But keep in mind that orchards take time and effort, including pruning, staking, timely harvesting, and protecting fruits from birds and other pests.

Enough room? Standard-size fruit trees can take up a good portion of your yard. If space is limited, select dwarf trees. Apple, pear, cherry, peach, nectarine, and plum trees are all available grafted onto dwarfing rootstock that restricts their size. They will still bear full-size fruit.

Beauty and bounty. While fruit trees are functional, they can also be decorative. Apples, crabapples, pears, and cherries make particularly attractive landscape specimens when in full flower.

Fruit trees are graded by height and trunk thickness and sold by age. Always go with the "A," or best, grade stock—it costs only a bit more. One-year trees are easier to transport, plant, and prune; 2- and 3-year trees will bear fruit sooner.

The right site. Choose a location with full sun and good air circulation for your orchard. A gentle south-facing slope with quick-draining soil is ideal.

A caution. If you locate the orchard on a slope, make sure there are no walls, hedges, tree rows, or other obstructions at the bottom. These will impede the flow of cold air and allow frost to settle around the trees—deadly to spring blooms. If you can't remove the obstacle, consider making an opening to let the air flow through.

Dig first. Have planting holes ready for your trees. Dig each about 3 feet wide and 2 feet deep and roughen the sides of the holes so that roots can penetrate. Incorporate compost or leaf mold with the backfill. Gardeners in the North can prepare a hole in fall for spring planting; just refill the hole with the amended soil and cover with a board until spring.

Raise the roots. Fruit trees can't tolerate wet feet. To promote drainage in damp soil, plant trees on mounds so that the crowns are 4 to 8 inches above ground level. Be sure each mound is at least a few feet wide so that it won't dry out in summer.

Tidy up roots. For bare-root trees, soak the roots in water for an hour before plant-

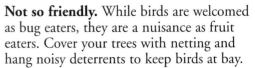

ing, then cut off any broken roots ½ inch above the damage. For trees with a root ball, carefully remove the container (usually burlap or wire) and prune damaged roots without disturbing the soil. Exposing healthy tissue will encourage rooting.

Spread 4 to 6 inches of compost, rotted manure, or other organic mulch around the tree. Keep it 1 foot away from the trunk to deny rodents a hiding place and to promote air circulation.

Keep in mind that some fruit trees need a partner for pollination. Plant compatible cultivars near each other to ensure fruit set.

Encourage bees to pollinate your orchard by installing a couple of bee hives. Use only the approved hives with removable frames. You can also invite bees by interplanting with specimens that attract them, such as lamb's ears, thyme, or bee balm.

Attract beneficials too. Encourage predator insects, like parasitic wasps and ladybugs, to visit the orchard by planting mint, Queen Anne's lace, catmint, yarrow, and other favorite food sources in a nearby bed.

Never use sprays at blossom time, since these may harm the bees and other insects that pollinate or benefit the trees.

Orchard helpers. Chickens can be a great help in the orchard. Let them roam freely beneath the trees, dining on insects and insect-infested fruits.

No better insurance. One of the most effective insect foes is the titmouse. Provide a birdhouse that has an opening of 1 to 1¼ inches in diameter to keep the sparrows away. Also lure birds to your yard with feeders in the winter—but not during growing season—and with birdbaths.

Not so friendly. While birds are welcomed as bug eaters, they are a nuisance as fruit eaters. Cover your trees with netting and hang noisy deterrents to keep birds at bay.

Wrap tree trunks with plastic guards to protect against sunscald, nicks from lawn equipment, and rodents who like to nibble on bark. Choose the type that expands as your tree grows and has ventilation holes.

Horticultural oil is effective for pest control on fruit trees. Use the heavier kind, called dormant oil, before trees leaf out to suffocate overwintering insects. Use the lighter oil—known as summer oil—during the growing season.

Good housekeeping. Always clean up leaves, fruits, and other debris around trees to discourage pests. Prune and destroy any diseased fruits or foliage. And monitor trees often for signs of problems, treating insects or diseases promptly.

▷ **Apple Trees, Apricot Trees, Cherry Trees, Citrus Fruits, Espaliers, Grafting, Harvesting, Peach Trees, Pear Trees, Plum Trees, Thinning**

ORCHIDS

Hard to grow? Orchids are commonly perceived as delicate and demanding. But thanks to modern cultural techniques, home gardeners can grow these exotic beauties with only moderate effort.

Most orchids require a warm environment (60°–80°F), high humidity, 12 to 14 hours of light daily, protection from direct summer sun, and good air circulation.

The two types. Terrestrial orchids grow in the ground; most are hardy enough to be raised outdoors in the North. Tropical orchids are tender and primarily epiphytic—that is, their roots thrive in organic matter lodged in tree limbs or rocks and are exposed to the air. Grow tropicals outdoors in warm climates; in cold areas, raise them in a greenhouse, solarium, windowsill, or window-mounted mini greenhouse.

TERRESTRIAL ORCHIDS

For success outdoors, plant each specimen in an environment that resembles its native habitat, such as a bog, woodland, or meadow. Provide winter protection with a heavy mulch of leaves or peat moss.

Never collect terrestrial orchids from the wild; buy only from nurseries. Look for healthy, established specimens that are ready to flower. Seedlings may not adjust to your garden and can take years to bloom.

The best choices for outdoors are the grass pink orchid *(Calopogon tuberosus),* calypso orchid *(Calypso bulbosa),* and lady's slipper *(Cypredium* spp.*).* They are hardy to –20°F.

TROPICAL ORCHIDS

Pot tropical orchids in a special medium that allows quick drainage and air circulation; they will not survive in a typical potting soil. Orchid fiber may include fir bark, sphagnum moss, tree fern fiber, perlite, and

A colorful tangle of orchids can become an exotic botanical attraction on a porch, patio, or deck.

charcoal. Use plastic pots with drainage holes; clay pots dry out too quickly.

For the best blooms and growth, apply a special orchid fertilizer once every 2 to 3 weeks.

Provide good air circulation; it's essential for healthy orchids. If you can't open a window, use a small oscillating fan, directing it away from the plants.

Orchids love humidity. Set them atop a tray of damp pebbles, keeping the base of the pots out of the water. You can also mist them lightly each morning.

Water in the morning whenever the potting fiber looks dry—but never make it soggy. While you can water once a week most of the year, you may need to do it daily in summer. Use 60° to 70°F water.

Repot orchids every 2 years, once the fiber breaks down or the plant outgrows its container. The best time to transplant is after the plant has flowered.

Groom orchids when you repot them. Prune off any dead roots with clean, sterile scissors. Divide overgrown specimens so that each new orchid plant has three or more pseudobulbs—the swollen stems— and some new growth.

Telltale roots. Orchid roots are a good indicator of the plant's health. They should be firm and white, with green tips. Soft brown roots may mean the orchid has received excess food or too much or too little water. It also may mean the potting medium has decayed and needs to be changed.

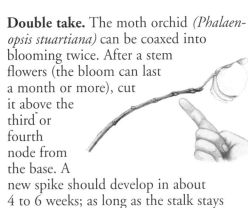

Double take. The moth orchid *(Phalaenopsis stuartiana)* can be coaxed into blooming twice. After a stem flowers (the bloom can last a month or more), cut it above the third or fourth node from the base. A new spike should develop in about 4 to 6 weeks; as long as the stalk stays green, there's a chance for it to rebloom.

Buying orchids as cut flowers may seem extravagant, but they are a thrifty choice in the long run—the blooms can last up to 7 weeks, depending on the variety. Change the water in their vase every 2 days, trimming the stem ends at the same time.

The easiest tropical orchids to grow at home are the cattleyas, epidendrums, lycastes, oncidiums, paphiopedilum, and phalaenopsis; these rarely grow more than 30 inches tall. All will thrive at normal room temperatures and moderate humidity (30 to 40 percent). Pot them in orchid fiber and place in any window except one with a north-facing exposure.

▷ **Houseplants, Native Plants**

ORGANIC FERTILIZERS

What are they? Organic fertilizers are garden foods derived from plants, animals, and minerals. They supply nutrients slowly, leach out gradually, and won't burn plants. They are also nontoxic to earthworms.

Food for the soil. Instead of feeding plants directly, organic fertilizers feed microorganisms in the soil, which break down the organic matter and release nutrients to plants.

Not a cure-all. As with chemical fertilizers, use organic ones to promote fertility—not to compensate for bad soil. Although some types, like manure, improve soil structure, no fertilizer can correct fundamental problems with drainage or tilth.

Buy organic fertilizers in garden shops or catalogs. Choose from complete fertilizers containing the three basic elements (nitrogen, phosphorus, and potassium) or special foods that supply one nutrient, like nitrogen-rich blood meal. With organic fertilizers, the sum of the N–P–K, or nutrient, ratio (such as 6–2–1) should not exceed 15.

Wet or dry. Some fertilizers, like bonemeal, are dry granules or powders; they can be spread on or dug into the soil. Others, like fish emulsion, are liquid; these are watered into the soil or sprayed directly on foliage.

Custom-made. You can mix your own fertilizers tailored to the needs of your soil. For an all-purpose fertilizer, for example, blend 2 parts blood meal, 3 parts bonemeal, and 6 parts greensand.

When to use. Apply fertilizers when you're preparing beds or holes for planting. With hardy trees, shrubs, and perennials, apply in early spring. For heavy feeders, you can also side-dress with light supplementary doses of fertilizer throughout the season.

⊰⊱ FEEDING YOUR GARDEN THE ORGANIC WAY ⊰⊱

While organic fertilizers often supply secondary nutrients and trace elements, including calcium and zinc, they are used primarily to provide nitrogen, phosphorus, and potassium. Select an all-purpose fertilizer that contains all three elements or use one of these single-nutrient types to correct a specific deficiency.

NITROGEN	Source	Nutrient rate	Application rate
Alfalfa meal	Alfalfa by-products	5%	5 pounds per 100 square feet
Blood meal	By-product of meat processing	15%	3 pounds per 100 square feet
Cottonseed meal	Dehulled cotton seed	6%	2–5 pounds per 100 square feet
Fish emulsion	By-product of fish processing	4%	20 parts to 1 part water
Fish meal	By-product of fish processing	10%	5 pounds per 100 square feet
Hoof and horn meal	By-product of meat processing	14%	4 pounds per 100 square feet
Leather dust	By-product of leather tanning	5–12%	½ pound per 100 square feet
Manure	Animal waste	2–13%	3–50 pounds per 100 square feet
Soybean meal	Soybean by-products	7%	5 pounds per 100 square feet
PHOSPHORUS			
Bird guano	Dried seabird manure	8%	3 pounds per 100 square feet
Bonemeal	By-product of meat processing	20%	3–5 pounds per 100 square feet
Rock phosphate	Washed, crushed limestone	33%	10 pounds per 100 square feet
POTASSIUM			
Granite dust	By-product of quarrying	5–7%	10 pounds per 100 square feet
Greensand	Marine sediment	3–5%	10 pounds per 100 square feet
Kelp meal	Processed seaweed	12%	1 pound per 100 square feet
Langbeinite	Mined mineral	22%	1 pound per 100 square feet
Liquid kelp	Extract of kelp meal	12%	25 parts to 1 part water
Wood ashes	Burnt wood	6–20%	1–2 pounds per 100 square feet

For acid lovers only. Cottonseed meal can lower soil pH. Use it only on plants that prefer acidic soil, like rhododendrons.

To brighten the hues of your hydrangea blooms, feed them with a dilute solution of blood meal. Stir about 1 ounce of blood meal into 5 gallons water and apply to the soil around plants. Repeat about 1 month later.

Banish bunnies from your garden by sprinkling blood meal around the plants. Be sure to replenish it after a rain.

Long-term benefits. Although greensand and granite dust yield their valuable potassium very slowly, they will endure in the soil for up to 10 years. Apply in the fall to beds being planted in spring. These two materials will also improve soil structure.

Sweeten acid soil with wood ash or rock phosphate. Either of these amendments will raise pH by at least one point.

Versatile kelp. Kelp meal and liquid kelp do more than simply providing potassium: they are also a source of chlorine, sodium, and the 50-odd other trace elements that plants need in minute quantities.

Dig it deep. Apply bonemeal close to the root zone, using the finest-ground product you can find. Work it into the holes when planting trees, shrubs, roses, and bulbs.
▷ **Ashes, Coffee Grounds, Fertilizer, Manure, Seaweed, Tea**

ORGANIC GARDENING

Garden with nature. The tenet of organic gardening is using nature as a guide and disturbing the environment as little as possible. It involves using preventive techniques to avoid problems and treating any pests, diseases, or nutrient deficiencies without synthetic chemicals. If you're not ready to truly "go organic," you might still try some of these gardening practices.

A healthy foundation. The basis of organic gardening is good soil. Have it tested and adjust the pH as needed. Use organic fertilizers and improve soil structure by incorporating compost, manure, or other organic matter. Guard against erosion with mulch.

Compost, compost, compost! It's the best way to provide organic matter to the soil and reduce the amount of garden waste flowing into landfills and dumps.

Be tolerant. Organic gardeners strive for optimum health, not cosmetic perfection. Learn to tolerate a few weeds or insect pests if they are not causing serious harm.

Plant good companions. Use certain plants to encourage growth of other plants and to repel or attract insects. Plant peanuts with squash, for example, to increase the crop yields of both. Use basil among ornamentals to discourage aphids. Growing yarrow near fruit trees will lure bees.

Away with weeds! Hand pick, hoe up, or smother weeds with mulch to keep them from harboring pests and diseases and robbing your plants of nutrients.

Prevent stress. Stressed specimens are vulnerable. To remedy, site plants in a spot that meets their growing needs, then keep them fed and watered. Set them at the recommended spacing to avoid root competition and promote air circulation. Protect them from air pollution as needed.

Shop smart. Buy plants, whether hybrid or open-pollinated types, that are resistant to pests and diseases and tolerant of the growing conditions in your garden.

PEST CONTROL
Preventive measures. Keep pests off plants with barriers. Use floating row covers, fine-mesh netting, burlap, cardboard, or aluminum foil. Even a circle of tar paper under a plant will keep some insects from doing damage or laying eggs.

Manual labor. Hand picking is often all that's needed to reduce insect populations. Pluck pests off plants and squash them. Or you can drop them in a pail of soapy water.

Lure beneficials. Plant food sources, such as angelica and morning glory, to attract ladybugs, lacewings, and other predators that eat fellow insects. Or buy beneficials from catalogs. As long as nectar and their favorite pests are available, they'll stick around.

Other helpers. Don't overlook the predators that devour pests, including birds, bats,

frogs, and lizards. Spiders are also good allies. Plant asters and goldenrod, which spiders like for their web sites; leave a patch of plant debris in a garden corner where spider eggs can overwinter.

Homemade sprays. You can brew your own pesticides in the kitchen by blending ½ cup hot peppers or garlic with 2 cups water and spraying it on infested plants. A strong stream of plain water is also effective in destroying aphids, mealybugs, and red spider mites.

Use biological controls, like *Bacillus thuringiensis,* and biological poisons, such as rotenone, to combat serious pest infestations.

DISEASE CONTROL
Keep it clean. Sanitary practices help prevent the spread of fungal, bacterial, and viral diseases. Wash tools in a solution of 2 tablespoons bleach to 1 quart water or wipe surfaces with isopropyl alcohol. Also keep the garden clean: remove infected plants and autumn debris, where diseases can lurk through winter.

Be diverse. Planting a wide range of specimens helps keep diseases from running rampant through the garden.

The way to water. Some soilborne diseases are spread when they are splashed on foliage during overhead watering. Use a soaker hose or drip irrigation and water only in the morning. Also use mulch to keep soil on the ground—not on plants.

There's no cure for bacterial and viral diseases; you must destroy the plants. You can control fungi, however, with nontoxic organic solutions made from baking soda, copper, sulfur, and lime.
▷ **Biological Controls, Companion Planting, Compost, Ladybugs, Organic Fertilizers**

THE GARDENER'S SHADOW

Organic gardeners like to quote an old Chinese proverb: "The best fertilizer in the garden may be the gardener's own shadow." It's their belief that the daily attendance of a living presence, as opposed to a chemical or artificial one, may be the best tonic growing plants can have.

ORNAMENTAL GRASSES

Not for the lawn. Related to the spreading lawn grasses, the ornamental varieties form large clumps with gracefully arching blades and delicate seed heads. They are at home in any garden—as a backdrop, edging, screen, ground cover, or accent specimen.

Learn the Latin name. Given the dizzying variety of ornamental grasses, avoid confusion when selecting them. Using the Latin name instead of the common one will ensure that you get exactly what you want.

DESIGN AND PLANTING

Where to plant. Most grasses, such as fountain grass *(Pennisetum spp.)* and pampas grass *(Cortaderia selloana)*, need full sun and moist, well-drained soil. Some, like gold hakone *(Hakonechloa macra* 'Aureola'*)* and moor grass *(Molinia caerulea)*, prefer shade. Bamboos dislike moist or wet areas,

Tipped with silvery-purple seed heads, the slender stems of fountain grass form a graceful foliage spray.

while the sedges *(Carex spp.)* and rushes *(Juncus spp.)* will thrive there.

Take a cue from nature when designing with ornamental grasses, which often grow in large drifts in the wild. Consider planting a sunny slope or field with masses of beardgrass *(Andropogon virginicus)* or switch grass *(Panicum virgatum)*.

Mix them in. The slender blades of ornamental grasses look especially striking when combined with plants boasting bold foliage or flowers. Mix blue oat grass *(Helictotrichon sempervirens)* with fothergilla and purple coneflowers. Or plant maiden grass *(Miscanthus sinensis* 'Gracillimus'*)* with black-eyed Susan and 'Autumn Joy' sedum.

Size them up. Use tall ornamental grasses—including zebra grass *(Miscanthus sinensis* 'Zebrina'*)* or ravenna grass *(Erianthus ravennae)*— at the back of the border or as a screen. Smaller grasses—such as blue fescue *(Festuca ovina* 'Glauca'*)* and Japanese blood grass *(Imperata cylindrica* var. *rubra)*—are ideal for edging beds or lining paths.

Fall fanfare. Many grasses are at their peak in autumn, when their stems are burnished copper and almond and topped with colorful seed heads. Emphasize their beauty by combining grasses with such late-flowering plants as asters, goldenrod, blackberry lily, and Japanese anemone.

Dramatic lighting. Let the sun illuminate grasses from the back or side for a spectacular effect. Plant wild-oat grass *(Chasmanthium latifolium)* in a west-facing garden so that the setting sun can play off the dainty seed heads. Or use feather-reed grass *(Calamagrostis × acutiflora* 'Karl Foerster'*)* in a border on the south side of your yard; the sun will spotlight its feathery spikes.

A solo act. With its tall stature—up to 12 feet—and large silver or pale pink plumes, pampas grass shares the stage with

no one. Plant it prominently as a specimen. While the species is hardy only to 20°F, gardeners in cooler climates can try 'Andes Silver' and the smaller (6-foot) 'Pumila,' which are hardy to about 5° to 10°F.

Queen of the Nile. An exotic choice for Southern gardens is papyrus *(Cyperus papyrus)*, prized for its threadlike stems and umbrella-shaped flower clusters. In warm areas, plant this Egyptian native in full sun and rich, moist soil; it thrives in shallow pools. In cold climates, plant it in a pot and submerge in a deep pool. When temperatures dip below 40°F, bring the plant inside to a greenhouse or sun room. Set the pot in a decorative container or large urn filled with water.

Beware of speedy spreaders. Unless you need ground covered quickly, avoid the vigorous grasses. Ribbon grass *(Phalaris arundinacea* var. *picta)*, kuma bamboo *(Sasa veitchii)*, and golden grove bamboo *(Phyllostachys aureosulcata)* are all rampant creepers. For erosion control on dry sites, use blue lyme grass *(Elymus racemosus* 'Glaucus'*)*. To bind the banks of a stream, try manna grass *(Glyceria maxima)*.

MAINTENANCE

Cut down clumps in early spring so that new shoots can emerge. Use a pruning saw or electric hedge trimmer to cut large clumps 6 inches above the soil. With small clumps, snip with shears to about 2 inches. Wear gloves; grass blades can be sharp.

Feed sparingly. Some grasses, such as gold hakone, appreciate rich soil. But most others will produce soft, unmanageable growth if given too much fertilizer.

Lift and separate. To divide grasses, lift a clump with a spade or fork in early spring. Divide small clumps by hand or with a

❧▐ PLAYING WITH COLOR ▐❧

Not all grasses are green. Many are either colored or variegated with a different hue. Try these varieties for subtle color in the garden.

Blue *Agropyron magellanicum; Festuca ovina* 'Elijah's Blue' (left); *Festuca amethystina; Elymus glaucus; Helictotrichon sempervirens; Sorghastrum nutans* 'Sioux Blue.'

Red *Imperata cylindrica* 'Red Baron' (right); *Miscanthus sinensis* 'Purpurascens'; *Panicum virgatum* 'Haense Herms, 'Squaw,' or 'Warrior'; *Pennisetum setaceum* 'Rubrum.'

White *Arundo donax* 'Variegata'; *Calamagrostis arundinacea* 'Overdam'; *Carex morrowii* 'Variegata'; *Miscanthus sinensis* 'Cabaret,' 'Cosmopolitan,' or 'Morning Light.'

Yellow *Alopecurus pratensis* 'Aureus' or 'Aureovariegatus'; *Carex elata* 'Bowles Golden'; *Glyceria maxima* 'Variegata'; *Hakonechloa macra* 'Aureola'; *Miscanthus sinensis* 'Strictus' or 'Goldfeder'; *Millium effusum* 'Aureum.'

knife; divide large ones with a sharp spade or an ax. Transplant the smaller pieces.
▷ **Bamboo**

ORNAMENTAL VEGETABLES

Favorites for fall. Gourds are one of the most popular vegetables grown for their decorative value. Harvest these cucumber cousins in autumn for their bright-colored shells—in yellow, orange, and green—and their odd shapes, from turbans to penguins.

The handsome artichoke. The silver-gray, serrated leaves of the artichoke contrast well with flowering bedding plants. You can grow it for the value of its foliage alone, without regard to its climate needs.

Autumn accents. With their ruffled foliage veined in rose, pink, purple, or cream-white, ornamental cabbage and kale are cold-hardy specimens that will adorn the garden well into winter. Plant them after summer flowers fade—along paths or in borders or tubs. For extra color, team them with fall bloomers like chrysanthemums, asters, and October daphne. Good choices include eye-catching 'Dynasty Pink' cabbage and 'Cherry Gateau' kale.

Homegrown bowls. Cut away the centers of ornamental cabbage and kale to make serving bowls for salads or dips. You can also peel off the outer leaves and arrange them as a liner on a serving plate.

Colorful corn. Grow ornamental corn for its prettily patterned kernels—ideal in autumn displays. Try 'Rainbow Inca' for red, blue, and orange kernels or 'Oaxacan Green' for emerald ones. 'Strawberry Popcorn' produces berry-shaped ears with tiny red kernels. Also try 'Red Stalker' corn for its red-purple stalks.

Good eating, good looking. Many common edible vegetables are attractive enough to be used as ornamentals. Use 'Tequila Sunrise' or 'Chocolate Bell' peppers and 'Violet Queen' cauliflower for their fruits. For textured or colorful leaves, plant ruby chard, savoy cabbages, or 'Red Sail' lettuce.
▷ **Gourds, Vegetable Gardens**

ORNAMENTS

Accessorize your garden as you would your home: the possibilities are limited only by your imagination. In addition to such traditional ornaments as pots, statuary, birdbaths, and sundials, you might use mirrored globes, wind chimes, abstract sculpture, baskets, whirligigs, grapevine wreaths, or decorative wall plaques.

Consider style. Match the ornament to the style of your garden. Classical statuary, for

An ornamental urn can punctuate a garden design and provide a visual pause in a sea of green.

example, looks best in a formal garden, while a folk-art whirligig or whimsical birdhouse betters suits a cottage garden.

Proper perspective. Place large ornaments where they can be appreciated at a distance. Site small ones for viewing up close.

A bee skep—the straw hive once used for beekeeping—makes an ideal ornament in an herb garden. Make sure it has no opening for bees to enter: you probably don't want a colony living in your garden, and skeps are not the most sanitary of hives.

Backdrops. Make a piece of sculpture stand out by planting evergreens as a backdrop. Good choices are yew or boxwood hedges, bamboo, small conifers, or ferns.

Pot within a pot. Ornamental urns seldom have drainage holes. To ensure proper drainage, set a potted plant inside the urn and prop it up on an overturned pot or bricks.

PALMS

A tropical touch. Because palms are native to the tropics, even the hardiest specimens can't tolerate temperatures lower than 20°F. Grow these stately trees in the garden only in the warmest climates. Otherwise, there are numerous species suited to pot culture.

Starting from seed. Soak fresh seed in lukewarm water for 24 hours before planting. Sow in a mix of equal parts sand and potting mix to a depth equal to the seed's height. Keep the soil warm and moist and the surrounding air humid. And be patient: it can take from a month to a year for the seed to sprout.

Stop transplant shock. Make transplanting fragile seedlings easier by sowing seed in plastic bottles cut off at the neck and perforated on the bottom. Once sprouts develop, slit open the container and gently remove the seedling for transplanting.

Prickly palms. To prevent injury to pets and people, locate the spiny-trunked needle palm and the sharp-leaved saw palmetto in low-traffic areas of the yard.

Transplant palms only at the start of the growing season. In dry areas, water the soil 2 days before digging up the tree. Have the planting hole prepared so that you can set in the tree immediately. Bury the trunk a little deeper than before to aid stability and root development. Water well until the plant is reestablished.

When potting palms, always use deep containers. The strong palm roots push down through the soil and can lift the tree out of the pot once they hit the bottom.

Freshen the soil of potted palms every 2 years. Carefully dig out the top 3 to 4 inches of soil, discard, and replace with new soil. Doing so enables the plant to stay in the same pot for many years.

If foliage yellows on indoor plants, the cause may be dry air. Increase moisture with a humidifier or by setting the pot in a pan of moistened pebbles. Trim back yellowed ends diagonally with scissors, leaving just a little of the damage to avoid cutting into healthy tissue. Also try growing varieties that require less humidity, such as the miniature date palm, fan palm, or sentry palm.

The Canary Islands palm soars to 60 feet and boasts up to 100 feathery fronds measuring 20 feet long.

Prune off dead or damaged leaf stalks flush with the trunk; use a pruning saw. The palm will look neat and tidy and there will be no hiding places for pests and diseases.

⊰ A PALM SAMPLER ⊱

The best choices for growing outdoors are the king palm (*Archontophoenix cunninghamiana*), queen palm (*Arecastrum romanzoffianum*), jelly palm (*Butia capitata*), Canary Islands palm (*Phoenix canariensis*), windmill palm (*Trachycarpus fortunei*), coconut palm (*Cocos nucifera*), and fan palms (*Washingtonia* spp.).

Smaller palms appropriate as houseplants include the parlor palm (*Chamaedorea elegans*), sentry palm (*Howea forsterana*), Chinese fan palm (*Livistona chinensis*), miniature date palm (*Phoenix roebelenii*), and lady palm (*Rhapis excelsa*).

PANTYHOSE

Store bulbs and seeds in pantyhose hung from a beam or pipe well above the ground. Rodents are repelled by synthetic fibers and will leave your stock alone.

Keep onions and garlic in pantyhose after they have been cured. Drop a bulb down a leg and tie a knot; continue with the rest of your bulbs. Hang the hose top from a hook in a cool, dark, well-ventilated place and snip off a bulb from the bottom as needed.

A stocking cap. Cover fruits and vegetables individually with legs cut from pantyhose. Slip a "cap" over the fruit and close the open end with twine (the toe forms the other end). The covering will repel birds, insects, and rodents and will stretch along with the growing fruit. The cap works well on tomatoes, apples, pears, eggplant, peppers, and grapes. For cabbage or broccoli, put the cap over the whole plant.

Rot-resistant ties. Cut hose crosswise into circles of the desired width and use them to tie trees, stems, and vines to stakes with a figure-eight loop. The soft, durable ties won't damage tender plant growth and are easy to snip off and remove at season's end.

Easier pickings. Make a fruit picker by attaching a hoop of stiff wire to the end of a pole. Stretch a leg of pantyhose around the hoop and secure it. The net is handy for reaching fruits from high branches—and won't bruise soft fruit skins.

The perfect tea bag. Turn pantyhose into a "tea bag" when making manure or compost tea. Cut off two legs and fit one inside the other. Fill the bag with rotted manure or compost, knot the top, and place in a container of water; about one shovelful is enough for a barrel. Let it steep for a week and apply full strength or diluted to your plants.

If you collect rainwater from downspouts, put an old piece of pantyhose between any two sections of the pipe at an easy-to-reach place. The water will be free of debris. Just be sure to clean the trap often to prevent clogging.

An improvised filter. Porous pantyhose make an ideal filter. Use it to strain fertilizer, pesticide, or fungicide solutions into a sprayer. If you keep bees, you can filter honey from the extractor; just make sure the pantyhose is very clean.

Deterring deer. To help keep deer out of the garden, fill pantyhose feet with bars of strong-smelling soap, mothballs, or clippings of human hair from the barbershop. Hang from stakes throughout the garden. While nothing can deter truly determined deer, the odors will repel casual browsers.
▷ **Protection, Spraying**

PARSLEY

A slow starter. Parsley seeds can take 6 weeks to sprout and need moisture to break dormancy. Speed germination by soaking the seeds in lukewarm water for several hours before sowing.

To ease handling of the tiny seeds, dry them off and mix them with sand or dried coffee grounds. Sow them outdoors in ¼ inch of soil and cover the row with a board to keep seeds moist and cool. Lift the board daily to check for sprouts; they should emerge in about a week.

Good companions. Sow some radish seed in the furrow with the parsley. Radishes sprout first, marking the row so that you won't disturb the parsley seed while hoeing.

Sowing indoors? If so, you can transplant the seedlings when they have two sets of true leaves. Tap the plants from the pots carefully—parsley has a long tap root and dislikes too much handling.

For fresh parsley all winter, sow seed in October. In the North, sow in pots and keep them in a sunny window. In the South, sow them in the garden; parsley grows best in warm and hot climates through the fall and winter.

Plant a strawberry pot. Fill the pot with soil to just below the first hole. Insert the first plant through the top of the pot, lay it on its side, and pull the foliage through the hole. Cover roots with soil and repeat with the remaining holes.

Keep leaves clean. Mulch parsley plants with straw to keep soil from splashing on the leaves during rainstorms or watering. To dislodge any grit before using parsley, swish harvested stems in cool water.

Going on vacation? Before you leave, cut parsley tops and freeze them for later use. Water the remaining stems well with dilute manure tea; new leaves will begin growing while you're away.

Save the scent. To preserve the delicate oils that impart flavor, freeze parsley in plastic bags just after harvest. Chop the leaves first or gather sprigs in bunches with a rubber band. When you need parsley, simply rub the bag on the outside to crumble the leaves, then scoop them out. You can also store stems by standing them upright in a glass of water.

A cure for puffy eyes. Don't discard parsley seeds that you didn't sow—use them in a refreshing compress. Mix 1 tablespoon of seeds with 1 cup boiling water; let cool. Soak a washcloth in the infusion, wring out till damp, and fold it in thirds lengthwise. Lie down, place it over your eyes, and relax.
▷ **Herbs**

PATHS

What's the use? When designing a path, consider how it will be used and select a material accordingly. A high-traffic connector between the house and driveway, for example, would call for a stone or brick path. A little-used woodland walk might be covered with pine needles or moss.

Straight or sinuous. A linear path looks formal and is best used in structured gardens, perhaps running between double borders or raised beds. A curved path is more relaxed; it works well in naturalistic settings, such as cottage or woodland gardens.

Beautify with blooms. Soften path edges by lining them with colorful borders of flowers. Select low-maintenance plants of medium height and a mounding or sprawling habit. Good choices include lavender, cranesbills, aubrieta, baby's breath, candytuft, coral bells, fringed bleeding heart, and astilbe.

A stone carpet. Turn a stepping stone or gravel path into a mini flower bed by tucking in plants among the stones. Use ground-hugging specimens that will appreciate the radiant heat and fill in quickly. Try aubrieta, alyssum, thyme, bellflower, creeping phlox, and ajuga.

Grass paths are an elegant, if high-maintenance, choice in regions with sufficient rainfall. They can make a small yard look larger by extending the lawn into the garden and help link the lawn with ornamental beds. Reduce wear and tear in the most heavily trafficked areas by laying a few flat paving stones at foot-step intervals. Set them deep enough so that a mower can pass over them easily.

In your flower beds, place stepping stones in among the plantings. They will keep your feet clean and dry and prevent soil compaction when you are doing maintenance—and will quickly be hidden beneath the growing foliage.

Proper pacing. To plan a stepping stone path, walk with a normal stride and mark your foot fall with sand or sticks. Lay down the stones and walk again: if they're too far apart, your stride will seem awkward; if too close, you'll feel as if you're standing still. Adjust the spacing, then set the stones in their permanent positions.

A clever clover path. Dutch white clover provides a resilient path between rows in the vegetable garden and serves a second purpose: when tilled under at season's end, it will add valuable nitrogen to the soil.

Safe footing. Logs cut horizontally into stepping "stones" make good use of felled trees and are a natural for a rustic path. But they can become slippery when wet. Before setting them in the ground, nail or staple fine metal screening to the top surface to provide traction. Choose screening that blends with the wood.

No artificial lighting? Line a path with large white stones. During the growing season, plant edgings of white or pastel flowers, which will seem to glow at twilight.

Thwart weeds. For paths of gravel, river stone, shredded bark, or other loose particles, work a weed suppressant into the soil and use a geotextile weed mat as an underlay. It will not only prevent weeds from pushing their way through the paving material but will also prevent the surface from sinking into the mud when it rains.

Prevent puddles. When building a paving stone or brick path, make sure the sides slope slightly away from the middle. This will allow water to run off onto an adjacent lawn or flower bed.
▷ **Bricks, Paving Stones**

PATIOS

The transition zone. The patio is an exterior living space that links your house and garden, creating a transition between indoors and out. Select a uniform style for the patio surface, furniture, planting containers, and plants that will harmonize with the overall look of your property.

Simpler is better. Use restraint when selecting surface materials for the patio. A single material—perhaps with one or two accents—will provide unity and balance. If you have a brick house, for example, consider a bluestone patio with brick edging. With a stucco house, you could use concrete pavers accented with quarry tiles.

Grade for drainage. Make sure the patio slopes away from the house so that water can drain freely; a fall of 1 inch for every 6 feet is usually enough.

Smother weeds. If you're decking the patio with wood planks, spread a permeable geotextile fabric underneath. It will keep weeds in check while letting water and air reach the soil, preventing the wood from rotting.

Plan for lighting. Make your patio liveable after sunset by installing both general and accent lighting. Use brighter lights for dining and seating areas and dimmer lights to outline patio edges and adjoining paths.

Screen your patio. If you need privacy or shelter from the wind, edge the patio with tall shrubs, such as cherry laurel, oak-leaf hydrangea, juniper, arborvitae, euonymus, or broom. Another alternative is to erect a sturdy latticework fence and plant it with quick-growing vines.

Soften the edges. Surrounding the patio with smaller shrubs will keep the view open to the landscape and minimize the hard paved edges. Good choices include thread-leaf cypress, boxwood, Japanese holly, leucothoe, and skimmia. Don't use any prickly plants, like barberry, near the patio.

A garden amphitheater. If your patio is sunken or at the bottom of a slope, surround it with a terraced garden. Use complementary materials for stairs, paths, and retaining walls and plant the beds with a variety of trees, shrubs, flowers, and ground covers.

Minimize mess. Keep plants with messy fruits or seed pods far away from the patio. Fruits like cherry, mulberry, and crabapple will stain the patio surface and furniture, while debris like acorns and catkins will need to be swept up.

South-facing patios may need to be shaded for comfort in high summer. Install a living umbrella by leaving a hole in the center of the patio and planting it with a pretty shade tree. Select a specimen that has a tall trunk, high branches, and deep roots that won't eventually raise the paving materials. In hot climates, consider installing a pergola over part of the patio.

Improve acoustics. Muffle noise as it bounces off the house by training climbing vines up the walls. As a bonus, the plants will keep the house cooler in summer and lower your air-conditioning bills.

From the ground up. When greening up your patio, plant in levels. On the floor, use pots and planting boxes. Or you can remove some of the surface material at random locations and plant the spaces with low-growing, mounding specimens. At eye level, use baskets hung on tripods or wall brackets. Add a sense of height to the patio by training climbers up a trellis or wall.

Clear the decks. Keep containers and plants out of high-traffic lanes, where they may be stepped on or knocked over. Also keep them away from furniture and access areas to the patio, such as paths or doors.

Plant for winter too. If your patio is visible from a room that you use often during winter, don't leave it bare. Plant a few attractive broad-leaf evergreens or conifers to enhance your view.

In the North, make sure you use all-weather planters for perennial vines, evergreen trees, or other hardy specimens that will remain outdoors over the winter.

If weeds pop up between patio pavers, stones, or bricks, kill them with boiling water instead of herbicide. The scalding heat will get rid of dandelions, crabgrass, clover, plantains, and other unwelcome visitors that often take root in paving spaces.

Seating space. On small patios with little room for seating furniture, build a low wall around the perimeter. Top it with flat, smooth stone or bricks to make it a comfortable place to perch.

A favorite activity. Most patios would be incomplete without a barbecue. Just make sure you locate it in a safe place—on a level surface so that it won't tip and far enough away from your house so that flying embers won't cause damage.

▷ **Paving Stones**

PAVING STONES

PURCHASING

Take your pick. Paving materials for paths and patios include brick, flagstone, slate, bluestone, cobblestone, concrete or clay pavers, granite setts, Belgian block, and ceramic tile. Select a surface that will provide the durability you need and will harmonize with your garden style.

The wet test. Spray a paving stone with water before buying. You can test the slipperiness and see how the stone changes color when wet.

Uneven surfaces, like those formed with Belgian block or cobblestone, are attractively rustic but hard on the feet. For high-traffic areas, choose a smooth, level surface instead, such as brick, pavers, or bluestone.

INSTALLATION

Make a base. Prepare the ground properly before setting down paving materials. Dig to a depth of about 6 inches and tamp the soil absolutely level; be sure to slant the surface away from any buildings to allow for water runoff. Then lay down 3 to 4 inches of gravel and top with a 2-inch layer of sand.

On the level. Don't just "eyeball" the installation of paving stones. Mark off straight edges with stakes and string. Always use a level when preparing the base and setting down the stones.

Keep them stable. You can install paving stones in a bed of either mortar or sand. Mortar is best for holding small, light, or irregularly shaped materials in place. It is also good if you have clay or sticky soil or live in a cold climate where frost heaves are common. Sand is a good choice in mild climates and for holding large, heavy materials.

To set in sand, lay stones either butted together or spaced with a gap of up to ½ inch on all sides. Pour sand on top and work it into the cracks well with a broom; water in to settle the sand. Once the stones are dry, add more sand and sweep again until the cracks are filled flush; water in. The more sand packed into the joints, the tighter the hold will be.

To set stones in mortar, first spread strips of mortar over the base where the stone edges will sit. Lay down the stones, leaving a ½-inch space between them; if necessary, use pre-made spacers to insure evenness. Tamp stones into the mortar and check for levelness. Then fill joints with more mortar, removing the spacers before it hardens. Smooth and recess the joints slightly by running the rounded end of a stick or paintbrush over them. Also remove any excess mortar from the stone surface.

A green alternative. Instead of sand or mortar, fill the spaces between stones with a mix of one part sand to one part compost. Plant with pearlwort, moss, mother-of-thyme, or another low-growing ground cover for an attractive "joint" that won't need mowing or maintenance.

MAINTENANCE

Stop slippage. Although moss and lichens are attractive on paving stones, they can be slippery and dangerous. Remove them by scrubbing with a stiff brush or treating with a nonstaining chemical eradicant.

A simple herbicide. To destroy weeds that crop up between paving stones, drench with boiling water or with a solution of 3 ounces salt dissolved in a gallon of water.
▷ **Bricks, Paths, Patios**

PEACH TREES

Where they thrive. Peaches are temperate-zone trees, growing well along both coasts, around the Great Lakes, and southwest of the Rockies. While some peaches require a period of cold dormancy before flowering, others are "low-chill" types that don't need and won't tolerate a harsh winter.

Select peaches according to your climate and the type of fruit you prefer: clingstone flesh is hard to pry from the pit, while the flesh of freestones comes away easily. Both kinds are either yellow or white.

Another consideration is the plant's resistance to pests and disease. Look for cultivars that won't be afflicted with brown rot, leaf curl, leaf spot, canker disease, or borers—all serious peach problems.

Pick your spot. Peaches need excellent drainage, full sun, and protection from wind. If late-spring cold snaps are common, plant your trees on a north-facing slope, where frostbitten buds will have a chance to thaw gradually before being exposed to the sun.

Winters too cold? You can still grow the so-called "patio peaches." These genetic dwarfs never grow taller than 3 feet, so you can raise them in tubs and move them to a sheltered location for the winter.

For a reliable harvest, plant new trees every 5 years. Peach trees live only 10 to 15 years, and the new trees will begin producing just as the old trees are fading.

MAINTENANCE

Pamper your peaches. Keep the trees well watered during the growing season; they need about 3 inches of water each month. Spread an organic mulch or compost at the tree base, keeping it 1 foot from the trunk. After the petals drop, feed with 10–10–10 as growth begins in spring and spread 2 cups of bonemeal outward to the dripline.

For the best peaches, thin fruits early, allowing 6 to 8 inches between each.

Look for the red. Wait to prune until the flower buds are just starting to show red. You'll easily be able to spot which branches will yield fruit and which have suffered winter damage. Pruning wounds will also heal more rapidly at this time.

Prune peaches more severely than most other fruit trees to increase fruit quality and promote growth. Remove any limbs that form a narrow angle and train to create a spreading shape with an open center.

"Fishbone" pruning. Select branches that are a year old—recognizable by their red-

dish color. Cut off at the base any shoots that point straight up or down, as well as any weak branches. This will leave vigorous shoots that are nearly horizontal—resembling the shape of a fishbone.

Banish borers. A gummy substance at the trunk base is a sign of peach tree borers. Poke wire into their holes to kill them. Or place a ring of mothballs on the soil around the trunk in late summer, before the soil cools below 60°F. Mound a thin layer of soil over the mothballs and against the trunk; after 1 month, level the soil.

Protect against leaf curl, which causes leaves to blister and drop. In mid-fall and again when buds begin to swell, spray with Bordeaux mixture or lime-sulfur. Apply to the entire tree, getting into all crevices. Remove and destroy any affected leaves.

Harvest when ripe, as green peaches won't mature off the tree. Select fruits that are slightly soft but still firm, have good color, and come free from the stem with a twist. Let them ripen further at room temperature for three days. Don't fret about a split pit or a little mold on the seed; the flavor and quality of the flesh will be unaffected.
▷ **Orchards**

> ### A PEACH SAMPLER
>
> **'Babcock'** White flesh; excellent flavor; good for the West
>
> **'Elberta'** A classic; yellow flesh; a good "keeper"; resists borers; widely adapted
>
> **'Garden Sun'** Yellow flesh; freestone; dwarf to 5 feet; good for canning
>
> **'Indian Blood'** Crimson skin and rose-gold flesh; clingstone; firm, fine-grained fruit
>
> **'La Seliana'** Yellow flesh; freestone; late-season fruit; adapted to the South
>
> **'Orange Cling'** Yellow flesh; clingstone; large, late-season fruit; good for canning
>
> **'Redhaven'** Yellow flesh with red, fuzzless skin; freestone; very juicy; good for the Northeast

---

PEAR TREES

European or Asian? European pear species boast buttery-smooth fruits, but may become afflicted with fire blight. The Asian species have small, crisp, somewhat gritty fruits but are more resistant to disease.

PLANTING

Don't play with fire. Fire blight is the most destructive problem affecting pears. Select a variety that is blight resistant and

---

> ### A PEAR SAMPLER
>
> **'Beurre Bosc'** European; russet skin; rich, fine-grained flesh; top quality; stores well
>
> **'Clapp's Favorite'** European; large yellow pear with red blush; sweet, juicy; very productive
>
> **'Hosui'** Asian; round, golden-brown fruit; very juicy; mild taste with a tang; easy to grow
>
> **'Moonglow'** European; gold skin with creamy flesh; big crop; excellent blight resistance
>
> **'Seckel'** European; small fruit with copper skin; sweet and spicy taste; good blight resistance
>
> **'Ya Li'** Asian; sweet fruit; good resistance to fire blight; ideal for warm climates

prune off any damaged tree parts in the dormant season to stop the blight's spread.

A pair of pears. Pears require cross-pollination to produce fruit, so always plant two compatible varieties. 'Bartlett,' 'Conference,' and 'Doyenné du Comice' are good pollinators and yield delectable fruits.

No room? If you have room for only one pear tree, select one with several varieties grafted onto a single rootstock. Your tree will be self-pollinating and bear different kinds of pears at different times.

A dwarf pear bonus. Minimize your pruning by growing a grafted dwarf pear. It needs only light grooming to keep its shape. Just snip any branches that point downward.

Pears need full sun and appreciate good garden loam, although they will tolerate heavier, poor-draining soil better than other fruits. In the East and Midwest, they can even be planted in the lawn as a shade tree.

MAINTENANCE

Hold the nitro. Feed pears sparingly with nitrogen; it stimulates succulent new shoots susceptible to fire blight. On trees 3 years and older, use only enough 5–10–5 to produce 6 to 12 inches of growth each season.

Poky producers. Pears first bear fruit after they are 3 years old. To encourage fruiting, bend upright branches down with strings or weights until they are just above horizontal, with little or no arching.

Thin fruits 6 weeks after bloom, after most of the immature fruits have already dropped. Thin multiple clusters to a single fruit and leave 6 to 8 inches between fruits.

Halve it. Instead of cutting pears off at the stem when thinning, snip the nut-size fruits in half with pruners. This prevents sap from rushing to the remaining fruits, which can cause them to drop.

HARVEST

For perfect pears, pick when the fruit is slightly underripe and just turning a lighter green. Then let them ripen for a few days at 65° to 70°F.

Two tests. Press the flesh at the base of the stem; when it gives, the pear is ready for picking. You can also check by lifting the fruit against the curve of the stem: harvest when the stem breaks easily from the branch spur right at the slight swelling.

A longer life. Pears will last longer if you dip the stems in melted paraffin or wax. Let dry; they'll ripen over several weeks.
▷ **Orchards**

PEAS

Cool veggies. Peas prefer cool weather and stop maturing once temperatures reach 70°F. In the North, plant as soon as the soil can be worked in spring; in the South, plant in fall. Sow seed ½ inch deep and 2 inches apart in rows that are 3 feet apart.

Treat pea seeds with a bacterial inoculant powder to help them fix nitrogen from the air. Doing so will increase your crop yields.

A pea tepee. A decorative and practical way to plant peas is in a ring around a tepee. Use slender tree branches with plenty of twigs. Push 5-foot-tall stakes about 1 foot into the soil.

Other supports. Give tall vining varieties an arbor to climb on. Support dwarf or midsize bush plants with netting, string, or a chicken-wire trellis that is 4 feet tall. Or grow them along a chain-link fence.

⚘ A PEA SAMPLER ⚘

Peas come in three forms: garden peas (also called shelling peas), snap peas, and snow peas—the latter two with crisp, edible pods. Select from dwarf, midsize, or tall types and early, mid-season, or late varieties—peas mature between 55 and 70 days.

Tasty garden peas include 'Little Marvel,' 'Lincoln,' 'Green Arrow,' 'Maestro,' and 'Alaska.' For crisp, sweet snap peas, grow 'Sugar Snap,' 'Sugar Ann,' or 'Sugar Daddy.' Tender snow peas include 'Dwarf Gray Sugar,' 'Snowbird,' and 'Oregon Sugar Pod II.'

A prelude for corn. Because peas will fix nitrogen in the soil, they are a good crop to plant before rotating corn or other heavy feeders in the same garden space.

The pea weevil is a common pest. Dust dampened or dew-laden foliage with lime or rotenone to repel the tiny brown beetles.

Pea pickin'. Harvest shelling and snap peas about 3 weeks after blossoms appear; the pods will be plump and bumpy. Pick snow peas when the pods are still flat. Snip or gently pull the pods from their stalks.

The sweetest peas are those eaten immediately; the sugar turns quickly to starch.
▷ **Vegetable Gardens**

PEAT MOSS

The magic moss. Derived from partly decayed sphagnum moss, peat has many garden uses. It loosens and aerates soil—making it ideal for potting mixes—and helps retain moisture. It also works well as a mulch and makes an excellent insulator.

Dig in. Peat moss is sold dried and pressed in plastic-covered bales and can be hard to scoop out. Loosen with a hand cultivator before digging in with a shovel.

Fight the heat. Potted plants dry out quickly in summer. Put them in a container filled with peat moss to insulate them.

Protect tender plants in a peat-moss jacket. Ring the plant with a wire cage

and line with plastic. Shovel in dry peat to cover the plant. Tent the top loosely with a plastic sheet to shed water but permit air flow.

The peat paradox. Though peat moss is very moisture retentive, it is slow to absorb water when completely dry. Moisten it thoroughly before using as a soil amendment or mulch, then keep it moist.

How much moss for mulch? A 6-cubic-foot bale of peat moss will cover about 300 square feet when spread 1 inch deep.

Start bulbs in the bag. Give dahlias and other summer-flowering bulbs a head start by planting them in a bag of peat outdoors. Cut open the bag, wet well, and nestle the bulbs in the peat. If a cold spell threatens, cover the opening with a board.

Storing tubers. After lifting the tubers of tender plants for the winter, bury them in a tray of dry peat moss. It absorbs moisture without letting the tubers dry out.

A hit with heath. Because peat moss is acidic, it is ideal for heath, heather, and their other family members: rhododendrons, mountain laurel, and blueberries. Dig plenty of moist peat into the planting hole and mix more into the backfill.
▷ **Planting, Alkaline Soil**

PEONIES

Terrible travelers. Peonies like to stay put, so select their location carefully and prepare their beds to last for years. Pick a sunny to partially shaded spot that is protected from wind. Dig to a depth of 12 inches and amend the soil generously with compost or well-rotted manure; the soil should be slightly acidic and quick draining. Mix a few handfuls of bonemeal into each hole.

Cover their eyes. Plant peonies in autumn, when their "eyes"—little red buds on the crown—are visible. Set the eyes 1 to 2 inches below the soil line, but no deeper; otherwise the plant will never bloom.

A classic combo. Interplant peonies with irises for a stunning show in late spring. Pair crimson peonies with bright yellow or purple irises for a hot mix. For a subtle look, use white or pink peonies with pastel irises.

Use a green screen. Help prevent peonies' heavy blooms from snapping in the wind by shielding the plants with an evergreen hedge. A bonus: The flowers will sparkle all the more before the dark green backdrop.

Support peonies. To keep the blossoms from falling over, let peonies grow through the metal support rings available at garden centers. Or make your own: cut a circle from a piece of large-mesh grill and attach it securely to a thick bamboo stake. Position the ring close to the ground as growth begins and raise it gradually as the stems get taller.

A string fence. To keep a row of peonies looking neat and natural, support them

Protected from wind by an evergreen hedge, a luxuriant tree peony unfolds its ruffly flowers.

with a string fence. Place green stakes at the ends and in the middle of the row. Run soft green twine between the stakes at two or three different heights. Be sure to set up the fence early—before the buds break.

Beware of blight. Botrytis blight makes peony shoots and leaves appear burned and causes buds to shrivel. Remove and destroy all damaged plant parts and spray with Bordeaux mixture in early spring. Cut back shoots in fall and clean up any debris.

Dramatic cut flowers. For displaying peonies indoors, select stems with buds that are just opening—the striking blooms will unfold in a few days. And cut the stems with only a few sets of leaves. The plants need the foliage to produce food for the following year.

If you must move peonies, transplant them in early fall. Lift the clump carefully with a fork and divide the roots into pieces with a knife or by hand, making sure that each has three to five eyes. Replant the divisions immediately in amended soil, with the tips of the eyes no deeper than 2 inches below soil level; water well. After the ground has frozen solid, spread a thick but airy mulch of hay, shredded oak leaves, or evergreen branches over the planting bed.

▷ **Flower Beds**

PEPPERS

Don't plant peppers where you previously grew potatoes, eggplants, or tomatoes. All of these members of the nightshade family are prone to the same soilborne diseases.

These tropical natives need warmth to thrive. Start seed indoors 8 weeks before you want to set out plants and keep them at about 70°F. Transplant outdoors a month after the last frost, once the soil temperature reaches at least 65°F.

Dig deep. Peppers like a well-aerated bed. Turn soil to 1 foot deep and amend with 20 pounds of compost per 100 feet of row.

Sun-shy seedlings. Transplant peppers in late afternoon or on a cloudy day to protect young leaves from scorch. In hot areas, shade the top growth beneath an upside-down cardboard box propped up at one end until plants are established.

Pale peppers? If you amended the soil well with compost, peppers generally don't need fertilizer. If leaves are pale, however, the plants may be suffering from a nutritional deficiency. Spray weekly with a mixture of kelp and fish emulsion until they bloom.

The way to water. Peppers need even, moderate moisture around their roots. Watering overhead

when plants are in bloom will wash away pollen, resulting in no fruits. Water only with a drip irrigation system or soaker hose.

Spread a thick but light mulch, such as grass clippings or hay, to conserve moisture, but keep it a few inches from the plant base. Good mulching is especially important once the peppers bear fruit—the heavy plants tend to topple over, and mulch will keep them clean.

Pick a peck of peppers by cutting—not pulling—the ripe fruits from plants, taking about ½ inch of stem.

A pepper rainbow. Harvest most fruits when they are still green. While leaving a few peppers on the plant slows production, the remaining fruits will become sweeter and change color to red, yellow, or orange depending on the variety.

If frost threatens, harvest any ripe peppers and cover the plants with blankets. The protection should keep the peppers producing for another week or so.
▷ **Chilies, Vegetable Gardens**

PERENNIALS

What are they? Perennials are herbaceous plants with soft, nonwoody stems that live for more than one season. The top growth dies back each winter but the roots survive to send up new shoots in spring. Although some perennials will last only a few years, others can survive for decades.

The exceptions. A few perennials, including santolina, lavender, and Russian sage, have semi-woody stems, but they are too insubstantial to be considered shrubs.

An elegant interplay of colors, textures, heights, and shapes marks the well-composed perennial garden.

The tender types. Some perennials, such as wax begonia, zonal geraniums, alstroemeria, and calla lily are not hardy and must be grown as annuals in cold climates. But they will return year after year in hot areas.

PURCHASING

Save money with seeds. While perennial plants are available from garden centers and catalogs, you'll save money—and enjoy a greater choice of plants—by raising perennials from seed. Start them in pots or a nursery bed; once they develop a set of true leaves, they are ready for the garden. Most perennials will bloom in about 2 years.

Flowers for free. If you need to cover an area quickly and economically, purchase perennials that reseed readily. Good self-sowers include yarrow, columbine, lamb's ears, bellflower, and pulmonaria. Also collect plant seed in fall and keep your eyes open for any volunteers for transplanting.

Consider your site. Most perennials require full sun and moist, well-drained soil. Select specimens that will thrive in your garden—whether it's boggy or dry, shaded or sunny, windblown or protected.

Learn to love leaves. Because perennials bloom for a brief period, select plants with attractive foliage. Bergenia, plumbago, and many sedums have waxy leaves. Monkshood, bleeding heart, coralbells, and cranesbills exhibit "cut" leaves. Iris, tradescantia, and daylilies have grasslike blades. Yarrow and chamomile offer lacy fernlike foliage, while lady's mantle and ligularia have saucer-shaped leaves.

Double your pleasure. Some perennials bloom twice per season, either naturally or after being cut back. Among those to plant for a double dose of blooms are 'Miss Lingard' phlox, Siberian iris, snowdrop anemone, dwarf baby's breath, lythrum, and cranesbills.

PLANTING

Draw a plan. A perennial will occupy its spot for many years, so plan carefully before you plant. Draw a small plan on graft paper. Arrange plants in combinations that show their flowers and foliage to best advantage, and remember that perennials look best when planted in drifts. Vary the number in each drift and intersperse with larger accent plants.

Hide the fast faders. Tuck plants whose foliage withers after blooming, such as poppies, bluebells, and bleeding heart, behind specimens that maintain their good looks, like iberis, hosta, or lamb's ears.

When to plant. In regions with cold, wet winters or heavy soil, plant perennials in spring once the soil warms. Where winters are mild or soil is light, plant in autumn.

Prepare the soil thoroughly, so the plants' long-lived roots will have a good home. Turn the soil over to at least 1 foot and incorporate plenty of organic matter to ensure good water and air circulation.

MAINTENANCE

Soak, don't spray. The most effective way to water perennials, which need about 1 inch of water weekly, is with a drip system or soaker hose. The soft stems may flop over if they are watered from above.

Mulch the beds year-round with an attractive organic mulch. It's the best way to suppress weeds, retain moisture, and prevent frost heaving over the winter.

Pinch them back. Keep perennials bushy and compact and prevent tall stems from toppling by pinching out the stem tips.

A constant chore. Deadhead your perennials religiously to keep the plants vigorous. Just snip or snap the spent flowers off the stems. However, don't deadhead any plants whose seed you want to collect for propagation or whose seed heads provide winter interest.

Put them to bed. Winterize your perennial garden by removing any dead flowers or foliage in autumn. After a hard freeze, cut back all stems to ground level and add extra mulch.

❧ A PERENNIAL SAMPLER ❧

There are thousands of perennials to choose from—one for every site, style, and level of gardening skill. The following are easy-to-grow plants, arranged by bloom time.

Spring Ajuga, arabis, basket-of-gold, bergenia, bleeding heart, columbine, coralbells, euphorbia, foamflower, Jacob's ladder, lady's mantle, leopard's bane, peony, poppy, primrose, pulmonaria, thrift, violet

Summer Acanthus, astilbe, baby's breath, bee balm, bellflower, blanket flower, catmint, coneflower, coreopsis, cranesbill, daylily, delphinium, dianthus, goat's beard, hosta, iris, lavender, loosestrife, lupine, monkshood, penstemon, phlox, veronica, yarrow

Fall Aster, boltonia, chrysanthemum, cimicifuga, Japanese anemone, goldenrod, lobelia, toad lily

▷ **Color, Flower Beds**

Inspiring designs from the past

Whether planted for utility or pleasure, gardens through the ages have exhibited a broad range of styles, influenced by environmental and philosophical upheavals but invariably linked to the efforts of earlier cultures. In medieval Europe, for example, the monks in cloistered monasteries kept alive the Greek and Roman traditions of cultivating herbs for medicine and food. Later, when the turmoil of medieval conflicts subsided, gardening evolved into an art form. This was most evident in Elizabethan England, with the dedicated manipulation of plants into formally manicured, highly specific shapes—topiary, espalier, and knot designs. The French carried this style to even stricter disciplines in their mirror-image parterres, allées radiating from a central axis, and trees in vases.

European settlers soon brought to the New World the gardening traditions of their homeland. Yet survival in this harsh new environment ensured that the household gardens of early New England would be largely functional.

By the 19th century ornamental gardening was back in vogue. In America a moneyed class built grand houses with landscapes to match. Their lush Victorian "carpet bedding" perfectly exemplified the Gilded Age: an era of overindulgence, even in gardening. The early 20th century, however, kindled an interest in more subtle—yet splendid—perennial borders, as popularized in English gardens by Gertrude Jekyll.

Whether fueled by necessity or by indulgence, the gardens that have gone before can inspire and enchant us.

A MEDIEVAL PHYSIC GARDEN

In the monasteries of medieval Europe, herbs and flowers were cultivated solely for their healing properties. They were used in fresh or dry forms or were distilled; the essential oils then went into the making of tinctures, ointments, and other medicines. The monks' knowledge of medicinal herbs was drawn from the writings of the first-century Greek physician Dioscorides, whose *Materia Medica* listed more than 500 plants that were believed useful for a variety of ailments.

The typical medieval physic garden was enclosed within the monastery's cloistered walls. Square or rectangular beds were divided by narrow paths and separated by a wide central path. Individual beds were small, for ease of maintenance, and were usually confined to the culture of a single species. Some of those species are listed here.

Borage *Borago officinalis*
Chamomile *Anthemis nobilis*
Eyebright *Euphrasia officinalis*
Fennel *Foeniculum vulgare*
Hyssop *Hyssopus officinalis*
Lavender *Lavandula officinalis*
Parsley *Petroselinium crispum*
Rosemary *Rosmarinus officinalis*
Rue *Ruta graveolens*
Sage *Salvia officinalis*
Tansy *Tanacetum vulgare*
Thyme *Thymus serphyllum*

AN ELIZABETHAN PLEASURE GARDEN

"Pleasaunce" gardens were highly favored in England during the reign of Queen Elizabeth I (1558–1603). These carefully planned outdoor rooms reflected the order and neatness so important in the daily life of the time. In contrast, however, were the facets of the garden that existed purely to delight the senses.

A typical Elizabethan garden was enclosed by tall hedges meticulously woven together. Ornamented rails surrounded the inner garden, where individual beds, planted with sweet herbs, flowers, and fruit trees, were arranged in perfectly symmetrical mirrored halves.

We know much about the plants grown at the time through the writings of Shakespeare. The plants that follow are among those recorded in his works.

Bay *Laurus nobilis*
Clove pink *Dianthus caryophyllus*
Eglantine rose *Rosa eglanteria*
Lavender *Lavandula angustifolia*
Pot marigold
    Calendula officinalis
Primrose *Primula veris*
Rue *Ruta graveolens*
Sweet marjoram
    Majorana hortensis
Woodbine honeysuckle
    Lonicera periclymenum

A COLONIAL HOUSEHOLD GARDEN

The gardens of 17th-century New England were grown more for utility than pleasure. A settler of modest means would organize a garden for small crops near the house, growing there what was needed for the household—food, flavoring, medicine, and dyestuff. Crops that needed more space were located farther away, where soil and exposure were better.

Like those of medieval Europe, Colonial household gardens were comprised of square or rectangular beds (often raised) separated by narrow paths and enclosed by pale or picket fencing. Useful flowering plants, herbs, small fruits, and vegetables were grown together with little concern for height or balance. Extremely fragrant plants, however, were planted in a separate area—the prevailing belief being that the perfume might permeate the soil and taint the rest of the crops.

The plants in the following list were taken from the writings of John Josselyn, who, in his *New England Rarities* (1673), described in detail the gardens of the New World.

Coriander *Coriandrum sativum*
Feverfew *Chrysanthemum parthenium*
Houseleek *Sempervivum tenctorum*
Lavender cotton *Santolina chamaecyparrisus*
Lettuce *Lactusa sativa*

Parsley *Petroselium crispum*
Pot marigold *Calendula officinalis*
Sorrel *Rumex acetosa*
Winter savory *Satureja montana*

HIGH VICTORIAN CARPET BEDDING

By the late 19th century, flower beds with a single species had fallen out of fashion. Favored instead was a form of mass planting aptly called "carpet bedding." Elaborate patterns were created with low-growing, boldly colored plants, which formed a dense carpet. At times the patterns had a patriotic or other symbolic theme, although geometric or concentric designs were more common. Beds were sometimes planted into a slope so that the pattern could be more fully appreciated.

Literally thousands of plants were used in the carpet beds of parks and municipalities. Home-owners sought to adapt such plantings to fit their own front yards. Their designs changed with the plants each season: hybridization and plant explorations around the globe meant that there were more varieties to choose from than ever before. The exotic plants that grew year-round in conservatories could now take their place outdoors in the summer plantings of any private home.

The plants in the following list were among the most commonly used in late-19th- and early-20th-century carpet bedding designs.

Banana plant *Musa ensete*
Canna *Canna ehmanni*
Coleus *Coleus* spp.
Dwarf blue ageratum *Ageratum* spp.
Geranium *Pelargonium* spp.
Golden feverfew *Chrysanthemum parthenium* var. *aureum*

Pansy *Viola tricolor* var. *hortensis*
Scarlet salvia *Salvia splendens*
Stonecrop sedum *Sedum acre*
Sweet alyssum *Lobularia maritima*
Tulips *Tulipa* spp.

PERIOD GARDENS

PERSPECTIVE

Reflections of grandeur. The mirror image created by a small body of water can change your perspective—making even a tiny garden appear more spacious. In a small area, install an elongated pool in the foreground. On a patio or roof deck, fill a large tub with water and install aquatic plants around its edges.

Out of bounds. Extend the perspective of your garden by highlighting a feature outside your property—perhaps a hill ablaze with fall colors or a distant church steeple. Frame the vista with a pair of ornamental trees, a gap in a fence, or an archway.

Create the illusion of depth by making a visual pathway that leads to a focal point. A row of shrubs, a strip of lawn, or a long flower bed composed of one bold color can all draw attention to a spectacular specimen plant or landscape feature in the distance.

Two for one. In a small or mid-sized space, create two gardens in one by installing a low wall or row of plantings. It not only makes the area seem larger but adds visual interest.
▷ **Landscaping**

PESTICIDES

No garden is pest-free. But a well-tended garden contains a balance of beneficial predators and healthy, resistant plants—along with a tolerable number of undesirable insects and other pests. Use pesticides only if an infestation is causing damage and can't be otherwise controlled. Start with the least toxic substance possible and move gradually to stronger measures as needed.

What they're made of. Pesticides are derived from a range of organic and synthetic sources and are available in liquid or dry form. Many gardeners prefer organic types, which are made from bacteria, viruses, fungi, fatty acids, minerals, oils, and plants; they decompose quickly into nontoxic substances that won't harm the environment.

How they work. Pesticides are generally sprayed or dusted on plants or soil, where they suffocate, paralyze, or poison insects on contact or by ingestion. You must completely cover the affected plant or soil surface, including leaf undersides.

Systemic insecticides are absorbed by the plant and circulated by its sap, and can't be washed away by rain. Pests are killed when they feed on any part of the plant.

Know your enemy. Be sure to identify the pest correctly and choose the appropriate pesticide. Find out about its life cycle and habits so you can treat it effectively.

Be kind to bees. Many pesticides harm bees and other desirable insects. Try to use the most "specific" substance possible—one that targets the pest you want to destroy—and don't apply a bee-killing pesticide during bloom time, when bees are most active.

USING PESTICIDES SAFELY

▷ Always read pesticide labels carefully and follow the directions on handling, use, and storage to the letter.

▷ Apply pesticides on a dry, calm day with moderate temperatures and low humidity.

▷ Always keep children and pets away from pesticides while they're being applied and until they have dried or settled completely.

▷ Cover as much of your skin as possible. Wear rubber gloves, long-sleeved shirt and pants, eye protection, and a dust mask. Avoid touching your face or eyes.

▷ Never eat, drink, or smoke while handling pesticides. Avoid inhaling powders or sprays.

▷ Don't allow pesticides to contaminate ponds, streams, or swimming pools.

▷ Don't apply a pesticide to food crops unless the label states that it is safe to do so.

▷ Clean all equipment carefully after application. Wash your hands and face thoroughly with soap. Launder clothing separately.

▷ Keep pesticides in their original packaging and store them in a secure, dry, cool place.

▷ Repeat applications only as needed and as indicated on the product label.

Horticultural oils, which include dormant oil and summer oil, are used to smother eggs and developing insects on trees and ornamentals. Use the heavier dormant oil in late winter or early spring, once temperatures are over 40°F, but before plants leaf out. Use the lighter summer oils any time the temperature is below 85°F.

Insecticidal soap is one of the best cures for soft-bodied pests like aphids, mites, and leaf miners. It is safe on most plants and is nontoxic to beneficial insects and animals. But don't spray it in direct sun, in extreme heat, or during drought.

Brew your own insecticidal soap by mixing 2 teaspoons dishwashing liquid with a few drops of vegetable oil and 1 gallon water. Use a plastic spray bottle to apply—but wash it thoroughly if it held household cleansers.

More home brew. Make "bug juice" by collecting ½ cup of the pest you want to kill; mash them with 2 cups water and a few drops liquid dish soap. Strain and spray on plants affected with that particular pest.

HOW TO AVOID PESTICIDE USE

▷ Start with healthy plants adapted to your site and encourage diversity in the garden.

▷ Practice good housekeeping by deadheading spent flowers and clearing away debris—thus denying pests a place to hide and nest.

▷ Monitor the garden constantly for evidence of pest damage so you can stop a problem before it becomes an infestation.

▷ Use mechanical controls, such as barriers, traps, hand-picking, and floating row covers

▷ Enlist such allies as chickens, frogs, birds, ducks, lizards, spiders, ladybugs, and bats—all predators that feast on garden pests.

Ay, caramba! Mix ½ cup hot chili peppers in 2 cups water and a few drops vegetable oil in a blender. Strain and spray on plants.

Test first. Some pesticides can scorch, discolor, or damage foliage. Always test the substance first on a small, inconspicuous part of the plant. Wait for a few days—if the growth remains healthy, use the pesticide on the entire plant.

Reserve a sprayer, either a hose-end or portable type, exclusively for pesticides; don't use it for herbicides or fungicides. Label it clearly with an indelible marker and clean it out thoroughly after each use.

Bottle it up. Prevent pets, birds, and children from touching a bait-type pesticide by placing it in a one-pint plastic bottle. Bury the bottle in the ground so that its top is right at the soil line. Pests are small enough to crawl in and reach the bait, but critters and kids are not.

▷ **Biological Controls, Spraying**

PETUNIAS

Tiny petunia seed needs extra attention. About 10 weeks before the last frost, sow indoors in a tray prepared with fine soil on top. Press the seeds well into the soil, but don't cover, and water from below. Plant out after danger of frost in soil amended with compost or rotted manure.

Please pinch the petunias. When seedlings are 6 inches tall, pinch the stem tips to encourage side branching.

⊰I A PETUNIA SAMPLER I⊱

These indispensable annuals come in most solid colors and numerous bicolors that have contrasting veins, edges, center stars, or stripes. Petunias bear either single, trumpet-shaped blooms or ruffled double blooms.

Of the two main types, grandifloras have fewer but larger flowers. Use them in hanging baskets, along paths, or in planters, where they will spill over the edges. The Cascade, Supercascade, Magic, and Supermagic series have single flowers; doubles include 'Circus,' 'Blue Danube,' and 'Purple Pirouette.'

Multifloras produce masses of smaller flowers and are more compact. Because they are more resistant to diseases, they are good for open borders and in humid climates. For singles, try the Joy, Pearls, or Plum series; for doubles, grow the Tart or Delight series.

Avoid spatters. Mulch petunias well so that mud won't splash up and mar the flowers when it rains.

A midsummer pick-me-up. Petunias get leggy in the middle of summer. Cut back the stems to 6 inches and give the plants extra fertilizer and water. Within a few weeks, they'll be blooming again.

No smoking. Petunias are particularly susceptible to tobacco mosaic virus. If you smoke, do so away from the plants. And always wash smoke or tobacco residue from your hands before touching petunias.

Look like rain? Then shield your petunias—even the sturdiest ones can be flattened by a downpour or a powerful squirt from the hose. Simply cover them with cardboard boxes or a plastic sheet draped over stakes to keep it off the plants.

▷ **Flower Beds**

PHOSPHORUS

Where to get it. Synthetic sources of phosphorus are superphosphate and diammonium phosphate. Organic sources include bonemeal, rock phosphate, and guano.

Feeling blue? Plants suffering from lack of phosphorus develop a bluish cast. Leaves may also turn a dark, dull green on top and bronze-purple on the undersides. Stems remain thin and may turn purplish. For a quick boost, spray plants weekly as needed with fish emulsion; it has about 5 percent phosphorus that is immediately available to plants.

A slow worker. Phosphorus moves downward in soil extremely slowly. When it is applied in liquid form to the surface, it remains at the top inch or so; in dry fertilizers, it remains near the granules. For this reason, make sure you apply phosphorus around the root zone.

Unfriendly soils. Phosphorus becomes less available to plants in acidic and cold, wet soils. This is critical in spring, when young roots are trying to get established. Watch for symptoms of deficiency and add phosphorus as needed. You can also sweeten acid soil with wood ash to a pH of about 6.5 and warm it with black plastic mulch.

The finer, the better. Bonemeal is a slow-release source of phosphorus, remaining in the soil for up to a year. Buy steamed, crushed bonemeal that is finely ground so that soil microorganisms can break it down more readily.

Rock vs. collodial. Rock phosphate is washed, crushed limestone and contains about 33 percent phosphorus. It releases the nutrient slowly and will work in acidic soil. Collodial phosphate is the residue left from washing limestone and comes in small particles. It contains about 20 percent phosphorus, some of which is available immediately; it works best in neutral soil.

If you go overboard and end up with excess phosphorus, don't add any source of the nutrient for 2 years. Work in extra nitrogen and potassium to balance it out.
▷ **Fertilizer, Organic Fertilizers**

PINCHING

Confused? The terms "pinching," "pinching back," "pinching off," and "pinching out" are interchangeable. All refer to removing the growing stem tip or a bud—usually about a half inch of growth—to spur compact, bushy plants and more buds.

For big blooms on dahlias, pinch out the side shoots to train it to a single stem. When buds appear, remove the lateral ones on the main cluster, leaving only the central bud. With chrysanthemums, start pinching out the stem tips when the plants are 8 inches tall and continue until mid-July, when the buds form.

On rose standards, keep the trunk tidy and direct the energy to the top growth by pinching or cutting out any little buds that form along the stem.

Big and beautiful. Eggplants and peppers often sprout many flowers that, if left alone, will make many small fruits. Pinch back some of the flowers so that the plant will expend its energy on producing larger fruits instead.

Double duty. Pinching back can also help eliminate colonies of aphids. These common pests often cluster on the stem ends of beans, roses, and many ornamentals.

⇥ PLANTS TO PINCH BACK ⇤

ORNAMENTAL PLANTS

Begonia	New York aster
Black-eyed Susan	Nicotiana
Bougainvillea	Pansy
Carnation	Peony
Chrysanthemum	Petunia
Coleus	Phlox
Dahlia	Poinsettia
Fuchsia	Salvia
Helenium	Snapdragon
Impatiens	Star jasmine
Jade plant	Sweet pea
Marguerite	Verbena
Marigold	Zonal geraniums

EDIBLE PLANTS

Basil	Peppers
Beans	Pumpkin
Chervil	Rosemary
Eggplant	Sage
Grapes	Squash
Melon	Strawberry
Mint	Tarragon
Oregano	Tomato

Nip it in the bud. Remove developing buds from the lower trunk of cherry, plum, and apple trees before they form branches. If the shoots are soft enough, simply pinch them off; carefully cut older shoots away with a pruning knife.

Variegated plants, with leaves marked in white, pink, or yellow, sometimes send out leaves of solid green. Pinch these back to the main stem; otherwise, the entire plant may revert to green.
▷ **Pruning**

PLANTERS

Take your pick. Planters for container plants come in such a wide variety of shapes and sizes—from the ornate to the starkly plain—that you can always find one suited to any site in your yard.

The right size. Container plants need sufficient space to develop strong root systems. For shallow-rooted annuals, herbs, and vegetables, use planters that are 8 to 10 inches deep. For taller shrubs, small trees, and climbers, use planters that are at least 12 to 16 inches deep.

Drill for drainage. Most manufactured planters have drainage holes. If needed, you can drill holes easily into wood, fiberglass, plastic, and even concrete containers—tubs, troughs, and window boxes, for example. Use a ¼-inch drill bit and drill at a slow speed to avoid cracking fragile materials; be sure to use a masonry bit for concrete.

A good foundation. Spread a layer of gravel or ceramic pot shards over the bottom. Cover with a very fine screen or a weed mat before adding potting mix to prevent the soil from washing out.

A weighty subject. Stabilize the planter for large or top-heavy plants by placing a few flat, heavy stones in the bottom.

Retaining water. The soil in planters dries out very quickly, especially in full sun. To help it retain moisture, add pumice or water-absorbing soil polymers to the potting mix; they swell with water, then release it slowly and evenly.

Lighten the load. For a balcony or roof garden, where weight might be a problem, fill your planters with a lighter-weight soil-less potting mix.

Top dressing. To renew the soil in a planter without repotting, carefully scrape off the top 2 to 4 inches of soil and replace it with a rich, new mixture. Mulch with compost, then water; nutrients from these new layers will seep down to the roots.

When repotting or replanting, empty the container completely and wash it with a solution of one part household bleach in nine parts water. Remove any mineral deposits with a mild vinegar solution. Then rinse the planter thoroughly with water.

Prop up your planter. Don't set planters directly on the patio. Not only will a concrete, brick, or stone surface radiate heat through the planter—which dries the soil and could harm the roots—but the planter won't be able to drain properly. Prop the planter atop a few small wooden blocks.

Winter protection. Use plastic, wood, or fiberglass planters if you intend to leave them out year-round in a cold climate. Protect both plant and container by wrapping wire mesh loosely around the planter; fill the space with plastic packing peanuts, plastic bubble wrap, or dead leaves.

Easy moves. If your planter doesn't have wheels, you can move it on a "conveyor belt" of round logs or pipes. Keep the planter rolling by continually bringing the last log to the front. If you can lift the planter, you can also transport it in a child's wagon.

▷ **Pots**

PLANTING

Think ahead. Choose planting sites and prepare planting holes in advance. The job will go faster on planting day, and your plants won't need to remain in their containers any longer than necessary.

The right site. Make sure the location you choose meets the plant's cultural requirements and will permit the specimen to reach its mature height and spread.

Rotate vegetables. When planning a vegetable garden, keep in mind what plants occupied which spots the previous year and rotate crops accordingly; you'll avoid soil-borne disease. Tomatoes, for example, are susceptible to verticillium wilt, which remains in the soil and attacks future crops.

Help young plants get off to a good start. Set them out on a cloudy day or in late afternoon, so that the delicate leaves won't scorch. Keep them well watered until they're established; young roots have difficulty drawing enough moisture from the soil.

In the bag. Before setting out small plants in a windy or exposed area, first put the plant in a paper bag containing good soil. Then set the bag in the ground, leaving 2 inches of the rim above soil level. The seedling will be sheltered, and as it grows, the paper will decay and let the roots reach into the surrounding soil.

Treating peat pots. When setting out plants that have been grown in peat pots, rip off the rim and the bottom of the pot. Leave the rest intact; it will protect the roots and eventually break down in the soil.

TIMING IS EVERYTHING

▷ Wait until the soil reaches at least 40°F before planting. Roots cannot grow in cold soil.
▷ Let the soil dry out. Don't rush to plant right after a rain—working soggy soil destroys its structure, and roots can rot in waterlogged soil.
▷ Check the last frost date. Wait until the danger of frost has passed before planting out any tender specimens or young seedlings.
▷ Don't plant when pests are at their most active. During a rainy spring, for example, leave seedlings in their pots a little longer to keep them from being eaten by slugs.

Plant at the proper depth. Never set a plant significantly higher or lower in the soil than the depth at which it was previously grown. A notable exception is the tomato, which can be planted deeply; it produces new roots along the stems.

Easy exit. Never pull a plant out of its pot by the stem. Coax it out by running a knife around the inside of the container, staying close to the sides. Turn the pot on its side and tap the rim and base with a mallet. The plant should slide out easily. If not, break a clay pot with a hammer or cut open a plastic one with shears.

Loosen the roots of a container-grown plant before planting. Tease the roots apart with your fingers; if they are tightly wound, use a trowel or a kitchen fork. Place the plant in the hole and spread the roots in all directions before backfilling.

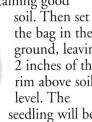

Accept no substitutes. Double check with your nursery that the material wrapped around your balled-and-burlapped tree or shrub is actual burlap. Some suppliers use a plastic mesh that resembles burlap but won't break down in the soil, thus severely inhibiting root growth. Always remove any synthetic burlap from the root ball before planting.

The real thing. If the root ball of the plant is wrapped in natural burlap, you can leave the covering in place when planting. Simply remove any twine and loosen the burlap around the stem, folding it back several inches to expose the top of the root ball. This will keep the burlap from wicking moisture away from the roots.

A new way to plant? The latest research on planting trees recommends against amending the soil; instead, the tree roots should become accustomed to the native soil while they are still young. To plant, dig a hole three times wider than the root ball, but no deeper (most roots don't penetrate more than 18 inches into the soil). Fill in the hole, water deeply, and mulch.

All alone... and a tree to plant. It's difficult to hold a tree upright while shoveling soil around the roots. To keep the stem steady, tie a long, sturdy piece of wood to the trunk at the soil line. Put the tree in place and backfill; remove the block when you're finished.

Turn, turn, turn. Once you've set a shrub or tree in its hole at the proper depth, stand back and look it over. Make sure the stem is straight up and down and that the prettiest, fullest side of the plant is most visible. Rotate the plant around in the hole and level it with a little soil under the root ball as needed.

Give it a shake. When planting a bare-root tree or shrub, give it an occasional shake as you add backfill. This will help the soil filter down between the roots and fill in evenly around them.

Get the air out. To eliminate air pockets when planting bare-root plants, make a mound of soil in the planting hole. Spread the roots out over the mound and fill in the hole halfway with soil. Add water to the top of the hole; let it drain out to settle the soil. Tamp lightly with your hands, then continue adding soil to the top the hole. Water again and mulch.
▷ **Staking**

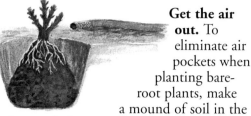

PLUM TREES

A quartet of plums. The most widely grown types of plums include European, damson, Japanese, and American. They vary widely in cold hardiness, pollination requirements, and disease resistance, so select a species appropriate to your site.

Early bloomers. Because plum trees, especially Japanese plums, bloom early in spring, the blossoms—and your crop—can be lost to a late frost. Plant the trees on a north-facing slope for protection.

Poor competitors. Shallow-rooted plum trees can't tolerate much competition, even from grass. If you plant a plum on the lawn, keep the soil beneath it free from grass or weeds out to the dripline; mulch with organic matter.

Plums like it rich. These heavy bearers need plenty of organic matter and fertilizer for maximum fruiting. Dress with 2 cups of bonemeal and 1 cup alfalfa meal each year, adding extra nitrogen if growth is not vigorous. Spread 10 pounds of compost from the trunk to the dripline annually.

Flowers, but no fruit? For best production, plum trees need cross-pollination, generally from a member of their own species (such as damson or Japanese). Check with the nursery about the requirements for your tree.

Watch for black knot, a fungal disease that causes black lumps on branches. Prune out and destroy infected wood. Or select a disease-resistant cultivar.

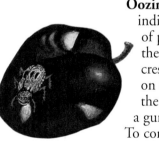

Oozing plums may indicate the presence of plum curculios; the beetle leaves a crescent-shaped scar on the fruit, and the grubs secrete a gummy substance. To control the pests, spread a sheet under the tree around bloom time and shake the tree: the insects will drop off. Also destroy all infected fruit, hang green sticky-ball traps, and spray with rotenone after petal fall.

Pick plums for eating fresh when they are fully ripe; the fruit should have good color and be soft. Pick fruit for cooking when they are slightly underripe.

Make prunes. Certain European varieties, including 'Italian Prune' and 'Stanley,' are prune plums—small, oval fruits with a high sugar content. They are not only sweet to eat fresh but are also suited to drying. Split the plums lengthwise and lay them on a screen. Cover with cheesecloth to protect from insects and dust; set outdoors in the sun.

▷ **Orchards**

⋙ A PLUM SAMPLER ⋘

'Blue Damson' Damson; blue-purple skin; tangy flesh; small, plentiful fruits; good for jam

'Burbank' Japanese; purple skin with amber flesh; sweet flavor; widely adapted

'Green Gage' A European classic; smooth, lime-green skin and amber flesh; rich flavor

'Ozark Premier' Japanese; red skin and juicy, tangy flesh; disease resistant and hardy

'Santa Rosa' Japanese; crimson skin and red, fine-textured flesh; grows fast and fruits early

'Shiro' Japanese; golden skin and flesh; excellent mild flavor; very productive

'Stanley' European; oval prune plum; blue skin and firm amber flesh; very juicy

'Superior' Japanese-American hybrid; large red juicy fruits; cold-hardy and vigorous

POLE BEANS

Good for small gardens. Since pole beans grow vertically, they take up little ground space and can fit in even small plots.

Starts slower, lasts longer. Pole beans take longer to mature than bush beans—usually about 65 days—but will produce for up to 12 weeks. Select from early-, mid-, and late-season varieties to time the harvest.

Be direct. Start seed directly outdoors 3 weeks after the last frost. Sow 2 inches deep and 6 inches apart in rows spaced according to the type of support you choose.

A string trellis. One popular support is a trellis formed with string slung in upside-down "V's" over a cross pole and secured in the ground with spikes. Use untreated twine; at season's end, clip the strings and toss them with the vines into the compost.

The tent technique. Form X-shaped supports with pairs of stakes spread 6 feet apart at the base; secure to a cross pole with cord. If a cold snap threatens, drape plastic tarps on the sides and ends.

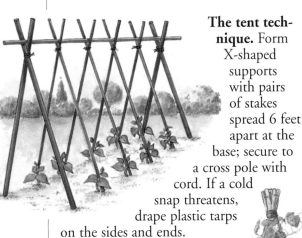

Playtime! Train your pole beans on a tripod constructed from 10-foot bamboo poles tied at the top with cord. Kids love bean tepees—and they can pick and eat fresh beans while they're playing inside.

Extra-long beans.
The 'Yard Long' variety, also known as the asparagus bean, can boast pods that grow up to 3 feet long. But they taste best if harvested at about 18 inches.
▷ **Vegetable Gardens**

❧ A POLE BEAN SAMPLER ❧

Although pole beans are usually slightly less tender than bush beans, many gardeners consider them more flavorful. The heirloom 'Kentucky Wonder' is still one of the most popular; its meaty yellow form is 'Kentucky Wonder Wax.' Excellent for canning is another old standard, 'Blue Lake,' with juicy, fleshy pods. 'Emerite' is a vigorous variety with long, slender pods and crisp-tender texture. The richly-flavored 'Romano,' also called the Italian pole bean, is broad and flat; it matures a little earlier than other varieties.

If you want pole beans for shelling and drying, try 'Oregon Giant.' For lima beans, grow the heirloom 'King of the Garden,' yielding a big crop of plump beans late in the season.

POLLINATION

The basics. Pollination involves the transfer of pollen from the male stamen of the flower to the female pistil and results in the setting of seed. To produce fruit, many garden plants require pollination, which is generally done by insects, bees, and wind.

Self-fertile vs. self-sterile. Some plants, such as tomatoes and raspberries, can pollinate themselves; these are called self-fertile or self-pollinating. Self-sterile plants require pollination from another plant or another variety; examples of those needing cross-pollination include sweet cherries, pears, and most nut trees.

Check for compatibility. Not all varieties of the same plant can cross-pollinate. Always check with the nursery to see if the variety you want to grow as a pollinator is compatible with your other plants.

Watch your timing. Make sure that your compatible plants will flower at the same time so that the pollen will be available. Also check that the pollinator plant flowers regularly; some varieties of apple and pear, for example, bloom only every 2 years.

The easy way. If you have only one tree that needs cross-pollination, consider grafting a branch from a pollinator variety onto the tree. This single branch will provide all the pollen needed. You can also purchase mixed-variety trees, which have several varieties already grafted onto the rootstock.

To ensure distribution of pollen, position a pollinator tree in the center of the trees

that need pollination. In a row planting or orchard, position the pollinator at the end of a row facing the prevailing wind.

Mixing peas and beans. Plant some sweet peas (the flowers, not the veggies) near your pole beans. The plants will climb together, and pollinating insects attracted by the pea flowers will fertilize the beans.

Separate sweet and hot peppers. If cross-pollination occurs, you may find your sweet peppers become too hot to handle.

Shake your tomatoes. Even though tomatoes are self-fertile, they need help releasing their pollen. Just shake the plant or its stake to ensure the transfer of pollen.

Take it off. If you're using a floating row cover to protect your vegetables from pests, remove it when the plants are in flower so that pollinating bees can do their work.

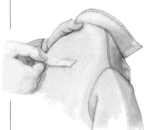

Treating pollen stains. If pollen brushes off on your clothes, don't try to wash or rub it out; remove it with the sticky side of masking tape. Or wait until the pollen is dry, then shake the clothes. To avoid pollen stains from cut flowers, snip off the stamen with scissors once the flowers open.

▷ **Orchards, Nut Trees**

POLLUTION

Limit garden garbage. Reduce pollution by keeping garden debris out of the trash —compost it instead. Dispose of pesticide and other chemical containers properly.

Buy green. Buy garden products that don't pollute. Try organic fertilizers and pesticides, which won't harm the environment after they break down.

Prevent runoff. When using fertilizer, don't let it spill onto paved surfaces or into gutters; runoff washed by rain can end up polluting streams and lakes with phosphates. Properly applied fertilizer binds to the soil and does no damage.

Stop the noise. Are you adding to noise pollution with your garden equipment? Use a manual mower or trimmer whenever practical. Make sure the muffler on gas-powered tools is working. Buy the quietest leaf blower or chain saw available.

Stamp out fires. Don't burn yard wastes even if it's permitted in your area. Compost healthy plant debris, put diseased plants in the trash, and chip or shred large branches.

⊶ POLLUTION-TOLERANT PLANTS ↝

TREES

Crab apple *Malus* spp.
European birch *Betula pendula*
Ginkgo *Ginkgo biloba*
Golden raintree *Koelreuteria paniculata*
Gray birch *Betula populifolia*
Hawthorn *Crataegus* spp.
Littleleaf linden *Tilia cordata*
Maple *Acer* spp.
Red oak *Quercus rubra*
Pear *Pyrus* spp.
Southern magnolia *Magnolia grandiflora*
Sweet gum *Liquidambar styraciflua*
Tulip tree *Liriodendron tulipifera*

SHRUBS

Arborvitae *Arborvitae* spp.
Cotoneaster *Cotoneaster* spp.
Forsythia *Forsythia* spp.
Japanese kerria *Kerria japonica*
Juniper *Juniperus* spp.
Privet *Ligustrum* spp.
Russian olive *Elaeagnus angustifolia*
Tatarian dogwood *Cornus alba*
Spirea *Spirea* spp.
Viburnum *Viburnum* spp.

Spray it away.
If the plants are exposed to car emissions, soot, smoke, or other pollutants, give them a regular misting with the hose to clean their foliage.

Go easy on the salt. If you use salt to melt snow and ice, keep it away from plants— it inhibits water uptake. And watch plants near a road where salt was used: if they seem to be suffering from drought even if receiving sufficient water, soak them thoroughly to leach out salt.

Get the lead out. If you think your garden soil may have become contaminated with lead from paint residues, auto emissions, or pesticides, have it tested before growing edibles or letting children play in the yard.

Plant a tree—especially if you live in an urban area. Tree leaves are natural air filters, absorbing chemical impurities that help create air pollution and releasing oxygen. They also trap dust, fumes, and odors and reduce the temperatures of "heat islands," which contribute to smog buildup.

Clear indoor air, too. Plants help improve air quality in the house. The foliage and roots filter such household pollutants as benzene and tobacco smoke.

Reduce indoor stress. Houseplants will suffer if the air is smoky, stagnant, or dry. Ferns, begonias, cyclamens, and zebra plants are particularly sensitive. Plants better able to resist pollution include cast-iron plant, bromeliads, grape ivy, ficus, snake plants, and philodendrons. Except on coldest winter days, open the windows daily to let in plenty of fresh air.

Watch for signs of pollution damage, which are easily confused with other problems. Plants affected by ozone develop stippled leaves resembling phosphorus deficiency. Removing sensitive plants from areas with heavy exposure to pollution is generally the only solution.

▷ **City Gardens**

POND LIFE

Beautiful and fascinating. The life in a pond provides not only visual pleasure but also an ongoing education. The interaction between aquatic animals and plants is a lesson in the natural balance necessary for a healthy ecosystem.

Goldfish, or koi, are the most common fish for ponds. They live in water between 30° and 90°F and swim near the surface. If you live in a warm or hot climate, you can try more exotic types, but be careful not to mix too many different species.

A proper introduction. Don't just plunk your fish into your pond. Instead, let them adjust to their new surroundings. Float the unopened plastic bag containing the fish on the pond for 1 hour. Then open it gently and set the fish free.

Don't overstock. Each fish needs a certain quantity of water to live. Calculate the required minimum by multiplying the length of the fish by five: a 4-inch-long goldfish, for example, needs at least 20 gallons of water. Another way to gauge is to allow 1 square foot of pond surface area per 1 inch of fish. And remember that too much water is better than too many fish!

Pond frozen? Fish become semi-dormant in winter, but they still must breathe. If the pond surface freezes for weeks, toxic gases in the water can build to harmful levels. Make a vent in the ice by heating a saucepan of water and setting it on top; repeat to melt as needed. You can also buy an electric deicer, which ensures an opening in the ice at all times.

Watch their diet. Encourage fish to eat insects—especially mosquito eggs and larvae—by letting them fend for themselves in summer. In spring and fall, feed them as long as the temperature is about 50°F. In winter, don't feed them at all. Never overfeed; excess food in the water upsets the pond's balance and can cause algae.

If aphids attack your plants, place plastic mesh over the leaves to sink them into the water; fish will find the pests an unexpected treat. After the leaves have been nibbled clean, remove the mesh.

Protect young plants. Fish graze on the young oxygenating plants underwater. Before you submerge the plants, encase them in a weighted cage of wire or plastic mesh. By the time leaves grow through the mesh holes, the plants will be established enough to withstand the interference.

A snail's place. Once your fish and plants are established, introduce a few trapdoor or ramshorn snails. These scavengers are good pond cleaners and still another component of a naturally balanced pond.

Noisy neighbors. Despite their nighttime croaking, frogs and toads are a welcome addition to the pond; they eat insects and are entertaining to watch. But don't let the population get out of control: tadpoles feed on aquatic plants. Keep their numbers in check by scooping the frogs' clear, jellylike eggs out of the water each spring.

Turtles from pet stores are foreign and don't belong in your pond. Never set them loose outdoors—they can spread disease and endanger native species.

Make way for ducks. If you want to introduce ducks to your pond, wait until the plants are well established. The pond should measure at least 160 square feet and be deep enough for ducks to submerge themselves completely. You can try to limit their wandering by providing a sheltered nesting area for them.

The down side to ducks. Although agreeable to watch and fun to feed, ducks and geese can become a nuisance. They eat and trample plants, while their droppings and feathers will litter the yard.

Migrating birds that use your pond as a rest stop on their travels usually aren't a nuisance. It is only when the fowl decide to make your property their permanent home that problems may arise.
▷ **Ponds, Water Plants**

PONDS

Make it fit in. Don't place your pond in the middle of the lawn; select a location where it can be incorporated gracefully into the landscape. In a formal garden, for example, consider using a symmetrical pond as a centerpiece. For a naturalistic look, site a free-form pond in a secluded spot—perhaps at the end of a path.

Level it off. If you're installing your own pond, make sure that the hole and ground around it are absolutely level. To give the

POND OPTIONS

There are typically four types of ponds used in landscaping. Earthen ponds are simply excavated holes filled with water; try this type only if your soil is thick enough to prevent the water from draining away. Concrete ponds can be formed in any shape and are durable; they are costly, however, and frost-heaving in cold climates can make them crack and leak. PVC-lined ponds comprise simply a plastic sheet spread over a hole; they are inexpensive but last only 10 years or so. Preformed fiberglass ponds are also inexpensive and are very durable—even in the cold. A disadvantage is their limited number of shapes and sizes.

walls extra strength, be sure that the sides slope down evenly to the center.

Nearby trees may block the sun needed by aquatic plants and litter the water with leaves in autumn. If you like the look of a pond in a leafy glade, choose evergreen trees and shrubs and site them far enough away so that they won't cast shade and their roots won't eventually weaken pond walls.

Line with sand. For the best fit, line the hole with ½ to 1 inch of damp sand before installing a PVC or fiberglass pond. It's also easier to fit a PVC liner in warm weather, when the plastic is more pliable.

Pick a color—but think first. A black liner will make a pond appear very deep, even bottomless; it also intensifies reflections. Gray or natural stone colors create a neutral backdrop for plants. Don't use white liners, which will soon look dirty, and beware of blue: it looks unnatural and is best reserved for swimming pools.

Mask the rough edges of a pond liner with a combination of plants and edging. Brick edging gives a neat look to formal ponds. For a naturalistic pond, use stones.

Fill gently. When filling a pond, fit a sock over the hose end to reduce the force of the water; secure it with a rubber band. Or let the hose run into a pail set in the pond; thread the hose between the pail rim and handle and fasten it with wire.

Top it up. Add water to the pond regularly in summer to counteract evaporation.

Too deep for plants? To give water plants more height, stack flat stones or bricks on the bottom of the pond as pedestals.

Limit algae by growing floating plants like water lilies; they block the sun that algae need for growth. The plants should cover two-thirds of the water surface.

Prevent ice damage. Frozen water expands and puts pressure on the pond sides. In late fall, place sealed, empty plastic bottles in the water; weight the necks with stones tied to strings. The ice will press on these flexible air pockets instead of the liner. You can also use rubber balls or floating logs.

No room? Create a mini pond with half a barrel or another watertight container. Use only small aquatic plants that are suited to tub culture.

A placid pond, well sited and complemented with ornamental plants, is a dandy addition to the landscape.

▷ **Pond Life, Water Plants**

POPLAR

Populous poplars. Members of the genus *Populus,* which includes poplars, aspens, and cottonwoods, are among the most widely distributed trees in North America. They are particularly valued in the Plains states, since they can withstand wind, drought, and temperature extremes.

Fast to start, fast to finish. Poplars are an obvious choice if you need to install a quick-growing screen: many varieties will grow as fast as 4 feet per year. Keep in mind, however, that poplars are generally weak-limbed and prone to canker disease; for this reason, they are seldom permanent garden features.

Good substitutes. While the graceful, slender Lombardy poplar *(P. nigra* 'Italica'*)* has been grown and admired for centuries, it is the most susceptible to canker disease. Plant the hardier pyramidal white poplar *(P. alba* 'Pyramidalis'*)* or upright European aspen *(P. tremula* 'Erecta'*)* instead.

What they like. These trees do best in very moist soil and full sun. They are also heavy feeders, so keep them well fertilized with 10–10–10 and mulch with compost.

Rambling roots. All poplars have shallow, invasive root systems that can lift paving and clog drains. Keep them at least 100 feet away from buildings, roads, sidewalks, storm drains, and sewer lines.

Scarred branches? The grubs of the poplar curculio tunnel into the branches and twigs of poplars, leaving conspicuous scars. To treat, prune out any affected wood and spray the tree with carbaryl or rotenone.
▷ **Aspen, Trees**

POPPIES

Papery beauties. The poppy family *(Papaver)* includes 50 species of annuals and perennials with crinkled, cuplike blooms reminiscent of crepe paper. They come in numerous shades, both solid and bicolor, and in single or double form.

Grow poppies in full sun in rich, very well-drained soil; standing water around the roots, especially in winter, can be fatal. Sow seed directly, since the poppy's long taproot makes it difficult to transplant.

Keep friends close. For all the beauty of their blossoms, poppies have coarse, hairy foliage that some find unappealing; they also go dormant after bloom. Plant poppies behind other ornamentals that will shield their leaves and fill in the gaps once they fade.

The showiest poppy is the Oriental *(P. orientale)*, whose flowers can grow to 10 inches and show black blotches at the base of red, orange, pink, or violet petals.

The corn poppy, or Flanders poppy *(P. rhoes)*, is the dainty but hardy annual that turns the fields of Europe into seas of scarlet in spring. Now naturalized in this country, corn poppies self-sow readily, so plant them where they can spread.

For pastel shades, grow Shirley poppies, a strain developed from corn poppies. Go with the single-flowered form for delicate blooms; use the double types for full, ruffled flowers that resemble peonies.

Demanding but rewarding. The Iceland poppy *(P. nudicale)*, a biennial grown as an annual, is the hardest to grow. But its silky petals are the most intensely colored and seem to glow with an inner light. This heavy bloomer—with up to 50 flowers per plant—is ideal for cutting. Sow in late summer for blooms the following year.
▷ **Flower Beds**

PORCHES

A pleasant ambience. Coordinating your porch furniture and plants will create a more inviting environment.

Rattan or wicker pieces look best with exotic tropicals like palms, hibiscus, and oleanders; ferns are also a nice complement. Sleek contemporary furniture, on the other hand, looks more at home with terra-cotta planters filled with brightly colored summer annuals and flowering shrubs.

Open or enclosed? For an open porch, metal, resin, or tropical-hardwood furniture will stand up to the elements better than rattan or wicker. Grow annuals and peren-

Peonies, lady's mantle, and cranesbills front this casual, friendly porch. Up the post twines clematis 'Picadilly.'

nials in pots or plant a climber to cover the railings. An enclosed porch is safe for painted wood or antique furniture and lets you grow tender plants all year long.

Year-round residents. For open porches, choose plants from subtropical and Mediterranean areas. They will be happy at temperatures as low as 40°F, unlike the delicate tropical beauties that require more heat.

Allow for air. Both you and your plants will be more comfortable if the porch is well-ventilated. Make sure a breeze can move through; if not, install an overhead paddle fan to keep the air circulating.

Watering porch plants. If you have many, install a spigot close to the porch to make watering easier. Make sure any rugs and mats on the porch are water resistant.

Give plants a lift. Use tables, étagères, tiered plant stands, hanging baskets, and cradle or trough planters to raise plants off the ground. Small pots will be more visible, and you'll be making better use of porch

space. Raised plants will also appreciate the improved circulation; this is especially important for begonias, African violets, and other humidity-sensitive specimens.

A vacation for houseplants. Putting houseplants on the porch in summer gives them a break and affords more protection than they would have in the yard. Place small plants on shelves and large ones on the floor. Locate all where they will get bright and indirect light, but no direct sunlight, from midmorning to late afternoon.

Overwintering. An enclosed porch is a good place to store tender plants during cold winters. But you'll need to use a space heater or move plants to a warmer location if the temperature dips close to freezing. Or you can insulate porch windows with triple glass panes or removable plastic sheets.

Water sparingly in winter, since most plants go through a dormant period that lasts several months. Let the soil in their pots dry out completely between waterings.
▷ **Furniture**

What letter? Potassium, also called potash, is listed on fertilizer labels by its chemical symbol: "K." It's the third essential nutrient, indicated last in the N–P–K ratio.

What it does. Potassium is required for proper growth of fruits and flowers, ensuring good size, color, and number. It helps plants build proteins and sugars and also aids plants in taking in other nutrients and withstanding the cold.

Warning signs. Plants need potassium when the leaves turn grayish, yellow, mottled, or brown and the edges curl; lower stem leaves are affected first. Symptoms usually occur late in the season, when potassium is used by developing fruits.

Quick fixes. For a fast solution, spray plants with fish emulsion or liquid kelp. Or side-dress plants with wood ashes, which can contain up to 20 percent potassium.

Keep ashes dry. Almost all the potassium content will leach out of wood ashes when they are exposed to rain. Cover them with a tarp to keep them dry until use.

Root crops are heavy potassium users, so dig in a source of the nutrient before planting. But check on the plant's pH preference before using ashes, which lower acidity.

Boost your spuds. Spread chopped leaves of faded larkspur or comfrey in the furrows around potato mounds. Or water young plants with a potassium-rich tea made by

steeping about 4 ounces of the leaves in 1 quart water for a month.

Discover langbeinite. This little-known mineral is a rich potash source, with about 22 percent potassium, 22 percent sulfur, and 11 percent magnesium—hence "Sul-Po-Mag," its shorthand trade name.

Greensand and granite dust are good organic sources of potassium; both are slow acting and long lasting. Dig them into soil in fall so they'll be available when you plant in spring; they'll last for up to 10 years.

The richest source? The synthetic fertilizers potassium chloride (62 percent) and potassium sulfate (48 percent) are highest in potassium. Both act extremely fast.
▷ **Ashes, Fertilizer, Organic Fertilizers**

POTATOES

PLANTING

Buy by climate. Potatoes prefer cool weather and can't tolerate hot, dry soil. In areas with mild summers, grow long-maturing types. In hotter regions you'll have better success with earlier varieties.

Get certified. Never use potatoes grown the previous year for seed potatoes—they can harbor diseases. And don't plant store-bought spuds; they are usually treated with a sprouting inhibitor. Plant only certified disease-free seed potatoes, or "spud buds," from a reliable source.

Double your pleasure. If you live in a warm or hot climate, plant potatoes twice: in late winter for a spring crop and in late summer for a fall crop.

In cold climates, plant about 4 weeks before the last frost; the soil should be dry and at least 40°F. Plant early-, mid-, and late-season potatoes for a long harvest.

> ❧ **A POTATO SAMPLER** ❧
>
> Pick a potato geared to your needs: some are better suited for baking than for salads. And branch out and be adventurous: besides red- or brown-jacketed potatoes with white flesh, there are many colorful alternatives.
>
> For tan-skinned bakers with fluffy white flesh, grow 'White Cobbler,' 'Frontier,' or 'Russet Burbank.' Tender-skinned red varieties, ideal for boiling, include 'Red Pontiac' and 'Norland.' Preferred for salads are 'Russian Banana' and 'Giant Peanut' fingerlings.
>
> To harvest potatoes that look and taste already buttered, grow 'Yellow Finn' or 'Yukon Gold.' Pretty and peculiar, with blue skin and flesh, are 'Purple Peruvian' and 'All Blue.'

Loosen soil to a depth of 1 foot and incorporate about 2 pounds of compost for every 10 feet of row. Dig in 5–10–15 fertilizer a few days before planting.

One potato, two potato. Count on harvesting about 4 pounds of potatoes per plant. A 15-foot row will yield 50 pounds.

A bulb planter doubles as the perfect planting tool. Level the bed and make sure it is slightly moist. Make a hole 8 inches deep every 12 inches along the row (note that many planters are calibrated). Set in a piece of seed potato with three eyes: the indents where the sprouts grow. Then backfill the hole with soil from the bulb planter.

Make a mound. In heavy soil, plant potatoes in hills measuring 3 feet wide by 6 inches tall. Set the seed potatoes 6 inches apart around the center of the hill and cover with several inches of soil.

MAINTENANCE

Keep out light. As plants grow, keep mounding soil or compost up around them to prevent sun from reaching the tubers. Light turns potatoes green and causes solanine, a mildly toxic substance, to develop.

Side-dress spuds with a little potassium nitrate when they reach 8 inches tall.

Keep them cool. Make sure you keep the soil moist, especially in warm weather. Provide 1 to 1½ inches of water weekly and mulch with compost or straw.

Disease control. Keep diseases from the tubers by pulling off any infected leaves. To keep the tubers from being disturbed, place your feet astride the plant as you grab the leaves. Wait a week before harvesting the potatoes to make sure that no disease spores are still present.

Prevent common scab, which disfigures the potato tubers, by keeping the soil slightly acid and well-watered.

HARVESTING

Harvest potatoes when the foliage withers and dies. Rub the tuber skin lightly with your finger; it should be firm and resist peeling.

A special tool. Use a grub hoe, available at some garden centers, to dig up your tubers—its wide, curved tines minimize the risk of injuring potato skins. Simply plunge it into the soil at the base of each hill and pull up.

Wait for a cloudy day. To prevent the formation of solanine and its telltale green coloration, don't expose the potatoes to sunlight when they are harvested or stored.

Cure potatoes for at least a week. Brush off the soil but don't wash them and spread them in a single layer in a dark place at around 60°F. Then store in a dry, dark, airy place with a temperature of 40°F. Check regularly for rotting potatoes and discard.

Tubers too sweet? If so, you may be storing them at too low a temperature.
▷ **Potassium, Vegetable Gardens**

POTPOURRI

New life for dying blooms. Make use of faded flowers with potpourri, a spice- and oil-scented blend of dried petals, leaves, and other plant materials. You may already have potpourri ingredients in the garden. Or you can grow a special potpourri plot.

What to use. The best potpourri plants include lavender, rose, larkspur, chrysanthemum, pinks, yarrow, peony, bachelor's button, calendula, pansy, lemon balm, chamomile, lamb's ears, and scented geraniums. All are easy to grow and retain their color when dried.

Go foraging. Collect potpourri ingredients while out walking in the woods. Seed pods, evergreen cones, and the berries of holly and pyracantha make pretty additions.

Exotic mixers. For variation, supplement homegrown ingredients with such store-bought materials as myrrh, sandalwood chips, patchouli, or eucalyptus.

For fruity potpourri, toss in thin slices of dried apple (dry in the oven for an hour at 100°F). Or add dried citrus peel; cut strips from lemons, oranges, or limes and let them dry in a bowl for 2 weeks. To add spice, use cinnamon sticks, whole cloves, anise seed, bay leaf, and juniper berries.

Essential oils are bottled in vials and sold at craft stores and health food stores. Add the oil of your choice—from woodsy bal-

sam to sweet wisteria—to enhance the scents of other ingredients.

Fixatives prolong potpourri fragrance. Among the choices are orrisroot, oak moss, amber, vetiver, and frankincense. Look for them where essential oils are sold.

Mixing bowls. Glass, ceramic, or wood are best for mixing potpourri; they won't react with the oils. Never use metal bowls.

The easiest way to make potpourri is to use all dry ingredients except for the oils. First, mix the fixative with essential oils in a bowl; stir with a chopstick, cover, and set aside to blend for several days. Then stir in the dry ingredients with a chopstick, taking care not to crush the flowers. Cover and set aside for a month, stirring occasionally. Unseal; if the scent is weak, add more essential oils.

The moist method. Making potpourri from partly dried plant materials is time consuming, but the fragrance lasts longer. Let materials dry for a few days until limp and leathery. Place a layer in the bottom of a bowl and cover with coarse salt. Alternate layers of materials and salt, then cover with a flat dish and weigh down with a stone. Store in a dry place until the mixture achieves a cakelike consistency— usually about 3 weeks. Remove the weight, crumble the mixture, and add oils and a fixative; blend with a wooden spoon. Cover the bowl, let age in a dark, cool place for 6 months, then it's ready to use. Because moist potpourri is not as attractive as dried, it is best used for sachets.

The dried flowers of bachelor's button, chamomile, rose, and calendula are classic potpourri ingredients.

Stuff a hanky. A linen handkerchief, or a piece of any loosely woven natural fabric, makes an ideal sachet. Just fill with potpourri, gather up the ends with ribbon, and let the scent perfume drawers, closets, and pillowcases. If you sew up the sachet instead of tying it, you can even toss it into the clothes dryer.

For sweet-smelling showers, hang a sachet behind the shower head or on the back of the bathroom door. The steam from the shower will release the scent.

'Tis the season. While potpourris are usually made from flowers, you can also create a winter recipe from seasonal materials. Combine conifer needles, bayberries, and boxwood or holly leaves with cedarwood chips and pinecones. Scent with an essential oil like balsam or myrrh.

To refresh potpourri's scent, sprinkle it with a few drops of essential oil or brandy.
▷ **Fragrance, Lavender**

POTS

Terra-cotta pots are the standard choice, and for good reason: because they're more absorbent than other pots, they are the best for herbs and other plants that prefer dry, light soil. Just be sure to wet them before using for the first time; doing so means the water for a newly potted plant will be absorbed by the soil instead of the pot. Immerse the pots in a tub of water until air bubbles no longer rise to the surface.

Color me blue? To relieve the sameness of terra-cotta pots in groups, paint them different colors with acrylic-based paint. For herbs, choose pastel hues and use a marker to write the herb's name on the pot.

To clean lime deposits or fertilizer-salt residue from terra-cotta pots, scrub the surface with a stiff pot-scrubber brush. For heavy buildups, use a solution of muriatic acid and water, carefully following the manufacturer's instructions. Wash the pot thoroughly and let it soak in plain water for several hours before refilling.

Strawberry pots can use additional help with drainage. Fill the bottom with a few inches of fine gravel, then slip in a length of plastic pipe or the cardboard tube from a roll of paper towels. Fill the tube with gravel and surround it with potting mix. Gently withdraw the tube, leaving the column of gravel in place.

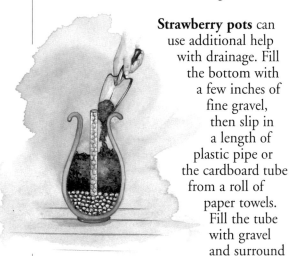

No drainage hole? If you want to use a favorite urn and can't safely drill a drainage hole, fill the bottom with gravel or styrofoam peanuts and cover with plastic mesh before adding soil. And don't overwater!

Hang your flowerpots.
Turn terra-cotta pots into hanging baskets by making a cradle: simply link three metal chains together and thread them through a hook. Alternatively, you can make a "swing" with a piece of wood.

Pot upon pot. In a greenhouse, place delicate potted plants, such as begonias or cyclamen, on inverted empty pots of the same size. Raised high, they will have better air circulation, and their fragile leaves won't touch the wet table after waterings.

Light vs. dark. In warm climates, paint pots white on the outside; in cool climates, paint them black. White pots absorb less heat and are best for plants that require cool roots, including clematis, delphiniums, primroses, and ferns.

Padded pots.
In cold-winter areas, insulate outdoor pots with plastic bubble wrap to keep plants' roots from repeated freezing and thawing.

Mix and match. Instead of planting several species in one large pot, plant them individually in 4-inch pots that you can sink into the potting mix. You'll be able to replace plants at will—adding seasonal color or removing faded flowers—without damaging the roots of the others.

No more room in peat pots? If your plants have outgrown their peat pots and you want to keep them potted instead of bedding them out, make slits down the sides of the pots and set each one inside a larger soil-filled container.

Plastic pots—the kind with holes around the bottom—make good fertilizer spreaders for areas too small or inaccessible for a drop spreader. Fit one pot inside the other and fill with fertilizer, misaligning the holes. To use, swivel the pots to line up the holes, then shake over the area to be fed.

▷ **Planters, Repotting**

POTTING MIXES

Keep it fresh. You don't necessarily have to repot a plant to keep its potting mix fresh. To give the soil new life, remove an inch or two from the surface of the old potting mix and use a fresh mixture to refill to the original level. You can also incorporate a slow-release fertilizer at the same time.

Soil lite. Give plants grown in a soilless potting medium, such as peat moss, a lot of water and extra fertilizer. They need it.

⤳ A POTTING MIX PRIMER ⤲

▷ **Potting soil** usually contains equal parts loamy topsoil, sphagnum moss or peat moss, and either perlite, vermiculite, or sand. It should be clean and nutrient-rich.

▷ **Soilless potting mix** is usually peat-based and also contains sphagnum moss, perlite, or vermiculite. Use it in planters when weight is a consideration or if a plant needs an especially light growing medium.

▷ **Seed-starting mix** has a light texture, retains water well, and is sterilized to prevent fungus diseases. Its main ingredients are soil, sand, and peat. It is low in nutrients.

▷ **Propagating mix** is used for rooting cuttings and has peat, perlite, or sand as a base. It drains well but is nutrient-poor.

▷ **Planting mix** generally refers to outdoor soil mixes for in-ground planting.

▷ **Compost** is the name given to potting mix in some gardening books and magazines—especially those of British origin.

▷ **Specialized mixes** contain ingredients that mimic conditions favored by certain plants, such as rock plants, azaleas, or orchids.

Shake it up. When preparing a potting mix, fill a heavy plastic trash bag halfway with the ingredients. Then close the bag and shake it at least 10 times. To keep dust down, let the mixture settle for a few seconds before opening the bag.

Have a large pot? If so, you can make up the mix in place. Add each ingredient in small increments, mixing well with your hands each time.

Soil savers. Always make more potting mix than you need. Stored in a labeled plastic bag or a plastic bucket with a lid, organic mix will stay fresh for several months—and will come in handy for small planting tasks.
▷ **Repotting**

POWER TOOLS

Do you need one? Before you buy a power tool, realistically gauge your needs. If a task is small or performed only once each season, a good-quality hand tool may do the job as well—and at less expense. Remember that you can also rent power tools.

Rent early. If you're renting tools not readily found in the typical garden toolshed, reserve them in advance. Shredders, for example, are in great demand in fall.

Never buy a tool unless its on–off switch is well-marked and easily reached.

⤳ PROS AND CONS ⤲

Power tools run on gas, electricity, or batteries. Before you decide which kind to buy, consider their disadvantages as well as the benefits.

GASOLINE-POWERED TOOLS

▷ Powerful and long-lived.
▷ Noisy, large, and heavy.
▷ A fire risk; must not be stored near gas appliances with a pilot light or open flame.
▷ Mechanical complexity means more maintenance and potentially more problems and repairs.
▷ Carbon monoxide is a danger; never start the engine inside a garage.

ELECTRIC-POWERED TOOLS

▷ Energy efficient, but less powerful than gas-powered tools.
▷ Less noisy than gas-powered tools.
▷ Limited by the length of the power cord.
▷ Ground Fault Interrupter outlets required.
▷ Generally for smaller jobs; may overheat if used for more demanding tasks.

BATTERY-POWERED TOOLS

▷ Energy efficient, but less powerful than gas or electric tools.
▷ Quietest type of power tool.
▷ Battery charge has a limited life; battery must be recharged overnight.

How many amps? Check the amperage rating for any electric tool before connecting an extension cord (the rating will be given on the tool itself). Unless you use an extension cord of sufficient gauge for the amperage, you risk having the tool's motor burn out.

Safety first. When any gas-powered tool is not in use, be sure to disconnect the spark plug cable. You'll never have to worry about an accidental start-up.

Take care with tillers. Tilling with a power tiller can do more harm than good if re-

⊰❘ POWER TOOLS FOR GARDENERS ❘⊱

TOOL	OPTIONS	PURPOSE
Blower	Gas, electric, and battery models	Cleaning up grass after mowing or edging. Also blows leaves into a pile for disposal.
Chain saw	Gas and electric models	Removing branches over 6 inches in diameter. Cutting small trees or firewood.
Edger	Gas, electric, and battery models	Cutting edges along walkways, driveways, and planting beds.
Hedge trimmer	Gas, electric, and battery models	Trimming shrubs and hedges. Forming hedges into formal shapes or topiary.
Lawn mower	Gas, electric, and battery models; mulching and riding types also available	Mowing grass to specific heights. Collecting and recycling grass clippings. May also be used as a leaf shredder.
Shredder	Gas and electric models	For chopping up leaves and other garden debris.
String trimmer	Gas, electric, and battery models	For trimming grass and weeds from areas that can't be reached with a mower.
Tiller, mini	Gas, electric, and battery models	Tilling and cultivating small planting beds. Attachments allow for dethatching or aerating lawns, edging borders, and trimming hedges.
Tiller, standard	Gas and electric models. May have front-, back- or center-mounted tines	Tilling and cultivating medium and large planting beds. Also used to break up lawn for replanting.

peated every year at the same depth: a layer of hardpan may form directly underneath the level of the tines. To prevent the problem, try tilling manually every third year.

Not just for tilling. A tiller with a furrowing attachment and hilling wings can easily build raised planting beds. Stake walkways of two tiller-widths and set the wings at the highest setting. Soil will be mounded up and can be leveled off with a rake.

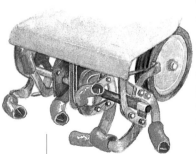

The cutting edge. To prevent injuries in the garage or basement, cut short lengths of garden hose and slip them over the ends of exposed tines before storing your tiller.

String-trimmer rules. Keep these trimmers away from the base of trees and shrubs; the whirling string can damage delicate bark.

Instead, trim by hand with an edger. And never cut back poison ivy or poison oak with a string trimmer! Contact with the airborne particles can cause a skin reaction.

▷ **Chain Saws, Mowing, Pruning Tools**

PRESERVES

Make your own pectin. Apples naturally contain this setting agent. If your jellies aren't setting up properly, place a cheesecloth sack filled with the apple parts that have the highest pectin content—peelings, cores, and

seeds—into the pan. Other good pectin sources include crab apples, true quince, and the Japanese quince.

A hint of almond adds a pleasing bitterness to apricot jam. Throw in some peeled (blanched) almonds to cook along with the apricots—about 10 almonds are enough to flavor five to six jars of jam.

TAKE PRECAUTIONS

Canning must be carried out with scrupulous care to prevent bacterial contamination and spoilage. Most spoilage causes only minor illness at worst, but one type of contamination—botulism—is extremely dangerous and often fatal. Use a water bath to can acidic foods such as pickles, fruits, jams, and jellies. Use a pressure canner for non-acidic foods, including vegetables and meat. To be safe, follow the instructions to the letter and check the seals on canning lids before storing. Store where temperatures stay between 50° and 70°F (a basement or pantry, for example). Before serving preserved food, carefully check the jar. Discard a jar if the contents seem foamy or discolored, if the lid bulges or is misshapen, or if the rim is leaking. Odd odors, mold, or spurting liquid are also warnings to steer clear.

Boiling jelly. Hot jelly will be easier to put in jars if you pour it into a pitcher first. Be sure to use Pyrex or other heat-resistant glass.

Is jam ready? Pour ½ tablespoon of boiling jam onto a plate; let it cool. Slant the plate. If the jam doesn't slide, it's ready to be put up. If it slides easily, cook it a bit longer.

If jam is crystallizing, the fruit you used probably did not contain enough acid. Cook it again, adding lemon juice or tea.

Keep beets red. Certain beets lose their color during canning and can stain cookware. Try a dark-colored variety, such as 'Detroit Dark Red,' for better color retention and less dye. Harvest the beets young, then cook them in their skins immediately.

Homegrown capers. Pickle the tightly closed flower buds of nasturtiums in vinegar. Use as a condiment for smoked fish.

Chow-chow. Use your surplus vegetables to make this savory pickle relish. Simmer finely chopped cabbage, tomatoes, onions, and peppers in vinegar and pickling spices; process in a water bath.

Homemade cornichons. You can duplicate the little French cornichons available in many gourmet produce stores by picking or buying Kirby pickling cucumbers when they are young and small. Wrap them in a towel with salt and leave them hanging up overnight. The next day, pack them in jars with your favorite vinegar, brine, and spice mixture; process as you would other pickles.

Keep the heat on. Don't let hot-packed jars cool before processing in a water bath canner. Once they lose their heat, they can crack when submerged in the hot water.

Head space. Always leave space at the top of the jar while processing, especially when raw packing. Overfilled jars can explode.

A tight seal. Boil rubber seals for a few minutes just before closing the jars. Listen for the telltale pop that lets you know that the jars are sealing. Recheck all jars the day after canning. If there is a slight depression in the lid and the jars give off a light "ping" when tapped, they are firmly sealed.

Altitude affects processing times. Add one minute of processing for every 1,000-foot rise above sea level.

Easy peeling. You can slip tomatoes right out of their skins if you plunge them into boiling water for 5 seconds. The same treatment works for peaches, apricots, peppers, and onions.

Preserves make thoughtful gifts for friends.

AMERICA'S FAVORITE CONDIMENT

Salsa, the Mexican mix of tomatoes, peppers, onions, and spices, can be processed in a water bath canner if it has enough lemon juice or 5-percent-acid vinegar to keep it acidic.

Cooked Salsa

Heat 1 large, chopped onion in 1 tablespoon olive oil. Add 1 cup diced sweet pepper, 1 finely chopped serrano or jalepeño pepper, and four minced garlic cloves. Cook until peppers are soft. Add seven peeled, seeded, and chopped Roma tomatoes, 2 tablespoons red wine vinegar, 1 teaspoon salt, and ¾ teaspoon ground cumin. Cook until thickened. Add ¼ cup chopped cilantro and cook for one more minute. To put up, leave ¼ inch of head space in the jars; process for 10 minutes.

▷ **Cucumbers, Freezing Food**

PRIMROSES

Commonly called... Most *Primula* species are called primrose, but this genus also includes the buttercup, oxlip, polyanthus, and cowslip. Primroses are usually listed in catalogs simply by the common species name, such as Japanese or English, while the polyanthus and pruhonicensis hybrids include many named cultivars.

What they like. Primroses prefer partial shade and cannot tolerate full sun in summer. They also need a cool spring, a mild summer, and consistently moist soil.

Happy marriages. Early-flowering polyanthus primroses make fine companions for delicate spring flowers such as forget-me-nots and narcissus. The moisture-loving candelabra primrose, which flowers later, will look its best with ferns or astilbes or as an underplanting for rhododendrons.

❧ A PRIMROSE SAMPLER ❧

Choose species by their use and the kind of culture they prefer. Note the adaptability of the English primrose and the new hybrids.

FOR POTTED PLANTS AND BEDDING

Auricula primrose *Primula auricula*
English primrose *P. vulgaris*
Fairy primrose *P. malacoides*
German primrose *P. obconica*
P. prunhonicensis hybrids

FOR DAMP BEDS AND WOODLANDS

Bulles primrose *Primula × bulleesiana*
Candelabra primrose *P. japonica*
Cowslip *P. veris*
English primrose *P. vulgaris*
Japanese star primrose *P. sieboldii*
P. pruhonicensis hybrids

FOR ROCK GARDENS

Auricula primrose *Primula auricula*
Cowslip *P. veris*
Drumstick primrose *P. denticulata*
English primrose *P. vulgaris*
P. pruhonicensis hybrids

Originating in the Alps, auricula primroses have a distinctive shape and come in many colors.

Mixed blessings. Planting different strains of polyanthus primroses close together will result in seedlings of different colors next year; they hybridize easily. Although the new plants will bear little resemblance to their parents, they will still be attractive.

A rock garden favorite. The drumstick, or Himalayan, primrose has round clusters of ½-inch lavender, purple, or white blossoms and is the first primrose to bloom in the spring. It performs best when planted in the moist spaces between rocks, where the roots will remain cool.

Two for wildflower gardens. If you live in a temperate region and can grow a deciduous woodland meadow, add English primroses and cowslips. Both are charmers in this setting and bloom in early spring.

Colonized candelabras. In damp places, don't rush to remove the spent flowers of candelabra primroses. Left alone to set and spread their seed, they will colonize. In a few years you'll have a collection of pink, crimson, and white flowers.

A disappearing act. Don't be disappointed if the Japanese star primrose disappears in the summer. The plant dies down to avoid summer's heat—but will come back the following spring to bloom again. It is particularly lovely in dappled shade.

Taking cuttings. Old primroses with rhizomatous roots can be propagated by cutting off portions of the rhizomes in 2-inch lengths. Lay the cuttings horizontally in a

box filled with peat and sand, covering them with the mixture about ⅜ inch deep. Keep them in a cold frame during the winter. The new plants will flower in the following season.

If you have patience, try starting different types from seed. Sow them in the fall in pots or small seed flats, then overwinter them in a cold frame. The cold period will break dormancy, and they should germinate in the spring. Keep in mind that fresh seed germinates more readily than old seed.

POTTED PRIMROSES

A warning. Some primroses, especially the German species—can cause skin irritations. They are usually sold as container plants for indoor decoration but may also be treated as bedding annuals outdoors. Wear gloves when handling. Or, if you like the look of the German primrose, substitute the dainty fairy primrose—similar but safe.

Outdoor types. Potted primroses and the many strains of polyanthus will grow indoors, but they are much happier outside and will flower longer in a window box or on the patio. If a cold snap strikes, protect

the plants by putting a cardboard box or a sheet of plastic over them. Lift the cover during the day to give the plants light. Remove the cover completely as soon as the weather turns warmer.

After they bloom, transplant the primroses from your patio containers or window boxes into the garden, where they will flower for several years.

Prolong flowering indoors by keeping potted primroses in a room whose temperature is no higher than 50° to 60°F. Or you can put them on a balcony overnight. Every 2 weeks, give them a little flowering-plant fertilizer that has been diluted to half the recommended strength.

A moist place. To maintain the moisture a potted primrose needs, place it inside a larger pot filled with damp peat moss. Water the peat regularly but not to excess.

A prop for primroses. Keep the stems of cut primroses from bending over by standing them in a tall, narrow-necked vase. Alternatively, gently tie the stems together below the flowers.
▷ **Flower Beds**

PRIVACY

A good-neighbor fence. If you're putting up a fence for privacy, find one that looks appealing from both sides—your neighbors will likely appreciate the thoughtfulness. Attractive alternatives are a vine-covered lattice or a row of container plants placed in front of a louvered screen.

A single flowering tree or a dense evergreen, such as spruce or fir, can be strategically located to screen a deck, picnic area, or patio from the view of passersby.

A deciduous hedge will keep a patio or porch screened from view as well as cool in the summer. It will also allow welcome winter sunshine to reach the house.

New heights. For extra privacy, extend the height of a low wall by building a partial trellis on top. Then plant climbers like English ivy or clematis to

fill in the trellis. If your wall is on a porch or patio, grow plants in containers and train them toward the trellis with supports.

A private cul-de-sac. If you want to create a quiet corner hidden from view in a large open yard, plant a garden "room" of boxwood or yew hedges. Line up plants in a U-shape or as a square with a "doorway."

The view from above. If you live in an apartment building, you can gain shade, rain protection, and privacy from upstairs neighbors by erecting a pergola, or "living roof": latticework blanketed with a leafy climber such as laburnum, clematis, climbing roses, or a grapevine.

Private and safe. To make sure no prying eyes can get close to your windows, plant spiny shrubs just underneath; the sharp points will discourage the most nimble intruders. Good choices include pyracantha, roses, and spine-tipped yuccas and agaves.

PLANTS FOR PRIVACY

Even though a plant with an open habit can provide some visual screening, the best planting for privacy is a densely foliaged hedge. Effective evergreens include hemlock, holly, pittosporum, Portugal laurel, and yew. Among the deciduous plants that will screen well— even when leafless—are barberry, photinia, red-twig dogwood, and trifoliate orange.

Trees that are branched to the base can be planted in rows to form a screen; try arborvitae, hornbeam, Leyland cypress, and podocarpus. Vines that will turn open fences into screens include *Clematis armandii*, climbing roses, honeysuckle, ivy, and morning glory.

▷ **Fences, Noise**

Creative gifts from the garden

For those who like to make things, a garden's marvelous bounty continues well past the growing season. To the creative eye, a few dried flowers, seed pods, cones, berries, gourds, leaves, and twigs are the raw material for charming home decor and ingenious gifts.

Many of the projects on these four pages were inspired by the interesting shapes and textures to be found in the backyard. A simple bottle gourd, for example, makes a perfect birdhouse. Dried seed pods can be added to berries, thistles, and cones to decorate napkin rings made of twisted vines. A pruned branch is ideal material from which to fashion rustic wooden buttons for a favorite shirt or blouse.

Other projects require items from a hobby shop—a silk tabletop Christmas tree, for example, which is a good foil for dried flower and cone decorations. A new basket can be embellished and filled with gifts. If you already enjoy the craft of paper-making, you can add more color and texture to your cards and notes with flower petals and leaves. If you like wonderfully scented soaps, you'll learn how to make your own by combining recycled soap scraps with essential oils distilled from your own herb garden and flower beds.

Look around in your garden. You may see the makings of the projects shown here or something entirely different—perhaps a dried herbal wreath for the kitchen or an evergreen swag to go around the front door. Craft shops, often associated with nurseries, and florist supply shops carry many items that will make your work easier.

GOURD BIRDHOUSES

Bottle gourds with long necks make fine birdhouses. Depending on a gourd's size, it can accommodate a family of nuthatches or wrens. A fellow bird lover might appreciate this simple project as a gift.

1. Pick suitable gourds when the stem ends dry. Put each gourd in a string or mesh bag and hang it in a cool—but above-freezing—dry place for several months to dry out thoroughly.

2. With the gourd in a padded vise, make a small hole at the top with a nail or variable speed drill on a slow setting. You will later thread a loop of twine through this hole to hang the birdhouse.

3. Cut a hole 1 to 1½ inches in diameter in the gourd's bulge with a keyhole saw or a hole saw attachment on your drill. Scrape out the dried seeds and membrane with a spoon.

4. For the perch, cut a ¼-inch dowel long enough to pass through the gourd and extend 3 inches on either side. Drill a 5/16-inch hole on either side of the gourd just below the large opening in front and at the same level in back. Insert the dowel through both holes.

5. To make a hanger, insert a loop of heavy twine, knotted at the end, through the top hole. Coat the gourd with polyurethane. Let it dry before you hang the new birdhouse outside on a tree limb.

A CHRISTMAS TREE

A silk Christmas tree, with soft, light-reflective needles and a sturdy wire frame, makes a handsome background for pinecones, acorns, seed pods, and dried flowers. The trees are available in many sizes at craft stores. Pick the size to suit your need; then collect materials in a proper scale for decorating it.

1. Using a hot glue gun, attach the dried cones, pods, and flowers, distributing them evenly around the tree.

2. Think of yellow or white flowers or pods as Christmas tree lights and place them accordingly.

3. Display your tree on its tiny log stand or wrap a remnant of vintage lace around the bottom. For a country look, use your glue gun to attach dried moss to the base and scatter a few tiny acorns or cones in the moss.

TWIG BUTTONS

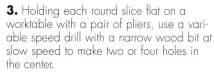

It's easy to create a distinctive look for a shirt, sweater, hat, jacket, or coat with buttons cut from tree branches.

1. With a pruning saw, cut a small branch—the diameter will be the size of the buttons from a tree. Use a sharp saw to avoid damaging the tree.

2. Put the branch into a vise and slice it into rounds with a sharp hand saw. Make chunky slices for coat and jacket buttons and thin slices for dress and blouse buttons.

3. Holding each round slice flat on a worktable with a pair of pliers, use a variable speed drill with a narrow wood bit at slow speed to make two or four holes in the center.

4. Sand the surface of each button with 300-grit paper. Leave the bark on if you like its rugged look. Otherwise, remove and then sand the button's edges.

5. Working in a well-ventilated area, finish buttons with two coats of clear polyurethane. Let the first coat dry completely before applying the second one.

Optional finishes Paint small flowers, dots, geometric shapes, or seasonal icons such as Christmas trees, valentine hearts, or Halloween bats on the buttons. Use acrylic paint and let it dry completely before applying the polyurethane. Paint the buttons solid colors, mixing and matching shades to coordinate with the colors of a jacket or shirt fabric.

PROJECTS & CRAFTS

PROJECTS & CRAFTS

GIFT BASKETS

You can quickly dress up an inexpensive basket to make an eye-catching container for gifts from your garden or kitchen. The basket will be prettier than wrapping paper—and far more useful after the gift has been removed.

1. Set your basket and materials—Spanish or dried green moss and dried seed pods, cones, and flowers—on newspaper so that you can easily discard glue spills and debris. Using a glue gun, attach a thick layer of moss around the rim of the basket to hold the other decorations.

2. Apply the flowers, cones, and pods to the moss in a pleasing pattern, dabbing the backs of the dried materials first with hot glue from the glue gun; then press them into the moss. You can make a scented basket by adding dried flowers from a potpourri.

3. The finished basket makes a pretty carrier for scented soaps, small loaves of bread, or several jars of your best preserves.

ADORNING HOMEMADE PAPER

If you're already a paper maker, proceed as usual. Otherwise, pick up a paper-making kit at a craft store and simply follow the directions. Adding embellishments from the garden, such as flower petals, herb leaves, grasses, and vegetable peels, will give your homemade papers a distinctive look.

1. Gather various pickings from the garden that will add texture or color to the finished paper. A few blades of grass, for example, will give it a flecked look. Spinach will tint paper green; marigolds will color it yellow. Lavender adds a subtle texture, a hint of color, and a pleasant scent.

2. While processing the paper mixture in a blender or food processor, add small pieces of spinach through the feeder, one piece at at time, and check the results before adding another. Too much may make the paper too dark or mottled. If using marigolds, add one flower head at a time.

3. When the paper is formed but still wet, press on a small segment of fern or a well-shaped leaf for an etched decoration. Or embed a very thin sprig of arborvitae in the surface. Experiment with color, texture, and impressions. The results may even be worth framing for display.

VINE NAPKIN RINGS

To fashion unique napkin rings for special dinner parties, gather sections of deciduous vines in the fall. Good choices for this project are grapevine, honeysuckle, trumpet vine, and wisteria.

1. Wrap a length of vine around the fingers of one hand three or four times to make a ring shape with an inside diameter of about 1½ inches. Use wire twist-ties to hold the shape temporarily.

2. Tie the ring shape in four places with thin, pliable sections of vine. Wrap the vine around 3 or 4 times before knotting it. Let the rings dry out in a cool, dry place for a week or more.

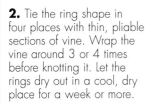

3. Decorate each napkin ring on one side with tiny dried flowers, nuts, pods, and pinecones. Apply these with a glue gun and allow them to dry thoroughly before inserting the napkins.

SCENTED SOAPS

You can enjoy the fresh aromas of herbs and flowers all year long by preserving each essence in oil and then using the oils to scent home-made bars or balls of soap.

ESSENTIAL OILS

Cut fresh, unblemished leaves from lavender, spearmint, peppermint, lemon verbena, lemon balm, or chamomile—or pull petals from calendula or rose flowers. Place about 4 ounces (½ cup, tightly packed) of a single herb's leaves or a flower's petals in a lidded glass jar with 4 ounces of good olive oil. Keep the jar in a cool, dark place for about 3 weeks. Strain the now aromatic oil to remove the plant material. Use the oil to scent potpourri and handmade soap. Also, a drop or two added to a bath makes it more refreshing.

1. To make new soap, collect slivers of used soap, then grate and melt them in a stainless steel or enamel pan (not aluminum) over low heat, stirring regularly.

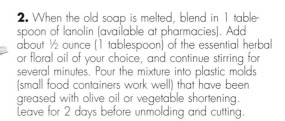

2. When the old soap is melted, blend in 1 tablespoon of lanolin (available at pharmacies). Add about ½ ounce (1 tablespoon) of the essential herbal or floral oil of your choice, and continue stirring for several minutes. Pour the mixture into plastic molds (small food containers work well) that have been greased with olive oil or vegetable shortening. Leave for 2 days before unmolding and cutting.

3. Cut the still-pliable new soap into cakes with a knife or make soap balls by working small amounts of the fresh soap into individual spheres with your hands. Pack the new soap bars or rounds into a decorated basket or wrap them in tissue paper before giving them to friends.

PROJECTS & CRAFTS

PROPAGATION

Stocking up. Propagating new plants is an inexpensive way to increase your garden stock. The most common method is to root cuttings, for which you need only a sharp knife, covered flats or pots, and rooting hormone powder. You can also propagate by layering, grafting, and dividing.

Propagation by cuttings simply involves removing part of a parent plant and rooting it. If cuttings are taken from healthy plants and have warmth, moisture, and a suitable growing medium, you can have new plants at very little cost.

A balancing act. The leaves left on cuttings are needed to nourish the developing roots. At the same time, too much foliage will demand more from the stem of the cutting than it can provide before the new roots begin to develop. Keep things balanced by

removing the lower leaves and any flower buds. As the roots develop, new leaves will quickly appear. In the case of large-leaved plants, such as hydrangeas, it's a good idea to cut the leaves in half.

A do-it-yourself propagator. Fill an old plastic tray with soil and insert your cuttings. Remove the hooks from three coathangers and bend the wires into hoops. Anchor the hoops in the soil at each end and in the middle of the tray. Then cover the tray with a clear piece of plastic, punching pinholes for ventilation.

Pot up cuttings quickly after the roots emerge. If the roots become entangled, separate them by gently immersing in a bucket of water and swishing them around.

Propagating in water. The stems of some houseplants and half-hardy perennials, such as impatiens, will root in a glass of water. Cover the filled glass with a piece of aluminum foil and push the cuttings gently through, making sure that any leaves remain above the foil. Keep the water topped up and replace it completely if it turns green. When roots appear, pot the cuttings in very moist potting mix; cuttings rooted in water can be slow to thrive.

A clean cut. Make sure to trim your cutting with a very sharp knife or razor blade before you insert it into a potting medium. Ragged cuts can cause rotting.

Root cuttings. Some plants with fleshy roots—including daylilies, sumac, and yucca—can be propagated from root cuttings. When the plant is fully

⊱ SEASONAL CUTTINGS ⊰

Softwood cuttings are taken in early spring and summer and are used to propagate most shrubs, trees, and herbaceous perennials.

Semihardwood cuttings of firmer growth are taken after the growing season but before dormancy—usually in late summer. These are also called semiripe cuttings

Hardwood cuttings are vigorous woody stems that have just completed their first season's growth. These cuttings are taken in late fall and early winter.

Root cuttings of trees, shrubs, and some herbaceous perennials should be taken while the plant is dormant.

Leaf cuttings of succulents, as well as indoor plants including African violets, gloxinia, and begonias, can be done at any time of year.

dormant, lift it from the ground and cut back any top growth. Wash the roots, remove young ones (cutting them close to the crown), and return the parent plant to its original place in the garden. Cut  2-inch sections from the young roots and insert them in a pot filled with sandy potting mix, pushing them down until their tops are level with the surface. Do not water them until the shoots appear.

Coming up roses. Heirloom, English, miniature, and many modern roses are good candidates for cuttings because they grow well on their own roots and don't necessarily need grafting. Pick healthy, new-growth stems after they have finished blooming. Cut with at least four leaflets intact. They will root in a few weeks.

Offsets. Bulbs and corms will form smaller offspring— tiny versions of themselves called bulblets or cormels. For narcissus and tulips, break off the offsets by hand and replant. For gladiolus corms, first let the corm dry out; then twist off the cormels. Store over winter and plant out in spring.

Cacti and succulents. To avoid rot, allow the base of any succulent cutting to dry or heal over before inserting it in a rooting medium—preferably cactus soil.

Ready to go. The "chicks" of hens-and-chicks *(Echiveria)* produce offshoots complete with their own roots. Simply break away the offsets and repot them in cactus soil.

Heel cuttings. Stem cuttings with a heel can be taken from softwood, semihardwood, hardwood, or evergreen stems. Remove a suitable sideshoot  from the parent plant by holding it between thumb and forefinger and pulling down sharply; then trim the heel and remove the lower leaves. Dip the basal cut in hormone rooting powder and tap gently to remove the excess. Insert the cutting in a small pot of potting mix or an equal mixture of peat and coarse sand. Shape one end of a length of sturdy wire

into a circle and insert the other end into the potting soil; the support will prevent the plastic from coming into contact with the leaves. Cover the pot with a plastic bag to prevent moisture loss.

Head down. Propagate *Cyperus* varieties, such as the umbrella palm and papyrus, by cutting off one of the heads and trimming back the leaves. Place the cutting upside down in water. New  shoots will appear between the leaves within a few weeks. You can then put the new plants in pots right side up.

Rooting outdoors. Hardwood cuttings from some plants, such as buddleias and roses, can be rooted in the shade of shrubs or perennials that get regular irrigation. Protect the cuttings with upturned glass jars, removing the jars when watering.

A wet moving day. Transplant cuttings to the planting bed on a rainy or overcast day. You'll minimize their shock of adapting to a new, sunny environment.

▷ **Begonias, Dividing, Grafting, Layering, Potting Mixes, Rooting Hormones**

PROTECTION

FROM THE ELEMENTS

Overheating. As the days get warmer in late spring and early summer, keep in mind that protective coverings can become mini saunas and wilt the plants they're meant to protect. Remove the coverings during warm days.

Cuttings and seedlings in pots can be protected with a plastic bag or the top half of a plastic soda bottle placed over the plants. Remove the cap on the bottle for ventilation.

Quick 'n' easy. Protect small plants or seedlings from frost by covering each with an upturned flower pot filled with dried leaves and straw. Clay or terra-cotta gutter pipes, also stuffed with leaves or straw, can be equally effective for rows of plants.

Stackable covers. A wooden frame, two crossed hoops of wire, and a covering of clear plastic make a lightweight cover for

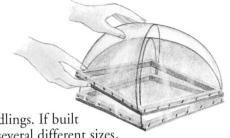

seedlings. If built in several different sizes, the covers can be used for numerous plants and stacked for easy storage.

Radiant heat. Fill plastic milk jugs with water and place them in planting beds among your seedlings. The sun heats the water-filled jugs during the day; at night, these homemade heaters radiate warmth, keeping delicate plants warm.

Sunscald. In the North, the summer sun can damage thin-barked maple or apple trees. Likewise, winter sun may crack the bark when frost sets in. Protect young trees by wrapping the trunks with burlap or the specially designed paper tape available from garden centers.

Standard procedure. Trees and shrubs that have been trained or grafted to grow on a single stem are known as standards. Protect the crown of leaves in winter by pulling a burlap sack down over the top and criss-crossing a cord around the sack several times. Tie the cord around the trunk and secure it tightly.

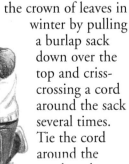

When the wind blows, protect young plants by hammering a few stakes around the plant and wrapping a barrier of burlap or a spun-bonded fabric around the stakes.

Blanket coverage. Drape sheets of plastic or drop cloths over flower and vegetable beds to protect against frost. Insulate further with a loose blanket of dry leaves under the covering.

Hot stuff. Among the commercial devices designed to protect seedlings from frost are "hotkaps." These inexpensive paper domes offer frost protection—but, unlike plastic coverings, are ventilated to keep the plant cool in the midday heat. The Wall-O-Water, a teepee-shaped contraption that encircles the plant, allows gardeners to plant weeks earlier than usual. Heat captured from the sun is warmed by water in plastic protectors, which keep growing plants toasty on cold nights. The device works particularly well with tomatoes, squash, and roses.

Floating row covers offer growing plants protection from the elements and pests.

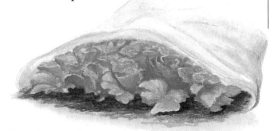

Lay these light-weight spun-bonded fabrics loosely over newly planted crops so that the plants will have room to grow. Secure with scoopfuls of soil at the edges. Row covers are especially effective for low, spreading self-pollinators such as spinach and lettuce.

A climbing vine on the wall of your house can do double duty as an insulating agent, helping to keep the house cool in summer.

FROM PESTS
A cunning trap. Your homemade covers can double as a trap for pests. Hide slug or rodent bait under the cover, propping up the edge slightly with a stone or shard of pottery. The pests will be able to find the bait, but it will be safely out of the reach of pets and birds.

Homemade pest barriers can be fashioned from old nylons or pantyhose. Simply cut the fabric into sections and tie the tops to create single-plant protective "caps." Slip the caps over your vegetable plants and pull the bottoms closed. The hose will expand as the plant grows.

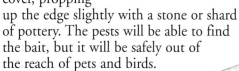

▷ **Cold Frames, Exposure, Frost, Netting**

PRUNING

A little goes a long way. If you prune trees and shrubs when they are young, shaping them as they grow, they will need less pruning as they mature.

Work with it. Unless you want a formal or exaggerated look, it's best to work with the tree's natural framework and growth pattern. A tree that is allowed to develop with its natural architecture will be more structurally sound than if it is trained into an unnatural shape.

Pruning tools. A complete set of trimming tools includes hand pruners, a pair of loppers, and a pruning saw to handle large branches. Hedge clippers are best for shearing dense plants that have smaller leaves and branches. A sharp, curved knife is needed for trimming cuttings and grafting. Disinfect tools with a solution of 1 part chlorine bleach or alcohol to 9 parts water. Remove rust with

---

〰 PRUNING TERMS 〰

Don't be confused by the many methods of pruning. Below is a guide to the various terms.

Deadheading Removing the spent blossoms of flowering plants to encourage continued blooming. Also gives a neater look.

Heading back Cutting back the main branches of a tree or shrub by at least half their length. This method stimulates new growth.

Limbing up Removing the lower branches of mature trees.

Pinching Removing the growing tip of a plant to encourage the formation of bushy growth and improved blooming.

Pollarding Specialized form of pruning to develop a formal shape or restrict the crown of a mature tree.

Thinning out Removing entire branches flush with the trunk or with a lateral branch. This method does not stimulate new growth.

Topping Drastic cutting back of large branches on a mature tree, often accompanied by shearing. This practice is no longer recommended.

Shearing A smooth cut across a flat plane—as with a hedge—to stimulate bushy growth.

---

a light solvent and steel wool. Sharpen blades with a stone or file.

The best time. The ideal time to prune most plants is at the end of the dormant season, just as growth begins. An exception is flowering shrubs. Prune shrubs that bloom in spring after they flower. Late-flowering shrubs that bloom on wood produced the same year can be pruned before growth starts in the spring. Another exception: mature fruit trees. Remove any weak, broken, or diseased branches in summer.

Conifers require specific pruning techniques. Don't cut back firs, spruces, pines, or other needle-leaf conifers. Just use your fingers to pinch off half of each "candle"—a new shoot with growth buds—before it turns green in spring. Take care not to remove the entire candle; doing so would stop any further growth of the branch.

Newly planted hedges can tolerate a severe pruning after the first year of growth. The hedge will thicken out much more quickly as each shrub pushes out vigorous new

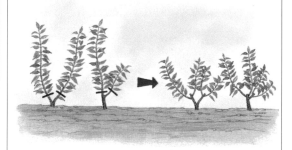

shoots. To ensure that the plants are good and healthy before you prune them, first feed them commercial shrub fertilizer, preferably with an NPK rating of 1–2–2.

Prepare your hedges. During dry spells, water any older hedges that you plan to rejuvenate so that the plants are in good shape when you prune. Fertilize with a commercially available shrub fertilizer immediately after cutting, and water it in.

Citrus plants respond to heading back by sending out vigorous new growth below the cut. This can lead to an unbalanced shape, so look carefully before you cut. The best way to maintain an even size is to thin out the branches. Be sure to cut them off flush with the point where they are attached to another branch.

Check your roses. If you see a small hole in a stalk, an insect borer has burrowed its way inside, where it can damage the plant. Prune off the stalk from below the hole.

Be gentle with trees. A soft approach to trees is better than a heavy-handed one. Instead of severely pruning a specimen all at one time—

called topping—prune over a 3- to 5-year period. This allows for the removal of only a few branches at a time, thereby retaining the tree's outline and its energy-producing leaves. Topping can also expose the inner branches and trunk to sunscald.

Certain shrubs, including forsythia, shrubby dogwoods, deutzia, and kerria, produce new canes from the base. To prune, select entire stems for removal instead of cutting long stems in half. Pruning away older canes allows the new growth more room to develop.

Flush for success. Pruning cuts on woody growth should be flush with the "branch collar"—that is, the cuts should not take off the swollen area where the branch joins the trunk or a larger limb. It will produce callusing wood to heal the cut.

Can the paint. Hold off on treating pruning cuts on young trees with wound paint. Instead, let the tree heal itself; it forms a natural protective layer inside cuts and wounds. Painting only encourages decay.

Outward and upward. Always prune to an outward-facing bud. The new branches will expand and open the tree. Buds or branches facing inward will grow the same way, cluttering up the plant and making pest control more difficult.

Easy does it. After transplanting or repotting a shrub, don't be tempted to cut it back hard. Instead, simply prune out any diseased, weak, or damaged branches and any

stubs left from broken branches. Give the transplant time to adjust to its new environment before trying to reshape it.

Make a safety sling. Before making the first cuts through the branch of a large tree, prevent damage to whatever lies below by looping a sturdy rope over a higher branch and tying it securely to the branch to be pruned. As you cut the successive sections away, a helper holding the rope below can gently lower the newly pruned branches to the ground.

Lawns beneath trees can suffer from fungal diseases encouraged by the shade and lack of air circulation. Before taking drastic measures, prune off the tree's lower branches and watch your lawn improve.

▷ **Hedges, Pruning Tools**

PRUNING TOOLS

Tools for cutting range from small hand shears used for ornamentals and hedges to pruning saws for cutting the branches off trees. Loppers are suited to jobs too large for shears and too small for saws. Power hedge trimmers are also available.

HAND PRUNERS

The best choice. Curved bypass shears give the cleanest cut. Check to make sure they have a sturdy frame, a spiral-type spring between the handles, replaceable blades, and a nonslip grip. Those with a thumb-operated

lock allow you to pocket the shears between cuts. Check that the pair is made by a reputable manufacturer who can supply replacement parts if needed.

What to avoid. Shears with lightweight folded metal frames are likely to twist under heavy loads. Those with a forged metal blade instead of replaceable blades can be sharpened, but will become useless if the blade is nicked or chipped.

Anvil shears have a cutting blade that is pushed against a metal sole, or anvil. On the plus side, they cost less than bypass shears and are less likely to twist when cutting larger branches. On the down side, they can crush the wood as they cut—and also leave a stub.

The kindest cut. When pruning a branch, hold the shears so that the upper blade is toward the part of the branch to remain on the plant. This way, any damage that might occur will be on the pruned branch instead of the one on the plant.

Small hands? If your hands are small, use short, lightweight shears. Lefthanders can find specially-made ones, with an inverted blade, counter blade, and locking clip.

Loppers are used for cutting branches too large or tough for shears but not large enough for a saw. Avoid using an anvil model except for cutting dead wood. Investing in a sturdy bypass model with a forged tempered steel blade will pay off for this often grueling work.

Maintain your shears for long-term use. If properly cared for, they take less effort to use and make a cleaner cut. Regularly lubricate the pivot area with light machine oil or petroleum jelly to ensure smooth operation. Clean sap off blades with light oil and steel wool. Regularly sharpen the blade with a fine file or stone and replace the blade when it becomes worn.

Keep them clean.
Spray your pruning tools with a disinfectant to kill any viruses that may have tainted the blades. Unclean blades will spread disease.

PRUNING SAWS

Use a bow saw for heavy-duty cutting: tree trunks, main branches, and logs. The teeth cut on both push and pull strokes, while the handle allows clearance to cut 8 inches deep.

A regular pruning saw is good for cutting branches 1 to 5 inches in diameter. The teeth cut on the pull stroke.

Tight spaces? Some pruning saws have curved, slender 14-inch blades that make it easier to prune branches in confined spaces. The teeth cut deeply into the wood on the pull stroke with little effort. Many have a handle that can be attached to a pole, thus extending their reach.

Pole pruners, ranging from 6 to 12 feet long, free you of having to use a ladder—but they are useful only for branches about 1 inch thick. Some come in one piece, while others have poles of interlocking pieces.

HEDGE TRIMMERS

Rev it up. Use a power hedge trimmer to make conifer, hornbeam, boxwood, and privet hedges shapely. For broad-leaf species like laurel, use pruning shears so as not to damage the foliage.

Take it easy. It's easy to over-prune with a hedge trimmer. Trim lightly at first and go over the hedge a second time only if needed.

Clean the blades and eliminate sticky resin or sap with a brush dipped in gasoline or turpentine. Oil afterward with light machine oil.

Store between seasons. Store a hedge trimmer blade in a plastic sheath after oiling well. It won't rust and will be ready to use when you next need it.

⇥CHOOSING POWER TRIMMERS⇤

Electric Less expensive, practically maintenance free, and lightweight. The only hitch? Keeping the cord out of the way.

Cordless Powered by a rechargeable battery, these will operate from 30 minutes to 1 hour, depending on the model. Ideal for small hedges and topiaries that need regular care.

Gas-powered models More powerful than electric, they are also more maneuverable. But they also cost more and make more noise.

Single or double blade? The single blade gives the machine more power—you can cut branches up to an inch in diameter. Double blades allow you to trim back and forth, resulting in a faster, more regular trim.

Short or long blade? Short blades (12 to 16 inches) are more maneuverable and lighter. Long blades (22 to 30 inches) offer flatter trims, especially on the vertical sections of a hedge—but expert technique is needed to use a blade longer than 20 inches.

Cord concerns. To avoid cutting the electric cord, buy one that is brightly colored. Or tie colorful strips of cloth or plastic along the cord to make it easier to spot. Hold the cord over your shoulder when working or use a special safety harness.

Sharpen regularly. Sharp blades cut neatly without shredding stems and foliage. Sharpen after every 10 hours of work.

Prevent accidents by wearing clothing that fits snugly so that nothing will be caught in the blade. When lowering the trimmer to your side, be careful not to hit your leg or catch your clothing.

After pruning a hedge with power shears, follow up with a pair of hand hedge shears to do the fine detail work.

The right mix. Be sure to use the proper gasoline-oil mixture in gasoline-powered hedge shears. Using the wrong mixture will shorten the life of the tool and reduce its operating efficiency.

▷ **Hedges, Power Tools**

PUMPKINS

Not just for pies. The pumpkin is one of the most versatile members of the gourd, or cucurbit, family. It is not only used for pies and soups but also has seeds that make tasty snacks when dried and roasted. But the pumpkin really comes into its own as a symbol of the witching season, when the plump orange fruits are transformed into Halloween jack-o-lanterns.

Pumpkins love summer. Most varieties require about 110 frost-free days. In northern states it's best to start seed indoors, preferably under lights, 3 weeks before the last frost date. To ensure against frost damage after planting out, shield tender seedlings with a cloche or other protective device.

Direct sowing. After the last frost of spring, make shallow depressions in the soil and place 5 or 6 seeds in each one, spacing seeds 6 inches apart. When several true leaves have appeared, thin to two or three

RECORDS TO BEAT

If you want to grow the biggest pumpkin in your neighborhood—perhaps even the country—choose one of the Cucurbita maxima species. 'Mammoth Gold' will tip the scales at 100 pounds; 'Big Moon' may hit 200 pounds; and 'Atlantic Giant' will grow to a whopping 400 pounds. The latter holds the world record. Growing champions takes time: at least 120 days. Soil should be rich, with plenty of potassium. Most vines send out secondary root systems; these you should side-dress with fertilizer. Let the plant form three fruits and then cut off two, leaving the best to grow to maximum size.

plants per hill. Pinch off the ends of the vines after a few fruits have formed.

Pest control. As soon as the seed is sown, it's a good idea to cover the row with a floating row cover. This will moderate the chancy spring weather and keep out the cucumber beetle, a serious pest.

Save space by growing pumpkins on a trellis. As they reach full size they'll need support. An easy way is to slip them into old pantyhose and tie it to the lathes.

Don't lift by the stem when harvesting; if the stem breaks off, fungi and bacteria may enter, hastening spoilage. Wait until the vine dies to harvest—but remove the fruits immediately if frost threatens.

Cure harvested pumpkins for a week in a dry place at a temperature of about 75°F. To kill bacteria and fungi on the skin, dip the pumpkin in a weak chlorine solution (1 part bleach to 10 parts water). Store in an unheated attic away from dampness.

An old "swamp Yankee" hint from New England says that pouring ½ cup of cream around each plant every 3 weeks gives the fruits a soft, creamy orange color.

▷ **Vegetable Gardens**

QUINCE

The two quinces. With forsythia, the flowering quince *(Chaenomeles speciosa)* is one of the first shrubs to burst into bloom in the spring. It is grown for the ornamental value of both its flowers, which resemble apple blossoms, and its yellow fruits, which are fragrant but lack taste. The true quince *(Cydonia oblonga)* is a much larger plant grown mainly for its fruits, which can be cooked with meat or made into jelly.

FRUITING QUINCE
What to grow. The pear-shaped summer fruits of the popular 'Vranja' cultivar are preceded in late spring by white or pale pink flowers. The fruits are golden yellow. The spreading tree grows to about 15 feet, as does the similar 'Lusitanica.'

Feed and mulch. Quince trees do best in good, moist loam but will survive in any garden soil. In colder climates, plant them in a sunny, sheltered corner. Keep the trees healthy and productive by working bonemeal (4½ ounces per square yard) into the surrounding soil in late winter. Apply a mulch of well-rotted compost in spring.

Picking and storing. Harvest fruits of *C. oblonga* in fall before the first frost. By this time, they may be ripe and yellow or still green, depending on the variety. Store in a dry, frost-free place; within 4 to 8 weeks, the green ones will ripen and turn yellow. Store quinces well away from other fruits, which can become tainted by their exceptionally strong aroma.

A common blight. Watch out for blackened leaves and curled shoot tips on quince trees—a symptom of fire blight, which can kill the plant. Prune out infected parts only during the dormant season and dip your pruning shears into alcohol between cuts. Burn the infected prunings.

Cook quinces in syrup and store them in freezer tubs. They make a delicious filling for pies and topping for ice cream.

Quince jelly. Just like apples, quince are so loaded with pectin that you don't have to add any when making quince jelly. They are useful combined with fruits that have a low-pectin content, including blueberries, blackberries, raspberries, and grapes.

Fun with grafting. You can make one or two branches of your quince tree bear pears instead of quinces. Use whip-and-tongue or cleft grafts with scions of pear varieties like 'Anjou' or 'Comice.'

FLOWERING QUINCE
Shape as you please. To encourage a flowering quince bush to grow into a tree shape, allow only one stem to grow from ground level; this stem will become the future trunk. Cut away any low stems that try to grow. To grow flowering quince as a bush, let all of the stems grow more freely.

As a freestanding bush, flowering quince needs only light pruning in the early summer to control its size.

A stunning hedge. Trim flowering quince, with its colorful blooms, into an eye-catching hedge. Its thorny

'Nicoline' flowering quince has striking red blooms.

branches also make it a natural barrier against intruders of the four-legged kind.

Espaliered quince. Flowering quince is a perfect candidate for training against a fence or wall. Its spring flowers will be followed by ornamental fruits in summer.

For a fragrant pomander, stick whole cloves, stalk end first, into the fruits, then hang them in a closet. The fruit will dry and give off a spicy fragrance.

A FLOWERING QUINCE SAMPLER

The most widely grown cultivars are those of *Chaenomeles speciosa* (also called Japanese quince), 6- to 10-foot shrubs with bow-shaped flowers borne in small clusters. 'Cameo' sports peach-pink flowers, while 'Spitfire' provides a brilliant red display. For pure white blooms, try 'Nivalis.' A spreading dwarf cultivar is the crimson 'Rubra Grandiflora.'

A smaller species of flowering quince is *C.x superba*, which grows 5 feet tall. Good choices include the multicolored 'Crimson and Gold,' the white-flowered 'Jet Trail,' and the spreading dwarf 'Knap Hill Scarlet.'

▷ **Espaliers, Grafting, Shrubs, Trees**

RABBITS

AS PESTS

The right fence. Keep rabbits out of your planting beds by installing a 2- to 3-foot-tall fence of 1½-inch wire mesh on wood

supports. Extend the mesh 8 to 12 inches deep in the soil so that even the most determined diggers can't tunnel underneath.

Commercial taste repellents, including No Nib'l and Ropel, are available at some garden centers and hardware stores. Apply by dusting or spraying them on plants.

Repel with smells that rabbits dislike. One such odoriferous cure is blood meal, which is also an excellent high-nitrogen fertilizer. You can even try leaving out an old pair of smelly sneakers, strategically placed. Be aware, however, that odor repellents are usually less effective than taste repellents.

Use decoys. Run a length of old hose between your rows—rabbits may think it's a snake. Move any decoys around frequently or they will lose their effect.

Plant borders. Plant a clover border around the vegetable garden; rabbits love clover and may prefer it to your edibles. Or border beds with plants rabbits hate, such as marigolds, globe thistle, catmint, and black-eyed Susans. The castor bean plant works too, but make sure that children can't get to the poisonous seeds.

Protect plants at risk. Rabbits like beans, carrots, lettuce, peas, the tender shoots of ornamentals, and even the bark of trees—especially the apple. Use a blender to make a homemade repellent: 1 quart water, two to four hot peppers, and three to five cloves of garlic. Strain it into a sprayer and apply. As a bonus, this mixture also repels grasshoppers, aphids, and thrips. Don't forget to thoroughly wash treated vegetables before cooking and serving.

A natural repellent. Sprinkle black pepper over and around plants of special interest to rabbits. It's organic, safe, and inexpensive.

Save cabbages from hungry rabbits by planting shallots, onions, leeks, garlic, and other onion relatives between the rows.

Shelter strawberries, a favorite food of rabbits, by placing fine polypropylene bird netting over your strawberry patch. Use the ¾-inch size and double it over.

Protect the bark of young trees. Wrap the bottom 18 inches of trunk with commercial tree wrap, burlap, or wire mesh. For protection in winter, wrap 18 inches higher than your anticipated snowfall; rabbits will climb snow banks to reach the bark.

AS PETS

Give them range. Instead of confining a pet rabbit to a hutch, build a large pen with firmly anchored posts and 6-foot-high wire mesh that extends about 8 inches into the soil. Use a 1½-inch mesh to keep out vermin. To keep the rabbit from digging warrens, as it does in the wild, place a little house inside the pen; it will shelter your pet from the elements. Let the door face south; rabbits don't like cold.

Plant mint around the pen to keep flies away from your pet on hot summer days.

Recycle rabbit droppings to use as fertilizer; they're a good source of nitrogen. Make a manure tea by soaking the droppings in a bucket of water for 1 week. Use about 2 ounces for 3 gallons of water.
▷ **Bark, Rodents**

RADISHES

A good indicator. Sow radish seed in with slow-germinating seed like that of carrots, beets, and Swiss chard. Quick to sprout, radishes will mark off the rows in a matter of days, making sure that you don't disturb the slower-germinating seeds while hoeing. The radishes will quickly be ready for harvest, freeing up space for the other crop.

Succession planting. Don't sow a whole packet of radish seed all at once. Ensure a longer harvest by sowing a third or a quarter of the packet every 10 to 15 days.

Encourage fast growth by giving radishes plenty of water; they can't tolerate drought conditions or heat waves. Sow them where they'll have partial shade at the hottest times of the day—planting near climbing beans or corn is ideal. If no shade is available, mulch the crop so that it stays cool. Or use a summer-weight floating row cover. The right conditions will result in crunchy radishes that aren't too peppery hot.

The right depth. You can simply sow the seeds of round radishes on the soil surface. Long radish seeds, however, should be buried about ¾ inch deep to make sure that the roots grow long and regularly-shaped.

Don't throw away the tops. Rich in vitamins and minerals, radish greens have proven to be beneficial for the lower urinary tract. Harvest young greens only and add them to garden salads for a touch of peppery flavor. Mature radish greens should be used solely for soups.

A common pest. Fight turnip flies by protecting radish rows with a floating row cover. Only the early-maturing radishes,

harvested in late April and the beginning of May, are safe from attack.
▷ **Vegetable Gardens**

RASPBERRIES

Thwart virus. Check at the nursery to make sure your new raspberry plants have been certified as virus-free. Don't let roots dry out before planting. Plant a few inches deeper than they were in their pots and cut them back to about 6 inches. Cultivate carefully; injured roots can admit virus.

Double your pleasure. Plant everbearing raspberries instead of the standard single-crop varieties. You'll reap a small crop in June and a larger crop in October.

A combo hedge. To get a protective yet productive hedge, mix single-crop and double-crop raspberries with blackberries. Add a climbing vine like trumpet honeysuckle to lace the canes together. The plants create a prickly barrier while providing a season-long berry harvest.

Too little space? Tie two raspberry bushes around a stake about 5 feet tall. Gather the branches together gently with strips of soft cloth, making sure to leave space between the canes for air circulation.

How to prune. To prune June-bearing single-crop varieties, cut the second-year canes, which have borne fruit and are turning brown and dry, to the ground. At the same time, cut back any first-year canes that have yet to bear fruit to a height of about 4 feet; these will branch out and produce fruit the following year. To prune everbearing raspberries, cut all canes that have borne fruit back to 4 feet.

Give them support. To keep long canes from touching the ground or blowing about in the wind, build a support. Drive

sturdy posts 2 to 2½ feet into the ground, then stretch wire between them at knee- and chest-height. There is usually no need to attach the canes to the wires.

Watch for dry spells, which can decrease the crop and the size of the berries. Keep your raspberry bushes well-irrigated at such times, watering in the evening.

Probable pests. Japanese beetles love raspberries; pick off the pests and crush them. Aphids can be controlled by a heavy spray from a garden hose or an application of insecticidal soap. Spray fruit worms, which eat the buds, with carbaryl or rotenone.

Good housekeeping. Raspberries are also vulnerable to many diseases, especially in warm climates. Pick up any canes that are diseased or winter-killed and burn them. Remove nearby wild bramble bushes to allow air to circulate freely.

Easy fire-starters. Don't discard hard, dry raspberry bush canes after you've pruned them off. They will become excellent kindling for your fireplace.
▷ **Birds, Netting**

RED SPIDER MITES

Common pests. These mites—also called two-spotted spider mites, red mites, and simply spider mites—have a wide range of targets, attacking fruit trees, shrubs, house-plants, and greenhouse plants.

Signs of trouble. Although the mites are nearly invisible to the naked eye, they make themselves known by tiny webs on the un-dersides of leaves, as well as damaged leaves that are curled and grayish; the leaves later become speckled with yellow and brown spots. If the infestation is severe, leaves and buds will fall off and the plant will die.

A spider mite test. Hold a sheet of white paper under a plant and tap the leaves gently. Any red spider mites will show up on the paper as little moving dots.

Favorite outdoor targets are cucumbers, beans, and strawberries. Hawthorns, rose bushes, and other shrubs are also affected.

In fruit trees. Red spider mites are often found in fruit trees; among their favorites are the apple, plum, and peach. From November to April, look for the pests' brownish-red eggs, which can be found near the buds. From May to September, look for adult mites; their presence is indi-cated by the tree's bronzing foliage.

Use natural predators such as ladybugs, green lacewings, or *Amblyseius californicus* (a predator mite) to control infestation.

Wet your plants. Red spider mites thrive in dry, dusty conditions, which some mite predators dislike. Invite predators by mist-ing plants with a stream of cold water early in the morning, repeating every 3 days. Keep the plant's roots slightly moist.

A buttermilk bath. Many gardeners swear by a buttermilk spray as a defense against mites. Mix ½ cup of buttermilk, 3½ cups of wheat flour, and 5 gallons of water.

Don't handle clean plants after you've touched infested ones. You may transfer the mites from one plant to another.
▷ **Pesticides**

REPOTTING

When to repot? Repotting can be done at any time, especially if a plant is suffering. But the best time to perform the task is just before growth begins—in most cases, spring; just remember that not all plants have the same growing cycle.

Four signals. It's time to repot if new leaves or stems grow slowly, even with the application of fertilizers; if the soil dries out very quickly; if water doesn't percolate into the soil easily; and if roots start coming out of the drainage hole.

Another test. Pull the plant gently from the pot and inspect the roots. If they are tightly coiled, the plant may be potbound.

Some plants, however, prefer this condi-tion; clivia and agapanthus are examples.

Starting up. Use a pot slightly larger in diameter than the original. Clean it well. If it's a new terra-cotta pot, soak it first.

Taking out. If the plant you're replanting is dry, water it several hours before you remove it from the pot. If you must break a pot to release stubborn plants, hit it as few times as possible to avoid damaging roots.

Once the plant is out, eliminate as much of the old soil as possible. Use a fork or pointed stick to pick away between roots, taking care not to damage them.

Putting in. Put a handful of soil in the bottom of the pot. Position the plant in the new pot at about the same height as in the previous pot; if the leaves are sturdy, you can hold the plant by its foliage. Fill in the empty space between the pot and the root clump, firming the soil with your fingers as you go. Tap the pot several times on the surface of the table and add more soil if necessary. Water the plant and place it in the shade; leave for about 1 week before putting it back in its usual spot. Expect the plant to start growing again in 1 to 2 weeks.

To fertilize or not? Fertilizer isn't needed for the first 6 months if the new potting mix has sufficient nutrients. If not, fertilize about 2 weeks after repotting with an all-purpose houseplant fertilizer.

Stop cats from digging. If your feline companion likes to scratch in the soil of newly potted plants, hide a couple of mothballs in the soil. Some of these pets' favorite plants are ferns, bamboo, catmint, and schefflera (umbrella plant).

Temperamental sorts. Some houseplants, such as the weeping fig *(Ficus benjamina)*, can be traumatized by repotting, suffering leaf drop and arrested growth. If you buy one of these difficult specimens and don't like the pot it's in, simply slip the old pot into a larger, more attractive one.

▷ **Bleach, Pots, Potting Mixes**

RHODODENDRONS

A home gardener's favorite. The genus *Rhododendron* encompasses a huge variety of plants—both deciduous and evergreen, from tree-size to dwarf. Rhododendrons are distinguished by their handsome foliage and glorious blooms in a variety of colors.

Size up the size. Although most rhododendrons measure between 5 and 8 feet tall when mature, some varieties have enormous flowers and can grow as high as 80 feet in the wild. Other species, like *Rhododendron yakusimanum* and its cultivars, are dwarf shrubs perfectly suited for containers and rock gardens.

PLANTING
What they like. Rhododendrons prefer acidic, moist, well-drained soil. Dig a hole twice as wide and deep as the root ball and toss a couple of handfuls of gypsum into the planting hole to promote drainage—especially in clayey soil. Mix the backfill thoroughly with well-rotted manure, peat moss, or compost. Make sure to put plenty of this nutritious mix in the top foot of soil, where the roots tend to grow.

Remove the burlap. While you can install some balled-and-burlapped plants with the natural burlap left around the root ball, it is not recommended for rhododendrons. The fabric can wick moisture away from the shallow roots. What's more, some "burlap" contains synthetic fibers that don't decompose and can inhibit root growth.

Soil too heavy? If so, plant rhododendrons in a raised bed or a mound. When mounding, cover the root ball completely with soil and mulch just to the crown.

New plants from cuttings. Though most rhododendron species can be propagated from cuttings, some of the large-leaved species can take up to 6 months. Take cuttings from new growth, treat with a rooting hormone, and insert into a peat container of potting soil. Place under glass and mist frequently to maintain 100 percent humidity. Don't overheat: place the cuttings out of the sun. Plant out the following spring.

Beware of deep shade. Semi-shade is more suitable than full shade for rhododendrons, since exposure to sun for about half the day promotes abundant flowering. On the other hand, too much scorching sunlight and dryness at the roots are detrimental.

Avoiding competition. Don't plant rhododendrons near surface-rooting trees, like birches, elms, and poplars. Both trees and rhododendrons will suffer from the ensuing competition between their roots. Deep-rooting trees, such as oaks, pines, and dogwoods, won't compete with rhododendrons.

MAINTENANCE
Cultivate with care. Because rhododendrons have shallow feeder roots, cultivate around them with extreme care. Spread 2 to 3 inches of mulch to prevent weeds.

The blooms of rhododendron 'Scintillation' are so profuse that they almost obscure the foliage. Because this cultivar can grow 12 feet tall and spread to 15 feet, it is best planted away from the foundation of the house.

A RHODODENDRON SAMPLER

As one of the largest plant genuses on earth, the rhododendron offers a rewarding range of choices. Select plants from the many species by size, cold hardiness, and flower color.

Canary rhododendron (R. lutescens) Evergreen; 15 feet; hardy to 5°F; fragrant lemon-yellow flowers with green throats

Carolina rhododendron (R. carolinianum) Evergreen; 6 feet; hardy to −10°F; white or rose-purple blooms

Korean rhododendron (R. mucronulatum) Deciduous; leaves turn bronze in fall; 8 feet; hardy to −20°F; pink or rose-purple blooms

P.J.M. hybrid rhododendron (R. carolinianum x R. dauricum) Evergreen; leaves go purple in fall; 6 feet; hardy to −5°F; lavender blooms

Rosebay rhododendron (R. maximum) Evergreen; to 36 feet; hardy to −30°F; purplish-pink to white flowers

Yako rhododendron (R. yakusimanum) Evergreen; 3 feet; hardy to −5°F; pink blooms

Also use mulch to retain moisture and shield the roots from heat and sun.

Encourage acid conditions. Feed planting beds with acid-forming fertilizer. Use compost made from materials that become acidic as they decompose. When mulching, use an acidic mulch of pine needles, shredded pine bark, or shredded oak leaves.

Water well during dry spells. Rhododendrons like moisture and won't tolerate drought for prolonged periods. Water thoroughly if it hasn't rained for 10 to 14 days, but don't let the soil become soggy. Refrain from watering heavily late in the season; this may promote new growth too tender to withstand winter freezes.

Drooping leaves in warm weather may indicate root rot (while rhododendrons crave moisture, their roots can't tolerate standing water). To save the plant, dig it up, gently shake the dirt from its root ball, and put it in the shade for several days, letting the roots dry out. Remove damaged roots that have turned black. Before

replanting, redig the hole and discard the soil. Or dig a new hole; slash the sides of the hole with the shovel, dig in a couple of handfuls of gypsum to promote drainage, and use garden soil amended with compost or well-rotted manure for the backfill.

Deadhead gently. Remove the spent blossoms as soon as possible so that the plant expends its energy on forming next year's buds, not seeds. Either snap the clusters off with your fingers or nip them with shears. Be careful: the tiny flower and leaf buds are located right beneath the old flower head. If you injure them there will be no growth the following year.

Groom lightly. Rhododendrons don't need regular pruning, although you can prune young specimens lightly to encourage a bushy shape. Keep in mind, however, that rhododendrons won't produce new growth below a cut where no buds or shoots are visible along the branch. Always cut back just to a bud, which is found right above the leaf cluster.

A second life. If an old rhododendron has grown leggy or sparse, remove lower branches to form more of a tree shape. Lop branches off at the stem and lightly prune some of the top growth. Keep the plant well mulched and watered, since the roots will be exposed to more sunlight and heat.

A living mulch. Underplant your rhododendrons with low-growing, shade-loving

woodland perennials like creeping phlox, foamflower, trillium, and ferns. They will not only keep roots cool but also provide a colorful carpet.

Constant color. Keep your rhododendron alive with color by planting a large-flowered hybrid clematis, such as 'Nellie Moser' or 'Niobe,' to climb up through its branches and adorn the shrubs after the rhododendron blooms fade.

Leaching lime. If you plant near a house or foundation made of brick and mortar, the soil around rhododendrons will eventually become more alkaline as lime leaches from the building. Compensate by treating the soil with peat moss, ferrous sulfate, or other acid-forming material.

First aid for cold damage. Wrap a rhododendron's splitting bark with strips of cloth to encourage the shrub to repair the damage. Ridge up a generous layer of mulch around the base of the plant.

Watch for lacebugs. These pests suck plant juices, leaving whitish or rusty speckles on the leaves and sticky black spots on the undersides. Dislodge them with a stream of water and spray with insecticidal soap.

▷ **Azaleas, Rooting Hormones, Shrubs**

RHUBARB

For a heartier harvest, prune off rhubarb flowers as soon as they form. The ornamental spikes—prized for their beauty by some gardeners—draw nutrients from the stalks.

Red alert. Rhubarb stalks are ready to pull when they are 1 to 1½ feet long. The newly developing stalks of the deepest red usually have the best flavor. Pulling season is over when emerging stalks stay small.

Spare the knife. When harvesting, never cut a rhubarb stalk off the plant. The remaining stub will bleed and invite rot. Instead, hold the stalk near the base and give it a slight twist as you pull it away.

Staying power. A well-tended rhubarb plant, started from seed or a root crown, can be harvested for 50 or more years.

A remedy for clubroot. When transplanting cabbage family plants, slip a few slices of rhubarb into soil near the roots. The oxalic acid in rhubarb can check the growth of the cabbage-harming fungi that are common in poorly drained or acid soil.

A warning. Eat rhubarb stalks only. Trim off the leaves well below the leaf joint.

Rhubarb leaves contain high levels of oxalic acid, which can contribute to kidney problems in susceptible people.

Soften the bite. To take the acidic bite out of rhubarb, soak peeled stalks in cold water for several hours. Or blanch them in boiling water before cooking.

🐟 A RHUBARB SAMPLER 🐟

'MacDonald' is the elder statesman of rhubarb varieties and is still a popular choice; it has bright red stalks and excellent flavor. 'Valentine' has broad, deep-red stalks that grow to 22 inches and retain their color when cooked. 'Starkrimson' is a less acidic rhubarb and is prized for its sweetness and deep red color.

▷ **Aphids, Vegetable Gardens**

ROCK GARDENS

A garden of stone. Rock gardens are modeled on the high-mountain terrain, where colonies of alpine wildflowers and shrubs thrive on the cool, sunny, arid stone slopes. You can create one by planting around an existing stone ledge or installing a special rock bed. You don't need to build a mini Matterhorn—just burying a few stones in part of your garden can achieve the right look.

If you're lucky enough to have a stone outcrop, you have the foundation for a rock garden. Clear away any unwanted vegetation, including roots. Replace heavy or rich soil with a light, quick-draining mix of builder's sand, gravel, compost, and loam. Add the mix to even the shallow crevices, where you can tuck in tiny plants.

Deep pockets. If the planting pockets in the stone aren't deep enough for plants to take root, make an extension. Use rocks with a matching texture and color, stacking them at the top or sides of the crevice.

No rock outcrop? Build your own. Select a sunny site, preferably in a naturalistic area where a rugged rock garden will blend in. An existing slope is ideal—especially if it faces east, west, northeast, or northwest.

Selecting stone. Help your garden fit into the landscape by using a type of rock found in your yard or region; granite, limestone, sandstone, and gneiss are common native stones. Use the same stone type throughout the garden for uniformity. Arrange the rock clusters in odd numbers, which are easier to group than even numbers.

Plant stones firmly. Don't just plop rocks on the ground—they'll look unnatural and be unstable. Bury them one-third to one-half in the soil. Dig a pocket for each rock and spread a light soil mix around the spot where it will sit. Set the stone in the pocket with the broadest side down. Slant it so that it tips back toward the soil instead of pointing downward; this helps retain water around plants and prevent erosion. Tamp in the stone and spread more soil mix, filling crevices to eliminate air pockets. On a steep slope, use the largest stones for the base and add more stones above. Leave flatter areas relatively open, with only a few small rocks, to allow for large drifts of plants.

Build a boulder. To make a group of small rocks look like a natural rock outcrop, arrange them close together and fill the gaps with soil mix. Several angular granite rocks fitted together can resemble a large, frost-shattered boulder once plants begin to spill out of the crevices.

The layered look. Sedimentary rocks, such as sandstone and limestone, have horizontal striations, or layers. To achieve the look of a natural outcrop, set the rocks with their layers running parallel. You can break the monotony of the horizontal pattern by tilting a rock vertically against the base row, as though it had tumbled there naturally.

To go a-wandering through your rock garden—both for maintenance and the pleasure of viewing the dainty plants up close—be sure to include paths and, if needed, steps. Preformed concrete blocks with an imitation granite face make inexpensive risers for a stone staircase, while flat fieldstones will provide sturdy treads.

Create a stone "stream"—a special type of rock garden that resembles a dry creekbed. Arrange rounded rocks along a flat contour in the garden to make them appear as if left behind by moving water. Tuck low-growing, mat-forming plants at random between the rocks to suggest a sense of flow.

A welcome transformation. Rock gardens are ideal for transforming steep, unmowable slopes, like those beside a garage or basement door, into a showpiece. If a retaining wall isn't already in place, build one with stone; this will ease maintenance and prevent soil from washing onto any paved area below. Work back from the wall when arranging the rocks, leaving planting pockets for spreading rock plants, which will spill decoratively over the wall.

An easy mini garden. Even if space is limited, you can enjoy a scaled-down rock garden—perhaps by the house entryway or off the terrace. Dig out the site, stripping any sod or removing paving. Spread a layer of gravel for drainage, then make a raised bed with a mixture of fine gravel, coarse sand, and compost. Top the bed with several rocks and surround it with a dry stone wall. Tuck rock garden plants into the wall crevices and atop the bed.

Rocks don't grow on trees. If you need a large quantity to build your garden, start hunting. Visit road and housing construction sites—builders are often happy to get rid of stones. Also contact quarries, utility companies, and your municipality.

A recipe for rocks. For homemade stones, make a mixture of one part each sand or perlite, dry peat, and Portland cement. Add water until the mixture attains the consistency of cottage cheese. Dig shallow depressions in the soil to serve as molds and pour in the mixture. To make planting pockets, cover the ends of thick dowels with plastic wrap and insert them into the mix. Remove the dowels and let the new "rocks" dry for several days before using them in the garden.

▷ **Landscaping, Rock Plants, Slopes**

ROCK PLANTS

What are they? The plants used in rock gardens are traditionally alpine plants that grow at high elevations—tough, hardy, often brilliantly colored wildflowers, along with ground covers and shrubs. But you can use any slow- and low-growing plants to complement these mountain natives.

PURCHASING

For the widest choice of plants and seeds, try local or mail-order specialty nurseries. Wildflower, rock garden, and native-plant societies are also good sources.

Little invaders. Purchase a limited number of quick spreaders, like snow-in-summer and crocus. Not only will they multiply freely on their own, but they may take over the garden.

A masterful mix. To ensure visual interest, buy a variety of plants that have different growth habits. Mix spreading and creeping specimens with trailing and upright plants that will draw the eye to the vertical plane. You can also mix bright, hot-colored flowers with softer pastels.

Go for the green. Adding plenty of dwarf conifers and other low-growing evergreen shrubs to the garden provides structure and texture, breaks up expanses of color during bloom time, and offers refreshing green foliage all year.

PLANTING

The right soil. Adapted to harsh conditions, rock plants are accustomed to poor, thin, quick-draining soil. Heavy soil will suffocate the roots, while rich soil promotes lush growth that may succumb to frost. Make a mix of coarse sand, compost or leaf mold, and fine gravel. Add peat moss for acid lovers or lime for alkaline lovers.

Highlighting. The shape of a dwarf conifer can be dramatized by planting

GOOD CHOICES FOR ROCK GARDENS

Bedeck your rock garden with traditional alpine plants—hardy wildflowers, ground covers, and shrubs that live in the mountains—as well as any low-growing annuals, perennials, bulbs, and shrubs that offer the same delicate appearance. The plants should also be slow growers, reducing pruning chores. If you have a sun-drenched site, you can pick from numerous mountain natives; if your site is shady, fill it with woodland plants. In either environment, add dwarf varieties of shrubs for structure and foliage.

Sun-loving perennials	Arabis, basket-of-gold, cactuses, candytuft, coral bells, cranesbills, edelweiss, gentian, ice plant, mother-of-thyme, maiden pink, moss phlox, rock rose, sedums, sempervivums, shooting star, snow-in-summer, stonecress, wooly yarrow
Shade-loving perennials	Astilbe, bellflower, columbine, corydalis, crested iris, epimedium, ferns, foamflower, fringed bleeding heart, blue and creeping phlox, primroses, saxifrage, violets
Bulbs	Crocus, cyclamen, dog-tooth violet, glory-of-the-snow, coral and nodding lilies, snowdrop, snowflake, scilla, Turkish and waterlily tulips
Shrubs	Azalea, broom, 'Crimson Pygmy' and Wilson barberries, bearberry, creeping and rock-spray cotoneasters, cryptomeria, rose daphne, false cypress, heaths and heathers, Japanese holly, juniper, potentilla, bird's-nest spruce, Japanese yew

it in front of a large, light-colored rock wall, which will set off its dark green silhouette.

Control aggression. Plant any specimens with aggressive tendencies in their own pocket to keep them contained; rock crevices form natural barriers against spreading roots. Use such invasive plants only to fill spots in the garden where little else will grow.

Where to put plants? Everywhere. Rock gardens allow you to plant both horizontally and vertically. Tuck tufts of plants into crevices. Let spreading, mat-forming plants form drifts over flat areas. Plant trailing or creeping types like sedum or hens-and-chicks to spill over edges.

MAINTENANCE

How to water. While many rock garden plants are drought resistant, they appreciate deep watering during long dry spells. Use a wand attachment on the hose to spray water gently into a pocket. To water a large planting area, use a sprinkler or a soaker hose to avoid disturbing plants.

Pruning and grooming. Keep rock plants bushy and compact: tall, spindly specimens will look out of character. In late summer, shear back any sprawling tufts, keeping the cuts somewhat uneven—a manicured mound looks artificial. Deadhead faded blooms, prune damaged stems, and lift poor performers.

Winter cover. Use straw, evergreen branches, or row covers to protect tender plants from winter damage. You can also purchase microfoam blankets at garden centers.

If rodents are a problem, place a few poison pellets under the covers as well.

Rocky mulch. Retain moisture, suppress weeds, and protect roots by mulching with coarse gravel. Spread 2 inches of rock chips under each plant crown.

Feed lightly with a high-potassium fertilizer, such as 5–10–5, to strengthen rock plant roots. Either spray with a liquid food or spread dry fertilizer, digging it gently into the soil.

A tableware tool. An old kitchen fork makes an ideal cultivator. It can help aerate soil without traumatizing roots and lets you get into tight spaces to dig out weeds.

Tired soil. Plants grown in rock pockets eventually exhaust the soil and begin to fail. Simply lift them out, refill the crevice with a light soil mix, and replant. Spray gently with a high-potassium liquid food.
▷ **Dwarfs, Rock Gardens**

RODENTS

A garlic barrier. Protect a favorite stand of flowers or vegetables from hungry rabbits, moles, gophers, squirrels, shrews, and voles by encircling it with garlic plants.

Many other plants besides garlic, including spurge and fritillaria, are known to have

FRIENDS OR FOES?

Don't panic if you spy a small, mouselike creature in your garden—chances are good that it's harmless. If it has a long, pointed muzzle and tiny eyes, it may not be a true rodent at all but a helpful insect-eating shrew. A similar-size animal with big black eyes, prominent ears, and a long tail is probably a field mouse, an inoffensive grain eater. If, however, the creature has small eyes, a rounded muzzle, barely visible ears, and a short tail, it is likely a field vole, a rapacious rodent that can devastate your garden.

Shrew

Field Mouse

Field Vole

animal-repellent properties. Unlike garlic, however, most cannot protect other plants. Rodents won't eat these "repellents" but will still eat your crops.

Good vibrations. Ultrasonic pest deterrents emit high-frequency sound waves that drive rodents from the garden. Powered by solar panels or batteries, they are normally used above ground—except for the mole-repelling model, which gives off underground vibrations. You'll find the appliances in garden stores and catalogs.

An organic repellent. If your vegetable garden or lawn shows signs of field vole infestation, try a fertilizer with a base of castor oil meal. This organic but poisonous product enriches the soil and discourages rodents. Distribute several handfuls per square yard and water it in; the effects of the repellent will last for several months.

A bulb screen. Use ½-inch-grid wire mesh to keep rodents away from your flowering bulbs. For individual bulbs, use wire-mesh baskets; in mass plantings, lay a sheet of wire mesh on the ground, edges turned down, before filling the bed with soil.

A gravel barrier. Rodents that tunnel won't penetrate a wall of gravel. You can fortify a small garden plot against the intruders by digging a trench 6 to 8 inches deep and 1 foot wide around the perimeter of the plot and filling it to the top with small pebbles or crushed gravel.

Grounding a groundhog. If these marmot rodents, also called woodchucks, are on your property, plant a decoy crop of lettuce near the entrance to their tunnel. With luck, you'll keep them satisfied eating "their" lettuce instead of yours.

A sly measure. The fumes of fox urine concentrate, which you can purchase at hunting stores, will discourage groundhogs from entering your garden. Be careful where you sprinkle this substance, however; the smell is so disagreeable that you won't want it close to the house.
▷ **Chipmunks, Gophers, Moles, Rabbits, Squirrels**

ROOTING HORMONES

What are they? Propagation with plant cuttings is more successful when you use a synthetic rooting hormone, which works like a plant's natural hormones. Hormone powders come in varying strengths—weak ones for softwood and herbaceous stems and strong ones for hardwood cuttings.

A homemade version. Willows give off indolebutyric acid, a natural rooting hormone. Soak pieces of willow bark in rainwater for 2 days and water cuttings with the solution. It doesn't keep, so make it fresh as needed.

Don't overdo it. Too much hormone powder can cause rot. To avoid overdosing, stick the base of a cutting into the powder and then tap it with your finger to knock off the excess.

Rooting rhododendrons. Certain large-leaved species of rhododenron, including *R. minus* 'Scintillation,' are fairly difficult to propagate; roots form in the stem and are then stopped by the bark layer, which is sensitive to hormones. To remedy, make a vertical wound on one side of the cutting with a grafting knife, lift or remove the flap of bark, and treat only the exposed stem with hormone powder. Roots will grow from the callus tissue around the wound.
▷ **Propagation**

ROSEMARY

Garden or pot? A Mediterranean native, rosemary makes a good shrub in Southern California and climates with dry summers and mild winters. Its hardiness in other warm and hot climates depends on light protection; cold, dry winds will quickly dehydrate the leaves. In cold and temperate areas, rosemary is best grown in pots.

⊰‖ A ROSEMARY SAMPLER ‖⊱

Upright forms of this aromatiic perennial shrub can grow up to 10 feet tall and make handsome evergreen hedges. Try 'Tuscan Blue,' with large needlelike foliage, or 'Majorca Pink,' with pink flowers on long branches. Spreading forms of rosemary make good ground covers and spill prettily over walls. Try 'Prostratus,' with deep blue flowers blooming all year long.

Light, well-drained soil is essential for rosemary, especially for container-grown plants; waterlogged soil will cause woodiness and death. Plants also need full sun. Feed in only very poor soils, and lightly.

Shapely plants. Fast growing and tough, rosemary is ideal for simple topiary shapes. To make a tree, choose a plant with a straight central stalk. Prune the lower branches repeatedly until the plant reaches the desired height (you can use the cuttings in cooking). Count on 4 to 4½ feet of growth in 2 years. Then trim the head into a ball, cone, or any shape you like. Clip rosemary anytime except during periods of stress caused by temperature extremes.

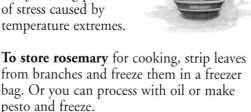

To store rosemary for cooking, strip leaves from branches and freeze them in a freezer bag. Or you can process with oil or make pesto and freeze.

On the barbecue. Tossing rosemary sprigs on the coals or grate of the barbecue during the last 10 minutes of cooking imparts a wonderful flavor and aroma to lamb, veal, or chicken. Rosemary branches can be used as shish kabob sticks; they can also be tied together to make an aromatic brush for applying sauce to the meat as it cooks.
▷ **Herbs**

ROSES

PLANTING

Mail-order roses. Rose bushes are usually shipped bare-root. Just before planting, rehydrate roots by soaking them in a bucket of water overnight. If you can't plant right away, open the container and moisten the roots. Reclose and store it for up to 2 weeks in a cool, dark place where the temperature stays an even 35° to 40°F.

Do not disturb. Nursery-bought roses are already planted in pots or boxes. So as not to disturb the roots, cut out the bottom of the container and set the still-packaged root ball into the planting hole. Slit one side of the container and gently remove it before backfilling the hole with soil or compost enriched with peat moss.

A drainage test. Dig a hole 18 inches deep at the desired planting spot and fill it with water. If the water is gone within 2 hours, the site is suitable for roses. If water is still standing after 2 hours, build a raised bed for your bushes.

In northern gardens, plant grafted nursery-bought rose bushes deep to protect the graft union from winter cold. Make sure the union is 1 or 2 inches below the soil surface.

In southern gardens, plant nursery-bought roses so that the graft union sits an inch or more above ground level. This placement discourages the cultivated canes from forming their own roots and rejecting the grafted ones.

Sun time. Most roses grow best where they get at least 6 hours a day of direct sun.

Good company. Planted near rose bushes, lavender drives away aphids; sage, hyssop, and thyme deter caterpillars; French marigolds may discourage nematodes.

For spring color, plant early bulbs such as narcissus, grape hyacinth, or crocus under the roses. The plants will bloom and go dormant before the rose leaves can shade them.

Orientation. Canes on a new rose bush sprout mainly from one side of the bud union. To produce a well-shaped mature bush, place the new rose in the planting hole with the sprouting side facing north. Equal growth on the other side of the bush will be stimulated by its southern exposure.

MAINTENANCE

Water requirements. In hot, dry weather, roses need an inch of water a week, either from rain or the hose. Use a bubbler (available at garden centers) on the hose so that the water seeps into the soil around the rose's roots without wetting foliage; damp leaves will invite fungus diseases.

Deadheading. To keep modern hybrid tea and floribunda roses blooming throughout the growing season, remove fading flowers before the seeds, or rose hips, can form.

As the petals start to drop, cut off the flower just above the fourth leaf cluster; ideally, the cluster should be outward-facing, with five leaflets. A new flowering stem will sprout from the base of the topmost remaining leaf.

Growing climbers? Climbing roses will flower more profusely if you train them to follow a horizontal line along a trellis or frame while the canes are still young and supple. Forming an arch by fastening the end of a cane to a peg in the ground will encourage even more blooms.

The second blooming. To stimulate the continued flowering of everblooming roses throughout the summer, drench the roots of each bush with 2 to 4 tablespoons brewer's yeast dissolved in 2 gallons water immediately after the first blooming.

Eliminate suckers. When rose varieties are grafted onto another rootstock variety, the rootstock will occasionally send out vigorous shoots. These undesirable shoots, or suckers, should be pruned out, as they can eventually choke out the parent plant.

Remedy low iron levels. Yellowed leaves with dark green veins are a symptom of chlorosis, a condition caused by an iron deficiency. Apply a fertilizer containing chelated iron, but first test your soil: to keep iron from "locking up," the soil's pH must be between 5.5 and 6.5. If the pH is higher, apply sulfur; if lower, apply lime.

Propagation. Take cuttings in June from a vigorous pencil-thick cane; one bearing a bloom is at the right stage of maturity. Cut the cane into 6- to 8-inch lengths, making sure that each one has at least three leaves. Without damaging the buds at their bases, trim off all but the top leaf on each. Cut a cross into the base of each cutting with a

---

❧ A ROSE SAMPLER ❧

Modern roses are hybrids that combine the winter hardiness of wild northern species with the lush everblooming habits of their southern relatives. Hybrid tea roses produce large individual flowers; floribundas bear blossoms in clusters. Climbing roses, despite the name, need to be tied to a support.

HYBRID TEA ROSES

'Chrysler Imperial' and 'Mr. Lincoln' (red)
'Color Magic' and 'Duet' (pink)
'King's Ransom' and 'Sunbright' (yellow)
'Honor' and 'Pristine' (white)

FLORIBUNDAS

'Europeana' and 'Showbiz' (red)
'Betty Prior' and 'Cherish' (pink)
'Sun Flare' (yellow)
'Evening Star' and 'Iceberg' (white)

CLIMBERS

'Blaze' and 'Don Juan' (red)
'Galway Bay' and 'New Dawn' (pink)
'Golden Showers' (yellow)
'City of York' and 'White Dawn' (white)
'America' and 'Joseph's Coat' (orange blend)

⇥ THREE WAYS TO PRUNE ROSES ↞

SEVERE PRUNING

Severe pruning of everblooming roses produces fewer but larger flowers. This method renews old and overgrown rose bushes and is appropriate for newly transplanted bushes. Cut three to six canes to about 6 inches in height and cut the other canes to the ground.

MODERATE PRUNING

This is the standard method of pruning for established specimens of everblooming hybrid tea roses and floribunda roses; it usually produces a large crop of good-quality flowers. Cut back the strongest canes to half their height; trim back less vigorous canes by only a third.

LIGHT PRUNING

Light pruning helps rose bushes facing difficult growing conditions, such as poor sandy soil or heavily polluted air. Cut back all canes by a quarter. This method suits old-fashioned, once-blooming roses and the most vigorous of the modern everbloomers, such as 'Queen Elizabeth' and 'Swarthmore.'

sharp knife and slip a grain of rice into the center of the cut. To keep the grain in place, bind the cutting's base (but not too tightly) with twine. Stand the cutting in water overnight, then pot it in a mix of equal parts sand and soil. Water the pot thoroughly and set it in a cool and bright but shaded spot. Keep each pot well watered. The cuttings should root in 2 to 3 weeks.

The right pruning tools. For the cleanest, least traumatic cuts on rose canes, use a sharp pair of bypass, or scissors-type, pruning shears; anvil-type shears can do damage. To prune the largest canes on your bushes, use long-handled lopping shears.

Timing. Modern everblooming roses, such as hybrid teas and floribundas, are pruned to best effect in early spring, just as the leaf buds swell. Roses that flower once a year should be pruned just after blooming.

Prune everbloomers by removing any dead or damaged canes. Then take out any canes that grow in toward the center of the bush and any that cross and rub each other. Cut off the suckers that sprout from below the graft union. Choose three to six of the strongest canes to keep, and cut all the other canes off at ground level. Then trim the remaining canes to the desired height.

Prune once-blooming roses as you would any flowering shrub to create an open, balanced framework of sturdy branches. To keep the growth compact, cut back each cane by a quarter.

Keep it clean. Rake up pruned clippings and dispose of them, since they may harbor disease spores or insect eggs and larvae. For the same reason, rake up and dispose of fallen rose leaves in autumn.

A winter sleeve. Standard roses, often called "tree roses," are actually rose bushes grafted onto long rootstock trunks. To protect the graft union over the winter, simply cut off the sleeve of an old sweater or sweatshirt. Prune back the rose's top growth in late fall so that you can slip the sleeve over the branches and around the graft union on the trunk below. Then stuff the sleeve with peat moss, dry leaves, or straw for insulation; tie a plastic bag over it to keep out ice and snow. Remove the sleeve in early spring.

A baking soda cure. At the first sign of black spot—a common leaf disease for roses in humid weather—mix 2 teaspoons baking soda and a few drops of liquid soap with 1 gallon of water. Spray the whole bush with the mixture. Reapply the mixture every 4 to 5 days until the spots disappear and the weather becomes drier.

INDOORS

Recut the stem when a rosebud's first petal opens so that it can take up fresh water.

A longer life. Cut roses will last longer if you remove the leaves and thorns that lie underwater in the vase; the stripping process creates more stem openings for water to enter.

A pick-me-up. Cut roses with drooping heads can often be revived by soaking their stems in hot water for a few minutes.

▷ **Drying, Shrubs**

Discover the beloved heirlooms

With a history that reaches back some 5,000 years, the rose is one of the oldest garden flowers. Its enduring popularity is in large part due to its diversity: over the centuries, gardeners crossed many different wild species to produce a dozen or more distinct breeds, or "classes," of domesticated roses. Known as heirloom, or "old garden roses," these floral antiques offer exciting and useful alternatives to the modern hybrid roses.

To qualify as an heirloom, a cultivar must belong to a rose group that originated before 1867, the year the first hybrid tea rose was introduced. Because of their diverse parentage, heirloom roses have the ability to adapt to a wide range of climate and soil conditions. In the northern states, heirloom gallica roses are hardy and reliable, while in the humid Southeast, vintage tea roses—an ancestor of the hybrid teas—outperform their descendants.

Heirloom roses offer a diversity of beauty as well. Some bear small, simple five-petalled flowers, while others produce huge ruffled blooms as wide as 6 inches across. The old roses tend to be more fragrant than modern roses, and their graceful forms integrate easily into mixed garden plantings.

As a rule, heirloom roses do not rebloom as freely as hybrid teas, and many types bloom only once a year, flowering for a period of several weeks from early to mid summer. Frequently, however, the once-blooming kinds bear more blossoms during their briefer season than a hybrid tea does over the course of a whole summer.

GALLICA ROSES

'Rosa Mundi'

Gallica roses have an impressive pedigree. When Julius Caesar settled a wreath of roses over his brow—to mask his receding hairline—it was likely gallica roses that he wore. Portraits of gallicas appear etched on the walls of Roman ruins, and medieval monks used gallica petals to perfume soaps and salves. This venerable class is especially well suited to modern gardens. Gallica roses tend to be compact—the bushes commonly grow just 3 to 4 feet tall—and are especially cold hardy and disease resistant. They thrive on poor soil and flower just once each season, bearing heavy crops of medium-size perfumed rosettes that range in color from red to pink to white.

SELECTED CULTIVARS
'Cardinal de Richelieu' (velvety purple flowers)
'Charles de Mills' (maroon flowers)
'Empress Josephine' (almost thornless, deep pink flowers)
'Rosa Mundi' (striped pink and white flowers)
'Tuscany' (maroon-crimson flowers with golden stamens at their centers)

DAMASK ROSES

'Madame Hardy'

Legend has it that crusaders returning home found the ancestors of this class of roses growing around Damascus and brought the plants back to Europe. Fact or not, by the mid-16th century, damask roses had become a fixture in Western gardens. Today literally thousands of damask rose bushes blanket Bulgaria's Valley of the Roses, where the blossoms are gathered by hand and processed to produce attar of roses for perfumes. Damasks form large, sprawling bushes and produce gray-green foliage and intensely fragrant double flowers. They tolerate poor soil and are reliably winter hardy in all but the coldest regions. Most damasks bloom only once a year, though a few cultivars, known as autumn damasks, rebloom in early fall.

SELECTED CULTIVARS
'Celsiana' (pink flowers with yellow centers)
'Damascena Bifera' (fragrant, loose-petalled pink flowers; reblooming)
'Léda' (compact shrub; grows to 3 feet tall; white blooms edged with carmine)
'Madame Hardy' (white blooms with green button at center)

A white heirloom rose (left) tumbles over the fence of a Texas cottage garden, where red and pink China roses 'Archduke Charles' and 'Old Blush' mix comfortably with lamb's-ears, mealy-cup sage, and pinks.

CENTIFOLIA ROSES

'Fantin-Latour'

In days gone by, the nickname for these enormous, full-bodied flowers was "cabbage rose." Indeed, the word centifolia is from the Latin for "hundred-petalled."

Another ancient class, centifolias are said to have bloomed in the garden of King Midas. But their true heyday was the Victorian era, when European gardeners treasured them for the lush elaboration of their blossoms. Centifolias make large bushes of gracefully arching canes that commonly reach a height and spread of 5 feet or more. The canes, which are very thorny, may need support. Most centifolias flower only once a year, though some cultivars will rebloom sparingly after their principal early-summer flush of flowers.

The blossoms range in color from white to deep rose and have a characteristically spicy fragrance.

SELECTED CULTIVARS
'Bullata' (pink flowers of globular or cabbagelike form; fragrant)
'Fantin-Latour' (large shrub; clusters of pink cup-shaped blossoms that grow to 4 inches across)
'La Rubanée' (4-inch cupped flowers striped purplish-crimson and white)
'Robert le Diable' (compact shrub; grows to 3 feet; blossoms fade from violet-purple to crimson and lilac; late flowering)

CHINA ROSES

'Old Blush'

Chinese gardeners had been growing the ancestors of the China roses for millenia when peripatetic Western merchants began sending them home to Europe sometime in the 18th century. These roses attracted considerable attention at the time because of the reliability with which they rebloomed throughout the warm-weather months. Later, they adapted beautifully to southeastern North America, where their high tolerance for heat and humidity and their ability to withstand drought rapidly made them a local favorite.

China roses commonly form dense, twiggy shrubs of small to moderate size. They adapt well to planting in mixed borders and do beautifully on their own as a flowering landscape shrub.

SELECTED CULTIVARS
'Cramoisi Supérieur' (large clusters of cupped red flowers)
'Fortune's Double Yellow' (a climber that grows to 15 feet or more; fragrant yellow to red-gold flowers)
'Mutabilis' (shrub; grows to 3 feet; flame-red buds that open yellow, then darken through copper-pink to copper-crimson)
'Old Blush' (shrub; grows to 4 to 5 feet; loose, pale pink flowers)

MOSS ROSES

'Common Moss'

In the waning days of the 18th century, a spontaneous mutation occurred in a European garden. From this accident of nature blossomed an unusual rose, bearing buds that appeared to be encrusted with balsamic-scented moss. The globular pink flowers were sweetly fragrant and opened over a long season—up to 2 months long. Commonly known as the moss rose, this plant rapidly won popularity throughout Europe.

The first moss rose, as well as the others that were eventually bred from it, typically form compact, cold-hardy bushes that will grow up to 4 to 5 feet high; most varieties bloom once a year, but a few occasionally rebloom. The blossoms of the moss rose are medium- to large-size and are known to exude an exceptionally fragrant perfume. The calyx and stems are blanketed with the furry, mosslike growth that gave this unusual plant its name.

SELECTED CULTIVARS
'Alfred de Dalmas' (cupped, blush-pink blossoms; reblooms)
'Common Moss' (pink, globular, perfumed blooms)
'Deuil de Paul Fontaine' (compact shrub; grows to 4 feet or less; crimson to almost black flowers; sometimes reblooms)
'Salet' (pink, perfumed flowers; reblooms)

TEA ROSES

'Marie Van Houtte'

A common sight in the American South, the large, flower-laden tea rose can be spotted spilling out over old cemetery fences and blanketing abandoned homes. Though Asian in origin, these roses are supremely well adapted to the climates and soils of the southeastern states.

Tea roses are said to have traveled to the West in the ships of 19th-century tea merchants. Enthusiastic rebloomers, tea roses flower heavily in spring and fall and intermittently through the southern summers. The shrubs tend to be large and upright in form, with bronzed foliage and heavy, nodded blossoms that range in color from pure white to crimson or yellow; indeed, the teas offer the clearest yellows found among the heirloom roses. Some tea roses actually do have a fragrance like that of tea leaves. Many demonstrate an outstanding resistance to black spot.

SELECTED CULTIVARS
'Catherine Mermet' (large, pale pink blossoms; outstanding disease resistance)
'Duchesse de Brabant' (compact shrub; rose-pink tulip-form blossoms)
'Marie Van Houtte' (large, globular lemon-yellow flowers)
'Monsieur Tillier' (compact shrub; grows 3 to 6 feet; fragrant carmine flowers)
'Sombreuil' (climbing shrub; grows 8 to 10 feet; creamy white, saucer-shaped flowers)

ROSES

SAGE

Sun lovers. Like many Mediterranean herbs, garden sage (*Salvia* spp.) loves sun and well-drained soil. Water young plants well, then keep on the dry side. In humid heat, try a gravel mulch to keep roots cool.

Harvest hints. Cut fresh sprigs as needed. For drying, cut off no more than a third of any individual plant. Strip leaves and lay them out on paper towels until dry. Store in a dark, tightly sealed container.

Garden sage has a variety of culinary uses. Place a few sprigs under a roast before putting it in the oven. Sprinkle some chopped leaves on a pizza before adding

⮞ A SAGE SAMPLER ⮜

Garden sage *Salvia officianalis* is woody and hardy, with soft grey-green foliage; it is the most familiar of the culinary sages. 'Aurea' has gold and green leaves; 'Purpurea' has purple foliage; 'Icterina' has yellowish foliage blotched with green. All grow to 2½ feet.

Pineapple sage *S. elegans* earns its name with its distinctive fragrance. It bears brilliant red flowers. Add leaves and flowers to fruit salads, jams, and tea. It grows to 3 feet.

Scarlet salvia *S. splendens* is a long-blooming mainstay of the annual bed. Hybrids come in pink, purple, or ivory. It grows up to 3 feet.

Silver sage *S. argentea* is grown for its decorative foliage—broad, scallop-edged leaves covered with silvery down. Its blooms are white to lavender. It grows to 2 feet.

toppings, or use in cheese dishes. Also put young leaves in vegetables, salads, and soups.

Sage tea has an honorable history as an antiseptic mouthwash and digestive aid. Indeed, an old adage holds that "no man need be ill if sage grows in his garden."

Ornamental sages, including scarlet salvia and silver sage, are used only for decorative purposes. If growing the former, be aware that its brilliant red color looks best against a palette of green leaves, rather than mixed with such vibrantly colored plants as marigolds and zinnias.

Sage advice. Catalogs often describe sages as short-lived perennials or half-hardy annuals. In fact, some "annuals" may survive mild winters, while extreme cold or hot, humid conditions may kill some "perennials." In cold areas, prune plants in the spring to shape them and remove dead growth. In most Southern gardens, it's best to treat sage as an annual.

For wreaths and arrangements, cut back flowering stems of garden sage. Secure a bunch with a rubber band and hang it upside down in a cool place to dry.
▷ **Herbs**

SALAD GREENS

Hanging salads. Plant a hanging basket with salad greens and herbs for a cook's garden right outside the kitchen door. It's out of reach of slugs and caterpillars, too.

WILD SALADS

You might not want them growing rampant in your garden, but some greens gathered from the wild will add interest and zest to salads. Avoid gathering them at the edges of roadways or other polluted areas and never pick and eat a plant that you have not identified. Among the wild edibles are chickweed, dandelion, ground elder, wild garlic, lamb's lettuce, sheep sorrel, and purslane. Nettles are also edible, but never as salad; they lose their sting only when cooked.

Plant salad greens in good, well-drained soil—preferably in raised beds. Cool-season crops need especially good drainage around their roots, which can easily rot.

Even-steven. Use a fine sifter to evenly distribute potting soil or sterile germinating mix over the tiny seeds of most greens.

Salad for months. In cool climates, make successive sowings of salad crops from March to October. Plant each new row as the first reaches about an inch in height. In warm climates, plant in fall after the nights cool; greens will grow through a mild winter. If nights get too cool in early spring or late fall, protect crops from frost and wind with floating row covers.

Scorching sun harms leafy greens, causing many to bolt or taste bitter. As heat increases, water more regularly and cover plants with shade netting over wire hoops.

Mixed greens. Create your own version of the gourmet mixture called mesclun from leftover seed packets of lettuce, chicory, escarole, chervil, garden cress, and arugula. Sow them densely and harvest the leaves when young and tender.

Uniform moisture is the secret to regular growth and crisp, well-formed leaves. Mulch plants with a layer of straw or hay and keep them well watered.

Do be fresh. Harvest the leaves from your greens often. Be sure to pick them from the outside so that the young inner leaves will keep growing and developing.
▷ **Endive, Lettuce, Vegetable Gardens**

SAND

Coarse is just fine. Add only coarse builder's sand to potting mixes—and only when recommended. Fine sand mixed with clay soil will make it stickier. Sand is often too heavy to mix with soil for containers that might be moved from place to place; use perlite or vermiculite instead.

Starting seeds. Seal small quantities of seed in a plastic bag with a handful of moist sand and place in the refrigerator. When sprouts appear—30 to 120 days, depending on the plants—remove and plant them out.

Cold treatment. For the seeds of herbaceous perennials, trees, and shrubs that need cold, moist weather before they will germinate, fill a container with alternating layers of sand and seed. Bury it in the garden and keep moist until early spring.

Sand and seed. When planting a wildflower bed, add the wildflower seed to a bucket of sand and mix it thoroughly. Then broadcast the sand-seed mixture by hand over the prepared beds. The seed will be evenly distributed.

Create drainage for cuttings by filling the first few inches of their containers or planting holes with sand. Fill in with rooting mix and insert the cutting just as far down as the sand extends.

A sandy row cover.
Put a thin layer of sand over freshly sown seed rows in the vegetable garden. It will prevent rain from forming the hard crust of soil that is difficult for emerging seedlings to penetrate.

Tool saver. Keep your hand tools—pruners, weeders, trowels, and knives—in a bucket of sand with a little light oil mixed in. The sand helps keep the metal surfaces clean, while the oil lubricates them and keeps them free of rust.

Ballast. Weigh down narrow containers, such as bud vases, with some sand in the bottom. In a transparent container, use layers of different colors.
▷ **Potting Mixes**

SANDY SOIL

Poor nutrition. Sandy soil often lacks vital nutrients. Moreover, nutrients tend to leach out quickly. You can fortify such soil with "green manures"—fast-growing, one-season plants. Sow buckwheat, clover, or oats and allow them to grow for 6 months, then till them into the soil. Also helpful are organic fertilizers, slow-release inorganic fertilizers or frequent, light applications of liquid fertilizers.

Partners in grime. To improve the ability of sandy soil to hold both water and nutrients, have a landscape supplier deliver a truckload of dry clay. Apply a 1-inch layer to the soil, then till in the clay to a depth of several inches.

Pining for food and water. If you have a ready source of surplus pine logs you can slow water drainage and the leaching of nutrients from sandy soil with this trick. Bury the logs 3 feet under rows of acid-loving plants like tomatoes or blueberries. As the soft wood decays, it will slow drainage and add nutrients.

Short and sweet. Unlike those in heavy soils, plants growing in sandy soils usually

benefit from shorter, more frequent waterings. Soaker hoses and drip-irrigation systems are the easiest and most water-thrifty forms of irrigation.

▷ **Drainage, Seashore Gardens, Soil**

SAWDUST

A nitrogen thief. Because fresh sawdust robs nitrogen from the soil as it decomposes, it's best to compost sawdust first, along with other organic matter. If you do use raw sawdust as a mulch, first add some ammonium sulphate, blood meal, or cottonseed meal to provide extra nitrogen.

Wood shops and local cabinetmakers are good sources of sawdust. Be careful which wood they have been using, however: walnut, cedar, and chemically treated wood should not be spread around the garden.

Strawberries like the acidity of a sawdust mulch. It can also keep slugs away. Raise the foliage and apply several inches around the base of the stems.

A fine blend. Chicken manure and sawdust complement each other when composted. The acidity of the sawdust is neutralized by the alkalinity of the chicken manure. Add them to the compost heap in alternating layers.

Store root crops, such as celeriac, beets, carrots, and turnips in a box filled with fresh sawdust. They should be kept cool and dry in a root cellar or basement.

SCARECROWS

Don't wait until the crops are ripe before installing scarecrows—birds will already be familiar with your crops and will be more difficult to deter.

A wise move. An owl or falcon perched atop a roof or fence can deter many destructive birds. Inflatable or solid plastic bird replicas are sold through specialty catalogs and at garden centers.

The straw man. Enlist the help of children to make an old-fashioned scarecrow stuffed with straw. It will be more effective if you hang streamers of shiny or reflective material from the scarecrow's arms. Keep birds wary by frequently changing the scarecrow's location, pose, and clothing.

Scaredy-cats. Black metal cats with glowing eyes can keep birds and squirrels at bay.

Make your own from stiff cardboard, gluing on some brightly colored beads for sparkling eyes.

Beak-busters. Paint a few dozen walnut shells bright red and scatter them through the strawberry patch before the berries have ripened. By the time the fruit is ready for harvest, local birds will have learned to stay away from these unpalatable red globes.

SEASHORE GARDENS

Keep soil moist and stable with a decorative, but heavy, mulch of gravel, stones,

wood chips, or compost. Avoid lightweight mulches such as peat moss or straw.

Constant winds are an unavoidable feature of all seaside gardens. To provide young shrubs with a much-needed windbreak until they have become established, tie plastic screening between sturdy stakes.

Brace taller trees with three wire cables. To avoid damaging the bark, secure a piece of rubber hose around the trunk and attach the wires to it; then drive three stakes into the ground around the tree and secure the other end of the wires to them.

No salt. Saltwater spray is a serious problem for evergreens. Wash them down regularly with a forcible stream of fresh water from a hose.

If seawater floods the lawn, let the grass dry out completely, then spread lime (2½ to 5 pounds per 100 square feet) and water in thoroughly. Don't despair if the grass dies down; if the roots are healthy, the lawn will recover the following spring. If the roots were injured, however, the lawn will need to be reseeded.

Hold it steady. Stabilize sand dunes by planting beach grasses. Protect them with windbreaks for the first year; when they become established, they will reduce erosion. The most effective anchors include wild-oat grass, wild rye or lyme grass, switch grass, canary grass, and cord grass or marsh grass.

A blustery day. To block prevailing winds and salt spray, install a windbreak of board fencing or a double row of suitable seaside shrubs. As a general rule of thumb, a hedge protects for a distance equal to 20 times its height, so a row of shrubs 15 feet high on its leeward side will protect a garden about 300 feet wide.

❧ GOOD CHOICES FOR SEASHORE GARDENS ❦

The unique conditions along a shoreline—constant winds, salt spray, and generally thin, sandy soil—call for particularly hardy plants that can withstand the harsh environment.

GROUND COVERS AND VINES

Bearberry, Carolina yellow jasmine (*Gelsemium sempervirens*), honeysuckle (*Lonicera heckrottii*), lowbush blueberry, shore juniper, trumpet vine (*Campsis radicans*)

ORNAMENTALS

Baptisia, blanket flower, butterfly weed, coreopsis, daylilys, helichrysum, nasturtium, nicotiana, portulaca, santolina, sea holly (*Eryngium maritimum*), sea lavender (*Limonium* spp.), sedum, sunrose (*Helianthemum* spp.)

SHRUBS

Abelia, bayberry, big-leaf hydrangea, broom, California privet (*Ligustrum ovalifolium*), cotoneaster, Japanese barberry, manzanita, rugosa rose, Southern yew, summersweet, thorny elaeagnus, wax myrtle, yucca

TREES

American arborvitae, American holly, Austrian pine, California bay, false cypress, coast live oak, hawthorn, shore pine (*Pinus contorta*), Monterey cypress, Norfolk Island pine, Scotch pine

SEAWEED

A shot of boron. Brown, corky spots in the pulp of apples indicate a lack of boron, a nutrient present in seaweed. To remedy the problem, apply a seaweed mulch to the base of your apple trees throughout the growing season.

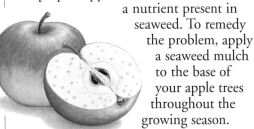

Help from kelp. A type of seaweed, kelp contains trace elements and minerals that promote blossoming, help plants absorb water, and give them greater tolerance to cold. It also improves soil structure. Apply kelp supplements in conjunction with a balanced fertilizer once or twice a month during the growing season.

When to collect. Seaweed fanciers will find the best pickings right after a storm, when most seaweed washes ashore. It's best to collect and use it as soon as possible. Wash off all the salt, chop the seaweed into small pieces, and dig it into the soil while the nutrients are still fresh.

SEEDS

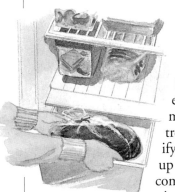

A cold treatment. Stratification is the name given to the process of inducing seeds to emerge from dormancy through cold treatment. To stratify, soak the seeds for up to 24 hours and combine them with a mix of moist peat and sand in a plastic bag. Place the mixture in the refrigerator and keep at a temperature of 34° to 41°F for 4 to 12 weeks.

Scarification. Some seeds have hard coverings that must be penetrated before they will germinate. This treatment—called scarification—can be done in one of two ways, depending on the size of the seed. Large seeds can be nicked with a sharp file or rubbed with fine sandpaper or an emery board until the coat is broken; this is where the new sprout will start. Seeds too small to nick are soaked overnight in a hot-water bath. Place the seeds in a container and pour water heated to about 190°F over them, in a water-to-seed ratio of 6:1. After 24 hours, remove the seeds and sow immediately without drying.

Good old seed. To test old seed for viability, pour it into a glass of water. Seeds that fall to the bottom have a good chance of growing. Discard those that float to the top.

Another test. Place 30-odd seeds left over from last year's packet between two moist paper towels for a few days. Remoisten the towels often and lift a corner to check for germination. Use the percentage of germinated seed as a guide for how much to sow.

Nice and cozy. The tops of water heaters or refrigerators make a perfect place to set a seed flat if their temperature matches that needed for germination—75°F for asparagus, lettuce, and peas, for example.

Treat seeds for fungus. To protect gathered seeds from many of the various fungal and bacterial diseases, soak them in hot water (125°F) for 30 minutes. Coating seeds with a small amount of a fungicide, like captan, helps deter damping off.

⊰ SPEEDING GERMINATION ⊱

Stratification and scarification make it possible to speed the germination of certain seeds.

Seeds to stratify
Aconite, bells of Ireland, bleeding heart, columbine, cotoneaster, daylily, euonymus, gas plant, hellebore, hickory, holly, juniper, lavender, *Lathyrus* spp., lupines, *Meconopsis* spp., peony, phlox, *Primula*, species roses, serviceberry, trillium, *Viola* spp.

Seeds to scarify
Apple, beans, beets, canna, carrots, celery, honey locust, impatiens, laburnum, lupin, mimosa, morning glory, pansy, parsley, peas, stone fruits, sweet peas

---

Be crafty. Garden seed that is no longer viable can be used to make mosaic patterns, suitable for jewelry and pictures. Use white glue to affix the seeds and cover with a coating of clear shellac. Choose large and small seeds with colorful shapes and patterns, including corn and beans.
▷ **Hybrids, Sowing**

SEED STORAGE

No surprises! Don't save the seeds from hybrid varieties. Offspring from hybrids won't breed true to their parents' traits.

Leave a little for Mother Nature. When collecting seeds in the wild, always leave enough seed on the plant so that it can continue developing in its native habitat.

Pick a pod. Remove the entire seed head or pod from a plant and store it in a dry place. To prepare the seeds for planting, open the pod and pour the seeds onto a piece of paper.

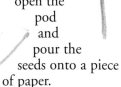

A slimy coating? Ferment tomato and cucumber seeds to remove their slimy coating and kill fungal spores. Squeeze seeds and juice from several fruits into a plastic carton and leave at room temperature with the lid ajar for 4 days, until mold develops. Then rinse the seeds clean in a sieve, drain, and spread them on a plate to dry.

Careful with the okra. Wear gloves when picking dry okra seed pods. They contain an irritant that can cause a skin rash.

Hard to get. Eggplant, pepper, tomatillo, and cherry tomato seeds can be hard to extract. Chop the fruit, put into a blender with water, and pulverize. Let stand until the good seeds settle to the bottom; pour off the pulp, then pour the seeds into a sieve, drain, and dry them on a plate.

All species roses can be reliably grown from seed; garden hybrids will not breed true. Allow the hips to ripen fully (the fleshy interior should be dry), then slit open to remove the seed. Another method is to remove the seed pod and stratify it whole, then remove the seeds when ready to plant.

Leftovers. Most seed packets contain more seed than you can use in one season. To store for the following year, carefully fold over the tops of packets and place in a plastic or wooden file box. Use index cards or dividers to categorize the seeds.

Keep seeds dry by mixing them with a desiccant such as silica gel at about a 1:1 ratio. The color-indicating silica gel turns deep blue when completely dry; as it absorbs moisture it turns pink. Alternatively,

mix powdered milk with the seeds or add a dessicant sachet from a medicine bottle.

SHADE

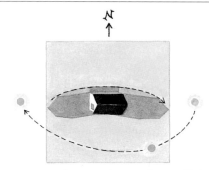

In summer, the sun rises and sets slightly north of an east-west line. The north side of a structure that lies east to west will be in shade at midday and receives weak light in the early morning and late afternoon.

In winter, the sun rises and sets well to the south of the east-west line, casting long shadows on the north side of the house. This limits the kinds of plants and trees that will do well in that part of the yard.

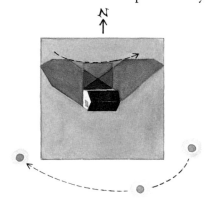

Don't fight it. Most yards are subject to some shade. Instead of trying to eliminate or modify it or trying to grow sun-loving plants, raise an attractive, diverse garden of shade lovers. They often have bolder and more colorful foliage than sun plants.

Plant in layers, just as nature does in the woodland. With the taller trees providing the "ceiling," use ground covers, bulbs, and perennials for the "floor." At the middle level, plant shrubs and small, open trees.

Open and airy. Plant shade lovers under small-leaved, open-branching trees, such as redbud, birch, and Japanese maple. Sufficient light can penetrate the top growth, and air can circulate around the tree.

A tough spot. Grass won't grow in the deep shade beneath densely branched trees. Use a ground cover, a moss, or an attractive year-round mulch instead. Open the area to more light by pruning branches on the lower trunk and thinning out the canopy.

A light in the dark. To lighten up deep shade, use plants with variegated leaves or bright blooms; they will seem to shine in the shade. Try coleus, pulmonaria, ivy, hakone, hosta, or Solomon's seal for foliage. For flowers, grow violets, impatiens, cyclamen, golden star, or bleeding heart.

Round out the season. Many shade plants bloom in early spring, before the trees leaf out and block the sun. For color in the garden throughout summer and fall, add a mix of annuals and later-blooming perennials and shrubs—perhaps astilbe and hydrangeas.

Prevent rot. Shaded areas stay damp longer than sunny ones and can become a breeding ground for diseases. Amend the soil so that it is very well drained and let it dry between waterings. Promote air circulation by spacing plants slightly apart. Clean up diseased foliage and autumn debris promptly.

Watch for scorch. The foliage on some shade lovers can be burned by excess sun.

Don't plant sensitive specimens where they will be exposed to too much light.

Compensate for competition. If your shade plants are located near trees, you'll need to give them extra fertilizer and water—especially during a drought. The greedy tree roots will rob the plants of needed nutrients and moisture.

Brighten up walls and fences in shady areas. Give them a coat of white paint or whitewash so that they reflect more light.

Too much sun? Shield delicate seedlings and new transplants with a lattice panel, mesh screen, or shade cloth attached to a frame. Move it as needed, depending on the sun's angle.

Tortoise and hare. Plant a pergola with both fast-growing annual and slower perennial vines. As the perennial matures, the annual offers color and shade.
▷ **Climbers, Moss, Trees**

❈ GOOD CHOICES FOR SHADY GARDENS ❈

When selecting plants, keep in mind the level of shade the specimen prefers. While ferns, for example, can tolerate deep shade, a Japanese maple or daylily needs only light shade.

Trees	Dogwood, dove tree, hemlock, Japanese maple, podocarpus, redbud, serviceberry, Carolina silverbell, Japanese snowbell, sourwood, stewartia, yew
Shrubs	Abelia, aucuba, azalea, camellia, daphne, enkianthus, fatsia, fothergilla, holly, hydrangea, kerria, leucothoe, mountain laurel, Oregon grape-holly, pieris, privet, rhododendron, sarcococca, skimmia, wintergreen, witch hazel
Ground covers and vines	Ajuga, ferns, climbing hydrangea, honeysuckle, houttuynia, goutweed, ivy, lily-of-the-valley, pachysandra, periwinkle, star jasmine, wild ginger, wintercreeper
Annuals and biennials	Begonia, browallia, Canterbury bells, clarkia, coleus, cup flower, forget-me-not, foxglove, fuchsia, impatiens, monkey flower, nicotiana, wishbone flower
Perennials	Astilbe, bleeding heart, blue star, bugbane, columbine, cranesbill, crested iris, epimedium, false indigo, foamflower, goatsbeard, globeflower, hellebore, hosta, Jacob's ladder, Japanese anemone, ligularia, lobelia, monkshood, creeping and wild blue phlox, primrose, pulmonaria, Solomon's seal, sweet woodruff, tradescantia, trillium, Virginia bluebells, violet
Bulbs	Allium, anemone, caladium, camassia, checkered lily, cyclamen, dogtooth violet, kaffir lily, squill, snowdrop, snowflake, tuberous begonias, winter aconite

SHAPE

Analyze from every angle. Consider not only a plant's overall silhouette but also the form of its leaves, stems, and flowers. This will aid you when designing and pruning.

Buy right. If you want a globe-shaped plant, buy one. Otherwise you'll have to constantly prune a plant of another shape to force into the desired form. To learn the natural shape of a mature plant, look at pictures in catalogs or ask at your nursery.

Mix it up. Combine plants with complementary shapes. A weeping tree, for example, will shine when underplanted with mounding shrubs. A ground cover with broad oval leaves pairs well with a perennial that has small, feathery foliage or flowers.

A tall pyramid shape, as formed by this tulip tree, creates a soaring punctuation mark in the garden.

Get help. Even if you have a good eye, a template can be helpful when you're pruning to maintain plant shape—especially if you want a perfectly clipped form. To trim a globe, for example, make an arch of stiff wire and attach it to the plant crown. Clip away growth that falls outside the template, rotating it around the plant as your work.

Spreading out. To encourage a tree or shrub that has a weeping growth habit to spread out in an open fashion, trim branches each year just above a shoot that points away from the crown.

Shaping a column. When pruning a plant with a columnar habit, don't remove the buds from the vertical stems; doing so will encourage the growth of lateral stems. Instead, prune the oblique stems to maintain the natural silhouette.

Repeating shapes will add structure to the garden. In a long border, for example, plant groups of mounding shrubs at equal intervals to create smaller sections visually while tying the entire design together. You can also be playful with recurring shapes by making "echoes." Plant a conical conifer at the center of a triangular bed or grow lollipop-shaped alliums around the base of a tree trained as a standard.

Patio picking. Grow a dwarf apple tree shaped to a central leader. 'Garden Delicious' and 'McIntosh' are good candidates for this treatment. When the tree is dormant, prune back the side branches but leave the spurs that will bear fruit. Once the tree reaches the desired height, cut back new growth on the leader in late spring to ½ inch above a bud.

Unusual shapes make good specimens, but use plants with striking profiles sparingly so as not to dilute the effect. One blue Atlas cedar, weeping beech, or Harry Lauder's walking stick is enough for any yard.

The spikes and spheres of yuccas and agaves aren't confined to arid climates. Some species will grow outdoors in cooler regions or can be grown in pots and overwintered indoors.

Herb topiary. To create the characteristic shape of a standard, select a plant with a straight main stem; myrtle, bay, basil, and scented geraniums are good choices. Trim off the lower branches and pinch the top growth into a sphere. To keep the stem straight and bud-free, enclose it in

FLOWER CLUSTER SHAPES

Flower clusters come in a number of shapes, the names of which can be confusing.

Umbel Each flower head rises from a central point (allium, angelica, dill, fennel, sweet alyssum)

Corymb Flower stalks grow from different points; blooms from the edge in (viburnum)

Cyme Multibranched cluster; blooms from the center out (forget-me-not, heliotrope)

Panicle Loose cluster; blooms from the bottom up (goatsbeard, astilbe, baby's breath)

Raceme Clusters of blooms arranged along stem on short stalks (hosta, red-hot poker, delphinium)

a tube split lenghwise. Use a drinking straw or a section of garden hose.

▷ **Espaliers, Pruning, Topiary**

SHRUBS

In the landscape. Shrubs are versatile woody plants that fill the middle ground between trees and flowers. You can use them in foundation plantings, grouped as shrub borders and hedges, interplanted in flower beds, or highlighted as specimens.

Look for many talents. Some shrubs bloom in spring and early summer, then offer little else. Choose varieties that have many talents: interesting fruits, fall color, attractive bark, and a pleasing silhouette, even when bare. Good choices for a long-

term display include barberry, euonymus, leucothoe, pieris, privet, mahonia, nandina, rhus, snowberry, and viburnum.

Times to plant. Install container-grown and balled-and-burlapped shrubs in early spring or fall, when dormant. Plant bare-root specimens only in spring. Needle-leaf evergreens can be planted in late summer.

Fertilize each spring with a complete food, like 10–10–10. Use an acid-forming fertilizer for acid-loving shrubs, like pieris.

Reduce weeding in large shrub plantings with a geotextile weed mat covered with an organic mulch. Cut out a circle around each shrub trunk to allow for fertilizing. And never use black plastic mulch; it will suffocate the roots.

Cover your bases. Instead of using mulch, cover the soil around shrubs with a shade-tolerant, shallow-rooted ground cover. Try periwinkle, pachysandra, American barrenwort, foam-flower, or star jasmine.

The lonely look. In foundation plantings and borders, avoid using a single row of shrubs; they will look forlorn. Add depth by planting in layers, from tall shrubs at the back to the ground-huggers in front.

Great gound covers. Spreading shrubs, especially evergreens, are ideal for blanketing a slope or large expanse. Try the prostrate forms of cotoneaster, junipers, bearberry, holly, and pyracantha.

Avoid hardwork. Match a shrub's cultural and space requirements to the proposed planting site. This will save you years of struggle to keep a plant healthy and will mean less pruning to keep it in bounds.

Nice habits. Take a plant's natural profile into account when designing with shrubs. Upright and pyramidal shapes are rigid and more formal, while mounding, weeping, and spreading habits appear more relaxed.

Look at the leaves, the shrub's dominant feature. Consider color, which ranges from burgundy to gold to blue-gray to all shades of green. Also look at leaf shape, texture, and growth habit on the stem.

Pruning methods vary from shrub to shrub, depending in part on their flowering habits. Ask the nursery for the proper way and time to prune a particular specimen. A rule of thumb is to always follow the natural shape of the plant; don't just shear away unless you're trimming a hedge or topiary. Cut back to an outward-facing bud or remove the whole stem at the base.

Be nosy. Monitor the stems and leaves of your shrubs regularly for signs of pests or diseases. Because of a shrub's larger size, it's often harder to detect problems at an early stage than it is on smaller flowers.

❧ COMMON SHRUB PROBLEMS ❧

OVERALL DECLINE OR DAMAGE

▷ The site doesn't suit the shrub's needs for light, water, soil type, and pH.

▷ The site doesn't suit the shrub's tolerance of temperature extremes, wind, or pollution.

▷ The planting depth is improper.

▷ The roots have been burned by herbicide, fertilizer, or road salt.

▷ Pests or diseases have attacked leaves and shoots.

▷ Moisture is excessive or too little.

NO BLOOMS OR FRUITS

▷ The shrub has not become sufficiently established to produce fruits.

▷ Pruning was done at the wrong time.

▷ High-ntirogen fertilizer was overapplied.

▷ Frost nipped the shrub at bud formation.

▷ The shrub lacked a pollinating variety or there were no insects to effect pollination.

▷ The buds or flowers were eaten by birds, animals, or insects

▷ The shrub was affected by problems such as petal blight or canker disease.

▷ **Azaleas, Barberry, Boxwood, Camellias, Fuchsias, Gardenias, Hedges, Hibiscus, Holly, Hydrangeas, Laurel, Lilacs, Oleander, Quince, Rhododendrons, Roses, Standards, Yew**

SLOPES

To measure a slope's rise, rest a sighting level on a 5-foot rod at the base; 50 feet up the slope, have a helper hold another 5-foot rod. Sight a horizontal line to the second rod, marking where the line hits the second rod. The distance from the mark to the top of the rod is the rise. With rods 50 feet apart, every foot of rise equals a grade of 2 percent. A grade over 3 percent is subject to erosion; a grade over 10 percent needs terraces and retaining walls.

How does your garden lie? If the grade is less than 3 percent, the orientation of planting rows makes little difference. On steeper slopes, however, rows should run parallel with the slope instead of up and down.

When you construct terraces or retaining walls, follow the natural contours of the hillside.

Rock solid. To ensure stability when building a masonry retaining wall, slant it back into the slope 1 inch for every 1 foot of rise. In cold areas, extend the

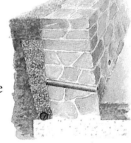

concrete footing into the soil well below the frost line. Provide "weep holes" for water to drain through.

Weave a wall. Make a rustic retaining wall to hold soil on a steep slope. Drive wooden stakes into the soil 3 to 4 feet apart, leaving 2 to 3 feet above ground. Strip thin, straight branches of their foliage and weave between the stakes, making sure the bottom row has good contact with the ground. Replace the branches when they begin to rot or look ragged.

Keep it moving. Make sure water and cold air can drain down the slope and dissipate. Don't create any depressions in the soil where water can collect. And don't plant any dense hedges—frost will settle in front of them and harm the plants.

To hold soil back while plants fill in, cover the slope with black plastic mulch or a geotextile weed mat. Poke holes through the material and set in the plants. Spread an organic mulch around the plants.

Nature's little helpers. Plant a slope with strong-rooted, low-growing, spreading specimens—preferably evergreen. Their roots will bind the soil, and the top growth will provide a low-maintenance ground cover for an awkward spot. Be sure to select

⊰ SLOPE SPECIMENS ⊱

When it comes to plants for slopes, the lower-growing, the better. Select shrubs, perennials, ground covers, and vines whose stems grow no taller than 1 foot upright.

Bearberry	Lily-of-the-valley
Low-bush blueberry	Creeping mahonia
Carmel creeper	Pachysandra
Cotoneaster	Periwinkle
Daylily	Rock rose
Goutweed	Creeping rosemary
Ice plant	Solomon's seal
Ivy	St. John's wort
Honeysuckle	Star jasmine
Juniper	Wintercreeper

plants suited to the light conditions on the slope.

Minimize water runoff by mounding up the soil on the downhill side of each plant to form a basin, which will retain moisture.

An ideal opportunity. Slopes invite rock gardens. The stones serve as retaining walls, and traditional rock plants are ground hugging and resilient.

Water slopes with a drip irrigation system or a soaker hose to avoid runoff. You will also be spared hauling hoses up the hill.

Good for goats. Unless you have these "living lawn mowers," don't plant grass on a steep slope; it's too hard to cut. If the grade is less than 15 percent, you can give it a try. Use sod instead of seed, laying the strips across the slope—not up and down. Peg in place until the roots develop.

▷ **Geotextiles, Ground Covers, Rock Gardens**

SLUGS & SNAILS

Natural predators. Blackbirds, ducks, frogs and toads, lizards, and snakes all consider slugs and brown snails a delicacy.

The infallible beer trap. Slugs and snails find the yeast in beer irresistible. Bury a container half filled with the brew where they can easily climb into it and die; the alcohol destroys their body tissue. Dump the container and add new beer every day.

Plants they hate. Plants that are reputed to repel snails include azaleas, apricot, basil, beans, California poppies, corn, chard, daffodils, fennel, fuchsias, grapes, ginger, holly, parsley, Peruvian lily, pumpkins, plum, rhododendrons, rhubarb, sage, and Swedish ivy.

Plants they love. These gastropod gourmands take a special liking to the following: dahlias, delphiniums, hostas, lupines, marigolds, zinnias, and almost any flower or vegetable seedling.

A sugar shack. Dissolve a teaspoon each of jam, sugar, and lemon juice in a glass of water; pour the mixture into a can with 2 or 3 openings cut in the side; push the sharp metal edges inward. Attracted by the sweets, slugs will climb in and be killed by the acidic lemon juice.

Protect young plants by encircling them with a sandpaper collar. Either cut your own or use a sandpaper collar for a drill disc; the rough surface will discourage the soft-bodied pests.

Barriers of sand or ash should be several inches deep and encircle the plant entirely. During periods of severe slug infestation, avoid mulching plants with straw, leaves, compost, or other organic materials. In addition to hiding in these mulches, the pests will likely lay their eggs there.

Night stalking. Slugs and snails are nocturnal. After dark, hunt in their favorite feeding places, armed with a flashlight and a salt shaker or a bucket of salty water. Salted slugs and snails don't survive.

The grapefruit diet. Upturned half-grapefruit rinds can serve as lethal traps before being discarded; the juice is acidic.

⊱ SLUG STOPPERS ⊰

Environmentally conscious gardeners have tried every conceivable material to deter slugs and snails from favored plants. Following are some that are said to be effective.

Ashes (hardwood)	Lime
Bark (particularly pine)	Quackgrass
Charcoal	Sand
Cinders	Sandpaper
Copper	(drill disc "collars")
Diatomaceous earth	Sawdust
Eggshells	Tobacco stem meal
Gravel	Thorns
Hair	Wood or bark chips

Keep bait dry. Put baits like metaldehyde in sections of plastic soda bottles. Moisture can cause fungus growth, making the bait less appealing.

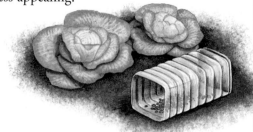

Wormwood *(Artemisia absinthium)* brewed into a tea and sprayed at the base of plants provides protection from slugs and snails. But take note: wormwood is also dangerous to humans.

▷ **Ashes, Pesticides**

SNOW

No flat tops. Hedges sheared to a flat top may accumulate enough snow to cause branches to split or collapse under the weight. In heavy snowfall areas, protect hedges by shearing them to an arched peak.

Snow mold is a fungal turfgrass disease that appears after snow has melted. To prevent it, cut back on nitrogen fertilizer in the fall and clear away melting snow as quickly as you can in spring.

A useful signal. Areas of early melting snow can indicate microclimates in your garden where tender plants have the best chance of survival and where seedlings and transplants will be safe from a late frost.

Like other hardy plants, witch hazel 'Sunburst' benefits from an insulating layer of dry snow.

Don't salt the snow. Salty runoff can harm your plants. Instead of road salt, sprinkle wood ashes, sand, gravel, sawdust, or fertilizer on walks and driveways.
▷ **Frost**

SOIL

The most fundamental element in the garden is soil: the very foundation for all plants. The gardener's job is to see to it that soil is healthy and in the best possible condition.

EVALUATING SOIL
Composition. Soil is made up of inorganic particles—sand, silt, and clay—as well as organic matter, air, and water. Soil quality depends on the proportion of these components and the activity of the attendant microorganisms, earthworms, and fungus.

Acidity and alkalinity in soil are measured on the pH scale, which runs from 0 (pure acid) to 14 (pure alkaline). From the neutral point of 7, the numbers increase or decrease geometrically: thus a pH of 5 is 10 times more acid than a pH of 6.

A test-kit substitute. For a quick pH test, buy litmus paper, sold at most pharmacies; it should come with a color scale. Mix distilled water and soil in a clean cup until a moist paste forms. Then insert the litmus paper. To find the pH, match the paper's final color to the scale.

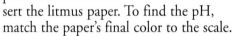

Analyze structure and texture. Texture refers to the amount of sand, silt, and clay in the soil, while structure refers to how the components clump together. To test structure, rub a pinch of moist soil between thumb and forefinger. Soil that's too sandy feels gritty. Silty soil feels smooth and slick, while clayey soil feels sticky and rolls up easily. For ideal "loam," with a mealy feel, the soil should contain up to 50 percent sand, between 25 and 50 percent silt, and up to 25 percent clay.

A texture test. Lightly squeeze a handful of moist soil. If the clump crumbles apart, the soil is sandy. If it forms a sticky ball, it is clayey. If the soil ends up as a spongy ball, you have loam.

Test for tilth, which refers to the soil's fitness for cultivation. Drop a spadeful of moist soil on a hard surface: if it breaks into ½-inch-diameter crumbs, the soil has good tilth and is ready for planting. If the soil breaks into clods, it is too heavily compacted and needs amending.

⚞ AMENDING SOIL pH ⚟

Use this guide as a starting point in adjusting the pH of 100 square feet of average soil by one unit. Soils that are rich in organic matter may need up to 50 percent more amendment, while nutrient-poor soils require less.

CLAY SOIL

To raise 1 point: 8 lbs. ground limestone
To lower 1 point: 6 ½ lbs. aluminum sulfate

SANDY SOIL

To raise 1 point: 3–4 lbs. ground limestone
To lower 1 point: 2 ½ lbs. aluminum sulfate

LOAM

To raise 1 point: 6 lbs. ground limestone
To lower 1 point: 6 ½ lbs. aluminum sulfate

Rich or lean? A "rich" soil teems with 13 of the nutrients plants need for growth, including trace elements. "Lean" or "light" refers to a soil that is low in fertility.

MANAGING SOIL
Tread lightly. Don't walk on, work in, or drive machinery over wet soil. Also refrain from excessive tilling. Doing either can damage soil structure, compacting the pores so that air and water won't be able to move through.

Add organic matter. The single most important way to improve all soils is by adding organic matter. Work 1 to 4 inches of rotted manure, compost, chopped leaves, or other source into the soil each year to produce rich, crumbly humus. Turn it in deeply: digging or tilling the soil adds oxygen, which microorganisms need to break down organic matter and release nutrients.

Give it a try. You can purchase biological soil conditioners from organic-gardening catalogs. Although unproven, these products are said to increase the activity of soil microorganisms in improving soil structure and breaking down organic matter.
▷ **Acid Soil, Alkaline Soil, Clay Soil, Drainage, Earthworms, Organic Fertilizers, Sandy Soil**

SOWING

The easy way. Commercial seed tape comes with seeds affixed at the appropriate spacing. Simply cut the tape to the length of the row, firm it in, and keep it moist; it will gradually decompose in the soil.

They come alive at night. The seeds of some plants, including cornflowers, forget-me-nots, coriander, delphiniums, larkspur, nemesia, phlox, parsley, and many vegetables, germinate only in darkness. Place folded newspapers over seed trays or a peat moss mulch over seed furrows.

Bad back? Avoid bending over by distributing seeds through a plastic tube. Pack down the soil with your heel.

TRANSPLANTING

How deep? Despite some exceptions, such as tomatoes and eggplants, most seedlings should be planted no deeper than they were in the seedbed or flat. After planting, make a slight depression around each seedling. This holds water long enough to ensure that it goes directly to the roots.

Only the strong survive. Thin seedlings thoroughly before planting out. Pick out the obvious weaklings after the first set of true leaves appears.

Reduce transplant shock for seedlings grown in a flat by cutting squares around each plant—just like cutting a cake—a week before planting them out.

▷ **Potting Mixes, Seeds, Transplanting**

INDOORS

Anything goes. Almost any container can be used for seed-starting: pots, flats, a milk jug, even an egg carton. It needs drainage holes and must be clean. To sterilize the container, soak overnight in a solution of 2 tablespoons household bleach to 1 quart water.

Ready to go. Bury peat pots, newspaper cones, and eggshells directly in the soil when the seedlings they contain have two true leaves; these containers will slowly decompose.

It's so fine. To distribute tiny seeds more evenly, simply put them in a clean salt shaker or a folded piece of paper.

Now you're cookin'! To prevent such soil-borne diseases as damping off, sterilize your homemade potting mix. Either put slightly moist mix in an ovenproof tray and cover it with aluminum foil or use a broiler bag. Bake for 35 to 45 minutes at 180°F. Keep the kitchen windows open; the cooking soil can have an unpleasant smell.

OUTDOORS

Firm soil. Pack down the soil on just-sown seed. In the garden, step down on a board or press the flat side of a hoe on the seed rows. In pots, press down gently with the palm of your hand or an empty pot.

SPADING

The right tool. Unlike the scoop-bladed shovel, a spade has a flat, rectangular blade. It is used to cut an edge on beds and lawns, strip sod, dig holes, chop roots, and pry up rocks. A second tool, the spading fork, has 4 flat tines as opposed to the curved tines of pitchforks. It is used for turning over and aerating soil or compost, mixing in soil amendments, lifting clumps and bulbs for division, and harvesting root crops.

Suit yourself. Choose a tool of a size and weight that feels comfortable: handles on spades and forks range from 27 to 39 inches long. Tall gardeners can spare their backs by using longer-handled tools, while short gardeners may find smaller styles—including the lightweight border spade and border fork—easier to work with.

Quality features. Look for a sturdy, D-shaped handle; it can be made of wood, metal, or plastic. The blade should be forged from a single piece of steel and have solid-socket construction where it meets the shaft. Also look for a smooth, rounded shoulder along the top of the blade, which will protect your foot when you press down. A spading fork should have broad, flat, stable tines with V-shaped ends.

Proper footwork. Wear heavy-soled shoes to make it easier on your feet when digging with a spade or shovel. And never stomp on the tool head, no matter how hard the soil. Instead, press it steadily into the ground with your foot, leaning in with your body weight.

Be kind to your back. Stand up straight when pushing the tool in the ground and as you draw the handle toward your body

to loosen the soil. Bend your knees and lift the load with your upper body, supporting the handle shaft against your thigh for leverage. With heavy loads, don't twist at the hips when depositing soil to the side; instead, turn your body to face the pile.

A head start. Spade up the soil in autumn and leave big clods in place throughout the winter. Rain, snow, and the alternate freezing and thawing of the soil will help break up any clumps by spring.

Spade for the long term. You can limit your spading to every 5 years or so by digging deeply, incorporating plenty of organic matter, and spreading mulch. And don't walk directly on spaded soil—lay down a plank path to keep the ground from becoming compacted.

When turning over large areas, use a tiller to do the heaviest work. Finish by hand, using a fork to break up any clods, remove stones, and dig up roots.

Sharpen your spade so that it makes a good, clean "bite." Use a flat file, drawing it smoothly down the original bevel from top to bottom; don't saw back and forth. File until the edge is evenly tapered and any nicks are removed. Make only a shallow bevel, since a blade that has been honed knife-sharp will chip. When finished, run the file along the back of the edge to remove the burr that has built up.

Clean your tools between uses. Rub off debris with a piece of burlap, a coarse cloth, or even a dry corncob. Use steel wool or a wire brush to loosen encrusted dirt. Wipe metal surfaces lightly with oil. Before storing tools for the winter, also wipe wooden handles with linseed oil.

Bang out dings. If a corner of the spade blade has been bent by hitting a rock, hammer it back into shape while holding it against a flat surface. File a new bevel on the dull edge.

Straighten a bent tine. Drive a sturdy metal pipe—3 feet long and an inch in diameter—into the ground so that it protrudes about 10 inches above the soil. Slide the damaged tine into the pipe and press slowly until it returns to its original position.

A temporary fix. To mend a split handle, spread wood glue on the split and press the two sides together; tape tightly. Drill several holes through the handle and fasten with round-headed bolts; secure with washers and nuts. This repair should last until you finish the job, but you'll have to buy a new handle.

SPINACH

Keep it cool. Heat makes spinach bolt. In warm and hot climates, plant in the fall for harvests in winter and early spring. In cold and temperate areas, plant a spring crop as soon as the soil can be worked or anytime before daytime temperatures reach 70°F; start a fall crop in August. To overwinter, use row covers or straw mulch.

A SPINACH STAND-IN

Gardeners in hot climates can grow New Zealand spinach (*Tetragonia tetragonioides*), a trailing plant with fleshy, juicy leaves that resemble those of true spinach. It won't bolt in the heat, is relatively undisturbed by pests and diseases, and, in frost-free areas, will grow as a perennial. Grow in sandy soil with plenty of moisture, spacing plants 2 feet apart in rows that are 3 feet apart. Harvest the tender tips often and prepare as you would spinach.

Rapid risers. Spinach matures quickly, needing only about 40 days until harvest. Sow short rows every 2 weeks to ensure a steady supply of tender young leaves.

Grow some shade. Help spinach stay cool by planting it at the base of corn, squash, beans, or peas—any tall or trellis-grown plant that will block out some of the sun but still allow for good air circulation.

Sow shallow. Place seeds ¼ inch deep and 1 inch apart in a neutral soil enriched with compost or manure; thin to between 3 and 6 inches apart when seedlings reach 1 inch tall. Instead of discarding the tiny plants, add them to a salad.

Basic care. Keep plants well fed and watered. Fertilize with 1 tablespoon fish emulsion mixed with 1 gallon water. Use about 1 cup per 1-foot row once the leaves emerge and feed weekly until plants are 3 inches tall; then feed a few more times during the season. Provide constant moisture to keep spinach from bolting.

Look for leaf miners, whose larvae tunnel inside the spinach leaves. If you find trails on the leaves or eggs underneath, pick and destroy the foliage; don't compost it. Treat plants with pyrethrin and till the bed under at season's end.

Cut or pinch the leaves to harvest instead of pulling them. Once the central seed stalk forms with the warmer weather, cut the whole plant back to the soil line.

⇥ A SPINACH SAMPLER ⇤

A versatile vegetable for salads, soups, and side dishes, spinach is a relatively carefree home crop. Try 'Melody,' with smooth, dark green leaves, for high productivity and no bitter taste. 'Avon' has succulent, semi-crinkly leaves and good heat tolerance. 'Tyee' is mildew resistant and suitable for planting in the damp, cold conditions of fall. 'Bloomsdale Longstanding' and 'Cold Resistant Savoy' both have crinkled leaves and will tolerate cold.

▷ **Vegetable Gardens**

SPRAYING

Ways to spray. A portable tank or a hose-end sprayer is used outdoors to apply fertilizer, pesticide, herbicide, and other liquids. A hand-held, trigger-grip sprayer, also called a mister, is used to squirt water on plants inside the house and greenhouse.

SPRAYING

Sprayer styles. There are many styles of tank sprayers for home gardens, ranging in capacity from 1 to 5 gallons. The most common type is the compression sprayer, which works with air pressure built up by intermittently pumping a plunger. Another type is the knapsack sprayer; the pressure needed to expel the contents is maintained by pumping a lever continuously.

Stainless steel or plastic? While both types of tank resist corrosion, translucent plastic lets you to see when to refill; but it can absorb chemicals. Stainless steel is heavier and opaque—but durable and nonabsorbent.

A warning. Reserve a separate sprayer for herbicides, and never use it to spray fertilizer or pesticides on desirable specimens—no matter how well you've cleaned it.

Measure and mix. Use only the amount of chemicals recommended by the manufacturer for a specific application and dilute with water in the proper proportion. To mix, close the lid tightly and shake well. To keep the chemicals from settling out, shake the tank several times as you work.

When filling a sprayer with manure tea or other solution with a solid component, strain through a doubled-up pair of pantyhose legs. Lower the toe into the tank and secure the top over the opening with a rubber band. Pour in the mixture; the liquid will flow through, and any nozzle-clogging particles will be trapped. Remove the strainer before spraying.

Adjust the squirt. Close down the nozzle to emit a thin stream for spot treatments. Open it to a full spray for a large area; for complete coverage, use a steady sweeping motion, back and forth.

A little goes a long way. Don't spray to the point where plants are drenched and dripping; overspraying is wasteful and can harm your plants. Apply a fine, even mist.

Spray when it's calm. Wind can carry the spray where you don't want it to go—onto plants, people, or pets. Always keep your skin covered with protective clothing in case a breeze kicks up.

Rinse after use. Before putting the sprayer away or using it with a different chemical, rinse it thoroughly. Pour clean water in the tank, shake, and squirt it through the nozzle. Empty and repeat twice.

A clogged nozzle? An obstructed nozzle won't deliver the correct dose of chemicals to the plants. Poke with a thin nail or a length of wire to clear out any sediment.

No muss, no fuss. The easiest way to treat large areas is with a hose-end sprayer. A chemical is placed in a glass or plastic reservoir, whose top attaches to a hose; the water pressure draws up, dilutes, and disperses the solution. Be sure to use only those concentrates specified for hose-end applicators and to adjust the sprayer settings for the proper dosage.

MISTING

Why mist? Contrary to lore, squirting foliage with water is not an efficient way to increase humidity for houseplants. Misting does help keep leaves clean and fresh and is a good way to add moisture to tender cuttings.

Plastic misters, sold at garden centers and hardware stores, are preferable to recycled spray bottles, in which chemical traces of your household cleansers may remain.

Use soft water (water low in minerals) so that it won't spot the foliage. Let the water stand until it reaches room temperature.

Mist in the morning, when the temperature is rising. Move the plants out of full sun before spraying; the water intensifies sunlight and can burn the foliage.

A group shower. Group together plants that enjoy being spritzed. Keep them separate from cacti and such fuzzy-leaved specimens as African violets, gloxinias, and gynuras, whose foliage will discolor if wet.

Keep flowers dry when misting. Shield the blooms with a piece of cardboard and wet only the foliage.

Prevent water stains on windowsills or furniture by putting houseplants in the bathtub for misting. If a plant is too large to easily move, spread a plastic drop cloth under it.

▷ **Pesticides**

SQUASH

Native Americans. Squash are ancient indigenous food crops and comprise two distinct types. Summer squash are bushy plants with soft-skin fruits. Winter squash grow on vines and have a hard rind.

All squash like rich soil and plenty of sunshine. Prepare for planting by digging a hole large enough to hold a bushel of cow manure or compost; dump it in and top off with 3 inches of good garden loam.

Where to plant. Don't place where squash and its relatives have been grown in the past year or so. Interplant with radishes or basil to repel borers and beetles.

For best germination, sow seed when the soil temperature is 60°F or above.

No need to feed. If you've amended the soil with manure, don't add fertilizer during the growing season. If not, incorporate a 5–10–10 at planting time and side-dress each plant when it starts to vine.

Squash's best friend. Black plastic mulch isn't pretty, but squash love it anyway. Use it to raise soil temperature, conserve moisture, reduce weeds, and deter pests.

Bug borers. Place aluminum foil under squash plants to reflect light and confuse the squash borer moth, who lays her eggs at the base of the stem. If you do see eggs, simply scrape them off. The squash species *Cucurbita moschata,* which includes the 'Butternut' variety, is resistant to borers.

Minimize mildew by allowing for good air circulation. At the first sign of fungus, spray with a solution of 1 teaspoon baking soda mixed in 1 quart water; add ¼ teaspoon cooking oil or soap to help it stick.

Fruitless flowers. Don't be alarmed if some of the flowers don't set fruit. Squash produce male and female flowers on the same plant, but only the females bear fruit after being pollinated by bees. You'll recognize the females by their short stems and a small bulge—the young squash— below the vase-shaped blossom.

SUMMER SQUASH

Family planning. Yellow crookneck and straightneck, zucchini, and scallop (also called patty pan) squash are notoriously prolific. Plan on only one plant per person.

Pack them in. Plant in rows, sowing about three seeds per foot, then thin to 18 inches apart. The close spacing reduces yield per plant but will increase it per square foot.

AN UNUSUAL SQUASH

Spaghetti squash, or vegetable spaghetti, is a large, oblong winter squash with a yellow-orange rind. It is grown for its unusual flesh—crisp and starchy, yet mildly sweet. When cooked, it comes away from the rind in long, thin strands that resemble spaghetti. Prepare it with butter and cheese or a tomato sauce, as you would pasta. Try 'Orangetti' for good productivity; one plant per family is adequate.

The smaller, the better. Harvest summer squash when it is still immature—no more than 6 inches long, with tender skin. Do the thumbnail test: the skin should be soft and easily pierced when pressed. Pick regularly to encourage productivity.

WINTER SQUASH

Plant in hills, sowing five seeds in each and thinning to the best three seedlings. Be sure to allow at least 6 to 8 feet around the hill for the vines to spread.

To save space, pinch off the vine ends after enough fruit has set and turn the tips of the vines back toward the hill. Or train the plants on a trellis or tripod, supporting the fruits in a sling of pantyhose or soft cloth—perhaps an old bed sheet. Keeping them off the ground also exposes the fruits to more sun, prevents rotting, and makes harvesting easier.

⊁ A SQUASH SAMPLER ⊱

Dozens of squash cultivars are available. Listed below are a few proven favorites.

SUMMER SQUASH

'Aristocrat' Green zucchini; short maturity time

'Early Summer' Yellow crookneck; solid, meaty flesh; bumpy skin

'Gold Rush' Yellow zucchini; tender skin; prolific grower

'Peter Pan' Green scallop; juicy, meaty flesh

'Seneca Prolific' Yellow straightneck; early cultivar; heavy yield

'Sunburst' Yellow scallop; buttery, nutty flavor

WINTER SQUASH

'Blue Hubbard' Blue-gray rind; smooth yellow-orange flesh

'Buttercup' Turban-shaped; dry, buttery flesh

'Jersey Golden Acorn' Gold flesh; stores well

'Waltham Butternut' Pear-shaped; sweet orange flesh; small seed cavity

---

Harvest winter squash once the rinds are firm and the vines begin to shrivel. Cut the stem about 2 inches above the fruit. While no squash is frost hardy, don't worry about cool fall nights—they bring out the sugars in the flesh and produce the sweet flavor.

Curing squash. If the fruit has not quite matured by harvest time, cure it at 80°F for about ten days. Then wash the rind with a solution of one part chlorine bleach to 10 parts water, dry, and store in a cool dark place; they will last for several months. Check often for soft spots—a sign of rot.
▷ **Vegetable Gardens, Zucchini**

SQUIRRELS

Omnivorous and wily, squirrels are difficult to keep away from your trees, vegetables, and bulbs. You may have to employ several different strategies repeatedly until you've had success.

Pepper your corn with cayenne or black pepper to prevent squirrels from nibbling. Sprinkle it liberally on the soil, stalks, and ears; repeat after a rain.

Nuts for nuts. Squirrels are so fond of nut meats, especially filberts and walnuts, that they can empty a whole tree in short order. To make nuts less accessible, prune the lowest branches to at least 6 feet above the ground; then band the trunk with a 2-inch-wide piece of aluminum roof flashing. Adjust the flashing as needed to allow for tree growth.

Agile jumpers. Make sure that trees you want to protect are 10 to 12 feet away from other trees so that squirrels can't leap from limb to limb. Prune back surrounding tree branches as necessary.

Wrap it up. Swathe sunflower heads and avocado fruits with netting, cheesecloth, or pantyhose to protect them, although a persistent squirrel might chew right through.

Make a walk-in tomato cage 6 feet tall and wide and 10 feet long with wooden supports and chicken wire. Be sure to bury the wire 6 inches deep to deter burrowers.

Cover crocus bulbs, which are a favorite squirrel snack. Lay a piece of ½-inch wire mesh over the bed and tuck the edges securely down into the soil.

Pie plates don't work. Some gardeners place foil pie pans on both sides of a bird feeder suspended on a wire as barriers. The squirrels soon learn, however, to jiggle the wire and spill seed on the ground instead.

Spray tactics. Try using a scent repellent, like those formulated for deer. Spray it around garden beds, trees, and bird feeders. You can also soak flower bulbs in a repellent before planting them.

Use a humane box trap about 8 inches high and wide and 2 feet long to catch squirrels. Wear rubber gloves when handling it to mask your scent and place it in a sheltered area. Bait with peanut butter, nut meats, sunflower seeds, melon rinds, oats,

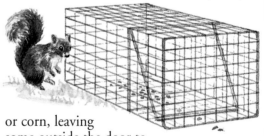

or corn, leaving some outside the door to entice them. Ask your local Cooperative Extension Service agent or animal control officer where to release the squirrels.

Don't overdo it. Never resort to poisons or inhumane leg-hold traps to rid your yard of squirrels; they can just as easily harm children and pets.
▷ **Birds, Rodents**

STAKING

Don't wait to stake new plants until they grow. Some grow surprisingly fast, and it can be difficult to put supports in place once plants start to sprawl.

The best stakes are made from naturally rot-resistant wood that will last longer than just one season. Good choices include redwood, cypress, red cedar, chestnut, and hazelnut. Metal stakes can also be used.

Eye protectors. Stake tops are often danger-ously sharp. Cover them with pieces of sponge or cork, old tennis balls with holes cut in them, small terra-cotta figurines, or even balls of modeling clay, which can then be imaginatively shaped.

Natural stakes. Instead of using tradi-tional, rigid pole stakes, try sticking stripped branches, chosen for their appealing shapes, into the ground right next to the plants that need support.

Three fine ties. Tree ties must be weatherproof and tight enough to fight the wind but loose enough to prevent injury to the plant. Three good materials to use are a pair of old stock-ings or panty-hose, adjust-able plastic ties with buckles, and a wide band of thick rubber held in place with wrapped wire. Remove the stakes from most trees after the tree's first year in the ground.

Practical ties. Pick up a roll of green Velcro in a gardening store. Velcro holds the plant firmly to the stake and blends in with the foliage. Velcro is extremely durable and can be reused in the garden for years.

For invisible staking, paint stakes green, use green ties, and, when needed for extra support, use pieces of green nylon netting.

Heavily flowered stems such as irises, delphiniums, gladiolus, or chrysanthemums may need staking. Stick a bamboo pole firmly into the ground and tie on the stem with

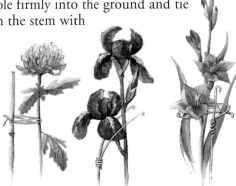

soft string wrapped in a figure eight. Drive a metal pole into the ground next to the stalk and rest the stem in a fork. Or attach the flowering stem to a nearby metal stake with a small loop of smooth round wire.

Plant stakes with trees.
When given firm support, a freshly planted tree puts down new roots more quickly and grows faster. Place the stake in the

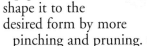

planting hole before refilling it so that the stake can't damage the roots. Pound the stake in a little deeper to be sure it's secure, then attach the young tree to it.

Don't tie too tightly. Slight movements caused by the wind help newly planted trees develop stronger, thicker trunks.

Pull stakes more easily by first driving them in a bit farther with a few taps of a hammer or mallet. They'll come right out.
▷ **Pantyhose**

STANDARDS

A manmade plant form. A standard is created by carefully pruning and training a shrub to grow into a small tree, about 3 to 4 feet tall, with a single trunk. The top is usually clipped into a sphere or cone shape.

Standard procedure.
Select a shrub with at least one straight vertical stem. Prune off all other low-growing stems and tie the selected one to a durable stake. When the plant is tall enough, pinch off the tip to make the top bushy. As the top grows, shape it to the desired form by more pinching and pruning. Carefully remove all unwanted buds that sprout along the main stem or trunk.

Plant prominently. Since standards are unusual and eye-catching, they deserve a special place in the landscape. Use them to line a walkway, or you can plant one on each side of a doorway, beside a gate, or at both ends of a garden bench.

Reliable plants for training as standards include azaleas, bay, boxwood, fuchsias, lan-tana, rosemary, and all the small-leaf hollies.

Climbing honeysuckle is easy to train. This honeysuckle standard is both decorative and fragrant.

A triple trunk. This interesting effect can easily be created with three flexible *Ficus benjamina* plants grown in the same pot. When they are 15 to 18 inches tall, cut off all lateral branches and carefully braid the three stripped stems. As they grow, the stems will thicken and wind together to form a sturdy handsome standard with a single trunk.
▷**Pruning**

STEPS

The foolproof formula for garden steps is based on the average length of the stride while walking. The proper proportion of tread (flat surface) to riser

(the vertical) is simply stated: Twice the height of the riser, plus the depth of the tread, should equal 26 inches. A 4-inch riser, for example, calls for an 18-inch tread, a 5-inch riser has a 16-inch tread, and a 6-inch riser has a 14-inch tread. The steepest practical step is an 8-inch riser with a 10-inch tread.

Make an estimate first. Before building steps, calculate roughly how many will be needed to get from one level to the next.

On steep slopes, lay out the steps so that they zigzag up diagonally, following the natural contours of the slope. Steps can be tiring and even dangerous if too steep.

If your slope is gradual, plan for a series of steps—7 to 8 steps each series maximum—linked by extra-wide landings, which should be at least 3 times the width of the regular steps' treads.

Slippery when wet. Logs, smooth stones, and slates are poor choices for steps because they can become slick in rain or snow. Instead, select materials with naturally rough surfaces. Where your garden receives full sunlight all winter, make your steps of dark stone, which will dry more quickly and absorb heat to melt ice or snow. Keep in mind that stones that get full sun in the summer will be hot to step on.

Rock solid. When making steps of flat stones or precast concrete, make sure that they are stable by using masonry or stone for risers and bedding them firmly on sand. Slope

treads slightly so that rainwater and snowmelt will drain off automatically.

A green staircase carpeted with creeping thyme, bentgrass, creeping phlox, or moss can be created with honeycombed concrete paving stones. Fill in and around the stones with soil for the plants, which will also stabilize the steps. Steps of this material will also be stable because of the stones' size and weight. Maintain plants by hand trimming.

Economical steps can easily be made by cutting them into the soil and packing them down thoroughly. Face risers with a material that will help keep them stable, such as log rounds, and cover the treads with crushed gravel.

Arrange bricks on firm ground on a bed of coarse sand. Bricks come in different sizes and shapes and offer a wide choice of step designs.

Install steps for easier maintenance of a steep rock garden. Give the steps a natural appearance by random placement, with narrow paths between small landings. Choose natural materials that will blend easily into the garden.

Camouflage old concrete steps or plain-looking new steps with long planters filled with your favorite annual and perennial flowers and herbs—or even salad greens.

On a very gradual slope, install steps by digging out a series of raised large landings, each deep enough to allow several strides to be taken between the risers.

Easy risers.
Railroad ties or landscape timbers made from rot-resistant or treated wood make excellent risers for steps. Their dimensions—7 to 8 inches square—are perfect as is. They can be sawed into two or three pieces as needed.

Soften the edges of stairways that appear too wide by planting fast-growing, sprawling plants alongside. Ivy, lavender, nasturtiums, and other plants with attractive foliage and blooms are good choices. Blooming vines such as clematis, wisteria, and honeysuckle can be trained to grow along treads and handrails.

Create a flowered stairway by making pockets of earth in the steps. Treat this stairway as a kind of unique multilevel rock garden. Plant perennial flowers such as periwinkles, saxifrage, cranesbills, or lavender in the pockets.

A handy ramp. If the steps are wide enough (more than 3 feet) and not too steep (18 inches high maximum), set up a ramp to accommodate a wheelbarrow anytime one is needed. Use a sturdy 2 by 10 or 2 by 12 piece of solid lumber laid flat against the front edges of all the steps.

Materials and placement are crucial factors in making sure that steps will add beauty to a hillside garden. Gather flat fieldstones or purchase them at a garden center and arrange and install them to follow the natural contours of the garden.
▷ **Slopes**

STONES

As natural ornaments in the garden, unusual, eye-catching stones work well. Simply place a few selected for their unique size, shape, or color in among the plants, or alongside a bench or well-traveled path.

For attractive—and effective—edging, use a row of fieldstones alongside a planting bed to mark the transition from lawn to ornamentals. The stones will also keep the mulch off the grass.

Make a large stone look natural by digging a shallow hole where you want it and burying the bottom third underground. Once plants fill in around it, the stone will appear as if it has always been there.

Leave them be. Don't move any big stones that might be in your garden beds. Save yourself needless digging and straining and use them as natural centerpieces for creeping, sprawling, or trailing plants.

Move huge stones by rolling them along on top of 5 or 6 smooth logs or large metal pipes. Move the last log or pipe up to the front as you move forward. Another trick: slide stones along on top of a slick sheet of strong, thick plastic.

A stone mulch. A mulch of small stones or gravel is good for plant roots because it helps hold moisture in the soil. The stones also collect the sun's heat during the day and release it at night. Use stone mulch to extend the growing season for fruiting vines and rows of vegetables. Stone mulch can also help plants survive cold winters.

Stones hold heat. In cooler northern regions or at higher altitudes, plant vegetables on a south-facing slope in front of a wide, low wall over which you can spread the vines and stems. Some plants that appreciate this extra warmth include tomatoes, zucchini, melons, and pumpkins.

Stop weeds and other plants from engulfing stepping-stones by laying the stones on top of a plant-smothering layer—such as thick newspapers or a geotextile fabric—covered with an inch or two of sand. Weeds won't take root in the sand, and the pathway will have a neater appearance—with much less maintenance.

Prevent weeds and mower damage by putting attractive stones over a layer of landscape cloth around the base of a favorite tree. Use one of the spun-bonded geotextile fabrics, which lets water through.

A protective layer. Spread small stones or gravel under the foliage of sprawling and climbing plants. Shielded from muddy soil and hungry slugs, the foliage will stay cleaner and fresher-looking, particularly during the wetter times of the year.

As a place to stand when watering, hoeing, spraying, or doing other maintenance jobs, install flat stones in flower beds. This also keeps the soil from being compacted and plants from being crushed. The edges will be softened by the foliage and blooms.
▷ **Paths, Rock Gardens, Walls**

STORING

Natural pest repellents. Place fresh bay leaves and peeled garlic cloves in various places throughout the storage area.

Right sides up. On storage trays and drying racks, be sure to put apples stem-down and pears stem-up. Make sure that none of the pieces of fruit are touching.

Disinfect yearly, well before the harvest, to kill germs, mold spores, and other harmful fungi. Take advantage of summer, when the area is empty, to wash walls with lime and to wipe down drying racks and shelves. Use a solution of 2 tablespoons of household bleach to 1 quart water. Then ventilate the room completely.

Store squash and pumpkins with an inch of stem left on. Place them on shelves padded with straw or hang them up in nets in a cool place above freezing. Their solid skin allows storage for several months. Be sure they don't touch one another.

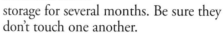

Save hot peppers. Allow them to ripen fully on the vine, then string them and hang them up to dry. In the arid Southwest, garlands of dried hot peppers are hung outdoors on houses as attractive, natural, and useful ornaments.

Keep potatoes in the dark. They will keep for the whole winter if stored in total darkness at about 40°F or a bit cooler. Place in slatted bins or mesh bags kept 2 or 3 inches above the floor for better air circulation. Don't pile more than 18 inches deep. Eat any potatoes damaged even slightly during harvest, since they won't last.

Sweet potatoes must be cured to keep well. Ideally they should be left in moist conditions at 85°F for 5 to 7 days after harvest. Then store at about 50°F and 80 percent humidity. Don't touch or move sweet potatoes until it's time to use them.

Bury other root vegetables such as carrots, turnips, beets, and rutabagas in cases filled with slightly moist, clean sand. Store them in layers. Carrots and parsnips can also be left in the ground, mulched heavily, and dug up all winter as needed.

Don't store Jerusalem artichokes. As soon as these tubers are out of the ground, they begin to dry out and shrivel up. Leave them underground and harvest as needed.

Store beans on a dry day. Use clean, dry containers with airtight lids and be sure that the beans are also completely dry. If the containers are filled and sealed on a day with low humidity, mold is less likely to develop.

Green tomatoes can be picked whenever frost threatens, wrapped in newspaper, and stored for up to 2 months until ripe.

Wrap cabbage tightly in newspaper when storing to hold in both moisture and odor. If nearby fruit starts to taste like cabbage, move your cabbage elsewhere.

Keep fruit away from vegetables. Gases released by ripening apples and other fruit often cause potatoes, turnips, and other vegetables to overripen and start sprouting.

Install a thermometer in the storage area and try to prevent temperatures from fluctuating too widely or from going below freezing. Good ventilation is also important but is difficult to achieve when trying to maintain a constant temperature.

A handy chute. Transport sand down to a basement or root cellar more easily by using a leftover piece of gutter pipe stuck down through a basement window. Position each storage box so it can be filled directly at the bottom of the pipe.
▷ **Drying, Freezing, Pantyhose, Preserves**

STRAWBERRIES

PURCHASING

How much is enough? For a family of four, plant about a dozen June-bearing strawberries, which fruit only once, and a dozen everbearing types, which produce crops in spring and late summer. Each plant yields from a cup to a pint per year.

Check the neck. Whether you're buying bare-root plants in spring or potted ones any time in season, look for a healthy, rot-free crown, or neck, where the flower buds and fruits will form. Spotless green leaves and whitish roots also indicate plant vigor.

Guard against virus by buying certified disease-free stock; strawberries are particularly susceptible to these diseases. Always select varieties adapted to your area.

PLANTING

The right soil. Strawberries like it rich, acidic, and well-drained. In early spring, prepare a thoroughly tilled, well-weeded bed amended with plenty of humus, compost, or aged manure.

Blanket the bed 4 to 8 weeks before planting time with a sheet of black or clear plastic mulch. The heat of sunlight will "solarize" the soil, inhibiting weed growth. To plant, slice crosses in the covering 12 to 18 inches apart and set in the plants.

Overcast days are the best time to plant, even though strawberries love the sun; they will be less stressed. Soak their roots in water for several hours beforehand.

Neither deep nor shallow. Strawberries are fussy about their depth in the soil. Plant so that the crown is just above grade.

If planted too deep, the plants will rot; if too shallow, they'll dry out.

A root boost. To help strawberries develop a strong root system, dig a hole about 6 inches wide and a few inches deeper than the roots. Mound soil in the center of the hole and spread the roots evenly over the top. If the roots are too long, never fold them up; snip with scissors instead.

A depth test. To make sure that the plants are set at the proper depth, water in thoroughly and note any settling of the soil. If the crowns sink, dig up the plants and raise; if they are protruding, add more soil to cover. Check again after the first rainfall.

Berries on the balcony. Keep strawberries close at hand for munching by planting them in containers for the terrace. If you don't have an actual strawberry pot, use any tub or barrel with holes in its sides, where you can tuck in plants. To water evenly, insert a perforated pipe down the center of the pot;

it can be left in or filled with gravel, which stays in place when the pipe is pulled out.

Keep moving. Once an existing strawberry bed becomes less productive, start a new one in another part of the garden. But don't choose a spot where tomatoes, peppers, or potatoes have been grown in the last 3 years; strawberries are prone to the same soilborne diseases that attack these vegetables.

MAINTENANCE

After the first flowering, mulch with straw, shredded pine bark, or pine needles to keep fruits from touching the soil. You can also use plastic collars.

A morning shower. Strawberries need to be kept moist. But take care: water only in the morning so that the plants can dry before sundown.

Take a pinch. Get young plants off to a good start and ensure bountiful harvests in succeeding years by pinching off the flower buds the first season. With June-bearing strawberries, this means forfeiting fruit; on everbearing plants, removing the buds through July 1 stimulates the late-summer crop.

Feed in summer by digging in compost enriched with blood meal and hoof-and-horn meal; use about 2 to 3 bushels per 100 square feet. Add a little nitrogen-rich fertilizer if you notice that the leaves are yellowing.

Speed the harvest. Strawberries will ripen and be ready to pick sooner if you protect the beds with plastic tunnels or row covers very early in spring.

A LITTLE HISTORY

Known since ancient Roman times, strawberries grow wild in temperate regions across America and Europe. Today's cultivated varieties are descended from a mid-18th-century hybrid of two species that are native to the Americas and prized for their large, prolific fruits. Curiously, the new plant was developed in France, where indigenous strawberries are smaller. After the French hybrid arrived on this continent, it became well established in home and commercial gardens by 1825. The first American cultivar, called 'Hovey,' was raised 13 years later by a fruit grower of that name in Massachusetts.

⊱| A STRAWBERRY SAMPLER |⊰

June-bearing strawberries produce fruits in early summer. One of the first to mature is 'Earliglow,' firm and sweet. 'Surecrop' is prized for its dependability, while 'Honeoye' ranks high for its excellent flavor. Later in June comes 'Sparkle,' which grows well in all but the hottest climates. For good disease-resistance, choose 'Guardian.'

Popular everbearing varieties include 'Ogallala,' a drought-resistant cultivar for cool climates; it has an appealing wild strawberry flavor. Heavy-bearing 'Ozark Beauty' keeps well and is suited to warm climates. 'Day-Neutral' is a popular Midwestern choice.

Lesser known are the alpine strawberries, which produce small but intensely scented fruits. 'Alexandria' boasts juicy fruits that are large for their type. 'Alpine Yellow' has small golden fruits. An alpine with exceptional flavor is 'Baron Solemacher,' while the runnerless 'Reugen Improved' makes a neat border.

Pick strawberries when they are still about 25 percent white. They'll turn berry-red in a day, and you'll avoid the risk of having overripe fruit rot on the vine if rain delays harvesting. For best flavor, always take the whole stem and handle the tender fruits gently to minimize bruising.

Store ripe berries unwashed in the refrigerator; wash and remove the stems and caps only just before using. Wet strawberries spoil quickly, even if kept chilled.

Thwart thieving birds by stretching nets over the rows when the berries begin to redden. You can also set up wires that whir in the wind; twist the wires slightly so that they vibrate and "sing" even louder.

A garden renewal. As strawberries age, they weaken, falling prey to diseases and pests. Each year, pull out and destroy the oldest plants and add an equal number of new ones in fresh soil. With June-bearing types, you can also renovate your strawberry bed immediately after harvest by burning off the old foliage or clipping it 3 inches above the crown.

Examine plants regularly for signs of insect infestation or disease and treat accordingly. Red, yellow, or purple foliage may indicate aphids, spider mites, mildew, or a virus. A fuzzy mold on fruits is a fungus.

The next generation. Help young runners put down roots by pinning them directly to the soil with 4-inch lengths of wire bent in a "U"; shape the wire around a broom handle held in a vise. You can also bury 3-inch pots in the soil at grade level and peg the runners over them. Cut the runner from its parent 6 weeks later and wait another week to transplant it in fresh soil.

Cold comfort. In areas with hard freezes, mulch after the first frost with several inches of straw, hay, or other coarse material. Remove the next spring after all danger of frost has passed.
▷ **Netting, Pots, Vegetable Gardens**

STUMPS & DEAD TREES

STUMPS
Let it be. Unless you want to replant an area around a stump or the stump is in a prominent sightline, leave it in place. The easiest solution is to simply hide it with a ground cover such as ajuga or periwinkle.

Snap any suckers. A freshly cut stump will periodically send up new growth from its roots. Pull off or cut back these sucker shoots at their base and daub the wound with a herbicide. Killing the stump will also prevent suckers from forming.

Using herbicides. Destroy stumps with any brush-killing product, such as sulfur chlorate, 2,4-D + triclopyr, or ammonium sulphamate. But first check with your state environmental office to make sure that their use is legal in your area. To kill the stump, drill several holes in its top surface and pour in the solution. You can also paint all exposed areas of the stump with the herbicide.

Effective but smelly. If you're not in a hurry to remove a stump, a slow but easy way to destroy it is to drill a 2-inch-diameter hole in its center and fill it with 3 ½ ounces of saltpeter (potassium nitrate). Plug the hole with a cork and let the saltpeter penetrate for 10 to 12 months. Reopen the hole, pour in kerosene, and set the stump on fire; the smell will be unpleasant, so avoid inhaling the fumes. The flames spread slowly, turning the roots to ashes. After the embers have cooled, clean up any remains.

Can't burn? If local ordinances prohibit open burning, use any commercial solution with a bacterial or fungal inoculant, which will slowly destroy the wood.

Keep a safe distance. Be careful when using brush-killers or other herbicides on stumps that are close to desirable plants. Some trees, including many magnolia species, are so sensitive that they can be damaged even without direct contact with these chemicals. Cover a treated stump with a plastic bag or tarp to prevent runoff from rain. And don't replant in the immediate vicinity for at least 12 weeks.

Read carefully. Stump- and brush-killing products are noxious, so be sure to read and follow the manufacturers' recommendations thoroughly for safe handling. And always don protective clothing, including vinyl gloves and goggles.

Small stumps can be removed by hand, but doing so requires elbow grease and patience. Leave about a foot of trunk when cutting down the tree. Dig a trench around it, loosening the roots with a spade; chop any tough ones with an ax. Keep working on the roots and rocking the trunk back and forth until the stump can be lifted out.

A natural pedestal. Use an uprooted stump as a stand for a sundial or other garden ornament. Place the stump in the spot of your choice, leaving its roots exposed. Top with an ornament. The pedestal will look especially at home in an informal herb or cottage-style garden.

A rustic planter. If you've re-moved a stump or find one that's been uprooted by nature, use it as a whimsical container. Cut the stump about 6 inches above the point where the roots flare. Set it in the ground cut-side down in a level spot, burying it slightly for stability. Fill the "bowl" inside the roots with potting soil, and add plants. Keep it fed and watered as you would any container specimen.

DEAD TRUNKS

An overlooked treasure. A dead tree need not be an eyesore. It will attract birds, such as woodpeckers, owls, and nuthatches, for nesting and feeding and will provide a habitat for mice, snakes, and other creatures. It can also serve as a natu-ralistic backdrop or a sculptural sup-port for living plants.

Safety first. Evaluate the risks a dead tree would pose if allowed to stand. Could it topple or drop a limb on a building,

utility line, or other structure? Does it over-hang a walkway, terrace, or area where people might gather? If so, cut it down.

Recycle. Once a dead tree has fallen, use it to line a rustic path or edge a naturalistic garden bed. Or place it beside a pond as shelter for frogs and newts. Or turn a good-size trunk into a bench: cut two equal slices crosswise for legs and top it with a seat sawn in half lengthwise.

An imposing support. Give a dead tree new life by letting climbers clamber over it. Cut off the thin lower branches and plant a self-supporting vine in several places around the trunk. Try English ivy, Boston ivy, winter creeper, Virginia creeper, trumpet creeper, or climbing hydrangea. But take note: once a tree is covered, you'll no longer be able to inspect it for weakness; for this reason, don't use dead trees close to public areas.

Tree trimming. Drill cavities in the trunk or use existing crevices as planting pockets. Fill with soil and tuck in trailing flowers; you may have to cut the root balls to make them fit. Try honeysuckle, ivy-leaf gera-nium, rose verbena, or Cape plumbago. Water as needed and feed lightly.

Sitting pretty. A trunk cut horizontally a foot or so from the ground can serve as a harmonious pedestal for a basket or pot of plants. Select specimens that will cascade attrac-tively over the sides. If necessary, anchor the planter with a heavy stone. Or drive a nail through the bottom into the stump.

A natural flowerpot.

Unless nature has already done it for you, hollow out the interior of a trunk with an ax or auger until you've made a basin; coat the sides with a layer of clay. Drill a downward-slanting drainage hole at the base. Fill the cavity with soil and plant with trailing specimens.

▷ **Benches, Undergrowth**

SUCKERS

What are they? A sucker is a vertical shoot that grows from either the plant roots or stems where no buds are visible. It should not be confused with the shoots that grow from lateral buds when a stem tip is removed. Suckers arising from the roots are called root suckers, while those arising from the trunk or branches are called water sprouts.

A telltale sign. You can identify a sucker by its leaves: they are usually smaller and sparser than those on a regular stem.

Spreading shrubs. Some plants, including lilacs, forsythia, and raspberries, spread by root suckers. To multiply them, pull back the soil around the suckers in fall, during dormancy. If the roots look pest- and dis-ease-free, sever the suckers, with roots attached, from the parent clump. Cut back about half the top growth and transplant. Remove and destroy any unhealthy suckers or those not needed for propagation.

Take it off. Remove a sucker by pulling it off as close to its base as possible, even if you need to dig up soil to do so. Pull carefully, taking care not to damage the surrounding tissue, and slice away any remaining nub with a knife to leave a smooth surface. Rub out any regrowth with your fingers before it has a chance to develop. On older, established plants, use a small amount of growth retardant or brush-killer, like ammonium sulfamate, on the wound.

Pull, don't prune. Cutting off suckers stimulates regrowth. Cut only if pulling or snapping would damage the parent plant.

On trees and roses— especially those grafted onto the rootstock of a related species— remove root suckers as soon as they appear. They compete with the main stem and divert nutrients away from the top growth.

Protective mulch. Discourage sucker formation by mulching plant roots; any damage to roots can stimulate sprouting.

On grafted stock. Never transplant suckers from a grafted tree or shrub. Suckers form on the rootstock of these plants and will reproduce with the characteristics of the rootstock, not of the desirable cultivar.

A positive. As a last resort, save a favorite old tree by "topping" it: cutting back old branches severely. This will spur water sprout growth. Select the most vigorous and well-placed sprouts to form the new "scaffold" of the tree, then remove the rest.

▷ **Pruning, Stumps & Dead Trees, Tomatoes**

SWEET POTATOES

A sweet-tasting tuber. Related to the morning glory, the sweet potato is a tender tropical vine that performs best in regions with long, hot summers. It needs full sun and about 120 days of warm temperatures.

Getting the slip. Sweet potatoes are grown from slips, or sprouted cuttings; you can buy them at garden centers or from catalogs—or grow your own. About 4 to 6 weeks before planting time, place a sweet potato on a bed of sand and cover it with moist sand. Keep at 75°F until sprouts are about 6 inches tall and have roots and a few leaves. This "seed potato" will produce 10 to 20 plants.

Do the twist. Some gardeners remove the new shoots and their roots by pulling or twisting them off. Others prefer cutting, which inhibits transfer of any diseases or pests.

Hold off. Wait 3 to 5 days before planting slips; little root hairs will develop and help ensure survival. Also wait until the soil temperature reaches at least 65°F.

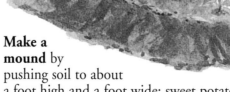

Make a mound by pushing soil to about a foot high and a foot wide; sweet potatoes will appreciate the good drainage. Plant the slips 4 inches deep at 12-inch intervals. Spacing at 15-inch intervals encourages early production.

Room to grow. The slips develop best in sandy loam, where they can expand with

less effort than in clay. To promote root production instead of vine growth, loosen the soil well and dig in a low-nitrogen fertilizer like 8–24–24 before planting.

Keep young plants moist, even though sweet potatoes need less water once they're established. Watering is especially important in fast-draining sandy soils, as is a midseason drink of liquid fertilizer; a good choice is liquid seaweed extract.

Weed carefully until plants become established; the shallow roots won't tolerate disturbance. Once the vines cover the soil, they will shade out weed seedlings, making heavy maintenance unnecessary.

Harvest time. Depending on the variety, tubers can be harvested 3 to 4 months after planting. In cold regions, the tubers are ready when frost blackens the vines.

Thin skin. Sweet potatoes are subject to bruising, which shortens their shelf life. Dig them up carefully with a spading fork. To help "set" the skin and make the tubers less susceptible, remove the vines a week before harvesting.

Brush but don't wash the soil off the potatoes before storing them. Clean with water just before you're ready to cook them; otherwise they will spoil.

Let them cure. To prolong storage life, cure sweet potato tubers by exposing them to high temperatures (85° to 95°F) and high humidity for a week immediately after harvest. You can use either a cold frame or a heated room for this treatment.

Long keepers. Tubers will keep 4 to 5 months if stored in a cool place (55° to 65°F). Don't let the tubers touch or they will rot. Never store in the refrigerator.

Outdoor storage is possible in warm climates. Place the tubers between layers of straw and cover with corn shucks.

Everybody loves sweet potatoes, including the sweet potato weevil. This common pest  chews the leaves and bores into the tubers. To discourage infestation, keep the soil clear of debris. Spray with pyrethrum or methoxychor when pests are active and destroy any infected plants.

Sweeter 'n sweeter. If you let the tubers sit for 2 months before cooking, more of the starch will convert to sugar. Your sweet potatoes will be all the more tasty.

Don't zap. Sweet potatoes baked in the oven will have a richer flavor than those cooked in the microwave.
▷ **Vegetable Gardens**

SWIMMING POOLS

Here to stay. Because an in-ground swimming pool is a dominant, permanent feature, choose its location with utmost care. In warm climates, where the pool is used year-round, consider integrating it into the landscape. In cold climates, you may want to separate it from the rest of the yard behind a fence or screen so that it won't seem desolate in winter and fall.

CHLORINE AND PLANTS

While some plants, such as boxwood, yew, and periwinkle, can't tolerate exposure to chlorine, many others will survive the occasional splash. As a rule, use small-leaved specimens so that foliage marred by chlorine spots can be removed without detracting from the overall look or health of the plant. Chlorine-tolerant plants include coreopsis, catmint, baby's breath, salvia, Russian sage, and yarrow.

Choose a style. You can complement—or contrast—the style of the pool with that of your house and landscape. A severely angular pool adds formality, while a free-form, curvilinear pool offers a more relaxed look.

Call City Hall. Before construction, obtain all necessary permits and observe local regulations. Many communities, for instance, require security fencing around open pools.

Block wind. Protect the pool from prevailing winds by planting an evergreen screen. Avoid plants that will shed leaves during the season when the pool is in use. Alternatively, site your pool on the opposite side of a building or build a high fence.

Design the pool area with amenities that will make it more enjoyable. Allow space for lounging furniture, and perhaps include dressing rooms or a storage chest for pool supplies. Shade a sitting area, but not the water, with small trees or an umbrella.

Play it safe. Cover the pool when it's not being used with a tarp or net. It should be sturdy enough to support a person without sinking and be easy to install and remove. Tarps also help prevent water evaporation and heat loss and keep out debris.

No slipping. To prevent accidents, choose a nonskid surface—such as textured concrete—for the apron around the pool. Have it slope away from the pool so that runoff from the surrounding area won't 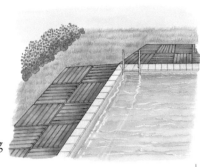 contaminate the pool water. Scrub with a stiff brush if it becomes slippery from algae.

Poolside plantings. Key the gardens around the pool to the rest of the landscape. For formal settings, arrange stately plants in well-trimmed borders; perhaps include a manicured lawn and straight paths. For an informal look, create a naturalistic garden with native plants in curving beds.

Clean companions. Select plant materials that won't drop leaves, fruit, or other litter. Ornamental grasses and evergreen shrubs are good choices. If you insist on using "messy" specimens, plant them in containers that can be moved away from the pool when they are ready to shed.

No bees, please. Never use flowers attractive to bees around a pool. Avoid lamb's ears, cleome, anise hyssop, loosestrife, New England aster, butterfly weed, and baptisia. Also avoid plants with thorns, bristles, or spines—all are unfriendly to the exposed skin generally found at poolside.

A hot spot. Because the water and pool apron radiate heat and light, choose plants that can withstand the intense conditions.

An old wading pool can find new uses in the garden. Fill it with a heavy load, such as stones, mulch, compost, or a large transplant, and slide it to the desired location. You can also use it to mix and store soil or, come winter, to coil garden hoses in it.
▷ **Landscaping, Paving Stones, Yucca**

SWISS CHARD

A big eater. The more fertilizer and compost you give chard, the more it will grow. Dig in plenty of well-aged manure before planting. Once plants are 6 inches tall, feed with 5–10–5 fertilizer every month or so, using 3 ounces per 10-foot row.

The best tool for harvesting chard is your hands; simply break off the stem at its base. Don't use a knife, which might injure the inner stems and prevent further growth.

Prolong the harvest by picking the outer leaves, a few at a time, after the plants grow

---

⤞ A SWISS CHARD SAMPLER ⇐

Swiss chard is grown for both its central stem and leaves. Stem chards have broad stalks; the leaves are stripped from the stems, which are eaten like celery or asparagus. Leaf chards have narrow stalks; the whole tops, or just the leaves, are used like spinach or salad greens.

'Lucullus' and 'Monstruoso' are stem-chard varieties that are very productive and suitable for stir-fry or crudités.

The best leaf chards are 'Perpetual Spinach,' which offers fine-textured leaves and a long harvest period, and 'Fordhook Giant,' with its thick, dark green leaves and prolific yield even in hot weather.

For beauty and bounty, select 'Rhubarb Chard' and 'Charlotte'—two highly ornamental varieties with tender leaves and stunning ruby-red stalks and veins.

---

to 10 inches. A biennial that won't bolt in heat, Swiss chard will continue developing new leaves from the central stem all summer into autumn.

In mild-winter regions, leave chard in the ground and it will send up tender young leaves the next spring. Protect the crowns with a deep layer of straw or other mulch if temperatures dip below 20°F; even if tops die back, the plant should bounce back.

Eliminate weeding by mulching with black plastic; space plants 1 foot apart. Alternatively, you can cover the soil well with compost.

Not only edible, red chard is also ornamental, sporting crimson stalks and crinkly green leaves laced with crimson veins. Plant among flowers, herbs, and other showy vegetables like flowering kale. Red chard sparkles when cloaked in autumn frost.
▷ **Vegetable Gardens**

SYCAMORE

A tree by any other name. The sycamore (*Platanus occidentalis*) goes by a number of names: plane tree, American plane tree, buttonwood, buttonball, Eastern sycamore, and shagbark sycamore. Other species include the London plane tree (*P. × acerifolia*), the Oriental plane tree (*P. orientalis*), and the California plane tree (*P. racemosa*).

A tall order. One of America's largest deciduous natives, the sycamore will soar to heights up to 120 feet. Use it as an accent specimen on an open lawn. Its spreading crown makes it an ideal shade tree.

Keep it moist. Growing naturally on stream banks and bottomlands, sycamores

---

prefer a deep, moist soil. But these hardy giants are surprisingly tolerant of harsh conditions, even thriving along urban streets. Site them in full sun.

A saving grace. While sycamores are messy, always dropping twigs, leaves, and their buttonball fruits, their unusual mottled bark is a fine compensation. Flakes of grayish-tan bark peel off in irregular patches to reveal a creamy underbark.

Winter in spring. If your sycamore looks as bare in May as it did in December, it may be suffering from anthracnose, a serious blight that scorches the leaves and causes defoliation. Thoroughly clear away all infected leaves and twigs and treat with a copper- or sulfur-based fungicide.

More platanus plagues. If you see a white-peppered effect on the upper surface of the leaves, the sycamore lace bug is in residence. Spray with malathion to control. Various scale insects are also occasional pests. Spray with a dormant oil in fall; if young crawlers are seen, use malathion.
▷ **Trees**

The flaking green and white bark of the sycamore can give the impression of dappled sunlight.

TARRAGON

Buy plants, not seeds. Tarragon seed in packets is that of Russian tarragon— a less aromatic variety than French tarragon, whose seeds are sterile. For the true anise-scented herb with a "bite," buy plants of *Artemisia dracunculus* var. *sativa*. Not all garden centers distinguish between the two, so take care when buying. French tarragon has a strong, sweet smell; test by crushing a leaf between your fingers.

Annual or perennial? Because tarragon needs winter dormancy, it is treated as an annual in warm and hot climates; grow it elsewhere as a perennial. Its basic needs, however, remain the same: extremely well-drained, loose soil and plenty of light.

A regular haircut. Tarragon likes to be snipped, so don't be afraid to cut back the tips; it keeps the plants full and bushy.

The little dragon. The herb's name is related to the Latin word for "dragon"— a reference to its serpentlike root system. Divide plants in spring every 2 years to untangle the roots and keep them vigorous.

For extra flavor, steep tarragon sprigs in white wine vinegar. You can leave them in or strain them out after a month or so.
▷ **Herbs**

TEA

Grass aid. Repair bare spots on the lawn with a teabag patch. Place a moist used teabag on the spot and sow with grass seed; the bag provides moisture and gradually decomposes. Some gardeners also soak grass seed in liquid tea before sowing it.

Tea mulch. Dump used tea leaves or teabags on the soil in pots or window boxes and cover with a mulch of pebbles or shredded bark. As you water, nutrients from the decomposing leaves will leach down into the soil.

A tea party for plants. Leave a used teabag or tea dregs in water overnight and serve the brew to azaleas, ferns, hydrangeas, and other acid-loving plants. Use only tea that hasn't been mixed with sugar or cream.

Root reservoirs. Put two or three used teabags in the bottom of a pot, placing them on top of the drainage layer of pebbles or shards. The bags will retain water and keep roots moist.

TERRARIUMS

How they work. Plants will grow indefinitely in sealed glass containers because of the greenhouse effect. Water evaporates from the soil and provides humidity; droplets then condense on the sides of the glass and roll down the sides into the potting mix, bringing moisture to the roots.

Grow a bottle garden. True terrariums are available as plastic or alloy-framed models or as more expensive brass-framed or leaded glass models, often with automatic ventilation controls. But you can grow a bottle garden in any glass or plastic vessel.

Container choices. A fishbowl, large food canister, glass jug, brandy snifter, or pitcher will work fine as long as it is transparent and waterproof. If it doesn't have a cork or lid, stretch plastic wrap across the top and trim the excess neatly with a razor blade.

What to grow? The best plants for bottle gardens are those that like low light and high humidity. Select either one showy specimen large enough to fill the container or mix plants with different shapes and textures. Use dwarf or slow-growing plants that have the same cultural requirements.

Getting started. First, wash the container with a solution of household bleach and water to prevent the growth of molds and fungi. Rinse well and dry thoroughly.

The layered look. Build up the planting medium in layers. Start with some sphagnum moss, then add a little fine gravel or sand mixed with a little horticultural charcoal. Top with a sterile, peat-based potting mix—about ½ inch for small bottles and 2 to 3 inches for larger containers.

A paper funnel makes it easy to fill a jug or bottle without getting the sides dirty. Simply roll up butcher paper or sheets of newspaper into a funnel and pour potting mix and drainage materials through.

Three planting steps. A few simple household utensils are all you need to place plants in a narrow-necked bottle or jug. Use a fork taped to a stick to make the planting holes.  Use tweezers, tongs, or a wire with a loop at one end to set in the plants. For tamping down the potting mix, you can use a cork or empty thread spool wedged firmly on a chopstick.

Cover your container with its lid, a cork, plastic wrap, or a piece of glass to trap moisture and create condensation.

Proper placement. Put the container in indirect sunlight or place it under a fluorescent light for 12 hours daily. Turn it regularly to keep plants growing evenly.

When to water. It is natural for tiny water droplets to form on the inside of the glass.

⊰ TERRARIUM PLANTS ⊱

If you're growing woodland plants, keep your terrarium "cool" by placing it where the temperature is no more than 70°F. For a "warm" terrarium, suitable for tropical specimens, keep the surrounding temperature at about 75°F.

COOL TERRARIUMS	WARM TERRARIUMS
Evergreen seedlings	Anthurium
Ferns	Baby's-tears
Hepatica	Begonias
Moneywort	Caladium
Mosses	Creeping fig
Partridge-berry	Croton
Pipsissewa	Fittonia
Saxifrage	Peperomias
Violets	Prayer plant
Wintergreen	Sedums

When the droplets disappear, additional water may be needed. Add a tablespoonful at a time until the potting mix is evenly moistened.

Too much condensation? If the glass becomes so foggy that it obscures your plants, there is an overbalance of moisture to soil. Wipe out the excess moisture and leave the top off the container overnight.

Hold the food. Don't fertilize bottle garden plants the first year. Thereafter, feed very lightly, diluting an all-purpose houseplant fertilizer to about ⅛ strength. If plants grow too large, prune them, transfer them to a larger vessel, or replace them.

THINNING

What is it? Thinning is the gardener's way of helping nature assure the survival of the fittest. By removing small, deformed, or overcrowded seedlings or fruits you help healthy, vigorous specimens perform better.

SEEDLINGS

Don't overseed. Doing so simply means more thinning. If the seeds are small and difficult to sow at the desired spacing, mix with sand to "dilute" them. You can also buy seeds encased in easy-to-handle clay pellets or attached to biodegradable tape.

Wait for true leaves. Thin most seedlings when the first set of true leaves appears. With leaf lettuce and greens, wait until the thinnings are large enough to eat.

Water first. Before thinning, dampen the soil and let it sit for an hour; this aids plant removal and limits damage to nearby roots. Loosen roots from the soil with a knife or small trowel and lift out the seedlings. Water the remaining plants to settle the soil that was disturbed around their roots. If you choose, pot or replant the lifted seedlings instead of discarding them.

Simply snip. If you don't want to save and replant thinnings, make the job easier— and less damaging to the remaining seedlings—by cutting off the excess plants with scissors or pinching them off; the soil will stay undisturbed.

FRUITS

June drop is the name for the natural thinning that occurs in early summer, when fruits that are diseased, pest-infested, or overcrowded fall from the tree. Weak fruits and those developed from the last flowers to open will be the first to drop.

Lend a hand. If June drop isn't enough, you'll need to intervene. On many new plants, including strawberries, grapes, and apples, you should thin out all young fruits the first year to help strengthen roots and stems. On established plants, thin to encourage larger fruits and to reduce stress on the branches caused by excess weight.

Thin your pears. To thin pears, which bear fruit on short twigs (called spurs), leave no more than one or two fruits on each spur.

Thin your peaches. To thin out peaches, which bear fruit on longer twigs, be sure to leave no more than one fruit every 4 to 6 inches. This rule of thumb applies to apples as well.

Thin early. Late thinning will reduce the strain on the branches but it won't improve the size and quality of the remaining fruits.

THYME

Time with thyme. For a clever garden showpiece, create a living sundial with thyme. Mark out a circle and divide it into 12 equal wedges, like a pie. Alternate three or four thyme varieties, planting each wedge separately. For a working sundial, make sure that the 12-o'clock position is oriented north. Install a gnomon, or pointer, to cast a shadow—perhaps a pretty birdhouse. Set stones around the perimeter to mark the hours.

The many kinds. Common thyme is the classic garden herb, but you can also grow varieties that smell of lemon, caraway, or nutmeg. Silver thyme has leaves banded in white, and woolly thyme has fuzzy foliage.

Mother-of-thyme is a common name for several species that self-sow readily after blooming: *Thymus praecox* ssp. *articus, T. pulegiodes,* and *T. serpyllum.*

Warmth-loving thyme thrives in well-drained soil and full sun. Plant it around a stone or brick path so that it can take advantage of the reflected heat and light. You can also tuck it into a stone wall, which provides extra warmth and quick drainage.

Keep it neat. For bushy plants, prune back the stems in spring if you live in a cool climate; in warm areas, prune in fall. Replace plants when they start to die back in the center—usually after 3 to 5 years.

A creeping carpet. Some thyme varieties, including caraway and coconut, are ground-hugging evergreens and like to sprawl. Use as a soft edging for borders or a fragrant filler between stepping-stones.

In the kitchen drop whole sprigs in soups, stews, or sauces; the tiny leaves will cook off in a few minutes. Before adding, discard any woody growth, which can be bitter.

Pretty flowers. Using thyme for cooking means pruning off most of the blooms. If you want to admire the bountiful little blossoms, plant a thyme border or combine them with your ornamentals.

Bee friendly. Thyme flowers, which bloom in white, lavender, pink, and magenta, lure bees. Place thyme wherever you need plants pollinated or want to watch bees at work.

Make a sachet. Wrap dried thyme in handkerchiefs or tea napkins and place in drawers, closets, and bookshelves. It adds a fresh aroma and also repels silverfish and other household pests.
▷ **Herbs**

TICKS

What are they? Ticks are parasites related to mites and spiders. They need blood to complete their life cycle and feed on many warm-blooded hosts, humans included.

Know their hangouts. The deer tick favors shady, damp areas in the garden, especially at the edges of woods and fields. The dog tick lives in fields and sunny, open areas near tree groves; it is active in warm weather and crawls to find a host.

Control measures. Use an approved insecticide recommended to treat tick infestations outdoors. Because ticks are carried by animals, however, no pesticide can provide complete control.

Reduce wildlife activity. Clean up woodpiles, hedgerows, brush, leaves, and weed patches to discourage animals. Clean up spilled seeds from the bird feeder and stop feeding birds between April and late fall.

Dress for success. When you're working in the garden around tall grass or densely planted trees, wear a hat, long sleeves, lace-up shoes or boots, and long pants with the cuffs tucked into your socks. Spray your clothes with tick repellent and wear light colors to make detection easier.

Check it out. Look over your clothing frequently while you're gardening and check your body thoroughly once you finish. Deer ticks are as tiny as a freckle and hard to spot; dog ticks are larger—about the size of a match head. Both like to burrow in along the hairline, so run your fingers along the back of your neck, around your ears, and above your forehead.

Proper removal. Remove a tick immediately—but don't bother trying to make it withdraw with oil, alcohol, salt, or a flame. Instead, grasp it as close to your skin as possible with tweezers (never your fingers) and gently pull outwards. Be careful not to squeeze its body, which could release fluids. Try your best to remove the tick with its mouthparts intact.

Wash the bite with antibacterial soap and swab with iodine or hydrogen peroxide. It may take weeks for the bite to heal.

Save the tick. Keep any tick you remove in a tightly closed jar. If you develop any symptoms of a tick-borne disease, the tick may need to be examined.
▷ **Pesticides**

TOMATOES

PURCHASING

The two types. Tomatoes are classified as either determinate or indeterminate. The first is a bush type and needs no staking; the fruits form at the stem tips, and all mature around the same time. The second is the vining type, which requires pruning and staking; fruits grow along the stem and keep developing until halted by frost.

What do the letters mean? Tomatoes have been developed to resist specific problems, and the letters after the variety names indicate which pests and diseases the plant can withstand. "F" is for fusarium wilt, "N" is for nematodes, "V" is for verticillium wilt, and "T" is for tobacco mosaic virus.

Plan on two plants per person for general consumption. If you intend to can and freeze the tomatoes, add a few more.

PLANTING

A good start. Sow tomato seed about 8 weeks before the first frost-free date. Use a seed-starting mix and place four or five seeds in each pot. Tomato seeds need temperatures around 75°F to germinate.

A LITTLE HISTORY

A nightshade cousin, the tomato was long believed poisonous—or at the very least unpalatable. Legend holds that it was shunned in America until an eccentric gentleman of Salem, New Jersey, took it upon himself to popularize the fruit. Why the wealthy Robert Gibbon Johnson decided to pursue his peculiar quest may never be known, but in 1820 he promised to prove the tomato harmless. Standing before an assembled crowd of dubious townfolk at the courthouse, he consumed a basketful of the vile fruit. It was claimed that after he suffered no ill effects, the tomato was accepted at last. Some food historians have boldly embellished the event to include marching bands and thousands of spectators, some of whom fainted.

Cool them off. Once the second set of true leaves form, move the plants to a cooler environment—55° to 65°F at night. Keep them moist and fertilize with manure tea or fish emulsion weekly. This treatment lets plants develop slowly and prevents them from becoming lanky.

Don't delay. Tomatoes are ready to set out when they have five to seven leaves. Plants that have already produced flowers or fruit may have a more difficult period of adjustment.

Heat relief. If you live in a hot region, stagger the planting dates so that you won't lose the entire crop if a heat wave strikes. To help shade them, interplant tomatoes among taller crops, such as corn.

In cold climates, place your tomatoes by a wall or the side of the house that faces south or west; it will absorb the sun's heat during the day and radiate it at night.

Make it rich. Tomatoes prefer well-drained soil with plenty of organic matter and a near-neutral pH. Dig a hole 1 foot wide and put in a layer of compost or well-rotted manure mixed with a handful of bonemeal and 1 teaspoon Epsom salts.

Novel additions. Fresh banana peels will act as a kind of slow-release fertilizer in the planting hole, providing potassium and trace elements. Some gardeners even put a dead fish in the bottom of the hole. In hot climates, do as old-timers did and place a 5-inch layer of corn cobs at the bottom; it is said to conserve moisture.

Space them well. For best results, space tomatoes 2 feet apart, with 3 to 4 feet between rows. Even though plants can be grown closer together, in typical garden soil their yields won't be as high; they will also be harder to prune and fertilize.

Bury them deep. The soil should reach to the first set of true leaves; additional roots will form along the buried part of the stem.

Trench-plant leggy seedlings or any that have been grown in tall containers. Lay the root ball on its side in a rectangular hole dug to a depth of at least 6 inches. Hold the stem erect while covering the root ball and the lower part of the stem with soil.

Give support. Stake indeterminate tomatoes by installing a 6-foot stake before planting; place it 4 inches from the hole and drive it 1 foot deep. Alternatively, use steel-mesh cages, stretch a chicken-wire trellis along the row, or let vines climb on strings suspended from an overhead wire.

Tying techniques. Loosely hold plant stems to the supports with figure-eight loops of soft twine every foot or so. You can also use soft cloth or pantyhose—they're gentler on the stems and will provide more support for heavy vines.

A central feeder. Tomatoes will feed as needed if planted around a nutrient supply. Dig a hole 10 inches deep and 3 feet wide. Encircle the hole with a 2-foot-tall mesh

cylinder and fill with well-rotted manure or compost. Then plant six tomatoes around it—either in cages 1 foot away or just next to the cylinder, tying them on for support. Water cylinder contents regularly.

MAINTENANCE

Limit nitrogen. Use fertilizer low in nitrogen, such as 4–8–4; too much nitrogen promotes foliage growth and makes fruits watery and bland. Once the fruit is set, side-dress lightly every 4 to 6 weeks.

Mulch plants 2 to 3 inches deep with hay, straw, buckwheat hulls, or shredded leaves to conserve moisture and suffocate weeds. Apply after the soil is already warm.

Water with sugar. When the fruits begin showing color, add a spoonful of sugar to their water—the tomatoes will be sweeter and juicier. But go easy: minimizing water while fruits ripen enhances their flavor.

Water with eggs. Once every 7 to 14 days, crush some eggshells in a blender and add them to the water for your tomatoes; about 6 shells per quart is enough. The extra calcium aids growth at the leaf tips and blossom ends and prevents blossom-end rot.

Prune your plants by pinching out the suckers between the main stems and the branches. The suckers can be rooted in pots and transplanted to the garden to provide a second crop of tomatoes.

Compensate for blossom drop, which often occurs in cool, wet weather or on hot, windy days, by helping the remaining

A TOMATO SAMPLER

STANDARD SIZE	COLOR	TYPE	FRUIT SIZE	DAYS TO HARVEST
'Better Boy' VFN	red	indeterminate hybrid	12 oz.	72 days
'Celebrity' VFNT	red	determinate hybrid	7 oz.	70 days
'Early Girl' VF	red	indeterminate hybrid	4–6 oz.	58 days
'Golden Jubilee'	orange	indeterminate standard	8 oz.	72 days
BEEFSTEAK				
'Beefmaster' VFN	red	indeterminate hybrid	1–2 lb.	80 days
'Ponderosa Pink'	rose-pink	indeterminate heirloom	1 lb.	90 days
'Supersteak' VFN	red	indeterminate hybrid	1–2 lb.	80 days
CHERRY				
'Sun Gold'	orange	indeterminate hybrid	1¼ in.	57 days
'Sweet 100'	red	indeterminate hybrid	1 in.	66 days
'Yellow Pear'	yellow	indeterminate heirloom	2 in.	76 days
PLUM				
'Italian Gold'	yellow	determinate hybrid	3 in.	70 days
'Roma' VF	red	determinate standard	3 in.	75 days

blossoms set fruit. On a day that's warm, calm, and dry, aid pollination by gently shaking the plant or tapping its stake.

Thwart aphids. You can protect tomatoes from aphids by surrounding plants with aluminum foil, shiny side up. As a bonus, the radiant heat will speed ripening of the fruits by about 2 weeks.

Cold nights? Keep plants cozy by flanking each one with two flat stones or tiles. They hold the sun's heat during the day and radiate it at night. You can also surround each plant with a manufactured self-standing plastic sleeve filled with water.

More heaters. Cover your tomatoes with plastic film laid over wire wickets; make sure the plastic is tall enough so that plants won't touch it. Close off the ends and secure to the ground with wire stakes.

Nipped in the bud. About 3 weeks before the first frost, remove all flowers and any fruits that have not yet reached a quarter of their mature size; they won't mature before the season is over and will divert nutrients from fruits that are more developed.

HARVESTING

Vine-ripened flavor. For the best taste, pick tomatoes when they are nearly or fully ripe; they should have even color and be firm but not hard. And don't leave overripe fruits on the vine—they decrease overall productivity and may spread disease.

Never the fridge! Always keep tomatoes at room temperature, shoulders up. Putting them in the refrigerator stops the ripening process cold.

One last try. After the first light frost, pick all the fruits. Let immature fruits that have begun to "pale out" ripen in indirect light at a temperature of 70° to 80°F. Be aware that small, green tomatoes will not ripen satisfactorily; use them instead for preserves, pickles, or relishes.
▷ **Vegetable Gardens**

The right tools for the job

Every gardener should have a shed's worth of useful tools—many of them indispensable. When you purchase your own, always buy quality, even if it seems expensive. In the long run, you'll actually save money, since well-made tools have a longer life. Better design can also make high-quality tools much easier to handle and more efficient to use.

When it comes to tools for working the soil, it's better to buy those with blades forged from a single piece of steel than the cheaper folded steel models. Handles made from ash, hickory, or even tubular steel or fiberglass are preferable to those made from beechwood or pine. As for pruning shears, the best are rarely the fanciest and often are not the most expensive. If possible, purchase pruners that can be disassembled, cleaned and sharpened easily, and have replaceable blades.

Choose tools that match your height and strength, making sure that the handle is the correct length and the tool is a comfortable weight. Before buying, test each model for its heft and feel to see which one suits you best.

After every use, your tools should be put away dry, their blades and handles wiped clean. Hoes, weeders, spades, shovels, and trowels work better if their edges are kept keen with a small stone or pocket file. Pruning shears also need regular sharpening. Dull tools are, at best, tiring to use; at their worst, they may cause unnecessary damage to the plants they are meant for. Always keep them sharp, and use them with care.

TOOLS

PREPARING THE SOIL

Spading tools
For loose or light soils, use a flat spade. For heavy or compacted soils, use a spading fork.

Metal grading rake
For leveling beds and removing clumps of soil and stones.

Gas-powered tiller
Unless the garden has a large acreage, it makes more sense to rent this expensive tool than to purchase one.

MAINTENANCE, WEEDING, AND TREATMENT

Hand cultivator
A short-handled tool for cultivating tight spaces.

Weeder
For digging out weeds and their roots.

Three-tined cultivator
For weeding and loosening the soil between rows and around individual plants.

Draw hoe
Used to loosen the soil around plants and for cutting weeds.

Scuffle hoe
For cutting off weeds at their roots and loosening the surface of the soil.

Fan rake
The basic fan rake with spring-steel tines, used for collecting fallen leaves and fine raking of the soil.

Hand-cranked spreader
For distributing fertilizer or small seeds evenly over small to medium-size areas.

Border rake
A narrow fan rake used for removing leaves and debris from between plants.

Tank sprayer
For applying pesticides and other liquids. Several models and sizes.

SEEDING, PLANTING AND WATERING

Cord and stakes
For easy sowing and planting in perfectly straight rows.

Trowel
For planting bulbs, potting, and transplanting plants.

Dibble
For making planting holes for small bare-root plants.

Measuring stick
For regular spacing of rows and individual plants.

Watering can
For taking water to plants. Buy two, of different sizes.

MAKING AND SPREADING COMPOST

Compost bin
For transforming kitchen scraps and garden waste into a fertile soil amendment.

Shovel
For handling compost and manure.

Fork
For turning the compost heap and piling up any fresh materials.

Within a humble shed lie the gardener's true essentials. Climbing roses transform this toolshed into an attractive garden feature.

STAKING, TRIMMING, HARVESTING, AND PRUNING

Clippers
For hedge trimming. Choose a model with shock-absorbing handles.

Pruning shears
For cutting small branches and flowers. Several models and sizes.

Lopping shears
For pruning branches too large for shears but too small for a saw.

Pruning knife
For cutting and grafting small branches.

Folding saw
Used in tight places; won't damage a pocket if properly closed.

Pruning saw
For medium branches.

Hatchet
Use the blade for sharpening stakes and the back of the head for driving them.

Bow-frame pruning saw
Easier to handle when cutting large branches.

Fruit picker
For harvesting fruit from tall trees. Buy one with a light handle (bamboo or aluminum) that is 10 feet long.

TOOLS

TOPIARY

An age-old art. Topiary is the tradition of sculpting plants into specific shapes, such as geometric figures, animals, and objects. There are two techniques for creating topiary: you can train plants into desired forms with pruning or grow them over a framework, clipping them into shape as needed.

Loosen up. While some topiary shapes, such as spirals and standards, are quite formal, others are fun and fanciful. Add a touch of whimsy to your garden by growing a big topiary bird or bunny. Or select a shape with personal meaning: an avid angler might sculpt a fish, for example.

Where to put them? Use topiary to frame an entry door, line a path, or create a garden centerpiece. You can even turn a hedge into topiary by clipping part of the top into shapes—perhaps cones or globes.

PLANTING
Good candidates. The best specimens for garden topiary are evergreen trees, shrubs, and herbs. They should have strong, woody stems and small, dense leaves and be able to withstand regular pruning. In the North,

try yew, privet, boxwood, ivy, Japanese holly, germander, and euonymus. In warm climates, use yaupon holly, myrtle, bay laurel, pittosporum, rosemary, and fig.

Start slow. A good choice for beginners is a geometric figure. Make a framework by pounding wooden or plastic stakes into the ground around a young shrub. Form wire mesh into the desired shape around the stakes. As the plant grows, clip any shoots

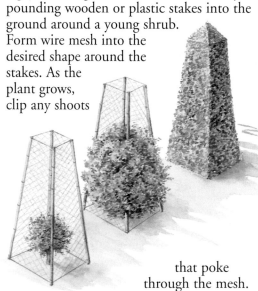

that poke through the mesh. Once the shrub has filled the "mold," remove the mesh. Shear the plant regularly to maintain its shape.

Grow a faux flowerpot by planting a hedge around a shrub trained into a tree shape, called a standard. Create the standard by removing shoots along the stem and snipping the top into a globe; stake the stem. For the "pot," plant low-growing, mounding shrubs in a ring around the standard. When they are about one third as tall as the standard's stem, clip them into a flowerpot shape. Remove the stake from the standard and keep all the plants trimmed.

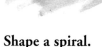

Shape a spiral.
Select a shrub with a columnar habit, such as English yew (*Taxus baccata* 'Fastigiata'). Plant a dense, 2-foot-tall specimen in rich soil and stake with a 5-foot pole to keep the main stem vertical. The next year, begin shaping by trimming all lateral branches to produce a neat column about 4 inches in diameter. Continue training to a column until the shrub is 5 feet tall and 8 inches around. To create the spiral, begin pruning at the base. Make the first ring the longest; the spaces between rings should decrease toward the

top. Don't fret if the spiral is scrawny at first—the shrub will fill in and be kept in shape by clipping. Take out the stake when the form is established.

A perching peacock. Invite a topiary bird to sit on top of an established hedge. Select a spot with strong stems and let some grow out when you trim the hedge. Install a stake that is a little taller than the projected height of the figure's back. Shape a bird "skeleton" from pieces of wire and attach it to the stake. Tie shoots from the hedge onto the frame at regular intervals; prune as needed. To form the tail, bend a long shoot downward with a weighted string.

Sheepish shrubbery. You can turn your garden into a "ranch" with topiary animals. To create a sheep, plant four shrubs where you want the animal's feet to stand and stake them firmly. Form a wire frame into the profile of a sheep and attach it to the stakes; the "belly" should be about 1 foot from the ground. As the shrubs grow, tie the new shoots onto the frame and prune any wayward stems. After the frame has filled in, let shoots grow out for the ears and tail. You can train them downward by tying them to a peg in the ground. Keep the plant neatly trimmed.

MAINTENANCE

Bind them gently. Be sure to use soft twine, preferably colored green, to tie young shoots onto stakes and wire frames. Check the ties periodically and loosen any that are constricting growth.

Soak and spritz. Water the soil around topiaries as you would for any free-growing plant, especially during dry spells. Also mist the foliage gently to keep it clean and fresh.

Add moss for moisture. For small topiary figures, pack the inside of the wire structure with sphagnum moss. This will retain moisture and let clinging plants like ivy or euonymus send out roots for a firmer hold.

Feed in early spring with a slow-release complete fertilizer, using about 2 ounces per square yard; later, supplement with

lighter meals as needed. Young plants may require extra nitrogen to produce shoots, but don't force growth on mature specimens—it only leads to extra pruning.

Trimming topiary. For young plants that are still being trained into a shape, prune back half of the new shoots around the base yearly to prevent legginess. Once the shrub begins filling in, trim lightly but regularly—especially in spring and after flowering—to maintain fullness and shape. The frequency depends on the plant's growth rate and the intricacy of the design. But don't prune late in the season, when soft new growth may be damaged by frost.

Mind your shears. Be sure that your pruning shears are sharp: they must slice the stems instead of crushing them. Take small cuts at first, then observe the results. Use guides, like levels or stakes, even if you have a good eye. Cut from the top down and the center out, working on both sides so that the trimming is symmetrical.

Easy cleanup. A tarp spread under the shrubbery when pruning will save you from raking up the clippings. Just bundle them up and take them to the compost pile.

Head off competition. Don't let grass and weeds encroach on the shrubs' roots; they steal nutrients and limit growth. Instead, spread an attractive year-round mulch, like shredded bark, around the plants. It will limit competitors and enhance the topiary.

A snow shield. Protect topiary from snow and ice buildup, which can destroy the carefully tended shapes, by erecting a wire mesh shield over the plants. Cover the mesh with burlap and brush off any accumulation as soon as possible.

TABLETOP TOPIARY

Bring it indoors. Topiary isn't limited to the garden. You can train houseplants and herbs into pretty shapes as decorations for tabletops, windowsills, and mantels.

Herbal standards. Train fragrant woody herbs into treelike standards; good choices include thyme, rosemary, lavender, lemon verbena, bay, and scented geraniums. Use a young potted plant with a straight stem; stake it. Keep pruning the lower lateral branches and pinching the growth to form a crown. When the crown fills in, trim to a globe. If the crown opens up and loses its shape, move the plant into brighter light.

Outline with ivy. Ivy, jasmine, and other small-leaved climbers can be trained over wire frames into a variety of shapes— hearts, arches, or cones. Make a wire frame or buy one from a garden or florist shop; it should be twice as tall as the plant's pot. Insert its base firmly in the soil around the plant. Wind one plant stem around one wire of the frame; repeat with the remaining stems. Don't force it: if a stem is stiff, tie it in place with soft green twine until it conforms to the shape. Pinch or snip any stems that grow out of place.

Stuff it with sphagnum. Fill a wire form in a desired shape with a mix of soil and sphagnum moss; mist with water to moisten. Plant ivy or creeping fig around the base of the form. The stems will climb up the wire and root in the stuffing. Peg stems into the mix with florist pins or old-fashioned bobby pins.

Keep the soil moist and feed with liquid houseplant fertilizer diluted by half.

Healthy rotation. Most tabletop topiaries require sun, so place them in a south- or west-facing window; give them a quarter turn every few days so they develop evenly. If you want to use topiary to decorate a dining table or mantel, grow "twins"— while one is on display, the other can be sunning in a window. You can also set your plants outdoors once the weather warms.
▷ **Bay Trees, Espaliers, Hedges, Laurel, Pruning, Rosemary**

TOXIC PLANTS

Pretty poisons. Hundreds of plants have toxic parts, whether their fruits, flowers, foliage, or roots. While some are infamous noxious weeds, like poison ivy, many others—from azaleas to tomatoes—are common ornamental and food plants. Learn to recognize and avoid all specimens that are toxic to touch or eat. And be sure to keep children and pets away from them as well.

Leaves of three, let it be. One of the most common toxic plants east of the Rockies is poison ivy *(Rhus radicans)*, recognized by its clusters of three leaflets that turn red in fall. The creeping vine bears small white flowers in spring and white, waxy berries through winter. A resin in the sap, called urushiol, causes an itchy rash on contact with any part of the plant. Even smoke from burning the plants is an irritant.

The Western cousin of poison ivy is Pacific poison oak *(R. diversiloba)*. It, too, contains urushiol, has three toothed leaves, and causes skin irritation. This pest grows as a vine or,

more commonly, as a shrub. A second type of poison oak *(R. toxicodendron)* is native to the Southeastern United States.

A serious threat. Poison sumac *(R. vernix)*, which grows in the East and Midwest, is perhaps the most toxic, causing severe inflammation on contact. Usually found in freshwater swamps, the shrub has smooth, elliptical, pointy-tipped leaves that grow in clusters of up to 13.

Protect yourself. If there's a chance you'll come in contact with a toxic plant, wear a long-sleeved shirt, long pants, gloves, socks, and lace-up shoes. Goggles will keep you from touching your eyes with tainted gloves.

There's no cure for the inflammation once you've come in contact with toxic plants. Try to limit an outbreak by washing skin immediately after exposure with

---

DANGERS IN THE GARDEN

Like potatoes? Stick to the tubers, because the leaves are poisonous. Pruning rue? Touching the foliage may result in a skin rash. These are but two of the common garden plants that cause problems on contact or ingestion. Take precautions when working around irritant plants and inform your children of the danger.

Plants that cause irritation Amaryllis, carnation, cyclamen, daisy, fig, four-o'clock, geranium, rue, stinging nettle, tulip bulbs

Plants with poisonous foliage Buttercup, datura, delphinium, diffenbachia, euphorbia, foxglove, iris, monkshood, oleander, philodendron, poinsettia, potato, rhubarb, rue, tomato

Plants with poisonous fruits Castor bean, daphne, euonymus, holly, ivy, lupine, mayapple, pyracantha, wisteria, yew

Plants with all poisonous parts Azalea, bleeding heart, boxwood, crocus, chrysanthemum, daffodil, hydrangea, lily-of-the-valley, mountain laurel, rhododendron, sweet pea

brown soap (such as Fels-Naptha); rinse it off. Lather again, leaving a thick soap paste on your skin for 5 minutes; then rinse thoroughly. Treat any blistering with calamine or hydrocortisone.

Fido, too? Pets can also develop an allergic skin reaction, so don't let them romp near toxic plants. If they've been exposed, bathe them with soap and water; wear rubber gloves when washing them.

Wipe them out. Don't try to pull up toxic plants—even with your skin protected. If you find a small patch, smother it under newspapers or black plastic. For large areas, eradicate with a systemic herbicide, such as amitrole, glyphosate, or 2, 4–D + triclopyr.
▷ **Edible Flowers**

TRACE ELEMENTS

Little essentials. Trace elements are nutrients required for plant health—but only in tiny amounts. Also called micronutrients, they include boron, chlorine, copper, iron, manganese, molybdenum, and zinc.

Where to find them. Complete fertilizers usually contain trace elements to prevent deficiencies. You can also buy individual micronutrient fertilizers, such as chelate of iron or zinc sulfate, at garden centers.

A bonus. Many organic fertilizers are rich in trace minerals; using them will guard against deficiencies. Wood ashes, kelp meal, kelp extract, granite dust, rock phosphate, guano, and greensand are all good sources.

Diagnosing deficiencies of trace elements is tricky. Common symptoms, such as discolored leaves or stunted growth, could be caused by other factors as well. If you are unsure, have the soil or plant analyzed by your local Cooperative Extension Service or a private laboratory before treating with fertilizers. The margin between too much and too little of these nutrients is slim.

A good clue. Trace element shortages often appear in leaves as chlorosis—the yellowing of leaf tissue between the veins. Plants with a shortage of zinc show symptoms on the older, lower leaves. Those with a shortage of iron, manganese, or molybdenum show chlorosis on the young upper leaves.

Be discriminating. After you determine which element the plant needs, apply just that one. Otherwise, the amount of the other nutrients might rise to toxic levels.
▷ **Fertilizer, Organic Fertilizers**

TRANSPLANTING

Take it easy. Whether you're setting out pot-grown seedlings in a bed or moving an overgrown shrub, handle plants with extreme care; they don't like being uprooted and moved to a new home any more than you do! To minimize transplant shock, plan your course of action, have planting holes ready, and allow plenty of time.

Start small. Whenever practical, transplant a specimen while it is still small. Doing so will mean less work for you and a quicker recovery for the plant.

Save the soil. Try to keep as much soil around the roots as you can—plants will have an easier time taking up water and nutrients until they're reestablished in their new surroundings.

Pamper the roots. When digging up a plant, take care not to injure the roots. Mist the roots or wrap them in damp burlap to keep them moist while the plant remains out of the ground. Limit the amount of time they are exposed to the air and protect them from sun and wind.

Watch the weather. Transplant on a cool, overcast—even drizzly—day or late in the afternoon so plants don't suffer in the heat and light. Keep new transplants shaded for the first week or so if it's sunny.

SEEDLINGS

Feed and water first. Several days before transplanting seedlings, feed with a complete liquid fertilizer. Then water them a few hours before moving them.

Transplant timing. Plan to move seedlings after the first set of true leaves has emerged. Don't wait too long; developing seedlings will crowd each other out in the container.

Harden them off. Tender seedlings started indoors must be toughened for outdoor conditions. Two weeks before you want to transplant, withhold food and limit watering. A week later, set the seedlings in their containers in a sheltered spot outside for one hour; increase their exposure daily until they're out for a full day.

Handle with care. Lift seedlings out of their containers with a small, narrow trowel or an ice cream stick; be sure to keep soil around the roots. Support the root ball on the tool and hold the plant by a side leaf—never by the stem or top.

Tricky transplants. Plants with taproots, like parsley and poppy, resent transplanting. If you must start seedlings inside, sow them in 4-inch pots and keep all the soil around the roots when transplanting. Another trick: cut the top off an eggshell, fill with soil, and sow a seed in it. To transplant, simply set the whole shell in the bed.

A handy carry-case. If you need to travel with seedlings, perhaps taking the transplants to a community garden or a weekend house, sow them in egg cartons. When it's time to go, close the lids for protection; reopen them once you reach your destination.

❧ TRANSPLANTING DEPTHS ❦

Though most transplants need the same depth they had in the container, there are exceptions.

SURFACE

Cover plants with soil just to the growing point or crown; some seedlings may wilt a bit before regaining vigor. Use for artichokes, beets, chicory, lettuce, and strawberries.

DEEP

Set plants in the soil up to the base of their first set of leaves. Use for cabbages, cucumbers, melons, and zucchini.

VERY DEEP

Bury the stem and the first set of leaves in the soil. Use for eggplants, leeks, sweet peppers, and tomatoes.

A homemade dibble. Nail rows of corks onto a board at regular intervals. When you're ready to transplant, press the board cork-side down into the soil. You'll have perfectly spaced planting holes for seedlings.

Transplant care. Water plants frequently, using a fine spray, and feed lightly. Shade any wilted seedlings from sun. Watch for late frosts and provide adequate protection.

TREES AND SHRUBS

Move a woody plant only when it's dormant—either early in spring or in fall, after the leaves drop.

Dig like a pro. Nurseries use a trenching, or tree, spade with a tapered, extended steel blade—about 15 inches long—for transplanting. The spade cuts cleanly through established roots and lets you dig deeply.

Start digging out the transplant beneath the dripline, at least 2 feet from the stem or trunk. Dig a trench 2 feet deep all the way around, then start working your spade in under the root ball. Don't try to lift the plant right away—keep prying the spade under the roots and rocking the plant away from you until it comes free.

Prepare older specimens in spring for transplanting in fall. With a sharp spade, cut a trench 6 inches wide and 1½ feet deep around the dripline. This severs the lateral roots and encourages growth of shallow feeder roots, which will help the plant readjust quickly. Fill the trench with sphagnum moss mixed with soil. Water the plant well through the summer; dig up and relocate in autumn.

How big? To judge the size of the root ball before digging up a plant, figure as follows: the ball measures about 12 inches wide for every inch of trunk diameter. For example, a shrub whose stem is 2 inches in diameter will have a root ball at least 24 inches wide.

Wrap the roots. To help keep the root ball intact and make it easier to move, wrap it in burlap while it's still in the hole. Rock the plant to one side and tuck the fabric in under the roots; tip it in the opposite direction and pull up the burlap around the root ball. Tie it around the trunk or stem with heavy twine.

To carry a heavy tree, wrap a piece of burlap around the trunk just above the root ball. Attach a wooden pole on each side of the trunk with cord. The poles make sturdy handles for two people to lift and transport the tree to its new location.

An hourglass figure. Trees and shrubs will recover more quickly from transplanting if you prune back one-quarter to one-third of the top growth. The reduced foliage mass loses less moisture and places fewer demands on the roots. Think of an hourglass shape: the amount of growth above ground should be roughly equivalent to the root growth below ground.

Water is essential—both to keep the disturbed roots moist until they can take up water from the soil and to eliminate air pockets. Soak the base of the plant once a week through the growing season if rainfall is insufficient. Let the soil dry slightly between waterings so roots don't rot. Mulch well to retain moisture.

Stake for stability. A newly transplanted tree needs support until its roots can take hold. Drive the stake into the hole after transplanting but before backfilling so that you make sure to site it away from the roots. Attach the tree to the stake with a rubber or webbing strap.

Transplant in trouble? Prune foliage by a further 15 percent to reduce stress on the roots. Keep thoroughly watered and mulch with compost or well-rotted manure. Wind paper tree wrap around the trunk to limit moisture loss. Check for and eliminate any air pockets in the soil.

▷ **Planting, Pruning, Shrubs, Spading, Staking, Trees**

TRANSPORTING PLANTS

Avoid extremes. Whether you're moving your own plants or having plants shipped from a mail-order nursery, wait for mild weather. Exposure to temperature extremes can endanger a plant's survival.

The best time to move? Trees, shrubs, and perennials are best moved in their dormant period—in early spring or late fall.

Take care when bare. When transporting bare-root plants, don't let the roots dry out. Wrap the roots in damp paper towels or burlap and place in a plastic bag. Or pack them in moist peat moss or sawdust wrapped in newspaper or plastic.

Driving with daisies. In summer, place plants in the trunk—it's shielded from sun and is often cooler than the passenger compartment. In cold weather, let plants ride in the heated car with you.

Heavy hauling. When hauling a tree on the roof of your car, first bind the top growth close to the trunk; wrap in a spiral with strong cord. Place it with the root ball or container facing front so that the tree catches less wind. If the plant extends beyond the rear of the car, attach a red flag to the end as a warning to other drivers.

No fast corners. Driving with top-heavy container plants? Wedge them securely in place and take it easy around corners—the pots can easily tip over. Spread a tarp or an old shower curtain under them just in case.

No tight squeezes. Transport small plants in containers roomy enough to accommodate them. To conserve moisture, wrap each plant in several layers of damp—not wet—newspaper and seal it in a plastic bag or a water-resistant box. On long trips, open the containers every evening to let the plants air out and to discourage rot.

Protecting bouquets. Wrap cut flowers in damp newspaper, leaving the top open for air circulation. For added protection, you can stand them in a pail, place them in an unsealed plastic bag, or wrap them in aluminum foil. Never place flowers in the back window of the car—they could cook in the sun.

CUTTINGS

On the road? If, while traveling, you collect cuttings to take home, enclose them in a plastic bag with a bit of moist facial tissue, paper towel, or newspaper. Better still, keep them fresh in an ice chest or a thermos with a few ice cubes. If you have access to a refrigerator when you stop for the night, place the cuttings inside—but don't forget them!

Post it. To send cuttings by mail, roll them first in moist, absorbent paper, then a sheet of plastic. Place them in a rigid, unbendable package: a styrofoam box is ideal.

Make your own container to transport cuttings. Cut off the top of a plastic jug or soft-drink bottle and place moist sphagnum moss or florist's oasis in the bottom. Insert the cuttings into the damp material.

For short trips, use a chopstick to poke holes in a raw potato, then insert your cuttings; they'll stay moist for a few hours.

▷ **Transplanting, Trees**

TREES

PURCHASING

Something for everyone. Trees come in 20,000 kinds—from desert palms to river birches to mountain pines. The trick is to select a tree with the size, shape, color, growth habit, and cultural requirements that are right for your garden.

Know your needs. What do you want from a tree? Shade in summer or color in autumn? A hard-working windbreak or an easy-care foundation planting? Choose a species that meets your needs instead of forcing one into a role that doesn't suit it.

Know your tree's needs for light, soil, and moisture and its tolerance of cold, heat, wind, pests, and diseases. Make sure it will thrive in your garden before purchasing.

From little acorns ... Always consider a tree's ultimate height and spread. And don't forget its root mass, which can reach three times the size of the canopy. Before bringing that sweet little sapling home from the nursery, select a spot where it can develop without encroaching on power lines, build-

ings, driveways or walkways, underground pipes, or neighboring plants.

Scout around. While your local nursery will surely stock a selection of old favorites suited to your area, you may need to look in catalogs for new or rare varieties.

Small but sturdy. Don't select the tallest, biggest tree you can find unless you need to fill in a spot immediately. Look for a small, young one with a sturdy trunk, well-formed branches, and no signs of pests or diseases. It will cost less, make moving and planting easier, and adjust more readily to its new home than an older tree would.

Buying bare-root. In early spring, when trees are dormant, you can buy bare-root deciduous trees. They are usually less costly and easier to handle than container-grown or balled-and-burlapped trees. You can also examine their roots, which should be fibrous, moist, and flexible. Be aware, however, that bare-root trees need more care at first and sometimes develop more slowly.

Avoid bare-root evergreens, both needle- and broad-leaf. Because their leaves con-stantly lose moisture, their roots must be kept moist in soil. Look for container-grown or balled-and-burlapped trees.

Size it up. If you want to estimate the height of an established tree, insert a stick vertically

into the ground near the tree on a sunny day. Measure the shadow of the stick, then that of the tree. Multiply height of the stick by the length of the tree's shadow and divide that number by the length of the stick's shadow. The final number will be the height of the tree.

Naughty girls. The female trees of some species have unattractive habits and are best avoided. Flowers of the female poplar, for example, can cause allergies. The female ginkgo produces foul-smelling fruits.

Small garden? If so, buy a tree that stays small at maturity, such as redbud, crab apple, dogwood, or paperbark maple. You'll be spared the constant pruning required to keep a large tree in bounds.

Shade lovers. While most trees need full sun, some tolerate or even prefer shade. Look for dogwood, serviceberry, stewartia, redbud, sourwood, Carolina silverbell, Japanese snowbell, or threadleaf maple.

The tropical touch. If you live in a cold climate and yearn to grow a palm, citrus, or other tender tree, choose a variety suited to tub culture. Buy the tree after all danger of frost has passed and set it on the porch or patio for the summer. Then bring it indoors to overwinter in a sunny window.

DESIGN

Soften the hard angles of building corners and mark the ends of foundation beds with trees. But keep scale in mind: a towering spruce would dwarf a small Cape Cod house, while a dainty dogwood would be overshadowed by a stately Tudor.

Special specimens. If you want to show-case a tree as a single specimen, select one that offers more than one season of beauty. A tree with flaking bark, pretty leaves, col-orful fruits or fall foliage, and a pleasing sil-houette works harder in the landscape than a dazzling spring bloomer that soon fades.

Look out the window. Consider not only how your tree will look outdoors but also how it will be viewed from inside. If you use the tree to block an unattractive vista, however, don't place it where it will com-pletely obstruct your sightline.

Group dynamics. When combining several trees, keep in mind their overall shape.

Trees with complementary silhouettes, such as round and umbrella forms or narrow pyramids and columns, mix more pleasingly than trees with contrasting form.

A dummy tree. Having trouble envisioning how a tree will look in its proposed site or where it will cast its shade? You can erect a dummy tree by sticking a spring rake through the top of a step ladder, then raising the handle as needed. Move the "tree" around and watch the shade pattern until you find the right location.

Neatness counts. Plant only tidy trees near decks, driveways, entryways, and patios. You'll be spared the mess of fruits, seed pods, bark, petals, or twigs.

Screening with trees. For an attractive privacy screen, don't create a straight line with one type of tree. Mix two or three trees with complementary shapes and foliage, arranging them in a balanced design along a slightly curving line.

Nature's air conditioner. Shade trees are invaluable for shielding houses from heat. Locate open-branched deciduous trees on the southern or western exposure so that their limbs block high-angled summer sun. But don't use densely branched deciduous or evergreen trees, which won't allow low-angled winter sun to penetrate.

Let roots roam. Underground barriers are ineffective for poplars, beeches, and other trees with invasive roots. Instead, site these trees where their roots can spread unimpeded. Keep them away from paved areas and don't underplant with grass or ground covers, which can't compete for nutrients.

Going solo. Deep shade and root competition make the area under a tree inhospitable for many plants. If you want to site a tree in the lawn, surround the base with mulch instead of grass. If you must plant under a tree, use shallow ground covers, bulbs, or prostrate shrubs that can tolerate the special conditions. Then give them a boost with extra moisture and fertilizer.

PLANTING

Timing. Plant trees at least 4 weeks before the temperature of the top 8 inches of soil falls below 40°F. Plant deciduous trees in early spring or late fall, when they are dormant; their roots will become established before the leaves start needing water and nutrients. Evergreens can be planted when only partly dormant, often in late summer.

Follow the old adage: never plant a five-dollar tree in a five-cent hole! Dig the hole large enough to allow you to spread out the roots of a bare-root tree or to fill in around the soil ball of others—usually three times wider than the root spread but no deeper. If you disturb the base of the hole, the soil may settle and cause the tree to sink.

Pierce the sides of the planting hole with a spading fork or spade and roughen the soil with a hand cultivator. The tree roots will be able to penetrate more easily.

Don't bother. Current thinking holds that because roots can spread more than 50 feet at a tree's maturity, it's neither practical nor wise to amend soil in the planting hole or backfill. Select a tree that will thrive in the chosen site and leave the native soil as is.

To position your tree, place a stick or tool handle across the hole to mark the ground level. Never plant the trunk-root juncture deeper than it was at the nursery. Turn the tree in the hole until the trunk is straight and the most attractive side is on view.

In heavy soil, raise a tree several inches above grade level by digging a shallower hole. Then pack and slope the backfill amply over the roots. Cover with mulch.

Cut it out. Don't yank a tiny sapling out of its container. Instead, cut away the pot with a utility knife. After placing the plant in the hole, gently spread the roots away from the root ball. Snip off any girdling roots around the trunk.

Balled-and-burlapped? If so, put the tree in the hole with the burlap intact. Once the tree is at the proper level, remove the burlap completely—but only if it is synthetic fabric. If it is natural burlap, you can either remove it or just cut away the sides.

Soak a bare-root tree for up to 24 hours before planting. Make a mound of soil in the planting hole and spread the roots over it, being sure that the root-trunk line is even with the grade level. Place half the backfill in the hole and water it in to settle the soil. Then add the remainder.

Install stakes just after planting to keep the tree trunk straight and stable while the roots grow.

But don't stake too rigidly—the tree needs to bend naturally in the wind. Loosen the wires or ties as needed and remove the stake after the first year.

Keep the canopy. The old practice of cutting back one-third of the foliage at planting time is no longer recommended—the tree needs its leaves to produce food. But do prune out any dead, diseased, or damaged shoots, as well as branches growing in an undesirable location or direction.

MAINTENANCE

Water attentively. Young trees need plenty of water until the roots are established. When they mature, water them deeply so that moisture soaks the roots. When rainfall is low, use a soaker hose around the base of the tree or let water run very slowly out of the hose end for several hours. If the soil or mulch is disturbed by the water flow, turn the pressure down to a trickle.

Multipurpose mulch. Mulch not only retains moisture and suppresses weeds but also keeps potentially damaging lawn-care equipment at a safe distance. Use a year-round organic material like shredded bark or wood chips—not fresh grass clippings

In the gray of January, winter lays bare the tree as sculpture: a consummate study in composition and form.

or sawdust. Spread it around the base of the tree, starting 6 inches from the trunk and keeping it only 2 to 4 inches deep; if deeper, it may suffocate the roots.

Protect young trees from windburn and sunscald. Wind paper tree wrap around the trunk or erect a burlap or canvas screen that reaches as high as the lowest limbs.

Feeding trees. Putting fertilizer in the planting hole can harm the roots of young trees. Do, however, feed developing and mature trees. Apply 1 to 2 pounds of fertilizer per inch of trunk diameter; use a compound like 10–6–4. If your soil is low in phosphorus and potassium, use 10–10–10.

Drill holes. Apply fertilizer outward to the drip line and down to the root zone by drilling holes in the soil. Feed in early spring and, if needed, again in late fall.

Prevent nibbling by rabbits, mice, and other pests that find tree bark toothsome. Wrap the trunk with small-mesh wire or a perforated plastic guard about 2 feet high.

Let it be. Unless you're creating topiary, let a tree be itself: its natural shape is part of its beauty. Prune only to stimulate natural growth patterns. You should also remove any limbs that interfere with others or that form a narrow crotch (less than 90°).

Avoid accidents. Promptly prune off any dead, diseased, or damaged limbs, which can easily fall and cause injury. But take note: because of their huge size, some older specimens can be difficult—and dangerous—to handle. If you need to prune large limbs, transplant an established tree, or remove a dead tree, don't attempt it yourself. Hire an arborist to do it for you.

Start a rap sheet. If one of your trees has recurring problems with pests or diseases, keep a file on it. Record when the incident occurred, the symptoms noted, and the measures that were taken to correct them—whether successful or not.

▷ **Ash, Aspen, Bark, Beech, Christmas Trees, Conifers, Eucalyptus, Evergreens, Flowering Trees, Leaves, Magnolia, Maple, Nut Trees, Palms, Poplar, Stumps & Dead Trees, Sycamore**

A WHOLE NEW LOOK

If an old conifer gets leggy, don't reach for the chain saw. You can turn it into an interesting specimen—by "cloud" pruning, Japanese-style. Select a few well-placed branches with good foliage growth on the ends. Remove twigs and branches along the lower stems and prune the tops into fluffy, elliptical shapes. The foliage will appear to be floating like clouds above the tree.

TRELLISES

Transform a blank wall into a vertical garden with a trellis covered with climbers. You can select the traditional latticework panels or a fan shape. Or try a more fanciful type: some sculptural trellises are designed with tops that resemble the sun, a flower, a heart, a fountain, or leaf clusters.

Choosing materials. Redwood, cypress, and cedar trellises are rot resistant, will age to gray, and don't require painting. Iron and steel trellises are good for heavy plants; look for a rust-proof finish. For low maintenance, try a plastic, fiberglass, or enameled aluminum trellis in colors of white, green, or brown. In the vegetable garden, use a netting or wire trellis to support pole beans and other climbers.

One size fits all. An expandable plastic trellis with riveted joints can be contracted or stretched, accordionlike, to fit any space.

Not just for walls. A freestanding trellis needs sturdy legs that can extend 12 to 18 inches into the ground: it has to support not only the structure but also the plants.

A bamboo curtain. Use bamboo poles for a lightweight but sturdy trellis; it looks

especially nice in a Japanese-style garden. Fasten the poles together by crisscrossing waterproof nylon cord over the joints.

When building your own latticework, use a wooden spacer to keep the pattern even. Also use rust-resistant, galvanized nails; they won't bleed onto the wood and mar the trellis.

Air space. Attach furring strips vertically to the wall before hanging a trellis to create at least 3 inches of space between the trellis and the wall. The gap will give plant stems room to grow behind the

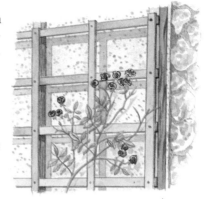

trellis, let water evaporate from the wall, and increase air circulation around plants.

Plan ahead. Attach the trellis to the furring strips with hooks and eyes instead of screws. If you need to paint or repair the wall, you can easily lift off the trellis.

The right trellis. Make sure your trellis and plant can coexist. Clinging vines, like ivy and trumpet vine, don't need a trellis—their stems can adhere to any surface. "Grabbers," such as clematis, have tendrils that need to coil around thin supports. Twining and sprawling plants, like honeysuckle and roses, require a sturdy trellis and should be trained on it with soft twine ties.
▷ **Arbors, Climbers, Espaliers**

TULIPS

PURCHASING

"Firm and fat" is how a healthy, quality tulip bulb should appear. Don't worry if the papery outer layer is tattered, but avoid bulbs with soft spots, bruises, or nicks.

Hybrid or species? The stately tulips that herald spring are hybrids—the result of 300 years of breeding. They offer the widest range of colors and flower forms but can suffer in hot summers and fail to bloom reliably after the first year. Species (or botanical) tulips are the wild European and Asian natives. They are smaller and hardier than the hybrids and will naturalize in the right spot for years of bloom.

Bulb hunting. Come fall, garden centers are stocked full of tulip bulbs—but often with only the most popular varieties. For species tulips and lesser-known hybrids, seek out catalogs from specialty bulb growers, who are more likely to carry rarities.

On the wild side. Species tulips usually have open, starlike blooms with a "wild" look that recalls their native mountain habitats. Use them in informal sites like rock gardens and give them room to spread. Try *Tulipa batalinii, T. clusiana, T eichleri, T. humilis, T. praestans,* and *T. turkestanica.*

Golden oldies. In addition to the new varieties introduced each year, you can buy a number of tulips that have been grown for centuries. Look for *T. tarda* (c.1590), *T. clusiana* (1606), 'Zomerschoon' (1620), and 'Keizerskroon' (1750).

An artistic touch. The Rembrandt tulip, named for the Dutch painter, has blooms that are streaked and flushed with a second color. While this feature was originally caused by an aphid-borne virus, it has been duplicated genetically and safely in modern Rembrandt tulips.

A LITTLE HISTORY

"Tulipmania" was the name given to the tulip-growing frenzy that swept Europe in the 17th century. The seed of this phenomenon was sown in the mid-1500's, when native tulip bulbs were imported from Turkey to the imperial gardens of Emperor Ferdinand I of Vienna. From there, a royal botanist who had zealously bred the unusual new plants carted his tulip bulbs to Holland, where, in 1593, they debuted in the botanical gardens. It has been said that the flowers were so coveted by the public that all 600 bulbs were stolen—and all in one night. Thereafter, the passion for tulips increased, peaking in 1637, when three Rembrandt tulip bulbs commanded the equivalent of $25,000.

⇥ A SEASON OF TULIP BLOOMS ⇤

To prolong the thrill of seeing tulips in bloom, plant cultivars that flower at different times. There is no dearth of choices: the tulip industry produces 1½ billion bulbs in more than 3,000 varieties annually.

	Class	Height	Description	Varieties
EARLY	Kaufmanniana	4–8 in.	Flat, star-shaped blooms	'Daylight,' 'Heart's Delight'
EARLY	Single early	6–15 in.	Six-petaled, cup-shaped blooms	'Apricot Beauty,' 'Bellona'
EARLY	Double early	8–12 in.	Ruffled, peonylike bloom	'Electra,' 'Monte Carlo'
MID-SEASON	Fosteriana	10–18 in.	Very large, cup-shaped bloom	'Yellow Emperor,' 'Purissima'
MID-SEASON	Triumph	16–24 in.	Cup-shaped blooms	'Aureola,' 'Peerless Pink'
MID-SEASON	Darwin hybrids	22–30 in.	Large, egg-shaped blooms	'Apeldoorn,' 'Elizabeth Arden'
MID-SEASON	Greigii	8–16 in.	Midsize blooms with dark center	'Cape Cod,' 'Red Riding Hood'
LATE	Single late	18–36 in.	Oval-shaped blooms	'Mrs. John T. Sheepers,' 'Sorbet'
LATE	Lily-flowered	15–30 in.	Pointed, reflexed petals	'Aladdin,' 'Ballade,' West Point'
LATE	Fringed	8–30 in.	Incised petals, open blooms	'Blue Heron,' 'Burgundy Lace'
LATE	Viridiflora	16–24 in.	Greenish blooms, curved petals	'Groenland,' 'Spring Green'
LATE	Rembrandt	15–20 in.	Streaked, flushed bicolor petals	'Cordell Hull,' 'Zomerschoon'
LATE	Parrot	15–24 in.	Large blooms, scalloped petals	'Black Parrot,' 'Estella Rijnveld'
LATE	Double late	18–24 in.	Large, ruffled, peonylike blooms	'Angelique,' 'Mount Tacoma'

A true exotic. Need an eye-catching tulip for a special location? Look for *T. acuminata,* the fireflame tulip. The red-streaked yellow petals roll up vertically into thin, irregular shapes that resemble tongues of fire.

Too hot for tulips? Most tulips need a period of cold dormancy for best bloom. But some will perform well in warm climates without needing to be chilled. Try *T. sylvestris, T. bakeri* 'Lilac Wonder,' 'Blue Parrot,' 'White Triumphator,' or 'Sweet Harmony.'

PLANTING

The right soil. While tulips can usually adjust to many soil types, they grow best in rich, quick-draining loam. To condition the soil, turn in compost or very well-rotted manure to a depth of 8 to 12 inches. Add bonemeal to the planting hole or bed.

The right spacing. Plant hybrid tulips with 6 inches of soil above the bulb tips. In light, sandy soil, set them 8 inches deep to ensure strong roots and good support for the stems; in heavy soil, plant only 4 to 5 inches deep. For species tulips, plant the bulbs at a depth 2½ times their diameter but no less than 4 inches deep. Space all tulips 6 to 8 inches apart.

Rigid or random. For lining a path, tulips look best in a single row—like a rank of soldiers. For a naturalistic look, let the bulbs fall where they may. But don't just toss them over your shoulder: put them in a bucket and spill them over the ground.

Protect from rodents. Plant bulbs in the wire-mesh cages sold at garden centers to keep gophers, moles, and voles at bay.

Shade and shelter. Plant tulips in a sunny location; light afternoon shade will help the blooms last longer. And make sure the plants are sheltered from wind; a strong breeze can snap the top-heavy stems.

Planting time. In cold climates, plant the bulbs between late September and the first frost, while the soil is still workable and roots can develop. In warm areas, wait until early December, when the ground is cooler.

A good combo. Underplant tulips with low-growing flowers or ground covers that blossom simultaneously, such as forget-me-not, wallflowers, chamomile, or sweet alyssum. The long-stemmed tulips will emerge from a frothy bed of blooms.

MAINTENANCE

A measure of water. Don't let the soil around tulips dry out. As a rule, water to a depth of 1 inch each week.

Feed the sprouts. Once tulips emerge in spring, sprinkle a little 5–10–5 fertilizer on the soil around them and dig in lightly.

Early-flowering tulips will grow under deciduous trees, basking in sun before the trees leaf out.

The first cut. On hybrid tulips, snip off spent flowers just below the bloom; leave the foliage in place to manufacture food for the bulb, so it can rebloom the next year. On species tulips, don't cut the heads off; let them go to seed and spread.

Clip again. Once a tulip's foliage has yellowed—usually in midsummer—cut it off and add it to the compost pile. In the meantime, hide the withering leaves by planting taller-growing annuals in front.

A second-year slump is common for some tulips; not every variety is a reliable repeat bloomer, even in ideal conditions. Lift the bulbs at season's end and discard. Or replant in an inconspicuous spot, where their less-than-perfect blooms won't matter.

For long-lasting bouquets, cut tulips in the morning. Select fairly tight buds with good color on the upper two-thirds; buds that are cut too green won't open. Before putting them in a vase, recut the stems at an angle while you hold them underwater.

Beware when handling cut tulips; the sap can cause a rash on sensitive skin.

In the vase. Give tulips plenty of room in the vase—the blooms can expand as much as 50 percent. And place the arrangement where it gets even lighting, since tulip blossoms will bend toward a light source.
▷ **Bulbs, Cut Flowers, Flower Beds**

TURNIPS

To avoid tough turnips, plant them in spring 3 weeks before the last frost or in fall, 2 months before the first frost. These cool-weather vegetables can tolerate cold if well mulched, but they turn woody and bitter in temperatures over 75°F.

✧ A TURNIP SAMPLER ✧

Turnips, rutabagas, and kohlrabi are all members of the cabbage family. The first two are true root vegetables; kohlrabi bulbs, which grow on top of the soil, are swellings in the stems. Popular turnip varieties include 'Tokyo Cross', 'Hakurei,' 'Market Express,' 'Gilfeather,' and 'Purple Top White Globe.' Prized for their greens are 'Seven Top' and 'Shogrin.' For tasty rutabagas, try 'Purple Top,' 'Marian,' and 'Canadian Gem.' Widely grown kohlrobi varieties include 'Grand Duke,' 'Early White Vienna,' 'Express Forcer,' and 'Kolpak.'

Plant turnips in rich, loose soil amended with any organic matter except manure, which turnips don't like. If needed, adjust the soil pH to a range of 5.5 to 6.8.

A bonus crop. Sow seed 1 inch apart in rows 1 to 1½ feet apart. When you thin plants to 4 inches apart, save the thinnings: you can use the tender little bulbs and leaf tops either raw or cooked.

Crave greens? Grow a turnip variety bred for its tasty leaves. To keep them coming, snip with shears to 1 inch above the ground when the tops reach 6 inches tall.

Provide shade for young plants by sowing seeds close to corn plants or trellis-grown pole beans, cucumbers, or squash.

Harvest turnips in spring when they reach golfball size. In warm climates, pull up the fall crop as you need it. In cold areas, harvest the plants and remove the tops, leaving a bit of stem. Don't wash off the soil, and store the bulbs in a cool, dark place.
▷ **Greens, Vegetable Gardens**

UNDERGROWTH

Starting from scratch. When clearing overgrown ground to plant a new garden bed or lawn, extraordinary measures may be required to rid the area of stubborn weeds, brush, brambles, and vines.

Mechanical means. You can rent heavy-duty tools designed specifically for cutting through undergrowth. A brush trimmer is similar to a string trimmer but has a toothed metal blade instead of a filament line; use it for woody growth 1 to 2 inches thick. For dense grass with brambles, you'll need a "brush hog," which resembles a lawn mower with a large front cutting deck.

A slow death. An easy way to clear undergrowth from a small area is by smothering it. Cut down all the vegetation in spring. Cover the ground with black plastic and anchor the edges with boards or stones. At summer's end, remove the plastic and spade up any remaining plants.

Wear them down. Repeated cuttings will eventually weaken plants by denying them the chance to manufacture food. The best time to cut back brambles is late June; you may have to cut them over several years.

HERBICIDE	TARGET PLANTS	WHEN TO USE	EFFECT
2,4–D	Spreading woody plants like brambles; most broad-leaf herbaceous plants	Use on emerging or actively growing plants or on freshly cut stumps	Selective systemic herbicide; won't harm grass, but keep away from ornamentals and food crops
Triclopyr	Broad-leaf and woody vines and shrubs; poison ivy; tree stumps	Use on actively growing plants or on freshly cut stumps	Selective systemic herbicide; often used in combination with 2,4–D; won't harm grass, but keep away from desirable plants; takes 2 to 6 weeks to work
Glyphosate	Grass; wide range of herbaceous weeds; some woody weeds	Use on actively growing plants; woody weeds may need repeat treatments at 30-day intervals	Nonselective systemic herbicide; will destroy any plant it touches but is inactive in soil; not effective on heavy or deep-rooted growth

Table title: **⚜ BRUSH-KILLING HERBICIDES ⚜**

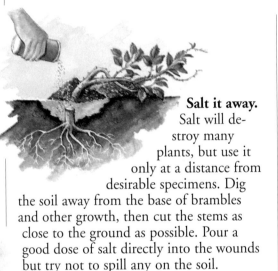

Salt it away. Salt will destroy many plants, but use it only at a distance from desirable specimens. Dig the soil away from the base of brambles and other growth, then cut the stems as close to the ground as possible. Pour a good dose of salt directly into the wounds but try not to spill any on the soil.

The last resort. Use herbicides to clear undergrowth that won't respond to cutting, pulling, or smothering—or those that shouldn't be touched, like poison ivy. First try organic herbicides made from fatty acids, not chemicals; they work on many weeds on contact and are the least toxic.

Synthetic herbicides. Use a selective herbicide, which is less likely to cause harm if it drifts onto desirable plants or is carried by runoff. A systemic product will circulate through the plant and won't affect the surrounding soil—but check the label for warnings: with some products, you may not be able to replant the soil for a while.

No digging required. To destroy the occasional persistent weed that reappears after you've removed the undergrowth—a tuft of thistle, for example—cut it back to the ground in early spring. When it regrows, remove the bottom from a screw-top plastic seltzer bottle and place it over the plant. Spray herbicide through the bottle's opening and screw on the top. Wait a couple of weeks and repeat the treatment if needed.
▷ **Stumps & Dead Trees, Toxic Plants, Weeds**

UNUSUAL PLANTS

Don't overdo it. Unusual plants are best used with discrimination. Planting a select few will enhance the garden; planting a yardful can be gaudy and detract from the beauty of an individual specimen.

ORIGINS
A tall order. If you long for a plant with a color that doesn't occur naturally, be patient: since such plants are the result of breeders' efforts to develop a particular

trait, it takes time for new varieties to be propagated in quantity for sale. What's more, the plants are usually sold only in a few nurseries or catalogs when introduced.

A valuable find. Some rare plants result from mutations. If you spot a mutant specimen—called a "rogue" or "sport"—in your garden, propagate it to preserve the desired new trait. It could be valuable.

Eureka! Plant hunters still roam remote areas of the world in search of new plants, and their discoveries sometimes find their way into the horticultural trade. Scan specialty catalogs and keep your eye out for these new introductions.

FRUITS AND VEGETABLES

A twining spinach. Malabar spinach is a trailing green vegetable with juicy leaves that taste like true spinach.

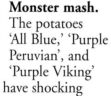

Monster mash. The potatoes 'All Blue,' 'Purple Peruvian', and 'Purple Viking' have shocking bluish-purple flesh.

Easter eggplants. The 'Easter Egg' eggplant bears ivory egg-shaped fruits about 2 inches long. Also look for the colorful 'Turkish Orange,' 'Rosa Bianca,' and 'Neon' eggplants.

FLOWERS

A rare chartreuse. When buying zinnia seeds, look for 'Envy' —a double-flowered cultivar with yellow-green blooms that are almost iridescent.

Sunflower shorties. For sunflowers with petite stems—only 2 feet tall—yet full-size, 10-inch blooms, grow 'Sunspot.'

A blue rose? Sadly, plant breeders have yet to come up with one. But *Eustoma grandiflorum* 'Blue Rose' is a close second. The blooms form in ruffled double rosettes in a deep, dusky blue. Native to the Southwest and Mexico, eustoma is commonly known as prairie gentian.

Pick a jewel. In late summer, the Chinese forget-me-not *(Cynoglossum amabile)* boasts tiny flowers of a blue as intense as that of lapis-lazuli. One variety, 'Blue Showers,' bears turquoise blooms.

Black drama. Several unusual cultivars of common plants have purple or maroon blooms so dark that they appear to be black. Look for 'Queen of the Night' tulips, 'Pennie Black' nemophila, 'Black Magic' violets, and 'Black Swan' iris.

Chocolate cosmos. The velvety petals of *Cosmos atrosanguineus* are actually dark burgundy but emit the distinctive aroma of cocoa.

Living stones. Lithops are bizarre round succulents with an amazing resemblance to stones. They bloom with small dandelionlike flowers from November to January.

Party lights. Chinese lantern *(Physalis alkekengi)* bears fruit in puffy, heart-shaped orange husks that look like paper lanterns.

TREES, SHRUBS, AND GROUND COVERS

Flaky trees. An especially impressive peeler is the white ironbark *(Eucalyptus leucoxylon)*, whose white and bluish bark separates

from the trunk in big, irregular sheets; it grows well in Southern California and similar climates. The more adaptable paperbark maple *(Acer griseum)* sheds its brown bark in thin sheets that curl away from the trunk.

A graceful exotic. A small tree from the Middle East, the Persian parrotia *(Parrotia persica)* has a graceful branching habit and striking amber, crimson, and gold autumn foliage. The bark on older trees flakes away in patches, creating a patterned effect.

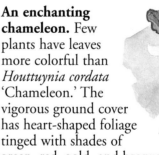

An enchanting chameleon. Few plants have leaves more colorful than *Houttuynia cordata* 'Chameleon.' The vigorous ground cover has heart-shaped foliage tinged with shades of green, red, gold, and bronze. A moisture lover, it also makes a good bog plant.

Brilliant twigs for winter. Red- and yellow-twig dogwoods are shrubs, not trees. They are most valued for the striking color of their bare twigs—particularly vivid against a background of winter snow. For brilliant red, grow 'Sibirica.' A popular yellow-twig type is 'Flaviramea.'

A changeable rug. The Siberian carpet cypress *(Microbiota decussata)* is an extremely cold-hardy (to -40°F) shrub that grows only 2 feet high but 15 feet wide. Shade-tolerant, this evergreen will turn coppery in winter if grown in full sun.
▷ **Ornamental Vegetables**

VACATIONS

OUTDOORS

Pre-trip preparations. During the growing season, weed and cultivate around plants before going away. Also deadhead spent flowers, make sure any stakes are firmly in place, treat for pests and disease, and mulch around plants to conserve soil moisture.

Pick vegetables that are ready. Then eat, can, freeze, or give away your harvest. Water well and mulch before leaving.

Provide protection. If you'll be gone during cold weather, make sure that tender plants have protection from frost, wind, and snow. Use floating row covers, extra mulch, and burlap screens as shields.

Keep patio plants moist while you're away. Dig a trench in a shady corner of the garden and set in the pots; then refill it with soil. Water the plants thoroughly and mulch with damp peat moss to retain moisture.

Long time gone? If so, you may need to enlist a "gardensitter" to water your plants, pick vegetables, deadhead blooms, and generally keep an eye on the yard.

INDOORS

Houseplant care. Water your houseplants, then group them in a kitchen sink or bathtub near a sunny window; line the surface with a large plastic sheet. Surround the pots with peat moss and soak it well. Your plants will stay moist for up to 3 weeks.

Make an indoor greenhouse with a plastic bag. Water a potted plant thoroughly and let it drain. Put a handful of gravel in the bottom of the bag to absorb any excess moisture, then place the plant on top. Tie the bag loosely, leaving a small gap for ventilation. Place the plant in indirect light. Humidity inside the bag will keep the soil moist for 2 weeks.

A slow drip. Cut the bottom off a small plastic bottle and stuff a cotton cloth into the neck. Turn the bottle upside down and insert the neck into the soil of a houseplant that you've just watered; tie the bottle to a stake for extra support. Fill the bottle with water. Water will gradually drip through the cloth and be absorbed by the soil.

▷ **Frost, Protection, Watering**

VEGETABLE GARDENS

PLANNING

The sunniest spot in your yard is the best place to stake out your plot. Most vegetables need a minimum of 6 hours of sun daily.

Watering. Because vegetables like plenty of moisture, site your plot near a water source. But take note: vegetables hate standing water. Keep them away from any low spots and rain runoff, where water can collect.

Strip the soil. When preparing a new bed, skim off the top 2 inches of soil or sod and add it to the compost. Removing this topmost layer will eliminate weeds for years.

A good home. For maximum results, give vegetables the best possible home while they live their short, intense lives. Each year, till or spade 2 or 3 inches of compost or rotted manure about 8 inches deep into the soil until it is loose and friable. Work in a complete fertilizer and, if necessary, amend the soil pH to around 6.0 to 7.0.

Rows or beds? Decide what kind of plot you want. Rows are easy to tend and allow air to circulate but are less efficient than beds in their use of space. Beds, on the other hand, permit intensive planting and therefore higher yields. A disadvantage is that beds take more time to prepare, are more awkward to tend, and have poorer air circulation.

Easy access. To make tending beds easier, keep them no wider than the spread of your arms—about 4 feet. Design a

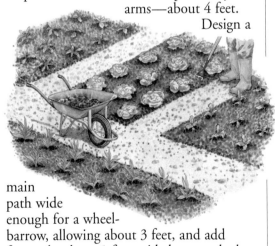

main path wide enough for a wheelbarrow, allowing about 3 feet, and add footpaths about 1 foot wide between beds. To suppress weeds and provide a clean place to walk, keep paths covered with straw, chopped leaves, boards, or bricks.

No room? If space is limited for a separate plot, combine vegetables with your flowers. Some veggies, like ruby chard, purple broccoli, and scarlet runner beans, are handsome enough to hold their own.

Leave room for blooms. Flowers in the vegetable garden not only make it a more pleasant place to work but also have their uses. Many types attract beneficial insects like bees, ladybugs, and lacewings, while others may repel pests. Try butterfly weed, French marigolds, or fennel. For a bonus, plant edible flowers like nasturtiums and violets.

Small-garden strategies. Plant vertical crops, like pole beans and squash, which take up little ground space. Or plant dwarf varieties, such as 'Tom Thumb Midget' lettuce and 'Tiny Dill' cucumbers. Or create a patio garden, using the dwarf varieties specially bred for containers: tomatoes, cabbages, cucumbers, melons, and more.

BUYING

How much to plant? Deciding how many plants to grow depends on how you use your garden. If you're keen on canning and freezing, add more plants than you would need for eating fresh. But be careful not to overplant any prolific producers, like summer squash and tomatoes.

Expand your horizons. Look for a few unusual vegetables, including imported and heirloom varieties, to add to your mainstays. Be adventurous and try out a new cultivar each year—particularly with tomatoes, which come in countless varieties.

WHY GROW YOUR OWN?

If you've ever sunk your teeth into the still-warm skin of a sun-ripened tomato right off the vine, you know the answer—incomparable flavor. Corn tastes sweeter, radishes snappier, and beans crisper when they are harvested from your own garden. Homegrown vegetables also retain their vitamins and minerals, can mean significant savings in the family food bill, and give you the chance to try unusual or heirloom varieties that you won't find at the local market.

Consider your conditions. In areas with short growing seasons, buy fast-maturing or cold-tolerant vegetables. In warm and hot climates, buy heat-tolerant varieties so that you can enjoy cool-weather favorites like lettuce. Also buy plants that are resistant to diseases common in your region.

PLANTING

Sun lovers. For maximum sun, try laying out rows east to west, following the sun's transit. Plants in north-to-south rows may get too much shade as the sun passes over.

For high yields, use space wisely. After harvesting a cool-weather crop (peas or spinach, for example), replant the space with a warm-weather vegetable (green beans or summer squash). Interplant quick growers (radishes) with slower ones (tomatoes); the short-term crop will be up and out before the slow grower can crowd or shade it.

With poor keepers, such as lettuce, don't plant all at once. Instead, plant short rows at 1-week intervals. Doing so means you'll have fresh pickings throughout the season.

The far side. Reserve the north end of your garden for perennial vegetables, such as asparagus, and tall, shade-casting plants, like corn. The rest of the space will be freed up for its yearly soil preparation and stay sunny through the growing season.

Crop rotation is essential for preventing a buildup of harmful soilborne microbes that prefer certain plants. For this reason, don't plant a vegetable or a member of its family in the same place year after year. Instead, divide the garden into sections and move the plants from one area to another. As a general rule, a plant should be replanted in its original spot only every 3 or 4 years.

Another advantage. Rotate crops to help balance soil nutrients between light and heavy feeders. An example: the first year, plant peas, which fix nitrogen in the soil. The next year, follow with nitrogen lovers such as cabbage and broccoli.

⇥ THE VEGETABLE FAMILY TREE ⇤

Like all living things, vegetables belong to families. Knowing which plants are kindred will come in handy when rotating your crops.

Allium family *Amaryllidaceae*
Garlic, leeks, onions

Brassica or mustard family *Cruciferae*
Broccoli, Brussels sprouts, cabbage, kale, cauliflower, radishes, turnips

Carrot family *Umbelliferae*
Carrots, celery, parsley

Cucurbit family *Cucurbitaceae*
Cucumbers, gourds, melons, pumpkins, squash

Goosefoot family *Chenopodiaceae*
Beets, spinach, Swiss chard

Legume family *Leguminosae*
Beans, lentils, peas

Nightshade family *Solanaceae*
Eggplant, peppers, potatoes, tomatoes

Sunflower family *Compositae*
Artichokes, Jerusalem artichokes, lettuce

MAINTENANCE

Weekly weeding. Vegetables can't tolerate competition from weeds. Monitor the garden weekly to pull up any invaders and mulch the soil well to suppress them.

A dry spell? Vegetables need an inch of water per week, whether from rainfall or watering. Moisture needs are most critical for leafy crops as they approach maturity, for fruiting vegetables as they set blooms (but not as the fruit ripens), and for root crops as the roots start to expand. Water young vegetables lightly but frequently, never letting their soil dry out completely.

A mid-season snack. Slow-maturing vegetables often benefit from a supplemental feeding halfway through the growing season. Side-dress lightly with a complete fertilizer, water with manure tea, or spray with a foliar food such as kelp extract.

▷ **Compost, Dwarfs, Fertilizer, Freezing Food, Frost, Hybrids, Mulch, Organic Gardening, Pesticides, Pollination, Preserves, Protection, Scarecrows, Seeds, Seed Storage, Thinning, Transplanting, Watering, Weeds**

Timeless heirlooms for your table

Many heirloom vegetables—commonly defined as any open-pollinated variety in cultivation prior to 1940—existed before the discovery of the New World. To grow them today is to be in touch with the family traditions of our ancestors, who diligently saved the seeds of their crops and passed them on.

Unlike modern cultivars, these mainstays of 19th- and early-20th-century gardens often go by different names. (For example, Ponderosa Pink, a tomato variety that dates from the 1890's and is still seen in catalogs, has been variously known as Majestic, Colossal, and Peak of Perfection.) Heirlooms also offer a greater variety of sizes, shapes, colors, and tastes than the uniform hybridized varieties that are bred to meet the needs of commercial growers. Although these living antiques tend to ripen more slowly, they have robust flavor and keep well; gardeners of old pickled, dried, and stored their harvest in preparation for winter.

Preservation of heirloom vegetables goes beyond personal gratification. Because they evolved before the advent of modern chemical pesticides and fertilizers, their genetically coded resistance to certain pests and diseases provides a rich storehouse of possibilities for plant breeders against the risks of increased uniformity. Maintaining this fragile link with our past by preserving heirloom plants is a way of assuring that genetic diversity is preserved for the future. To find these treasured vegetables for yourself, look to seed exchange societies, local botanical gardens, and catalogs—even the Internet.

BEANS

Heirloom beans, some of which were cultivated before the 1600's, exhibit a remarkable palette of colors. One of the oldest, the scarlet runner bean, has 1-inch seeds marked with black on purple. Like other climbing varieties, it ripens over a long season. The venerable Jacob's cattle bean (left), white with red spots, is named for the biblical Jacob, who inherited his father's spotted cattle; it has a pleasantly peppery flavor. Bush varieties yield prolific dry beans for soups and baking. One, the soldier bean, is creamy white, with a red mark that was said to resemble a soldier in uniform.

HEIRLOOM BEANS
Asparagus *Vigna unguiculata*
Yard Long
Bush *Phaseolus vulgaris*
Black Valentine Stringless
Dwarf Horticultural
(Wren's Egg)
French Horticultural
Jacob's Cattle
Low's Champion
Pencil Pod Wax
Soldier
Vermont Cranberry
Pole *Phaseolus vulgaris*
Genuine Cornfield
Kentucky Wonder
(Old Homestead)
King of the Garden Lima
Sieva Lima
Speckled Cranberry
(Wren's Egg)
Runner *Phaseolus coccineus*
Scarlet Runner (pre-1750)

Antique varieties of beans come in a colorful mix of shapes and types.

BEETS

With a lineage that dates back to the first century A.D., beets were brought to America by early European settlers. Many of the older varieties adapt easily to a wide range of conditions. One vintage beet, the large Early Blood Turnip, has a fine grain and sweet flavor, making it a superior storage vegetable. Lutz Green Leaf is also a flavorful winter-storage beet and is prized for its fine, leafy greens. Chioggia (above) is a scarlet Italian heirloom with a cross section of concentric red and white rings. Two mid-season red beets, Crosby Egyptian and Detroit Dark Red, were developed in the late 19th century; both have been refined over the years to take advantage of their quality for both canning and eating fresh.

HEIRLOOM BEETS	
Chioggia	Early Blood Turnip
Crosby's Egyptian	Lutz Green Leaf
Detroit Dark Red	

CABBAGES

So popular were cabbages in the mid-19th century that Fearing Burr's *Field and Garden Vegetables of America*, published in 1865, described 25 varieties. Included were the fragrant, conical-headed Early Jersey Wakefield and the hefty 10- to 15-pound Premium Flat Dutch, with its flat-topped head; both are popular in home gardens today. The solid, tightly packed heads of Mammoth Red Rock (above), Danish Ballhead, and the Dutch varieties are resistant to damage by the common cabbage looper.

HEIRLOOM CABBAGES	
Danish Ballhead	Mammoth Red Rock
Early Flat Dutch	Premium Flat Dutch
Early Jersey Wakefield	Winningstadt

CARROTS

The cultivated varieties familiar to us today were bred from the yellow- and white-rooted carrots that were commonly known in Europe until orange-rooted varieties came into favor in the 18th century. Nearly all modern carrots are descended from two types: the large, tapered, long-rooted winter varieties selected from the Long Orange Carrot (above); and the earlier-maturing, shorter, blunt-rooted types developed from the Horn Carrot. These two parent varieties are recorded as early as the 1600's and were among the first vegetables introduced into North America by early colonists. Properly harvested, vintage carrots will stay crisp and sweet in winter storage.

> **HEIRLOOM CARROTS**
> Chantenay Red Core
> Danvers Half Long
> Early Scarlet Horn
> Long Orange
> Oxheart (Guernade)

CORN

Early European settlers found American Indian tribes cultivating varieties of the grain they called maize, or "our life." The earliest corns in cultivation were the hard-grained flint and dent types grown for grinding into cornmeal. In times when winter storage was a critical concern, sweet corn varieties for fresh boiling and roasting played a secondary role.

Of all the garden vegetables, sweet corn has undergone the greatest changes in the past 50 years. Plant breeding has succeeded in increasing the sugar content and retarding the conversion of sugar to starch—resulting in the creation of modern "supersweet" hybrids. The old adage, "Don't pick your corn until the water is boiling" can be ignored with these new varieties, which are well-suited to the needs of commercial growing and longer shelf life. But older home gardeners may recall with nostalgia the robust flavor of roasted ears of Golden Bantam (left) or Country Gentleman.

Another difference is the modern hybrid's lack of natural resistance to disease—a reality that was brought home dramatically in 1970, when a blight wiped out 15 percent of the U.S. corn crop. In contrast, the American Indians and farmers who grew corn before the advent of hybrids took advantage of the natural selection that occurs when corn varieties cross-pollinate.

Vintage corns offer a wide choice of colors, tastes, and plant types. Such colorful varieties as Black Mexican, Hopi Blue, Anasazi, and Mandan Bride are not only decorative but also nutritious and flavorful.

HEIRLOOM CORNS	HEIRLOOM POPCORNS
Black Mexican	Lady Finger
Bloody Butcher	Pennsylvania Butterflavored
Country Gentleman	
Golden Bantam	**HEIRLOOM FLOUR CORNS**
Luther Hill White	Anasazi Traditional
Six Shooter	Hopi Blue Flint
Stowell's Evergreen	Hopi Yellow
	Mandan Bride

CUCUMBERS

Among the oldest cultivated vegetables in the world, cucumbers, or "cowcumbers," as they were sometimes called, were common in colonial American gardens. But because of their susceptibility to such diseases as cucumber mosaic and bacterial wilt, many vintage cucumbers have not survived. The varieties that prevailed, like Longfellow, Lemon, White Wonder, and Early Cluster (above), allow the home gardener to experience a much broader range of sizes, colors, and flavors than is offered on supermarket shelves.

For pickles, home canners can take advantage of the abundant harvest, convenient size, and keeping quality of heirlooms such as Boston Pickler. One of the best pickling varieties is the West India Gherkin, an African cucumber relative with melon-leaved vines and small fruits; it was introduced into North America via the slave trade. A few hills planted with this hardy, highly resistant variety will produce enough fruit to fill a pickle crock in a single harvest.

> **HEIRLOOM CUCUMBERS**
> Boothby's Blond
> Boston Pickling
> Early Cluster (Russian)
> Improved Long Green
> Longfellow
> West India Gherkin
> White Wonder

MELONS

With the advent of the modern transportation methods that carried ripe melons to distant markets without spoilage, many home gardeners gave up the cultivation of these tender fruits. The needs of market growers and shippers for tougher melons dominated the 20th-century seed industry and, as a result, many of the sweeter, more delicate varieties became extinct or rare. The vintage muskmelons and watermelons that survive offer superior flavor and aroma when eaten fresh, at peak ripeness.

Though most melon varieties are grown for fresh eating, the Citron Preserving Melon is cooked in a spicy sugar syrup to preserve it, then used as a condiment or as a substitute for citron in fruitcakes. Another type, the Cassaba (below), was listed in catalogs in the late 19th century but did not become popular until the 1920's.

With the exception of Moon and Stars, a dark-green Amish heirloom ornamented with yellow markings, the varieties shown here ripen in under 90 days—making them suitable for northern growing seasons, even when sown directly in the garden.

HEIRLOOM MUSKMELONS	HEIRLOOM WATERMELONS
Cassaba	Citron Preserving Melon
Hale's Best	Ice Cream
Jenny Lind	Kleckley Sweets (Monte Cristo)
Nutmeg	Moon and Stars
Rocky Ford (Eden Gem)	Mountain Hoosier
	Nancy
	Strawberry
	Tom Watson

VINTAGE VEGETABLES

ONIONS

Heirloom onion varieties offer home gardeners a wide variety of colors, sizes, and flavors as well as excellent keeping quality in winter.

Red Wethersfield, the classic hamburger onion, was developed in the eponymus Connecticut town prior to 1830, when onion-growing was a major industry there. Two others, the Potato and Egyptian onions, are curiosities. The Potato Onion is a multiplier variety that grows and produces much in the manner of shallots, while the Egyptian (left), also called the Top Onion, bears clusters of small onions that perch atop its leaves.

HEIRLOOM ONIONS
Egyptian (Top Onion)
London Flag Leek
Red Wethersfield
Scotland Leek
Southport Red Globe
Southport White Globe
Southport Yellow Globe
White Portugal
Yellow Potato Onion

ROOT VEGETABLES

Root vegetables were popular in 18th- and 19th-century gardens but later went out of fashion—a shame, considering their unique taste. The parsnip (far left) adds hearty flavor to soups and stews. Scorzonera (middle) and salsify (right) are both known as the "vegetable oyster"; when boiled and mashed, they have a flavor that resembles that of the shellfish. All three of these hardy roots are at their peak when left to overwinter in the ground for harvest in early spring.

HEIRLOOM PARSNIPS, SCORZONERA, AND SALSIFY
Student Parsnip
Hollow Crown Parsnip
Scorzonera (no named varieties)
Mammoth Sandwich Island Salsify

PEAS

Peas are one of the most ancient of vegetables, with evidence of their cultivation dating back to 7000 B.C. The oldest pea varieties were the starchier, smooth-seeded types that gardeners stored dry and ate as a cereal food, which they called "pease porridge." The rise in popularity of fresh, or English, peas occurred in the mid-1700's, when the sweeter, wrinkle-seeded varieties developed. Alaska, Thomas Laxton, and Little Marvel remain popular early-maturing varieties. Lincoln and Wando, both heat-tolerant types, extend the season. All are good for freezing.

Edible podded peas, like Dwarf Gray Sugar and Mammoth Melting Sugar, date from the 1500's.

HEIRLOOM PEAS
Alaska
Alderman (Tall Telephone) (left)
Dwarf Gray Sugar
Lincoln
Little Marvel
Mammoth Melting Sugar
Thomas Laxton
Wando

POTATOES

The potato originated in South America, from whence Spanish explorers introduced it to Europe.

The history of this vegetable's importance in Ireland is legendary and graphically illustrates the need to maintain genetic diversity. The potatoes grown in 19th-century Ireland were descended from a few varieties brought there by Sir Walter Raleigh on his return from the New World. Lacking inbuilt resistance to the diseases of this new land, the tubers succumbed to the great potato blight of the 1840's—and famine ensued.

Nevertheless, numerous heirloom potato varieties have survived in America, largely due to the efforts of home gardeners, who saved tubers of their own family favorites.

Heirloom potatoes come in a wide array of colors and shapes. Old standards such as Burbank—developed by horticulturalist Luther Burbank—Green Mountain, Irish Cobbler, and Katahdin are reliable, white-fleshed varieties that store well. Modern gardeners can enjoy collecting red, blue, and violet potatoes. A group planting of these colored heirlooms can even yield a red, white, and blue potato salad for the Fourth of July.

HEIRLOOM POTATOES
Blue/purple varieties
Caribe
Cowhorn
Fenton Blue

Fingerlings
Anna Cheeka's Ozette
Banana
Lady Finger
Russian

Red/pink varieties
Early Ohio
Early Rose
Garnet Chile

Standard
Burbank
Green Mountain
Irish Cobbler
Katahdin

PUMPKINS

Actually a winter squash, the round, orange vegetable that is cultivated for autumn pies and decorative jack-o'lanterns is known in America as the pumpkin. Among the heirlooms are Connecticut Field (far right), a traditional jack-o'-lantern choice; it is directly descended from pumpkins grown by American Indians. The beautiful scarlet Rouge Vif D'Etampes, developed in France in the late 19th century, is the classic Cinderella pumpkin. The smaller New England Pie, with its sweet flesh, is a long-standing favorite for holiday desserts. More unusual are the various buff-colored Cheese pumpkins, which are flattened like a wheel of cheese.

HEIRLOOM PUMPKINS
Connecticut Field
Landreth Cheese
Magdalena Big Cheese
New England Pie
Rouge Vif D'Etampes

RADISHES

Historically, the radish was more important in garden culture than it is at present. The Egyptians inscribed radishes on pyramid walls, and the Greeks offered radishes made of gold to Apollo.

Nineteenth-century gardeners grew spring radishes—sown as soon as the ground could be worked—and planted fall varieties for winter root-cellar storage. Today heirloom radishes can be found in round and cylindrical shapes, small to large sizes, and an assortment of colors, including scarlet, white, pink, and black.

HEIRLOOM RADISHES

Spring varieties
Early Scarlet Turnip
French Breakfast (above left)
White Icicle

Winter varieties
China Rose
Long Black Spanish
Round Black Spanish (below left)

SALAD GREENS

Until the mid-19th century, lettuce, spinach, and cresses were more often brought to the table cooked than used raw. Recipes of the time called for stewing and serving as an accompaniment for meat dishes.

Modern gardeners can choose greens with a range of colors, including the red-tinged leaves of Deer Tongue and Rouge d'Hiver lettuces. For single-serving-size heads, try Tennis Ball and Tom Thumb. A planting of winter-hardy Corn Salad in late summer or early fall keeps the table supplied with fresh greens. An heirloom spinach, Bloomsdale Long Standing, introduced before 1915, remains prized for its heat tolerance.

HEIRLOOM LETTUCES
Black Seeded Simpson
Corn Salad (Fetticus)
Deer Tongue
Oakleaf
Paris Island Cos (above left)
Rouge D'Hiver
Tennis Ball
Tom Thumb

HEIRLOOM SPINACH
Bloomsdale Long Standing
New Zealand Spinach
Prickly Seeded Spinach

Heirloom varieties of lettuce and spinach offer unequaled flavor.

SQUASH

Native to the New World, summer and winter squashes vary in size from modest crooknecks to 40-pound Boston Marrows. The creamy White Bush Scallop squash is noted in accounts of European explorers from the 1500's. Cushaw and White Jonathan winter squashes, with thick, meaty necks, are good pie vegetables. Turk's Turbans (above) are fine baking squashes. Good storage squashes include the Neck Pumpkin, the Hubbard varieties, and Sweet Keeper.

HEIRLOOM SQUASH

Summer bush varieties
Early Yellow Crookneck
White Bush Scallop
Yellow Bush Scallop

Long-vining winter varieties
Boston Marrow
Green Striped Cushaw
Hubbard (True Green, Golden, Warted, and Blue)
Neck Pumpkin
Seminole
Tennessee Sweet Potato
Turk's Turban
White Jonathan

TOMATOES

Yellow and Red Pear tomatoes are among the handful of named tomato varieties dating to the early 19th century. Most other heirloom tomatoes, like Ponderosa (1891) and Abraham Lincoln (1923), date from the late 19th century to the 1930's. Victory garden favorites Rutgers and Marglobe are all-purpose types suitable for canning. Mortgage Lifter and Oxheart produce large fruits with thick, meaty walls. For variety, the purple and striped tomatoes add exotic color to summer salads.

HEIRLOOM TOMATOES
Abraham Lincoln
Amish Paste
Arkansas Traveler
Big Rainbow (striped)
Brandywine (left rear)
Burbank
German Johnson
Marglobe
Mortgage Lifter (Radiator Charlie)
Old Fashioned Red Cherry
Oxheart
Ponderosa Pink (Colossal)
Prudens Purple (left front)
Red and Yellow Pear
Rutgers

TURNIPS AND RUTABAGAS

Dinnertime staples during the Middle Ages, these ancient vegetables were brought to the New World with the earliest explorers. The turnips Purple Top White Globe and Purple Top Strapleaf date from the mid 19th century. White Egg has fine-grained white flesh and a pale green crown. All are sweet and crisp when grown quickly. Rutabagas, also known as yellow Swedish winter turnips, were popular root vegetables in the 19th century; slow growers, they should be harvested after frost in the fall.

HEIRLOOM TURNIPS
Purple Top Strapleaf
Purple Top White Globe (far left)
White Egg

HEIRLOOM RUTABAGAS
American Purple Top (left)
Gilfeather

WALLS

Why a wall? Whether you need to mark a boundary, highlight a border, or hold back a slope, a wall adds structure and texture to the garden. Select a material, such as stone or brick, that fits your style and budget. While you can build one yourself, hire a professional for a wall over 3 feet tall or if don't want to deal with mortar. Also check with your building inspector—there may be restrictions on wall size and location.

DRY STONE WALLS

Building your own. A dry, or mortarless, stone wall is the most popular type and is not difficult to build. All you need is stone, a few tools, patience, and a strong back. Figure on 300 pounds of stone for each 2½ cubic feet of wall surface. Use flat, angular, medium-size stones for the wall body. To ensure stability, add some small wedges to fill in crevices and lay several long "tie stones" perpendicular to the lengthwise course.

To shape a stone, first score it with a cold chisel, then lay it on a support and tap with a sledge or mallet until the excess breaks off. For safety, wear goggles and heavy gloves.

Dimensions. Make the width of the wall about one-third of its height; a wall that is 3 feet tall would be 12 inches wide. Set the wall on a gravel foundation that is 1 foot wider than the wall and extends 6 to 12 inches below ground level.

The one-over-two rule. Set each stone of a top course so that it covers the space between two stones below it. Use a cord strung between two stakes as a guide to keep the course straight; check it with a level. Raise the cord each time you begin a course.

A retaining wall needs a slight backward slope, called "batter," so that it can withstand pressure from the earth behind it. Slant the wall 1 inch for every 1 foot in height. Check the angle with a wooden "batter frame" and a plumb bob.

WALL PLANTINGS

Grow a vertical garden. The face and top of a dry stone wall are perfect spots to site trailing or climbing specimens like sweet peas and creeping phlox, which will cascade prettily down the sides.

Starting from seed. Enclose a seed inside a small ball of moist soil. Pack it into a crevice between stones and add

more soil if possible. Keep moist by spritzing with water until the seed germinates and roots become established.

Planting in pockets. If you've left gaps for plants in a new stone wall, you're all set to begin. If you're planting in an existing wall, you'll have to scoop out some of the soil around stones to create a pocket. Add a little soil to the hole and use a chopstick to tuck in the plant roots, dividing them if needed for fit. Firm with more soil mixed with sphagnum moss. Spritz with water to keep moist until roots are established. Spray with liquid fertilizer diluted by half, but don't force growth too quickly.

⇥ A FLOWERING STONE WALL ↤

Some flowering plants are made to order for display on a stone wall. They will soften its heavy look and integrate it with the garden.

PLANTS FOR WALL POCKETS

Basket-of-gold	Sandwort
Bellflowers	Sedums
Candytuft	Sempervivums
Creeping penstemon	Showy primrose
Draba	Soapwort
Forget-me-nots	Thyme
Plumbago	Veronica
Rock jasmine	Violets

PLANTS FOR WALL TOPS

Arrow broom	Rock cress
Catmint	Rock rose
Corydalis	Saxifrage
Cranesbills	Sun rose
Creeping baby's breath	Sweet peas
Creeping phlox	Threadleaf coreopsis
Lavender	Thrift
Moss pink	Wallcress

Mind the microclimate around a wall when selecting plants. The leeward side receives less rain than the windward side. It is also subject to downdrafts as wind is forced over the solid surface, then pulled down. A sunny south-facing wall is good for heat-loving plants, while the north side is better for those that prefer a cool environment.

The weathered look. Give your new stone wall a patina of age by encouraging moss to grow there. Spray the stone with a mixture of 2 cups each chopped moss and buttermilk and 2 tablespoons of corn syrup.

OTHER GARDEN WALLS

Bricklaying is an art. If you want to tackle a brick wall yourself, be sure to keep the wall level and plumb—checking often with a string guide, level, and bob. If you set a brick too high, tamp it into the mortar with the trowel handle. If a brick is not plumb, don't wriggle it around in the mortar; remove it, scrape it off, and reset it.

For a professional finish, use a pointing trowel to bevel the mortar on a brick wall while it's still moist. Give horizontal joints a slight downward slope so they shed water.

Let water drain from a retaining wall built of landscape ties by drilling "weep holes." Use a drill bit at least 1 inch longer than the width of the ties.

Use riprap. To prevent erosion on a moderate slope, construct a retaining wall of riprap—the name

⊱ CHOOSING WALL MATERIALS ⊰

Concrete blocks are relatively inexpensive and easy to work with, but they're heavy and look utilitarian. Dress up the sides with paint or stucco and the top with terra-cotta roof tiles.

Bricks are available in numerous colors, shapes, and textures and offer a tidy, formal look. Use ordinary bricks where they will not be seen and "facing" bricks for the visible surfaces.

Landscape ties are a good, economical choice for low retaining walls and raised beds. They are also easy to handle: simply overlap the corners and secure with galvanized metal pins.

---

given rubble of concrete, brick, and stone. Simply pack the chunks into the soil and plant around them; the plant roots will soon bind the soil around the rubble.

Tone it down. If you cover a cement block wall with masonry paint, which is usually white, keep in mind that it will radiate heat and cause intense glare. Cool it down by planting a climbing vine at the base. English ivy and climbing hydrangea will adhere to the wall; for twining vines like clematis, you'll need to install a trellis first.

A clever cover-up. Conceal an unsightly wall by turning it into a shelter for stacks of firewood. Add a small lean-to with a tile roof to protect the logs from rain.

▷ **Fences, Laws, Moss, Slopes**

WASPS & HORNETS

A hardworking family. Wasps comprise a large family of insects that includes hornets and yellow jackets. All are fierce predators of many common garden pests. Some members of the family, unfortunately, also damage fruit and have a painful sting.

STINGING WASPS

Bag it. Wasps find ripe fruit irresistible. Provide protection by covering fruits with muslin or pantyhose tied at both ends.

Bottled up. Cut the top off a plastic bottle and invert it inside the base to make a funnel; secure with tape if needed. Pour sugared water into the bottle and hang it in a tree. The wasps will climb in to reach the liquid and will either drown or be unable to climb out.

⊱ AVOIDING STINGS ⊰

▷ Don't use scented products, such as perfume, sunscreen, or hairspray.

▷ Don't wear light blue or yellow clothing.

▷ Work in the garden in the morning or evening, when wasps are less active.

▷ Pick fruit when it's ripe—don't leave it on plants or the ground.

▷ Close all garbage cans securely. Don't leave food or drinks out in the open.

▷ Distract wasps by placing a piece of meat or fruit or a saucer of beer at the periphery of your garden or picnic area.

▷ Don't panic—running, flailing, and screaming only agitates wasps.

✺ A GUIDE TO BENEFICIAL WASPS ✺

WASP TYPE	TARGET PESTS	DESCRIPTION
Brachonid	Aphids, codling moths, cutworms, gypsy moths, tent caterpillars, tomato hornworms	Adults ¹⁄₁₆ to ¼ inch long; yellow-red to black; prefer warm weather
Chalcid	Aphids, beetles, caterpillars, leafhoppers, mealybugs, moths, scale, whiteflies	Adults about ¹⁄₁₆ inch long; gold or black; found across North America
Encarsia	Whiteflies	Adults less than ¹⁄₁₆ inch long; used in greenhouses; not hardy below 65°F
Ichneumonid	Borers, cutworms, tent caterpillars, sawflies, webworms	Adults ¹⁄₁₆ to 2 inches long; red-orange; streamlined; able to attack larger larvae
Trichogramma	Armyworms, borers, cabbage loopers, gypsy moths, mealybugs, whiteflies	Adults less than ¹⁄₁₆ inch long; prey on the eggs of more than 200 pests

Let them gorge. Tie a piece of fruit to a stick and suspend it over a bucket of soapy water. Wasps will flock to the bait, eat, and fall to the water too engorged to float. The soap breaks surface tension and keeps the wasps from treading water.

Get them stuck. Sprinkle flypaper with granulated sugar. Hang the strips in fruit trees or wherever you want to trap wasps.

Good riddance. Yellow jacket wasps sometimes build an underground nest with a single entrance. To get rid of the pests, use malathion or carbaryl: simply apply a few squirts into the nest door, then quickly block it with a shovelful of dirt. This treatment works best at night, when the wasps are sluggish. If the wasps are still visible a week later, repeat the treatment.

Bear with them. Yellow jackets and other wasps prey on the larvae of flies, beetle grubs, ants, and caterpillars. If you think their benefit to your garden outweighs the risk of getting stung, don't destroy their papery nests—unless you or someone in your family is allergic to insect bites.

BENEFICIAL WASPS

Tiny helpers. Beneficial wasps are so small —usually less than ¼ inch long—that you might not be able to see them. But you can sometimes find their handiwork. All beneficial wasps are parasitoids: they lay their

eggs on an insect host, usually on eggs or larvae. The developing wasps then form cocoons on the host. If you see a grub or caterpillar with small, ricelike pouches on it, you have beneficial wasps in your garden.

Where to buy them. You can purchase wasp eggs from mail-order insectaries and through some gardening catalogs. Follow the accompanying directions for releasing them: some wasps should be set loose over a period of several weeks. Also be sure that host pests are present in your garden.

Double trouble. Beneficial wasps are most effective when pest populations are low to moderate. Treat severe infestations first with an organic insecticide, then release the wasps 2 weeks later.

Be a good host. Encourage beneficial wasps to stick around by growing the adults' favorite nectar sources. They are especially partial to goldenrod, clover, coreopsis, marguerite, sunflowers, yarrow, coriander, parsley, and tansy.

▷ **Biological Controls, Pesticides, Whiteflies**

WATER BARRELS

Free water. Collect rain and melted snow for use in the garden—it will come in handy during dry spells. Use a wine barrel, trash can, or any watertight container. You can also look in catalogs for special rain barrels with a lid molded to accept a downspout and a spigot for drawing off water.

For crystal-clear water, use a barrel made of an opaque material; otherwise light will penetrate and encourage algae growth. Also cover the container with a lid or board to keep out insects, debris, and pollutants.

A water diverter fitted between two sections of downspout channels water to the barrel as needed. When the barrel is full, flip up the diverter to make gutters work as usual.

Raise your barrel up on bricks or blocks so that you have enough room to draw water from the spigot into a pail. Cover the surrounding ground with gravel or a single layer of bricks—if water splashes out, it won't disturb the soil.

Bury it. If you want to hide the barrel, set it in the ground under a downspout. Position it so that the rim is about an inch above soil level and you can cover the top to keep out debris. When you need water, scoop it out in a bucket or siphon it out with a hose.

▷ **Pantyhose, Watering, Xeriscaping**

WATER PLANTS

The crowning touch. Water plants bring life, color, and beauty to a pond. If your local nursery doesn't carry a good selection, make the extra effort to seek out aquatics. Check in gardening magazines for specialty growers and catalogs. Ask a botanical garden or horticultural society for sources.

Consider your space. Each plant needs a minimum amount of space to thrive. Plan on three to six submerged plants per square foot of surface area. Cover half to two-thirds of the pond with surface plants.

A must-have. No water garden is complete without water lilies. Tropical varieties bear the showiest blooms but tolerate cold only to 40°F. Hardy types have a more subtle appearance but can overwinter outdoors as long as their roots are below the ice level.

For big ponds only. The exotic water platters *(Victoria* spp.)—puckered green saucers with purplish undersides and pink blooms —can reach 6 feet across. Grow only in large ponds and in water 75°F or warmer.

Wait a week after you fill your pond before adding plants. This will allow the water to warm and any chlorine to dissipate.

Newly purchased plants may harbor pest eggs or larvae. Rinse the plants in a stream of water, then immerse the roots in a container of water for 2 weeks. Add to the garden once you're sure the plants are uncontaminated.

Sink or swim. To get a submerged plant into deep water, wrap the roots in a strip of sod tied with twine; weight with a pebble. Toss the plant in the water—it will sink and settle on the bottom.

✺PLANTING A WATER GARDEN✺

Plant your water garden in levels. Some specimens must be completely submerged, while others need their roots underwater and their foliage above the surface. Still others live in the shallows at water's edge.

Submerged plants add a sense of depth to the pond and provide shelter for fish, frogs, and snails. They also absorb minerals and pollutants and release oxygen—keeping the water clean and algae-free.

Surface plants have leaves that float on the pond. They keep water cool, slow evaporation, and offer a resting place for frogs and dragonflies. They reduce algae by preventing light from reaching the water.

Emergent plants root in shallow water or the saturated soil at pond margins. They help hold the soil, provide a frame around the pond, and serve as a habitat for frogs and waterfowl.

Use a basket. Plant a surface plant in a plastic or wire basket with a stable base; line with a permeable fabric to hold in soil. Fill to 1 inch below the rim with garden soil mixed with well-rotted manure. Set in the plant so that its crown is just at soil level; top with 1 inch of gravel. Place the basket at the proper depth for the leaves to float.

Getting centered. To add a plant basket in the middle of a deep pond, wind two long ropes around the rim. Working with a partner, pull the ropes taut to suspend the basket over the water. Lower it into place, then slack off on the cord, letting the plant settle in its new position.

Anchor emergent plants in the soil around ponds or in shallow water. If the muck doesn't hold them down, pin the rootballs carefully with U-shaped wires. Alternatively, set stones around the stems until the roots take hold.

No pond scum. Discourage algae growth by removing all yellowed plant foliage and spent flowers. Cut back on fish food and be sure that garden fertilizer doesn't run off into the pond. Add submerged plants to filter the water. Copper sulfate will control severe algae, but it can also harm plants and fish.

Winter care. Hardy plants can withstand the cold as long as their roots don't freeze. If there's a chance the water will

❧❘ PLANTS FOR WATER GARDENS ❘❦

SUBMERGED PLANTS

Arrowhead *Sagittaria latofolia*
Elodea *Elodea* or *Anacharis canadensis*
Fanwort *Cabomba caroliniana*
Hornwort *Ceratophyllum demersum*
Parrotfeather *Myriophyllum aquaticum*
Sword plants *Echinodorus* spp.

SURFACE PLANTS

Azolla *Azolla caroliniana*
Bladderwort *Utricularia vulgaris*
Riccia *Riccia fluitans*
Salvinia *Salvinia rotundifolia*
Water chestnut *Trapa natans*
Water fern *Ceratopteris pteridoides*
Water lilies *Nymphaea* spp.
Water hyacinth *Eichhornia crassipes*
Water lettuce *Pistia stratiotes*
Water platters *Victoria* spp.
Water poppy *Hydrocleys nymphoides*
Water snowflake *Nymphoides indica*

EMERGENT PLANTS

Arrow arum *Peltandra virginica*
Cattails *Typha* spp.
Flowering rush *Butomus umbellatus*
Lotus *Nelumbo* spp.
Marsh marigold *Caltha palustris*
Pickerel rush *Pontederia cordata*
Sweet flag *Acorus* spp.
Water arum *Calla palustris*
Water irises *Iris pseudacorus, I. versicolor*

freeze down to the pond bottom, lift the plants—especially any tropical specimens. Then store the plants in a cool, frost-free place and keep their soil moist.

A carefree life. Water plants are remarkably untroubled by pests. Squirt off any aphids with a strong stream of water; fish will eat them. If you spot any trails left by leaf miners, cut off the affected foliage. And watch for delta moth larvae, which float on bits of leaves on the surface; simply scoop them out with a net.

Leaf spots are usually caused by fungal diseases. Spray the foliage of affected plants with Bordeaux mixture and remove and destroy infected leaves and stems.
▷ **Pond Life, Ponds**

WATERING

Rule Number 1. Water deeply but infrequently. This delivers moisture down to the plant root zone—usually between 6 and 18 inches deep—and encourages deeper roots, which in turn need less water. One inch of water penetrates about 12 inches in sandy soil but only 4 inches in clay after 24 hours.

An exception to the rule.
The roots of young plants are shallow. Water them lightly and more often than mature plants.

Rule Number 2. Water in the morning. Less moisture will evaporate at the cooler temperatures. Plants will also be able to dry before nightfall—discouraging foliage diseases.

Keep leaves dry. Water only the soil around plants that are prone to fungal infections; these include roses, lilac, phlox, and squash. Getting the foliage wet with overhead watering can cause mildew, as well as fungus and other diseases.

Getting misty. Water both the roots and foliage of evergreens. Their leaves will appreciate having dust and dirt washed away.

A false alarm. Plants often wilt in intense sun, but may not need watering. To avoid overwatering, wait until the next morning. If the plants are still droopy, water then.

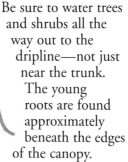

Going to the limit.
Be sure to water trees and shrubs all the way out to the dripline—not just near the trunk. The young roots are found approximately beneath the edges of the canopy.

Roof watering. In arid areas, don't waste a drop of precious water. Locate your foundation plants in the center of broad, shallow depressions, then direct water from the gutter downspouts into the trenches.

Make a custom waterer for a specimen plant. Perforate a 1-gallon plastic jug and bury it near the plant with its spout right at soil level. Fill the jug with water; it will seep out slowly and keep the roots moist.

CONTAINER PLANTS

Use rainwater or melted snow for greenhouse and indoor plants—especially the delicate ones, like orchids. This free water is softer than tap water and free of soil-borne pollutants.

Save the mineral-rich water in which eggs or vegetables were cooked. Allow it to cool, then use it to water potted plants.

Let it sit. Allow water to come to room temperature before using it on houseplants.

Water savers. Use absorbent soil polymers to reduce the need for watering. Add them to the soil when potting up plants. For established plants, insert a straw deep in the soil and drop in a half-dozen crystals. Pull out the straw and repeat several times.

Plant sitters. If you can't water your plants for several days, set up an automatic irrigation system. Place a few pots in a larger container and pack peat moss around them. Saturate the peat moss; it will slowly humidify and water the potted plants. You can also insert one end of a strip of capillary matting into a potted plant and the other in a pan of water.

EQUIPMENT

The right hose. When buying garden hose, look for three- or four-ply vinyl, nylon, or rubber that is reinforced with mesh and rated for high water pressure (up to 500 pounds per square inch). Also look for heavy-duty cast brass couplings.

No-kink storage. Always coil up a hose after use—either over a hose hanger, around a hose reel, or in a cut-down plastic garbage can. It will keep the hose from becoming riddled with unwieldy kinks.

Protect your plants. Dragging a hose through the garden can crush your plants. Run the hose around guides: use either wood or metal stakes or manufactured guides with a lip that prevents the hose from slipping up over the top.

Four in one. If you have only one outside tap and need to hook up several hoses, buy a distributor device. It threads onto the tap and has four connectors for adding hoses.

Oscillating sprinklers can cover large areas—but 25 percent of the water may evaporate before reaching the soil.

A magic wand. Can't reach to water your hanging baskets? Buy a spray wand. The long, light pipe with a rosette head attaches to a hose and extends your reach by 3 feet.

A soaker hose is made from canvas or perforated plastic and seeps or sprinkles water along its entire length, wetting the soil 2 feet on either side. It is especially useful for vegetable garden rows. If you use it for trees and shrubs, circle it around the plant along the dripline. The hose can also be buried up to 1 foot deep; you can leave it in the soil indefinitely.

Low-volume irrigation systems slowly apply water directly to the ground, with no runoff and less evaporation. Water penetration can be controlled by varying the delivery of gallons per hour (gph).

Drip irrigation, using a network of plastic tubes with emitters that drip or spray water along their length, is the most efficient low-volume system. Start with a small kit, sold at garden centers and through catalogs.

▷ **Drought, Water Barrels, Xeriscaping**

WEEDS

What are they? A weed is any plant—even an ornamental—that grows where it's unwanted. Common weeds are fast-growing, resilient nuisances that not only make the garden look unsightly but also steal nutrients from your cultivated plants and serve as hosts for pests and diseases.

How they grow. Weeds can be annual, biennial, or perennial. Annuals and biennials reproduce only by setting seed—but a single plant can yield more than 10,000 seeds. Perennials also spread by roots and stems.

PREVENTION
Shade them out. Weed seeds need light to germinate. To shade the soil around your plants, keep it covered with organic mulch, black plastic or paper mulch, layers of wet newspaper, or a geotextile weed mat.

Build a shield. Use edging materials like bricks or underground barriers of metal or plastic around garden beds. This will keep lawn grass and perennial weeds from creeping into flower beds and vegetable plots.

Solarizing the soil means letting the sun do the weeding work for you. Till up the soil and water it. Lay a sheet of clear plastic over the area, anchor the edges with stones, and wait 4 to 6 weeks: the sun's heat will "cook" weed seeds. If any weeds are found after you lift the cover, rake them up lightly without disturbing the soil.

Till twice. Till the soil the first time to bring buried weed seeds up to the surface, where they can germinate. Wait 2 weeks. Till again, this time with the tiller at a shallower setting. The second tilling will chop up the weeds without exposing more seeds.

Be careful with compost. Toss into the pile any weeds that have not yet bloomed; they have no seeds to spread. Add weeds that have set seed only if the pile heats up

---

⚜ THE TEN LEAST WANTED ⚜

WEED	DESCRIPTION	CONTROL/HERBICIDE
Bindweed	Perennial vine; pointed leaves; twines on plants	Cultivation/2,4–D
Canada thistle	Perennial; lobed, spiny leaves; wide-spreading roots	Mowing/2,4–D; glyphosate
Chickweed	Annual; floppy stems and leaves; blankets the ground	Hand pulling/MCPP; DCPA
Crabgrass	Annual; coarse-textured grass; invades lawns	Mowing/DCPA
Dallisgrass	Perennial; long, coarse grass stems; invades lawns	Cultivation/glyphosate
Dandelion	Perennial; toothed leaves; yellow blooms; in lawns	Hand pulling/2,4–D
Ground ivy	Perennial; lobed, mintlike leaves; creeping habit	Cultivation/2,4–D; triclopyr
Nutsedge	Perennial; grasslike leaves; triangular stems	Cultivation/methanearsonate
Plantain	Perennial; broad round leaves; ground hugging	Hand pulling/2,4–D; MCPP
Purslane	Annual; succulent leaves; purple stems; forms mat	Cultivation/DCPA; 2,4–D

---

to 200°F—the temperature needed to kill seeds. Or start a separate compost pile for weeds; use this compost only in deep planting holes, where seeds can't germinate.

Keep soil covered. Don't let soil remain bare for any length of time—weeds will move right in. If you regrade or remove plantings, blanket the soil with a cover crop, ground cover, mulch, or grass.

Don't mow too short. Letting grass grow to the recommended height shades out weed seeds. It also spurs root growth, which crowds out any emerging weeds.

CONTROL
Slow on the trigger. Don't automatically reach for the sprayer to treat lawn and garden weeds. A combination of elbow grease, ingenuity, and tools will usually do the job.

Buy a dandelion digger, which has a sharp, notched end that will pry up stubborn weeds with taproots. You can also buy weeding tools with hoe-like blades and short handles; they're good for slicing weeds off below the surface.

Water before weeding. Weeds are easier to pull with their root systems intact if the soil is moist. Also, neighboring plants are less likely to be disturbed or damaged.

A close shave. Use a hoe to shave the tops off weed seedlings by keeping the head parallel to the ground and pulling shallowly in the soil. Digging down can bring weed seeds to the surface and compact soil.

Take it all. Be sure to remove any part of the weed that can regenerate. Wild garlic grass will regrow from little bulblets, plantains have persistent taproots, and quackgrass can resprout from its deep, spreading root system.

Sprinkle salt on weeds that sprout in paved areas or wild patches. But don't use it around your desirable plants.

Pour it on. Drench weeds growing up through the cracks in paving stones or bricks with boiling water. Some old-time gardeners insist that water from boiled potatoes is even more effective.

HERBICIDES

Start gently. Always try a product with low toxicity, such as an organic herbicidal soap, before using harsher poisons.

Keep cans separate. Reserve a single watering can, a sprayer, and measuring implements for using only with herbicides.

Direct focus. Be extremely careful when applying herbicides. Direct the product only at the weeds—not at desirable plants. Also make sure that there are no obstructions in a sprayer nozzle that could cause liquid herbicide to squirt out at an angle. Wait for a calm day to apply the chemicals so that wind doesn't carry the spray or granules to an unintended location.

Be weather-wise. Herbicides work best when temperatures are mild (70° to 80°F) and the soil is moist. Don't apply sprays before a rain, which will wash them away.

An ounce of prevention. Use a pre-emergent herbicide on the lawn to keep weeds from sprouting and work it into cultivated soil before installing plants. It's especially useful in new patches of ground cover.

❧| HERBICIDE LINGO |❧

Learning the language of herbicide labels lets you buy the product appropriate to your task.

Selective herbicides (2,4–D; methanearsonate) destroy only certain types of plants but leave others unaffected.

Nonselective herbicides (glyphosate) will destroy any plant it touches.

Contact herbicides (diquat) act only on plant foliage that they touch.

Systemic herbicides (triclopyr; dicamba) are absorbed by the roots or foliage and spread through the plant.

Pre-emergent herbicides (DCPA, trifluralin dichlobenil) are applied to lawns or cultivated soil to prevent weed seeds from germinating.

Post-emergent herbicides (MCPP, MCPA, fluazifop-butyl) are applied to weeds that are already growing.

Toxic-free zone. Because a tree's roots are concentrated under the canopy, don't use herbicides to kill any weeds there. Instead, remove the weeds manually and cover the soil with an organic mulch.

Don't risk runaways. Take care when applying herbicides on the top of a slope if desirable plants are located below. Water runoff could carry the poisons where you don't want them to go.

You've poisoned a plant by accident? If so, water it immediately and thoroughly to flush out the chemicals. Continue watering daily for a week to limit the damage.
▷ **Geotextiles, Invasive Plants, Mowing, Spraying, Toxic Plants, Undergrowth**

WHITEFLIES

Know your enemy. Tiny whitefly adults (about ¹⁄₁₆ inch long) resemble moths with white, powdery wings. Shake the stems of a plant you suspect is infested. If a white cloud rises, the plant has whiteflies.

Watch for whiteflies outdoors as soon as the weather warms; they attack many vegetables and ornamentals. Indoors, look for them in fall, when they come in from the cold; they particularly like chrysanthemums and poinsettias. Affected plants have yellowing, sticky foliage and may become covered with a black mold that grows on the honeydew secreted by whiteflies.

Attract and repel. Nicotiana or catnip (*Nepeta cataria*) lure whiteflies away from other plants, where you can destroy them. To repel, try marigolds or nasturtiums.

Choose a cure. Control whiteflies by wiping plant leaves with cotton dipped in diluted rubbing alcohol. Or spray with insecticidal soap, pyrethrum, or garlic cloves mashed in water.

Smoke them out. Rid a greenhouse of whiteflies by burning dry oak leaves in a clay flowerpot. Place the pot on damp soil or another fireproof surface and close all of the air vents. Let the leaves burn for about 30 minutes, adding more if needed.

Suck them up. Use a small hand-held vacuum to scour whiteflies off leaves—or even out of the air—as they hover over plants.

A welcome wasp. The wasp *Encarsia formosa* attacks and destroys whitefly larvae; it works best in the greenhouse. Lacewings and ladybugs are also good predators.

Try seaweed. Dig kelp meal into the soil around infested plants and spray the foliage as needed with liquid kelp.

Sticky traps. To monitor for whiteflies and reduce their numbers, hang a yellow card covered with an adhesive, such as Tangletrap, over infested plants or seed flats; whiteflies will fly up and get stuck. The larger the card, the better—a yellow file folder is ideal.
▷ **Garlic, Pesticides, Wasps & Hornets**

A vibrant touch of the wild

The joy of gardening with wildflowers comes from creating landscapes that reflect the natural beauty of the varied parts of our country. A garden made up of plants native to a particular region becomes a living testament to the diversity of the American landscape.

Like any other kind of gardening, growing wildflowers requires work and care, including soil preparation, watering, and maintenance. Although native plants as a whole tend to be hardier and more robust than many of our cultivated plants, they perform well only if you follow the old gardening rule of putting the right plant in the right place. To take advantage of the innate hardiness of these plants, it is important to place them in their accustomed environment—a meadow for sun-loving plants, for example, or a shady glen for woodland wildflowers.

Some gardeners shy away from wildflowers because they fear they may look "too messy." But many of our native species are ideal for using in a wide variety of landscapes: some plantings can even have a manicured, formal look if they are carefully maintained.

As the popularity of wildflowers has increased, so too has the abuse of native plant populations. The lure of the wildflower has resulted in the collection of thousands of wild plants for selling through the nursery trade— a plight that will ease only when there is no longer a market for these illegally collected species. Be an informed consumer and make sure that the native plants you purchase have been grown in a nursery, not dug in the wild.

WILDFLOWER MEADOW

Ox-eye daisy

A meadow is a grassland area that supports a profusion of wildflowers. Even though transforming a pasture or an expanse of lawn into a meadow is an idea that has gained favor of late, it has also resulted in much frustration among gardeners. But with proper seed bed preparation, sufficient water and weed control, and the use of plants native to your own region, a wildflower meadow can be an excellent, easy-care alternative to high-maintenance turf or flower beds.

Plant a meadow in spring or fall—just before the rainy season. Start your site preparation 6 weeks before planting, tilling the area 6 to 8 inches deep. Wait 3 weeks for any weeds to germinate, then apply a general herbicide to eradicate them; wait another 2 weeks for the herbicide to dissipate. Sow the wildflower seeds

New England aster

evenly, using the recommended rate. Rake them into the soil lightly and tamp down with a roller or board. Water regularly between rains until plants are mature. Once the meadow is established, weed out intruders and reseed bare spots with your favorite flowers. Mow meadows to a height of 6 to 8 inches in late fall.

Wildflowers that will grow in most areas of the country are suggested below. All need at least 6 to 8 hours of sunlight a day.

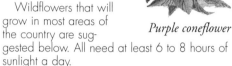

Purple coneflower

Annual coreopsis *Coreopsis tinctoria*
Black-eyed Susan *Rudbeckia hirta*
Butterfly weed *Asclepias tuberosa*
California poppy *Eschscholzia californica*
Goldenrod *Solidago odora*
Indian blanket *Gaillardia pulchella*
Lance-leaved coreopsis *Coreopsis lanceolata*
New England aster *Aster novae-angliae*
Ox-eye daisy *Chrysanthemum leucanthemum*
Purple coneflower *Echinacea purpuea*
Swamp sunflower *Helianthus angustifolius*

DECIDUOUS WOODLAND

Nothing announces spring's arrival more beautifully than the pastel petals of delicate woodland plants found on the forest floor. Your own woodland garden should match the conditions found in a natural wooded site: shaded protection from the summer sun; rich, moist soil with a high proportion

Virginia bluebell

of humus; leaf litter for mulch; and dappled sunlight in the spring, which will bring out the best blooms as the plants begin to peek aboveground. Most woodland plants prefer acid soil; to provide it, work chopped oak leaves or compost into the soil before planting.

Although sun-loving wildflowers are easily grown

Monkshood

from seed, most woodland plants grow slowly; it is usually preferable to use small, nursery-grown plants to establish your woodland garden.

The woodland plants listed below are native to many regions of the country. All require moist, slightly acidic soil and moderate watering.

FOR THE EAST
Bloodroot *Sanguinaria canadensis*
Columbine *Aquilegia canadensis*
Foamflower *Tiarella cordifolia*
Mayapple *Podophyllum peltatum*
Solomon's seal *Polygonatum biflorum*
Spring beauty *Claytonia virginica*
Trout lily *Erythronium americanum*
Virginia bluebell *Mertensia virginica*
Wild geranium *Geranium maculatum*
Wild ginger *Asarum canadense*

FOR THE WEST
Columbine *Aquilegia formosa*
Fawn lilies *Erythronium oregonum*
Monkshood *Aconitum columbianum*
Twinflower *Linnaea borealis*
Wild ginger *Asarum caudatum*

ROCK GARDEN

Cascading over boulders or tucked into rocky crevices, hardy wildflowers add a variety of colors and shapes to a sunny rock garden. A multitude of plants—from tiny alpine flowers to low-growing coastal shrubs—can survive the rigorous environment of a rock garden, with its shallow beds,

Shooting star

gravelly soil, and scant protection from the elements.

A slope or hillside provides a natural spot to establish a rock garden, particularly if your yard has natural rocky outcrops or ledges. When choosing plants, mimic a natural area as closely

Iris douglasiana

as possible; include not only tiny, ground-hugging wildflowers but dwarf conifers and branching shrubs as well.

The native plants listed below are recommended for sunny rock gardens in most parts of the country. If you can't find certain plants through the nursery trade, try collecting seeds from plants you admire in the wild.

FOR THE EAST
Firepink *Silene virginica*
Fringed gentian *Gentiana crinita*
Iris *Iris cristata*
Phlox *Phlox pilosa*
Shooting star *Dodecatheon meadia*
Wild lupine *Lupinus perennis*

FOR THE WEST
Iris *Iris douglasiana*
Lupine *Lupinus nanus*
Penstemon *Penstemon davidsonii*
Phlox *Phlox nana, Phlox hoodii*
Shooting star *Dodecatheon alpinum*
Sulphur flower *Erigonum umbellatum*

WILDFLOWER GARDENS

WILDFLOWER GARDENS

BOG GARDEN

COASTAL GARDEN

The edge of a pond or swamp provides a unique environment for any number of lovely native plants, including marsh marigolds (above).

Cardinal flower

If you don't have a natural bog site, you can create one. Dig out the soil to a depth of about 9 inches. Remove any large branches, sharp stones, and rubble, then line the hole with heavy black plastic. Scatter pebbles over the plastic on the bottom of the bog and then shovel in the backfill after enriching it with compost or well-rotted manure. Keep the area thoroughly watered during dry weather.

Because bog

Canada lily

plants are not true water plants, they don't like to be submerged; instead, make sure their heads are in the sun and their feet are kept wet.

The plants listed below are found in boggy areas all over the country. If you have a large site, add tall plants to attract nesting marsh birds; be aware, however, that one such choice—the common cattail—is such a vigorous grower that it may take over the garden.

Canada lily *Lilium canadense*
Cardinal flower *Lobelia cardinalis*
Cattail *Typha latifolia*
Cinnamon fern *Osmunda cinnamomea*
Iris *Iris* spp.
Joe-pye weed *Eupatorium maculatum*
Marsh marigold *Caltha palustrus*
Royal fern *Osmunda regalis*
Skunk cabbage *Symplocarpus foetidus*
Swamp geum *Geum rivale*
Swamp milkweed *Asclepias incarnata*
Wild calla *Calla palustrus*

Seashores offer challenging environmental conditions for the gardener. High winds, salt spray, occasional salt-water, and poor, alkaline soil make living conditions difficult for growing plants.

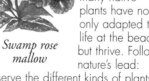

Swamp rose mallow

Nevertheless, many native plants have not only adapted to life at the beach, but thrive. Follow nature's lead: observe the different kinds of plants that grow in your area, as well as their locations. Small spreading grasses and wildflowers, for example, grow closest to the open beach, with shrubs and trees found farther back.

Seaside plants play an important role in stabilizing sandy soils and stemming erosion. For this reason, provide plant coverage for as much bare ground as possible.

FOR THE EAST
Beach head iris *Iris Hookeri* or *I. Setosa*
Beach pea *Lathyrus japonicus*
Bluff wallflower *Erysimum franciscanum*
Indian blanket *Gaillardia pulchella*
Leopard's bane *Arnica acaulis*
Sand verbena *Abronia umbellata*
Sea lavender *Limonium carolinianum*
Seaside goldenrod *Solidago sempervirens*
Swamp rose mallow *Hibiscus palustris*
Wax myrtle *Myrica cerifera*

FOR THE WEST
Farewell-to-spring *Clarkia amoena*
Iris *Iris douglasiana*
Mule ears *Wyethia angustifolia*
Wax myrtle *Myrica californica*
Wild peony *Paeonia californica*

Seaside goldenrod

PRAIRIE RESTORATION

DESERT

American prairies once stretched from the Rockies east to Ohio and Kentucky. Today only small pockets of original prairie remain. These areas, found in cemeteries or along old railways, are reminders of the beauty of this once-vast land of rolling grasses and colorful wildflowers.

Prairie smoke

Although most gardeners lack the resources to reproduce large prairie areas, it is possible to plant a small prairie garden. The key is to use only those native plants that have a proven ability to thrive in your region. To plant, choose an area that gets at least 6 to 8 hours of sun a day. Work the soil until it is loose enough to create a seed bed, then sow seeds in spring or fall. Keep

Switch grass

the bed watered until plants are well established—usually 2 to 3 weeks. Keep invasive weeds under control: they can destroy the delicate balance of the prairie plant community.

Fires were an integral part of prairie life; where legal, controlled burning every 3 to 4 years is still an effective method of controlling weeds and improving the soil. Good prairie garden choices are listed below.

FLOWERS

Beardtongue *Penstemon digitalis*
Black-eyed Susan *Rudbeckia hirta*
Ironweed *Vernonia altissima*
Pasque flower *Anemone patens*
Phlox *Phlox pilosa*
Prairie coneflower *Ratibida columnaris*
Prairie gayfeather *Liatris pycnostachya*
Prairie goldenrod *Solidago pallida*
Prairie smoke *Geum triflorum*

GRASSES

Big bluestem *Andropogon gerardii*
Side oats grama *Bouteloua curtipendula*
Switch grass *Panicum virgatum*

The desert is one of the most inhospitable places on earth: an environment of extremes of temperature, long periods of drought, and strong, merciless winds. The fact that beautiful, exotic flora can thrive in this climate is a never-ending miracle.

Blazing star

A gardener can never tame the desert but can learn to work with it. If you live in a desert region, grow the native plants that thrive there, which have learned to adapt to these extraordinarily difficult conditions.

Because desert soils are often saline, it's advisable to perform a soil test before you plant. If soil proves to be high in salt, water heavily at

Moth mullein

planting time and again 3 or 4 times a year afterwards; doing so helps leach the salt out of the soil.

It is best to transplant nursery-grown seedlings of native desert plants into the garden. If these aren't avaiable through the nursery trade, buy or collect seed from the plants native to your region, then grow them indoors until they are ready to set out in the garden.

The plants listed below are adaptable to many desert environments.

Barrel cactus *Ferocactus acanthodes*
Blazing star *Mentzelia lindleyi*
Century plant *Agave parviflora*
Coral bean *Erythrina flabelliformis*
Desert marigold *Baileya multiradiata*
Moth mullein *Verbascum blattaria*
Pink sand verbena *Abronia umbellata*
Prickly pear cactus *Opuntia* spp.
Queen of the night *Peniocereus greggii*
Saguaro cactus *Carnegiea gigante*
Sulphur flower *Eriogonum umbellatum*
Yucca *Yucca schidigera*

WILDFLOWER GARDENS

WIND

A temporary solution. To protect plants from wind damage during a storm, make a windbreak out of plastic screening. You can buy it by the roll from a lumberyard or garden supply store. Install stakes or posts on the windward side of the garden and tie or

staple the screening to them. A simple windbreak of this sort can reduce the force of the wind by as much as 60 percent.

The double whammy. Another windbreak, 15 feet windward of the first, can reduce wind force an additional 75 percent.

Know its reach. A windbreak can shelter a distance 10 times its height. A 3-foot-high wall protects plants 30 feet away. A 5-foot stand of evergreens will reduce wind velocity for a distance of about 50 feet.

For a permanent windbreak in a cold climate, plant trees and shrubs in two or more rows. To create a natural look, plant in a slightly curved row instead of a straight line. Space tall, dense evergreens, such as

WHAT NOT TO PLANT

If you live in a windy area, you can avoid problems and disappointments by not planting the following types of trees and shrubs.

▷ Large-leaved specimens like catalpa, paulownia, and rhododendron. The leaves are apt to be badly torn by a windstorm.

▷ Brittle trees such as silver maple, poplar, or Siberian elm; they can crack in heavy winds.

▷ Pollen-producing trees such as hickorys, oaks, and elms; the wind can widely distribute allergy-causing pollen.

▷ "Messy" trees like poplars and willows; the seed pods they shed will become a nuisance on a nearby patio or terrace.

Douglas fir or spruce, as a background and fill in the front with flowering shrubs—perhaps lilacs, hydrangeas, or crape myrtles. This living screen will protect downwind garden plants from winter cold and keep them from drying out.

Lower bills! An evergreen windbreak on the side of the house that faces prevailing winds can reduce heating costs by as much as 20 percent. The dense row of trees slows cold breezes before they can penetrate openings around window and door frames.

Use deciduous trees to shield a cold or temperate garden on the south side. In full leaf they will provide summer wind protection for flowers, vegetables, and fruits. In winter, when the branches are bare, they will allow the sun into a chilly garden.

Save the trees. When landscaping a new yard, keep as many of the existing trees as you can for wind protection. If you decide to replace old trees with new ones, do it gradually over a few years.

Will deep planting help? Not in all cases, since many plants won't tolerate it. Instead of trying to anchor your plants, plant at the recommended depth and support tall specimens with stakes or cages. As extra insurance, erect a barrier on the windward side.

Bundle baby trees. To minimize wind damage, cover the trunks of newly planted trees with commercial tree wrap, available at garden centers, or strips of burlap. The wrapping can be removed after the trees are established—usually within a year.

Let it through. In areas where high windstorms are common, prune deciduous trees so that strong winds can pass through their branches without doing damage. Remove the small interior branches to allow space for the wind. Carefully executed, such pruning can also enhance the appearance of the tree.
▷ **Balcony Gardens, Exposure, Protection**

WINDOW BOXES

PURCHASING
Wood's the word. Boxes made of cedar or other weather-resistant lumber insulate plant roots from heat and cold better than metal or plastic. Paint them a light color on the outside to reflect heat. Treat the inside to protect the wood against the rotting and warping that results from contact with wet soil; use a copper-based product, such as Cuprinol, which won't harm the plants.

Insulation for metal boxes. Before filling a metal box with soil, insert a sheet of styrofoam on the side exposed to afternoon sun. Or you can set a smaller box inside the larger one and pack the space between the two with peat moss. Keeping the soil cool will promote more vigorous growth.

❧ SEASONAL CHOICES ❧

Flowers are the stars of window boxes in spring and summer. In fall, other additions provide interest, while in winter you can create a display with cut branches and ornaments.

EARLY SPRING

Crocus	Hyacinth
English primrose	*Narcissus cyclamineus*
Glory-of-the-snow	Sweet violet

SUMMER

Annual salvia	Impatiens
Cascading lobelia	Ivy
Cascading petunias	Miniature
Geraniums	snapdragons

FALL

Bittersweet	Ornamental kale
Colchicum	Ornamental corn
Chrysanthemums	Sedum
Dried flowers	Small pumpkins

WINTER

Evergreen foliage	Pinecones wired to
Christmas ornaments	branches
Holly branches	Strung cranberries

Heavy but tough. Boxes of cast cement are heavy, but are well insulated and almost indestructible. Make sure they have good drainage and are securely fastened.

Proper drainage. Drainage holes should be 6 to 9 inches apart and about ½ inch in diameter. Line the box bottom with an inch or so of lightweight material, such as crushed brick bits or styrofoam peanuts.

The right size. Window boxes that are too large can become too soil-heavy, while those too small won't let the plants develop and thrive. The ideal box is 3 to 4 feet long, 10 inches wide, and 8 inches deep. The wooden boards should be at least 1 inch thick to prevent warping.

PLANTING

Make a light mix. Plain garden soil is too heavy and drains too slowly for a window box. Prepare your own mix by combining equal parts of garden soil, peat moss, and perlite; add a slow-release fertilizer. Or use one of the packaged soilless mixes sold at nurseries and garden centers.

Consider all dimensions for window box plantings, choosing varieties that will add height, fullness, and depth. Cascading or trailing plants such as periwinkle, petunia, and nasturtium are particularly attractive additions and will soften the box edges.

Which window? Almost any window is a candidate for a window box if the box can be secured to the sill and you can tend it easily from inside the house. Choose plants appropriate for the exposure—full sun, partial shade, or full shade.

For shady windows, pick proven shade-tolerant plants. Try primroses, crocuses, daffodils, pansies, periwinkle, ivy, winter jasmine, and dwarf rhododendrons in the spring. Summer possibilities include begonias, trailing lobelia, fuchsias, impatiens, asparagus and other ferns, grasses, strawberry begonias, and hydrangeas.

Plant small conifers in the back of flower boxes on exposed, wind-prone balconies or terraces. Place the conifers to face the wind so that they'll protect the more delicate plants in front.

A kitchen window box. If the exposure is sunny, you can grow herbs such as thyme, chives, parsley, sage, or sorrel just outside the kitchen window. If the window box is at least 16 inches deep, you can also plant lettuce and dwarf varieties of beans, cabbage, and other vegetables.

Flowers hard to reach? Choose self-cleaning plants for your box. Flowers that simply drop by themselves—impatiens, nasturtiums, and certain varieties of ivy and geraniums—will save you the chore of deadheading.

MAINTENANCE

Watering tips. To encourage deep rooting, water window box plants until the water drains out of the bottom. On hot, windy days, when evaporation is high, a box may need watering both morning and night. When you water at night, be sure to wet only the soil and not the foliage.

Feeding. In the close quarters of a window box, plants compete for the available nutrients in the soil and rapidly deplete the supply. Apply a complete fertilizer regularly; a water-soluble type is a good choice.

Change the soil. Because a window box's soil quickly becomes exhausted, it needs annual replacement. Remove the old soil in your boxes every spring and mix a new batch, tailoring the planting medium to the plants you've chosen to grow.

A refresher for houseplants. In the warmer months, take your indoor houseplants outdoors to occupy the window boxes on the shady side of the house.
▷ **Dwarfs, Hanging Baskets, Planters**

WIRE

A coat hanger hook. Use a wire cutter to cut off the hook of a hanger at its base, then secure it to the end of a pole or broomstick with duct tape. Use it to pull the vines out of trees or to pull down any out-of-reach branches on fruit trees.

A coat hanger cold frame. To protect potted cuttings, bend two 12-inch sections of hanger wire into arcs. Cross them and insert into the pot, leaving headroom for the cuttings and their future growth. Cover the wire frame with shade cloth or a plastic bag. Set the pot in a shady spot and water as needed.

Wire for cut flowers. To keep long-stemmed flowers upright, insert green florist's wire into the stems to stiffen them. Alternatively, crumple a piece of chicken wire into a ball and put it into the vase.

A durable trellis. A trellis made of wire strung on wall nails is stronger than string and lasts from season to season. You can train an annual vine to the same piece of wire fencing year after year.

Use wire fencing—preferably with a 4-inch mesh—to tie up tomatoes, pole beans, and cucumbers in the vegetable garden.

Extend a fence. Keep burrowing animals from attacking your garden by extending your fence with an equal length of chicken wire. Dig a narrow trench and set in the wire, attaching it to the bottom of the above-ground fencing with plastic ties, then refill the trench.
▷ **Espaliers, Trellises**

WISTERIA

Pretty but pushy. Wisteria is a fast-growing climbing vine that produces heavily scented cascades of white or lavender blooms in late spring. But it is also a willful beauty that can quickly outgrow its bounds and latch onto gutters, shingles, and shutters. Be aware that wisteria can literally pull apart all but the strongest trellis.

A good spot. Don't plant wisteria near your house, trees, or utility lines, where it could become a nuisance. Instead, train it to twine along a strong fence or over a stone wall.

Feed young wisteria extra fertilizer to help it become established. Mature plants bloom better without supplements.

Pruning schedule. Regular and careful pruning not only keeps wisteria contained but also promotes next year's blooms. Clip after flowering

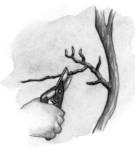

in summer by cutting off the long, stringy shoots to 6 inches, leaving six leaves (the buds form on short spurs); prune again in winter, shortening the shoots to 3 inches with three buds. Also snip off any side shoots emerging from the base of the trunk.

Train as a tree. You can train wisteria as a standard by staking it upright and pruning the top heavily for years. The stem will eventually grow to trunklike proportions.

Root-prune wisteria vines that fail to flower; forcing roots to branch out encourages flower bud formation. Use a spade to cut a circle about 4 feet in diameter (smaller for young vines) and 2 to 3 feet deep around the trunk, cutting off any roots you encounter there.

A different spin. Chinese and American wisterias twine up a support from left to right; Japanese and Formosan wisterias twine from right to left.

◈ A WISTERIA SAMPLER ◈

Japanese wisteria is the most fragrant and has flower clusters that open first at the base and then gradually to the tip. An old favorite is 'Longissima,' with flowers in white or violet. Chinese wisteria is less fragrant but blooms more spectacularly: the flowers open on the cluster all at one time. Try the lovely violet 'Caroline.'

▷ **Climbers, Standards**

XERISCAPING

What is it? *Xeros* is the Greek word for dry: thus "xeriscaping," landscaping that requires very little, if any, supplementary water. Ideally, a xeriscape garden is built with plants that naturally thrive on the normal rainfall of the region.

Savings. Xeriscaping saves in two ways. After your plants have become "conditioned"—usually about 2 years—you won't have to spend time watering. A drip irrigation system will also save on water bills.

PLANNING

Not all desert. Xeriscaping doesn't limit your garden to cacti and rocks. On the contrary, a well-designed xeriscape can be eye-catching and lush all year. If you limit the size of the garden, you can set aside a small portion for vegetable and cutting gardens, which demand more water.

Go easy on the gravel. Avoid desert xeriscapes with large areas of gravel and only a few succulents for interest. Such a

ⅷGOOD CHOICES FOR ARID CLIMATESⅷ

Whether your xeriscape garden is in a warm or cold part of the country, you can pick dryland species and others—both native and exotic—that will adapt well to xeriscaping. Start with the list below.

WARM CLIMATES

EVERGREEN TREES	DECIDUOUS TREES	SHRUBS	PERENNIALS
Afghan pine	Crape myrtle	Bird of paradise	African iris
Eucalyptus	Desert willow	Fairy duster	Alyssum
Holly oak	Jacaranda	Indigo bush	Aspidistra
Scotch pine	Olive	Natal plum	Autumn sage
Sweet acacia	Palo verde	Oleander	California poppy
Wright's acacia		Texas ranger (*Leucophyllum frutescens*)	Lantana
			Lavender cotton
			Rosemary
			Verbena

COLD CLIMATES

EVERGREEN TREES	DECIDUOUS TREES	SHRUBS	PERENNIALS
Austrian pine	Black locust	Adam's-needle yucca	Aster
Eastern red cedar	Bur oak (*Quercus macrocarpa*)	Amur privet	Columbine
Ponderosa pine	Golden-rain tree (*Koelreuteria paniculata*)	Butterfly bush	Evening primrose
Scotch pine		Cotoneaster	Flax
	Green ash	Japanese barberry	Snow-in-summer
	White ash	Littleleaf mock orange	Yarrow
		Pyracantha	
		Rugosa rose	

spare layout offers no respite from the sun; in fact, it raises temperature by radiating heat back into the environment.

A welcome relief. A trickling fountain is a refreshing addition to a xeriscape garden in the hot, dry areas of the Southwest. Even the sound of splashing water is restful. A recirculating pump keeps water use to a minimum.

Lawn is allowed. Lawns require more water than most ground covers, but you can save water by confining your turf to a single focal point off the patio or between flower beds. Choose dryland grass species that need less water—tall fescues, blue grama, and buffalo grass; adjust your mower so that you don't cut the blades too short. Elsewhere in the garden, replace your lawn with drought-tolerant ground covers, such as common yarrow, Portuguese broom, and sea thrift.

Annuals adaptable to xeriscaping in both warm and cold climates include marigolds, cockscomb, African daisy, dusty miller, gazania, moss rose, sunflowers, and zinnias.

PLANTING

Establishing plants. Hill soil around the base of new trees and shrubs to create a water-catching basin. Water infrequently and deeply to encourage deep roots. After 2 years, you can knock down the basins and install a low-volume irrigation system.

Raise them high. Dryland plants do best in raised beds that shed excess water. Work with the plant's natural defense against drought by mixing an absorbent amendment like pumice into the bed. After a rain, plants will absorb water released by the pumice long after the soil has dried.

Peat moss worked into the soil will make bare-root dryland plants root faster.

Zone your xeriscape garden according to the water needs of the plants. Group those that need more moisture, for example, where they can benefit from the runoff water from downspouts, driveways, and patios. Put plants that don't need full sun under the dappled shade of tall trees; this will keep down the soil temperature and minimize the need for water.

Planting rules. Put plants in the ground just before the rainy season to take advantage of whatever natural precipitation you get. Space them far enough apart so that roots will have plenty of room to spread and won't have to compete for moisture.

MAINTENANCE

Use mulch. By keeping soil temperatures cool, a 2- or 3-inch layer of organic mulch significantly reduces water loss.

Low-volume irrigation systems operate at low pressure and deliver a low but steady amount of water. They include soaker hoses, controlled drip emitters, miniature sprayers and sprinklers, and root irrigators that soak the soil beneath the surface.

Install a timer. Electronic timers are available that will water your garden whether you're at home or away. Invest in one and hook it up to your low-volume system.

▷ **Cacti & Succulents, Drought, Heat, Watering**

YEW

An all-round favorite. Yews *(Taxus* spp.) are among the world's most popular needle-leaf evergreens. Hundreds of species and cultivars are available, ranging in size from 40-foot columnar trees to sturdy, dense shrubs good for hedges and 2-foot spreading shrubs wider than they are tall.

No wet feet. Yews are accommodating plants that grow in sun or shade, tolerate temperatures as low as -30°F, and rebound from drastic pruning. If their roots sit in soggy soil, however, they turn yellow, drop their needles, and die. Nor do yews like the humidity of a subtropical climate.

A natural hedge. Instead of pruning a yew hedge into a formal, rigid shape, you can let it go natural. In either case, check to make sure that the cultivar you choose won't grow too large in the long run.

Time to prune. Cut back either in early spring, before new growth starts, or in late summer, after new growth hardens off.

🦜 A YEW SAMPLER 🦜

The English yew *(Taxus baccata)* is the least hardy species but has many cultivars excellent for warm climates. The Japanese yew *(T. cuspidata)* is more adaptable; cultivars range from the 1-foot-high 'Aurescens' to the 40-foot pyramidal 'Capitata.' *T. × media* is a hybrid of English and Japanese yews and has the largest choice of cultivars. Try 'Hicksii,' which grows into a narrow, tall tree, or the popular 'Densiformis,' a thick shrub ideal for hedges.

Propagating yews. New plants can be rooted from hardwood cuttings taken in fall or early winter. Dip cuttings in a strong rooting hormone, shake, and insert them in moist sand or a peat and perlite mixture at room temperature. Water only when the medium dries out. Rooting should occur within 2 to 3 months.

▷ **Hedges, Shrubs**

YUCCA

Tough and resilient, the yucca can put up with drought, heat, cold, and poor soil and still produce spectacular creamy white flowers once a year. Its many varieties are grown in gardens, on patios and terraces, and in sunrooms throughout every part of the country; some species are hardy to 0°F.

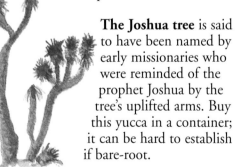

A polite pool pal. Because yucca leaves die down and remain attached to the trunk, they won't fall off and dirty the water of swimming pools and ponds.

The Joshua tree is said to have been named by early missionaries who were reminded of the prophet Joshua by the tree's uplifted arms. Buy this yucca in a container; it can be hard to establish if bare-root.

Dry leaf tips? Don't worry. They are common to yuccas and do not indicate an illness or infestation.

A healthy yucca has no spots on the leaves at its center. If you do see spots, they indicate bugs or fungus. Treat by spraying the plant with malathion or a fungicide.

Watering. When temperatures rise above 85°F, you can give yuccas a little water and watch them thrive. When the weather cools, however, water only every 2 weeks.
▷ **Cacti & Succulents**

ZINNIAS

An easy annual. Sow zinnias in peat pots about 4 weeks before the last frost is predicted; seeds will sprout in 4 to 5 days. Harden off the seedlings for a few days in a cold frame or other sheltered place before setting them out. Then plant, peat pots and all, directly in the ground; zinnias don't like to have their roots disturbed.

Thin them out. When seedlings have three pairs of leaves, thin them out. Remove the weakest seedlings, leaving 6 inches between smallest varieties, 10 inches between medium-size ones, and 18 inches between the tallest types.

"Cut-and-come again" was an old name used for zinnas, which respond enthusiastically to cutting. Deadheading fading flowers and cutting fresh ones for

display will keep the plants amazingly prolific. Choose buds that are just about to open and cut them early in the day. Before putting them in a vase, strip off the lower leaves, which can quickly deteriorate.

Don't wet the leaves. Zinnas like moist soil but are subject to mildew. To prevent the problem, keep the leaves dry.

Apply a 5–10–5 fertilizer, scratching it carefully into the soil around the plants. It will improve the quality of the blooms and increase their number.

A hidden enemy. Stalk borers may tunnel into zinnias. Cut open the affected stems and dig out the intruders. If treated right away, the plant will probably survive.

▷ **Flower Beds**

ZUCCHINI

Prepare yourself. Zucchini are famous for producing more squash than even a large family can use. If your climate is conducive to such a surplus, take extra produce to a soup kitchen or share it with your friends.

To get an early crop, sow zucchini indoors in late April in the North or 3 weeks earlier in the South. Transplant

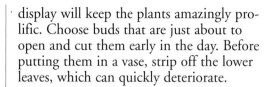
the seedlings to a sunny part of the garden a month later to be ready for a harvest by the fourth of July.

When to harvest. Pick fruits when they measure from 4 to 6 inches long. Once they've grown past 8 inches, their skin hardens and their flesh is full of seeds.

Bush-type plants, such as 'Ambassador,' 'Aristocrat,' 'Butterstick,' and 'Seneca Milano,' take up less room than the older vining varieties and don't need staking. Other popular compact types are 'Long Green Striped' and 'Zucchini Select.'

Round zucchini. Scan your catalogs for 'Ronde de Nice,' a round heirloom variety the size of a tennis ball. It makes a unique side dish when stuffed with bread crumbs.

Try courgettes. Zucchini are called courgettes in much of the world. In America, the term is usually applied to baby zucchini, whether young fruits or dwarf cultivars. Harvest courgettes at 2 to 3 inches with the flowers still attached; slit them lengthwise and sauté lightly. Look for 'Type 1406,' a seedless Swiss variety.
▷ **Squash, Vegetable Gardens**

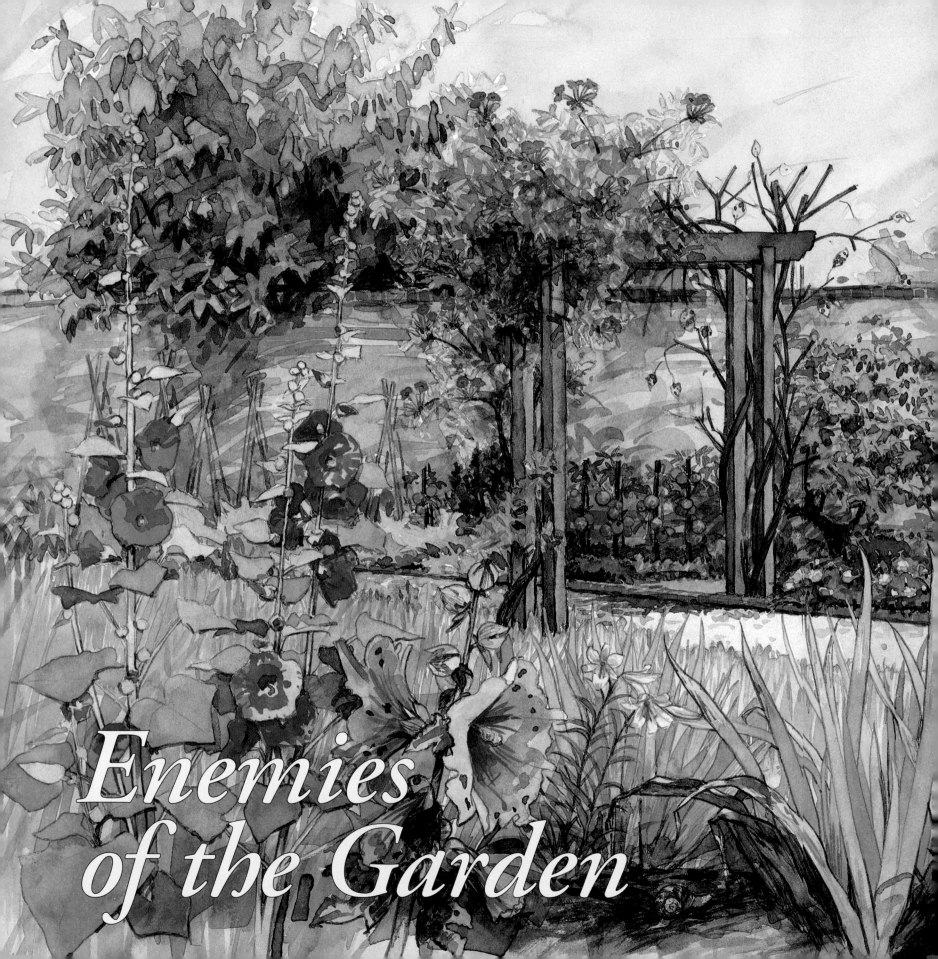

*Enemies
of the Garden*

Meet the enemies of your garden: the pests and diseases that can wreak havoc on growing plants. But you need not suffer these unwelcome visitors gladly. For nearly every blight or mold or hungry caterpillar there exists a viable deterrent. Keep in mind that time of year, climate, and location can determine whether a pest will show up at all; check with your local Cooperative Extension Service to learn which problems are most likely to occur in your area.

The following pages help you identify common intruders in gardens and tell you how to control them; each is keyed to one of the symbols shown below. When a quick solution is called for, don't be afraid to use the recommended pesticides: all lean toward the environmentally friendly. Just follow the manufacturer's instructions to the letter and keep containers stored safely away.

Disease

Pest

Physiological disorder

LEAVES WITH VISIBLE PESTS

DISFIGURED LEAVES

APHIDS

Everywhere in the garden, orchard, and greenhouse

Plants affected Many—especially roses, fruit trees, artichokes, beans, cabbage, and lettuce.

Symptoms and causes Colonies of small black, green, pink, brown, yellow, or grayish globular insects—most without wings—can be found under leaves or at the ends of branches. Infestation is promoted by new or rapid growth of plants.

Treatments As a preventive, apply only a moderate amount of nitrogen fertilizer. Spray with pyrethrum, rotenone, malathion, or insecticidal soap. Do not treat if ladybugs or aphid lions (lacewing larvae) are present; instead, pinch off or prune affected parts. Washing foliage during watering will also reduce aphid populations. Monitor with yellow adhesive traps.

WHITEFLIES

Common indoors in the North, outdoors in the South

Plants affected Many ornamental plants; green peppers, tomatoes, eggplant, cabbage, geraniums.

Symptoms and causes Look for small white-winged flies on the undersides of leaves or fluttering about the plants. High humidity and warm temperatures promote infestation. Plants from commercial greenhouses are usually the source.

Treatments Check nursery-bought plants for infestation. Spray with insecticidal soap or pyrethrin and repeat as needed. Monitor with yellow traps coated with an adhesive such as Tangletrap. In a greenhouse, introduce their natural enemy, *Encarsia formosa,* a parasitic wasp.

LEAF-CURLING PLUM APHIDS

Look for visible pests and honeydew

Plants affected Plum trees.

Symptoms Young leaves are curled up; aphids are present on the undersides. Honeydew secreted by aphids is present on leaves.

Treatments As soon as symptoms appear, spray with malathion, rotenone, or insecticidal soap. The removal of young, aphid-infested plant shoots on the inside of the tree will reduce future aphid populations.

SCALE INSECTS

Found on fruit trees and other trees and shrubs

Plants affected Many trees and shrubs—especially lilacs, cotoneaster, euonymus, magnolias, and pines.

Symptoms and causes Look for small brown, gray, or whitish shields that are flat or globular, circular or elongated, and waxy or floury; they will be especially visible on young shoots and leaves. Wingless females are carried to new plants by the wind or on birds' feet.

Treatments Late in the dormant season, spray with dormant oil; if young crawlers are present, spray with malathion. Indoor plants can be treated by using a soapy sponge on leaves and stems; rinse plants after application.

MEALYBUGS

Among the most damaging pests on flowers and shrubs

Plants affected Houseplants and many fruit trees, vegetables, and shrubs.

Symptoms Look for small pink insects or white, cottony masses on leaf axils. Sooty mold (p.342) grows on the sticky gel exuded by the bugs.

Treatments Isolate newly purchased plants until you are sure they are free of mealybugs. Use a cotton swab dipped in a solution of rubbing alcohol and water to remove any you see. Alternatively, wipe the leaves with a sponge soaked in soapy water, then rinse off with water.

BLACK CHERRY APHIDS

Often found on young cherry trees

Plants affected Fruiting and ornamental cherries.

Symptoms Black aphids can be found on the undersides of leaves. Sooty mold (p. 342) and honeydew make the foliage sticky and give it a dull blackish color.

Treatments As soon as symptoms appear, spray with malathion, rotenone, or insecticidal soap. Do not treat if ladybugs or aphid lions (lacewing larvae) are present; instead, remove aphid-infested plant shoots on the inside of young trees to reduce the population.

CYCLAMEN MITES

Tiny arachnids that rarely cause serious damage

Plants affected Mainly begonias, dahlias, ferns, fuchsias, gerbera, potted cyclamen, gloxinia, geraniums, African violets, and other greenhouse plants. Also strawberries.

Symptoms Plant leaves are small, deformed, curled, or crumbly. They may blister and are often abnormally rolled up at the edges.

Treatments Check nursery-bought plants for infestation. Replace affected plants or spray with a dicofol-based miticide.

RUSSIAN HONEY-SUCKLE APHIDS

Evidenced by witches'-broom foliage

Plants affected Many honeysuckle species are susceptible.

Symptoms Diseased leaves are folded flat at mid-vein; tiny aphids appear inside the folds. In the fall and winter, the tops of honeysuckle shrubs turn brown, with a witches'-broom appearance.

Treatments Prune out dead foliage from the tops of shrubs to keep aphid eggs from overwintering. At the first sign of leaf-folding on terminal growth, begin spraying new foliage with an acephate insecticide. Repeat in 4 weeks.

GALL MITES

Strange little outgrowths on the leaves of trees

Plants affected Mainly linden and maple trees.

Symptoms and cause Galls appear as a small oval or spherical red rash erupting on the tops of leaves; they are caused by mite larvae inside. Gall mites feed throughout the summer and emerge from leaves in the fall.

Treatments The galls are more alarming than harmful. There is no need for treatment. You may cut off and destroy affected parts.

ROSE LEAFROLLERS

Evidenced by tattered or rolled foliage

Plants affected Roses.

Symptoms and cause Much or all of a leaf has been eaten, except for the main vein. Leaves may be rolled along their entire length. Caused by black-headed green larvae.

Treatments Spray bushes every 2 weeks in May with rotenone, Orthene, or an acephate insecticide. In June, remove and burn all infested leaves.

APPLE APHIDS

Look for visible pests and honeydew

Plants affected Mainly apple, pear, and hawthorn trees.

Symptoms Young leaves are blistered or curled and often have yellowish or reddish coloring. Aphids appear at the ends of plant shoots and on the undersides of leaves.

Treatments As soon as symptoms appear, spray with malathion, rotenone, or insecticidal soap. Use a dormant oil to control overwintering eggs on the twigs. The removal of young, aphid-infested plant shoots on the inside of the tree will reduce future aphid populations.

LEAF GALLS

Unpleasant-looking rashes on the leaves of trees and shrubs

Plants affected Oak trees and some species of roses and willows.

Symptoms and cause Galls resembling peas, cherries, silk buttons, or soapflakes are visible on the foliage. These outgrowths—sometimes solitary but often found in groups—are caused by microscopic fly larvae.

Treatment The galls are more alarming than harmful. There is no need for treatment. You may cut off and destroy affected parts.

FOLIAR NEMATODES

A leaf-infesting nematode species

Plants affected Mainly ferns, begonias, lilies, chrysanthemums, gloxinias, orchids, verbena, African violets.

Symptoms and cause Indications include discolored angular- to wedge-shaped blotches or stripes in leaves. Malformed or stunted growth is common; leaves may die, starting at the plant's base. The causal nematodes overwinter in dormant buds, growing points, and dead leaves.

Treatments Buy disease-free, certified transplants. When symptoms appear, remove and burn infected indoor plants; cut off and burn tops of outdoor plants at season's end. Apply dry mulch, avoid overhead watering, and eliminate weeds to prevent reinfection.

FUSARIUM WILT OR YELLOWS

Most prevalent in warm and hot climes

Plants affected Mainly cabbage, celery, peas, cucumbers, eggplant, melons, peppers, sweet potatoes, tomatoes, China asters, carnations, chrysanthemums, cyclamen, gladiolus, lilies, narcissus, petunias, sweetpeas, and zinnias.

Symptoms and cause Plants are usually stunted and turn yellow at the stem base. Foliage and flower heads wilt, wither, and die. Dark streaks appear in the vascular tissue when stems are cut lengthwise. The causal fungi are active at temperatures above 75°F.

Treatments There is no cure. Purchase and plant healthy stock in virus-free, fertile, well-drained soil. If possible, choose resistant varieties. Avoid using seeds of diseased plants.

OAK WILT

The most serious disease of oaks

Plants affected All oak trees, including tan-bark; most chestnut and chinquapin trees.

Symptoms and causes Leaves in the upper crown and on branch ends of red oaks and black oaks turn pale green, bronze, or tan. Leaves drop early. Dark streaks appear in sapwood. Some leaves of white oaks and bur oaks turn light brown and curl but don't drop. Fungus is spread by sap-feeding beetles and root grafts.

Treatments There is no cure. Avoid wounding trees while pruning; if wounds do occur, cover with tree-wound dressing. Prune oaks only in late fall or winter. Sever root grafts between diseased and healthy trees mechanically or chemically. Remove and burn or bury diseased oaks.

VERTICILLIUM WILT

A serious problem, primarily in the West

Plants affected Mainly eggplant, melons, okra, pepper, potatoes, tomatoes, raspberries, strawberries, carnations, China asters, chrysanthemums, geraniums, roses, maple trees, and redbuds.

Symptoms and cause Leaves on part of the plant are pale or will wither and die. Dark streaks often appear in vascular tissue when stems are cut lengthwise. The causal fungus thrives at 70°–75°F but is retarded at higher temperatures.

Treatments Control is difficult. Remove and destroy entire plant or affected parts if disease spreads. Grow resistant species of tomatoes and strawberries. Control weeds. Fertilize and water regularly to promote vigorous growth.

DUTCH ELM DISEASE

Has almost wiped out elm trees

Plants affected American and other elms.

Symptoms and causes Leaves wilt, turn yellow, then brown on whole branches. Entire tree may die in several weeks or months. Dark streaks form in outer sapwood of wilted branches. The causal fungus is transmitted by either elm bark beetles or root grafts of diseased stock.

Treatments A community-wide program is needed to remove all dead, weak, and dying elms. Burn all injured, weak, and dead wood from trees or from the ground. Treat sick elms by injecting the lower trunk with Arbortect or a carbendazim-based fungicide. Replant with a resistant variety or species of elm or another type of tree.

BACTERIAL WILT

Plants wilt and die for no apparent reason

Plants affected Mainly cabbage, cauliflower, beans, cucumbers, eggplant, muskmelons, peanuts, peppers, potatoes, sweet corn, tomatoes, canna, carnations, petunias, and wallflowers.

Symptoms and cause Plants are often stunted and droop, wilt, wither, and die. Caused by sticky masses of bacteria that enter through insect, mechanical, or nematode wounds, plugging water-conducting tissue.

Treatments Collect and burn any infected plants. Control insects. Select resistant varieties to plant, and rotate crops 2 to 6 years or longer, excluding susceptible crops and weeds. Grow garden plants in disease-free, well-drained, fertile soil.

PINE WILT DISEASE

A widespread problem—and growing worse

Plants affected Mostly two- and three-needle pines, especially Scotch. Very rarely found on other evergreens.

Symptoms and cause Needles change from healthy green to grayish green, then to brown. Trees die within a few weeks or months. The disease is caused by microscopic nematodes; the nematodes are transmitted by large sawyer beetles, which feed on pine shoot tips.

Treatments Prune dead branches from live trees. Promptly remove dead trees at the soil line or below and burn or bury the wood. Replace with spruce, Douglas fir, hemlock, or white pine.

LEAF CURL OR BLISTER

A major problem for peach trees

Plants affected Mainly peach, almond, apricot, cherry, plum, and nectarine trees.

Symptoms and cause Large reddish, yellowish, or purplish blisters form on puffy, puckered leaves, causing leaves to drop prematurely. The causal fungus overseasons in the bud scales.

Treatments Apply a single dormant oil spray in late fall, winter, or early spring before buds break open, using any fungicide in a multipurpose home fruit spray; apply when temperature is 40°F or above. Promote the regrowth of healthy foliage by regular fertilizing and watering.

CLUBROOT

Root is distorted by fungus

Plants affected Mainly cabbage, broccoli, cauliflower, Brussels sprouts, mustard, and turnips.

Symptoms and cause Leaves wilt, wither, and drop prematurely on hot, dry days. Plants remain stunted and yellowish due to masses of distorted, warty swellings on roots. The causal fungus can survive for more than 20 years in soil; it is disseminated by infected plants, manure, soil on shoes, and garden tools.

Treatments Set out only certified, healthy transplants. Destroy diseased plants and their roots. If necessary, apply fresh hydrated lime 6 weeks or more before planting to achieve a soil pH of at least 7.5; work into top 4 inches of soil.

ASTER YELLOWS

Plants are stunted and yellowish

Plants affected Mainly China asters, chrysanthemums, gladiolus, phlox, zinnias, carrots, celery, lettuce, onions, potatoes, and tomatoes.

Symptoms and causes Yellowing and stunting of young growth can occur. Plants also become stiff, with a tight curling and rosetting of leaves. Floral organs are distorted and rarely form seed; flower petals may be green. Carrot roots are hairy and bitter tasting. The disease is caused by mycoplasmalike (MLO) bacteria, which are transmitted by infected aster leafhoppers.

Treatments Control is difficult, so promptly destroy any infected plants. Grow indoor crops under tight cloth or wire screening. Weeding and an insecticide spray may prove effective.

LATE BLIGHT

A serious fungus in cool, wet climates

Plants affected Potatoes and tomatoes.

Symptoms and cause Leaves have blotches of dark green to black-purple and soon turn brown and die. A white mold appears on leaf undersides in cool, damp weather. Tomatoes are dark green, brown, or black and appear wrinkled or greasy. Potato tubers have brown spots and dry, reddish-brown stains; a reddish-brown stain appears in the flesh. The causal fungus is *Phytophthora*.

Treatments Apply fungicides containing Bravo, maneb, mancozeb, or copper before flowering or when damage is first seen; repeat every 7 to 10 days. Destroy any debris after harvest. Keep down weeds and control insects.

ROOT-KNOT NEMATODES

Galls on roots weaken plants

Plants affected Some 2,000 herbaceous plants.

Symptoms and cause Leaves are yellowish; plants lack vigor and are often stunted. In severe cases, plants wilt in dry weather, then recover briefly before withering and dying. Small to large galls cause roots to become swollen or distorted. The causal soilborne nematodes are generally found in light, sandy Southern soils and in indoor plants grown in non-steamed soil or soil mix.

Treatments Plant disease-free nursery stock, leaf and stem cuttings, and certified vegetable transplants. Keep weeds down, work well-decomposed compost into the soil, and fertilize and water regularly. Use Nemacur as a soil drench.

SOUTHERN BLIGHT

A serious problem in warm regions

Plants affected Many vegetables. Also irises, tulips, chrysanthemums, delphiniums, narcissus, and peanuts.

Symptoms and cause A girdling infection at or below the soil line causes lower leaves to turn yellow and wilt; shoots die back. A cottony mold grows over the crown, roots, and surrounding soil in damp weather. Small, white bodies (sclerotia) of the causal fungus turn dark brown to black and form on the infected tissue and nearby soil.

Treatments Solarize moist soil with transparent polyethylene plastic during the summer. Rotate susceptible plants with sweet corn and deeply bury surface debris. Before planting, apply a nitrogen fertilizer containing ammonium.

CHLOROSIS

Common where soil is rich in lime

Plants affected Mainly pin oaks, sweet gums, and pine trees. Also blueberries, strawberries, camellias, gardenias, hydrangeas, lilies, rhododendrons, and mountain laurel.

Symptoms and causes Young leaves turn light yellow to almost white. Discoloration is often caused by a lack of iron in the plant and excessive lime in the soil.

Treatments Avoid growing susceptible plants in soil with a pH of 6.0 to 7.0 or higher. Acidify the soil by working in regular amounts of sulfur (¾ pound per 100 square feet). Water several times, at 3-week intervals, with a solution of iron sulfate (3 tablespoons to 1 gallon). Or apply a commercial iron chelate compound used in alkaline soils.

MAGNESIUM DEFICIENCY

Not a problem in most garden soils

Plants affected Mainly apple, cherry, and peach trees. Also blueberries, grapes, potatoes, sweet potatoes, camellias, and roses.

Symptoms and causes Mature leaves and lower leaves turn yellow or bright red between the veins, which stay green. As the condition worsens, leaves become brown and wither. This deficiency is most common in deep, sandy, acid soils in wet seasons, and where sodium and potassium are excessive.

Treatments After a soil test, apply dolomitic limestone, magnesium-containing fertilizer, or Epsom salts in a regular fertilizer mix. Beginning in the spring, spray foliage with a magnesium sulfate solution (1½–2 tablespoons per gallon) at 10- to 15-day intervals. Spray three to five times.

PINE SHOOT MOTHS

Evidenced by stunted terminal growth

Plants affected Pine trees and shrubs.

Symptoms and cause New "candles" on pines turn pale green, twist or crook, then die. Severe infestations can prevent growth. The problem begins in spring, when moths lay eggs on the buds of new growth. Worms then hatch from the eggs; before maturing, they eat into the bases of new shoots.

Treatments The damaged candles on mature, full-size trees and shrubs can be pruned by hand or simply left alone. Spray young trees and shrubs at the first appearance of new damage—usually in June; use either dimethoate or acephate.

COLD INJURY

Affects several plants at the same time

Plants affected Mainly cucumbers, melons, peppers, tomatoes, morning glories, and sweet peas.

Symptoms and cause Young leaves on affected plants suddenly turn white or pale yellow in color. This ailment occurs in spring whenever nighttime temperatures drop close to 32°F.

Treatments Avoid cultivating during cold periods—especially when nights are clear—to prevent cooling the soil. Protect young plants by covering them with a cloche, plastic tunnel, or floating row cover. Fertilize and water to promote new growth.

NITROGEN DEFICIENCY

Plants become weak and pale

Plants affected Fruiting trees and bushes, shrubs, vegetables, and flowers.

Symptoms and cause Leaves and stems of affected plants do not develop fully. Young leaves are pale yellow-green and dry to a light brown. The cause is a lack of nitrogen in light soils that are low in organic matter.

Treatments Work well-decomposed compost or manure (6 pounds per 10 square feet) into the soil in the fall. In the spring, apply a high-nitrogen synthetic or organic fertilizer over the root zone and water in well.

PEAR LEAF BLISTER MITES

Red blisters on leaves

Plants affected Pear and mountain-ash trees.

Symptoms An abundance of pustules—green, brown, or sometimes red in color—appear on both sides of the leaves.

Treatments To prevent infestations, dust emerging foliage with sulfur or carbaryl. The damage from mites is rarely severe.

GALL ADELGIDS

Insects very similar to aphids

Plants affected Mainly pine, Douglas fir, larch, and spruce trees.

Symptoms and cause Undersides of needles and axils are infested by colonies of small, dark aphidlike insects that are partially covered with white waxy tufts. The needles turn yellow and are disfigured. On spruce trees, the damage resembles pineapple-shaped galls at the branch tips.

Treatments In the event of major infestation, spray in late fall with a dormant oil. Spray when aphids are present with malathion or diazinon.

RED OR TWO-SPOTTED SPIDER MITES

Microscopic specks on fine webbing

Plants affected Apple, peach, plum, and pear trees. Also houseplants, grapes, and conifers.

Symptoms and causes Leaves become finely mottled with bronze and gradually dry out. Light webbing and microscopic eight-legged spiders are seen on the undersides. Treatments using a non-miticide insecticide promote infestations, as do hot, dry conditions.

Treatments Avoid systemic insecticides. In the greenhouse, release a mite predator such as *Phytoseiulus persimilis*. Or spray with a dicofol or bifenthrin acaracide.

LEAF SCORCH

Margins of leaves are discolored

Plants affected Trees with tender foliage—especially beech, horse chestnut, and maple—and most indoor and greenhouse plants.

Symptoms and causes Edges of indoor or greenhouse plant leaves turn tan to completely brown; excessive sunlight and heat will scorch leaves. Chilly spring winds or hot, dry summer winds can cause leaf scorch in outdoor plants.

Treatments Plant in wind-protected sites. In the greenhouse, provide shade; indoors, put plants in a spot with less sunlight. Fertilize and water to increase vigor.

ONION THRIPS

Often called oat bugs or oat lice

Plants affected Onions, shallots, leeks, cabbage, and small grains such as oats.

Symptoms and cause Leaves are finely mottled and sometimes appear disfigured or shriveled, with a silvery appearance. Thrips increase in number under hot, dry conditions.

Treatments Spray and water plants frequently as a preventive measure. In case of an infestation, apply sprays containing carbaryl, malathion, or diazinon.

LEAFHOPPERS

Tiny, wedge-shaped insects are visible

Plants affected Rhododendrons, roses, asters, potatoes, snap beans, carrots. Also maple and redbud trees and many greenhouse plants.

Symptoms and cause Small white spots appear on the leaves, which subsequently become pale, with the edges turning brown and curling. Wedge-shaped insects can be observed sucking plant sap from foliage.

Treatments For major infestations, spray with carbaryl, rotenone, or malathion.

SOOTY MOLD

A black coating of fungus on foliage

Plants affected Mainly apple, citrus, plum, oak, linden, magnolia, and tulip trees. Also camellias, crape myrtles, gardenias, and roses.

Symptoms and cause A superficial dark brown to blackish growth covers leaves, fruits, and stems. Sooty mold fungi grow on honeydew secreted by sucking insects like aphids and scale insects.

Treatments Treat as for aphids, scales, and white-flies. Rubbing the affected areas with a cloth dipped in soapy or plain water will easily remove the mold.

ANTHRACNOSE

Fungi common during wet springs

Plants affected Ash, dogwood, linden, maple, oak, sycamore trees, and others.

Symptoms and cause Brownish areas, which may follow the veins, appear on leaves, often causing them to drop prematurely. Anthracnose diseases are the result of fungi that attack plants in damp weather.

Treatments Start with healthy plants. Keep them vigorous by properly fertilizing, watering, and pruning. Where feasible, spray foliage of small trees three or four times, 10 days apart, starting just as the buds are opening; use a fungicide that contains maneb, mancozeb, Daconil, Zyban, or Domain.

SCAB

Most serious disease to affect apple trees

Plants affected Mainly apple, crab apple, hickory, pecan, and pear trees. Also pyracanthas.

Symptoms and causes Crustlike areas develop on leaves, stems, and fruit, starting as olive-green but later turning a dark brown to blackish color. Scab fungi infect in damp weather.

Treatments Keep plants well-spaced, pruned, fertilized, and watered. Request resistant varieties when purchasing. During the growing season, spray three to six times, seven to 10 days apart, starting at budbreak. Apply a fungicide containing captan, Daconil, maneb, mancozeb, Zyban, or Domain. Follow local recommendations.

SPITTLEBUGS

"Spit" is repulsive but harmless

Plants affected Mainly lavender, chrysanthemums, roses, goldenrod, asters, willows, junipers, and strawberries.

Symptoms and cause Small insects, or nymphs, of spittlebug species are covered by frothy masses of "spit" and are found among the leaves. The nymphs come in many colors but are usually pink.

Treatments The nymphs do little damage, but the spitlike appearance can detract from a plant's appeal. Masses can be removed with a brush, broom, or strong stream of water.

ROSE BLACK SPOT

Most serious fungus disease for roses

Plants affected All species of roses.

Symptoms and cause Black roundish spots develop on leaves, which then turn yellow and drop prematurely. The causal fungus enters the leaf's underside.

Treatments Buy top-quality, disease-free plants of resistant varieties. Prune canes close to the ground in the fall, then burn discarded canes. Spray the foliage every 7 to 10 days, starting shortly after new growth appears. Use triforine, maneb, mancozeb, Daconil, Zyban, or Domain fungicides. Separate resistant varieties from susceptible ones.

RUST

Easily identifiable by powdery masses

Plants affected Mainly apples, crab apples, plums, pine, anemones, chrysanthemums, holly-hocks, roses, snapdragons, and sweet William. Also asparagus, beans, mint, and raspberries.

Symptoms and cause Yellow, orange, or brown powdery masses develop on affected leaves and stems, and sometimes on the flowers and fruit. Leaves wither and fall early. The causal fungi are active in damp weather.

Treatments Ask for resistant varieties. Space plants and grow in a sunny site. Spray at about 10-day intervals in warm, damp weather, treating as for rose black spot (p. 342). Follow local recommendations.

BOTRYTIS BLIGHT OR GRAY MOLD

A gray mold appears in damp weather

Plants affected Practically all flowering herbaceous and woody plants.

Symptoms and cause Spots that are tan to brown, followed by a fuzzy gray mold, form on succulent leaves, stems, buds, fruit, seedlings, and aging flowers. The causal botrytis fungi are active in damp, cloudy weather.

Treatments Space plants in well-drained soil in a sunny location. Carefully collect and destroy affected parts. Spray regularly with a fungicide containing Ornalin, Curalan, Daconil, Bravo, Zyban, mancozeb, Domain, or Chipco 26019. Follow local recommendations.

POWDERY MILDEW

A familiar problem for many gardeners

Plants affected Practically all fruits, vegetables, flowers, trees, and shrubs.

Symptoms and causes Superficial white coatings that are powdery to mealy appear on leaves, buds, shoots, flowers, and fruit. Powdery mildew fungi infect during warm, dry days and cool, damp nights wherever air circulation is poor.

Treatments Avoid overcrowding and damp, shady locations. Spray several times, 7 to 14 days apart, starting when mildew first appears. Use triforine, Bayleton, sulfur, Stripe, Zyban, Domain, or benomyl. Follow local recommendations. Give plants as much sun as possible.

VIRUS DISEASES

Degeneration occurs over months or years

Plants affected Practically all fruits, vegetables, flowers, trees, and shrubs.

Symptoms and cause Foliage is irregularly mottled with light and dark green or yellow stripes, blotches, or blisters. Leaves are often puckered, crinkled, curved, or cupped. Flowers may be deformed or show streaks and blotches. Plants may be stunted and bushy. Growth is poor and degenerates in succeeding years. Viruses are transmitted by sucking and biting insects and by propagating from infected plants or seeds.

Treatments There is no cure. Plant only resistant varieties of nursery stock and seed or plants certified free of viruses. Control insects. Pull up and burn diseased plants. Keep down weeds.

WHITE RUST

White pustules on lower leaf surfaces

Plants affected Mainly beets, broccoli, Brussels sprouts, cabbage, mustard, horseradish, spinach, and sweet potatoes. Also alyssum, candytufts, morning glory, and sweet alyssum.

Symptoms Pale yellow areas form on the leaf's top surface. Powdery, often glistening pustules develop on undersides of the leaves and sometimes on stems and flowers.

Treatments Start by using disease-free seed or plants. Carefully remove and destroy affected parts. Varieties differ in resistance, so check before buying. Not a very common problem.

SCLEROTINIA ROT, WHITE MOLD, OR WATERY SOFT ROT

A problem in damp weather and wet soil

Plants affected Mainly beans, cabbage, carrots, lettuce, and peas. Also chrysanthemums, dahlias, delphiniums, and narcissus.

Symptoms and cause Leaves and stems rot at the base and are covered with a fluffy white mold. The entire plant turns yellow and wilts. Bean-shaped black bodies (sclerotia) of the fungus form in the white mold and pith of infected stems. The fungus overwinters in soil and plant debris.

Treatments Rotate vegetables and flowers. Avoid overcrowding. Destroy diseased plants, including the roots.

DOWNY MILDEW

Most damaging in humid, mild weather

Plants affected Mainly grapevines, broccoli, cabbage, cauliflower, cucumbers, lettuce, melons, onions, peas. Also wallflowers.

Symptoms and cause Blotches on leaf tops change color from pale green to yellow and then brown. White to gray or purple mildew forms on the undersides of leaves, which may wilt and die. Mild, moist weather allows the fungi to thrive.

Treatments Fertilize with well-decomposed compost. Sow disease-free seed in well-drained soil. Plant resistant varieties of grapes, crucifers, and lettuce. As a preventive, spray in wet weather every 10 days with copper, maneb, mancozeb, Bravo, or Daconil fungicides. Thwart weeds. Destroy plant debris after harvest.

CATERPILLARS

Found everywhere in the garden

Plants affected Many garden, fruit, and ornamental plants or trees—especially cabbage, broccoli, apple trees, oaks, and pines.

Symptoms and cause Often more than one generation of these pests appears per year. Leaves are cut and tunneled through; sometimes they are completely eaten. Web nests may be present.

Treatments Treat with a spray or dust formulation of *Bacillus thuringiensis* (Bt) when feeding is first noticed. Sprays containing rotenone or carbaryl are also effective.

SLUGS AND SNAILS

Evidenced by slimy mucous trails

Plants affected Many—especially young tulips, hostas, lilies, sweet peas, delphiniums, lettuce, and strawberries.

Symptoms and causes Leaves are irregularly eaten. Mucouslike slime trails are visible. Humid conditions and damp mulch encourage infestation.

Treatments Spread metaldehyde-based attractant bait near infested plants. Slugs and snails are also attracted to beer—even when it is flat. Pour beer into containers placed firmly in the ground around plants; the pests will crawl in and drown. Empty and renew the contents every 3 days.

PLANT BUGS

Many species of juice-sucking insects

Plants affected Mainly apple and pear trees, dahlias, hydrangeas, cabbage, and beets.

Symptoms and cause Leaves are blistered with small holes or discolored spots and subsequently become deformed and wither. The pests responsible are also known as leaf bugs and are not a serious garden problem.

Treatments Spray with a rotenone- or carbaryl-based insecticide when bugs are numerous and causing damage.

BEAN LEAF BEETLES

Holes appear in new leaves

Plants affected Mainly garden beans, including snap, wax, and lima.

Symptoms and cause Irregular round holes appear in the first leaves of emerging bean plants. Various brown, tan, or red beetles, with or without spots, feed on plants. Beetles may be beneath leaves or found in or on soil.

Treatment If much of the foliage is damaged or missing, dust or spray with a carbaryl- or rotenone-based insecticide. One treatment per crop season is adequate.

CUCUMBER BEETLES

Yellow-and-black beetles eat holes in leaves

Plants affected Vine crops, including squash, pumpkins, melons, and cucumbers.

Symptoms and cause Beetles, which are striped or spotted yellow with black markings, feed on emerging plants or defoliate older plants. A bacterial wilt may also be transmitted to susceptible plants as beetles feed, causing the infected plants to suddenly wilt and die.

Treatments Dust or spray infested plants—especially cucumbers and melons—with rotenone or carbaryl as they grow. Repeat as necessary. Compost old vines or bury them after harvest.

WEBWORMS

Caterpillars feeding inside webbing

Plants affected Trees, shrubs, and herbaceous plants—especially apple, cherry, currant, holly, rose, privet, and honey locust.

Symptoms and cause Young leaves are eaten and drawn together with silk webbing, then rolled up.

Treatments Spray with *Bacillus thuringiensis* (Bt) or a carbaryl-based insecticide.

FLEA BEETLES

Look for shiny, hopping beetles

Plants affected Mainly cabbage, turnips, radishes, sugar beets, potatoes, eggplant, and horseradish. Also sweet alyssum.

Symptoms and cause Cotyledons and young leaves are pitted with tiny holes. Tiny hopping beetles that are shiny, bright, black or striped appear on the foliage. Infestations are most common under hot, dry conditions.

Treatments Water beds regularly and provide shade with a canopy. Spray or dust with a carbaryl-based insecticide.

APHIDS

These pests are almost impossible to avoid

Plants affected A wide variety, especially roses, beans, artichokes, and apple trees.

Symptoms and cause Colonies of aphids, also called plant lice, proliferate on young shoots. Honeydew and sooty mold are often present.

Treatments Wash off foliage with a stream of water. Remove excess infested foliage from a tree's interior. Spray with insecticidal soap, rotenone, or malathion.

COLORADO POTATO BEETLES

Sometimes alarming, yet very localized

Plants affected Mainly potatoes, tomatoes, and eggplant.

Symptoms and causes Leaves are partially or completely eaten by yellow and black striped beetles, as well as by yellow larvae with black spots.

Treatments If there are only a few infested plants, pick off and dispose of insects. Otherwise, dust or spray with carbaryl, rotenone, or *Bacillus thuringiensis* (Bt).

SHOT-HOLE DISEASE

A problem for many stone fruits

Plants affected Mainly peach, almond, apricot, cherry, plum, nectarine, and cherry laurel trees.

Symptoms and causes Small spots that are reddish to purple or brown or black in color first appear, then drop out of leaves, resulting in their shot-hole appearance. Leaves often turn yellow and wither. The problem is caused by various fungi, bacteria, and viruses or spray injury.

Treatments Prune, fertilize, and water to maintain vigor. Plant virus-free stock. A homemade fruit spray that contains captan or Daconil is a good preventive. Spray following local guidelines.

SOFT BROWN SCALE

Close to the same color as their host

Plants affected Mainly citrus trees, olive trees, and indoor and greenhouse plants. Also gardenias and oleander.

Symptoms and cause Old shoots usually are infested with colonies of immobile or slow-crawling insects that have a waxy brown or yellow scale or a shield-shaped shell.

Treatments Prune infested shoots. Treat with an insecticidal soap or malathion spray. Clean infested leaves and stems with a soapy cloth or sponge. Rinse with clean water afterward.

RODENTS

Rabbits, moles, gophers, and voles

Plants affected Young trees and vegetables, including cabbage, lettuce, and peas.

Symptoms Bark is eaten on the trunks of woody plants at or near ground level. Transplants and other vegetable plants are eaten.

Treatments Protect young trees with metal mesh wrapped around the trunk. Apply a thiram-based repellent on or near affected plants. Protect vegetables from feeding rodents with a buried fence around the border.

CUTWORMS

Plants chewed off at the soil line

Plants affected Mainly young plants, but also lettuce, chicory, tomatoes, and brassica crops.

Symptoms and cause Gray caterpillars attack plants by eating them at ground level; can be found curled up under the plants or in the soil.

Treatments Eliminate weeds. Use direct seeding rather than transplants. Spray with a *Bacillus thuringiensis* (Bt)-based insecticide. In addition, dust or spray with carbaryl at the base of plants.

EUROPEAN RED MITES

Early-season mites on trees

Plants affected Mainly apple, plum, peach, pear, and walnut trees.

Symptoms and cause Round eggs of brick-red color will be present on stems, limbs, in crotches, and near fruit buds.

Treatments A delayed dormant oil spray, containing paraffin, will smother overwintering red mite eggs on affected trees. Use sprays that contain a dicofol-based miticide on adult mites. Be aware that insecticides used to control pests also eliminate predator mites, which causes an increase in pest mites.

GUMMOSIS

Symptom of various stone fruit disorders

Plants affected Mainly apricot, cherry, peach, plum, and other *Prunus* species.

Symptoms and cause Viscous amber liquid oozes from wounds on branches and the trunk, eventually hardening. The gum is a sign of various disorders and diseases, including shot-hole disease (p. 345), bacterial canker, and borers.

Treatments Fertilize, water, and prune trees to maintain vigor. Control borers. Follow a routine fruit spray program to control diseases and insects.

WOOLLY APHIDS

Woolly patches appear on bark

Plants affected Mainly apple, hawthorn, mountain ash, and white pine trees. Also cotoneaster and pyracantha.

Symptoms and cause Branches become deformed. White woolly tufts appear on the trunk and branches.

Treatments Avoid planting susceptible varieties of apple. In the dormant season, spray with a dormant oil. During the growing season, spray with malathion or diazinon.

WOOD ROT OR DECAY

Eventually occurs in all older trees and shrubs

Plants attacked Older trees and shrubs.

Symptoms and cause Damage appears slowly over many years, with infection occurring through unprotected wounds. Indications are heartwood that becomes discolored, spongy, stringy, or crumbly. Additionally, wood rot fungi cause mushrooms or hoof- or shelf-shaped fruiting bodies to form over decayed wood.

Treatments Promptly smooth bark and wood wounds, then cover them with shellac. Keep plants vigorous by proper pruning, fertilizing, and watering.

BARK SPLITTING, FROST CRACK

A common problem with exposed, thin-barked trees

Plants affected Many broad-leaf and young fruit and ornamental trees situated in exposed, sunny sites.

Symptoms and cause The bark splits lengthwise on the trunk and major limbs on the south or southwest sides. The problem is often caused by warm and sunny winter days that are followed by rapid temperature drops at night.

Treatments Wrap young, thin-barked trees with tree-wrap tape, burlap, or white plastic wrap. Apply a coat of whitewash or tie a wide board upright on the south side. Fertilize in late fall or early spring based on results from a soil test.

WITCHES'-BROOM

Unnatural clusters of weak twigs appear

Plants affected Mainly hackberry, ash, cherry, birch, fir, and spruce trees.

Symptoms and causes Numerous compact, broomlike clusters of shoots form on trees. Leaves may be small, blistered, or upright and tend to die back on evergreens in winter. The problem is caused by fungi and mycoplasmalike organisms (MLOs), mites, and American or dwarf mistletoes.

Treatments Cutting affected branches several inches or more behind the broom cures trees of fungi and mistletoes but not of MLOs or mites, which can be controlled with a miticide. Start by planting certified, disease-free trees.

RASPBERRY ANTHRACNOSE

Most common on black raspberries

Plants affected Raspberries and other cane fruits.

Symptoms and causes Spots of reddish brown to purple form on young canes and fruit spurs; they eventually become sunken with light gray centers and purple margins. Canes may become gray-crusted, cracked, and subject to winter-kill. There are numerous causal fungi.

Treatments Spray with liquid lime-sulfur at budbreak before the leaflets are ⅜ inch long. Then apply a homemade fruit spray when shoots are 4 to 8 inches tall, just before and just after bloom. Cut and burn fruiting and weak canes after harvesting.

BLACK KNOT

May eventually kill or deform trees

Plants affected Mainly plum, apricot, and cherry trees.

Symptoms and cause Rough, black, elongated swellings appear on twigs, branches, and trunk. In spring the knots are covered by a velvety olive-green fungus. Trees gradually weaken and die.

Treatments Prune and burn infected twigs and branches during the dormant season; cut 4 to 6 inches behind a knot. Surgically remove knots on large limbs and trunk by cutting back several inches into healthy wood. Destroy wild plums, cherries, and unproductive fruit trees. Apply a multipurpose fruit spray before buds swell, when fruit buds show color, and once more when 90 percent of the petals have fallen.

MISTLETOE

Parasitic plant sucks sap from a tree

Plants affected Most broad-leaf trees.

Symptoms American or true mistletoes (used for Christmas greens) form leafy, evergreen masses that grow to about 3 feet in diameter. They can be found in trees as far north as southern New Jersey in the East and Oregon in the West, where winters are not severe. These parasitic plants also have scaly leaves.

Treatments If feasible, cut off any young infected branches about a foot beyond any sign of mistletoe. On older branches, cut out bark and wood a foot or more away from each infection. Prune before the berries ripen and are spread by birds.

CANKER DISEASE

A common cause of dieback and decline

Plants affected All woody plants.

Symptoms and causes Round to oval or elongated dead areas appear in the bark and girdle the twigs, branches, or trunk and admit canker fungi and bacteria. Affected parts wilt, wither, and die, starting at the tip of the shoot.

Treatments Grow hardy, well-adapted species. Start with vigorous, disease-free stock. Plant, prune, fertilize, and water properly in order to maintain good vigor. Prunings should be burned.

FIRE BLIGHT

A serious disease, easily transmitted

Plants affected Mainly apple, crab apple, pear, quince, hawthorn, and mountain ash trees. Also cotoneaster and pyracantha.

Symptoms and cause Shoot tips curve down to form "shepherd's crooks." Blossoms, leaves, fruit spurs, and fruit turn brown or black as if burned. Bark on branch and trunk cankers is discolored. The causal bacteria enter flowers or wounds and are transmitted by insects, rain, or pruning tools.

Treatments Grow resistant varieties of apple, crab apple, and pear. Grow resistant species of cotoneaster and pyracantha. Keep plants in a low to moderate state of vigor. Prune out infected parts only during the dormant season.

CROWN GALL, CANE GALL

Roundish knots, most near the soil line

Plants affected Mainly euonymus, brambles, grapes, fruit trees, nut trees, and roses.

Symptoms and cause Plants lack vigor and may be stunted; they may later wilt and die. Rough, irregular, soft and spongy (finally hard) black galls, up to several inches or more in diameter, usually form at or near the soil line, graft, or bud union. The causal bacterium enters through fresh wounds (those less than 24 hours old).

Treatments Carefully dig up and burn young and severely affected plants. Don't plant susceptible plants in the same location for at least 5 years. Plant only certified, disease-free stock that shows a smooth graft union and is free of suspicious overgrowths. Avoid wounding plants.

COLLAR ROT

Brown dry rot at the stem base

Plants affected Mainly African violets, gloxinia, primroses, sweet peas, beans, and tomatoes.

Symptoms and cause Plants lack vigor. Leaves may later yellow or wilt. Stem bases turn brown, after which the entire plant dies. This disease complex is caused by various soilborne fungi.

Treatments Exclude susceptible crops for at least 4 years from any diseased vegetable or flower beds. For potted plants, use only a disinfected potting mix. Or treat as for blackleg (p. 348).

DAMPING-OFF

An aptly named fungus infection

Plants affected All seedlings—especially beans, cabbages, eggplant, peppers, lettuce, onions, spinach, tomatoes, petunias, and snapdragons.

Symptoms and causes Seeds decay in soil. Most noticeable when seedlings wilt, collapse, and die shortly after emergence. This disease complex is caused by various seed- and soilborne fungi.

Treatments Sow plump, healthy, crack-free seed in either light, well-drained, well-prepared soil or in a sterile rooting medium. Do not water or fertilize excessively. Avoid overcrowding and poor air circulation.

BLACKLEG

Black rot at the stem base

Plants affected Mainly cabbage, broccoli, and other brassicas. Also geraniums.

Symptoms and causes Black, sometimes soft, rot at the base of stems. Leaves turn yellow or reddish and wither; the plant dies from infection by bacteria or fungi.

Treatments Start with certified-disease-free seed or plants. Avoid all types of injuries, poorly drained soil or soil mixes, overwatering, and overcrowding. Control insects as needed and destroy diseased plants.

TULIP FIRE, BOTRYTIS BLIGHT

The most serious disease of tulips

Plants affected Tulips.

Symptoms Leaves, stems, and flowers rot and are covered with a fuzzy gray mold in cool, damp weather.

Treatments Plant only healthy, blemish-free bulbs in deep, very well-drained fertile soil in a sunny spot. Exclude all tulips from diseased sites for 3 to 4 years. Destroy diseased plants, including bulbs. Spray several times at 5- to 10-day intervals with Daconil, Ornalin, Chipco 26019, or Curalan; start when leaves emerge.

DODDER

Orange-yellow vines strangle plants

Plants affected All herbaceous garden plants.

Symptoms and cause Slender orange-to-yellow "leafless" twining vines appear in tangled, yellowish-orange patches. These parasitic plants can reduce plant vigor and may kill plants.

Treatments If possible, start with seed that has been certified as contamination-free. Carefully remove and burn vines before the dodder forms seeds.

ROSE CHAFERS AND JAPANESE BEETLES

Shiny metallic beetles visible on plants

Plants affected Mainly roses and other flowering shrubs.

Symptoms and causes Petals and stamens are eaten by large, bright green or green- and copper-colored beetles with white spots. Rose chafer larvae live in the rotted material of hollow trees, while Japanese beetle larvae, also called white grubs, feed on the roots of mowed turfgrass.

Treatments Rose chafers can be collected by hand and disposed of. Japanese beetles can be effectively caught by attractant traps baited by both a food and a sex attractant bait. Japanese beetle larvae can be controlled with a soil drench of either diazinon or Dylox.

PLUM CURCULIO

"Snout" beetles scar new fruit

Plants affected Mainly apple, plum, cherry, peach, and pear trees.

Symptoms and cause Crescent-shaped scars form on new fruit soon after bloom. Damage is caused by the adult curculio during feeding and egg-laying. The eggs later hatch and resulting larvae feed in the fruit, causing it to drop.

Treatments Spray fruit trees with either carbaryl or phosmet just after petals drop to protect new fruit. Repeat every 2 weeks, for a total of two or three sprays.

VIRUS DISEASES OR FLOWER BREAKING

Flowers are deformed

Plants affected Mainly carnations, chrysanthemums, irises, lilies, orchids, stock, and tulips.

Symptoms and cause Flowers become deformed, develop abnormal color streaks and blotches, or fail to open. Problems are caused by viruses transmitted by sucking insects, especially aphids. The same viruses may cause a mosaic mottling or stunting (see Virus Disease, p. 343).

Treatments None. Promptly destroy diseased plants and replace with new, virus-free ones. Keep down weeds.

GRAY MOLD OR BOTRYTIS

A gray mold covers damp plants

Plants affected All flowering plants.

Symptoms and cause Flower buds may rot. Tan or brown spots and blotches form in flower petals. Flowers soon rot and turn brown. Affected parts are covered with a coarse, tan-to-gray mold in damp weather. The same fungi also infect leaves, stems, and ripening fruit (see Gray Mold, p. 351) and may cause damping-off (p. 348).

Treatments Carefully remove and burn any rotted buds and fading flowers before petals fall. Avoid overcrowding, overfertilizing, overhead watering, wet mulches, and planting in shady or low areas if air circulation is poor. Spray plants weekly in damp weather, starting when buds or flowers appear. Apply fungicide as for botrytis (p. 348).

CLIMBING CUTWORMS OR BEET ARMYWORMS

Can be very destructive

Plants affected Mainly roses, chrysanthemums, and geraniums. Also peach and apple trees.

Symptoms and cause Holes eaten in flower buds. Small to medium-size caterpillars are often seen.

Treatments When the first symptoms appear, spray with rotenone, *Bacillus thuringiensis* (Bt), or a carbaryl-based insecticide.

GLADIOLUS THRIPS

Silvery streaks or patches in flowers

Plants affected Mainly gladiolus and related plants.

Symptoms and cause Flowers become deformed and show small white patches. Yellow insects—small, fast-moving, and long—are visible.

Treatments Just before planting, dust corms with a rotenone-based product. If symptoms appear, spray with a pyrethrin- or rotenone-based insecticide or with diazinon or malathion.

ANTHRACNOSE

Sunken spots on fruit

Plants affected Mainly beans, cucumbers, melons, peppers, and tomatoes.

Symptoms and causes Light to dark brown sunken spots appear on fruits and pods. This complex of diseases is caused by fungi that attack in damp weather; some are seed-transmitted.

Treatments Start with healthy seed or transplants. Choose varieties that are described as resistant on packages or in catalogs. Plant in fertile, well-drained soil. Follow suggested fungicide spray programs for your area. Keep down weeds and control insect infestations.

BITTER PIT

An early-season pest

Plants affected Apple trees.

Symptoms and causes Small brown patches in the skin and outer flesh of apples, which may become bitter. Damage appears before or after harvest when fruit is stored. Caused by excessive nitrogen intake and a calcium deficiency, resulting in unbalanced fertility.

Treatments Fertilize based on a soil test. In acid or neutral soils, regularly add a fertilizer high in calcium. Apply calcium nitrate or calcium chloride in pest control sprays, starting when fruit are the size of grapes. Follow local recommendations.

RASPBERRY BEETLES OR FRUITWORMS

Larvae in wormy fruit

Plants affected Mainly raspberries, loganberries, and blackberries.

Symptoms and causes Small white larvae are seen feeding on fruit.

Treatments Soon after fruit set, check for gray-brown beetles by shaking plants; if beetles are present, spray with malathion or rotenone. To avoid killing bees, be sure that blooming has already occurred.

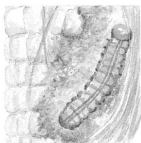

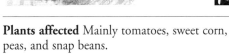

CORN EARWORMS OR TOMATO FRUITWORMS

Worms tunnel into tomatoes or corn ears

Plants affected Mainly tomatoes, sweet corn, peas, and snap beans.

Symptoms and cause Symptoms vary by plant. Insects eat holes into pea and bean pods at the site of seed and into tomatoes near the stem. Worms feed on the ear tip of sweet corn.

Treatments Early-ripening crops are less affected by this pest than late-season ones. Use either *Bacillus thuringiensis* (Bt) sprays or dusts on peas, beans, and tomatoes. Or use sprays containing rotenone or carbaryl. Repeated spraying of carbaryl every 2 to 3 days on the silks of sweet corn will prevent earworm damage.

SPLITTING AND CRACKING

Common when drought is followed by heavy rain

Plants affected Apples, cherries, pears, plums, tomatoes, and others.

Symptoms and cause Fruits split or crack as they approach harvest, then rot. Usually caused by abundant rainfall after an extended dry period.

Treatments Water if the soil is dry and rainfall averages less than 1 inch per week. Mulch tomato plants to help maintain uniform soil moisture.

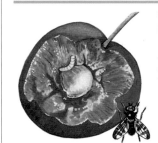

CHERRY FRUIT FLIES

Maggots in cherries

Plants affected Cherry trees.

Symptoms and cause Cherries are wormy at harvest time. Infested fruit turns brown and rots from the inside.

Treatments Soon after blossoming—but before the fruit changes color from green to white—hang yellow pieces of cardboard coated with Tangletrap to trap flies, if present. If flies are trapped or wormy fruit has been harvested in past years, spray fruit when the color changes from white to light red. Use an all-purpose fruit spray or carbaryl.

CODLING MOTHS

Source of the all-too-famous apple worm

Fruit affected Apples, pears, quinces, walnuts.

Symptoms and cause Fruit is eaten by a small white caterpillar. The opening of the tunnel is covered with brownish powder. The fruit often falls off well before ripening. Another generation of moths usually appears late in the season.

Treatments Monitor moth activity and check marble-size apples for worm entry holes. Protective sprays containing phosmet, carbaryl, or an all-purpose fruit spray will prevent injury from worms. A spraying schedule with 10- to 14-day intervals should be continued until 2 months past the apple bloom stage.

TARNISHED PLANT BUGS

An early-season pest

Plants affected Peaches, nectarines, apricots, plums, quinces, apples, and pears.

Symptoms and cause Small fruit, especially peaches, are attractive to these sap-feeding insects. Feeding causes a cat-facing or deformation of the growing fruit. Damaged areas appear as depressions covered by brown, corky tissue.

Treatments An all-purpose fruit spray or sprays containing phosmet or carbaryl will control this pest if applied when the young fruit appear on the tree. Repeat every 2 weeks for a total of three or four applications.

GRAY MOLD

A fungus encouraged by damp weather

Plants affected Mainly grapes, raspberries, strawberries, beans, peas, and tomatoes.

Symptoms and cause Ripe fruits are covered with a gray fuzzy mold. The causal fungus thrives in damp weather.

Treatments Space plants to avoid poor air circulation. Fertilize based on a soil test. Carefully collect and burn affected parts. Mulch strawberries with black plastic or organic material. Follow pest and disease spray programs for your area. Sulfur or benomyl are suggested fungicides (see Botrytis, p. 349). Treat from the beginning of blossoming for strawberries and raspberries and at the end of blossoming for grapes. Pick fruits carefully, frequently, and early in the day. Control weeds.

APPLE MAGGOTS

Brown "tracks" through apple

Fruit affected Apples and pears.

Symptoms and cause Apples at or near harvest appear bumpy or uneven. Trails inside ripened fruit are tunnels left by the legless maggots. Late in the season, flies sting the fruit skin and deposit an egg, which soon hatches.

Treatments To monitor the pests, hang red spheres covered with Tangletrap in trees as fruit begins to turn red. Then, if needed, spray with an all-purpose fruit spray or a carbaryl- or phosmet-based spray to control.

BROWN ROT

Very common on ripe stone fruits

Plants affected Tree fruits, especially cherries, peaches, plums, and nectarines.

Symptoms and cause Soft, brown, enlarging areas in ripe fruit. Diseased areas may later be covered by powdery tufts of gray or tan mold. Fruits shrivel and become hard, wrinkled mummies on the tree after leaves fall. The disease is caused by fungi that infect through skin punctures, cuts, and bruises.

Treatments Destroy rotted and mummified fruit. Prune annually to eliminate dead wood. Spray with a fungicide like Captan or benomyl, following recommended stone fruit spray schedules for your area.

GREENBACK OR POTASSIUM DEFICIENCY

Fruits ripen unevenly

Plants affected Tomatoes.

Symptoms and cause Hard patches of green or yellow color appear on ripening fruits, especially around the peduncle, causing fruits to ripen unevenly. Caused by a potassium deficiency.

Treatments Plant another variety. Conduct a soil test to see if you need to apply a fertilizer rich in potassium (K) and magnesium (Mg), and keep the soil mulched.

BLOSSOM-END ROT

Common after droughts

Plants affected Tomatoes, peppers, squash, pumpkins, and watermelons.

Symptoms and cause A sunken brown-to-black area develops on the blossom end of fruit. Caused by a lack of calcium in rapidly enlarging fruits.

Treatments Mulch under plants and water during dry periods to maintain uniform soil moisture and promote steady growth. Conduct a soil test to determine fertilizer needs.

CARROT RUST FLIES

A problem primarily in the Midwest

Plants affected Mainly carrots. Also parsley, celery, and fennel.

Symptoms and causes Foliage yellows and blackish tunnels appear on the surface of roots. The cause is two fold: small flies lay eggs at the base of top growth and maggots hatch and feed on the roots. The problem is of less concern in home gardens than in agriculture.

Treatments A soil drench with diazinon prior to planting will protect the roots from maggot feeding. Spraying top growth with rotenone or diazinon will reduce egg-laying flies. Fine netting placed over the soil and the tops of plants will prevent flies from laying eggs.

STEM AND BULB NEMATODES

Microscopic pests that infest the soil

Plants affected Many vegetables. Also hyacinths, irises, narcissus, tulips, and strawberries.

Symptoms and cause Plants lack vigor, leaves are commonly puffy or deformed, and bulbs are often soft and rotten. The problem is caused by microscopic nematodes found in soil and plant debris.

Treatments Plant only noninfected crops in infested areas for 3 years or longer. Plant only certified, heat-treated plants and bulbs in well-drained soil. Grow disease-free bulbs or seed in sterilized or clean soil. Keep down weeds.

FRUIT SPOTS AND ROTS

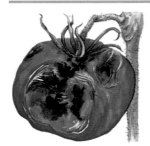

Common on ripening fruits

Plants affected All fruits and vegetables.

Symptoms and causes Ripening fruit develop spots, which often enlarge and merge; whole fruits may later rot and shrivel. Causes include numerous fungi and bacteria that attack following a wide variety of injuries. Fruits resting on moist soil are especially susceptible.

Treatments Follow suggested insect and disease spray programs for your area. Destroy affected leaves and fruit as they appear. Keep down weeds. Resistant varieties are available for certain diseases.

BULB ROT

Bulbs rot in soil or in storage

Plants affected All bulbs—especially onions, garlic, shallots, lilies, narcissus, and tulips.

Symptoms and causes Roots and bulbs can rot when in storage or in soil. Shoots either fail to emerge or turn yellow and die back. Caused by various bulb and soilborne fungi.

Treatments Carefully sort bulbs before planting or storing, making sure they are healthy and free of rot and blemishes; discard affected bulbs. Store healthy bulbs in a cool, aerated place.

ONION MAGGOTS

Not a serious pest

Plants affected Onions, leeks, and shallots.

Symptoms and cause Small maggots tunnel into young bulbs. Foliage withers and bulbs turn mushy before dying. Heavy, moist soil promotes this problem.

Treatments Do not add manure to soil before planting susceptible crops. Rotate crops and burn or bury infested plants. To kill maggots hatching from eggs laid at the base of new plants, drench soil with diazinon.

BAGWORMS

Rough bags shaped like spindles

Plants affected Many trees and shrubs, especially juniper and arborvitae.

Symptoms and cause Clusters of spindle-shaped sacks or bags, containing worm eggs, are seen. Defoliation occurs in the summer when eggs become worms that feed on the host plant's foliage. The bags are ½ to 1½ inches in length and remain attached to the trees throughout the fall, winter, and spring.

Treatments Light infestations can be removed by hand before eggs hatch. Spray *Bacillus thuringiensis* (Bt) on young worms and new bags, especially when the insect is feeding. Bagworm populations fluctuate as insect parasites attack them and reduce their numbers.

BULLFINCHES AND ROBINS

Birds that eat flower buds and fruit

Plants affected Pear, plum, apple, and cherry trees, blueberries, forsythia, flowering cherries, and others.

Symptoms and causes Flower buds are eaten in winter by bullfinches: bright red-breasted birds with a black crown and large beak. Orange-breasted robins feed on ripening fruit.

Treatments Protect bushes and low trees with netting.

FASCIATION

Appears alarming, but harmless

Plants affected Many herbaceous and woody plants.

Symptoms and causes Dwarfed, thin, flattened, ribbed, and sometimes curved shoots. Several stems may appear fused laterally. Apparently results from a genetic mutation or imbalance in growth-regulating hormones; possibly caused by absorption of a herbicide.

Treatments Remove all affected stems. The new shoots that develop later in the season or the following spring will be normal.

PINE SAWFLIES

Clusters of worms visible in foliage

Plants affected Pine trees and shrubs.

Symptoms and causes In early summer, clusters of dark green worms eat needles from the ends of pine branches. Severe needle removal can damage or deform pine trees. The worms hatch from overwintering eggs laid on pine needles and tend to feed in groups or clusters.

Treatments Worms on a single tree or a few small trees can be picked off by hand and destroyed. Control severe infestations with sprays containing carbaryl, malathion, acephate, or rotenone.

EARWIGS

Generally beneficial, but may cause minor plant damage

Plants affected Mainly clematis, chrysanthemums, dahlias, and gladiolus.

Symptoms and cause Petals are cut. Earwigs usually eat only small insects, such as aphids, but will sometimes consume petals.

Treatments Place traps consisting of flower pots, bags, or boxes filled with sawdust near susceptible plants. After a few days, when the earwigs have moved in, dust or spray with carbaryl or diazinon. Discard the containers after using.

CLEMATIS WILT AND BLIGHT

Uncommon, but can kill plants

Plant affected Clematis.

Symptoms and cause Foliage wilts, withers, and dies. The damage is the result of a stem canker at or near the soil line.

Treatments Remove and burn diseased stems, cutting well below the infected area. Start with disease-free plants or sow seed in a new location. Grow in fertile, moist, well-drained, neutral soil.

The Garden Calendar

There's a time to sow and a time to reap, but spring arrives considerably earlier in Miami than it does in Minneapolis. The proper time for gardeners to begin their work varies according to climate and the kinds of plants they choose. The Garden Calendar reminds you at a glance of those monthly garden tasks—whether seeding or feeding, pruning or mulching—no matter where you live or what you grow. Here you'll find short notes on what to do for your lawn, annuals, perennials and bulbs, vegetables and herbs, trees and shrubs, patio and container plants, and two all-time garden favorites—roses and tomatoes.

Each one of these handy checklists is divided into four broad climate zones— cold, temperate, warm, and hot—based on the U.S. Department of Agriculture's 10 hardiness zones (pp.10-11). Look to the zone that includes your locality and consult the columns that pertain to your needs. Then turn to the alphabetical Garden Dictionary on pp. 14-333 for relevant hints and tips on the best ways of carrying out the job.

JANUARY

TREES & SHRUBS

ANNUALS

PERENNIALS & BULBS

ROSES

COLD

TREES & SHRUBS
▷ After a heavy snowfall, watch for bark nibbled away by rodents. Protect stems and trunks with a wire-mesh collar. Leave prunings on top of the snow for the animals.
▷ Construct a buffer to protect plants growing near the road from salt spray when the roads are salted.

ANNUALS
▷ Review last season's notes to help plan successful spring plantings.
▷ Scan your new catalogs, garden books, and magazines for ideas and new plants suited to your area.
▷ Keep plants overwintering indoors cool. Water and fertilize sparingly.
▷ Save wood ashes from the fireplace to add potassium to beds just before they're planted in spring.

PERENNIALS & BULBS
▷ Check to see that winter mulch is still in place.
▷ Lay branches cut from the Christmas tree over loose mulch to keep it from blowing away.
▷ Scan your new catalogs, garden books, and magazines for ideas and new plants suited to your area.

ROSES
▷ Contact your local Cooperative Extension Service for latest recommendations on disease and pest control.
▷ Check dates on insecticides and fungicides, and replace any that are more than 2 years old. Write the date on new purchases.
▷ Request the latest catalogs from mail-order rose nurseries.

TEMPERATE

TREES & SHRUBS
▷ Leave any cold-damaged foliage on evergreen shrubs until spring.
▷ Remove with pruners the injured parts from yews, hemlocks, elms, and tulip trees, which are subject to damage from winter storms.

ANNUALS
▷ Review last season's notes to help plan successful spring plantings.
▷ Scan your new catalogs, garden books, and magazines for ideas and new plants suited to your area.
▷ Order seeds and supplies.
▷ Keep plants overwintering indoors cool. Water and fertilize sparingly.
▷ Save wood ashes from the fireplace.
▷ Test soil to determine the need for lime and fertilizer.

PERENNIALS & BULBS
▷ Check to see that winter mulch is still in place.
▷ Scan your new catalogs, garden books, and magazines for ideas and new plants suited to your area.
▷ Monitor the condition of plants in cold frames regularly and ventilate on warm days.
▷ Be prepared to protect tender early-flowering bulbs from sudden frosts and cold spells.

ROSES
▷ Contact your local Cooperative Extension Service for latest recommendations on disease and pest control.
▷ Check dates on insecticides and fungicides, and replace any that are more than 2 years old. Write the date on new purchases.
▷ Request the latest catalogs from mail-order rose nurseries.
▷ Water all roses deeply during any surprise thaws.
▷ Sharpen pruning tools.

WARM

TREES & SHRUBS
▷ Protect sago palms and other tropical shrubs by covering with burlap on the coldest nights.
▷ Prune crape myrtles, chaste trees, and pomegranates back to 1-inch branches to encourage larger flowers in summer.
▷ Leave any cold-damaged foliage on evergreen shrubs until spring.

ANNUALS
▷ Sow seeds of slow-growing annuals indoors and take cuttings from over-wintered plants.
▷ Keep annual beds free of weeds.
▷ Lightly fertilize winter annuals such as pansies, stocks, and snapdragons.
▷ Be prepared to protect tender plantings from frost.
▷ Test soil to determine the need for lime and fertilizer.
▷ Direct-seed half-hardy plants such as larkspurs, poppies, and cornflowers.

PERENNIALS & BULBS
▷ Scan your new catalogs, garden books, and magazines for ideas and new plants suited to your area.
▷ Start planning spring plantings.
▷ Prepare soil for spring plantings by adding organic matter, lime, and high-phosphate fertilizer as needed.
▷ Plant Oriental lilies as the bulbs become available.

ROSES
▷ Contact your local Cooperative Extension Service for latest recommendations on disease and pest control.
▷ Check dates on insecticides and fungicides, and replace any that are more than 2 years old. Write the date on new purchases.
▷ Prepare beds and dig planting holes for new roses.
▷ Sharpen pruning tools.

HOT

TREES & SHRUBS
▷ Wrap the growing points of young palms with foam rubber to protect from penetrating cold.
▷ Leave any cold-damaged foliage on evergreen shrubs until spring.
▷ Apply pre-emergent herbicides to prevent weeds from germinating around trees and shrubs in spring.

ANNUALS
▷ Keep winter plantings weeded, fertilized, and watered as needed.
▷ Deadhead winter annuals to rejuvenate and prolong flowering.
▷ Plan for summer plantings.
▷ Be prepared to protect tender plantings from frost in colder areas.

PERENNIALS & BULBS
▷ Scan your new catalogs, garden books, and magazines for ideas and new plants suited to your area.
▷ Plan for spring plantings.
▷ Divide and replant overgrown plants.
▷ Sow seeds for spring transplanting.
▷ Begin planting out gladiolus corms.
▷ Weed, water, and fertilize as needed.

ROSES
▷ Contact your local Cooperative Extension Service for latest recommendations on disease and pest control.
▷ Check dates on insecticides and fungicides, and replace any that are more than 2 years old. Write the date on new purchases.
▷ Prepare beds and dig planting holes for new roses.
▷ Water deeply in dry weather.
▷ Apply complete granular fertilizer.
▷ Spray for black spot and mildew.

 VEGETABLES & HERBS	 TOMATOES	 LAWNS	 PATIO & CONTAINER PLANTS	
▷ Read seed catalogs, review performance of all varieties grown last year, and plan for the next growing season. ▷ Take inventory of supplies, such as seeds, pots, flats, and potting soil. ▷ Test germination of leftover seeds in moistened paper towels. Discard bad seed. ▷ Buy a garden diary and resolve to write in it regularly this year. ▷ Save wood ashes from the fireplace to amend acid soil.	▷ Read seed catalogs, review performance of varieties grown last year, and plan for next growing season. ▷ Test germination of leftover seeds in moist paper towels. Discard bad seed. ▷ Place orders for seed and try a few new varieties, such as heirloom types from seed exchanges. ▷ Check supplies of pots, flats, fertilizer, and potting soil, and restock.	▷ Clean and oil mower. Sharpen the blade. Repair or replace worn parts. ▷ Rake up leaves and debris when lawn isn't under snow. ▷ Perform a soil test to learn nutrient needs for next season. ▷ Check for poor drainage areas to fix in spring. Snow mold fungus can be active all winter in poorly drained areas, even without snow cover.	▷ Protect winter-hardy outdoor plants from snow and ice damage. ▷ Provide cool conditions and good light for plants overwintering indoors. ▷ Water and fertilize overwintering plants sparingly to avoid forcing excessive growth. ▷ Read books, magazines, and catalogs for ideas for the new season.	**COLD**
▷ Read seed catalogs, review performance of all varieties grown last year, and plan for the next growing season. ▷ Take inventory of supplies such as seeds, pots, flats, and potting soil. ▷ Test germination of leftover seeds in moistened paper towels. Discard bad seed. ▷ Buy a garden diary and resolve to write in it regularly this year. ▷ Check stored vegetables and remove any that have spoiled.	▷ Read seed catalogs, review performance of varieties grown last year, and plan for next growing season. ▷ Test germination of leftover seeds in moist paper towels. Discard bad seed. ▷ Place orders for seed and try a few new varieties, such as heirloom types from seed exchanges. ▷ Check supplies of pots, flats, fertilizer, and potting soil, and restock.	▷ Clean and oil mower. Sharpen the blade. Repair or replace worn parts. ▷ Rake up leaves and debris when lawn isn't under snow. ▷ Perform a soil test to learn nutrient needs for next season. ▷ Check for poor drainage areas to fix in spring. Snow mold fungus can be active all winter in poorly drained areas, even without snow cover. ▷ Watch for fusarium patch disease throughout winter and spring.	▷ If soil isn't frozen, water outdoor container plants to prevent them from drying out in winter winds. ▷ Protect winter-hardy outdoor plants from snow and ice damage. ▷ Provide cool conditions and good light for plants overwintering indoors. ▷ Water and fertilize overwintering plants sparingly to avoid forcing excessive growth. ▷ Read books, magazines, and catalogs for ideas for the new season.	**TEMPERATE**
▷ Set out cool-season vegetable and herb transplants, and direct-seed parsley, cilantro, thyme, and chives. ▷ Plant pepper and eggplant seeds in a greenhouse or on a sunny windowsill for spring transplants. ▷ Plant peas in the garden. Also direct-seed mustard, turnips, carrots, beets, and radishes. ▷ Water and fertilize as needed. ▷ Add organic matter to soil. ▷ Watch out for cabbage loopers.	▷ Plant tomato seeds in a greenhouse, under grow lights, or on a sunny windowsill for spring transplants. Use sterile soilless mix. ▷ Prepare the tomato plot by tilling under any cover crop and by adding 2–4 pounds of complete fertilizer (12–24–12), depending on your soil analysis. ▷ Order floating row covers to wrap cages for wind and frost protection.	▷ Clean and oil mower. Sharpen the blade. Repair or replace worn parts. ▷ Keep lawn free of leaves and debris. ▷ Perform a soil test to learn nutrient needs for next season. ▷ Check for poor drainage areas to correct in spring. ▷ Watch for incidence of spring dead spot in Bermuda grass, caused by dry conditions.	▷ Water outdoor container plants to prevent drying out in winter winds. ▷ Pot spring-flowering shrubs such as camellias and azaleas in tubs. ▷ Begin putting out potted annuals for spring color in warmer areas. ▷ Start tuberous begonias, caladiums, and cannas indoors. ▷ Insulate planters containing tender-rooted plants in colder areas. ▷ Protect tender plants if frost threatens.	**WARM**
▷ Set out cool-season vegetable and herb transplants, and direct-seed parsley, cilantro, thyme, and chives. ▷ Plant pepper and eggplant seeds in a greenhouse or on a sunny windowsill for spring transplants. ▷ Plant peas in the garden. Also direct-seed mustard, turnips, carrots, beets, and radishes. ▷ Water and fertilize as needed. ▷ Add organic matter to soil. ▷ Watch out for cabbage loopers.	▷ Plant tomato seeds in a greenhouse, under grow lights, or on a sunny windowsill for spring transplants. Use sterile soilless mix. ▷ Prepare the tomato plot by tilling under any cover crop and adding 2–4 pounds of complete fertilizer (12–24–12), depending on your soil analysis. ▷ Order floating row covers to wrap cages for wind and frost protection.	▷ Clean and oil mower. Sharpen the blade. Repair or replace worn parts. ▷ Keep lawn free of leaves and debris. ▷ Perform a soil test to learn nutrient needs for next season. ▷ Check for poor drainage areas to correct in spring. ▷ Watch for incidence of spring dead spot in Bermuda grass, caused by dry conditions.	▷ Monitor plants daily for water needs and pest control. ▷ Pinch back and deadhead flowers as needed. ▷ Plant cool-season annuals such as calendulas, pansies, and stocks for late-winter and early-spring display. ▷ Plant spring-flowering shrubs such as azaleas, camellias, and gardenias. ▷ Try to prevent, but also be prepared to deal with, rainy-season diseases such as root rot.	**HOT**

JANUARY

FEBRUARY

| | TREES & SHRUBS  | ANNUALS  | PERENNIALS & BULBS  | ROSES  |

COLD

TREES & SHRUBS
▷ Remove with pruners the damaged parts of yews, hemlocks, elms, and tulip trees, which are subject to injury from late-winter storms.
▷ Complete a garden inventory and plan spring plantings.

ANNUALS
▷ Order seeds and supplies.
▷ Plan to try a few new varieties and combinations.
▷ Test soil to determine the need for lime and fertilizer.
▷ Save wood ashes from the fireplace to add potassium to beds before they're planted in the spring.

PERENNIALS & BULBS
▷ Draw up plans for spring plantings.
▷ Lay out locations of plants by height, color, texture of foliage, season of bloom, and adaptability to sun or shade.
▷ Check to see that winter mulch is still in place.
▷ Check plants in cold frames regularly. Ventilate on warm days.
▷ Look for snowdrops and winter aconite to bloom late this month.

ROSES
▷ Water roses deeply during any surprise thaws.
▷ Send in orders to the mail-order nurseries.
▷ Sharpen pruning tools.

TEMPERATE

TREES & SHRUBS
▷ Apply fertilizer to deciduous shrubs, trees, and hollies.
▷ Cut overgrown or misshapen lilacs to the ground.
▷ Snap off new "candles" from Scotch pines, firs, and other conifers to encourage a compact shape.
▷ Look for, remove, and destroy any bagworm cocoons in your trees.

ANNUALS
▷ Order seeds and supplies if not done already.
▷ Sow seeds of slow-growing annuals indoors late in the month.
▷ Take cuttings from overwintering plants when they're about 4 inches tall.
▷ Test soil if not previously done.
▷ Save wood ashes from the fireplace to add potassium to beds before they're planted in the spring.

PERENNIALS & BULBS
▷ Draw up plans for spring plantings.
▷ Lay out locations of plants by height, color, texture of foliage, season of bloom, and adaptability to sun or shade.
▷ Check to see that winter mulch is still in place.
▷ Check plants in cold frames regularly. Ventilate on warm days.
▷ Begin soil preparation as weather allows, adding needed amendments.
▷ Plant lilies as weather permits.

ROSES
▷ On sunny days, ventilate any roses that are overwintering in plastic-foam rose cones.
▷ As temperatures moderate, remove evergreen boughs or other protective coverings from miniature and ground-cover roses.
▷ If orders have not been sent to mail-order nurseries, send now.
▷ On a mild, still day, spray with dormant oil to kill overwintering insects, their eggs, and disease spores.

WARM

TREES & SHRUBS
▷ Apply dormant oil spray to camellias and evergreen hollies to eradicate scale insects and kill overwintering insect eggs.
▷ Prune shrubs like beautyberry, butterfly bush, and smoke bush to the ground to encourage summer flowers.
▷ Gather up camellia flowers as they fall to prevent pests from overwintering in them.
▷ Prune all fruit trees, evergreen shrubs, and other small trees.

ANNUALS
▷ Plant out started plants of hardier annuals.
▷ Prepare beds by adding organic matter, lime, and fertilizer as needed.
▷ Direct-seed marigolds and zinnias toward the end of the month.
▷ Weed, water, and fertilize winter plantings as needed.

PERENNIALS & BULBS
▷ Order new plants and plant them as soon as they arrive—especially lily bulbs.
▷ Divide and replant overgrown perennials.
▷ Prepare the soil for planting by adding organic matter, lime, and high-phosphate fertilizer as needed.
▷ Look for early crocus species to bloom.

ROSES
▷ Plant all kinds of new roses.
▷ Test soil pH. In the Southwest, soils are likely to be too alkaline and will require treatment with wettable sulfur.
▷ Water deeply in dry weather and apply a complete slow-release fertilizer at the end of the month.
▷ Prune back roses when emerging shoots are 1 inch long. Prune ever-blooming climbers lightly, leaving the main canes alone. Remove any winter-killed wood.

HOT

TREES & SHRUBS
▷ In hot, dry weather, control spider mites by spraying regularly with insecticidal soap.
▷ Apply dormant oil spray to evergreens to eradicate scale insects and kill overwintering insect eggs.
▷ Prune shrubs like beautyberry, butterfly bush, and smoke bush to the ground to encourage summer flowers.
▷ Take cuttings of woody plants.
▷ Prune yaupon hollies and other evergreens.

ANNUALS
▷ Direct-seed marigolds and zinnias.
▷ Set out plants that require warm soil, such as lantanas and periwinkles.
▷ Apply summer mulch to any established plantings.
▷ Be prepared to protect tender plants from sudden frosts.
▷ Weed, water, and fertilize winter plantings as needed.

PERENNIALS & BULBS
▷ Divide and replant overgrown perennials.
▷ Sow seeds for late-spring planting.
▷ Plant new permanent beds of summer-flowering bulbs.
▷ Weed, water, and fertilize as needed.

ROSES
▷ Plant container-grown roses.
▷ Spray for black spot and mildew.
▷ Water deeply in dry weather and apply a complete slow-release fertilizer to established—but not to new—roses.
▷ Control weeds through shallow cultivation of beds or hand-pulling. Rose roots can be damaged if cultivation goes deeper than 1 inch.
▷ Sharpen pruning tools.

VEGETABLES & HERBS	TOMATOES	LAWNS	PATIO & CONTAINER PLANTS	
▷ Lay out the garden on paper, rotate crops, and develop a planting schedule. Be realistic in evaluating time available for gardening. ▷ Order seeds, plants, and supplies. ▷ Start seeds of onions and leeks indoors and, later this month, cabbage-family crops. ▷ Check stored root vegetables for decay; use remaining crop as soon as possible.	▷ Shop local garden centers while their supplies are still adequate. ▷ Test grow lights over seed-starting benches, and replace as needed. ▷ Pick a sunny site for this year's tomato patch. Avoid any spot where solanaceous-family plants such as peppers, eggplant, potatoes, or tomatoes have been grown in the past 3 years. ▷ Buy new seed-starting flats or disinfect last year's with a bleach solution.	▷ Inventory your lawn supplies. List those needed for spring. ▷ Don't use salt to melt snow on walks and driveways near grass areas. ▷ Walk the lawn, noting bare and thin areas in need of overseeding in spring. ▷ Perform a soil test to determine nutrient needs, if not done already. ▷ Watch for red thread fungus disease throughout winter and spring.	▷ Protect winter-hardy outdoor plants from snow and ice damage. ▷ Provide cool conditions and good light for plants overwintering indoors. ▷ Water and fertilize overwintering plants sparingly to avoid forcing excessive growth. ▷ Continue planning, and place mail orders for spring delivery.	COLD
▷ Check stored root vegetables for decay; use remaining crop as soon as possible. ▷ Check tools and make needed repairs. Clean and sharpen blades. ▷ Start seeds of onions and leeks indoors. ▷ Watch for preseason sales at garden centers and load up on supplies while the store is well stocked.	▷ Shop local garden centers while their supplies are still adequate. ▷ Test grow lights over seed-starting benches, and replace as needed. ▷ Pick a sunny site for this year's tomato patch. Avoid any spot where solanaceous-family plants such as peppers, eggplant, potatoes, or tomatoes have been grown in the past 3 years. ▷ Buy new seed-starting flats or disinfect last year's with a bleach solution.	▷ Inventory your lawn supplies. List those needed for spring. ▷ Don't use salt to melt snow on walks and driveways near grass areas. ▷ Walk the lawn, noting bare and thin areas in need of overseeding in spring. ▷ Perform a soil test to determine nutrient needs, if not done already. ▷ Watch for red thread fungus disease throughout winter and spring.	▷ Protect winter-hardy outdoor plants from snow and ice damage. ▷ Provide cool conditions and good light for plants overwintering indoors. ▷ Gradually increase temperature, watering, and fertilizer. ▷ Pinch back or take cuttings from leggy overwintering plants. ▷ Prepare new planters, incorporating organic matter and sand or perlite. ▷ Start begonias and caladiums.	TEMPERATE
▷ Locate a good source of organic mulch; save newspapers to put underneath. ▷ Destroy any overwintering pests such as the leaf-footed bug. ▷ Plant potatoes around the first of the month. ▷ Begin planting warm-season crops like beans, corn, melons, and squash. ▷ Set out peppers and eggplants.	▷ Set out tomato plants. In areas of high rainfall (more than 30 inches per year), use raised beds. ▷ Keep transplants growing vigorously with weekly applications of a soluble fertilizer and regular watering. ▷ Wrap row covers around cages for wind and pest protection and to raise temperatures a few degrees.	▷ Inventory your lawn supplies. List those needed for spring. ▷ Perform a soil test to determine nutrient needs, if not done already. ▷ Watch for pythium blight fungus, which can infest warm-season grasses from now through late spring.	▷ Monitor all plantings daily. ▷ Pot spring-flowering annuals. ▷ Pot cool-treated spring bulbs. ▷ Pot annuals for spring color. ▷ Protect tender plants against any possible surprise frosts. ▷ Prune and reshape potted trees and shrubs while they're dormant.	WARM
▷ Locate a good source of organic mulch; save newspapers to put underneath. ▷ Destroy overwintering pests such as the leaf-footed bug. ▷ Plant potatoes around the first of the month. ▷ Begin planting warm-season crops like beans, corn, melons, and squash. ▷ Set out peppers and eggplants.	▷ Set out tomato plants. In areas of high rainfall (more than 30 inches per year), use raised beds. ▷ Keep transplants growing vigorously with weekly applications of a soluble fertilizer and regular watering. ▷ Wrap row covers around cages for wind and pest protection and to raise temperatures a few degrees.	▷ Inventory your lawn supplies. List those needed for spring. ▷ Perform a soil test to determine nutrient needs, if not done already. ▷ Watch for pythium blight fungus, which can infest warm-season grasses from now through late spring.	▷ Monitor all plantings daily. ▷ Pinch back and deadhead as needed. ▷ Fill in gaps with cool-season annuals such as calendulas, pansies, and stocks for late-winter and spring display. ▷ Plant precooled spring-flowering bulbs.	HOT

FEBRUARY

TREES & SHRUBS

ANNUALS

PERENNIALS & BULBS

ROSES

COLD

TREES & SHRUBS

▷ Root-prune conifers that you want to stay small, using a long-bladed spade.

▷ Prune deciduous plants now, while you can most easily see the trunk and branch structure.

▷ Apply dormant oil to lilacs before leaves appear, to prevent later scale infestation.

ANNUALS

▷ Complete spring planning.

▷ Fertilize overwintering plants so that they will produce enough growth for cuttings.

▷ Continue to save wood ashes.

▷ Test soil if not previously done.

PERENNIALS & BULBS

▷ Order spring plants and supplies.

▷ Check cold frames every day and ventilate as needed on warm days.

▷ Don't remove mulch from tulips or hyacinths until danger of frost is past.

▷ Apply high-phosphate fertilizer to beds and bulb plantings as needed.

ROSES

▷ On sunny days, ventilate roses over-wintering in plastic-foam cones.

▷ As temperatures moderate, remove evergreen boughs or other covering from ground-cover and miniature roses.

▷ On a mild, still day, spray roses with dormant oil to kill overwintering in-sects, their eggs, and disease spores.

TEMPERATE

▷ Remove supports from trees that have been in the ground a year.

▷ After forsythia, spirea, or other foun-tain-shaped, early-blossoming shrubs have flowered, cut ⅓ of the oldest canes to the ground.

▷ Apply fertilizer to all plants as soon as growth starts.

▷ Apply dormant oil to lilacs before leaves appear, to prevent later scale infestation.

▷ Start the seeds of slow-growing an-nuals indoors for summer blooms.

▷ Take cuttings for outdoor beds from plants overwintered indoors.

▷ Prepare beds by adding organic matter, lime, and fertilizer as needed.

▷ Plant out cold-resistant plants such as pansies at month's end.

▷ Order spring plants and supplies.

▷ Check cold frames every day and ventilate as needed on warm days.

▷ Remove winter mulch and begin soil preparation as weather permits.

▷ Apply high-phosphate fertilizer to all planting beds as needed.

▷ Divide and replant overgrown perennials not divided in the fall.

▷ Deadhead spring-flowering bulbs to prevent seed formation but don't remove any foliage until it has dried.

▷ As leaf buds swell and open, re-move winter protection from bushes.

▷ Test soil pH and amend as needed.

▷ Water deeply and apply a com-plete slow-release granular fertilizer.

▷ Check for borers and prune back stems to below borers' tunnels.

▷ Bring standard tree roses out of win-ter storage and plant. If bare-root bushes arrive too early to plant, store in a cool, dark spot and moisten.

WARM

▷ Start trees and shrubs from seed. An acorn planted now can reach 4 feet by late summer.

▷ After forsythia, spirea, or other foun-tain-shaped, early-blossoming shrubs have flowered, cut ⅓ of the oldest canes to the ground.

▷ Apply pre-emergent herbicides to prevent spring-germinating weeds.

▷ Fertilize most plants as soon as growth starts. Fertilize camellias after flowering.

▷ Protect all tender plants from any possible late frosts.

▷ Continue to plant out all summer annuals.

▷ Apply pre-emergent herbicides to prevent spring-germinating weeds.

▷ Weed, water, and fertilize as needed.

▷ Continue soil preparation, dividing, and new plantings.

▷ Water new plantings if the weather is dry.

▷ Apply pre-emergent herbicides to prevent spring-germinating weeds.

▷ Deadhead spring-flowering bulbs to prevent seed formation but don't remove any foliage until it has dried.

▷ Prune ever-blooming roses.

▷ Plant container-grown roses.

▷ Water deeply in dry weather and apply complete slow-release fertilizer to established—but not to new—roses.

▷ Begin weekly sprays to control black spot and mildew.

▷ Spray bushes with dormant oil to control scale, aphids, whiteflies, and spider mites.

▷ Sow seeds of shallow-rooted annu-als like portulacas as a living mulch.

HOT

▷ A few weeks after trees have pro-duced new leaves, prune to encour-age an open, spreading shape.

▷ Prune dead branches back to where new buds can be seen.

▷ Apply foliar fertilizer to newly emerging fronds of palms damaged by unusually cold weather.

▷ Prune young azaleas just after flow-ering to encourage compact growth.

▷ Fertilize most plants as soon as growth starts.

▷ Fill in beds with plantings of heat-loving annuals.

▷ Weed, water, and fertilize as needed.

▷ Watch for early signs of pests and diseases.

▷ Deadhead annuals to encourage continued flowering.

▷ Apply summer mulch to established plantings.

▷ Divide and replant overgrown perennials.

▷ Plant lilies and tuberous begonias for summer bloom.

▷ Weed, water, and fertilize as needed.

▷ Apply pre-emergent herbicides to prevent spring-germinating weeds.

▷ Prune ever-blooming roses.

▷ Plant container-grown roses.

▷ Water deeply in dry weather and apply complete slow-release fertilizer to established—but not to new—roses.

▷ Begin weekly sprays to control black spot and mildew.

▷ Control weeds through shallow cultivation or hand-pulling.

▷ Sow seeds of shallow-rooted annu-als like portulacas as a living mulch.

MARCH

VEGETABLES & HERBS

▷ Sow peppers, celery, and warm-weather crops in flats indoors on a bright windowsill or under lights. Speed germination with heating mats, which also help to prevent disease.

▷ On balmy days, finish any garden cleanup chores left from fall and prepare soil for planting.

▷ Late in the month, direct-seed hardy cold-tolerant vegetables such as spinach, peas, and radishes.

TOMATOES

▷ Test heating coils or mats before they are needed.

▷ Build new cages as needed.

▷ Check stakes for signs of rotting.

▷ Late in the month, start seeds of early varieties so that you'll be first on the block to pick ripe tomatoes. Plant a few extra seeds for insurance.

▷ Watch seedlings for early signs of damping off.

▷ Raise lights or lower growing shelves as seedlings get taller.

LAWNS

▷ Rake and mow before green-up to remove leaves and winter debris and to let the sun warm the soil.

▷ Correct grade in soggy areas.

▷ Aerate to improve air, water, and nutrient movement. Overseed with a variety suitable for your area. Then apply slow-release 4–1–2 fertilizer.

▷ Keep moist until seed sprouts. After 4–6 weeks, treat as established lawn.

▷ Don't apply herbicides for broad-leaf weed control for next 4 weeks.

PATIO & CONTAINER PLANTS

▷ Protect winter-hardy outdoor plants from snow and ice damage.

▷ Gradually increase temperature, watering, and fertilizer for plants over-wintering indoors as days lengthen.

▷ Pinch back straggly growth and take cuttings.

▷ Start tuberous begonias, caladiums, and cannas indoors.

▷ Prepare new planters, adding organic matter and sand or perlite.

COLD

▷ Sow peppers, celery, and warm-weather crops in flats indoors on a bright windowsill or under lights.

▷ On balmy days, finish any garden cleanup chores left from fall and prepare soil for planting.

▷ Late in the month, direct-seed cold-tolerant vegetables such as spinach, peas, and radishes.

▷ Be careful if you uncover tender perennial herbs. Late-spring cold spells can be severe.

▷ Start seeds of early varieties so that you'll be first on the block to pick ripe tomatoes. Plant a few extra seeds for insurance.

▷ Consider installing heating coils or mats to ensure germination.

▷ Apply fertilizers and compost to beds if soil and weather allow.

▷ Complete any garden cleanup overlooked or left undone last fall.

▷ Rake and mow before green-up to remove leaves and winter debris and to let the sun warm the soil.

▷ Correct grade in soggy areas.

▷ Aerate to improve air, water, and nutrient movement. Overseed with a variety suitable for your area. Then apply slow-release 4–1–2 fertilizer.

▷ Keep moist until seed sprouts. After 4–6 weeks, treat as established lawn.

▷ Don't apply herbicides for broad-leaf weed control for next 4 weeks.

▷ Bring spring bulbs out of storage for spring flowering.

▷ Start potting frost-tolerant plants such as pansies and stocks.

▷ Plant small containers indoors and let plants become established before putting them outdoors.

▷ Pinch back straggly growth and take cuttings.

▷ Monitor overwintering plants for optimum light, water, and fertilizer.

TEMPERATE

▷ Set out more peppers and eggplants. Seed beans, corn, cucumbers, melons, and squash.

▷ Foliar-feed with a hose-end fertilizer sprayer to keep plants growing.

▷ Set out transplants of oregano, sweet marjoram, savory, basil, rosemary, and other herbs.

▷ Install a low-volume irrigation system (drip or soaker hose) and mulch.

▷ Begin planting hot-weather vegetables like okra and sweet potatoes.

▷ Set out more tomato seedlings.

▷ Check plants daily for aphids and early blight fungus.

▷ Install a low-volume irrigation system (drip or soaker hose) and mulch.

▷ Water and fertilize as needed.

▷ Apply slow-release 4–1–2 fertilizer at recommended rates.

▷ If soil test indicated other nutrient deficiencies, apply what is required.

▷ Apply pre-emergent weed controls for annual weeds.

▷ Correct grade in soggy areas.

▷ Begin mowing Bermuda grass weekly with blade set at 1½ inches.

▷ Monitor plants daily for water needs and pest control.

▷ Pinch back straggly plants and deadhead spent flowers.

▷ Replace bulbs and winter annuals with heat-tolerant annuals or tropical plants that have colorful foliage.

WARM

▷ Finish warm-season plantings by mid-month. Set out more peppers and eggplants. Seed beans, corn, cucumbers, melons, and squash.

▷ Foliar-feed with a hose-end fertilizer sprayer to keep plants growing.

▷ Set out transplants of oregano, sweet marjoram, savory, basil, rosemary, and other herbs.

▷ Install a low-volume irrigation system (drip or soaker hose) and mulch.

▷ Begin planting hot-weather vegetables like okra and sweet potatoes.

▷ Set out the last of your tomato seedlings; later plantings won't set much fruit once night temperatures climb above 65°F.

▷ Check plants daily for aphids and early blight fungus.

▷ Install a low-volume irrigation system (drip or soaker hose) and mulch.

▷ Water and fertilize as needed.

▷ Apply slow-release 4–1–2 fertilizer at recommended rates.

▷ If soil test indicated other nutrient deficiencies, apply what is required.

▷ Apply pre-emergent weed controls for annual weeds.

▷ Correct grade in soggy areas.

▷ Begin mowing Bermuda grass weekly with blade set at 1½ inches.

▷ Monitor plants daily for water needs and pest control.

▷ Pinch straggly plants and deadhead spent flowers.

▷ Begin replacing fading cool-season annuals with those that love the heat, such as marigolds, portulacas, vincas, zinnias, and tropical foliage plants.

HOT

MARCH

TREES & SHRUBS	ANNUALS	PERENNIALS & BULBS	ROSES

COLD

TREES & SHRUBS
- Cut overgrown or misshapen lilacs to the ground.
- Apply fertilizer to deciduous shrubs, trees, and hollies.
- Prune apple and other fruit trees.
- After forsythia, spirea, or other fountain-shaped shrubs have flowered, cut ⅓ of the oldest canes to the ground.

ANNUALS
- Start seeds of remaining annuals indoors.
- Continue rooting cuttings of overwintered plants.
- Prepare beds by adding organic matter, lime, and fertilizer as needed.
- Plant out half-hardy plants after danger of severe weather has passed.

PERENNIALS & BULBS
- Speed up warming of the soil by removing winter mulch as plants begin to grow.
- Prepare planting beds, adding organic matter, lime, and fertilizer as needed.
- Purchase plants from local nurseries.
- Begin planting as weather permits.
- Divide and replant overgrown established plants if not done in the fall.

ROSES
- Remove mulch from beds so that soil can thaw and dry out.
- As leaf buds swell and open, remove winter protection and note which cultivars are most damaged.
- Apply complete slow-release fertilizer to established roses.
- Bring standard tree roses out of winter storage and replant. Plant bare-root roses as soon as soil can be worked.
- Test soil pH and amend as needed.

TEMPERATE

TREES & SHRUBS
- Apply 3–4 inches of organic mulch around new and established plants.
- Prune young azaleas, wisterias, and jasmines just after flowering to encourage compact growth. Remove dead and misshapen branches.
- Apply a high-nitrogen foliar fertilizer to evergreens with yellowing leaves.
- Pinch off contorted new growth on pines to remove pine shoot moths.

ANNUALS
- Continue preparing beds.
- Start seeds of fast-growing annuals such as zinnia indoors.
- Sow seeds of hardy annuals such as cornflower and larkspur outdoors.
- Apply pre-emergent herbicide to reduce spring-germinating weeds.
- Keep indoor seedlings and rooted cuttings cool. Give them plenty of light for bushy, compact growth.

PERENNIALS & BULBS
- Complete soil preparation, division, and planting.
- Weed, water, and fertilize as needed.
- Apply pre-emergent herbicide to reduce spring-germinating weeds.
- Watch for signs of pests and diseases.
- Don't remove foliage from spring-flowering bulbs until it has started to dry out on its own.

ROSES
- Prune ever-blooming roses.
- Plant bare-root roses. Plant container roses anytime until July.
- Apply complete slow-release fertilizer to established roses.
- Begin weekly sprays to control black spot and mildew.
- Lightly prune ever-blooming climbers, leaving main canes alone.
- Remove winter-killed wood from old garden roses but don't shape or thin at this time.

WARM

TREES & SHRUBS
- Apply 3–4 inches of organic mulch around new and established plants.
- Prune young azaleas, wisterias, and jasmines just after flowering to encourage compact growth. Remove dead and misshapen branches.
- Apply a high-nitrogen foliar fertilizer to evergreens with yellowing leaves.
- Prune hollies, nandinas, and mahonias to promote compact habit.
- Check fruit trees for fire blight and cut off infected branches.

ANNUALS
- Continue with early plantings.
- Apply pre-emergent herbicides to reduce spring-germinating weeds.
- Weed, water, and fertilize as needed.
- Watch for signs of pests and diseases.
- Deadhead winter plantings as needed to prolong blooming.

PERENNIALS & BULBS
- Complete soil preparation and planting.
- Plant begonia, canna, crinum, dahlia, lily of the Nile, montebretia, and gladiolus bulbs and corms.
- Weed, water, and fertilize as needed.
- Deadhead or cut back hard after flowering to promote plant vigor and rebloom.
- Watch for signs of pests and diseases.

ROSES
- Continue weekly sprays to control black spot and mildew.
- Plant container-grown roses.
- Apply complete fertilizer.
- Remove fading blossoms from ever-blooming types to promote rebloom.
- Flower buds that don't open may be a symptom of thrips. Apply proper insecticides as needed.
- Control aphids with insecticidal soap.

HOT

TREES & SHRUBS
- Transplant palms into holes slightly deeper than the previous holes and support with stakes.
- Old hedges and shaped shrubs may need severe pruning now to encourage vigorous growth and good flower set.
- Check fruit trees for fire blight and cut off infected branches.
- Control scale on citrus and other plants by spraying with lightweight summer oil.

ANNUALS
- As winter plantings are removed, add organic matter, lime, and fertilizer to garden beds as needed.
- Weed, water, and fertilize established plantings as needed.
- Watch for signs of pests and diseases.
- If not finished last month, apply summer mulch to the remaining plantings to keep soil cool and to conserve moisture.

PERENNIALS & BULBS
- Divide and replant overgrown perennials.
- Weed, water, fertilize, and deadhead as needed.
- Cut back or deadhead perennials after flowering to promote plant vigor and rebloom. Deadhead bulb flowers (not foliage) to prevent seed formation.
- Watch for signs of pests and diseases.

ROSES
- Renew mulch in rose beds.
- Water deeply in dry weather and apply complete slow-release fertilizer.
- Continue weekly sprays to control black spot and mildew.
- Flower buds that don't open may be a symptom of thrips. Apply proper insecticides as needed.
- Control weeds in beds through shallow cultivation or hand-pulling.

VEGETABLES & HERBS

▷ Begin tilling when the soil no longer makes a tight wet ball when squeezed in the hand.

▷ Direct-seed potatoes, onions, beets, radishes, cabbage, and spinach.

▷ Put out cabbage family plants started indoors and water with a high-phosphate starter fertilizer.

▷ Weed and water as needed.

▷ Harvest rhubarb and asparagus.

▷ Harvest asparagus, rhubarb, and chives.

▷ Plant out cabbage family, onions, and leeks.

▷ Direct-seed peas and continue succession plantings of lettuce, radishes, spinach, and onions.

▷ As soil warms, direct-seed beets, carrots, turnips, and other cool-season crops.

▷ Cut back overwintered sage and direct-seed or plant out other herbs.

▷ Continue to set out hot-weather herbs like basil and rosemary.

▷ Plant more hot-weather vegetables like okra and black-eyed peas.

▷ Plant bush beans and corn weekly to ensure a long harvest season.

▷ Foliar-feed or side-dress heavy feeders like corn and peppers with a complete fertilizer.

▷ Install low-volume irrigation (drip or soaker hose) and pile on 4–6 inches of organic mulch.

▷ Continue to set out hot-weather herbs like basil and rosemary.

▷ Plant more hot-weather vegetables like okra and black-eyed peas.

▷ Plant bush beans and corn weekly to ensure a long harvest season.

▷ Foliar-feed or side-dress heavy feeders like corn and peppers with a complete fertilizer.

▷ Install low-volume irrigation (drip or soaker hose) and pile on 4–6 inches of organic mulch.

TOMATOES

▷ Finish garden cleanup left over from last fall as needed.

▷ As weather and soil conditions allow, apply fertilizer and compost to garden beds.

▷ Work soil as it begins to dry out.

▷ Early seedlings sown indoors may need transplanting to individual pots.

▷ Sow main season varieties indoors about mid-month.

▷ Collect or buy mulch and store for application later in the season.

▷ Start main season varieties indoors now. There are usually 4–6 weeks of unpredictable weather left before they can be transplanted outdoors.

▷ Early seedlings sown indoors may need transplanting to individual pots.

▷ Finish incorporating fertilizer, compost, overwintered cover crops, or crop residues into the beds.

▷ Check and clean off last year's cages, trellises, stakes, and twine.

▷ Foliar-feed or side-dress tomatoes with a complete fertilizer.

▷ Remove row covers from cages and put aside for use with fall crop.

▷ Mulch plants heavily with alfalfa hay or other material.

▷ Break off a few lower leaves to improve circulation and reduce fungal diseases. Watch for early blight.

▷ Harvest fruit when it first shows pink to reduce insect and bird damage.

▷ Foliar-feed or side-dress tomatoes with a complete fertilizer.

▷ Remove row covers from cages and put aside for use with fall crop.

▷ Mulch plants heavily with alfalfa hay or other material.

▷ Break off a few lower leaves to improve circulation and reduce fungal diseases. Watch for early blight.

▷ Harvest fruit when it first shows pink to reduce insect and bird damage.

LAWNS

▷ Dethatch and aerate if not done earlier in spring or the previous fall.

▷ Apply a slow-release 3–1–2 fertilizer at the recommended rate.

▷ Overseed with a variety suitable for your area, if you didn't last month.

▷ Keep moist until seeds sprout. After 4–6 weeks, treat as an established lawn.

▷ Apply pre-emergent herbicides to established lawns.

▷ Dethatch and aerate if not done earlier in spring or the previous fall.

▷ Apply a slow-release 3–1–2 fertilizer at the recommended rate.

▷ Overseed with a variety suitable for your area, if you didn't last month.

▷ Keep moist until seeds sprout. After 4–6 weeks, treat as an established lawn.

▷ Apply pre-emergent herbicides to established lawns.

▷ Apply a slow-release 3–1–2 fertilizer at recommended rate, if not done earlier.

▷ Apply pre-emergent herbicides to established lawns.

▷ Begin sodding with Bermuda grass anytime now through October.

▷ Watch for diseases such as brown patch, pythium blight, and dollar spot.

▷ Watch for signs of cinch bugs, sod webworms, army worms, fire ants, mole crickets, and grubs.

▷ Establish regular mowing schedule.

▷ Apply a slow-release 3–1–2 fertilizer at recommended rate, if not done earlier.

▷ Apply pre-emergent herbicides to established lawns.

▷ Begin sodding with Bermuda grass anytime from now through October.

▷ Watch for signs of pests and diseases.

▷ Establish regular mowing schedule.

▷ Plant St. Augustine and centipede grasses using sprigs, sod, or plugs.

PATIO & CONTAINER PLANTS

▷ Bring pots of spring-flowering bulbs out of cool storage to start forcing blooms indoors.

▷ Start small container plants indoors to let them get established before moving them outside.

▷ Continue monitoring overwintering plants daily for needs.

▷ Continue pinching back straggly plants and deadheading spent blooms.

▷ Put out overwintered containers and those started indoors as the weather permits.

▷ Sink empty pots into large planters to hold seasonal plants such as spring bulbs and summer annuals.

▷ Fill gaps or replace winter plantings with those for spring and summer.

▷ Be prepared to protect tender plants from possible late frosts.

▷ Monitor plants daily for water needs and pest control.

▷ Pinch back straggly plants and deadhead spent flowers.

▷ Replace winter annuals with plants for summer.

▷ Pot tender bulbs such as tuberous begonias.

▷ Monitor plants daily for water needs and pest control.

▷ Pinch back straggly plants and deadhead spent flowers.

▷ Continue to replace cool-season plants with hot-season ones as needed.

▷ Watch for signs of pests and diseases.

COLD

TEMPERATE

WARM

HOT

APRIL

TREES & SHRUBS

ANNUALS

PERENNIALS & BULBS

ROSES

MAY

COLD

TREES & SHRUBS
- ▷ Apply 3–4 inches of mulch to shrub beds.
- ▷ Prune water sprouts from crab apples, Japanese magnolias, and other trees.
- ▷ Remove supports from trees that have been in the ground a year.
- ▷ Snap off new "candles" from Scotch pines, firs, and other conifers to encourage compact shape.

ANNUALS
- ▷ Plant out half-hardy annuals.
- ▷ Put out containers of seedlings on warm days to harden them off before transplanting.
- ▷ Apply pre-emergent herbicides to reduce spring-germinating weeds.
- ▷ Weed, water, and fertilize as needed.

PERENNIALS & BULBS
- ▷ Keep new plantings well watered.
- ▷ Apply water-soluble fertilizer to get new plantings off to a good start.
- ▷ Complete new plantings.
- ▷ Complete dividing and replanting of overgrown or crowded plants.
- ▷ Allow foliage of daffodils and other early-flowering spring bulbs to dry out before you remove it.

ROSES
- ▷ Plant bare-root roses. Plant container roses anytime from now until July.
- ▷ When shoots are 1-inch long, prune ever-blooming and mini roses.
- ▷ Lightly prune ever-blooming climbers, leaving main canes alone.
- ▷ Remove winter-killed wood from old garden roses. But don't thin or shape at this time.
- ▷ Feed established roses.
- ▷ Sow shallow-rooted annuals like portulacas as a living mulch in beds.

TEMPERATE

TREES & SHRUBS
- ▷ Prune tent caterpillar nests from trees and destroy them.
- ▷ Prune water sprouts from crab apples and other small trees.
- ▷ Prune suckers from the bases of crab apples and other trees.
- ▷ Apply granular fertilizer to crape myrtles and other blooming shrubs to encourage extra flowers.

ANNUALS
- ▷ Plant out remaining annuals when all danger of frost has passed.
- ▷ Weed, water, and fertilize as needed.
- ▷ Watch for signs of pests and diseases.
- ▷ Apply summer mulch around established plantings.

PERENNIALS & BULBS
- ▷ Apply summer mulch.
- ▷ Weed, water, and fertilize as needed.
- ▷ Deadhead or cut back perennials after flowering to promote plant vigor and rebloom.
- ▷ Continue deadheading spent bulb plant blooms to prevent seed formation.
- ▷ Watch for signs of pests and diseases.

ROSES
- ▷ Apply granular complete fertilizer to encourage extra flowers.
- ▷ Watch for mildew and aphids, and spray as needed.
- ▷ Water weekly in dry weather, applying 1 inch of water and taking care not to wet foliage.
- ▷ Sow shallow-rooted annuals like portulacas as a living mulch in beds.

WARM

TREES & SHRUBS
- ▷ Prune suckers that sprout from the bases of newly planted Japanese magnolias and other trees.
- ▷ Apply granular fertilizer to crape myrtles and other blooming shrubs to encourage extra flowers.
- ▷ Spray with insecticidal soap as needed to control whiteflies and black sooty mold.

ANNUALS
- ▷ As winter plantings are replaced, add organic matter, lime, and fertilizer as needed.
- ▷ Direct-seed annuals that require warm soil, such as zinnias.
- ▷ Weed, water, and fertilize as needed.
- ▷ Watch for signs of pests and diseases.
- ▷ Cut flowers early in the morning for longer-lasting arrangements.
- ▷ Apply summer mulch to beds.

PERENNIALS & BULBS
- ▷ Apply summer mulch to conserve soil moisture as hot weather arrives.
- ▷ Weed, water, and fertilize as needed.
- ▷ Deadhead or cut back perennials after flowering to promote plant vigor and rebloom.
- ▷ Deadhead spent bulb plant blooms to prevent seed formation.
- ▷ Watch for signs of pests and diseases.

ROSES
- ▷ Apply granular complete fertilizer to encourage extra flowers.
- ▷ Watch for mildew, rust, and aphids, and spray as needed.
- ▷ Water weekly and deeply in dry weather, applying 1 inch of water.
- ▷ Spread organic mulch such as shredded bark or pine straw.
- ▷ Continue spraying for black spot and powdery mildew.
- ▷ Above 85°F, dilute fungicidal sprays by ⅓ to avoid burning the foliage.

HOT

TREES & SHRUBS
- ▷ Lure May beetles off shrubs by putting out white buckets of water, lit with flashlights, at night.
- ▷ Spray insecticidal soap to control spider mites on crotons, azaleas, and camphor trees.
- ▷ Spray insecticidal soap to control whiteflies and black sooty mold.
- ▷ Prevent spider mites and thrips by spraying water on leaves daily.
- ▷ Prune seed heads from crape myrtles to encourage summer flowers.

ANNUALS
- ▷ Emphasize shade plantings for summer enjoyment.
- ▷ Deadhead flowers as needed to promote extended bloom.
- ▷ Weed, water, and fertilize as needed.
- ▷ Watch for signs of pests and diseases.
- ▷ Cut flowers early in the morning for longer-lasting arrangements.

PERENNIALS & BULBS
- ▷ Apply summer mulch to conserve soil moisture as hot weather arrives.
- ▷ Weed, water, and fertilize as needed.
- ▷ Deadhead or cut back perennials after flowering to promote plant vigor and rebloom.
- ▷ Deadhead spent bulb plant blooms to prevent seed formation.
- ▷ Watch for signs of pests and diseases.

ROSES
- ▷ Spray for black spot and mildew.
- ▷ Watch for spider mites and spray as needed.
- ▷ Fertilize established bushes with granular complete fertilizer.
- ▷ Control weeds through shallow cultivation or hand-pulling.
- ▷ Water deeply once or twice weekly in hot, dry weather.
- ▷ Above 85°F, dilute fungicidal sprays by ⅓ to avoid burning the foliage.

VEGETABLES & HERBS

▷ Sow cool-season vegetables early this month. Make succession plantings of radishes, lettuce, and spinach. Late in the month, direct-seed beans and other warm-weather crops.

▷ Transplant seedlings of cucumbers, melons, squash, and peppers. Water with a high-phosphate fertilizer. Plant through black plastic mulch and protect with floating row covers

▷ Weed and water as needed.

▷ Plant hardy herbs. Start basil inside.

▷ Plant hardy herbs. Start basil inside.

▷ Continue succession plantings of fast-growing plants like cilantro.

▷ Thin seedlings in planting rows and eat thinnings as baby greens.

▷ Transplant seedlings of cucumbers, melons, squash, and peppers. Water with a high-phosphate fertilizer. Plant through black plastic mulch and protect with floating row covers.

▷ Weed and water as needed.

▷ Sow corn, beans, and pumpkins.

▷ Now is the last chance to plant hot-weather vegetables like okra, black-eyed peas, and sweet potatoes.

▷ Plant hot-weather herbs like basil and rosemary.

▷ Watch for spider mites, squash vine borers, and stinkbugs.

▷ Water thoroughly, using a low-volume irrigation system. Soak soil 8–12 inches deep and don't water again until plants show slight signs of wilting.

▷ Now is the last chance to plant hot-weather vegetables like okra, black-eyed peas, and sweet potatoes.

▷ Plant hot-weather herbs like basil and rosemary.

▷ Watch for spider mites, squash vine borers, and stinkbugs.

▷ Water thoroughly, using a low-volume irrigation system. Soak soil 8–12 inches deep and don't water again until plants show slight signs of wilting.

TOMATOES

▷ Till bed regularly until transplant time to control weeds and aerate soil.

▷ Apply black or clear plastic mulch 1–2 weeks ahead of transplanting time to help warm the beds.

▷ Harden off plants in a cold frame or on an unheated porch 7–10 days before transplanting out.

▷ Apply high-phosphorus fertilizer at planting time.

▷ Be ready to protect transplants from surprise frosts.

▷ Start some late varieties now for an early fall crop.

▷ Keep seedlings short and stocky by providing high light intensity.

▷ Harden off plants in cold frames 1 week before transplanting out.

▷ Warm soil by applying black or clear plastic mulch to tomato beds.

▷ Risk first outdoor transplants in early to mid month. Be ready to protect from late frosts. By month's end, weather risks should be minimal.

▷ Watch for spider mites and blossom-end rot. Pick off any leaf-footed stinkbugs or apply a recommended insecticide.

▷ Fool birds with red Christmas-tree balls; one peck at the decoys and they'll leave the real tomatoes alone for a while. Harvest fruit as soon as it turns pink and ripen it fully indoors.

▷ Be aware that new fruit set will be minimal in high temperatures.

▷ Check irrigation system to be sure it's working properly.

▷ Watch for spider mites and blossom-end rot. Pick off any leaf-footed stinkbugs or apply a recommended insecticide.

▷ Fool birds with red Christmas-tree balls; one peck at the decoys and they'll leave the real tomatoes alone for a while. Harvest fruit when pink.

LAWNS

▷ Fertilize lightly if lawn has lost some color and is not growing well.

▷ Establish regular mowing schedule. Never cut more than ⅓ of the leaf.

▷ Watch for fungus diseases such as anthracnose, brown patch, dollar spot, helminthosporium, necrotic ring spot, and red thread.

▷ Watch for insect damage from cutworms, grubs, ants, and clover mites.

▷ Give 1 inch of water per week with one deep soaking if weather is dry.

▷ Fertilize lightly if lawn has lost some color and is not growing well.

▷ Establish regular mowing schedule. Never cut more than ⅓ of the leaf.

▷ Watch for signs of fungus diseases.

▷ Watch for insect damage from cutworms, grubs, ants, and clover mites.

▷ Give 1 inch of water per week with one deep soaking if weather is dry.

▷ Establish zoysia grass by sodding, plugging, or sprigging.

▷ Fertilize lightly if lawn has lost some color and is not growing well.

▷ Dethatch Bermuda grass lawns.

▷ Start Bermuda grass lawns from seed if night temperatures are above 65°F.

▷ Watch for fungus diseases such as anthracnose, brown patch, dollar spot, helminthosporium, necrotic ring spot, and red thread.

▷ Watch for insect damage.

▷ Apply post-emergent herbicides to control weeds in Bermuda grass.

▷ Fertilize lightly if lawn has lost some color and is not growing well.

▷ Dethatch Bermuda grass lawns.

▷ Start Bermuda grass from seed if night temperatures are above 65°F. Start Bahia grass from seed through July.

▷ Watch for fungus diseases such as brown patch, pythium blight, gray leaf spot, helminthosporium, and rusts.

▷ Watch for insect damage.

▷ Apply post-emergent herbicides to control weeds in Bermuda grass.

PATIO & CONTAINER PLANTS

▷ Put out overwintered or newly planted containers as weather permits.

▷ Sink empty pots into large planters to hold seasonal plants such as spring bulbs, summer annnuals, and fall mums.

▷ Be prepared to protect tender plants from surprise late frosts.

▷ Monitor plants daily for water needs and pest control.

▷ Pinch back straggly growth, and deadhead as needed.

▷ Replace spring bulbs with summer-blooming plants.

▷ Watch for signs of insects and diseases, discarding diseased plants and removing insects by hand if possible. Use insecticides only as a last resort.

▷ Monitor plants daily for water needs and pest control.

▷ Fill in gaps with tropical plants that have colorful foliage for a low-maintenance summer replacement.

▷ Pinch back straggly growth, and deadhead as needed.

▷ As the weather warms, watch for signs of insects and diseases, discarding diseased plants and removing insects by hand if possible. Use insecticides only as a last resort.

▷ Monitor plants daily for water needs and pest control.

▷ Pinch back straggly growth, and deadhead as needed.

▷ Pot heat-hardy annuals such as marigolds, periwinkle, and zinnias.

▷ Pot shrubs such as chenille plant, croton, and hibiscus in tubs for summer color.

COLD

TEMPERATE

WARM

HOT

MAY

TREES & SHRUBS	ANNUALS	PERENNIALS & BULBS	ROSES

COLD

TREES & SHRUBS
▷ Discourage sapsuckers by wrapping wire around the trunks of ashes, birches, and other susceptible trees.
▷ Lightly prune small trees to increase air circulation and control white powdery mildew on leaves.
▷ Prune juniper, yew, and hemlock hedges.

ANNUALS
▷ Plant out remaining annuals.
▷ Direct-seed annuals that require warm soil, such as zinnias.
▷ Weed, water, and fertilize as needed.
▷ Watch for signs of pests and diseases.
▷ Apply summer mulch.

PERENNIALS & BULBS
▷ Apply pre-emergent herbicide to control weeds.
▷ Apply summer mulch.
▷ Weed, water, and fertilize as needed.
▷ Deadhead to promote plant vigor and possible rebloom and to prevent seed formation on bulb plants.
▷ Watch for signs of pests and diseases.

ROSES
▷ Apply granular complete fertilizer to encourage extra flowers.
▷ Watch for aphids, Japanese beetles, spider mites, thrips and fungal diseases; spray as needed.
▷ Water weekly in dry weather, applying 1 inch of water and taking care not to wet foliage.
▷ Take cuttings to propagate new plants.
▷ Weed by hand or hoe shallowly to avoid damaging roots.

TEMPERATE

▷ Apply acid fertilizer to magnolias, rhododendrons, and other acid-loving plants.
▷ Water dogwoods before they begin to wilt during dry summers.
▷ Lightly prune small trees to increase air circulation and control white powdery mildew on leaves.
▷ Prune juniper, yew, and hemlock hedges.

▷ Plant to fill gaps in the beds or to replace plantings that have failed.
▷ Direct-seed annuals that require warm soil, such as zinnias.
▷ Weed, water, and fertilize as needed.
▷ Watch for signs of pests and diseases.
▷ Deadhead for extended flowering.
▷ Cut flowers in the early morning for longer-lasting arrangements.

▷ Start seeds for fall or spring planting.
▷ Weed, water, and fertilize as needed.
▷ Deadhead or cut back perennials after flowering to promote plant vigor and rebloom; deadhead bulb flowers to prevent seed formation.
▷ Remove foliage of spring-flowering bulbs when it is brown and dry. Leave green foliage alone.
▷ Watch for signs of pests and diseases.

▷ Continue watering whenever weather is dry. Mulch bare spots.
▷ Apply granular complete fertilizer.
▷ Watch for aphids, Japanese beetles, spider mites, thrips and fungal diseases; spray as needed.
▷ Cut fading flowers from modern ever-bloomers to encourage rebloom. Cut stems back to a leaf with 5 leaflets.
▷ Take cuttings for propagation.

WARM

▷ Prune to control the shape of evergreen shrubs and hedges.
▷ Monitor leaves for signs of wilting, and water plants if the ground is dry.
▷ Control spider mites on junipers by spraying with insecticidal soap.
▷ Take cuttings for propagation from both evergreen and deciduous shrubs.

▷ Plant to fill gaps in the beds or to replace plantings that have failed.
▷ Weed, water, and fertilize as needed.
▷ Watch for signs of pests and diseases.
▷ Deadhead for extended flowering.
▷ Cut flowers early in the morning for longer-lasting arrangements.

▷ Start seeds for fall planting.
▷ Weed, water, and fertilize as needed.
▷ Deadhead or cut back perennials after flowering to promote plant vigor and rebloom; deadhead bulb flowers to prevent seed formation.
▷ Watch for signs of pests and diseases, especially during humid weather.

▷ Watch for aphids, Japanese beetles, spider mites, thrips and fungal diseases; spray as needed.
▷ Water deeply and weekly in dry weather, twice a week if very hot.
▷ Prune spring-blooming old garden roses after main flush of flowers ends. Prune climbers, removing any old or failing canes and tying in new canes as replacements.

HOT

▷ Monitor hydrangeas for blight, which rots the stems at the base. Remove infected plants and apply a fungicide.
▷ Lightly prune small trees to improve air circulation and control white powdery mildew on leaves.
▷ Prune hedges and small shrubs.
▷ Apply fertilizer to all plants.

▷ Remove remaining winter annuals and replace with summer plantings.
▷ Solarize unplanted beds with clear plastic to control weeds and disease.
▷ Deadhead for extended flowering.
▷ Weed, water, and fertilize as needed.
▷ Watch for signs of pests and diseases, especially spider mites.
▷ Cut flowers early in the morning for longer-lasting arrangements.

▷ Apply summer mulch, if not done previously, to conserve moisture before hot, dry weather arrives.
▷ Weed, water, and fertilize as needed.
▷ Deadhead or cut back perennials after flowering to promote plant vigor and rebloom; deadhead bulb flowers to prevent seed formation.
▷ Watch for signs of pests and diseases.

▷ Monitor for blight, which rots stems at the base. Remove infected plants and apply a fungicide.
▷ Watch for aphids, Japanese beetles, spider mites, thrips and fungal diseases; spray as needed.
▷ Irrigate deeply twice weekly in hot, dry weather.
▷ Renew mulch as needed.

JUNE

VEGETABLES & HERBS

▷ Direct-seed cucumbers, melons, squash, and pumpkins. Water with a high-phosphorus fertilizer. Plant through black plastic mulch and protect with floating row covers.

▷ Sow bush beans every 2–4 weeks for continuous harvest.

▷ Start seeds of fall crops for transplanting as space opens up.

▷ Weed and water as needed.

▷ Plant out basil. Plant sweet potatoes and lima beans when the soil warms.

TOMATOES

▷ Finish planting out early this month.

▷ Remove row covers or other frost protection as plants begin to flower and set fruit.

▷ Begin to prune, tie, train, and cage plants as needed.

▷ After soil is warm, replace plastic mulch with organic mulch to prevent weeds and hold moisture.

▷ Water deeply during dry spells.

▷ Watch for signs of pests and diseases.

LAWNS

▷ Maintain a regular mowing and watering schedule to keep grass healthy. Leave the grass clippings on the lawn.

▷ Apply post-emergent herbicides as needed to control annual weeds.

▷ Watch for signs of fungus disease and insect damage. Apply the proper controls at the recommended rates.

PATIO & CONTAINER PLANTS

▷ Monitor plants daily for water needs and pest control.

▷ Apply water-soluble fertilizer or foliar feed to plants as needed for healthy vigor—usually every 2–4 weeks.

▷ Pinch back straggly plants and deadhead spent blooms to maintain a neat appearance.

▷ Replace seasonal and failed plants as needed.

▷ Plant out basil. Plant sweet potatoes and lima beans when the soil warms.

▷ Harvest vegetables and herbs as they mature. Cut back foliage by ⅓ on herbs; chives and parsley regrow if cut back even more. Replace spent plants with later crops or cover crops.

▷ Side-dress corn, vine crops, and other heavy feeders with fertilizer.

▷ Stop harvesting asparagus and rhubarb to let these plants grow and recharge their roots.

▷ Finish planting out early this month.

▷ For a large fall crop, plant some late-started seedlings by month's end.

▷ Begin to prune, tie, train, and cage plants as needed.

▷ After soil is warm, replace plastic mulch with organic mulch to prevent weeds and hold moisture.

▷ Water deeply during dry spells to help prevent blossom-end rot.

▷ Watch for signs of pests and diseases.

▷ Maintain a good mowing and watering schedule to keep grass healthy. Leave the grass clippings on the lawn.

▷ Apply post-emergent herbicides as needed to control annual weeds.

▷ Watch for signs of fungus disease and insect damage. Apply the proper controls at the recommended rates.

▷ Give zoysia grass a light application of slow-release fertilizer to keep it healthy over the summer.

▷ Monitor plants daily for water needs and pest control.

▷ Apply water-soluble fertilizer or foliar feed to plants as needed for healthy vigor—usually every 2–4 weeks.

▷ Pinch back straggly plants and deadhead spent blooms to maintain a neat appearance.

▷ Replace seasonal and failed plants as needed.

▷ Watch for powdery mildew fungus on squash and cucumbers.

▷ Watch for insect pests like stinkbugs and spider mites.

▷ This is the big harvest season. Pick early in the morning.

▷ If eggplants or cucumbers are bitter, it's a sign of plant stress. Keep watering and fertilizing as needed.

▷ Seed the fall tomato crop using early-maturing and cherry types.

▷ This is the end of the season. Pick what's left while still half green to limit insect and bird damage.

▷ Watch for leaf-footed stinkbugs, spider mites, leaf spot, and fruit rot.

▷ Maintain a good mowing and watering schedule to keep grass healthy. Leave the grass clippings on the lawn.

▷ Apply post-emergent herbicides as needed to control annual weeds.

▷ Watch for signs of fungus disease and insect damage. Apply the proper controls at the recommended rates.

▷ Give Bermuda grass a light application of slow-release fertilizer.

▷ Dethatch Bermuda grass anytime through July.

▷ Monitor plants daily for water needs and pest control.

▷ Apply water-soluble fertilizer or foliar feed to plants as needed for healthy vigor—usually every 2–4 weeks.

▷ Pinch back straggly plants and deadhead spent blooms to maintain a neat appearance.

▷ Replace seasonal and failed plants as needed.

▷ Watch for powdery mildew fungus on squash and cucumbers.

▷ Watch for insect pests like stinkbugs and spider mites.

▷ This is the major harvest season. Pick early in the morning.

▷ If eggplants or cucumbers are bitter, it's a sign of plant stress. Keep watering and fertilizing as needed.

▷ Cut okra daily to ensure tender pods.

▷ Seed the fall tomato crop using early-maturing and cherry types.

▷ This is the end of the season. Pick what's left while still half-green to limit insect and bird damage.

▷ Watch for leaf-footed stinkbugs, spider mites, leaf spot, and fruit rot.

▷ Maintain a regular mowing and watering schedule to keep grass healthy. Leave the grass clippings on the lawn.

▷ Apply fertilizers and herbicides only as needed during the summer months.

▷ Dethatch anytime through August to increase vigor and growth.

▷ Monitor plants daily for water needs and pest control.

▷ Apply water-soluble fertilizer or foliar feed to plants as needed for healthy vigor—usually every 2–4 weeks.

▷ Pinch back straggly plants and deadhead spent blooms to maintain a neat appearance.

▷ Replace seasonal and failed plants as needed.

▷ Emphasize shade plantings with begonias, browallias, and impatiens.

COLD

TEMPERATE

WARM

HOT

JUNE

TREES & SHRUBS	ANNUALS	PERENNIALS & BULBS	ROSES
COLD			
▷ Apply foliar fertilizer to new plants, especially if they start dropping leaves or if a wet summer has waterlogged the soil, inhibiting nutrient absorption. ▷ Control spider mites on junipers and other shrubs by spraying with insecticidal soap.	▷ To fill gaps in the beds, plant large nursery-grown specimens. ▷ Weed, water, and fertilize as needed. ▷ Deadhead to promote extended flowering. ▷ Watch for signs of pests and diseases, especially spider mites. ▷ Cut flowers early in the morning for longer-lasting arrangements.	▷ Apply mulch if not already done. ▷ Plan bulb orders for fall planting. ▷ Sow the seeds of perennials for fall or spring transplanting. ▷ Weed, water, and fertilize as needed. ▷ Deadhead or cut back after flowering to promote plant vigor and possible rebloom. ▷ Watch for signs of pests and diseases.	▷ Continue watering as needed. ▷ Apply granular complete fertilizer. ▷ Watch for mildew, Japanese beetles, and aphids. Spray as needed, diluting fungicides by ⅓ to prevent burning the foliage. ▷ Cut faded flowers from everbloomers to encourage rebloom; cut stems back to a leaf with 5 leaflets. ▷ Prune old garden roses after they bloom. Cut off failing old canes on climbers and tie in new ones.
TEMPERATE			
▷ Watch for and prune blight from cryptomerias, Douglas firs, and hemlocks. ▷ Apply foliar fertilizer to new plants, especially if they start dropping leaves or if a wet summer has waterlogged the soil, inhibiting nutrient absorption. ▷ Control spider mites on junipers and other shrubs by spraying with insecticidal soap.	▷ Sow the seeds of cool-season plants for fall and winter bloom. ▷ Weed, water, and fertilize as needed. ▷ Deadhead to promote extended flowering. ▷ Watch for signs of pests and diseases, especially spider mites. ▷ Cut flowers early in the morning for longer-lasting arrangements.	▷ Plan bulb orders for fall planting. ▷ Sow the seeds of perennials for fall or spring transplanting. ▷ Weed, water, and fertilize as needed. ▷ Deadhead or cut back after flowering to promote plant vigor and possible rebloom. ▷ Watch for signs of pests and diseases, especially spider mites; check for mildew on phlox and New England aster.	▷ Continue watering weekly as needed. ▷ Apply granular complete fertilizer. ▷ Watch for mildew, Japanese beetles, and aphids. Spray as needed, diluting fungicides by ⅓ to prevent burning the foliage. ▷ Prune old garden roses after they bloom. Cut off failing old canes on climbers and tie in new ones.
WARM			
▷ During dry summers, water dogwoods before they wilt. ▷ Apply foliar fertilizer to new plants, especially if they start dropping leaves or if a wet summer has waterlogged the soil, inhibiting nutrient absorption. ▷ Lightly prune small trees to improve air circulation and control white powdery mildew on leaves.	▷ Solarize unplanted beds under plastic to control weeds and diseases. ▷ Cut back tired annuals, and apply water-soluble fertilizer to rejuvenate. ▷ Weed, water, and fertilize as needed. ▷ Deadhead to promote extended flowering. ▷ Watch for signs of pests and diseases, especially spider mites. ▷ Cut flowers early in the morning for longer-lasting arrangements.	▷ Sow seeds of perennials for fall planting. ▷ Weed, water, and fertilize as needed. ▷ Deadhead or cut back after flowering to promote plant vigor and to prevent seed formation on bulbs. ▷ Watch for signs of pests and diseases, especially spider mites.	▷ Continue watering twice weekly as needed in hot, exposed areas. ▷ Apply granular complete fertilizer. ▷ Watch for mildew, spider mites, and aphids. Spray as needed, diluting fungicides by ⅓ to prevent burning the foliage.
HOT			
▷ Pinch back new growth on shrubs to ensure a thick, compact habit. ▷ Check crape myrtles and shrubs for foliage diseases. ▷ Monitor palms for yellow fronds due to nutrient deficiencies or pests.	▷ Solarize unplanted beds under plastic to control weeds and diseases. ▷ Cut back tired annuals, and apply water-soluble fertilizer to rejuvenate. ▷ Weed, water, and fertilize as needed. ▷ Deadhead to promote extended flowering. ▷ Watch for signs of pests and diseases, especially spider mites. ▷ Cut flowers early in the morning for longer-lasting arrangements.	▷ Pinch back fall-blooming perennials all month for compact growth and extra blooms. ▷ Weed, water, fertilize, and deadhead as needed. Remove dead foliage from bulbs but leave green foliage alone. ▷ Watch for signs of pests and diseases.	▷ Continue watering twice weekly as needed in hot, exposed areas. ▷ Renew mulch as needed. ▷ Watch for mildew, spider mites, and aphids. Spray as needed, diluting fungicides by ⅓ to prevent burning the foliage.

JULY

VEGETABLES & HERBS	**TOMATOES**	**LAWNS**	**PATIO & CONTAINER PLANTS**

COLD

VEGETABLES & HERBS

▷ Spring harvest peaks this month.

▷ Harvest herbs just before they flower for peak flavor. Preserve by chopping finely, pureeing in oil, and freezing or by drying whole.

▷ Harvest produce in the morning; clean and store as quickly as possible.

▷ Water and weed as needed. To conserve water and prevent leaf burn, don't water in the heat of the day.

▷ Direct-seed or transplant crops, such as cabbage, for the fall garden.

TOMATOES

▷ Continue to prune, tie, train, and cage plants weekly or as needed.

▷ Make sure cages are firmly anchored before plants get top-heavy.

▷ Water deeply during dry spells to maintain even moisture and reduce blossom-end rot and fruit cracking.

▷ Watch for diseases, particularly blight, on lower branches. Check for insects like hornworm caterpillars.

▷ Harvest first fruit.

LAWNS

▷ Check mower blade for sharpness; grass cut by a dull blade is susceptible to disease and insect damage.

▷ If water is restricted, let the lawn enter summer dormancy; it will likely recover when rains return.

▷ Minimize fertilizer use; nitrogen stimulation in hot weather makes turf more prone to disease.

▷ Watch for signs of fungus diseases. Use proper mowing and watering to minimize these problems.

PATIO & CONTAINER PLANTS

▷ Monitor plants daily for water needs and pest control.

▷ Apply water-soluble or foliar fertilizer to plants as needed for healthy vigor—usually every 2–4 weeks.

▷ Pinch back straggly plants and deadhead spent blooms to maintain neat appearance.

▷ Replace seasonal plants and failed or diseased plants.

TEMPERATE

VEGETABLES & HERBS

▷ Cultivate lightly to control weeds.

▷ Mulch to conserve moisture. Water in the morning, using drip irrigation if possible.

▷ Harvest mature crops and young shoots from herbs. Use or preserve as soon as possible for best nutrition and taste.

▷ Harvest snap beans regularly to encourage continued pod set.

TOMATOES

▷ Watch for ripening fruit. Heavy foliage can make it hard to spot.

▷ Continue to prune, tie, train, or cage plants as needed.

▷ Make sure cages are firmly anchored before plants get top-heavy.

▷ Water deeply during dry spells to maintain even moisture and reduce blossom-end rot and fruit cracking.

▷ Watch for diseases, particularly blight, on lower branches. Check for insects like hornworm caterpillars.

LAWNS

▷ Check mower blade for sharpness; grass cut by a dull blade is susceptible to disease and insect damage.

▷ If water is restricted, let the lawn enter summer dormancy; it will likely recover when rains return.

▷ Minimize fertilizer use; nitrogen stimulation in hot weather makes turf more prone to disease.

▷ Watch for signs of fungus diseases.

▷ Increase mowing height by an extra ½ inch during hot, dry periods.

PATIO & CONTAINER PLANTS

▷ Monitor plants daily for water needs and pest control.

▷ Apply water-soluble or foliar fertilizer to plants as needed for healthy vigor—usually every 2–4 weeks.

▷ Pinch back straggly plants and deadhead spent blooms to maintain neat appearance.

▷ Replace seasonal plants and failed or diseased plants.

WARM

VEGETABLES & HERBS

▷ Plant heat-tolerant crops like calabaza squash and yard-long beans.

▷ Use floating row covers to protect plants from the heat and to exclude insect pests.

▷ Solarize unplanted beds under plastic to reduce weeds, nematodes, and other pests.

▷ Harvest herbs just before they flower for peak flavor. Preserve by chopping finely, pureeing in oil, and freezing or by drying whole.

TOMATOES

▷ The first tomato harvest often ends this month, except for cherry tomatoes. Remove plants that are not setting fruit or that appear diseased.

▷ Put out transplants for a fall crop.

▷ Solarize unplanted beds under plastic to reduce weeds, nematodes, and other pests.

LAWNS

▷ Maintain regular mowing and watering schedule.

▷ If water is restricted, let the lawn enter summer dormancy; it will likely recover when rains return.

▷ Increase mowing height by an extra ½ inch during hot, dry periods.

▷ Seed, sprig, or sod Bermuda grass if not under water restrictions.

PATIO & CONTAINER PLANTS

▷ Monitor plants daily for water needs and pest control.

▷ Apply water-soluble or foliar fertilizer to plants as needed for healthy vigor—usually every 2–4 weeks.

▷ Pinch back straggly plants and deadhead spent blooms to maintain neat appearance.

▷ Replace seasonal plants and failed or diseased plants with new heat-tolerant plants.

HOT

VEGETABLES & HERBS

▷ Plant heat-tolerant crops like calabaza squash and yard-long beans.

▷ Use floating row covers to protect plants from the heat and to exclude insect pests.

▷ Solarize unplanted beds under plastic to reduce weeds, nematodes, and other pests.

▷ Harvest herbs just before they flower for peak flavor. Preserve by chopping finely, pureeing in oil, and freezing or by drying whole.

TOMATOES

▷ The first tomato harvest often ends this month, except for cherry tomatoes. Remove plants that are not setting fruit or that appear diseased.

▷ Plant seed for fall crop this month.

▷ Solarize unplanted beds under plastic to reduce weeds, nematodes, and other pests.

LAWNS

▷ Maintain regular mowing and watering schedule.

▷ If water is restricted, let the lawn enter summer dormancy; it will likely recover when rains return.

▷ Increase mowing height by an extra ½ inch during hot, dry periods.

▷ Seed Bahia grass. Sprig, sod, or plug St. Augustine and centipede grasses.

▷ Watch for signs of insect damage and fungus diseases.

PATIO & CONTAINER PLANTS

▷ Monitor plants daily for water needs and pest control.

▷ Apply water-soluble or foliar fertilizer to plants as needed for healthy vigor—usually every 2–4 weeks.

▷ Pinch back straggly plants and deadhead spent blooms to maintain a neat appearance.

▷ Replace seasonal plants and failed or diseased plants with new heat-tolerant plants.

JULY

AUGUST

 **TREES & SHRUBS**

 **ANNUALS**

 **PERENNIALS & BULBS**

 **ROSES**

COLD

TREES & SHRUBS
▷ Apply 3–4 inches of mulch around plants to prevent winter water loss and soil heaving.
▷ Take a garden inventory and remove plants that have not performed well.
▷ Collect a soil sample and have it tested for nutrient content.
▷ Plant woody ornamentals.

ANNUALS
▷ Cut back tired annuals and rejuvenate with water-soluble fertilizer.
▷ Weed, water, and fertilize as needed.
▷ Deadhead to promote extended flowering.
▷ Watch for signs of pests and diseases, especially spider mites.
▷ Cut flowers early in the morning for longer-lasting arrangements.

PERENNIALS & BULBS
▷ Deep watering is essential this month.
▷ Weed and fertilize as needed.
▷ Deadhead to promote plant vigor.
▷ Cut back unsightly bearded iris foliage.
▷ Divide or move bearded irises and Madonna lilies now that they are dormant.
▷ Watch for signs of pests and diseases.

ROSES
▷ Even if plants are still flowering, don't fertilize after the first week of the month. It may encourage tender new growth that is subject to winter burn.
▷ Cover planted cuttings with glass jars to keep them moist. Spray several times weekly.
▷ Stop deadheading spent blooms.
▷ Spray diluted fungicides as needed.
▷ Test the soil in the rose beds; the results will determine next year's fertilization plans.

TEMPERATE

TREES & SHRUBS
▷ Avoid pruning now; it may cause tender new growth that is subject to winter damage.
▷ Avoid fertilizing blooming shrubs to prevent tender new growth that is subject to winter damage.

ANNUALS
▷ Seed for fall transplants if not already done.
▷ Cut back tired annuals and rejuvenate with water-soluble fertilizer.
▷ Weed, water, and fertilize as needed.
▷ Deadhead to promote extended flowering.
▷ Watch for signs of pests and diseases, especially spider mites.
▷ Cut flowers early in the morning for longer-lasting arrangements.

PERENNIALS & BULBS
▷ Deep watering is essential this month.
▷ Weed and fertilize as needed.
▷ Deadhead to promote plant vigor.
▷ Cut back unsightly bearded iris foliage.
▷ Plant autumn-flowering crocuses and colchicums as soon as bulbs are available.
▷ Watch for signs of pests and diseases.

ROSES
▷ Even if plants are still flowering, don't fertilize after the first week of the month. It may encourage tender new growth that is subject to winter burn.
▷ Stop deadheading spent blooms.
▷ Spray diluted fungicides as needed.
▷ Test the soil in the rose beds; the results will determine next year's fertilization plans.
▷ Order bare-root roses from mail-order nurseries for fall planting.
▷ Water weekly during hot weather.

WARM

TREES & SHRUBS
▷ Prevent the production of palm and palmetto seedlings by pruning off immature seeds now. Use a saw to remove dead fronds flush with the trunk.
▷ Prune seed heads from crape myrtles to encourage a few more flowers in the fall.
▷ Keep berry-producing shrubs well watered through this dry month.

ANNUALS
▷ Start seed for fall transplants.
▷ Cut back tired annuals and rejuvenate with water-soluble fertilizer.
▷ Weed, water, and fertilize as needed.
▷ Deadhead to promote extended flowering.
▷ Watch for signs of pests and diseases, especially spider mites.
▷ Replace spent annuals with heat-loving transplants for fall blooms.

PERENNIALS & BULBS
▷ Weed, water, and fertilize as needed. Fertilize summer-flowering bulbs with 5–10–5 or bonemeal.
▷ Deadhead or cut back to promote plant vigor.
▷ Divide overgrown bulb clumps as foliage dies back. Replant before fall rains.
▷ Cut back unsightly bearded iris foliage.
▷ Watch for signs of pests and diseases.

ROSES
▷ Increase watering to twice weekly during heat and drought.
▷ Spray diluted fungicides as needed.
▷ Request new catalogs.
▷ Renew mulch as needed.
▷ At month's end, prune bushes by removing dead wood and shortening long canes by ⅓ for better fall bloom.
▷ Prune climbers by cutting back side shoots.

HOT

TREES & SHRUBS
▷ Shade tree trunks from hot sun if large branches have been broken off by storms.
▷ Cut back bougainvillea and other rampant shrubs.
▷ Apply foliar fertilizer to new plants, especially if they start dropping leaves or if a wet summer has waterlogged the soil, inhibiting nutrient absorption.
▷ Prevent the production of palm and palmetto seedlings by pruning off immature seeds now. Use a saw to remove dead fronds flush with the trunk.

ANNUALS
▷ Start seed for fall transplants.
▷ Cut back tired annuals and rejuvenate with water-soluble fertilizer.
▷ Weed, water, and fertilize as needed.
▷ Deadhead to promote extended flowering.
▷ Watch for signs of pests and diseases, especially spider mites.
▷ Replace spent annuals with heat-loving transplants for fall blooms.

PERENNIALS & BULBS
▷ Weed, water, fertilize, and deadhead as needed.
▷ Plant Dutch iris, freesia, Madonna lily, and other fall- and winter-flowering bulbs.
▷ Sow seeds for late-winter and early-spring plantings.
▷ Deadhead or cut back to promote plant vigor.

ROSES
▷ Water twice weekly as needed.
▷ Spray diluted fungicides as needed.
▷ Watch for spider mites.
▷ Control weeds by shallow cultivation or hand-pulling.
▷ Test soil and fertilize as needed.
▷ Prune bushes by removing dead wood and shortening long canes by ⅓ for better fall bloom.
▷ Prune climbers by cutting back side shoots.

		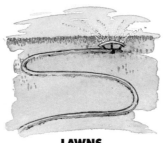	
VEGETABLES & HERBS	**TOMATOES**	**LAWNS**	**PATIO & CONTAINER PLANTS**

COLD

VEGETABLES & HERBS
- ▷ Harvest crops as they mature; pick herbs before they flower for best flavor. Use or preserve right after harvest for the best nutrition and taste.
- ▷ When the weather cools, plant out heat-sensitive seedlings and direct-seed fall crops as harvesting opens up space. Plant cover crops.
- ▷ Water as needed and mulch the soil.
- ▷ Watch for leaf diseases.
- ▷ Pull and compost large weeds.

TOMATOES
- ▷ Harvest fruit of heirloom and other open-pollinated varieties for seed saving. Choose perfect ripe fruit and double-check labels to avoid mix-ups.
- ▷ Leave hornworm caterpillars with white cocoons on their backs alone; the parasitic wasps that hatch from them help control future hornworms.
- ▷ Harvest fruit as close to fully ripe as possible. Eat or preserve right away.
- ▷ Pinch off plants with green fruit to hurry ripening before the first frost.

LAWNS
- ▷ Maintain mowing and watering schedule. Raise mower blade ½ inch.
- ▷ Assess lawn condition for possible fall renovation.
- ▷ Watch for signs of insect damage and fungus diseases; apply chemical controls as needed.
- ▷ Sod new lawn. Prepare site and lay sod within 24 hours of delivery.

PATIO & CONTAINER PLANTS
- ▷ Monitor plants daily for water needs and pest control.
- ▷ Apply water-soluble fertilizer as needed for healthy vigor—usually every 2–4 weeks.
- ▷ Pinch back straggly plants and deadhead spent blooms to maintain neat appearance.
- ▷ Replace summer annuals and failed or diseased plants with heat-tolerant foliage plants or fall bloomers.

TEMPERATE

VEGETABLES & HERBS
- ▷ Harvest crops as they mature; pick herbs before they flower for best flavor. Use or preserve right after harvest for the best nutrition and taste.
- ▷ When the weather cools, plant out heat-sensitive seedlings and direct-seed fall crops as harvesting opens up space. Plant cover crops.
- ▷ Water as needed and mulch the soil.
- ▷ Watch for beetles and disease.
- ▷ Pull and compost large weeds.

TOMATOES
- ▷ Harvest fruit as close to fully ripe as possible. Eat or preserve right away.
- ▷ If birds or other pests are damaging ripe fruit, pick earlier when blossom end turns pink and allow fruit to ripen indoors. Never refrigerate; an air-conditioned house, however, is ideal.
- ▷ Early varieties will finish producing this month. Compost fruitless plants. Later plantings will start ripening at the end of this month for another harvest.

LAWNS
- ▷ Maintain mowing and watering schedule. Raise mower blade ½ inch.
- ▷ Assess lawn condition for possible fall renovation.
- ▷ Watch for signs of insect damage and fungus diseases; apply chemical controls as needed.
- ▷ Sod new lawn. Prepare site and lay sod within 24 hours of delivery.
- ▷ Dethatch zoysia grass and apply slow-release fertilizer at recommended rate.

PATIO & CONTAINER PLANTS
- ▷ Monitor plants daily for water needs and pest control.
- ▷ Apply water-soluble fertilizer as needed for healthy vigor—usually every 2–4 weeks.
- ▷ Pinch back straggly plants and deadhead spent blooms to maintain neat appearance.
- ▷ Replace summer annuals and failed or diseased plants with heat-tolerant foliage plants or fall bloomers.

WARM

VEGETABLES & HERBS
- ▷ Plant peas, even if it seems too hot. They won't produce until temperatures cool in the fall.
- ▷ Plant bush beans weekly from now until mid-September.
- ▷ Use floating row covers to protect plants from heat and pests.
- ▷ Harvest herbs at their peak, just before they begin to flower, and use or preserve as soon as possible.

TOMATOES
- ▷ Use a complete foliar fertilizer on new transplants to encourage vigorous growth and early production.
- ▷ Set up and use a low-volume irrigation system on the new tomatoes. Mulch to conserve moisture.
- ▷ Watch for spider mites, which thrive in the heat of summer.

LAWNS
- ▷ Apply post-emergent herbicides to control annual weeds in Bermuda grass.
- ▷ Seed, sprig, or sod new Bermuda grass lawns.
- ▷ Maintain regular mowing and watering schedule.
- ▷ Assess lawn condition for possible fall renovation.
- ▷ Watch for signs of pests and diseases; apply controls as needed.

PATIO & CONTAINER PLANTS
- ▷ Monitor plants daily for water needs and pest control.
- ▷ Apply water-soluble fertilizer as needed for healthy vigor—usually every 2–4 weeks.
- ▷ Pinch back straggly plants and deadhead spent blooms to maintain neat appearance.
- ▷ Replace summer annuals and failed or diseased plants with heat-tolerant tropical foliage plants.

HOT

VEGETABLES & HERBS
- ▷ Plant peas, even if it seems too hot. They won't produce until temperatures cool in the fall.
- ▷ Plant bush beans weekly from now until mid-October.
- ▷ Use floating row covers to protect plants from heat and pests.
- ▷ Harvest herbs at their peak, just before they begin to flower, and use or preserve as soon as possible.

TOMATOES
- ▷ Set out fall transplants.
- ▷ Use a complete foliar fertilizer on new transplants to encourage vigorous growth and early production.
- ▷ Set up and use a low-volume irrigation system on the new tomatoes. Mulch to conserve moisture.
- ▷ Watch for spider mites, which thrive in the heat of summer.

LAWNS
- ▷ Apply post-emergent herbicides to control annual weeds in Bermuda grass.
- ▷ Seed, sprig, or sod new Bermuda grass lawns.
- ▷ Maintain regular mowing and watering schedule.
- ▷ Watch for signs of pests and diseases; apply controls as needed.
- ▷ Apply light fertilization to Bahia, St. Augustine, and centipede grasses.
- ▷ Dethatch, if not done earlier.

PATIO & CONTAINER PLANTS
- ▷ Monitor plants daily for water needs and pest control.
- ▷ Apply water-soluble fertilizer or foliar-feed plants as needed for healthy vigor—usually every 2–4 weeks.
- ▷ Pinch back straggly plants and deadhead spent blooms to maintain neat appearance.
- ▷ Replace summer annuals and failed or diseased plantings with heat-tolerant tropical foliage plants.
- ▷ Evaluate and plan for fall.

AUGUST

TREES & SHRUBS	ANNUALS	PERENNIALS & BULBS	ROSES

SEPTEMBER

COLD

TREES & SHRUBS
▷ Rake debris from shrub beds to eliminate overwintering insect eggs.
▷ Prune tent caterpillar nests from trees and destroy.

ANNUALS
▷ Water and weed until frost.
▷ Take cuttings from or move plants to be overwintered indoors before frost.
▷ Select the best flowers for drying.
▷ Protect tender plants from frost to prolong bloom.
▷ Take final performance notes.

PERENNIALS & BULBS
▷ Divide and replant perennials that have begun to crowd each other, especially bearded irises and daylilies.
▷ Plant new lily bulbs and spring-flowering bulbs right away for good root growth before the soil freezes.
▷ Weed, water, fertilize, and dead-head as needed.
▷ Watch for signs of pests and diseases.

ROSES
▷ Resume spraying with full-strength fungicides as needed as the weather cools.
▷ Water as needed; fall is often dry.
▷ Transplant rooted cuttings into a cold frame or protected nursery bed.
▷ Note which plants were weak growers and plan their replacements.
▷ Weed the beds.

TEMPERATE

TREES & SHRUBS
▷ Apply 3–4 inches of mulch to protect soil from drying winter winds.
▷ Plant woody ornamentals.

ANNUALS
▷ Water and weed as needed.
▷ Take cuttings or move plants to be overwintered indoors before frost.
▷ Select the best flowers for drying.
▷ Begin planting out winter-hardy plants such as pansies.

PERENNIALS & BULBS
▷ Transplant seedlings started in summer as space is available.
▷ Begin to divide and replant perennials that have begun to crowd each other, especially bearded irises and daylilies.
▷ Plant new lilies as soon as bulbs are available.
▷ Weed, water, and fertilize as needed.
▷ Watch for signs of pests and diseases.

ROSES
▷ Resume spraying with full-strength fungicides as needed as the weather cools.
▷ Water as needed; fall is often dry.
▷ Foliar-feed the ever-blooming types for better fall bloom.

WARM

TREES & SHRUBS
▷ Check fruit trees for fire blight and cut off any infected branches.
▷ Collect a soil sample and have it tested for nutrient content.
▷ Watch for caterpillar infestations on deciduous trees.

ANNUALS
▷ Sow the seeds of annuals for winter display.
▷ Water and weed as needed.
▷ Select the best flowers for drying.
▷ Watch for signs of pests and diseases.
▷ Cut back tired annuals and apply water-soluble fertilizer to prolong blooming.

PERENNIALS & BULBS
▷ Plant paperwhite narcissuses, bulbous irises, surprise or spider lilies, ranunculus, colchicums, and autumn-flowering crocuses.
▷ Cut back to promote plant vigor.
▷ Weed, water, fertilize, and dead-head as needed.
▷ Watch for signs of pests and diseases.

ROSES
▷ Apply the last feeding of complete fertilizer at mid-month.
▷ Order bare-root roses from mail-order nurseries for late fall or winter planting.
▷ Cultivate the soil in beds and sow the seeds of sweet alyssum as living mulch.

HOT

TREES & SHRUBS
▷ Collect a soil sample and have it tested for nutrient content.
▷ Apply sulfur to acid-loving ixoras, azaleas, and allamandas.
▷ Prune back any shrubs that are growing out of bounds.

ANNUALS
▷ Water, weed, and fertilize as needed.
▷ Sow the seeds of annuals for winter display.
▷ Watch for signs of pests and diseases.
▷ Cut back tired annuals and apply water-soluble fertilizer to prolong blooming.

PERENNIALS & BULBS
▷ Divide and replant overgrown bulb clumps before fall and winter rains.
▷ Sow seeds for late-winter and spring plantings.
▷ Cut plants back after flowering to rejuvenate. Remove dry tops from bulbs that are to be left in the ground.
▷ Weed, water, fertilize, and dead-head as needed.
▷ Watch for signs of pests and diseases.

ROSES
▷ Prune and fertilize roses that have made it through the summer.
▷ Water once or twice weekly as needed.
▷ Watch for black spot and mildew, and spray as needed.
▷ Control weeds with shallow cultivation or by hand-pulling.

 **VEGETABLES & HERBS**	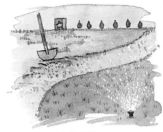 **TOMATOES**	 **LAWNS**	 **PATIO & CONTAINER PLANTS**	
▷ Make final plantings of short-season crops like radishes and lettuce. ▷ Prepare frost protection for tender plants and harvest frost-tender pumpkins, squash, and gourds early. ▷ Remove bottom leaves and growing point from Brussels sprouts spike to give maturing sprouts room and vigor. ▷ Pot up herb plants or start seeds for winter use and indoor growing. ▷ Greenhouse and sunroom gardeners should start seeds now.	▷ Late varieties are at peak production, but ripening slows as temperatures fall. ▷ Be prepared to battle any early frosts and protect productive plants. ▷ Harvest fruit as fully ripe as possible and eat or process right away. ▷ When a hard freeze threatens, harvest all fruit and put up tomato relish and green tomato pickles. ▷ Start removing cold-killed plants. ▷ Note in diary where tomatoes grew.	▷ Rake to remove thatch and weeds. ▷ Aerate if not done already or if soil seems hard and compacted. ▷ Apply 3–1–2 fertilizer at the recommended rate. Add powdered limestone if a pH test reveals acid soil. ▷ Sow seed over thin or bare spots, making passes from different directions. A light dressing of soil improves germination, and straw prevents erosion. ▷ Keep moist until the seeds sprout and develop a root system.	▷ Monitor plants daily for water and fertilizer needs and pest control. ▷ Replace summer seasonals with fall bloomers such as mums. ▷ Be prepared to protect tender plants from possible early frosts. ▷ Take cuttings of tender plants for overwintering indoors.	**COLD**
▷ Late plantings of sweet corn and winter squash reach their peak quality this month. Beware of earworms. ▷ Prepare frost protection for tender plants. Harvest frost-tender pumpkins, squash, and gourds late this month. ▷ Cover cropping should also peak this month. Plant oats or rye. ▷ Pot up herb plants or start seeds for winter use and indoor growing. ▷ Greenhouse and sunroom gardeners should start seeds now.	▷ June-planted varieties should be at peak production, though ripening slows as temperatures fall. Prune plants to discourage late fruit set. ▷ Prepare battle plan for early frosts now. Have old blankets handy to protect productive plants from light frosts. ▷ When a hard freeze threatens, harvest all fruit and put up tomato relish and green tomato pickles. ▷ Compost dead vegetation; plant winter cover crop of oats or rye.	▷ Rake to remove thatch and weeds. ▷ Aerate if not done already or if soil seems hard and compacted. ▷ Apply 3–1–2 fertilizer at the recommended rate. Add powdered limestone if a pH test reveals acid soil. ▷ Sow seed over thin or bare spots, making passes from different directions. A light dressing of soil improves germination, and straw prevents erosion. ▷ Keep moist until the seeds sprout and develop a root system.	▷ Monitor plants daily for water and fertilizer needs and pest control. ▷ Replace summer seasonals with fall bloomers such as mums. ▷ Be prepared to protect tender plants from surprise frosts. ▷ Take cuttings of tender plants for overwintering indoors.	**TEMPERATE**
▷ Set out transplants of cool-weather vegetables like lettuce, mustard, kale, turnips, cabbage, Swiss chard, and broccoli. ▷ Plant potatoes for fall production. ▷ Check early plantings of sweet potatoes for mature tubers. ▷ Add new mulch, and water thoroughly to soak the soil 8–12 inches deep. ▷ Watch for spider mite and stinkbug infestations.	▷ Use a complete foliar fertilizer to encourage vigorous growth and early production. ▷ Check plants daily for spider mites and leaf miners. ▷ Mulch plants with alfalfa hay, dried grass clippings, or other herbicide-free organic material. ▷ Remove the lower leaves on the fall plants to improve air circulation.	▷ Keep mowing and watering. ▷ Dethatch Bermuda grass. ▷ Apply 3–1–2 fertilizer at recommended rates on Bermuda and zoysia grasses. ▷ Apply pre-emergent herbicides on Bermuda grass as needed. ▷ Overseed Bermuda grass with perennial rye grass to keep lawn green through winter. Seed 6–8 weeks before frost and before Bermuda grass goes dormant.	▷ Monitor plants daily for water and fertilizer needs and pest control. ▷ Replace summer plants with fall and winter annuals as soon as cooler weather arrives. ▷ Continue pinching back and deadheading as needed. ▷ Prepare the soil in containers for new plantings by adding organic matter for better water retention and sand or perlite for good drainage.	**WARM**
▷ Direct-seed cool-weather vegetables like lettuce, mustard, kale, turnips, cabbage, Swiss chard, and broccoli. ▷ Plant potatoes for fall production. ▷ Check early plantings of sweet potatoes for mature tubers. ▷ Add new mulch, and water thoroughly to soak the soil 8–12 inches deep. ▷ Watch for spider mite and stinkbug infestations.	▷ Plant out more fall and winter tomato plants. ▷ Use a complete foliar fertilizer to encourage vigorous growth and early production. ▷ Check plants daily for spider mites and leaf miners. ▷ Mulch plants with alfalfa hay, dried grass clippings, or other herbicide-free organic material. ▷ Remove the lower leaves on fall plants to improve air circulation.	▷ Keep mowing and watering. ▷ Apply 3–1–2 fertilizer at the recommended rates for St. Augustine, Bahia, and centipede grasses.	▷ Monitor plants daily for water and fertilizer needs and pest control. Try to encourage summer plantings to last another month or two. ▷ Pinch back and deadhead as needed for health and appearance.	**HOT**

SEPTEMBER

OCTOBER

	TREES & SHRUBS	ANNUALS	PERENNIALS & BULBS	ROSES

COLD

TREES & SHRUBS
▷ Prepare tree peonies and other ornamentals that need protection from winter cold by surrounding them with boxes filled with leaves.
▷ Stake young or brittle plants to prevent snow damage.
▷ Remember to water plants in containers, which will dry out in winter winds.

ANNUALS
▷ Take final performance notes.
▷ Remove annuals killed by frost and begin fall cleanup of beds.
▷ Add weeds and other disease-free plant material to the compost pile.
▷ Add organic matter, lime, and ferti-lizer to beds, and turn them over.
▷ Shut off, drain, and repair any irrigation system before freezing weather begins.

PERENNIALS & BULBS
▷ Continue dividing and fall planting of herbaceous perennials.
▷ Finish planting spring-flowering bulbs.
▷ Plant seedlings started in summer.
▷ Clean up beds as plants freeze back and add the plant materials to the compost pile.
▷ Make notes on the season's performance.
▷ Apply high-phosphate fertilizer to beds as needed.

ROSES
▷ Stop fungicidal sprays. Store these and any leftover insecticides in a protected, well-ventilated place; extreme cold will destroy the chemicals.
▷ Plant spring bulbs like crocuses and snow drops in the rose beds for early spring color.
▷ Rake up fallen leaves, which may harbor pest eggs or disease.
▷ When tree roses are dormant, dig up and store. Prune bushes back by ⅓. Protect all roses for winter.

TEMPERATE

TREES & SHRUBS
▷ Stake new trees as high as possible and tie them loosely to encourage wind movement yet still protect them from damage.
▷ Continue planting new woody ornamentals.
▷ If you spot any scale insects on the backs of the leaves of broad-leaf evergreens, spray with dormant oil.

ANNUALS
▷ Take performance notes.
▷ Take cuttings from or move indoors any plants to be overwintered.
▷ Weed and water frost-resistant plants.
▷ Remove annuals killed by frost and begin fall cleanup in colder aeas.
▷ Add all weeds and disease-free plant materials to the compost pile.
▷ Begin planting out hardy plants for winter display, such as ornamental kales.

PERENNIALS & BULBS
▷ Continue dividing and fall planting of herbaceous perennials.
▷ Plant all spring-flowering bulbs.
▷ Water and weed as needed.
▷ Deadhead or cut back bloomed-out perennials.
▷ Clean up beds as plants freeze back in colder areas and add the plant materials to the compost pile.

ROSES
▷ Stop fungicidal sprays. Store these and any leftover insecticides in a protected, well-ventilated place; extreme cold will destroy the chemicals.
▷ Plant spring bulbs like crocuses and snow drops in the rose beds for early spring color.
▷ Plant bare-root roses in the cooler parts of this region.

WARM

TREES & SHRUBS
▷ Plant woody ornamentals.
▷ Avoid pruning now; it may encourage the tender new growth that is subject to winter damage.
▷ Use fallen leaves and pine straw as organic mulch around shrubs and trees.

ANNUALS
▷ Flush and repair any irrigation system as soon as the fall rains arrive.
▷ Continue to deadhead as needed.
▷ Weed, water, and fertilize as needed.
▷ Prepare the soil for fall plantings as space becomes available.
▷ Select and cut the best flowers for drying.

PERENNIALS & BULBS
▷ Divide overgrown and crowded plants, especially those having fleshy roots.
▷ Plant all spring-flowering bulbs.
▷ Water, weed, fertilize, and deadhead as needed.
▷ Watch for signs of pests and diseases.

ROSES
▷ Stop deadheading spent blooms.
▷ Foliar-feed roses with diluted fertilizer for better fall bloom.

HOT

TREES & SHRUBS
▷ Apply fertilizer to citrus trees and all shrubs.
▷ Apply 3–4 inches of organic mulch around plants.
▷ Watch for leaf spots and apply fungicide to control as needed.

ANNUALS
▷ Sow the seeds of annuals for winter display.
▷ Flush and repair any irrigation system as soon as the fall rains arrive.
▷ Continue to deadhead as needed.
▷ Weed, water, and fertilize as needed.
▷ Prepare the soil for fall and winter plantings as space opens up.

PERENNIALS & BULBS
▷ Divide and replant overgrown or crowded perennials.
▷ Plant prechilled spring-flowering bulbs.
▷ Test the soil, prepare beds, and make new plantings.
▷ Sow seeds for later plantings.
▷ Weed, water, fertilize, and deadhead as needed.
▷ Apply high-phosphate fertilizer to beds as needed.

ROSES
▷ Resume spraying with full-strength fungicides as needed as the weather cools.
▷ Water as needed; fall is often dry.
▷ Control weeds with shallow cultivation or by hand-pulling.
▷ Test the soil and fertilize as needed.
▷ Sow the seeds of sweet alyssum in the beds to provide a living mulch.

VEGETABLES & HERBS	**TOMATOES**	**LAWNS**	**PATIO & CONTAINER PLANTS**

COLD

VEGETABLES & HERBS

▷ Plant garlic for overwintering. Mulch after the ground freezes.

▷ As frost kills crops, continue garden cleanup. Compost shredded plant matter or till it into the soil.

▷ Gather the last harvest from the remaining crops. Fall carrots, leeks, and especially parsnips reach peak flavor in cool weather.

▷ Don't store apples with potatoes. Store pumpkins and squash without bruising skins. Store root crops in crates of sand.

TOMATOES

▷ When a hard freeze threatens, harvest all fruit and put up tomato relish and green tomato pickles.

▷ Remove dead plants, and compost them; any that are visibly diseased should be discarded or destroyed.

▷ Clean vines and foliage from cages, stakes, and trellises, and store the equipment for the winter.

▷ Collect piles of fall leaves, shred them with a lawn mower, and till them deeply into your garden beds.

LAWNS

▷ Establish or reseed the lawn with a variety suited to your area.

▷ Apply 3–1–2 fertilizer at recommended rates if not done already.

▷ Rake off leaves and other debris.

▷ Raise mower blade ½ inch above normal, and mow at new appropriate intervals.

▷ Apply broad-leaf weed controls, unless you have recently overseeded.

PATIO & CONTAINER PLANTS

▷ Remove frost-damaged plants and consider replacing them with hardy plants for winter interest, such as conifers with cold-tolerant roots.

▷ Plant spring-flowering bulbs in large planters and in smaller pots for insertion into planters in early spring.

▷ Bring in tender plants for overwintering. Small containers can be carried in and out for a time, depending on the weather.

TEMPERATE

VEGETABLES & HERBS

▷ Harvest and store late potatoes.

▷ Plant spinach and garlic. Plant cover crops for overwintering. Mulch after the ground freezes.

▷ As frost kills crops, begin garden cleanup. Compost shredded plant matter or till it into the soil.

▷ Collect as many fallen leaves as possible for mulch and composting.

▷ Keep tender vegetables productive as long as possible with cold frames, floating row covers, or other shelter.

TOMATOES

▷ Some plants may survive until mid-month. Once a freeze kills these late producers, begin the fall cleanup.

▷ Remove dead plants, and compost them; any that are visibly diseased should be discarded or destroyed.

▷ Clean vines and foliage from cages, stakes, and trellises, and store the equipment for the winter.

▷ When a hard freeze threatens, harvest all fruit and put up tomato relish and green tomato pickles.

LAWNS

▷ Establish or reseed the lawn with a variety suited to your area.

▷ Apply 3–1–2 fertilizer at recommended rates if not done already.

▷ Rake off leaves and other debris.

▷ Raise mower blade ½ inch above normal, and mow at new appropriate intervals.

▷ Apply broadleaf weed controls, unless you have recently overseeded.

PATIO & CONTAINER PLANTS

▷ Continue monitoring plants daily for water needs and pest control.

▷ Pot bulbs for spring bloom.

▷ Bring in tender plants for overwintering before they are killed by frost.

▷ Begin potting frost-tolerant plants such as ornamental kale and pansies for winter and early-spring interest.

WARM

VEGETABLES & HERBS

▷ Set out transplants of cool-weather vegetables like lettuce, mustard, kale, turnips, cabbage, Swiss chard, and broccoli, plus hard-to-seed herbs like parsley and chives.

▷ Sow the seeds of herbs like borage, cilantro, fennel, mint, oregano, and thyme.

▷ Watch for cabbage loopers, which love cool-weather leafy vegetables. Use Bt or other biological sprays.

TOMATOES

▷ Watch for leaf-footed stinkbugs.

▷ Start a compost pile with leaves, grass clippings, and manure.

▷ As harvest time nears, hang red Christmas tree balls to fool the birds.

▷ Compile your observations from the spring crop to help decide which varieties to plant next year.

LAWNS

▷ Apply 3–1–2 fertilizer at recommended rate for Bermuda grass if not done last month.

▷ Apply pre-emergent weed controls for annual weeds on established Bermuda grass.

▷ Overseed Bermuda grass lawns in the lower South and hot regions with perennial rye grass.

▷ Mow weekly until growth slows and stops.

PATIO & CONTAINER PLANTS

▷ Continue monitoring plants daily for water needs and pest control.

▷ Continue pinching back and deadheading as needed.

▷ Plant fall and winter annuals and bulbs for spring bloom.

▷ Replace dead or unsatisfactory trees and shrubs.

▷ Prepare the soil in containers by adding organic matter and sand or perlite before making new plantings.

HOT

VEGETABLES & HERBS

▷ Direct-seed cool-weather vegetables like lettuce, mustard, kale, turnips, cabbage, and broccoli.

▷ Sow the seeds of herbs like borage, cilantro, fennel, mint, oregano, and thyme.

▷ Set out transplants of parsley, chives, and other hard-to-seed herbs.

▷ Watch for cabbage loopers, which love cool-weather leafy vegetables. Use Bt or other biological sprays.

TOMATOES

▷ Set out the last batch of plants.

▷ Watch for leaf-footed stinkbugs.

▷ Start a compost pile with leaves, grass clippings, and manure.

▷ As harvest time nears, hang red ornaments to fool the birds.

▷ Compile your observations from the spring crop to help decide which varieties to plant next year.

LAWNS

▷ Apply 3–1–2 fertilizer at recommended rates for established Bahia, St. Augustine, and centipede grasses.

▷ Raise blade height ½ inch and mow every 2 weeks for St. Augustine grass.

▷ Raise blade height ½ inch and mow every 10 days for centipede grass.

PATIO & CONTAINER PLANTS

▷ Continue monitoring plants daily for water needs and pest control.

▷ Continue pinching back and deadheading as needed.

▷ After composting spent plants, prepare the soil in containers by adding organic matter and sand or perlite before making new plantings.

▷ Begin planting cool-season annuals such as calendulas, pansies, stocks, and ornamental kales for winter interest.

OCTOBER

NOVEMBER

TREES & SHRUBS

ANNUALS

PERENNIALS & BULBS

ROSES

COLD

TREES & SHRUBS
- ▷ Thoroughly water all trees and shrubs before the ground freezes.
- ▷ Spray evergreens with antitranspirants to prevent water loss.
- ▷ Apply whitewash or protective cloth around the trunks of young trees to prevent winter sunscald.

ANNUALS
- ▷ Continue garden cleanup and turn the compost pile.
- ▷ Complete soil preparation for spring.
- ▷ Clean, repair, and store tools, hoses, and other garden equipment.

PERENNIALS & BULBS
- ▷ Take soil samples before the ground freezes for testing.
- ▷ Finish garden cleanup, adding disease-free plant materials to the compost pile.
- ▷ Begin soil preparation for spring before the ground freezes.
- ▷ Water new bulb plantings if fall weather is dry.

ROSES
- ▷ Prepare new beds to be planted in the spring.
- ▷ Inspect and repair trellises and arbors.
- ▷ Cover the soil in rose beds with a mulch of dry fallen leaves.
- ▷ Cover miniature and ground-cover roses with evergreen boughs or other light protection.

TEMPERATE

TREES & SHRUBS
- ▷ Prune overgrown hollies by cutting the top branches to mere stubs while leaving lower branches longer. Use prunings for holiday decoration.
- ▷ Take a garden inventory and remove plants that have not performed well.
- ▷ Collect a soil sample and have it tested for nutrient content.

ANNUALS
- ▷ Continue garden cleanup and turn the compost pile.
- ▷ Complete soil preparation for fall or spring plantings.
- ▷ Begin to clean, repair, and store tools, hoses, and other garden equipment.
- ▷ Shut off, drain, and check irrigation equipment in colder areas.
- ▷ Complete performance notes.
- ▷ Complete planting of hardy plants for winter display.

PERENNIALS & BULBS
- ▷ Continue fall cleanup.
- ▷ Finish dividing and transplanting crowded plants.
- ▷ Finish planting spring-flowering bulbs.
- ▷ Apply high-phosphate fertilizer as needed.
- ▷ Prepare soil for spring plantings as space opens up in the beds.
- ▷ Fill in with hardy annuals for winter display.

ROSES
- ▷ After roses shed their leaves, cut the canes back by ½ to reduce winter damage.
- ▷ Dig up tree roses and lay them flat on the ground. Cover all parts with a foot of well-drained, sandy soil.
- ▷ Rake up rose leaves, which may harbor pest eggs or disease.
- ▷ Plant bare-root roses in the warmer parts of this region.
- ▷ Prepare new beds to be planted in the spring.

WARM

TREES & SHRUBS
- ▷ Stake new trees high on the trunk; tie them as loosely as possible to encourage wind movement while still protecting them from damage.
- ▷ Keep planting woody ornamentals.
- ▷ Control scale insects on the backs of the leaves of broad-leaved evergreens by spraying with dormant oil.
- ▷ Take a garden inventory and remove plants that have not performed well.

ANNUALS
- ▷ Protect tender plants from frost in colder areas to extend blooming.
- ▷ Remove all spent and frost-damaged plants, and prepare the soil for winter and spring planting.
- ▷ Add all weeds and disease-free plant materials to the compost pile.
- ▷ Take cuttings from or move indoors any plants to be saved or overwintered.

PERENNIALS & BULBS
- ▷ Sow seeds for spring planting.
- ▷ Finish planting spring-flowering bulbs.
- ▷ Clean up after any frosts in colder areas, adding disease-free plant materials to the compost pile.
- ▷ Fill in with hardy annuals for winter display.
- ▷ Watch for signs of pests and diseases.

ROSES
- ▷ Take cuttings for propagation.
- ▷ Transplant rooted cuttings from last year.
- ▷ Plant pansies and violas in the rose beds for winter color.
- ▷ Plant early spring-flowering bulbs in the rose beds.

HOT

TREES & SHRUBS
- ▷ Water newly planted palms and other plants.
- ▷ Apply a pre-emergent herbicide to keep weeds from sprouting in shrub beds.
- ▷ Prune storm-damaged plants.

ANNUALS
- ▷ Continue to remove tired summer plants and add disease-free ones to the compost pile.
- ▷ Prepare the soil and set out ornamental vegetables and other plants for winter display as the weather cools.
- ▷ Weed, water, and fertilize as needed.

PERENNIALS & BULBS
- ▷ Divide and replant overgrown or crowded perennials and bulbs.
- ▷ Plant agapanthus, amaryllis, montbretia, tigridia, watsonia, and lily bulbs for spring and summer bloom.
- ▷ Sow seeds for late-winter and early-spring plantings.
- ▷ Weed, water, fertilize, and deadhead as needed.
- ▷ Test the soil, prepare beds, and make new plantings.

ROSES
- ▷ Spray for black spot, mildew, and spider mites as needed.
- ▷ Plant container-grown roses for winter bloom.
- ▷ Water weekly during dry weather and twice weekly on exposed sites.
- ▷ Control weeds with shallow cultivation or by hand-pulling.

VEGETABLES & HERBS	TOMATOES	LAWNS	PATIO & CONTAINER PLANTS	

VEGETABLES & HERBS

▷ Mix fresh manure into all beds except those to be planted with root crops.

▷ Mulch the soil around perennial crops like asparagus and sage.

▷ Dig and store root crops in cool, moist sand.

▷ Clean up and store trellises, cages, bean poles, and stakes.

▷ Finish collecting fall leaves and tilling them into the soil; shredding speeds their decomposition.

▷ Finish fall harvesting. Mix fresh manure into all beds except those to be planted with root crops.

▷ Dig and store root crops in cool, moist sand.

▷ Clean up and store trellises, cages, bean poles, and stakes.

▷ Finish collecting fall leaves and tilling them into the soil; shredding speeds their decomposition.

▷ Where snowfall is erratic, place a snow fence to create insulating drifts.

▷ Harvest new potatoes by carefully digging near the surface. Save the deeper tubers for mature harvest in December.

▷ Watch for cabbage loopers.

▷ Add leaves, grass clippings, and manure to the compost pile, and turn it every 2 weeks. Add more manure and water if the pile won't heat up.

▷ Foliar-feed fall vegetables and herbs with a hose-end fertilizer sprayer.

▷ Harvest new potatoes by carefully digging near the surface. Save the deeper tubers for mature harvest in December.

▷ Watch for cabbage loopers.

▷ Add leaves, grass clippings, and manure to the compost pile, and turn it every 2 weeks. Add more manure and water if the pile won't heat up.

▷ Foliar-feed fall vegetables and herbs with a hose-end fertilizer sprayer.

TOMATOES

▷ Complete garden cleanup before the first snowstorms.

▷ As weather allows, till more fallen leaves into the soil.

▷ Incorporate manure, compost, and other needed amendments into the beds now to break down and mellow over the winter.

▷ Make sure tools and supplies are safely stored away for the winter.

▷ Complete garden cleanup before the fall rains arrive.

▷ As weather allows, collect, shred, and till fallen leaves into the soil.

▷ Incorporate manure, compost, and other needed amendments into the beds now to break down and mellow over the winter.

▷ Make sure tools and supplies are safely stored away for the winter.

▷ Be prepared to protect plants from early frosts.

▷ Harvest fruit as soon as it turns pink to limit insect and bird damage.

▷ Continue adding to the compost pile and turn it every 2 weeks. Add more manure and water if it won't heat up.

▷ Watch for leaf-footed stinkbugs.

▷ Plant empty areas with a cover crop of rye or oats to discourage nematodes.

▷ Harvest fruit as soon as it turns pink to limit insect and bird damage.

▷ Continue adding to the compost pile and turn it every 2 weeks. Add more manure and water if it won't heat up.

▷ Watch for leaf-footed stinkbugs.

▷ Plant empty areas with a cover crop of rye or oats to discourage nematodes.

LAWNS

▷ Rake up leaves and debris as needed.

▷ Mow newly overseeded grass at ½ inch above normal for a manicured appearance.

▷ Water if fall is dry.

▷ Trim tree limbs and prune shrubs over areas where grass had difficulty growing because of shade.

▷ Establish a new lawn with sod if the ground isn't frozen.

▷ Rake up leaves and debris as needed.

▷ Mow newly overseeded grass at ½ inch above normal for a manicured appearance.

▷ Water if fall is dry.

▷ Trim tree limbs and prune shrubs over areas where grass had difficulty growing because of shade.

▷ Establish a new lawn with sod if the ground isn't frozen.

▷ Apply pre-emergent herbicides.

▷ Apply fertilizer to Bermuda grass if not done already.

▷ Mow only as needed.

▷ Water if conditions are dry, particularly if lawn was overseeded with perennial ryegrass.

▷ Rake up leaves and other debris as needed.

▷ Mow only as needed.

▷ Apply post-emergent broad-leaf weed control at recommended rates.

PATIO & CONTAINER PLANTS

▷ Finish fall cleanup after killing frosts.

▷ Complete planting of all spring-blooming bulbs.

▷ Complete planting of hardy plants for winter display, including evergreens such as pines and spruces.

▷ Bury—or insulate by wrapping—containers of any root-tender but otherwise hardy plants.

▷ Keep all containers well watered until the soil freezes.

▷ Finish fall cleanup after killing frosts.

▷ Complete planting of all spring-blooming bulbs.

▷ Replace any remaining summer plants with those having winter and early-spring color or interest.

▷ Bring in the last tender plants for overwintering if not done already.

▷ Monitor plants daily for water needs and pest control.

▷ Pinch back and deadhead as needed.

▷ Continue planting cool-season annuals and replacing trees and shrubs as needed.

▷ Monitor plants daily for water needs and pest control.

▷ Pinch back and deadhead as needed.

▷ Continue planting cool-season annuals. Replace and plant new trees and shrubs in large permanent containers as needed or desired.

▷ Prune and shape permanent tree and shrub plantings.

COLD

TEMPERATE

WARM

HOT

NOVEMBER

TREES & SHRUBS

ANNUALS

PERENNIALS & BULBS

ROSES

DECEMBER

COLD

TREES & SHRUBS
- ▷ Leave cold-damaged foliage of evergreen shrubs on the plants until spring.
- ▷ Apply a granular complete fertilizer to shrub beds.
- ▷ Lightly prune conifers and hollies to provide greenery for the holidays.

ANNUALS
- ▷ Continue garden cleanup and turn the compost pile once more.
- ▷ Finish cleaning, repairing, and storing tools, hoses, and other garden equipment.
- ▷ Think about the year's successes, learn from the failures, and start dreaming about next season.

PERENNIALS & BULBS
- ▷ Complete fall cleanup and turn the compost pile.
- ▷ Clean, repair, and store tools, hoses, and other garden equipment.
- ▷ Drain any irrigation systems and make any needed repairs before freezing weather sets in.
- ▷ Apply winter mulch once the soil has begun to freeze.

ROSES
- ▷ Water standard roses stored in pots occasionally to keep the soil from drying out completely.
- ▷ Check on roses planted last spring or summer. If frost has heaved them up, replace the soil around the roots and bud union.
- ▷ Plan plantings for next year. Consider cold-hardy rugosas and old garden roses. Avoid any types observed last spring as prone to winter damage.

TEMPERATE

TREES & SHRUBS
- ▷ If your soil is too acid, add lime; because it moves slowly through the soil, it will reach your plants' roots when they need it in early spring.
- ▷ After heavy snowfalls, check young trees and shrubs for bark nibbled off by hungry rodents. Wrap trunks with wire mesh to protect them from further damage.

ANNUALS
- ▷ Continue garden cleanup and turn the compost pile.
- ▷ Weed, water, and fertilize winter display plantings.
- ▷ Clean, repair, and store tools, hoses, and other garden equipment.
- ▷ Think about the year's successes, learn from the failures, and start dreaming about next season.

PERENNIALS & BULBS
- ▷ Continue fall cleanup and turn the compost pile.
- ▷ Clean, repair, and store tools, hoses, and other garden equipment.
- ▷ Drain any irrigation systems and make any needed repairs before freezing weather sets in.
- ▷ Continue to fill in gaps with winter annuals as space is available.
- ▷ Apply winter mulch once the soil has begun to freeze.
- ▷ Water bulbs if weather is dry.

ROSES
- ▷ Water roses deeply during any periods of thaw.
- ▷ Check on roses planted during last spring. If frost has heaved them up, replace the soil around the roots and bud union.
- ▷ Inspect arbors and trellises; repair as needed.
- ▷ Cover miniature and ground-cover roses with a blanket of evergreen boughs or other light protection.

WARM

TREES & SHRUBS
- ▷ Mulch shrubs and trees to protect them from drying winter winds.
- ▷ If your soil is too acid, add lime; because it moves slowly through the soil, it will reach your plants' roots when they need it in early spring.
- ▷ Prune overgrown hollies by cutting top branches to mere stubs; leave lower branches longer. Use prunings for Christmas decorations.
- ▷ Watch for, cut off, and destroy any bagworm pouches.

ANNUALS
- ▷ Continue fall cleanup and soil preparation as summer annuals are removed.
- ▷ Continue planting ornamental vegetables and other winter plants.
- ▷ Weed, water, and fertilize winter plantings as needed.
- ▷ Protect tender plants against frost damage in colder areas.
- ▷ Turn the compost pile.

PERENNIALS & BULBS
- ▷ Plant amaryllis and tuberous begonias in warmer parts of this area.
- ▷ Sow seeds for spring plantings.
- ▷ Fill in with hardy annuals for winter color.
- ▷ Weed and water as needed.
- ▷ Watch for signs of pests and diseases.
- ▷ Cut plants back after frost, adding disease-free prunings to compost pile.
- ▷ Prepare the soil for spring.

ROSES
- ▷ Plant bare-root roses.
- ▷ Apply dormant oil to kill overwintering insects and eggs.
- ▷ Dig and prepare new rose beds and planting holes for late-winter or early-spring planting.
- ▷ Apply winter protection anywhere winter temperatures could drop below 20°F.

HOT

TREES & SHRUBS
- ▷ Take a garden inventory, and remove plants that have not performed well.
- ▷ Prune olive and other slow-growing trees to prevent heavy canopies subject to storm damage.
- ▷ Transplant deciduous trees like cassias and orchid trees.
- ▷ Stake new trees high on the trunk. Tie them as loosely as possible to encourage wind movement while still protecting them from damage.

ANNUALS
- ▷ Continue fall cleanup and soil preparation as summer annuals are removed.
- ▷ Continue planting ornamental vegetables and other winter plants.
- ▷ Weed, water, and fertilize as needed.
- ▷ Protect tender plants against frost damage in colder areas.
- ▷ Turn the compost pile.

PERENNIALS & BULBS
- ▷ Plant out gladiolus corms.
- ▷ Divide and replant overgrown or crowded perennials.
- ▷ Prepare beds; set out new plants.
- ▷ Sow seeds for spring plantings.
- ▷ Weed, water, and fertilize as needed.
- ▷ Cut plants back after blooming to rejuvenate.
- ▷ Be ready to protect tender bulb plants from surprise frosts.

ROSES
- ▷ Spray for black spot and mildew weekly or as needed.
- ▷ Prune roses late this month, cutting back canes by ⅓–½.
- ▷ Water deeply once a week in dry weather, twice weekly on exposed sites.
- ▷ Control weeds with shallow cultivation or by hand-pulling.

 VEGETABLES & HERBS	 TOMATOES	 LAWNS	 PATIO & CONTAINER PLANTS	
▷ Protect herbs that are not dependably hardy in your area with bags stuffed with straw or dead leaves. ▷ Monitor stored crops for spoilage. ▷ Harvest carrots, parsnips, and Jerusalem artichokes left in the garden anytime the soil is diggable. ▷ Fill in gaps in your garden journal now, while memories are fresh. Make an appraisal of the season and write down what worked and what didn't.	▷ Put up snow fencing on the windward side of the garden. It will collect extra moisture and insulate the ground with drifts of snow. ▷ Finish filling in the garden diary, noting failures, successes, and new varieties to try next year.	▷ Rake up leaves and other debris when lawn isn't under snow. ▷ Minimize salt deposits on areas near walks and driveways. ▷ Perform a soil test if not done recently, or send a soil sample to the Cooperative Extension Service or a private lab for analysis. ▷ Store mower (with its gas tank drained) with other lawn supplies in a secure, dry place.	▷ Continue watering until the soil freezes. ▷ Decorate all evergreens and their containers for the holidays. ▷ Review the season's successes and failures in preparation for the new planting season.	COLD
▷ Mulch tender herbs against cold. Hardy herbs may prefer nomulch. ▷ Finish cleaning up and composting any plants killed by cold weather. ▷ Monitor stored crops for spoilage. ▷ Harvest carrots, parsnips, and Jerusalem artichokes left in the garden anytime the soil is diggable. ▷ Fill in gaps in your garden journal now, while memories are fresh. Make an appraisal of the season and write down what worked and what didn't.	▷ Complete garden cleanup before the first snows arrive. ▷ As weather allows, keep tilling fallen leaves into the soil and incorporating manure, compost, and other needed amendments into the beds. ▷ Finish filling in the garden diary, noting failures, successes, and new varieties to try next year.	▷ Rake up leaves and other debris when lawn isn't under snow. ▷ Minimize salt deposits on areas near walks and driveways. ▷ Perform a soil test if not done recently, or send a soil sample to the Cooperative Extension Service or a private lab for analysis. ▷ Store mower (with its gas tank drained) with other lawn supplies in a secure, dry place.	▷ Continue watering until the soil freezes. ▷ Decorate evergreens and their containers for the holidays. ▷ Review the season's successes and failures in preparation for the new planting season. ▷ Pot evergreens with cold-tolerant roots, such as pines and junipers, for winter interest. ▷ Protect tender-rooted but otherwise hardy plants with insulated containers.	TEMPERATE
▷ Plan next season's vegetable and herb gardens. If possible, locate the herb garden near the kitchen so that it will be handy for cooking. ▷ Order seeds and plants for the spring garden. ▷ Set out cool-season herb transplants or direct-seed parsley, cilantro, and chives. ▷ Send a soil sample to the Cooperative Extension Service or a private lab for analysis.	▷ Plan next season's tomato patch. Remember to allow a minimum of feet between plants and 8–10 hours of full sun per day. ▷ Order seeds and plants for the spring garden. ▷ Prepare the soil by adding 2–6 inches of compost and working it in. ▷ Send a soil sample to the Cooperative Extension Service or a private lab for analysis.	▷ Apply post-emergent herbicides for annual grasses and broad-leaf weeds to help next year's Bermuda grass.	▷ Monitor plants daily for water needs and pest control. ▷ Continue with new plantings, both seasonal and permanent. ▷ Consider new plantings appropriate for seasonal holiday interest. ▷ Review the season's successes and failures in preparation for the new planting season.	WARM
▷ Plan next season's vegetable and herb gardens. If possible, locate the herb garden near the kitchen so that it will be handy for cooking. ▷ Order seeds and plants for the spring garden. ▷ Set out cool-season herb transplants or direct-seed parsley, cilantro, and chives. ▷ Send a soil sample to the Cooperative Extension Service or a private lab for analysis.	▷ Plant out another batch of transplants and be prepared to protect them from rare frosts. ▷ Plan next season's tomato patch. ▷ Order seeds and plants for the spring garden. ▷ Prepare the soil by adding 2–6 inches of compost and working it in. ▷ Send a soil sample to the Cooperative Extension Service or a private lab for analysis.	▷ Apply post-emergent herbicides for broad-leaf weeds at recommended rate to help next year's lawn.	▷ Monitor plants daily for water needs and pest control. ▷ Continue to fill gaps with new plantings of winter annuals and attractive foliage plants. ▷ Complete pruning and reshaping trees and shrubs. ▷ Review the season's successes and failures in preparation for the new planting season.	HOT

DECEMBER

GLOSSARY

Accent plant A plant used as a focal point in a yard or garden composition; generally of striking size, shape, or color.

Acid soil Soil with a pH value below 7; also called sour soil.

Adventitious Growing from places where growth does not normally occur. *Example:* adventitious roots growing from a buried stem.

Alkaline soil Soil with a pH value greater than 7; also called sweet soil.

Allée A tree-lined path or roadway, usually formal, with the trees trimmed to form green "walls."

Alpine A plant that grows in mountainous regions and is also suited to rock gardens.

Amendment A material added to the soil to improve its condition. *Examples:* lime, peat moss.

Annual A plant that completes its life cycle within one growing season.

Anther The functional part of a stamen, which produces and contains the pollen grains.

Arachnid One of a class of anthropods that includes spiders, mites, and ticks.

Axil The angle between a leaf and stem, from which arises further growth or flower buds.

Bactericide Any pesticide that kills bacteria.

Balled-and-burlapped Used to describe a nursery plant with its root ball wrapped in burlap for protection during transport or shipping.

Bare-root Used to describe a dormant nursery plant sold without soil around its roots.

Bedding Generally, a large planting area or bed containing a single variety to give uniform shape or create blocks of color.

Bedding plant A plant, with blooms or without, used for temporary garden display; usually an annual.

Beneficials Insects or plants that control harmful insects, increase the productivity or fertility of plants, or attract other aids to the garden.

Berm A mound of soil; a raised planting bed used as a landscape feature.

Biennial A plant that requires two growing seasons to complete its life cycle; leaves are formed the first year, flowers and seeds the following season. *Example:* foxglove.

Biological control Any living or biologically derived agent that controls garden pests and disease. *Example:* toads eating slugs and snails.

Blanching (1) Literally, "making white"—bleaching a growing vegetable, such as celery or cauliflower, by depriving it of light for a period of time. (2) Par-boiling fresh vegetables to prepare them for freezing.

Bog plants Plants whose preferred habitat is consistently damp or moist soil.

Bolt To go to seed prematurely; usually applied to vegetables, such as lettuce, and often caused by a cessation of normal growth due to drought, heat, or poor soil.

Brassica A member of the cabbage family, including broccoli, cauliflower, Brussels sprouts, collards, and kale.

Broadcast To scatter seed or fertilizer evenly over wide areas.

Broad-leaf A plant having broad, flat leaves as opposed to the needlelike leaves of conifers; usually deciduous.

Bromeliad A member of a family of tropical plants; usually rosetted with stiff leaves that form a central tube or cup.

Bulb A swollen underground stem where food is stored during a plant's dormant period.

Bulbil A tiny bulb developed aboveground on certain bulbous plants, as in the leaf axil of some lilies and in the flowerhead of various onions.

Bulblet A small bulb that grows on the roots of a parent bulb.

Calcareous Used to describe alkaline soils containing limestone.

Cambium In plants, a thin formative layer of tissue where new cells are produced.

Cane A slender woody stem, such as those of raspberry and blackberry bushes and bamboo.

Carpet bedding Massing bedding plants together to form dense areas of color or patterns.

Chlorosis A loss of chlorophyll caused by a lack of essential minerals, particularly iron; indicated by yellowing foliage.

Clay soil Heavy soil; often compacted and slow-draining.

Cloche A glass or plastic cover for protecting plants from cold and frost; usually bell-shaped.

Cold frame A bottomless box with a hinged plastic or glass top; used to harden off and protect plants from the cold.

Companion planting Interplanting of different plants considered to have a beneficial effect on one another.

Compost Rich organic matter created by the decomposition of plant remains and farm animal wastes; used as a soil amendment or as mulch.

Conifer Usually a cone-bearing plant with needlelike leaves; generally evergreen.

Corm The underground bulb-like stem-base of a flowering plant. *Example:* gladiolus.

Corolla The whorl of inner leaves in the petals of a flower.

Cotyledon The first leaf or set of leaves to emerge after a seed has germinated; also known as the seed leaf.

Cross-pollination Transfer of the pollen of one plant to the pistil of another.

Crown (1) The basal part of herbaceous perennials, from which both the stems and the roots grow. (2) The upper branches of a tree.

Cucurbit A member of the gourd family, including squash, cucumbers, and melons.

Culm A jointed stem or stalk, generally hollow, of ornamental grasses and bamboos.

Cultivar *(abbr.:* cv.*)* A named plant variety selected from the wild or a garden and cultivated by controlled propagation to preserve certain characteristics; distinguished in a plant's name by the use of single quotation marks. *Example: Thuja occidentalis* 'Gold King.'

Cutting A leaf, shoot, root, or bud that has been cut off a plant for use in propagation.

Deadheading The removal of faded flowers to discourage seed development and encourage more vigorous blooming.

Deciduous Nonevergreen trees and shrubs that shed their leaves at the end of the growing season and grow new foliage at the start of the next season.

Dividing The process of dividing a plant in order to propagate it, usually in early spring. Also called division.

Dolomitic limestone A form of limestone containing small amounts of magnesium.

Dormancy The cessation of a plant's growth for a rest period.

Drench Application of a pesticide to the roots of a plant.

Epiphyte A plant that grows above the ground on another plant and draws nourishment from the debris on the host plant and from air.

Espalier (1) A tree or bush pruned and trained to grow flat against a wall, trellis, or fence. (2) The training or support of such a plant.

Etiolation The long, thin, pale growth of a plant caused by the exclusion of light.

Evergreen A plant that bears foliage throughout the year.

F$_1$ hybrid A plant bred from two pure-breeding parents to produce a hardier and more productive offspring; will not breed true in next generation.

F$_2$ hybrid Offspring of an F$_1$ hybrid.

Family Botanically, a group of plant genuses having overall similar characteristics.

Filament On a flower, the anther-bearing stalk of a stamen.

Flat A shallow box or container in which seeds are sown for germination.

Floating row cover A lightweight woven or bonded fabric placed over planting rows as protection from frost or pests.

Floriferous Bearing flowers.

Forcing Inducing a plant to bloom or fruit sooner than it does naturally by manipulating light or temperature.

Foundation planting A planting around the base of a structure for decorative purposes.

Friable Easily crumbled, as soil.

Frost dam An obstacle on a slope that causes cold air to collect on the uphill side. *Examples:* a wall, hedge, or dense row of trees.

Fungicide Any substance used to kill or inhibit fungi growth.

Gall An abnormal outgrowth on a plant; caused by insects, bacteria, mites, or fungi.

Genus Botanically, a like group of plants within a family; composed of one or more species; the first word in the Latin name of a plant.

Geotextile Any of a wide variety of modern woven or bonded ground-cover plastics that allow water and air to pass through. Used for frost and pest protection, mulch, and erosion control.

Germinate To begin to grow; to sprout from seed.

Glauconite An iron potassium silicate present in greensand.

Grafting A method of propagation through the artificial union of the shoot of one plant (the scion) to the stem of another (the rootstock).

Gray water Household water, such as bathwater or dishwater; used for watering plants.

Greensand A sediment composed of grains of glauconite mingled with clay or sand; used as an organic fertilizer.

Habit The direction or shape a plant takes as it grows.

Harden off To gradually acclimatize seedlings or larger plants to cooler outside conditions before transplanting.

Hardiness A plant's ability to withstand unfavorable climatic conditions, particularly frost.

Hardpan A hard, dense lower layer of soil formed when minerals leach down and bind with soil particles; blocks drainage and inhibits root penetration.

Heeling in Planting in a temporary location.

Herbaceous Applies to any plant that has soft or tender upper growth rather than woody growth; can describe an annual, biennial, or perennial.

Herbicide A chemical used to control or kill weeds.

Hilling up Piling up soil around a plant as protection, to encourage stem development, or to blanch the stems.

Honeydew Excretion from aphids and scale insects.

Humus Nutrient-rich substance in soil resulting from the natural decomposition of animal and vegetable matter.

Hybrid A plant bred from the cross-fertilization of two or more genetically different parents, usually between species of the same genus.

Hydroponics The growing of plants in a soilless, nutrient-rich water solution.

Inflorescence (1) Flowering. (2) Flowers that grow in a group from a single axis.

Insecticidal soap An insecticide in a liquid soap base, generally applied by spraying.

Insecticide Any pesticide that kills insects.

Interplant To plant two or more types of plants together. *Examples:* mixing tall and short plants or mixing foliage plants with flowering plants.

Interspecific cross A hybrid whose parents are species within a particular genus.

Knot garden An elaborately designed formal garden with plants pruned into intricate patterns of open and closed knots, sometimes in a continuously weaving thread.

Lateral A side growth on a shoot or root.

Layering A method of propagating in which a stem, side shoot, or cane is made to form roots while still attached to the parent plant.

Leach To seep through soil out of the reach of plant roots; drainage of soluble nutrients downward from the surface.

Leader The main stem or branch of a plant.

Lime (1) One of several compounds containing calcium; derived from limestone. (2) A small green citrus fruit.

Limestone A rock consisting primarily of calcium carbonate; the source of compounds used as amendments for the soil.

Loam Soil that has a relatively equal balance of sand, silt, and clay and is also usually rich in humus; friable soil.

Medium The term used for soil mix in which plants are grown, potted, or propagated. Also called growing medium.

Microclimate A discrete physical area with a set of conditions different from those of the surrounding climate.

Miticide A pesticide that kills mites; also called acaracide.

Mulch A protective organic or manmade material applied to the soil surface; used to provide weed or pest control, conserve moisture, or keep soil cooler in summer and warmer in winter.

Node A stem joint, sometimes swollen, from which buds, shoots, and branches emerge.

Offset An offshoot that generally develops from the base of the parent plant.

Open-pollinated Used to describe a plant whose pollination has occurred naturally rather than by human manipulation.

Organic Derived from decomposed animal or plant matter.

Ornamental A plant grown strictly for its foliage or flowers; a fruit or vegetable plant that produces decorative but generally inedible fruits.

Overwintering Sheltering marginally hardy plants outdoors or bringing tender plants indoors during the winter.

Peat moss Partially decayed sphagnum moss used in potting media, soil amendments, and as a mulch.

Peduncle The stem or stalk of a single flower or the principal stem supporting a flower cluster.

Perennial (1) A flower that dies down to dormant roots over the winter and resumes new growth in the spring. (2) Any nonwoody plant that lives over several seasons.

Pergola A structure generally consisting of supporting rows of columns connected by an open or latticework roof.

Perlite Granular volcanic rock used to improve aeration in a growing medium.

Pesticide Any chemical, whether natural or synthetic, that controls or kills weeds, insects, or animal pests.

Petiole The stalk of a leaf.

pH The degree of acidity or alkalinity in the soil, measured numerically.

Pheromone traps Artificial scent lures that imitate the natural hormonal attractants of specific insect pests.

Pinching back Removing by hand the growing tip of a plant to stimulate production of side shoots or new buds. Also called pinching out.

Potpourri oil Essences or essential oils from flowers, barks, fruits, and leaves; used to add fragrance to potpourri.

Propagate To grow new plants from parent stock.

Pseudobulb A swollen growth resembling a bulb; found mainly on epiphytic orchids.

Raceme An unbranched elongated inflorescence with stemmed flowers.

Ramet An individual member of a group of plants all propagated from the same parent.

Rhizome A swollen underground stem that stores food and produces shoots and roots.

Root ball The roots and accompanying soil visible when a plant is taken out of its planting site and transported.

Rooting hormone A chemical substance used in propagation to encourage root formation.

Rootstock The section of a plant onto which the shoot or bud of another plant is grafted.

Runner A trailing stem that roots itself where a node makes contact with the soil.

Scale (1) Any thin, scalelike appendage on a plant, usually a leaf. (2) A widely diverse group of tiny sucking insects.

Scarification Nicking or applying a chemical treatment to a tough seed coat to induce speedier germination.

Scion A shoot or bud from one plant grafted onto the rootstock of another.

Seed head A dried cluster of ripened seeds.

Self-pollinating Self-fertilizing; a plant able to transfer pollen to itself.

Set (1) A small bulb, corm, or tuber used for propagation. (2) The stage when a flower has been fertilized and begins to produce fruit and seeds.

Sharp sand Coarse sand with sharp-edged grains, usually used as a soil amendment

Side-dress To spread or sprinkle fertilizer on the soil around a plant or alongside a row.

Side shoot A stem that arises from a main shoot.

Soilless mix A potting medium that contains no soil; usually a combination of peat moss, vermiculite, and fertilizer.

Species *(abbr.:* spp.*)* Botanically, a group of plants sharing at least one distinct trait that sets them apart from all others; a unit of classification that ranks immediately below genus; the second word in the Latin name of a plant.

Specimen plant A plant set apart from others in order to exhibit its striking appearance.

Sphagnum moss Moisture-retaining moss found in bogs and added to potting media.

Spores The dustlike reproductive cells of flowerless plants like ferns, fungi, and mosses.

Stamen On a flower, the male reproductive organ, consisting of the anther and usually a filament or stalk.

Standard (1) A tree or shrub trained or grafted to grow on a single stem and whose growth is concentrated in a crown of foliage. (2) A nonhybrid, open-pollinated plant.

Stipule A small leaflike structure at the base of a leaf stalk.

Stratification The exposure of hard-coated seeds to cold to improve or speed germination.

Succulents Plants that store water in their fleshy leaves or stems; includes cacti.

Sucker An undesirable shoot that arises from the roots or the leaf axil of a plant.

Systemic Used to describe a pesticide that is absorbed by a plant and enters its sap.

Taproot The main anchoring root of a plant.

Thinning out Removing surplus seedlings, flowers, or fruits so that the remaining ones grow more vigorously.

Tilth The condition or structure of the top layer of the soil.

Top-dress To apply fresh soil, compost, or fertilizer to the surface around a plant without working it into the soil.

Topiary Pruning trees and shrubs into ornamental shapes.

Topsoil The nutrient-rich topmost layer of soil.

Train To direct a plant to grow in a desired form.

Transplant To move a plant from one location to another, one pot to another, or from indoor flats to outdoor beds.

Tuber A thickened part of a stem or root where food is stored, generally underground. *Example:* potato.

Variegated On leaves, marked by striations or patterns in contrasting colors.

Variety *(abbr.:* var.*)* A distinct variation in a species, with a name of its own; often used interchangeably with cultivar.

Vermiculite A moisture-retaining mineral used to lighten soils and potting mixes.

Woody Used to describe certain types of plants, usually trees and shrubs, with hard stems or trunks that do not die back in winter.

Xeriscaping Landcaping method based on the use of low-volume irrigation systems and drought-adaptable plants.

INDEX

▷ An index entry followed immediately by a **boldface** page number refers to one of the 362 alphabetical entries or special features in the Garden Dictionary section.

▷ Page numbers preceded by the word "Enemies" refer to the Enemies of the Garden section. Those preceded by "Calendar" refer to the Garden Calendar section.

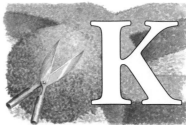

GARDENING INFORMATION SOURCES

As a gardener, your most valuable tool may be your telephone and the number of your local Cooperative Extension Service office. Located in every county in the U.S. by federal government decree, these offices and the agents who work there are available to answer your questions about plants, climate, cultivation, and pests.

Another rich local resource is your home state's land grant agricultural university and the regional plant and soil experts who work or teach there. They are usually more than willing to help any gardener in their state with a problem or question.

The associations and other groups listed on these two pages offer more specialized information, along with mountains of free or low-cost material on their particular horticultural interest. Many even send out cuttings and seeds for only the cost of shipping. If no phone or fax number is listed, you may assume that the organization would prefer to be contacted by mail.

All-America Gladiolus Selections
11734 Road 33½
Madera, CA 93638-8465
(209) 645-5329
Fax: (209) 645-1300

All-America Selections
1311 Butterfield Rd. Suite 310
Downer's Grove, IL 60515
(708) 963-0770
Fax: (708) 963-8864

American Association of Botanical Gardens and Arboreta
786 Church Road
Wayne, PA 19087
(610) 688-1120

American Bamboo Society
230 Quail Gardens Drive
Encinitas, CA 92024

American Begonia Society
157 Monument Road
Rio Dell, CA 95562-1617

American Bonsai Society
P.O. Box 1136
Puyallup, WA 98374-1136
(206) 841-8992

American Botanical Council
PO Box 201660
Austin, TX 78720
(512) 331-8868
Fax: (512) 331-1924

American Boxwood Society
HCR 60 Box 41T
Deerfield, VA 24432
(540) 939-4646

American Camellia Society
Massee Lane Gardens
One Massee Lane
Fort Valley, GA 31030
(912) 967-2722, 2358
Fax: (912) 967-2083

American Chestnut Foundation
469 Main Street, PO Box 4044
Bennington, VT 05201-4044
(802) 447-0110

American Community Gardening Association
315 Chestnut Street
Philadelphia, PA 19106-2777
(215) 922-2104
Fax: (215) 625-9392

American Conifer Society
827 Brooks Street
Ann Arbor, MI 48103-3161
(313) 665-8171
Fax: (313) 665-8720

American Daffodil Society
1686 Grey Fox Trails
Milford, OH 45150-1521
(513) 248-9137
Fax: (513) 248-0898

American Dahlia Society
16816 C R 10
Bristol, IN 46507
(219) 848-4888

American Fern Society
Milwaukee Public Museum
800 W. Wells Street
Milwaukee, WI 53233

American Herb Association
PO Box 1673
Nevada City, CA 95959-1673
(916) 265-9552

American Horticultural Society
7931 E. Boulevard Drive
Alexandria, VA 22308-9801
(800) 777-7931

American Iris Society
N75 W14257 N. Point Drive
Menomonee Falls, WI 53051
(414) 251-5292

American Orchid Society
6000 South Olive Avenue
W. Palm Beach, FL 33405
(407) 585-8666
Fax: (407) 585-0654

American Rhododendron Society
PO Box 1380
Gloucester, VA 23061-1380
(804) 693-4433

American Rose Society
PO Box 30,000
Shreveport, LA 71130-0030
(318) 938-5402
Fax: (318) 938-5405

American Willow Growers Network
RFD 1, Box 124A
South New Berlin, NY 13843
(607) 847-8264

Azalea Society of America
PO Box 34536
West Bethesda, MD 20827-0536

Bio-Dynamic Farming and Gardening Association
PO Box 550
Kimberton, PA 19442
(800) 516-7797
Fax: (610) 983-3196

Bonsai Clubs International
2636 W. Mission Road, # 277
Tallahassee, FL 32304-2556
(904) 862-8844
Fax: (904) 864-1410

Cactus and Succulent Society of America
1535 Reeves Street
Los Angeles, CA 90035

Elm Research Institute
PO Box 805
Harrisville, NH 03450
800-FOR-ELMS

FWH Seed Exchange
PO Box 651
Pauma Valley, CA 92061-0651

Gardenia Society of America
P. O. Box 879
Atwater, CA 95301

Herb Research Foundation
1007 Pearl Street, Suite 200
Boulder, CO 80302
(800) 748-2617

Herb Society of America
9019 Kirtland Chardon Road
Kirtland, OH 44094
(216) 256-0540

Heritage Rose Foundation
1512 Gorman Street
Raleigh, NC 27606-2919
(919) 834-2591

Hobby Greenhouse Association
8 Glen Terrace
Bedford, MA 01730-2048
(617) 275-0377

International Bulb Society
PO Box 92136
Pasadena, CA 91109-2136
(818) 337-2164

International Carnivorous Plant Society
c/o Fullerton Arboretum
Fullerton, CA 92634

International Geranium Society
PO Box 92734
Pasadena, CA 91109-2734
(818) 908-8867 (West Coast)
(405) 472-4203 (East Coast)

International Oak Society
PO Box 310
Pen Argyl, PA 18072-0310
(610) 588-1037

International Oleander Society
PO Box 3431
Galveston, TX 77552-0431

Lawn Institute
1501 Johnson Ferry Rd. NE #200
Marietta, GA 30062-6485
(770) 977-5492

Magnolia Society
6616 81st Street
Cabin John, MD 20818
(301) 320-4296

Marigold Society of America
PO Box 5112
New Britain, PA 18901
(215) 348-5273

Master Gardeners International
PO Box 526
Falls Church, VA 22040-0526
(703) 241-3769

National Council of State Garden Clubs
4401 Magnolia Avenue
St. Louis, MO 63110

National Fuchsia Society
11507 East 187th Street
Artesia, CA 90701-5603

National Gardening Association
180 Flynn Avenue
South Burlington, VT 05401
(802) 863-1308

National Pond Society
PO Box 449
Acworth, GA 30101
(800) 742-4701

National Wildflower Research Center
2600 F.M. 973 North
Austin, TX 78725-4201

North American Fruit Explorers
Route 1, Box 94
Chapin, IL 62628

North American Heather Society
E. 502 Haskell Hill Road
Shelton, WA 98584
(360) 427-5318

North American Lily Society
PO Box 272
Owatonna, MN 55060-0272
(507) 451-2170

North American Mycological Association (Mushrooms)
3556 Oakwood
Ann Arbor, MI 48104-5213
(313) 971-2552

North American Rock Garden Society
PO Box 67
Millwood, NY 10546
(914) 762-2948

Northern Nut Growers Association
9870 South Palmer Road
New Carlisle, Ohio 45344
(513) 878-2610

Seed Savers Exchange
3076 North Winn Road
Decorah, IA 52101
(319) 382-5990

Terrarium Association
PO Box 276
Newfane, VT 05345
(802) 365-4721

World Pumpkin Confederation
14050 Rt 62
Collins, NY 14034
(800) 449-5681
Fax: (716) 532-5690

ILLUSTRATORS

Isabelle Arslanian
Liliane Blondel
Sylvia Bokor
Bénédicte Carraz
Nicole Colin
Bruno Congar
Philippe Degrave
Paulette Dimier
William Fraschini
Lary Greiner/Graphic Chart and
    Map Co., Inc.
Nicole Gawsewitch
Michel Loppé
Régis Macioszczyk
Jean-Marc Pariselle
Anne Sarrazin
Michèle Trumel
Christine Wilson

PHOTO CREDITS

Cover Walter Chandoha; **2** Ping Amranand; **16** Lamontagne; **22** Jacana/D. Lecourt; **23** *left* Map/N: P. Mioulane; **23** *right* Michael S. Thompson; **24** *top* Richard Shiell; **24** *bottom left* Map/N: P. Mioulane; **24** *right* Map/N: P. Mioulane; **25** *left* Map/A. Descat; **25** *right* Ph. Perdereau; **29** Ping Amranand; **33** Grant Heilman: Lefever/Grushow; **34** Michael S. Thompson; **35** Lamontagne; **39** Lamontagne; **40** Lamontagne; **41** Lamontagne; **45** Grant Heilman/Jane Grushow; **48** Lamontagne; **55** Ping Amranand; **64** Lamontagne; **67** Lamontagne; **68** Charles Mann; **74** New York Botanical Garden/Bronx Green-Up; **77** Lamontagne; **82** Lamontagne; **88** Lamontagne; **91** Positive Images/Jerry Howard; **95** Michael S. Thompson; **100** Lamontagne; **105** Grant Heilman: Lefever/Grushow; **107** Lamontagne; **117** Lamontagne; **123** Map/N: P. Mioulane; **125** Charles Mann; **128** Lamontagne; **131** Harper Horticultural Slide Library/Pamela J. Harper; **132** Elvin McDonald; **140** Charles Mann; **142** Ph. Perdereau; **145** Lamontagne; **146-147** Walter Chandoha; **148-149** Karen Bussolini; **150** Garden Picture Library/John Glover; **152** Lamontagne; **154** Garden Picture Library/Ron Sutherland; **156** Lamontagne; **163** Garden Picture Library/Brigitte Thomas; **166** Ph. Perdereau; **170** Lamontagne; **172** David Schilling; **173** David Cavagnaro; **177** The Image Bank/P. Eden; **184** Lamontagne; **185** Lamontagne; **190** Derek Fell; **193** Michael S. Thompson; **195** Walter Chandoha; **199** Derek Fell; **202** Thomas E. Eltzroth; **203** Lamontagne; **204** Lamontagne; **211** Lamontagne; **213** Lamontagne; **214** *top* Sonja Bullaty & Angelo Lomeo; **214** *bottom* Postive Images/Lee Anne White; **215** Positive Images/Margaret Hensel; **225** Lamontagne; **227** Karen Bussolini; **229** Map/N: P. Mioulane; **233** J.C. Mayer-G. Lescanff;

234 Lamontagne; **237** Steven Mays; **238** Steven Mays; **239** Steven Mays; **247** Jerry Pavia; **251** Harper Horticultural Slide Library/Pamela J. Harper; **260** Suzanne Christopher; **268** Lamontagne; **273** Karen Bussolini; **280** Lamontagne; **288** Walter Chandoha; **295** Map/N: A. Descat; **304** Harper Horticultural Slide Library/Pamela J. Harper; **307** Lamontagne; **312** David Cavagnaro; **315** David Cavagnaro; **321** Map/N: P. Mioulane; **324** National Wildflower Research Center/Texas Department of Transportation; **325** Charles Mann; **326** National Wildflower Research Center/Doug Sherman; **327** National Wildflower Research Center/Jeanette Milne.

Engraved by
Applied Graphics Technologies
Carlstadt, NJ

Printed & bound by
R. R. Donnelley & Sons Company
Willard Manufacturing Division

1001 HINTS & TIPS FOR YOUR GARDEN is designed in QuarkXPress 3.31. Body text typeface is Adobe Garamond & Futura Light